Born in Bath on 22 January 1943, Michael Spicer was educated at Wellington College, where he was head boy. He subsequently read economics at Emmanuel College, Cambridge. In 1964 he joined the *Statist* journal and in 1965 was appointed by Edward Heath to re-establish contact between the Conservative Party and university academics. He fought Emanuel Shinwell at Easington in the 1966 general election (the youngest candidate in the country versus the oldest). He was elected to Parliament in February 1974 for the constituency of South Worcestershire, which later became West Worcestershire, from which he retired in 2010.

He was vice-chairman of the Conservative Party from 1981 to 1983 and deputy chairman from 1983 to 1984. He was minister variously for aviation (1984–7), electricity and coal (1987–90) and housing (1990). He was knighted in 1996. In 2001 he was elected chairman of the 1922 Committee (Conservative parliamentary party), a position he retained until 2010, when he was appointed to the House of Lords.

His hobbies include bridge, painting, writing novels and tennis (he captained the Lords and Commons Tennis Team between 1997 and 2007). He is married to Ann, and they have three children, Edward, Antonia and Annabel, and five grandchildren, Alexia, Harry, Ferdie, Edward and James. He lives in Worcestershire.

By the same author
Final Act, Severn House 1981
Prime Minister Spy, Severn House 1986
Cotswold Manners, Severn House 1989, St Martin's Press 1998
Cotswold Murders, St Martin's Press 1990, Constable 1991
Cotswold Mistress, St Martin's Press 1992, Constable 1992
A Treaty Too Far: A New Policy for Europe, Fourth Estate 1992
Cotswold Moles, St Martin's Press 1993
The Challenge from the East & The Rebirth of the West, St Martin's Press 1996

The Spicer Diaries

The Spicer Diaries

MICHAEL
SPICER

Biteback Publishing

First published in Great Britain in 2012 by
Biteback Publishing Ltd
Westminster Tower
3 Albert Embankment
London
SE1 7SP

ISBN 978-1-84954-238-8

10 9 8 7 6 5 4 3 2 1

A CIP catalogue record for this book is available from the British Library.

FRONT JACKET Portrait of Lord Spicer by Anastasia Pollard, RP 2009 winner of the Ondaatje Prize for Portraiture (in association with the Royal Society of Portrait Painters).

Set in Garamond and Baskerville

Printed and bound in Great Britain by
CPI Group (UK) Ltd, Croydon CR0 4YY

To my darling wife Ann, my son Edward and his wife Lulu, my daughters Antonia and Annabel and her husband Jonathan, and to my five grandchildren, Alexia, Harry, Ferdie, Edward and James.

Acknowledgements

My sincerest thanks in the production of this book go to its excellent editor, Sam Carter, and to the publisher, Iain Dale, whom I have known and admired for many years; to my close friends David Porter, chief executive of the Association of Electrical Producers, David Kleeman, my wise counsellor, Harriett Baldwin, my wonderful successor as Member of Parliament for West Worcestershire, and Henry Angest, Chairman of Arbuthnot Banking, all for kindly reading the book in draft and for making such helpful suggestions for its improvement; to my long-time friend and eminent New York publisher of six of my previous books, Tom Dunne, for agreeing to publish this one in America; to Margaret Bottomley, who features regularly in this book and who has helped me with every book I have written and particularly for transcribing the diaries; to Jessica Chessher (née Stewart) for having been such a loyal and efficient PA throughout the opposition years; and, of course, to my darling wife Ann for her copious and wise advice and for yet again putting up with my absence from the washing-up sink with the excuse for the umpteenth time that I was deeply involved in the book. Without Ann beside me, much of what follows would not have taken place.

Contents

Preface

For an autobiography to be bearable either its subject must be an historical colossus or it must be funny. My own career does not merit an
autobiography.

A diary is rather different. There is a salacious quality about a diary which
is not always apparent in the biography. But a diary has its limitations. Every
entry is a flash in time, sometimes deadly accurate but often only for a split
second. The diarist must be quick to judge and quick to take a view which
may change, probably will, a day, an hour, even a minute later.

I kept a diary of sorts on and off for some sixty years from the age of nine.
I stopped doing so at the point that this book ends.

I found reading my diaries more difficult than I did writing them. This is
because I wanted to change everything 'with the benefit of hindsight'; but I
did not, asking myself, 'Why should "insight" be the monopoly of old age?'
And so I have rarely substituted one set of words for another and then only to
make the meaning clearer, not to change the sense. I have cut the text where
its length made it tedious or to avoid breaking a confidence. Where the diary
is weak but the story is strong I have added a few words and made it clear
that I have done so. Indeed, the early chapters, although written in diary
form, have merely drawn on the various diaries for background. It is not until
Chapter 4 that the diary entries really take over.

Many of these entries were made as notes rather than as fully constructed
sentences. I publish them in the raw, with the obvious costs and benefits. The
book should probably have been called *The Spicer Notes*; *The Spicer Diaries*
sounds better. Nor was I as disciplined as others have been in 'writing up'
the diaries. I only made an entry when something genuinely interested me.
I have to admit that, during a half-century of political adventure, there was
much that did.

I was not at the height of events but I was at the bottom of many of them.
I played a part in the fall of Alec Douglas-Home and in his replacement with
Ted Heath, on whose staff I served in quite a central position during the
1960s when the Conservatives were in opposition. For a short, intense, time I
acted as Margaret Thatcher's parliamentary private secretary. As deputy chairman of the Conservative Party I was deeply involved in operations on the

night of the Brighton bomb. During the 1980s I was variously minister for aviation, electricity & coal and housing & planning. I chaired the rebellion against John Major's Maastricht Bill and tried unsuccessfully to organise the succession for Michael Howard. For nine years I chaired the parliamentary party (the 1922 Committee) under the leadership (briefly) of William Hague, of Iain Duncan Smith, of Michael Howard and of David Cameron.

I surfaced in the headlines on six occasions: when at the age of twenty I founded Pressure for Economic and Social Toryism (PEST); as minister for aviation when I supervised the aftermath of the disastrous crash of a Chinook helicopter off Shetland in 1986; when I introduced armed troops at London's airports; as minister for electricity when I offered the Americans the opportunity to invest in our nuclear power industry; during the Maastricht rebellion when I took the lead against John Major's government; and when as chairman of the 1922 Committee I presided over three changes to the leadership of the Conservative Party. Particular excitement was generated by my receipt in secret of letters from more than twenty-nine Conservative MPs, triggering the vote of confidence in Iain Duncan Smith.

This book is the story of my relationship with five Prime Ministers and four Conservative party leaders. Perhaps because there were so many of them, their heroic qualities are through my eyes tempered. It is not that I did not admire several of them; it is more that I have a Tawneyesque[*] rather than a Shakespearean view of history. That is to say, the past is explained to me more by the force of events than by heroic actions. Prime Ministers fill the needs of their time and work through the idiom of their age. To a lesser extent than they or their opponents believe do they themselves control and direct the affairs of men.

During the Falklands War, for instance, Margaret Thatcher showed enormous courage, powers of resilience and leadership and a remarkable steadfastness of purpose; but her actions were largely reactions to the buffeting of events, disastrous events in the early stages. Ultimately she was judged at the 1983 election not as a war leader but on the performance of the economy on her watch;[†] this in turn was substantially governed by the incidence of international economic movements. Even in the conduct of the war itself she was largely at the mercy of the Americans.

Nor was Thatcherism quite the aberration it has been cracked up to be.

---

[*] Cf. R. H. Tawney, *The Agrarian Problem in the Sixteenth Century*, Longmans, Green & Co., 1912.

[†] Just as in 1945 Churchill was judged for the past performance of his party and not as the victor over Nazi Germany.

For a start, it was always hard to define. Despite her rhetoric to the contrary, Thatcher herself had no doubts, for instance, about the capability of central government for doing good – and for doing so for 'our people', in other words on a selective basis. Thus people who owned their own homes, especially those who had recently bought them from the state, were to be given preferential treatment over those who rented or who were their landlords. As minister of housing, I did not wholly concur with this view. As recorded in her memoirs, this got me into a spot of bother with the Prime Minister.

She had little problem, either, with intervening and discriminating on matters to do with trade. Buying and selling with the likes of Mahathir's Malaysia was if possible to be avoided (as, indeed, was all trade with Europe); business with North America was to be encouraged. Best of all was to buy at home.

The paradoxes between what others defined as Thatcherism and what she meant in practice by it were legion (to the extent that a good A-level question might be 'Was Thatcher a Thatcherite?'). If London's airports had to be privatised as a monopoly, to maximise the takings for the state, so be it. If nuclear power needed to be retained in public ownership for its own protection, that is how it would be. If the privatisation of the coal mines was to be put off for fear of upsetting the miners, then the responsible parliamentary under-Secretary of State at the Department of Energy – Michael Spicer – would be given appropriate instructions to that effect.

The position she took on coal, especially towards the end of her administration, was of particular interest to me. Here is what she says in her autobiography: 'I never had regard for commercial aspects alone ... I felt a strong sense of obligation and loyalty to the Nottinghamshire miners who had stayed at work ... And second I also knew we might have to face another strike.'* My view is that she got this completely wrong. What the miners of both the UDM and the NUM were interested in by the time I was minister for coal at the end of the 1980s was the price of any shares going.† The significant point for the moment is that it illustrates – what shall we call it? – the subtlety of Thatcherism.

In so far as Thatcherism was definable in terms of a renewed emphasis on self-reliance, thrift, individual enterprise and social mobility on the basis of

---

* Margaret Thatcher, *The Downing Street Years*, HarperCollins, 1993.
† I learnt many years later that she had had similar reservations about John Moore's proposals when Secretary of State for Health & Social Services, for an insurance-based health service as per the French system, where the patient effectively holds the purse-strings (and makes the choices) with the financial support of the state.

merit, its roots lay deeper in history and were more widely scattered than her supporters, like me, proclaimed at the time. Thatcher may not have been quite 'Heath in drag' but neither was she the antithesis of Heath, as he, she and we supposed. From an at times close association with each, I track in the pages ahead the several similarities between them.

Each was openly elected by the Conservative parliamentary party; each symbolised a reaction against the 'magic circle' which had chosen Alec Douglas-Home. Each rose through the ranks of the party on merit. They both began as Prime Ministers with the radical intent to roll back the reach of central government.

Margaret Thatcher did indeed bring about substantive political change with the early abolition of prices and exchange controls and later the mass sale of council houses and the privatisation of the major utilities. Edward Heath, who was better prepared in opposition and more experienced than Margaret Thatcher, nevertheless went into reverse gear almost immediately with the nationalisation of Rolls-Royce, with a high-profile discriminatory and interventionist regional policy and with the attempted control of wages and prices. For her part Thatcher, while proclaiming herself to be 'not for turning', increasingly surrounded herself with people who espoused just that, until she put herself, her administration and all that it stood for on a course of self-destruction. By the late 1980s, in terms of real power, the Ridleys, the Parkinsons and the Tebbits had been replaced by the Pattens, the Clarkes and the Hurds. In large measure because of this, her fall became assured, as did the turbulence which followed at the top of the Conservative Party for the next fifteen years.

The Thatcher years were pivotal in the sense that they were both cause and effect of much that went on at the time. In the same way that the short ascendancy of Alec Douglas-Home explained her rise to power, so was the Thatcher administration a determinant of the succeeding premierships, including those of Brown and Blair. They each formed part of a chain.

John Major was particularly confused by his inheritance. On the one hand he was apparently Thatcher's choice as her successor; on the other, he was a proud member of the Blue Chip Club, dedicated to the reversal of all that she stood for. An interesting question is whether Major's attempts during the Maastricht debacle to appeal simultaneously to both sides was a conscious effort to divide and rule or the act of a man with split roots, vainly struggling to maintain some sort of control. I shall address this issue head on.

Tony Blair's half-way house between Thatcher and socialism might have worked. Initially, and before he became leader of the Labour Party, when I was pitted against him during the passage through Parliament of the 1987

Electricity Bill, he seemed to have the will and the energy genuinely to buck the pull of events; this unusual position seemed to desert him the moment he took office. Once safely deposited in Number 10 he attempted to emulate Thatcher as war leader but conducted a quasi-socialist economic policy which, in the hands of his successor, brought the country to its knees.

David Cameron looks as though he may be the first genuinely post-Thatcher leader. His premiership may come to be the first to be described in terms of factors largely outside the Thatcher legacy. He is already being required to deal directly with a series of strategic/global issues which have been rumbling around for several decades but which have not until now forced critical decisions: Is Islam to be confronted or appeased? Is it to be a friend or foe of the west? Can it absorb western concepts of plurality and democracy or will it be the western countries which will have to adapt most to become more disciplined? Do we link arms with the east (China, above all) in order to make a go of world trade or do we take the protectionist route of Europe and, under Barack Obama, of North America? How will Cameron square his decisions on these matters with the needs of the vast and increasingly isolated continent of Africa and with the renewed, possibly dangerous, ambitions of Russia? Will there continue to be an overlay of green policies or were these luxuries from a bygone age of plenty? Are the signposts for the future bedded in the recent past? Or are the waters now so uncharted that your guess is as good as mine about what will happen?

And then there is Europe. I tell the story in Part II of the tribulations that beset the Conservative Party in Parliament during the passage of the Bill to ratify the Treaty of Maastricht, by which a monetary union was established in Europe.

In this case hindsight does not apply. I was always clear that, if Maastricht went ahead, with or without British participation, the European Union would turn itself into a fiscal union (either with its own taxation and expenditure instruments or by submitting to German ones); and that it would use the European Court and the law of the Union to rule Britain as if she were in the Euro.

The choice for Britain would then be straightforward: either to join the emerging Federal State or to leave it. At the time of Maastricht, a small band of us helped to keep the options open for our country. I doubt that that trick can be worked again. The issue will now have to be addressed. This book is in part a contribution to the process of moving towards that decision.

Michael Spicer
Cropthorne, 2012

Part I

The Thatcher Years

Chapter 1

Alec Douglas-Home

I am born in Bath in the early hours of 22 January 1943 at my grandparents' home, Chota Koti (they had previously lived in India).* Nurse Skuse is in attendance. My father is not present; he is commanding the Second Battalion of the East Yorkshire Regiment in preparation for an eventual invasion of Europe.

Shortly after my birth my mother and I move to Weston-super-Mare to escape German bombing of the Admiralty buildings in Bath.

Until she left the service to have me, my mother, a woman of some beauty, had been a naval intelligence officer. Having made herself bilingual in German, she had in 1940 been in charge of a listening post in the south-east of England in anticipation of a German invasion.

My mother and father had known each other for less than a month before they were married in a ceremony over which raged the Battle of Britain, diverting to the skies the attention of the few guests present. My father, ten years older than my mother, had won her heart by bombarding her with a series of rather remarkable love letters, a flavour of which is as follows:

HQ 198, Home Forces
1.9.40

Sailor dear, what should I write to you about today? It is so lovely that we ought to take a couple of bath buns, our bathing gear and search the coast for a strip of sand clear of mines, burrow a hole, one for you and one for me, talk – sleep – bathe – talk – sleep – could anything be nicer ... What sort of books do BAs read in their spare time? And do they ever lower themselves so much as to hold hands in the pictures? ...

There is that ominous whirr whirr in the air again. They are late this morning. Are they over you much? ... Has your father asked any leading questions about my financial position? My pay as a Captain is about £420 a year from which income tax has to be deducted ... I don't know why I tell you all this because as yet you have not shown the slightest inclination to fall in with my wishes ... Would it break your heart if I were posted to Egypt? I might be you

---

* My maternal grandfather was a director of Bateman's opticians.

know because I hold a language qualification in Arabic. Isn't it time you told me something about yourself? ... Trevor Card took 'Winnie the Pooh' [the PM] all round the place the day before yesterday.

It was most amusing to hear first hand evidence of so interesting a character. I have ceased to love you until you condescend to love me a bit! I hate one sided correspondence...

Three days later, two and a half weeks after they had first met, my mother accepts my father's proposal on condition that they are married asap. Over the moon, my father nearly 'blows it'. In the excitement he mixes up lady friends. He cannot even remember the date when he writes the following.

198 Home Forces
Day, time or date unknown

You have got me so muddled that I have now gone and mixed my letters!!! Please return me a letter commencing 'Jean dear', 'Dear Jean', or 'Jean darling', or simply 'Darling Jean', which has got mixed up in one for you. And don't get excited about it. Jean is a perfectly respectable married woman with two children who I have known for twelve years and who I was asking to have you to stay in Camberley. Heaven knows what I said about you. Probably all frightfully sentimental. If you have been unlucky enough to read it in error, forget it and forgive a stupid and embarrassing blunder.

I enclose the letter written to you, apparently on Tuesday. Apropos of your wish to get married in a hurry, the sooner you marry me the better and get me under control. And, darling, whatever I do or say and however much I get tied up, I love you and you only and always, always will. I am rather miserable about this Jean business, so please write and say it's OK. And let's get married before I go to the Staff College, or we will have to wait until Xmas. Darling, I am miserable. Hardy.

My mother evidently forgives this minor indiscretion and on 7 September receives this telegram from my father:

DARLING I AM WILDLY EXCITED WILL TRY AND ARRANGE SPECIAL LICENCE WEDNESDAY STOP THINK REGISTRY OFFICE ONLY HOPE STOP BRIGADIER INSISTS I GO LONDON MONDAY STOP LONGING TO SEE YOU WILL TELEPHONE TOMORROW 0900 HOURS RED PERMITTING GOODNIGHT ALL MY LOVE HARDY

Someone pulls rank and a church is arranged. My mother drums up a fellow Wren, Marjorie Adams, to be her bridesmaid. On 8 September Marjorie wires:

YES HOW EXCITING WHERE AND WHO MARJORIE

In 1943, my mother, now a civilian, joins the two-hour ration queue for a morsel of fish, which I spit back in her face.

My father does not take his regiment onto the Normandy beaches on 6 June 1944. General Montgomery had issued an order that all battalion commanders must be under the age of forty and my father was born on 4 February 1903; so he returns to the General Staff with the rank of lieutenant colonel.

Once the war is over, my father is posted back to north Africa and commands a Sudanese Defence Force brigade from Asmara in Eritrea, where he is joined by my mother, me and my newly born sister, Angela Jane.* Our home in the capital, Asmara, is in the palace, which has its own zoo. We also have a house in the second biggest town, Keren, where on 9 December 1946 a guest for lunch is Compton Mackenzie, author of *Whisky Galore*. He wrote of his visit, 'We came back from the battlefield† to lunch with the Spicers. Towards the end of lunch a large but slim chocolate coloured ram came into the dining room to beg for cigarettes to eat. I gave him a cigar … Edgar was the name of this engaging animal.'‡

There is a picture of me at the time aged three, taking the salute beside my father as soldiers of the Sudanese Defence Force march by.

In 1948 we move from north Africa to Vienna, where my father is the deputy commander of the British garrison. In this capacity he gives permission to Carol Reed to film *The Third Man* on condition that 'the man with the zither' plays the film's theme tune at a party my father and mother throws at Rosen Villa in Ober St Veit, their new home, requisitioned from a Nazi family.

When my wife, Ann, and I visit the house some sixty years later, the daughter of the Nazi is still living there. As she opens the front door to me she says:

---

* Killed in a car crash in South Africa in 1973.
† Keren Heights, scene of a major battle between the British-led 4th and 5th Indian Divisions and the Italians in March 1941.
‡ Compton Mackenzie, *All Over the Place*, Chatto & Windus, 1948.

You, I feel sure, are the son of Herr General. You are most welcome. I always felt you would come back one day. Did you know that when your family left the house it was returned to us in perfect condition and with every item, down to a little box of thimbles, in exactly its right place?

As we leave, her two good-looking sons click their heels and give a short bow.

In Vienna my parents lead a very grand life. My sister and I are left in the capable hands of a professional governess, Frau Galvani, whom I convert into Hitler's mistress and mother of a British Prime Minister in my novel *Prime Minister Spy*.

After Vienna it is Hamburg, Hanover, Naples and finally, incongruously, Aldershot for my father and mother. As the years go by and the post-war army begins to shrink, my father's rank is reduced so that by the time we reach Aldershot in 1952, he no longer wears red tabs on his collar.

In Naples my father is the victim of some sort of administrative practical joke – either that or a cock-up. Having commanded brigades and occupation garrisons, he is put in charge of a NATO stores base. The supplies for which he is responsible evidently do not include uniforms. The men under his charge certainly have no standard military dress. When Field Marshal Montgomery pays the depot a surprise visit, they are lined up in every form of military attire – light khaki, dark khaki, whites, shorts, longs, fatigues, you name it. Monty is not best pleased and says so, despite the famed eccentricity of his own military clothes. The whole event is recorded by an anonymous cartoonist, who dresses his soldiers in everything from a Danish guard's full dress to oversized tropical kit.

My mother adores Naples, living as they do in the *palazzo* of a glamorous Italian aristocrat, Dickie Winspere, and enjoying the *dolce vita* of post-war Italy. She persuades my father to delay for six months his letter to the War Office requesting a transfer.

Eventually they return to England, where our army house in Aldershot is painted yellow on the outside to make use of the spare camouflage paint which is surplus to the requirements of the abortive attack on the Suez Canal.

At the age of nine I fall in love with the army and, disturbingly, with the gorgeously attractive Princess Margaret, who one ever-to-be-remembered day visits Mons Officer Cadet School, where my father ends his military career as deputy commandant.

From the age of eight my sister, Angela, and I commuted to boarding schools in Dorset; mine is called Dumpton and is located outside Wimborne

Minster. We are suitably labelled for travel while our parents are in Germany. It is not unknown for the labels to get mixed up and for a young commuter properly destined, for instance, for Hamburg to be despatched to Trieste or wherever, by mistake.

I am a precocious little boy, acting, producing and writing plays after the manner of Shakespeare and Agatha Christie. I play secret bridge in the maths classes, passing cards inside folded blotting paper; perhaps I am just a professional schoolboy, becoming as I do head of College at Wellington. An entry in my diary at the time indicates that, thankfully, there was another side to me. On 13 April 1959 I write, 'Went up [to London] with Chris Miers [who lived there] to get Brigitte Bardot's autograph for a bet … We were unsuccessful; however to begin with we were the only onlookers there.' She was filming early in the morning near Parliament and, I recollect, in a bad mood.

There is at this time a more profound episode in my life. It is described by Field Marshal Montgomery, no less, in his book *The Path to Leadership*:[*]

Then there is the story of the English schoolboy, aged 16, who had to write an essay on somebody he knew by reputation – and he selected me. He read all he could about me in the Press, much of it very uncomplimentary, and having described my army career, finished by saying I was a very unpleasant person – conceited, vain, ruthless, and so on. His father sent me the essay to read, which I did with interest! I then wrote to his father, saying that the boy should at least be fair; he had never met me, indeed had never seen me, and yet had made definite statements about my character. I suggested that he could have begun his critical remarks in this way: 'I have never met him but *it is reported* that he is…'

I asked the boy to visit me in my home, and he duly came. He was a delightful lad, very intelligent, and with a most attractive personality; we had an amusing talk and he is now one of the greatest of my young friends – and he visits me every time he returns from school for the holidays. I have persuaded him to go to Sandhurst and become a soldier – and he will make a good one.

I am the mysterious 'English schoolboy'.

The most relevant entries in my diary at the time are:

Friday 10 April 1959. Arrived at 3 o'clock. Met Monty, who was wearing a purple duffle coat and was standing in his garden. He said: 'You would like me to

---

[*] Montgomery of Alamein, *The Path to Leadership*, Collins, 1961.

show you round my home?' First of all he took me round his three caravans, which he had left in exactly the same state as they were at the German surrender on Lunenburg Heath. Showed me a picture of Rommel which he used to study before Alamein. Two caravans were captured from the enemy. Monty had a feeling that the one captured at Tunis was Rommel's. (He had to fight the government to be allowed to keep these caravans. They will be returned to the country when he dies.)

The third caravan – map caravan – is his own. No press are allowed in here. He showed me the place where there had been a light but George VI had bumped his head on it and had it removed…

Then we went indoors and had some tea.

Monday 28 December 1959. Arrived at 10 o'clock. Straight away was shown how to work the motor bike – what an excitement it was. At first just drove it around the drive. After lunch was allowed to use the gears in the road, having been shown how by Monty's chauffeur. Did this all afternoon. 7.00 p.m. went up to the flat which I had been lent and which was on the top floor. Dinner at 8.00. Afterwards listened to Monty's recent lecture at Oxford on the menace of China.

Next day, 29th, rode the bike home. Discovered with a shock that I have failed both English and History A levels … On returning to Monty I told him. He simply said, 'That's bad, very bad'. Left early on the 30th plus bicycle.

Tuesday 12 January 1960. Went with an uncertain mind as to what my future career was to be. Monty found this out when I mentioned at lunch that instead of going to Sandhurst I might go to Mons Officer Cadet School – which would mean I would only do a short service commission.

Monty was at first surprised – then indignant. If my object in life was to be a soldier – why a short service commission? I replied that I wanted to see what the army was like myself before I committed to it. 'Then your mind is not clear,' he said. I replied 'No', at which he was as near to becoming angry as I had seen him – said words to the effect that at 17 years it was an appalling state of affairs if a boy had not made up his mind.

I said my main objective was the university – Cambridge. Once I had got there I had the whole world in front of me. He said I must look further ahead and make up my mind what my career was to be. If my decision was the army then I should adopt the following policy: Main objective – army. Two ways of reaching this, (a) preferably university, (b) if not, via Sandhurst. But these last two were only two means – either left flanking movement or right for the main goal. I was to discuss this with my father when I returned home and was to come back to see him in the next holidays.

I don't join the army. Instead I go to Cambridge University to read economics.

July–August 1963
I am due to begin my third and final year at Emmanuel College, Cambridge, where I am reading economics. So far I have taken only a passing interest in politics, leading the debate in the Union on one or two minor occasions, and am certainly not politically well connected. I do not, for instance, know the leading Conservative lights like Michael Howard, John Selwyn Gummer and Kenneth Clarke,* though I am quite friendly with Norman Lamont.

I am much more involved in the Amateur Dramatic Club, whose star is Richard Eyre,† and with which I travel to the Soviet Union, writing sketches and playing Hamlet in front of one or two large audiences in Moscow, Kiev and Gurzuf on the Black Sea. Khrushchev is in charge and there is promise (false, as it turns out) of greater freedom in the USSR. Certainly there is a spreading barter culture. A pair of Marks & Spencer woollen socks brings you a fourth-class train ticket to the Black Sea.

When I return from Russia towards the end of the long summer vacation of 1963 I begin to take in what is happening on the political scene. The tribulations of the Conservative Party, especially, do begin to impress themselves on my consciousness.

I become, in particular, an avid reader of the weekly articles in the *Sunday Times* of William Rees-Mogg, whose theme is the compounding isolation of the Conservative Party, in government until 1964 and in opposition thereafter.

Sitting in the kitchen of my parents' house in Farnham, Surrey, contemplating the style and literature of the Campaign for Democratic Socialism (CDS), the Labour group which has developed a strong following on the left in Cambridge, I play with the words 'Campaign', 'Toryism', 'Pressure', 'Economic' and 'Social'. I come up with Pressure for Economic and Social Toryism – PEST. The mix of economics and politics has already begun to intrigue me.

In a scribbled note I claim that there are three factors which worry the members of PEST – never mind that there are no members. What is of

---

* Ken Clarke did remind me in later life that we met once in my rooms when he refused my invitation to him to join PEST.
† Later director of the National Theatre.

concern to them, I say, is first the intellectual and social isolation of the Tory Party; secondly the lack of coherence in 'progressive' Tory thought, especially in economic and social matters; and, finally, the lack of contact of the Tory Party with the universities. It could all be summed up in the phrase 'too much money chasing too few ideas'.

With these virtually meaningless generalisations safely preserved, I prepare my attack on the bastions of Cambridge University in general and the Cambridge University Conservative Association in particular. Of such coincidences are rebellions germinated.

Thursday 3 October 1963

My first practical move is to ask my mother to lend me an old sheet. The second is to paint on it 'Pressure for Economic and Social Toryism' (PEST). Armed with this materiel I set off for my third and final university year with the intent, no less, to put the Conservative Party back in touch with the people.

Saturday 5 October

The train from London Liverpool Street pulls onto the Cambridge platform twenty minutes late. I tug the hood of my black duffel coat over my forehead and ears. It is bitterly cold despite the time of year; with no obstacles to impede it, the wind blows straight from Siberia.

The train comes to a standstill and windows are pulled down. Female arms struggle to release outside door handles.

She steps neatly onto the platform, red wavy hair tied in a silk scarf, blue suit perfectly tailored, starkly contrasting with the jeans and chunky sweaters worn by the other weekend visitors. Her natural prettiness will develop with age into classical beauty like her New Zealander mother (granddaughter of Prime Minister Sir Joseph Ward) and like her Jerusalem-born grandmother.

Ann Hunter and I have known each other for about a year. We both come from Farnham in Surrey, where we met at a Sunday morning drinks party. She is a London fashion designer, not quite the typical Cambridge undergraduate 'bird'. Nor is the life she is now plunged into very typical of that to which she is accustomed in London.

As we walk for five minutes to my digs in Station Road, I pass on to Ann the information that the Freshers' Fair will open the next day and that PEST will be represented there with a stall at which members will be recruited in their droves.

There are two snags: one, PEST has at present no members except for me (and her if she wants to join) and, two, PEST has no stall. If she does decide to join, it will be her task tomorrow to secure a table and to pin up the sheet on which I have painted 'Pressure for Economic and Social Toryism'.

Ann asks why I could not secure the table myself. I point out that it would not look good if the chairman of this new national political force were spotted pinning up sheets and fighting for trestle tables at an undergraduate freshers' fair.

That evening we dine illegally* in my digs off sardines and toast, followed by a packet of dark chocolate digestive biscuits. 'Healthy diets' are for the distant future. Someone in the room next door plays what must be a recently purchased record of a new group from Liverpool called the Beatles. The distinctive nasal sounds easily penetrate the thin walls. At one point Joey Chinoy puts his handsome face round the door. 'The trouble with you English is that you are so damned middle class,' he says, and disappears down the stairs. Joey is from the upper reaches of society in Pakistan. As it is the first weekend of the new academic year he has forsworn his beloved polo for forty-eight hours.

Monday 6 October

The day dawns clear and frosty. I advise Ann to arrive at the Freshers' Fair in a taxi (for which I raid my allowance, provided by British Petroleum as part of a scholarship which I have been awarded). I will follow in an hour or so on foot.

When Ann arrives at the hall off Market Square, she is allocated a space and a trestle table. Luckily for Ann the areas beside her are already occupied by some nice young men from the Campaign for Nuclear Disarmament on one side and from the Communist Party of Great Britain on the other. In no time at all they have the PEST table up and the sheet pinned to the wall behind. They are also able to provide her with some plain paper and a pencil. PEST is in business.

Within minutes, John Barnes,† a fellow of Caius College and well-known university Conservative personality, approaches Ann. 'This seems interesting,' he says, looking her up and down. 'Tell me more about it.'

Ann blushes and hands him the grubby piece of paper on which is scribbled my single-paragraph PEST mantra. 'Definitely interesting,' he says. 'How much does it cost to join?' Ann blurts out, 'One shilling.' (I haven't

---

* Women were not allowed in men's colleges after 9.00 p.m.
† Lecturer in government, London School of Economics, 1964–2003.

given any thought to subs rates). 'You're on,' says Barnes, and so we recruit our first director of research.

During the day some fifty undergraduates sign up – no doubt in part because we are cheaper than the Cambridge University Conservative Association (CUCA). PEST is on its way to becoming, within six months, one of the largest political student groups in Cambridge and, within eighteen months, one of the largest student groups in the country, with twenty university branches. It takes off nationally when Alec Douglas-Home becomes Prime Minister and Rab Butler becomes its patron.

Rab has reservations about the word PEST. In a letter to me dated 15 February 1964 he writes:

> When I first heard the name PEST I thought it was rather witty, but I can quite see that not everyone would have the same idea and that it might provoke antagonistic reactions. I do not think it is too late to change. You can easily explain the move; but I am afraid I have no very helpful suggestion to make.

For a short while, when the Conservatives lose the general election on 15 October 1964 and a leadership struggle ensues, PEST was a household name, which we did not change despite Rab's entreaties.

Sunday 18 October 1964
In the *Sunday Times* William Rees-Mogg analyses the result of the preceding week's general election when Labour emerges as the largest party in Parliament, but with no overall majority.

> The Labour Party polled almost exactly the same number of votes as it did in 1959 ... the Liberal Party nearly doubled its vote ... the Conservative vote fell by a million and three-quarters ... People of the centre had come to believe that the Conservatives were too much in the hands of what might be termed the fuddy-duddy right.

The focus of Rees-Mogg's attack then switches to Sir Alec Douglas-Home:

> The fundamental issue is that his interests are so different from those of the average liberal voter. During the election it became apparent that Sir Alec was not interested in, and did not know much about, education, pensions, economics, house mortgages and the other home issues ... This was symbolised in his final television broadcast when he was repeatedly pictured reading

his notes on home affairs and then shown pushing his notes aside to launch with relief into foreign affairs. The voters the Conservatives lost did not believe the country could be run on this basis.

Finally, Rees-Mogg turns to the future:

> Faced with a Prime Minister who is as skilful a politician as Mr Wilson, the Conservative Party is now in an extremely perilous strategic situation ... It is always too late to remedy one's own mistakes but Sir Alec could now again exchange roles. He could again become king-maker, or at least supervisor of a legitimate process of election.

In other words, he should step down and a proper election should follow.

At the time this is written, I am assistant to Paul Bareau, editor in chief of the weekly *Statist*, rival to *The Economist*, owned by IPC. In this capacity, my first job since leaving university, I produce a substantial article every week with my own byline. More significantly, I also write, under the banner of PEST (now with branches at the universities of Cambridge, Oxford, London and Bristol), a pamphlet entitled *Will the Tories Lose?*.

On 3 January 1965 William Rees-Mogg publishes the pamphlet in its entirety over the two centre pages of the *Sunday Times*, with a lead story by the chief lobby correspondent, James Margach, on the front page. The impact of this is sensational. On the Monday the story leads in most of the national papers; it rumbles on for the rest of the week and beyond. The tone of the pamphlet strikes a national and international resonance.

The pamphlet opens with these words:

> We believe that unless there is a fundamental change of heart inside the Tory Party, there is now a strong possibility of another greater defeat at the next general election. In the following pages we are not always concerned with the facts, with what the Tory Party actually is, but with the image which it is presenting to the nation.
>
> The reason that Conservatives like to give for their defeat at the general election is that the country was tired of having the same faces around. The implied corollary to this is that as soon as we have had a brief spell of the alternative, we shall be refreshed and ready once more to welcome our true masters to their rightful seat of governance. The trouble with this argument is that it ignores the fact that 'desire for change' is not an independent factor; it is itself a result of rather more fundamental causes.

For several months PEST has been suggesting two prime reasons which would in the end directly contribute to the party's downfall. The first of these is the image which it gives of representing a narrow section of the community; and the second is what we have called 'intellectual sterility'.

After eight pages of analysis of contemporary policies under such headings as 'The Matchstick Economy' (Harold Wilson had accused Douglas-Home of having worked out his economics with matchsticks), the pamphlet turns to the leadership issue with the words 'It is emphatically not an attack on Sir Alec'. Emphatically it is. Indeed, the next sentence insists:

It is a condemnation of the choice and the forces which lie behind the choice, in constituencies, parliamentary backbenches and in the hierarchy of the party organisation itself. However well Sir Alec did in adapting to the role of Prime Minister, however liberal may be his own personal outlook, he symbolises forces which have little to do with the running of modern Britain.

The headlines the next day are typified by the *Daily Telegraph*'s 'Home must go says Tory "Ginger Group"'. The *Mail* runs a leader down the entire length of its broadsheet front page: 'These Pests (and more power to their pestiferous elbows) have come out with a pamphlet "Will the Tories Lose?". They think electoral defeat will be even worse next time unless there is a change of heart in the Party. We agree.' Charles Greville in the *Mail* and Ann Leslie in the *Express* writes personal sketches of me, now at the age of twenty-three.

The next day the *Mail* runs a front page cartoon by Jon of a shocked lady and her daughter – both in long evening dresses and in conversation with a chinless wonder in a dinner jacket – over the caption 'The four-letter word I used was PEST'. That evening, on the BBC's *Panorama* programme, I say, 'Sir Alec should go and must go'. Robin Day is the interviewer on this programme and Ted Heath the other guest. He defends Home weakly: 'Sir Alec has supported policies right up to the hilt which appeal to the great majority of the people of this country.'

I share a taxi with Heath on the way home and I say something to the effect that 'if our policies are so popular, presumably Alec lost the general election for reasons other than policy, i.e. because of himself'. Heath stared out of the taxi window and says nothing. The *Panorama* programme is used as a peg for more headlines on 5 January.

By the time PEST publishes its second pamphlet, *Call an End to Feeble Opposition*, on 24 April 1965, it has branches in twelve universities and a membership of over 1,000 students. I had resigned from *The Statist* and am running the organisation full time from 2 Observatory Gardens, off Kensington High Street. The main call of PEST at the time is for a new system for electing leaders through a ballot of Conservative MPs. In February 1965, the leadership rules are changed in precisely this way. Henceforward Conservative leaders would be chosen by a secret ballot of Tory MPs. In order to win, they required a 15 per cent lead of votes cast. Conduct of the ballot was to be the full responsibility of the chairman of the 1922 Committee and the leadership race could be triggered only by the resignation or the death of the leader. (Further changes in 1975 made it easier to challenge the leadership.)

Tuesday 6 July 1965
Twenty-five Conservative backbenchers request a vote on the leadership at a meeting of the 1922 Committee.

That weekend William Rees-Mogg wrote a piece entitled 'The right moment to change'. On 22 July Alec Douglas-Home announced his resignation at a meeting of the 1922 Committee. The vote for his successor took place on 27 July. 150 voted for Edward Heath, 133 for Reginald Maudling and 15 for Enoch Powell. Although this was not decisive, Maudling withdrew and Heath was declared the new leader of the Conservative Party.

PEST backed Heath against Maudling. Of the two, the former was not only the more active 'moderniser', he was also the future 'Selsdon man'.* In other words, he was to the right, certainly of his rival.

Arguably Margaret Thatcher, a full ten years later, took forward the position Heath adopted at the point that he inherited Home's mantle, although by the time she ousted him his position had changed dramatically.

Reflections
What in later life do I think of my actions, which helped, with a boost from William Rees-Mogg, to make life so uncomfortable for Alec Douglas-Home? Today, no doubt, I would empathise with Home to a far greater extent than I did in 1964. Even today, however, I would have to accept that – like John Major, who also took over the leadership of the party and the premiership of the country at one and the same time, and against whom I also rebelled

---

* The phrase 'Selsdon man' was coined by Harold Wilson and in the short term rebounded against him. Wilson's reference was to a shadow Cabinet policy conference chaired by Heath at Selsdon Park, Croydon, in January 1970, at which an avowedly right-wing election programme was agreed (focusing, for instance, on immigration, taxation and law and order).

– Home was at best the second choice of most people who were involved. Like Major, Home followed a class act in leadership, which he could not match. Like Major also, he pretended not to want the job while planning to challenge for it when the right moment came. Above all, he was never in tune with the wider electorate.

Today I do acknowledge that, again like Major, Home took over a rotten hand of cards. In each case, however, I believe there were people around him who would have played them better. That said, Rab Butler confessed to me when I visited him at his London home in Smith Square, on 9 February 1967: 'If I had got the top job I would probably have won the general election in 1964 and lost the next one far more heavily than Ted did; we would then have been out of office for years.'

Chapter 2

Edward Heath

August–September 1965

I receive the following letter from Edward Heath:

6 August 1965

Dear Michael

I am so sorry that I have been unable to take up the question of financial help for you with Mr X* yet, but as you will understand it has simply not been possible to deal with this in the last few days. I will try to take the matter up on my return from holiday.

I am afraid too that it will now no longer be possible for me to address your meeting at the Party Conference. As I am sure you will understand, as Party Leader I could not address any meetings at the Conference other than my main engagement. I will try to arrange another speaker for you,† but thought I ought to write at once to let you know my own position.

I was most interested to know your new plans for PEST. Perhaps we may have a chance some time later to discuss them.

Yours ever,
Edward Heath

This letter is followed by another dated 28 August.

Dear Michael

Thank you so much for your good wishes, which I appreciate immensely. I am most grateful to you for your message.‡

Yours sincerely,
Edward Heath

---

* I have deleted the name so as not to embarrass the individual concerned.
† Heath added in his own writing: 'Perhaps you can keep in touch with my office so that we get one you would like.'
‡ Heath added in his own writing: 'Please thank all PEST for me.'

PS [in his own hand] Perhaps we can have a word after the holidays about various aspects of the future.

I reply with a letter dated 20 September. This includes the words:

You kindly mentioned in your letter to me of August 28th that you would like a word with me about various aspects of PEST's future as soon as the holidays were over. Our plan is first to spread our network of formal and informal contacts essentially at the postgraduate level in the universities.

Following this I was invited to two meetings at 'F2', Heath's large Albany flat, where he typically held court in preference to the House of Commons or to Conservative Central Office. These meetings established that he would like to control the invasion of the university common rooms as an 'in-house' operation. He would like, in other words, to take me onto the Conservative Party's books.

I received the following letter, dated 7 February 1966, from Brendon Sewill, director of the Conservative Research Department:

Dear Michael

I am writing to confirm your appointment as a member of this Department as from 1 February 1966. The appointment will be initially for a probationary period of six months and your salary will be at an annual rate of £1,600. In addition, you will receive an expenses allowance of £150 a year to cover all entertainment expenses and travel in the London area. Travel outside London and hotel bills can be claimed separately.

We expect that you will be spending about half your time on the university work and about half on preparing material for speeches dealing with certain subjects – for instance, steel and international liquidity – in the Economic Section here.

We see the university exercise in the following broad terms: that you will spend a number of months exploring the scope for establishing closer and more effective links with senior members of the universities who are friendly towards the Conservative Party. As this work progresses, one would hope that it might in due course be formalised in a new organisation. When this is launched you will run it with the aid of voluntary help in the various universities. The body would include dons, postgraduate research students and graduates doing research in research institutions, but would not include graduates who are outside the academic world.

The objects are:

First, to keep the Party in touch with academic thinking if it is to draw in people and ideas for policy research work and other constructive contributions to current political activity.

Second, to keep universities in touch with party policy and thinking.

Third, to show the general public that the party is in touch with academic opinion and, in particular, to show academics that we are in touch with them and thus to influence them in a Conservative direction.

I am sure this work will be of great value to the Party and to this Department. We are glad to have you here and I am sure you will enjoy the work.

Yours sincerely

Brendon Sewill

With roughly the salary of an MP and at the age of twenty-three, I arrived at 24 Old Queen Street, then the home of the Conservative Research Department, to prepare for the task of reconnecting the official opposition with key academics in the universities. I joined an office which already included Christopher Patten, Mark Schreiber, Tony Newton, Norman Lamont, John Cope and other subsequently distinguished people. Tim Boswell and I arrived on the same day and shared a ground-floor room.

My arrival at the Conservative Party attracted the attention of the press. On 28 February the *Daily Telegraph* reported that

Mr Spicer was given the special task of compiling a comprehensive and up-to-date roll of Conservative sympathisers among the dons … The intention is to call upon them for studies which may form the basis of policy documents … A primary objective is to restore the traditional Tory image of intellectual superiority in the face of the idea propagated by Mr Wilson that Labour now has the monopoly of eggheads.

Julian Critchley, writing in the *Telegraph* on 7 March 1966, said, 'Mr Spicer has now been recruited to work for Central Office. His task is to tour the universities seeking out Tory dons who may at one time or another be persuaded to serve on the party's many policy committees.'

The appointment was seen rather differently by my contemporary Jonathan Aitken, who wrote as follows in his best-selling book, *The Young Meteors*:[*]

Michael Spicer, then a *Sunday Times* journalist, created an organisation called PEST (Pressure for Economic and Social Toryism). It was a highly successful

---

[*] Jonathan Aitken, *The Young Meteors*, Secker & Warburg, 1967.

thorn in the Tory Party's flesh, calling for many radical reforms, and incidentally making embarrassing and much-publicised demands for the removal of the then leader, Sir Alec Douglas-Home. Such independence could not go unchecked. Frontbenchers such as Iain Macleod and Sir Edward Boyle were soon appearing on PEST platforms, eulogising the organisation for its originality. Michael Spicer was quickly offered a place in the Research Department and a new job was specially created for him. PEST today is a pale shadow of its former self.

Whether or not the new job was specially created to keep me out of mischief, I plunged into it with zest. There were some twenty universities which I visited immediately.

It was all too much for the satirical magazine *Private Eye*. On 18 March 1966 it reprinted a lead article by Iain Sproat (a year later my best man) in the *Sunday Telegraph* headed 'Tory drive to recruit brains trust'. Underneath this, the *Eye* pronounced:

The group's leader ... announced: 'Good afternoon. We are here to recruit academic talent.' At this several fellows opened their eyes and enquired drowsily, 'What's the money like?' After a frank discussion of emoluments two Fellows, both nonagenarians engaged on research into mediaeval costume, agreed to join the preparation of new schemes for the modernisation of the Conservative Party's 'image'. Cheques were exchanged and other Fellows were woken by soft-footed menials bringing in the traditional afternoon port and grated walnuts.

Youngest parliamentary candidate

Coincidentally, just as this piece of vintage *Private Eye* hit the streets I took time out to fight a parliamentary seat at the general election, which fell on 31 March 1966. I need, therefore, to pause in the main narrative to say a word about how this came about.

Egged on by William Rees-Mogg, I began the search for a seat in Parliament in the autumn of 1965. 'The first thing to do is to fight a safe Labour seat at the general election,' William advised me over lunch at the Carlton Club earlier that year. 'If you have any connection there, I would go for somewhere in the north-east. I did.' (He fought Chester-le-Street at a by-election in 1956.) 'I found them wonderful people. There are even one or two Conservatives amongst them. As to getting adopted, there are so many vacancies for candidates that you choose them, rather than the other way round.'

'I do have connections in the region,' I said. 'My father is a Geordie; my grandfather ran a string of banks on Tyneside and was a trustee of the Sir James Knott Foundation [at the time the largest charitable fund in the north].'

'Then I should go ahead,' William advised.

September 1965

The Three Tuns Hotel is one of the two main hostelries which over many centuries have served visitors to the city of Durham. It is at the bottom of the town and is less posh than the County Hotel. Nor does it have the association with the National Union of Mineworkers that is the case with its rival, with its famous balcony past which the miners file in their thousands on Gala Day.

It is appropriate that the Conservatives, being such a minority force in the area, should choose the more modest Three Tuns in which to make the preliminary selection of candidates for the various Labour strongholds around the county of Durham.

I push open the only door I can find and enter a bar which is almost deserted. A small man in a flat cap is perched on his own in a corner of the room beside a round plastic table; in front of him sits a full pint of Newcastle Brown. I approach him. 'You don't happen to know where the Conservative meeting is taking place?' I ask. The man smiles. 'Why-aye, man, this is it.' He speaks in a lilting Geordie accent which I recognise from my father's frequent rendering of 'Blaydon Races' in the bath. 'Are there others expected?' I enquire. 'I hope so, pet. Otherwise we'll have to make do by ourselves. You are?' 'Spicer. Michael Spicer, one of the applicants to be candidate for a Durham county seat.' 'Looks like the only one at the moment.' 'I was told to report here for a preliminary meeting before the more formal one at Chester-le-Street tomorrow afternoon.'

At this point the door blows open and we are joined by a thick-set man dressed in a tweed suit with a bald head and a small moustache. 'I'm Freddie Woods,' he says, 'committee member from Easington'. His accent is less recognisable than the other man's, certainly not Geordie. 'Can I get you a beer? A pint of Vaux?' he asks. 'Thank you.' 'No one else coming?' Woods addresses his question to a boy who has suddenly appeared behind the bar.

When the Easington representative returns to our corner, he says, 'As no one else has turned up, we might as well get on with it. As I understand it, there are three seats going begging: Easington, Houghton-le-Spring and Chester-le-Street. Which one would you like?' Now he is speaking straight to me. 'What's the difference?' I ask warily. 'We've got Manny.' 'Manny?' 'Emanuel Shinwell, the oldest MP in the country and the wickedest. In his eighties, he is a total phoney, like the rest of the Labour Party up here. Changes into working man's clothes at the Grand at West Hartlepool whenever he pays one of his rare visits to the constituency. It's a one-party state here, you know, and it's totally corrupt. But you're not going to change it. It's the way it is. They weigh Labour votes here – too many to count.'

He pauses. I do not try to fill the silence because I can think of nothing to say. 'I'm biased, but I would go for Easington,' he says.

I look for a sign from the man in the cap. He seems to have gone into a trance and there is no help from that quarter. 'Easington it is,' I say. 'Right you are. Now I've met you I'll get together a welcoming party at Chester-le-Street tomorrow. There will be more of us than today. Durham city is a bit awkward for most of our folk; parking is difficult, too many hills; anyway, most of them don't have cars to get here in the first place. By the way, I think we have your details somewhere – probably at the Horden Club. I'm sure I've seen them. Quite impressive. We like the bright young men from London to cut their teeth up here; then when they become famous we feel good about it.'

The meeting the next day is meant to comprise representatives from each of the three vacant constituencies. In fact, only the people from Easington turn up, prompted to do so by Freddie Woods. There are the miner's wife Mrs Mills, the farmer's wife Mrs Bryden, Mrs Ritchie the lawyer's wife, and the wife of a retired naval officer, Mrs Lawson. Also present are Freddie Woods himself and a small man with a dark complexion, sunken eyes and a Glaswegian accent. He remains anonymous. For much of the time he stares at the open coal fire; every so often he sighs and says, 'It's a grand fire.'

Freddie Woods conducts the meeting efficiently; indeed, he despatches the main business within three minutes. He puffs out his chest and says in a voice which is inappropriately loud, 'In the absence of the group agent, who is no doubt working hard somewhere in the county [the man in question is an avid horserace-goer and this probably explains his absence], I call the meeting to order. No point in beating about the bush.' Patting me on the shoulder, he continues, 'This young man wants to get back to London by midnight. I think we're all agreed that he will make a good candidate for Easington and that we should recommend his adoption at the next meeting of our Executive committee, which will convene at the Horden Club on 12 October.'

Everyone claps and says 'Hear, hear', except for Pat Lawson, who says, 'What I bloody well need is a stiff gin and tonic; can I get you one, Michael?'

November 1965

I am formally adopted as prospective Conservative candidate for the Easington division on 11 November.

In my acceptance speech I open with the one about the Archbishop of Canterbury arriving in New York, to be met by a posse of journalists who ask him if he plans to visit any nightclubs while staying in the Big Apple. He replies: 'Are there any nightclubs in New York?' He is surprised by the billboards which emerge that evening throughout the city with the screaming headlines 'First question asked by Archbishop on arrival in New York: "Are there any nightclubs?"' This becomes my slightly tortuous way of indicating that I know a thing or two about the press.

I fought the general election in the two or three weeks leading up to polling day on 31 March 1966 under the red colours of my party in the north-east.* The contest between Shinwell and myself received some attention from the national press. On 18 March Michael Gay, writing in the *Daily Mail* under the headline 'David and Goliath' and a picture of my fiancée, Ann Hunter, and me (we married on 8 April 1967), said, 'At the politically tender age of 23, the youngest candidate in Britain has had the effrontery to challenge the oldest campaigner of them all, 82-year-old Mr Emanuel Shinwell ... His absence from the constituency indicates that he is not particularly worried about the opposition.' Nor had he much cause to be so. On 31 March Shinwell won by 24,747 votes, one of the highest majorities in the country. At the count he advised me to try somewhere else.

It was good of him to talk to me at all as we had almost come to blows on one occasion during the campaign. The incident occurred when one of his supporters snatched my microphone from me in the centre of Peterlee, shouting 'Tories are buggers'. The word 'bugger' has a special use in the north-east and occurs in almost every sentence used by Geordies requiring a pronoun. My friends and helpers from London were not aware of this nuance and joined in robustly with the ensuing melee.

Working for Heath

My main objective after the election was to follow Shinwell's advice and to try to get myself adopted for a winnable seat. I came close, losing by two votes at Falmouth & Camborne (December 1967) and as runner-up at South Cornwall (April 1968), but by the time of the 1970 election I was still fighting

---

* It may come as a surprise, but it is a fact that in the 1960s red was still the colour of the Conservatives in the north-east.

Easington. My new opponent, Jack Dormand, won on 18 June with a slightly lower share of the vote than Shinwell in 1966.

There is a direct tie-up between all this and Edward Heath. On two occasions Easington constituents wrote to him with serious complaints. I was asked to chase these up on his behalf.

The first such occasion concerned a threatened uprooting of two-thirds of the village of Station Town to make room for a new housing development. I was unable to do much to save these poor souls.

I did, however, with the backing of the Heath name, intervene successfully in the second matter. This concerned a Mr Smith of Brissago, Peterlee.

In a letter to Heath dated 1 September 1967, Mr Smith wrote, 'I first became aware of my problem in October 1965 when I was informed by the local petrol pump attendant that it was proposed to build a road through my five-year-old individualistically designed bungalow.'

When Mr Smith objected to the planning authority, he was offered compensation and an alternative site in the local scrapyard. The problem, according to Mr Smith, was that the compensation was totally inadequate in lieu of destroying his 'individualistically designed bungalow' and the site offered was an unfair swap for his present sea view. What Mr Smith did not say in his letter was that by making a fuss he lost his Labour Party membership card and that this put his job as a teacher on the line.

I went into action with the powers that be at County Hall on the orders of Mr Heath. As soon as it was known that I was working at the behest of the Leader of the Opposition, all resistance crumbled. Mr Smith was offered both compensation and an alternative site that he could live with. More importantly, his political credentials were restored. When I next met him in 1970 he was happily 'telling' against me on polling day at the general election. 'I'm so grateful to you, Michael,' he beamed. No wonder Andrew Cunningham* and T. Dan Smith† (two prominent members of the Labour Party in the north-east) found themselves in prison in 1974.

Corruption at this time in Labour circles was endemic. Exposing this is what made fighting a seat like Easington a worthwhile task for a Conservative candidate.

One reason why Heath was able to send me on various missions to the north is that I was now working closely for him in London. Although formally operating out of the Conservative Research Department, I was in direct contact with the leader. With the exception of the brief interlude

---

* Alderman Andrew Cunningham, chairman of the Durham Police Authority.
† Chairman, North East Development Council.

provided by the general election, I was also permanently on the road, visiting universities the length and breadth of the land. Every week I added another half-dozen or so names to my list. Many of these were well-known figures, world-class academics. Others, more junior, provided the 'link men' between the party and the university common rooms.

Not only did I list these names meticulously, I made copious notes on their expertise, personalities and political orientation.

After my first university call at Newcastle (10 February 1966) I wrote about Professor S. R. Dennison: 'Well-known economist; specialises in regional development; probably too senior to act as a link man.'

My notes on historian Robert Blake* at Oxford (visited 23 February 1966) cover a sheet of foolscap, quoting his views on what was holding back academics from supporting the Conservative Party and why this was a bad thing. Blake suggested that we set up a council of link men in Oxford.

Professor Asa Briggs at Sussex (visited 20 May 1966) pressed for Conservative MPs to visit his university.

Others, for instance Professor Wiseman, York (visited 24 May 1966), wanted to hold dinners for shadow Cabinet members to help 'construct a coherent philosophy for the Conservative Party'.

At Birmingham (visited 31 May 1966) I met Professor Alan Walters, who later became Margaret Thatcher's chief economic adviser.

Professor Bauer at the LSE (visited 3 June 1966) had very clear and controversial views about developing countries.

Professor Prest in Manchester (visited 4 July 1966) agreed to sponsor a dinner in Manchester.

At the Manchester Business School (also visited 4 July 1966) I met Professor D. C. Hague, joint author of a famous economics textbook,† who became a close friend and a member of the Prices Commission and, later, adviser to Margaret Thatcher's Policy Unit at 10 Downing Street; for this he received a knighthood, becoming Sir Douglas Hague.

The last university report I can find is dated 19 May 1967, by which time I had collected some 500 names of potential academic sympathisers.

The big question now was how best to involve this galaxy of very eminent potential advisers without upsetting any one of them. Some time later, writing in the *Daily Telegraph* on 26 June 1968, Anthony Lejeune put the question in a large centre page article like this:

---

*   Later Lord Blake, biographer of Disraeli.

†   Alfred W. Stonier and Douglas C. Hague, *A Textbook of Economic Theory*, Longmans, Green & Co., 1953.

Having found your intellectuals and entered into dialogue with them, how do you keep the relationship alive and make it fruitful? If they happen to be economists or political scientists or specialists in some other relevant discipline, they can be co-opted onto policy committees and recommended to television producers who want someone to balance a left-wing specialist. Mediaeval historians or Celtic archaeologists, however, are less readily employable. Last summer a Conservative seminar was attended by two or three hundred dons and there will be a seminar this year on technology.

Michael Spicer is probably correct in believing that … the Conservative Party needs intellectuals and needs the support of intellectuals … the Labour Party has visibly become in many ways 'the stupid party', tied to dogmas and shifts of expediency which are simply not intellectually defensible.

I was aware of the problem of what to do with my lists from the very beginning. No sooner was the 1966 general election out of the way than I began bombarding Heath with ideas as to how we might take matters forward. In a letter to him dated 4 April 1966 I asked:

As for the future, would it be a good idea to extend the type of network which we have been establishing in the universities to cover all 'expert' bodies and professions, such as architects, engineers, social scientists etc.?

This might result in the formation of an independent research unit whose function it would be to seek out, formalise and channel relevant advice. I feel that something more concrete is needed than the present arrangements for ad hoc liaison from the Research Department.

This was a bit cheeky given that I had only been in the Conservative Research Department for two months. Nevertheless the long-suffering Ted Heath wrote back to me in less than two weeks. In a letter dated 18 April, he said, 'I was interested to have your suggestions about an independent research unit, to build contacts with expert bodies and professions. We must discuss your ideas soon.'

In practice the next step was taken over a year later when I organised a conference on economic policy, chaired by Iain Macleod, the shadow Chancellor of the Exchequer, and attended by some 350 academics on 20 May 1967.

Angus Maude

The first serious attempt to systemise the arrangements was launched on 17 March 1967. After several conversations with Edward Heath, Angus Maude was appointed to head up a futuristic study of social and economic trends into the 1980s. I received the following letter dated 1 May from Brendon Sewill, director of the Conservative Research Department.

Dear Michael

I am writing to confirm your appointment in charge of our Systems Research Study of Social and Economic Trends into the 1980s. I am arranging for your salary to be increased to the rate of £1,900 a year, backdated to 1 April 1967, with increments of £100 on 1 January each year.

You will naturally be working closely with Angus Maude, putting him in touch with the appropriate academic experts, servicing his Steering Group, organising whatever studies are required and helping to draft the final report. At present I am hoping that you will be able to produce the report in about the autumn of 1968.

The study will clearly require the use of many modern techniques, including systems analysis. As you point out, however, we do not know enough about these new techniques to enable us to be precise at this stage about the type and amount of technical assistance that would be required. It would therefore be valuable for you to familiarise yourself with the particular scope and method of the various new techniques. Then after one or two meetings of the Steering Group it should be possible to obtain direct technical backing.

You should, however, regard the Angus Maude exercise as your main purpose: the application of new knowledge about new techniques to other aspects of party policy will be supplementary. In particular, this means that you must devote a major part of your energies this summer to getting the Angus Maude exercise into full operation.

While writing, I should congratulate you on the excellent work you have done in building up our contacts in universities. As I see it, the Angus Maude study of the 1980s follows naturally out of this work. It could provide a method of involving many of our academic friends in the formulation of policy and the wonderful source of new ideas about the future.

Although I am sure that the study of the 1980s will be very much a full time task, I would also like you so far as time permits to continue to expand our university contacts in the UK, to complete the record of these contacts and keep it up to date and continue to organise national dinners or seminars as appropriate.

I am certain that the study of the 1980s can be made a very impressive piece of work. It could have an important effect on the future of the Conservative Party and of our policies for the future of the country. It is a big opportunity for you and I hope you will make the most of it.

Yours,

Brendon Sewill

The Maude project made a big splash in the press. Writing the lead article in the *Daily Telegraph* on 17 March, Harry Boyne, the political correspondent, said, 'It is Mr Heath's firm conviction that post-war governments, including the Conservatives, have erred in failing to look and think far enough ahead. The "Britain in the 80s" survey is intended to repair this omission.'

It didn't work out. Maude, who was out of sorts with Ted Heath, was not the right man for the job. He was bored by it and was hard to pin down. He was much more interested in attacking Heath's 'materialistic' approach to economic growth (Maude didn't believe in growth). The climax of my frustration came when I organised a meeting of senior academics which Maude was meant to chair but to which he failed to turn up.

On 3 January 1968 the indefatigable Brendon Sewill wrote to me:

> I know, and share, your disappointment that the 1985 exercise has not worked out better from your point of view … You know that everyone here would be delighted if, at any time in the future, you can invent a new project which would give you an excuse to come back and join us again.

In truth, the breakdown of the Maude exercise, and my resignation from it, was not entirely Maude's fault.* My heart, too, was not in it. During the course of the previous two years I became increasingly interested in the new techniques being developed across the Atlantic for the collation and analysis of data to help make political decisions.

In the process of searching out new ways to proceed, I came into contact with Mervyn Pike, Member of Parliament for Melton Mowbray. Mervyn was assistant Postmaster General and a junior Home Office minister in the Macmillan administration. Under Heath she became a member of the shadow Cabinet in 1966 as shadow Secretary of State for Social Services. Perhaps because of her health, which by this time was poor, she left the shadow Cabinet in 1967. By the time I met her in the same year, she was restless and under-employed. She had also at that time considerable private means, which she had inherited through the family ownership of the second largest clay-mining company in the country, Watts Blake Bearn.

My interest in applying computer-based technology to policy-making

---

* It is ironic that the next occasion on which the task of preparing for government was undertaken systematically was under David Cameron, with Angus Maude's son, Francis, in charge. Prior to being asked to do this job Francis Maude, like his father, had been removed from a key position – in Francis's case the chairmanship of the party, and in Angus's the shadow ministership for colonial affairs.

fascinated her, though she would be the first to acknowledge that she was by no means versed in the subject herself. Her close friend Dame Susan Walker, who was one of the Conservative Party's most senior officials, was also increasingly involved. Together they brought enthusiasm, knowledge of the party, money and a highly influential network of friends in the United States.

Conservative Systems Research Centre

An undated letter from Mervyn Pike to me gives a flavour of her commitment to a project from which grew the formation of the Conservative Systems Research Centre, with Mervyn as its chairman and myself as its director. In part her letter reads:

> I have arranged to see Ted at 12.30 on Monday for a drink to tell him what I am up to and to arrange that he meets the three of us later in the week. Monday couldn't be a more awkward day as I am meant to be in the cattle market but thought I had better get him whilst the going was good.

At a meeting at 10 o'clock in the morning on 22 May 1968 in his flat in the Albany, Ted Heath formally agreed to the formation of the Conservative Systems Research Centre, with me as its director. A note in my diary for that day says, 'The meeting went extremely smoothly, I wonder whether too smoothly. Heath agreed to everything and told us to start with the tax exercises and then move into the public expenditure project. Afterwards Mervyn and I go to Fortnum's to celebrate with buns and coffee.'

I was right to be worried. I was setting up a brand new organisation outside the mainstream of the Conservative Research Department, which was run by Brendon Sewill under the overall direction of the formidable Sir Michael Fraser. The formation of CSRC was guaranteed to cause resentment in the official Research Department. What is more, Brian Reading, the party's chief economic adviser, questioned the theoretical justification for what we were doing.

A further note in my diary for 20 November 1968 reads, 'Mervyn made a telephone call to Heath in the light of Brian Reading's reservations. Heath seems to be backing us. This is the essential point. We can go forward fearlessly now.' However, the matter did not rest there. On 12 February 1969 at 3.00 p.m. a meeting was held between Douglas Hurd, the head of Heath's office, Brian Reading and myself. I was invited to defend my cause. The next day at 4.00 p.m. Heath became involved himself.

It is unsurprising that the first and, so far as I know, the only, attempt by a political party to use what are even now highly sophisticated computer techniques to analyse policy created this frisson. Even I, writing in the academic magazine *Technology & Society* on 2 October 1969, under the rather pretentious title of 'The Mathematics of Choice', stressed that the policy of a party would depend ultimately upon the values and interests it espoused. The 'What?' choice was for politicians; the 'How?' choice might be assisted by modern technology. 'This is of more than academic interest,' I wrote. 'The temptation for political parties – particularly in opposition – to promise something for everyone and to proclaim each item in the name of "philoso-phy" is very great; and they have succumbed liberally to this temptation.'

And so, with the assistance of some of the academics I had met, we began the process of placing on the computer the inter-relationships between expenditure and taxation policies and the resource limitations that would inevitably constrain the policies. We used the most advanced econometric techniques that were available, such as input/output analysis and linear programming. We set up shop in Mervyn's office at 1 Bridge Street, an old building looking out on Westminster Bridge which was later replaced by Portcullis House.

I was not totally starry eyed about what we were doing. In the winter edition of *Public Administration*, I wrote, 'The model forced a consideration of the opportunity costs/priorities attached to policy … The emphasis remained, however, on cost. The question of need and impact was largely ignored.' Moreover, I added, 'political action is largely a function of alliances of muddled objectives … Political parties do depend on the support of conflicting interest groups to achieve a majority.'* Despite these caveats, the show went on.

A major feature in the office was the physical presence of a new-generation screen-based computer terminal linked to a massive Control Data 6600 machine in Victoria. This was probably the first computer terminal ever to exist within the precincts of the Palace of Westminster. So advanced and, for its time, powerful was this technology that Heath agreed to open the extended Control Data facilities on 23 September 1969.

In the event, he had to switch his plans and on 10 September wrote to Mervyn as follows:

Dear Mervyn

I am so sorry that I have to let you down about coming to the Control Data offices on the 23rd. I now see that this is going to be a very busy day and I have to go off to Leeds for three days on the morning of the 24th.

---

* A view articulated at the time in Charles E. Lindblom, 'The Science of Muddling Through', *Public Administration Review* 19(2) (Spring 1959), pp. 79–88.

I understand that Iain* has said he will come in my place: I am so glad. Thank you for the report on the public expenditure and taxation models. I am glad to have this and will study it. When you are ready for the initial run please let my office know and if I possibly can I will come over to Bridge Street.

Yours,

Ted

Heath did visit us at Bridge Street. Following this he wrote a letter to me dated 15 April 1970:

Dear Michael

I should have written before to say how enjoyable and profitable my morning was with you all last Friday. Please thank everyone concerned.

I will further extend my knowledge of this field next Friday and I understand that you will join me at F2 early that morning to drive to ICL.

Yours,

Ted Heath

The visit to ICL merits a quick footnote. The company had two buildings on either side of Putney Bridge. I turned up at the wrong one, on the south bank. The building was completely deserted except for a cleaner, who told me everyone had gone to the other building to meet 'some bigwig or other who is having a look round'. I rushed across the bridge just in time to meet Heath as he arrived.

A few months later I accompanied Iain Macleod to the Control Data offices, as foreshadowed in Heath's letter to Mervyn. Iain put up a magnificent show on 23 September, saying that he had always been an unreconstructed admirer of Control Data technology. He could not express adequately how proud he was to launch its latest computer, which he knew to be the largest in the world.

Back at the House of Commons Iain and I passed one of his more senior MP colleagues, to whom he said: 'You will be pleased to know that I've just come back from some company called Control Data, about which I know not a sausage.'

Iain Macleod confided to me when I lunched with him at his house, The White Cottage, Potters Bar, on 24 September 1967 that he could never make up his mind in his youth whether to be an actor or a politician, 'between which there is not much difference'. On the same occasion he admitted to never holding surgeries, 'because they attract loonies like bees to a honeypot'.

---

* Iain Macleod.

It is with Iain also, together with Bill Shearman, our candidate in West Ham, and David Owen, then a health minister, that I helped to start Crisis at Christmas, now Crisis. We began with a march to draw attention to the plight of the homeless at Christmas. Rather surreally, this ended with us all sharing a large fish at a Chinese restaurant (a rare place at that time) in the East End.

The nature of the work at the Conservative Systems Research Centre reflected the approach of some of the burgeoning think tanks in the United States. I paid my first visit there in the autumn of 1969, for three weeks, sponsored by the Carnegie Corporation, with whom Professor Hague had close connections.

Often in politics the publicity for a venture as significant as what we were doing at the Systems Research Centre comes before the results are apparent. Not in this case. It was not until 26 May 1970 that Conservative Central Office issued a press release, which read:

'The Conservative Party's preparation for government is backed up by the most intensive research ever carried out by any political party in this country [probably not an exaggeration].

As part of this research, over the past few years a team of economists, mathematicians and computer experts have been creating a computerised policy information system. They have had the help of some of the most eminent academics in this field.

The system, which is in two parts, deals with taxation and public expenditure policy.

As foreshadowed by Mr Iain Macleod at the Conservative Party Conference in Blackpool in 1968, the tax model permits detailed examination of the effects of alternative taxation policies on prices and on the standard of living of 45 separate households ... price ranges are measured for 34 separate types of goods and for four special price indices. 1973/74 has been selected as the year in which the public expenditure model should examine alternative combinations and levels of expenditure saving policies under varying conditions. These policies have been assessed in terms of the demand they make on available budgetary and physical resources. Among the physical resources are 23 categories of commodities and imports and five categories of labour. The effects of these policies on prices and regional expenditure have also been included.

The value of this policy information system is threefold. First, it prevents inconsistencies between policies. Second, it indicates the range of conditions under which expenditure policies may be feasible. Third, it shows the range of policy choice offered to the party. The system, which is computerised, is flexible and dynamic.

Despite the fact that a general election was in the offing, and there were bigger news stories about, this press release generated media attention. *The Guardian*, for instance (hardly a friend of the Conservative Party), ran it over two columns on its front page. Near the end of this it mischievously said:

> With an engaging frankness which will probably endear him to Mr Wilson and Labour candidates everywhere, Mr Spicer goes on to say that 'the question is how do the Conservatives square these conflicting objectives and constraints? How do they intend to control public expenditure on the one hand and on the other to manage what appears to be an increasing budget?'

The Guardian predictably left out my answer to those questions. This is that the system 'forced' you to make choices and set priorities until the revenue constraints were met.

What all this goes to show is that under Ted Heath the Conservative Party prepared for office in a way that no other opposition has done either before or since. The techniques for analysing data were years in advance of their time and indeed the approach that lay behind their use has never been repeated. The resulting display of competence was undoubtedly a major contributor to the victory in 1970. However, it is not possible to argue from this that opposition parties should always go for the detailed approach to policy that was the case under Ted Heath. Tony Blair won a massive victory in 1997 with no policies at all. In 2010 there was little attempt by any of the parties to produce policies which would 'add up' to solving the £150 billion deficit. Nor is it the case that heavy preparation for government necessarily means that the right decisions are taken once the party in question gets into office.

The preparation for government undertaken by Ted Heath went, of course, much further than the project with which I was involved. The suite of offices next door to the one I occupied under Mervyn Pike's name in 1 Bridge Street was taken up by my colleague Mark Schreiber (now Lord Marlesford), who, with the patronage of Ernest Marples, was charged with the task of creating an administrative blueprint for government. It was Mark who, together with David Howell, invented the term 'war on waste'. Meanwhile in the Research Department very bright men, including Brian Reading, were preparing an economic game plan under the leadership of Iain Macleod.

It was all a massively impressive operation on several fronts. It was not, however, the precursor of a particularly effective administration. On the contrary, either through bad luck or ineptitude, the Heath government was thrown out of office at the end of its first term.

As for the 1970 general election itself, my one encounter with Heath during the campaign was at a Young Conservatives' barbecue in Richmond, Yorkshire, at the home of Tim Kitson, Heath's parliamentary private secretary. The evening was billed as informal and fun, with the attraction of a popular local band. The promise was that Heath would drop in for a few minutes. When I arrived, the barn in which the event was to take place was full of young people. Beer was in plentiful supply; the band was in good form and everyone was having a wonderful time.

Heath arrived earlier than expected. He was cheered and the band went silent. Heath immediately mounted the crude stage and began to deliver himself of the seven points (industrial relations, taxation, defence etc.) which had provided the backbone to his campaign. After twenty minutes of respectful silence, the cry went up: 'Give us back our band.' Totally unruffled, Heath completed a 45-minute oration and honour was satisfied, although the evening was not quite the same thereafter. Edifying it may have been. Fun it was not. Sensitivity to the mood of the moment was never a Heath trademark.

After Heath's electoral victory on 18 June 1970, our paths crossed only once again in any substantive way. I watched from a distance the transformation of a government whose objectives had been determined at the meeting at Selsdon Park into an interventionist, strike-ridden administration whose self-professed greatest achievement was the 1972 Treaty of Accession (to the European Common Market). Despite the preparation, perhaps precisely because in opposition there had been too much attention to detail, the Heath government turned out to be directionless and without a clear strategic purpose.

My time over the next four years was taken up in securing a winnable parliamentary seat and in setting up an economic consulting company called Economic Models Limited. After getting close in Thirsk & Malton, Chester, Ripon, Melton Mowbray, Braintree, Arundel and Tynemouth, I was finally selected in late December 1973 to fight South Worcestershire, following the sudden death of Sir Gerald Nabarro. My only connection with the constituency was that in 1967, on the advice and with the financial support of my father, Ann and I spent the first two nights of our honeymoon at the famous Lygon Arms hotel in Broadway. Other than that, all I knew about my new constituency was that to get to it you turned right halfway down the M4 and kept driving through the Cotswold Hills until you descended steeply at Broadway to the fields of leeks and fruit trees of the Vale of Evesham.

Ann was pregnant with our third child, Annabel (Edward was born on 16 January 1969 and Antonia on 26 September 1971), and did not come with me to the early rounds of the interviews for the candidacy. I was asked if I had any skeletons in the cupboard. I said, 'Mind your own business,' which was apparently the right answer, and I got the job.

My first task on New Year's Eve was to help welcome Prime Minister Heath to the constituency. He paid a lightning visit to give a pep talk at the memorial hall at Upton-upon-Severn to the party workers, who were about to launch into a by-election campaign. The gist of Heath's speech was that there was no way, no way at all, that the government would back off from the threatened miners' strike; nor would his administration abrogate responsibility by calling a general election, despite all that was being said to this effect in the press. It followed that within the next few weeks we in South Worcestershire would be fighting our by-election.

Heath rubbed in these sentiments when I met him after the speech in the home of the Conservative Association's chairman, Major Maurice Jewell. Heath was sitting in the corner of the room in a large leather chair beside an open fire. Outside in the drive police outriders were revving their engines and the Prime Minister's Humber was warming up for departure. Over a second glass of malt whisky, Heath relaxed and stressed to me that I would be in the heat of the kitchen as the miners' unrest worsened and the eyes of the world turned to us.

I told him that I could probably cope. 'The main thing', I said, 'is not to call a general election in the present atmosphere, especially if the miners go for an all-out strike – even if this means that I lose the by-election.'

Heath appeared to agree. It was the last serious conversation, after so many in the past ten years, that I had with him. In the following years we would avoid each other from opposite sides of the party's deep chasm on Europe.

The officers of my association were deeply concerned by what Heath had said. So worried were they that early in the new year they travelled to London to see Lord Carrington, the party chairman. They told him that a by-election in South Worcestershire would produce a debacle. 'The Liberals would pounce on our new candidate and it would be a rout,' my chairman warned.

Unbeknown to Major Jewell, the issue being debated amongst the people at the top of the party was not whether there would be an early general election, but when; a favoured date for many was 7 February. In the end this was ruled out by procrastination and the passage of time in favour of 28 February. The rest is history. It was not Ted Heath's finest hour.

Fall of the Heath government

Why did he change his mind? In his book *An End to Promises*,* Douglas Hurd, at the time Heath's political adviser, speculates on whether it was more to do with the quadrupling of oil prices and the prospect of an immediate recession than the threatening miners' strike. This may well be so. At the time it seemed as though Heath had simply been worn down by those around him who thought that he would win the argument about who governed Britain.

Whether or not the economy determined Heath's decision to go to the country, it certainly affected the outcome of the February election. Labour won with a majority of four over the Conservatives in a hung parliament.

My maiden speech on 9 May from the opposition back-benches I think captures the essence of what was going on in the economy. I spoke not only as a new Member of Parliament but also as the founder of Economic Models.

The constituency of Worcestershire South is large and far-flung. From the government scientists, pensioners and schoolmasters of Malvern in the west, to the market gardeners of the Vale of Evesham in the east, from the farmers in the northern part of the constituency on the boundaries of the City of Worcester to the hoteliers and coffee shop owners of Broadway in the foot of the Cotswolds to the south, my constituents have two characteristics in common. With very few exceptions they do not earn their living from big business. With even fewer exceptions they are not supported by big unions. My constituents do not belong to the big battalions. They are in-between people. They are almost to a man and to a woman members of the middle classes. In the mould of the British middle classes down the ages, they have a strict and I suppose some might say narrow code of conduct. It is based on private thrift, self-help and of public allegiance to an incorruptible and protective government. It is no mean ethic which has attracted the lifetime imagination of such master historians as R. H. Tawney and has contributed in good part to the character and living style of our nation.

It is these middle classes in my constituency who have been disillusioned, disabused and undermined by a continuous set of events over the last twenty years ... It is not hyperbole to suggest that the middle classes of my constituency are on the brink of revolt. They are outraged by current events. The main reasons are the rate of inflation, currently running, I believe, at around 20 per cent per annum...

To those Honourable Members who, if they were permitted to do so by convention, would accuse me of being alarmist, I offer two points ... First, it

---

* Douglas Hurd, *An End to Promises*, Collins, 1979.

is a historical fact that, with the exception of Iceland, no western country has suffered a rate of inflation of over 20 per cent and remained a democracy. It is well to remember that the middle classes, who in normal times are the sheet anchor of democracy, can be its greatest adversaries when they are whipped into fury, as in the case of Peronism, by perceived national failures or, more usually, by savage inflation. There is no need to remind the House that the pre-war fascism of Austria and Germany was not, as has been popularly supposed, the result of an alliance between business and the working movement. It was in essence a revolt of the middle classes, as was the Poujadist movement in France in the mid-1950s.

It is in this sense that what goes on in my constituency and, I believe, in surrounding constituencies has a wider significance. The British middle classes, traditionally loyal and providing the dynamo of our country, are today boiling over with anger…

The recent mass rallies in Malvern and Evesham, marches in Worcester and Solihull, the demagoguery, the anger and abuse which is hurled almost indiscriminately at any platform speaker who appears even remotely on behalf of the establishment, or the government, at any level, are the release of the pent-up anger and frustration of people who believe in the virtue of thrift but see the value of their savings declining by one fifth every year.

The member called to follow my speech was the future economic spokesman for the Liberal Party, John Pardoe, MP for North Cornwall. It is the tradition that the speaker who follows a maiden speech should say something nice about it. Pardoe certainly did that. Indeed, some might say he went over the top: 'I congratulate the Honourable Member for Worcestershire South on a notable maiden speech. It was not only a notable maiden speech, but a notable speech by any standard. It was one of the most penetrating economic speeches I have heard in the House for a long time.' My own view is that it is not only the first but also the best speech I made in the chamber of the House of Commons in my thirty-six years there.

The skill and the art of parliamentary debating are developed either before you enter the place or early on in your career as a Member of Parliament. As orators there are very few late developers. Although it has to be said that the ability to speak well, in particular on the floor of the House, is a useful asset, it is not the only or even the most important one required of a successful politician. Another is the capacity simply to hang around and to be available, to linger at the end of meetings. If you can't be a good speaker, be a good listener.

In my early years in Parliament I was neither. Having been elected, my main concern was to make money – at least enough of it not to have to depend on a parliamentary salary. In my case this meant being able to educate three children and buy a home in the constituency and one in London.

Chapter 3

Elmer B. Staats:
Comptroller General of the United States

The pay of an MP at the time was minimal, around £3,000 net, out of which he or she typically had to pay about £1,000 to make up a secretary's salary to £3,000 gross. The salary in 1974 – a time of galloping inflation – was roughly what I had been earning ten years earlier as a twenty-year-old employee of the Conservative Party. On this salary you had either to have an outside job, or you had private means, or you were very poor. I knew members of the Commons who lived in dormitories, bought oranges for breakfast, and hoped to be invited to open a restaurant at least once a week in return for a wholesome meal.

The way I made my family financially secure was to take to the market some of the ideas I had developed for the Conservative Party in opposition. I formed a consultancy company with two of my best economist friends, Professor Douglas Hague and Professor Jim Ball. Jim was developing with his assistant, Terry Burns, an econometric forecasting model which he ran through the London Business School.

In 1970 I named my company Economic Models Limited. Mervyn Pike was the chairman; second in command was Charles Stancomb, an old school chum who preceded me as head boy at Wellington. My close Cambridge friend and brilliant financial adviser David Kleeman joined the board. He did the same for my son Edward when he started a very similar company some thirty years later.

Economic Models set up shop at West Eaton Place, near Sloane Square, in the basement of a beautiful house with a pretty garden belonging to an architect; it was next door to where Mervyn lived when she was in London. The company was financed from the start on the back of one or two large contracts we collected, mainly in the United States, thanks largely to Mervyn's contacts there. For instance, she was very friendly with the top brass of the American Medical Association, for whom we undertook a highly lucrative piece of work comparing the British and American health systems.

At the same time we built an econometric model for the British Aircraft Corporation to provide them with the tool for deciding between building

Concorde and a competitor to the Boeing and Lockheed passenger aircrafts, the BAC 311. As economists we came out against Concorde and were promptly sacked. To compensate for this, we secured a contract in the north-east which required us to set up an office in Peterlee new town; we did this under the management of a brilliant young economist, Norman Glass.[*]

The income stream generated in particular by our American business enabled us to develop a core service of providing econometric models and forecasts. Our clients could access this service in off-peak time on a world-wide network provided via satellite and hosted by a fast computer system in the United States owned by General Electric. Quite uniquely, for a few years we provided what was in effect a personal computer service ten years before PCs were invented.

After a few years we moved into very grand offices in a seven-storey building, 30 Old Queen Street, almost next door to where I once worked for the Conservative Party. By this time we employed several very bright young econometricians. The money continued to flow in from America, to which eventually I commuted, often on a monthly basis, invariably flying on the Friday morning Concorde (ironic that we had advised its cancellation), arriving in New York at 9.00 a.m. and leaving on Saturday or Sunday to be in Parliament on Monday morning.

Life in New York was good, especially when Mervyn accompanied us. With a small office at 527 Madison Avenue, we lived in style in the Carlyle or the Stanhope Hotel, where we became quite friendly with legendary pianists such as Bobby Short and George Fayer.

There is one particular marketing venture in the United States which bears recording in some detail. Sitting on the twenty-fifth floor in our small Midtown New York office was our single full-time employee, a dark-haired lady of South American origin in her early thirties, whom I will call Dominique in order to save myself from the danger of being sued for defamation of character. (This is almost the only occasion in this book when I do not use a real name. The other relates to those whose letters to me triggered the vote of confidence in Iain Duncan Smith.) Dominique's job was to scout for business for us in the US and to carry out research tasks which needed to be completed on the spot. She had brought in no business herself after being in post for a year.

In the spring of 1973 we decided to launch a major marketing project in the US. For this purpose we hired the main banqueting suite in the Plaza Hotel, arguably the most prestigious marketing platform in America. We

---

[*] Later director of the National Centre for Social Research.

planned to fill this with 300–400 of the top business leaders on the east coast of the United States. The hook would be a presentation of Economic Models' prowess. The bait would be Elmer Staats.

Elmer Staats was Comptroller General of the United States, possibly the most powerful position in the American government besides that of President. Part of the basis of this power is that Comptroller General is one of the very few posts in Washington which is not necessarily in the gift of the President of the day. Supreme Court judges and the chairman of the Federal Reserve are in much the same position. The Comptroller General's job as head of the General Accounting Office (GAO) makes him more responsible to Congress than to the President, whose administration is subject to his or her constant probes and checks.

I knew Elmer when Nixon was head of state; he had been appointed by Lyndon Johnson. I met him through my association with a project looking at the accountability of governments on both sides of the Atlantic, sponsored by the Carnegie Corporation and run at the British end by Douglas Hague.

The joke is that Elmer was the only man in the world arrogant enough to spell his surname backwards the same way as he spelt it forwards. In reality, he was an extremely pleasant, modest, academic person. I dined at his home in Washington on 12 September 1969. Although he had remote-controlled garage doors (the first time I have ever seen these) his house was an integral part of rich suburbia, but no more. We met in his office and he drove me to his house himself. Despite appearances he was an extremely important person. Some measure of this is that his previous job was executive director of the National Security Council.

I invited him to speak at the Plaza lunch and he accepted. It was fixed that the United States Air Force would fly him from Washington to a secret Air Force base near New York and back so that he could return to his desk in the capital by 4.30 p.m. We did not know at the time that his speech would be the GAO's first public comment on the burgeoning Watergate crisis, which would ultimately destroy Richard Nixon.

Dominique's job was to lay on a suitably high-level audience for Elmer Staats. For this purpose we set up what was by our standards a massive budget to include, for instance, the purchase of the best available marketing list. Dominique was over the moon and was still bubbling with enthusiasm when I spoke to her on the telephone the night before Mervyn, Charles Stancomb, Terry Burns and I departed for New York on the eve of the lunch. 'Michael, this is going to be a very great occasion,' she said.

'I assume we will fill the dining room with top-grade people?' I asked.

'I promise you you will be surprised,' was her reply.

It was only as she greeted us at New York's John F. Kennedy airport that she told me, 'There was something wrong with the mail list and we have had nil response.' She was too devastated to tell me the truth in advance of our departure from London.

I did not take in the full significance of what she told me and said, 'Then we will need to collect people off the street, give them a free lunch – drunks, meths drinkers from Central Park, the lot. We have got to provide Staats with an audience.' It was a crazy idea of mine; there simply was not time. The lunch was twelve hours away. In any case, it is likely that even the meths drinkers in Central Park were aware of the fact that there is no such thing as a free lunch.

We drove straight from the airport to the Plaza Hotel and I found the banqueting manager. I assured him that we would pay as if there were 250 people in the room. Then I requested that a shield of flowers be placed at the front of the speaking platform in an attempt to hide the speaker from his 'audience'. I asked that the bright lights should be focused straight at the speaker and the rest turned out; finally, I requested that as many waiters and hotel staff as possible be collected and sat down in the room for the duration of our guest's speech.

Fortunately Elmer was late. When he did arrive I took him straight to the podium where he broke out into profuse apologies for his lateness. For this he was clapped and cheered by the waiters lurking in the darkened room. Elmer, now in the height of good spirits, delivered a speech which by 6.00 p.m. was blazoned from the billboards throughout the land, the first take by the government's Accounting Agency on the Watergate scandal.

Afterwards he wrote to me to thank me for laying on such a wonderful platform. He was either extremely polite or myopic. Economic Models was flooded out with letters from senior executives from all over the country asking why they had not been invited to such an important event.

Despite this excitement, Economic Models was a brake on my political career. Because I was running a commercial operation in London and New York I was not as available as I should have been in the House of Commons, although I was a regular member of Finance Bill standing committees. My frequent absence from Parliament, often abroad, is no doubt one reason why I was not as in touch as I should have been with the political demise of Ted Heath and with the waning of his strength within the parliamentary party.

The right wing of the party, in particular, was restless. In their view Heath had as Prime Minister deserted the original 'Selsdon agenda'. There was also the growing suspicion that what he had done in Europe went far deeper than merely attaching ourselves to a trade bloc, that the 1972

Act of Accession might have been the foundation for the surrender of the country's ability to govern itself.

Keith Joseph

The person first chosen to represent this growing disillusionment with Ted Heath was Keith Joseph, an attractive intellectual who was quickly perceived to be no more than that and certainly not to possess the singleness of purpose and the ruthlessness required of a leader.

At about this time, Keith paid a visit to my constituency to speak at a modest party wine and cheese event. When I met him at the station you would have thought he was about to address a meeting of the United Nations. In the car driving to the black and white cottage we had rented in Wick, just outside Pershore, his questions came thick and fast. How many people would be there? Would they be friendly? How often did we hold these meetings? Who had the previous speakers been? All this from one of the best-known politicians in the land. The whole process reached a climax when, the moment we reached the cottage, he demanded to use the bathroom; from this he emerged half an hour later with blood dripping from his face, which was patched with blobs of cotton wool – the apparent result of his attempt to shave himself.

The fact is that Keith, lovely man though he was, was not quite right for the top job. What I did not anticipate was the person who came forward to fill the gap.

Chapter 4

Margaret Thatcher, 1979–83: first term

From my personal point of view the fall of Edward Heath in February 1975 and the succession of Margaret Thatcher was a calamity. I voted for Heath in the first round, mainly on the grounds that as an army officer's son, you stand by the commanding officer. I watched Thatcher's acceptance speech on television with Ann in our bedroom at the Chewton Glen Hotel just outside New Milton in Hampshire, where Economic Models was organising yet another high-powered conference. I was under no illusion as to what her arrival meant for me. I did not know her and what she knew of me she did not trust. Even after I had acted as her parliamentary private secretary some ten years later, and had arguably become more of a Thatcherite than she was, she remained suspicious.

Cecil Parkinson in his autobiography puts it like this:[*]

> Michael Spicer, my PPS, had come with me from the Department of Trade into Central Office and I found him a valuable ally.
>
> Michael had already had a successful career as a computer specialist and had built up his own business and sold it. He is a very gifted person; a published novelist, a talented painter, and very competent, with an unfailing sense of humour. He is also extremely efficient and given a job to do does it very well. As a very young man he had fought two general elections against Emanuel Shinwell at Easington, County Durham. He had started Pressure for Economic & Social Toryism (PEST), which subsequently became the Tory Reform Group, and this earned him a reputation as a 'wet', which stuck with him long after he had become very dry. In fact, PEST probably earned its left wing label because it was youthful and anti-establishment, rather than because of any particular policy proposal. He upset the party establishment by attacking Alec Douglas-Home's selection for the leadership of the Conservative Party. Many of its publications were actually rather market-orientated, and it was always firmly opposed to the various bodged attempts to introduce any

---

[*] Cecil Parkinson, *Right at the Centre*, Weidenfeld & Nicolson, 1996

form of incomes policy. However, I have no doubt that Michael's involvement in PEST made Mrs Thatcher suspicious of him and I always felt that he would have been promoted into government much earlier but for this connection. Initially he worked as my Personal Assistant but three months after my appointment, when I reorganised the management of Central Office, at my request he was made a Vice-Chairman of the Party with responsibility to me for the day-to-day operations of the office.

Nigel Lawson

My interest in economics brought me into contact with one of Margaret Thatcher's chief lieutenants, Nigel Lawson, who was increasingly important as a spokesman on economic affairs. He consulted me at one point on whether I thought Professor Jim Ball (a director of Economic Models) would be suitable as chief economic adviser to a future Conservative government. I said something flippant like 'Terry Burns* would be cheaper'; what I did not anticipate is that Terry Burns it eventually was.

On one occasion Nigel Lawson objected to one of Economic Models' highly publicised economic forecasts of Britain's balance of payments deficit, unemployment and inflation. I felt I had to put up a show of confidence in our work and offered to take on a bet with him that we were right. The wager was written down in Nigel's hand in three columns. In the left-hand column was written, 'In 1978: Balance of Payments deficit on current account, Unemployment, Inflation.' My three forecasts (or, rather, those of Economic Models) were in the second column, Nigel's in the third. We both signed the document, although Nigel's signature has become rather faint.

I would not be telling the story if I had not won the bet.

When the Conservatives won the 1979 election I was made a parliamentary private secretary to Sally Oppenheim, minister of state at the Department of Trade and Industry. I was extremely fortunate to sell Economic Models at a good price to the Computer Science Corporation (CSC), on the west coast of America. With the proceeds I bought a house in Worcestershire and exchanged my house in Kennington for one in Westminster.

CSC resold Economic Models to McGraw Hill, who put it together with our main competitor, Data Resources Inc. It became the largest econometric company in the world, with branches in fifty-eight cities in North America, Europe, Australia and South Africa. After a short spell as a consultant, I broke

---

* Then statistical assistant to Professor Ball, mainly working on the LBS econometric forecasting model.

all contact with the company and sought fame, but not fortune, in the bowels of the first Thatcher administration.

Vice-chairman of the party

Six months into the Thatcher government it was decided that the two ministers of state at the DTI, Sally Oppenheim (consumer affairs) and Cecil Parkinson (trade), should share me as their parliamentary private secretary. The effect of this was that when Cecil was appointed chairman of the party in October 1981, I went with him to Central Office. Very soon I was made vice-chairman. The combination of this position in the party hierarchy and my growing friendship with Cecil meant that I began to move in circles which were close to the Prime Minister. This was particularly true in the New Year of 1982, when a deep freeze settled over the country. On 12 January the temperature in Cropthorne fell to minus 20 degrees Celsius and our Elizabethan house beside the river Avon was surrounded by two feet of snow.

Somewhat incongruously, the day before, Margaret Thatcher's son Mark went missing in the Sahara desert. The Prime Minister was distraught. Cecil summoned me to London 'to help out'. I left Cropthorne, which was now completely cut off to normal traffic, in a bread van. By the time I finally got to London, Mark had been found (if he had ever been properly lost). I went straight to the Prime Minister's flat in Number 10 and found her in tears with relief. My main task for the moment was to do what I could to prevent Mark 'giving exclusives to the press'.

However, my prime responsibilities were not at 10 Downing Street but at 32 Smith Square.* In his book *The Ultimate Spin Doctor: The Life and Fast Times of Tim Bell*,† Mark Hollingsworth wrote up Cecil's and my arrival at Conservative Central Office as follows:

> Cecil Parkinson decided that a strong dose of professionalism must be administered and that the Party's message should be projected more seriously. Suddenly, advertising was down-played and down-graded and the emphasis shifted to the press. The Party's communication strategy would now be run by an Inner Cabinet at Central Office and Saatchi's would be more accountable. Party funds were in short supply and Michael Spicer, a Tory MP who had been an economist, was made Deputy Chairman to bring fiscal prudence into the relationship between the party and Saatchi's. These requirements created

---

* Conservative Central Office premises 1958–2004.
† Mark Hollingsworth, *The Ultimate Spin Doctor: The Life and Fast Times of Tim Bell*, Coronet, 1997.

considerable tension between Central Office and Bell, who had enjoyed a high degree of autonomy under the previous regime.

It was not just our relationship with the advertising agency that Cecil and I had to tighten up. After two years in office we were faced with opinion polls which put us third behind Labour and the Liberals. There was a clear need to inject a new sense of urgency throughout Central Office. Departments were placed on a firm reporting structure supervised by a committee, which I chaired. The senior officials, such as Tony Garner, responded superbly and Sir Christopher Lawson, a senior executive at Mars and long-term friend of Cecil's, was brought in to direct the promotion of the party.

It was not, however, all Cromwellian austerity. Cecil infected the office with a good deal of laughter and there was a warm relationship between myself and the treasurer, Alistair McAlpine, whose office was down the passage from Cecil's and mine. Here champagne, high living and an extremely successful fund-raising operation were all in full swing. I controlled the spending of money, which Alistair was collecting in fistfuls. Frequently we met late at night, often at Annabel's, the fashionable nightclub, to compare how we were each doing. It was a dynamic, slightly bohemian and highly productive era in the party's history. Above all, there was a very tight chain of command between Number 10 and Conservative Central Office. The Parkinson–Thatcher alliance was at that time unshakeable. This further raised morale at Smith Square.

Practical joking was all the rage. An example of this occurred on 1 April 1982. I arrived that morning to find a rope and a hook on my desk. An accompanying note informed me that I was the fire officer for the floor and that as part of my duties I was to demonstrate to the rest of the staff how to escape from my window to the pavement below. I was to fix the hook and one end of the rope to the radiator, throw the other end out of the window and abseil down the wall outside. I picked up the note and immediately took it next door, where I confronted Cecil behind his desk. I told him that I did not see it as a part of my unpaid responsibilities to risk killing myself in the party's cause. In short, I refused to jump. Cecil took one look at the note and invited me to consider the significance of the date.

About five minutes later Cecil came into my room ablaze with excitement. He had received a letter from the British Olympic Association inviting him, as a Cambridge running blue, to carry the Olympic torch down The Mall. 'I should do it, don't you think?' he asked me. 'What is the date on the letter?' I responded. Fade of Parkinson smile.

All this was the work of his PA, the indispensable Shirley Oxenbury, in cahoots with her hilarious associate Alex Mennell.

It was not all laughs. Beneath the good humour – perhaps because of it – serious work was under way. One innovation I introduced into Conservative Central Office was a simple econometric model correlating forecasts of the economy with our position in the opinion polls. This was my last throw of the dice as an economist; fortunately it worked rather well. As we had assumed it would, the economy improved and so, as forecast, did our poll ranking. By the early spring of 1982 we overtook the Liberals and were catching up with Labour.

Cecil and I decided to go and boast about this to the Prime Minister. A meeting was fixed for Wednesday 31 March. At the last minute this was switched from Number 10 to her office behind the Speaker's chair in the House of Commons. The frenetic, exhilarating, but constant pace and direction of our life was about to receive a seismic shock.

Argentina had invaded the Falkland Islands and the British government was in a state of total disarray. My life would never be quite the same again. Around this time I began to keep fairly extensive notes of events which touch me; some of these are historically significant, as is the case, for instance, of the Falklands War, the Brighton bomb, the privatisation of electricity and the various Conservative leadership crises in the first decade of the twenty-first century.

These notes I now offer on a selective basis, adding the odd comment or additional narrative where I feel something important has been left out or needs emphasising. I begin by backtracking to the middle of January 1982.

Diary notes

Sunday 17 January 1982
Brian Walden, *Weekend World* programme, says on present polls the Alliance Party would win with 200 seats, Labour 180, Conservatives 120. 19 per cent of the electorate is prepared to change if we bring down unemployment but they do not see us as likely to do this.

Monday 18 January
Issue of the day: reappointment of Saatchi & Saatchi as advertising agency. I had been hoping for a rational appraisal of alternatives. This is pre-empted by PM, who comes on the phone in the middle of the meeting with S&S to express her wish that they should be reappointed.

Tuesday 19 January
Ann still in Cropthorne. We have a leak in the oil tank. What a winter this is.

Wednesday 20 January
Meeting with PM, chairman and Norman Fowler. Purpose: to discuss publication of four pamphlets to get our case going again. Need to stress independence, private initiative etc.

Thursday 21 January
Congregate outside PM's office in the House to discuss Hillhead by-election (plus chairman and Michael Ancram, chairman of Scotland). While we wait in the ante-room, Ian Gow (PM's PPS) comes out of PM's office to dictate Nicky Fairbairn's resignation letter as Solicitor General for Scotland. Nicky had been involved in a minor scandal over a girlfriend at Christmas. I suppose his dismissal was inevitable,* but how cruel that he was not allowed to write his own resignation letter. When I resign, or am pushed, I shall insist on writing my own letter.

Monday 25 January
Meeting with Michael Ancram, Cecil Parkinson, George Younger, in talks about when to hold Hillhead by-election.

Tuesday 26 January
I am beginning to get the measure of Central Office. Not a bad team.

Tuesday 2 February
Francis Pym has made a speech claiming that unemployment will be with us until the end of the century. Press very excited, especially as Downing Street press officer (Bernard Ingham) has been stirring it all up by saying PM v. upset (press agency tapes say PM blames Central Office for issuing the speech!).

Off to see Ian Gow with CP. Tell him CCO press officer actually improved Francis Pym's speech (from PM's point of view). Atmosphere at court fevered and very introverted.

Friday 5 February
For the first time I begin to wonder whether we can win the election, even though this is still theoretically over two years off. PM and CP spent two hours

---

* Actual cause: mishandling in the Commons of a rape case. Nicky spoke to the press first and then opened his statement to the Commons with the words 'With your Lordships' permission'. He was blindly repeating a statement that the Lord Advocate had just made to the House of Lords – and was ridiculed for it.

together last night. They talked about Francis Pym (leader of Commons) and whether she should sack Chief Whip etc. I am running Central Office while CP helps to rule the country.

Tuesday 16 February
Ted Heath comes up to me in the lobby. 'Why haven't you contacted me?' I don't have a proper answer.

Thursday 18 February
After 10.00 p.m. vote, invited to Ian Gow's room for a drink. Find Norman Lamont there with him. Conversation turns to what would happen if we do not get overall majority at next election. Gow speculates that PM would not compromise over proportional representation. Palace could invite Pym to form government. Norman Lamont and I argue she must be flexible to keep Conservative Party together and perhaps to prevent constitutional crisis over monarchy. Norman argues that we may have to deal with Labour.

11.30: Gow rings PM; says how good she was on TV. She asks him to come over for a chat. He carries great influence with her. (He says in response to Norman and me that he would not vote even with the PM if she compromised on proportional representation). Apparently he writes a v. robust letter to Tim Rathbone against PR 'at any cost'. Gow puts a copy of this into PM's box without showing it to her in advance. She writes 'superb' on top.

Monday 8 March
6.30: Drinks party in St Stephen's Club to say goodbye to the press officer, Sir Harry Boyne. Most of the lobby present. Also PM. Suggest to PM that nationalised industries need to be made more accountable. She says, 'You will never do that; the only answer is to abolish them.'

Saturday 27 March
Central Council meeting at Harrogate. Breakfast with CP. At dinner the night before Denis Thatcher kept on falling asleep. PM alternately frowned at him and ignored him. She was unusually relaxed. Talked about Common Market, Trident, law and order. Later given lift back to Worcestershire

by Edward du Cann,* now almost longest-serving chairman of 1922 Committee.

Monday 29 March
Dine in members' dining room with Francis Pym. He argues present radical 'sod the lot of them' style is not truly Conservative. We have always been evolutionist. We pull everyone together – at least when we are at our best, he says.

Afterwards taken by Peter Temple-Morris[†] to meet the young Shah of Iran at Julian Amery's house in Eaton Terrace. Winston Churchill there: v. friendly as we are giving him a job running the anti-CND campaign. WC v. workmanlike about it all. Shah pleasant young man. Everyone bows and curtsies to him. Goodness knows whether he will ever have a real court again. Julian Amery is one of the old patrons of the party – though I am told he has no ready cash.

The Falklands War

Wednesday 31 March 1982
After 10.00 p.m. vote, sit in Ian Gow's office outside PM's office with Norman Tebbit and Cecil Parkinson waiting to discuss proposed TU trust.[‡] Some civil servant comes out of the PM's office and starts to dictate message to naval commanders alerting them to stand by for engagement with Argentine navy over Falkland Islands.

---

[*] Sir Edward Du Cann was chairman of the 1922 Committee from 1972 to 1984. A former party chairman, he is probably best remembered for his part in securing the election which brought Margaret Thatcher to leadership of the Conservative Party. In 1974, under his chairmanship, the 1922 Executive decided to press Edward Heath to stand for re-election as leader of the Conservatives, who had suffered two general election defeats that year. Du Cann was himself seen as a potential leader, but the collapse of his company, Keyser Ullman, put paid to a leadership bid, leaving the way clear for Margaret Thatcher.

[†] MP for Leominster 1974–2001; joined Labour in 1998; created 2001 Lord Temple-Morris.

[‡] We had also planned to use this occasion to tell PM about our (predicted) rise in the polls. When it became apparent that the Argentines had attacked South Georgia, Cecil said: 'There are now two reasons why we should go and not trouble the PM – one, she is going to be very busy for a while and, two, our position in the polls is likely to collapse and our little presentation will be a bit redundant.'

Friday 2 April
Argentina invades Falkland Islands. Everyone at AGM (in Worcestershire) shocked. War fever is bursting out all over. Emergency session of Parliament fixed for next day.

Saturday 3 April
8.15 train for London. Bump into Nick Ridley in the House. NR was the minister responsible last year for the Falkland Islands. I think he has missed the mood of the country (popular press now screaming for war). So has the PM when she speaks in measured terms in the debate. Irony of ironies: the Labour Party and, more ominously, the SDP (especially David Owen) coming over as the nation's saviours. No doubt they will wriggle later.*

At backbench meeting after the debate Carrington (Foreign Secretary) especially weak. There could be trouble about the government surviving if there is a censure debate next week. All depends on how credible our armada turns out to be in rescuing the Falkland Islands. It all has the making of a heroic tragedy. Watch this space to see whether the PM is Iron Lady or made of aluminium netting. John Nott (Defence Secretary) and Carrington in deep trouble. Words like 'steaming' suddenly in fashion, as in 'Falkland Islands 24 days' "steaming" from Portsmouth'.

Sunday 4 April
Much more worried and less bellicose press. My mood is certainly changing. The government apparently means business with the fleet, which sails tomorrow. I can't see how the PM can survive. If we do not engage the Argentines, her position is impossible; if we do, there will be casualties and public opinion will turn against us. In this event, party may turn to Francis Pym, who is positioning himself to take over.

Monday 5 April
Entire FO ministerial team resigns.

Tuesday 6 April
Francis Pym Foreign Secretary. Fleet at sea.

---

* In his biography of Thatcher, Hugo Young sums up the Saturday debate rather neatly: 'At its start the war wasn't Thatcher's war but Parliament's.' Hugo Young, *One of Us*, Macmillan, 1989.

Wednesday 7 April
Debate on Falkland Islands calms nerves. Simultaneously we announce an exclusion zone 200 miles around Falkland Islands and indicate we will engage. Argentina also looks willing to talk.

Friday 9 April
I fly Concorde to New York to meet publishers (St Martin's Press). Americans v. sceptical about Britain's role/capacity/case for the Falkland Islands. Still seen as a legacy of empire. Reports in newspapers under headlines like 'Britain waives the rules'. Suggests loss of nerve back home. Bulletin on CBS last night suggested UK and Argentina have identical problems, e.g. inflation (fact: Argentina 150% inflation, UK 9% and falling. Fact: Argentina is a military dictatorship; we are still a democracy). Still the Americans are taking it seriously: 'What started as a Gilbertian farce is taking on the characteristic of a Shakespearian tragedy' – CBS.

At around midnight (London 5.00 a.m.) I pop into an Irish pub I know near my hotel (the Plaza). The only two people inside are the barman and a drunk propped up at the bar. In the corner a black-and-white TV set is crackling; through what appears to be a thick mist but what is in reality, I suspect, a defect of the TV, a series of ships can be seen dimly moving from left to right across the screen – the British fleet on its way to the Falklands. 'Bastards,' shouts the drunk. 'You have to be roight,' agrees the barman. They both look at me. It is not a safe moment to be English but, unable to retreat, I perch silently on the stool beside the drunken Irishman. 'Don't you want to know whoi I say they're bastards?' he asks me suspiciously. 'Of course,' I mumble in what I fervently hope passes for a Scottish accent. He doesn't appear to hear me. 'Because they always win. That's whoi.' I slurp the Guinness which has been put before me, develop a bad cough and make a cowardly departure. I certainly don't win that one.

Sunday 11 April (Easter Day)
US ambassador,* addressing UN, says Argentina 'not guilty of armed aggression because territory ownership is in dispute'. US commentators say not much hope of a compromise as each side is over-committed to its position. I am not sure this is true.

---

* Mrs Jeane Kirkpatrick.

Tuesday 13 April

Arrive back in London. Sam Brittan* rings to ask me to tell CP that in the light of new Argentine proposals it would be 'murder' if we start to shoot now. Tell CP, who passes it on to PM. CP hints SAS go in to South Georgia tonight. The die is cast. PM knows that 75 per cent of parliamentary party will ditch her if she gives up now. Leaving aside the question of whether we start a world war, there is no British interest at stake. We are in a 'no win' position. Either we retreat and government collapses, or we lose, or we win, which now looks like meaning that we attack the mainland bases. Do we have the hardware for this? Talked to Julian Amery and William Clark[†] in the smoking room. Right wing definitely wants war. Eerie watching talk of peace on TV when you know SAS is just about to go in.

11.00 p.m. Drive with CP to Sam Brittan's flat. Sam v. worried. Repeats 'You must find way of making peace'. Cecil reveals Cabinet other than Willie Whitelaw (deputy PM), Margaret Thatcher, himself and John Nott have no idea what is going on.[‡] On way back drop in at Ian Gow's place with CP. I say, 'It's no win, isn't it?'

CP says: 'I'm not so sure.'

Wednesday 21 April

General feeling on back benches, even amongst the 'wets', that we can gradually escalate war. CP very bullish. SAS have already gone in (while peace negotiations proceed); Ian Gow thinks 50:50 chance of peace.

Sunday 25 April

We have taken South Georgia. This is the moment to do a deal with Argentina and set up proper RN base at South Georgia.

Tuesday 27 April

It looks as though we are heading for an attack on the Falkland Islands. PM will not agree to further negotiations with UN. Labour Party withdrawing support. Michael Ancram says to me in the corridors: 'If she fails, she will

---

* Economics editor of the *Financial Times,* and author of several books on the politico-economic scene.

† MP for Nottingham South 1959–66, East Surrey 1970–74, Croydon South, 1974–92; created 1992 Lord Clark of Kempston.

‡ War Cabinet consists formally of PM, Whitelaw, Pym, Nott, Parkinson and Admiral of the Fleet Sir Terence Lewin, Chief of Defence Staff.

have to go – no general election.' CP v. bullish, as is John Nott when I dine with him in the members' dining room. His only worry is two Argie subs.

Friday 30 April
CP asks me to tour several south coast constituencies for him and on Sunday 2nd to do broadcast on *News at One* on BBC. As a member of the War Cabinet he does not think it appropriate for him to represent the party. Must be seen at present to be above party. We are, of course, now riding high in the opinion polls.

Monday 3 May
We sink an Argentine cruiser* with over 1,000 people on board. God knows what this is going to do to world opinion or, for that matter, to opinion in the House of Commons.

Thursday 6 May
Lunch with Cecil at Mimosa in Wilton Road. Our main force does not arrive until 19th. In the meantime we see what can be done to take out airbases etc. with SAS. Later in members' lobby, talk with CP and Winston Churchill. WC tells story of his grandfather's comment at Suez. 'I would not have had the guts to go in and, by God, I would have had even less guts to pull out halfway.' CP: 'Don't worry, we're not going to.'

Thursday 13 May 1982
CP more worried than before. Not quite sure what the problem is other than that he is a 'doer' rather than a backstairs discursive politician. He does not feel comfortable at Cabinet. Dislikes having to be assertive (so do I). 1922 Committee anxious and uncertain. Does not like severe terms already accepted by government. However, the military plan for the 19th still seems to be in place as per PM's speech at Perth.

Sunday 16 May
Apparently three days to go until we invade. I wonder whether history will say all these peace negotiations were a charade. Press v. mixed as to what we should do. Perry Worsthorne (right-wing journalist on *Sunday Telegraph*) says so long as they pull out we should make peace. That's a big 'if'. Most of press seems to want blood, as does the majority of the Tory Party. This week will

---

* The *General Belgrano*.

tell. Boating on the Avon at the bottom of our garden, with the girls, was a far cry from all this!

Monday 17 May
Dinner with CP and Ann (Spicer). Everything points to a decision having been made to go in. Looks as though decision was made on Sunday and that we are committed. Whatever the legal jargon, the British government doesn't trust the Argies to pull out, nor does the nation, nor does the Conservative Party. All very glorious. Hope to hell there is no military disaster. Looks as if the 19th will definitely be the day. Meanwhile I am minding the shop at Conservative Central Office.

Tuesday 18 May
Lunch in members' dining room with Michael Havers (Attorney General), who is now legal adviser to the War Cabinet. PM asked him to join on Saturday after she had checked out his views on the war. He is putting all sorts of Machiavellian sub-clauses into each 'final' proposal to the Argentines. Last night the decks were stripped for action in the War Cabinet. But this morning UN Secretary General has come in with some new proposals which are apparently unacceptable and will be turned down by PM. Best guess is we go in tomorrow.

End evening with PM herself, CP and Ian Gow. She actually said 'Within the confidence of us four'. PM tired but heroic. Claims everything that is said of FO is true. Also 'If Carrington is to come back, as Janet Young wants, she will have to make way for him'. I may not have much of an official position but am beginning to climb dangerously up the greasy pole.

Friday 21 May
Landing commences at San Carlos.

Monday 2 June
Gather we were very lucky to win Goose Green. Our intelligence was up the creek. We thought there were a third of the numbers. General* stuck on *QE2* before he could take command. PM up and down about Reagan and Mitterrand, according to CP. Mitterrand has stopped Exocet sales to Argentina so he is 'in' at the moment. PM off to France for weekend. I am off to stand in for CP at businessmen's lunch in Keswick.

---

*   Major General Sir Jeremy Moore RM, commander, British Task Force.

Saturday 14 June
British troops march into Stanley and Argentines surrender.

Friday 2 July
With PM at Conservative rally at Cheltenham racecourse. She makes an off-text phrase: 'Never mind about the art of the possible' – reference to R. A. Butler's book – 'what we want is the will to achieve the impossible.' 'As long as she doesn't try to walk on water,' says Nick Ridley, one of the local MPs.

Wednesday 14 July
Meeting in Geoffrey Howe's room. Geoffrey to become i/c policy groups. He will accept this only after PM has told other Cabinet colleagues. Later in the evening find a morose Nick Ridley. He was i/c Falkland Islands last year. They seem to prey on his conscience. His love for the PM seems to be wilting. 'She doesn't understand aristocrats [e.g. himself] and working class.' This could be worrying for the PM. When the right wing turns, watch out.

Monday 16 August
Sunset in Cornwall. Last day of 13-day holiday in Parkinsons' house in Constantine Bay. Politics a long way away, except that Central Office have been on the phone several times. CP in Bahamas so all problems coming to me. Many people think we should have used the 'Falklands factor' and gone to the country last month. I disagree. We must see out our term. When I get back I have to make a decision as to whether to buy 100 new computers to go into constituencies for direct mailing.

Reflections
Was there a 'Falklands factor'? Did Margaret Thatcher win the 1983 election on the back of her victory over the Argentines? I have never believed this to have been the case. Her political fortunes were recovering swiftly in the spring of 1982 from their low point in the second half of 1981. This had been predicted by the simple economic model I introduced into Conservative Central Office soon after I arrived there.

When the Argentines invaded, there was a sharp downturn in the government's stock in the polls; this recovered as soon as our military success began to unfold. By the end of hostilities the polls had returned to the trend which had been established before the war. Economics was, as usual, the prevailing force.

There has been academic research to confirm this. Writing in the *British Journal of Political Science* in 1987, David Sanders, Hugh Ward and David

Marsh from the Department of Government at the University of Essex and Tony Fletcher from BBC Television's Political Research Unit concluded that the 'Falklands effect' was largely spurious.* Instead, they attributed the dramatic increase in public support for Thatcher and her government in the year preceding the 1983 election almost entirely to the rapidly improving state of the British economy in the winter of 1982; this, in combination with tax cuts contained in the March 1982 Budget, fuelled a surge in voter confidence in the economy. Using a relatively simple model in which the performance of the economy together with personal economic expectations predicts government popularity in the polls, they concluded that 'over and above the effect of the various macro-economic variables, we have identified that the Falklands factor does not help us explain the overall variations in the popularity of Mrs Thatcher's first administration.' This research has its academic critics but, to me at least, it sounds plausible.

The general election: acting parliamentary private secretary to the Prime Minister

Thursday 9 September 1982
Walk with CP to Downing Street. Clear, hot September day. Hoped to discuss various party organisational matters, e.g. agents' salaries and direct mailing. CP's mind on Cabinet: nurses' pay. Shown Queen's Speech.

Tuesday 21 September
State Opening of Parliament. Walked with CP through police barriers from 32 Smith Square to the House. Lunch in members' dining room with John Nott. He claims that the Americans were very unreliable allies during the Falkland Islands crisis. They provided the kit but not political backing. I ask him if we trust them to service Trident. He said once we have got it, that's it. I asked him why the Americans let us have it. He says, 'That's a thought that has always interested me; presumably because they believe, like us, that two fingers on the trigger are a better deterrent to the Soviets than one.'

Monday 20 December
Stood in for CP at CCO office party. Main job to introduce PM to everyone. She was tired and therefore relaxed and at her most personable. For once

---

* David Sanders, Hugh Ward, David Marsh and Tony Fletcher, 'Government Popularity and the Falklands War: A Reassessment', *British Journal of Political Science* 17(3), pp. 281–313, 1987.

got on rather well with her. She actually touched my arm at one point! CP, however, still furious with her performance at Cabinet. She had complained he was taking a week's holiday over Christmas – skiing – whereas she claimed to be working herself the whole time.

Tuesday 28 December
CP wants Patrick Jenkin to be moved to Defence and Nigel Lawson to Industry ('What we need is a free trader there'), with Tom King to Energy. CP really could be a very good PM if he lasts the course. As PM he would pick a good team and motivate it.

Saturday 1 January 1983
Conservative Trade Unionists' Conference in Bristol. I am there as vice-chairman of the party. Suddenly find myself getting close to the PM. I am invited into her room with CP and Ian Gow. CP suggests she makes peace with Francis Pym. I say, 'The troops don't like it when the gods quarrel,' and she agrees. She says, 'Have you ever been nervous, Michael, before making a speech? I am terribly nervous.' She has a cold and is rather attractive with it.

Wednesday 5 January
Drive down to Chequers with CP for election planning meeting. PM in abrasive form. Clearly does not want a GE until 1984. Sit next to PM at lunch at her request. Why me? Answer: earlier in the day it had been decided that I should replace Ian Gow on her tours round the country when he is in his constituency. Norman Tebbit very much around; he is a favourite. He kept on warning me that unemployment would be the clinching issue. He sat on her other side.

Tuesday 11 January
Back in CCO. CP the day before in talks with Francis Pym, Michael Havers and Willie Whitelaw. Each gets at him to try to intervene with PM (at present in Falkland Islands) to make peace between PM and Pym. (As accurately reported by Hugo Young in the *Sunday Times*, the two are at each other's throats).

In the afternoon pound falls violently. CP onto the press: 'Don't panic – all our policies working; no immediate election'; is very refreshing. Tomorrow will tell whether we have a major crisis on our hands. 1 per cent rise in interest rates seems to have quietened the pound.

Wednesday 19 January
Walk back to Ian Gow with CP. Apparently PM has reconvened ODSA (Office for the Defence of the South Atlantic). She is obsessed by defence and the Falkland Islands. The quicker we get the election out of the way now the better.

Sunday 23 January
My fortieth birthday at Tower of London.* Afterwards Ma, Pearses, Bonases, Tebbits, Parkinsons, Clive Sinclair, to dinner at Athenaeum. Quite wonderful. Nicest night of my life. Clive Sinclair presents me with a six-figure cheque as a donation to the Conservative Party.

Thursday 27 January
Dinner à deux with Ian Gow to plan election tours with PM.

Monday 31 January
9.30 meeting with CP, PM and Ian Gow in PM's room in Commons. Discuss election date: June 1983, October 1983 or March 1984. Decide not to produce a pre-election advertising campaign – because (a) everyone expects it and (b) we do not want to be accused of stirring up an election. If we go we must be seen to be forced into it.

Sunday 6 February
My first speech to a large conference (2,000 Young Conservatives). Afterwards go backstage to be with PM. Extraordinary how nervous she becomes before these big set-piece occasions.

Monday 7 February
Meeting with PM, CP, IG, David Wolfson, at Number 10 further to discuss election. PM in v. bouncy form. I carried in a large poster rolled as a scroll.†
PM thought it ghastly. Said, 'That will have a swift death.' Talked seriously about June, even of a date. She said: 'Don't put it in your diary, Michael.' She clearly wants me to go on for longer. We were all swept out after an hour to make way for Michael Jopling (Chief Whip).

Tuesday 15 February
Reception for Central Office employees at Downing Street. Had to try to

---

*   I was permitted to give this party at the Royal Fusiliers' headquarters, Tower of London, because of my father's former connection with the regiment.
†   The poster has her with arms up in the air at the party conference.

introduce 250 people to PM. She was in v. good form. 'No election before we have had four years,' she says. Meanwhile, polls in the newspapers show us on average 10 per cent in the lead. It is a bit deceptive as the Alliance vote (still over 20 per cent) probably will bite into us on polling day. Also what about 3¼ million unemployed?

Wednesday 23 February
Reception at Number 10 for agents. Take Ann and manage to get her talking to PM, who made a magnificent little speech: 'Much history has been made in this room and with your help we will make much more yet.' She is always at her best when she is tired.

Thursday 10 March
4.30: Report to Number 10. Hand suitcase to Joe, PM's driver; wait in ante-room to Cabinet room for half an hour. PM in meeting with Francis Pym, Nigel Lawson, about UK attitude to OPEC prices. PM comes out at 5.30 and heads straight for the front door. I catch up with her. Suggest she brings a coat. She darts back to the lift to get one. We leave. She sits on the right, I am on the left in the back of the car, detective in front. I am going to be alone with her for the next twenty-four hours. Heading for Woodbridge. Pick up motorbike escort after an hour of heavy traffic. Discuss George Thomas (Speaker). PM wants to put him in the Lords and replace him with Francis Pym. Also would have preferred Willie Whitelaw to go to the Lords with a hereditary peerage. Make a phone call from the car from her to Central Office to stop a letter she has written to the candidates. Not happy with it. Too rushed.

Woodbridge Hotel v. comfortable. The manager shows her to her suite. I am in the room next to her. Uniformed and armed police in rooms down the passage. Meet area chairman for quiet private dinner. She then goes up to her room with a private secretary to look at Budget speech. I join them around 12.30 a.m. and drink with her until 1.00.

Friday 11 March
Up at 6.30. Bang on PM's door at 7.00 and carry her bags to the car. Set out for East Anglia at 8.10. (She and I alone in the back of the car.) At Felixstowe docks she climbs up an iron ladder. I go up behind her to prevent embarrassing pictures.

When we arrive at Robinson College, Cambridge, at 12.00 noon, a large crowd of hostile demonstrators. PM hardly glances at them. They almost break through police barriers. During the buffet lunch Special Branch ask her whether she would like to go out the back way. 'No, certainly not; we came in through the front door and we go out through the front.'

I must confess am in danger of becoming a devotee; really begin to warm to her as a person. Takes me, surprisingly, into her confidence about her colleagues. She finds this relaxing, I think.

Finally back at 9.00 p.m., she waves goodbye to me from steps of Chequers as if I were a personal friend who had known her for years. I take her official car back to London. It really was a very good day. God knows where it all leads. As a matter of fact it really doesn't matter. Maybe as you get older you learn to follow your nose.

Later reflections
The PM was in cracking good form when we arrived at Felixstowe docks – the most flourishing private port in the land. Mrs Thatcher spotted the crane immediately; when told that it was one of the tallest cranes in Europe, she became hell bent on climbing it – at least to the first level.

Leaving aside the fact that she would not meet a single voter on either the way up or the way down, forgetting for a moment the sheer physical hazard of climbing the vertical iron ladder, the immediate worry for her staff was that she was wearing a tight blue skirt and black stockings, with the world's press waiting at the bottom of the ladder. My job, when her determination to ascend became irresistible, was to put myself between the Prime Minister and every one of the fifty or so camera and TV lenses waiting to record the obvious images for immediate and lucrative distribution around the globe. On the way up, my task was relatively easy. I simply kept as close to her as was physically possible. On the way down I had the additional function of guiding the Prime Ministerial feet from one iron rung to another, while avoiding being photographed myself with eyes focused upwards.

To my knowledge no one quite got the picture they were looking for – so much so that one late arrival asked her to do it again. This time, with the help of a detective, I virtually carried her to the waiting car. By the time we got back to Chequers I felt I had earned the bottle of malt whisky which someone had given her and which she generously passed on to me.

Tuesday 15 March
Budget day: everyone expects giveaway Budget. In fact, they get a business-as-usual, steady-as-she-goes Budget. CP increasingly thinks we may go to next March or May before general election.

Friday 18 March
Am asked by PM's private secretary to travel down to her constituency with her in the back of the car. Wait in Number 10 ante-room to the Cabinet

room. King Hussein of Jordan comes by with Denis Thatcher, followed by PM. I walk down with her to the front door. One of the secretaries rushes up to me: 'Message from your son Edward. He is stuck at a bus stop at Tewkesbury.' I say he will have to wait until his mother comes. He must have given her the wrong time for the school bus to arrive from Milton Abbey. By now PM is in the car. I rush to join her in the back seat.

On the trip she says things are going well with the Arabs but badly with Europe, where there is a new push to get our money back.

While in the car with the PM she says, 'I think the election is going to be me against the rest of the world'. When preparing for PMQs on Thursday, she looked wistfully at the front page picture of herself in the _Telegraph_. 'Rather a nice picture of me, don't you think?' Everyone in politics has a certain vanity.

Monday 28 March
Long session with IG and CP. As is often the case, I walk CP home. One of the many things I have learnt from CP is always to laugh at other people's jokes.

Wednesday 6 April
Meet CP at 8.15 at Maunsel Street.* We plan to have a quiet dinner in preparation for a meeting the next day at Chequers. In the event, arrive at Overtons to find a Greek Cypriot, a restaurateur, who knows CP; he brings us champagne before dinner and invites us back to his restaurant afterwards (Elysee, a Greek restaurant in the Tottenham Court Road where people smash plates after dinner). Get home around 1.00 a.m.

Thursday 7 April
Perhaps because of the night before, confusion with CP about whose home to meet for drive to Chequers. CP thinks I am walking over to him. I think he is picking me up. Finally we leave London with CP at the wheel at 9.30 a.m. for 10.00 meeting at Chequers.

Arrive 10.25 to find PM in bad mood, not because of us but because Tories accused in morning radio programme of being anti-environment. We miss coffee and join Geoffrey Howe, PM, Tim Bell, Gordon Reece, David Wolfson, Ian Gow, Chris Lawson in the upper meeting room. PM all over the place. Finally we settle down when Chris Lawson presents options/difficult dates for GE. PM wants to talk about the _Today_ programme. She looks under strain to me. We move on to policy. She switches from policy to themes and

---

* My house in Westminster, in a very pretty street full of little front gardens, which leads to Vincent Square.

slogans. I say we should focus our policies towards creating more jobs in the manifesto. She says, 'We are.' Then she switches to her programme for the general election: 'Must go near military bases,' she says. 'Are we allowed to?' I ask. 'You completely miss the point,' she says. 'I don't mean into the camps, just go near.' We break for lunch.

Over the lunch table and into the afternoon we all settle down, including the PM. We begin to discuss GE options in detail: unemployment figures, replacing of Cruise missiles, other party conferences in September etc. A consensus builds up for early June (while we still lead in the polls). PM says, 'I must not be boxed in.'

Next day on the phone CP says he would not be surprised if she baulked at June. She can be very perverse, but noble and rather glorious. Just hope she can last the course and lead us to victory. She looked on this occasion as if she might be overdoing it. She never lets up. It must all sometimes be too much. I thought she looked a little frail and very taut. Much nervous energy. It cannot be good for her never to relax – even though she makes a virtue of it: 'I was the only one working over the Easter weekend'. 'What a lot of pessimists you are,' she retorts when Geoffrey Howe says, 'Must put on more human image for the party.' She is very concerned not to have hostile crowds outside her election meetings – even the youth rally we are planning for the final Sunday. So we agree not to use Albert Hall but to fix Wembley. 'And shouldn't we have it on the penultimate Sunday?' she asks. 'That's a bit pessimistic,' I say. The irony is lost. One wonders how long she can go on doing it.

Sunday 8 May
CP joins Willie Whitelaw, Ian Gow, Norman Tebbit and John Biffen with PM at Chequers to decide when to call GE. PM favours late June. Arguments against this:

1. Would mean calling Cardiff by-election (get SDP bandwagon going?) on Tuesday 10 May.
2. Looks as if we are dithering.
3. 17 June = inflation figures to which pension rises to be hitched.
4. Unemployment figures in June may be a problem.
5. All the CCO advice, including analysis of local elections, is to go quick.

Monday 9 May
I go round to Downing Street to discuss details of PM's next trip. She has such a bad cold she can hardly talk – quite worrying. CP says, 'It's nerves; she will throw it off when we get into the campaign.'

On Monday 9 May it was announced that the general election would be held on Thursday 9 June.

Tuesday 17 May
PM in for briefing at Central Office. Pre-election nerves.

Wednesday 18 May
Manifesto launch. PM very authoritative. Francis Pym asked about Argentina.

Thursday 19 May
I have good adoption meeting in Worcestershire. Roughly 170 people in Pershore. V. friendly.

Tuesday 24 May
Arrive Downing Street 7.45. Leave with PM 8.15 for CCO, then drive to Battersea heliport and thence to Dover to visit Peter Rees's constituency. Goodish day, slightly marred by CND protestors. On return to Number 10, PM goes off to BBC and has very tough interview,* but survives well. By car back to Number 10. I sit in front. 'Bloody Mafia,' exclaims Denis (re BBC). Then into family supper. Joined for dinner by David Wolfson and John Selwyn Gummer. Afterwards, dreary evening trying to write a speech for Harrogate.

Wednesday 25 May
Better day. Arrive Number 10 at 7.50. Straight up to flat. Edward du Cann, chairman of the Treasury select committee, has said government probably responsible for unemployment. Over to CCO with PM. She goes into a meeting with CP, Francis Pym, Heseltine etc. prior to press conference. I have to speak to du Cann to get him to release statement recanting and supporting HMG. I do this. PM much happier. Leave Gatwick via Victoria station. She says, 'Marvellous, Michael.' Rest of day in Norfolk villages; large crowd; PM in good form.

---

* On *Nationwide*, the PM was pressed about the sinking of the *Belgrano* by Mrs Diana Gould of Cirencester. In the car on the way back to Number 10 I am told to ring CP to say that the PM is minded after the election to abolish the BBC in its present form. CP's response on the phone is 'Have you people in Downing Street gone completely mad?' Judging from my expression the PM remarks, with I think a twinkle in her eye, 'I do not think the chairman of the party is totally on side on this one.' I have never been able to decide how serious this conversation really was.

Thursday 26 May
With PM in Yorkshire. Start day in bad sorts as she has been up until 3.00 a.m. writing speech for Harrogate. On the way back from Leeds, chat to Denis Thatcher. What a nice man he is. 'My job is to prevent the PM from developing delusions of grandeur like the others.' PM seems to be appreciative when I leave her at the airport: 'You have done a marvellous job.'

Thoughts at the end of the first week of the campaign:

Tories still have a big lead. When will the banana skins turn up? Labour collapsing.

PM glorious but totally mercurial. On Monday she had only 1½ hours' sleep. Hard task of how to calm her down.

Derek Howe is a tremendous PRO. He has only one problem, which is a paranoid hatred of the press. This can be an advantage, however, as he metaphorically clips them over the ear and tells them to clear off when they get out of hand.

On Wednesday I had to do my bit about getting du Cann to surrender. PM now sees him as a goody.

Tuesday 31 May – written some time after the event
The Prime Minister is sitting as we approach for landing at Edinburgh between me and David Wolfson. I am in the aisle seat, chatting to Denis Thatcher behind me, with his hands on a gin and tonic. I have half an ear open for the conversation that is going on between the Prime Minister and David Wolfson. At one point she indicates that she is not entirely content with the last sentence in the speech she is about to deliver.

Foolhardily I intervene to say that I too think that the sentence can be improved. At this point she shouts above the aircraft engine that she is sick of people around her criticising her speeches without having anything positive to contribute.

I scribble a couple of alternative last sentences. The Prime Minister tears them up, saying that they are ridiculous.

Carol Thatcher, who is part of the PM's team throughout the general election, describes the scene thus:[*]

The speech panic for the evening's address had begun on the plane, which had travelled up from London at lunchtime. David Wolfson, Michael Spicer and Mum had simultaneously fastened their seatbelts, snapped open briefcases

---

[*] Carol Thatcher, *Diary of an Election*, Sidgwick & Jackson, 1983.

and fished out copies of the speech. As we taxied out to take off they started axing sentences and sections.

Throughout the flight to Edinburgh Mum carried on scribbling amendments in the margins.

As the under-carriage touched the tarmac on the runway, the speech still hadn't got an ending which Mum considered suitably rousing. In a suite of the Caledonian Hotel she sat down to familiarise herself with the speech and to work on the last lines.

My own recollection is rather more dramatic. As we leave the aircraft, we are met on the tarmac by the Secretary of State for Scotland, George Younger. I manage to whisper to him that the Prime Minister is upset about her speech. She says she would like to go in the car by herself with Denis and will leave the Secretary of State for Scotland and her staff in a separate car to come up with a final sentence for the speech by the time we reach the centre of Edinburgh.

As we approach the hall where several thousand people are waiting for her, the street outside is lined, as it often is, with noisy hecklers on one side and crowds cheering on the other, a microcosm of the way she is received nationally. I am relatively calm and tell George Younger that this is not an untypical example of the way in which she hypes herself up before a speech. All we need to do is to come up with two or three alternative pieces of rhetoric with which she can end what she wants to say. We each scribble down our own sentence, which we present to her as alternatives when we reach the green room prior to her going on stage. These are torn to shreds and we have no speech.

The press officers are becoming extremely restless, as indeed is the very large press contingent who want to have an advance copy of what she is going to say. By the time Denis Thatcher intervenes we are well over fifteen minutes late on stage. What he says settles the matter immediately: 'Margaret, this is ridiculous. Let's go into the room without a final sentence.' She smiles and says, 'Good idea,' and we're on.

I do not think she fully forgives me for this incident.

The speech itself is a great success. She is certainly well and truly hyped up for it. At the end we head straight back to the airport and thence for an overnight stay in Inverness, where David Maclean* is cutting his teeth as our candidate. Tragically, as we leave the aircraft a local freelance photographer called Jimmy Anderson collapses and dies at the foot of the boarding steps.

Next day on to Manchester.

---

* Opposition Chief Whip, 2001–5.

Thursday 2 June

Alison Ward, PM's secretary, says the PM has not slept all night. When I go up to her flat at 8.00 a.m., I am told to come back in fifteen minutes. When I return she has gone with David Wolfson. I follow her to CCO in another car. Not a good start to the day.

Later when we get to Gatwick, on PM's orders, I make a phone call to CP at CCO to say, 'Don't run three-page ad. PM thinks it is too expensive.'* Plane held up for me. Police escort me back onto the tarmac. CP says he will see her later. Ring him again from the bus to make sure he knows that she is serious. PM starts complaining about organisation again (running one hour behind). I arrange to switch her from coach to car and drive with DT and MT. We catch up time. It does not endear me to Wolfson, who is left behind.

Back at Number 10. Stay for supper with PM cooked by Crawfie† – lasagne and home-made soup. CP arrives to talk to PM at 10.30 while Wolfson and I, Peter Morrison and Ferdinand Mount go through the West Midlands speech for the next day.

At around midnight CP and I go off to Saatchi's. The aborted ad is the main subject. Tim Bell fights hard. CP says come in tomorrow. I try to dissuade CP. 'If the PM thinks the decision has been made then it is final. Do you want to open it up?'

4.00 a.m. CP and daughter Mary, whom he has summoned to pick him up, drive home.

Monday 6 June

With PM in quick tour of two London marginals and then off to TV studio. She is in much better form. Seems to know that I am behind the youth rally. Lunch in her flat. Afternoon return to CCO.

Tuesday 7 June

Talk to Alison Ward on the phone. She was for nine years the Prime Minister's constituency secretary. We agree something must be done about the political side of Number 10 after polling day. Stephen Sherbourne should be

---

* This was a significant event, especially for me. The three-page advertisement included a blank page of 'Liberal Democrat policies'. The PM did not see or appreciate the joke. In her view a blank page was a waste of money, especially as we were winning anyway. Soon after polling day it was my job to ensure that the cost of the aborted advertisement was not included in Saatchi & Saatchi's final bill. As we will see, this caused me great difficulties.
† Cynthia Crawford, personal assistant to MT.

political secretary. Ann and I drive down to Worcestershire for evening meeting at Pershore.

Wednesday 8 June
Helicopter to the Isle of Wight, where Virginia Bottomley is the candidate. Have to show PM a gossip column piece in the *Sunday Times* where Virginia says MT not a person she would want to sit next to at dinner. PM deadpan on reading this. After we return to London, I take helicopter back to my constituency for eve of poll rally.

Thursday 9 June
Polling day.

Friday 10 June
The Conservatives are re-elected with a majority of 144.

Tuesday 14 June
Prime Minister writes to me as follows:

10 Downing Street
Personal [in her own hand-writing]

Dear Michael
    May I thank you most warmly for your splendid help during the General Election Campaign, not only at Central Office but acting as my PPS. It really was the most magnificent effort to do two jobs <u>and</u> fight a seat!
    During the last few years you have worked tirelessly at Central Office and I am most grateful for everything you have done; I know that the 'budget' there in the past couple of years has been met, and that this is in large part due to your own effort.
    Thank you so much,
    With every good wish to you and to Ann,
    Yours ever,
    Margaret

Reflections
How to sum up that brief period in 1983 when I worked very closely with Margaret Thatcher (there were times when there was no one else around except for me)?
    Reading the diaries for the first time in a quarter of a century, I am struck

by the contradictory flows running through my relationship with her. At times I was elated by her friendliness and warmth, at others dumbfounded by her coldness, not only to myself but on one occasion, as related in the next chapter, to my daughter. At one moment I was immensely impressed by her insight into the character of her colleagues, at another surprised by what appears to be her brusqueness and narrowness of judgement. On policy matters, on the other hand, her instant one-line pronouncements were invariably the product of deep thought and discussion. 'The best thing to do with nationalised industries is to abolish them' is an example.

She was more cautious – much more – about implementing her thoughts. Her unwillingness to privatise the nuclear energy industry, coal and rail are examples of this caution, to which I shall return later when I describe two cases for which I was the minister responsible.

My admiration for her did not develop into unbounded affection. I could never have wept before she spoke, as her real PPS, Ian Gow,[*] is reputed to have done. I sometimes worry about my lack of emotional commitment to her. Why, like some others of her devotees, is there never a glint in my eye as I recall her extraordinary achievements?

I have recently taken some comfort in all this from the memoirs of Ferdinand Mount, who was one of her speechwriters at the time I was working closely for her. Ferdinand wrote towards the end of his book *Cold Cream*:[†]

> She remained heroic, intolerable, often vindictive, even poisonous sometimes, but always heroic … It is easy to slip into thinking that some of the things she achieved could have been achieved in a kinder style and at a lesser cost. I rather doubt it. There are times when what is needed is not a beacon but a blow torch.

I cannot improve on this. It is how I feel. She was exactly the right person for the job that needed doing at the time.

What she did not have was a sense of historical continuity. She was especially uninterested in what and who would follow her. In so far as she had a chosen successor at the end of her first parliament, it was probably Cecil Parkinson. His position, however, changed rapidly at the start of her second administration.

I was close to Cecil at this time and had some insight into, not to say involvement in, his change of fortune. It is to this that I now turn.

---

[*] Ian Gow was murdered by an IRA bomb on 30 July 1990. Some time later a 'death list' was found on which my name appeared as another 'soft target' associated with Margaret Thatcher.

[†] Ferdinand Mount, *Cold Cream*, Bloomsbury, 2008.

Chapter 5

Cecil Parkinson: his resignation, 1983

In the run-up to the general election, Cecil Parkinson and I developed a habit of walking back from the House of Commons along the Embankment after the last vote. Typically we turned right at the roundabout at Lambeth Bridge. We walked up Horseferry Road. I left him at Maunsel Street. Cecil walked on to his house in Pimlico.

On one of these walks home, a week before polling day, CP told me about his relationship with Sara Keays and about her pregnancy with his child. He had decided not to trouble the PM with it until the polls were closed. Norman Tebbit was another person who knew.

Alistair McAlpine in his autobiography put the matter thus:[*]

> Towards the end of the campaign Cecil Parkinson told me that he had a problem. I had a feeling that all was not well and that his problem was serious. It was not, I was sure, the sort of problem that I needed to know about … Cecil is an outgoing sort of person … If Cecil was to tell me something in confidence I could be sure that I was not the only one to be told. The secret was sure to get out and I did not want to be suspected of leaking whatever it was Cecil was so keen to tell me … Cecil Parkinson does not intend to gossip or pass on remarks made in confidence. It is a fault that he cannot help, telling people stories that are interesting or funny …
>
> I have often wondered if it was after dining with Michael Spicer and myself that Parkinson got himself into the trouble that finished his chances of being Britain's Prime Minister. Spicer and I used to say that if we had lingered longer over the wine or Cecil had turned right at Vauxhall Bridge instead of left, he might be living in Number 10 today.

Saturday 11 June 1983
Two days after polling day.

Strange day. 10.15 round to Number 10 with Antonia, Annabel and Ann. Watch Trooping of the Colour. Direct access to our seats from a window in Number 10. For some reason which remains unknown to me, Denis

---

[*] Alistair McAlpine, *Once a Jolly Bagman*, Weidenfeld & Nicolson, 1997.

Thatcher has to clamber up scaffolding to join us. Afterwards reception of high commissioners, then a sit-down lunch with PM and others who have been involved with the tours, plus their families. Should have been a joyous occasion. My Annabel (aged nine) says 'Well done' to PM, who ignores her, unlike Mark Thatcher, who is very natural and easy with the children who are around. To an extent I take Mark as I find him.

CP suddenly tells me there has been a change of plan about me. I am no longer to go into the government immediately but to remain at CCO to help him. [I had assumed from several conversations with CP that I would be one of his ministers of state at the FO, probably doing Europe.] CP himself is not to get the FO but Trade & Industry. Implications of this take a while to sink in.

After lunch go back for coffee with CP at CCO, then drive with him in his Jaguar to meet his new private secretary at DTI. Afterwards I drive CP in his car back to Number 10. While parking his car in Downing Street, bump into PM back from the Palace. She waves to me from the door to come into Number 10. As I walk down the passage I ask her whether I am to be 'deputy chairman'. She says to check that with Alistair McAlpine (current deputy chairman). I say we can fudge it.

Dinner with Gow and CP to discuss implications. Go through new government list. Find there is a gap. 'Any ideas?' CP comes up with his current PPS, Bob Dunn. 'Good idea,' says Gow. 'He's in. I am sure I can sell it to the PM.'

Wednesday 6 July

12 noon: appointment with PM and CP at Number 10 to discuss future of chairmanship. She wants CP to stay for two years. Will this be possible? What about his personal problem? Also discuss Euro relations. Advise her to make it up with Henry Plumb.* She invites him to Chequers, plus me, plus Ann, plus CP, next Sunday.†

Thursday 7 July

Dinner with CP, Stephen Sherbourne, Peter Cropper,‡ Michael Allison, Michael Portillo, to discuss Number 10–CCO relations. These are improving fast. After dinner drive home with CP, who has lost his front door key. Go to my house for two hours while hopefully his daughter returns. She doesn't.

---

* Former chairman of National Farmers' Union and leader of Conservative MEPs.

† This must have been cancelled. I can find no record of its having taken place.

‡ Later special adviser to Nigel Lawson.

Eventually walk back with CP at 1.30 a.m. CP becoming more wrapped up in DTI.

Friday 15 July
Media meeting with PM. Topic: MPs' pay. Asks me to be ready to unleash National Union* on the 1922 Committee, which the night before had erupted at 4 per cent pay offer. Later in the morning, after a reception for the press who had travelled with us during the election, she calls Wolfson and me to say that one of du Cann's companies had given 4 per cent for each of four years. Du Cann formula immediately accepted by PM and I am asked to call off the hounds. I wonder if the MPs will buy it next Tuesday. It is all very up and down.†

Monday 18 July
Bump into Ted Heath in the smoking room. He calls me over. 'Hear you're going to be the next party chairman,' he says. 'Am I?' I reply. 'If you don't know, you probably are,' he guffaws. Conversation lapses to America's Cup.

Thursday 11 August
Travel to London from Evesham to settle Saatchi account for general election. Previous day had had a short talk with Tim Bell from Saatchi. They want to be paid in full, i.e. £3.1 million. I say I will settle immediately if we negotiate a settlement on the disputed amount. They are furious. I have the backing of the PM. After ten minutes they knock three-quarters of a million off the account. We settle. I ring the PM to tell her. She has been in hospital for an eye operation and sounds a bit low but says, 'Well done.' I use the opportunity to say that we must have a much more professional relationship with Saatchi. She says, 'Yes. Get alternative estimates in future.'

The Hollingsworth version of these events is as follows:‡

After the campaign, when Saatchi's bill arrived at Central Office, Spicer was astonished. 'What on earth is going on?' he asked Keith Britto. In his

---

* The Conservative voluntary body.
† Ironic, this, in view of the role I played later in life as 1922 Committee chairman.
‡ Mark Hollingsworth, *The Ultimate Spin Doctor: The Life and Fast Times of Tim Bell*, Coronet, 1997.

estimation, the 'amount due' of £3,624,000 was a massive £750,000 in excess of agreed budgets and included invoices for the ads for the last Sunday's papers that had been neither commissioned nor used ... but the Agency had included the full newspaper fees plus commission of 15 per cent. They also hinted strongly that as they were expanding corporately, they needed the money. However, Spicer, a hard-nosed economist, was adamant that the ads had not been authorised and that the money had not been spent. Therefore the invoice was not valid. Yet the Prime Minister backed the agency. She was grateful to Saatchi & Saatchi and would not query the invoice ... Eventually, after a series of tough meetings with Bell and Michael Dobbs, the party refused to pay the full amount and Saatchis wrote off £750,000 arrears.

Tuesday 6 September

Return to office to find CP problem now an incipient crisis. Sara's family now up in arms. Fixed to see PM at Chequers the next day.

Wednesday 7 September

5.00 p.m. Visit PM in her study. She looks frail after her eye operation. V. friendly but rather subdued. We begin talking straightaway about chairmanship issue. A number of points emerge. CP must go by party conference as chairman; another chairman must be appointed, possibly by next week. John Eden is her preferred choice. We agree on the need for a non-Cabinet stand-in. Tried to persuade her why I could fill the role as an executive type. May be getting somewhere. Meeting lasts 1½ hours. As I leave, Robin Butler, comes up to me with info of an emerging war in the Middle East. PM agrees to tell me before she approaches John Eden. I leave feeling door still just open and determined to fight on. Next stop Tebbit (only people she is talking to about this are me, Tebbit and Gow). The other question is will Parkinson remain as Secretary of State? She is inclined to give it a go because (a) she knew everything when she put him there and (b) Ann has stuck with him so who is to sit in judgement over him?

Thursday 8 September

9.30 a.m. Ring Tebbit. 'Can I come to see you? Make sure we are speaking with one voice to the PM.' 'Yes, 2.30.' Tebbit comes up with an idea: appoint me chairman of organisation to run CCO and appoint himself as chairman of policy with John Eden as vice-chairman reponsible for candidates. The advantages of this are it gives a positive reason for change and adds 'bottom' to my appointment (restricting me to organisation matters, e.g. modernising the party). I put this idea on the phone to the PM. She doesn't comment. Later I phone CP. He sounds very weak – wobbly about whether to stay as Secretary of State. I say he must. He says only if it is fun. Apparently Nigel Lawson (Chancellor of the Exchequer) rings to support what I say. Nigel is to see her tomorrow.

Friday 9 September
Tony Shrimsley rings me to say CP visited Chequers. She backs him as Secretary of State but the question of who is to become chairman is unresolved. Office of Chief Whip (John Wakeham) ring to ask whether I can see him on Monday.

Sunday 11 September
5.30 train for London. 7.45 arrive Gow's house in Kennington. Nice supper. Gow tries to persuade me to accept deputy chairmanship if I do not get the chairmanship. I dig in against this. PM rings. Nothing resolved after half an hour's conversation.

Monday 12 September
9.00 a.m. train to Alton in Hampshire to see Wakeham at his request. Gives me the 'What's best for you is to toe the line, my lad' treatment. 'If you play ball and accept deputy chairmanship, the PM has indicated she will invite you into her government in a year or so at a middle, i.e. minister of state, level.' Firm indication that I am not to be offered the chairmanship. Apparently I am in the doghouse for fighting my corner direct with PM. Return to CCO and write to her offering my services as chairman. In the evening talk to Cecil. He says, 'Strongly advise you to toe the line.'

Tuesday 13 September
Ring Gow. If the PM asks me herself to be the deputy I will do it. In the evening I am rung by Chief Whip. 'Please meet me tomorrow at 9.30.'

Wednesday 14 September
9.00 a.m. Arrive 12 Downing Street to see Chief Whip and Willie Whitelaw. Terrible shock to hear they will be appointing John Selwyn Gummer as chairman. PM wants me to stay on as deputy and will offer me another job later. I say I will do it if the PM sees me herself. Have had other promises of jobs. This time she must tell me herself. Whitelaw says that is reasonable. Leave them in a daze. Take advice from Mervyn Pike and Cecil Parkinson. 'Important you let her off the hook.'

3.15: See PM. I apologise that my suit smells of Dabitoff. This breaks the ice. She says, 'Do the honourable thing.' 'It is a good appointment,' she adds. 'I will offer you a job in due course. I consider deputy chairman as more important than a parliamentary under-secretary.'

Thursday 15 September

Tony Royle* says, 'It is bloody ridiculous. You must get out by the spring.'

I may have conceded prematurely. I will never know. PM and Tebbit agree the tragedy is Cecil Parkinson going. One leg out of three has gone. Tebbit twitching about Heseltine. If PM runs under a bus he sees himself as the only hope to prevent Heseltine taking over. Finally have been promised minister of stateship by both the PM and Chief Whip in a year's time.

Thursday 6 October

Wake up to hear the news that CP affair has finally broken out.

9.30: Go round to see CP at 1 Victoria Street [DTI offices]. He seems relieved that the boil has been lanced, also slightly amazed to find himself lead story in every national paper. He feels that if he keeps his head he will probably survive.

Friday 7 October

See PM at Number 10 at 8.45. She is in a good mood. Takes my advice not to appear on TV. We discuss CP. As long as he can stick it out himself, he will be OK. What about his family? She asks me to arrange for somebody to man Ann Parkinson's phone.

Leave Number 10 and talk to CP on the phone. He agrees that so far the press is OK except for *The Times* and the *Mail*. Determined to battle on. Ring Ann Parkinson to see if she would like someone to man her phone as suggested by PM. 'Yes please.' Eventually fix for Mark Pendlington, their constituency agent, to do this. Ann Parkinson asks, 'Can you find out if PM wants CP on platform for her speech at party conference?' Later in the afternoon told by Tessa at Number 10 that PM is thinking about this. Annie Page, my secretary, says, 'Loyalty one thing, blind loyalty another!'

Sunday 9 October

Alistair McAlpine to lunch at Cropthorne. He is determined to wage battle for CP at Blackpool. After lunch Alistair drives me to Blackpool. Slight mishap at a petrol station when he half-blinds himself with petrol in his eye.

---

* Created 1983 Lord Fanshawe of Richmond.

It is clearly a new experience for him to man the pump himself. Drive to the Imperial with Alistair. Sunday lobby journalists explain CP's bad Sunday press is due to the fact that John Gummer did not come to his defence at Friday briefing.

Monday 10 October
CP to appear that evening on *Panorama*. He is very upset about Sunday press. Feels he may have been let down by colleagues. Talked to Gummer at agents' lunch. He says he will be praising CP's work as chairman at press conference. This takes place at 6.30. Only real interest is the CP story. Gummer, Russell Sanderson (chairman of National Union) and I wade in for CP. Ring him at about midnight to tell him so. Shirley Oxenbury, Alex Mennell and Annie Page very much reassured.

Tuesday 11 October
John Selwyn Gummer cheered at party conference and then given a standing ovation for saying nice things about CP. I fall off the platform when speaking to 250 people at a meeting to discuss computers in constituencies. In the evening another large party (lobster and champagne) given by Alistair McAlpine. Talk to Margaret Tebbit. She says Norman in constant touch with CP. Tuesday *Times* has story that Cecil Parkinson was offered FO and that it had to be withdrawn.

Here is Alistair McAlpine's version of the events which now follow, to which I am too close to be fully objective about:[*]

> I cannot remember [a party conference] where so many Whips came to Blackpool on the day before the conference's opening, a day when normally nobody was about except the serried ranks of the press. Sadly, the Whips were not there to save Parkinson's career, rather to put an end to it. Michael Spicer set out to try and save him from having to make a ministerial resignation. Gummer (the Chairman) took Spicer's actions extremely badly and began to regale him and myself – I was in Gummer's sitting room at the time – with a litany of all the awful things that Ann Parkinson had said about Spicer ... These words fell on deaf ears. As Michael Spicer and the Parkinsons were exceptionally close friends, I was shocked that John Selwyn Gummer should repeat the contents of what was obviously a desperate outburst by Ann Parkinson delivered in a private conversation at a time when she was under immense

---

[*] Alistair McAlpine, *Once a Jolly Bagman*, Weidenfeld & Nicolson, 1997.

pressure. It was clear to me that the purpose of repeating that conversation was to alienate Michael Spicer from his friends, the Parkinsons.

Wednesday 12 October

Times story not too bad. Doesn't mention CP directly. All seems quiet again. Later that night, around 1.30, bumped into *Mirror* correspondent in the New Pembroke Hotel. They are out to get CP and are confident they will succeed.

Thursday 13 October

Ann Parkinson arrives by car. Lunch with *Times*. Sit next to Peter Stothard.* CP arrives at 12.00. Mobbed by press outside hotel.

Up to McAlpine's room. I advise Parkinson not to try any tricks at the conference: 'Keep the speech focused on your job at the department.' This he does quite competently; his greeting when he arrives on the platform and at the end of his speech is warm. The platform claps but doesn't rise to its feet.

At a press drinks party in Gummer's room, Peter Simmonds of the *Mail on Sunday* and Andrew Roth are convinced CP has no chance. Simmonds seems to know something and is catching the next train for London.

Downstairs in the bars all the talk is of CP. Simon Hoggart of *The Observer*, who last week wrote something to the effect that he had risen too fast, says he will try to get the other side of the story over, bringing in the fact that three years ago his daughter Mary was severely ill. He will also stress his wife's loyalty.

8.00 p.m. Dinner with John Carter and other big donors. Around 11.00 with Larry Lamb (editor of the *Express*) chez McAlpine. CP arrives around 11.30 at Alistair's apartment, tired, indiscreet and slightly tight. At 12.30 decides to go upstairs to bed. Asks Ann (Spicer) and me to come up with him to his room. We are worried about intruding but we go nevertheless. Spend about ten minutes with them.

As we leave his telephone rings (this is a fatal call from PM to say that Sara has gone public in *The Times* the next day). Downstairs in the lobby Peter Morrison, who has made an appalling speech to the conference, says, 'Parkinson must go.'

Upstairs to Alistair's room. Present: Annie Page, Robin Day and Geoffrey Parkhouse. Told that Ann Parkinson had arrived in great distress and hauled Alistair upstairs. Later he spent time with Parkinsons while they tried to sort out *Times* story and discuss it with PM. I went upstairs twice: first time because I heard CP's voice on the phone booming down the stairwell.

---

* Former editor of *The Times*.

Friday 14 October

7.00 a.m. Full story of Sara blasts off over all the news. CP's number seems to be up. Downstairs whips are running around and people are giving me a wide berth. Up to Alistair's, who is dressing. CP coming into breakfast.

8.30: Down to the National Union meeting. CP only mentioned by du Cann. Wakeham, Gummer say 'this' is all being dealt with. No one else comments. I get confirmation from David Hunt that CP has to go.

9.00: Back to Alistair's room. CP comes in. 'It's over.' Will be going, probably on Sunday. He is exhausted; doesn't look at me. I am off to find Heseltine to discuss what we are to say when we appear on radio programme. Tell him CP is going.

10.15: Reach studio. CP resignation now public. Ring Downing Street to check. 'Yes.' Heseltine comes on air and says nice things about 'his friend'. Somehow I get through the programme and one or two interviews on TV. Feeling numb and totally exhausted. Back to hotel with Heseltine (we had been down to the conference centre). Arrive hotel around 11.00. Mobbed by press for comment. 'Very sad; he was a good chairman; party will pull together.'

Up to Alistair's room. He had organised CP's escape. Learnt afterwards that PM was in tears. What a stalwart chap Alistair has turned out to be.

Back to conference centre for PM's speech – 'Let's not forget architect of the victory.' Long standing ovation. Back to tea with PM. Take Russell Sanderson plus John Carter. She is particularly nice to Ann and me. ('It is all done now. I tried to save him for as long as possible.')

Saturday 15 October

Press is hysterical. Ring CP. He still seems to be coping OK. Has invited press into his garage. Alistair seems to be organising his flight from the country.

Sunday 16 October

Press given more of his story but CP is quoted, 'My friends will keep quiet.' On the phone he sounds more depressed. The sooner he leaves the country the better.

Monday 17 October

Times leads with 'Thatcher pressed CP to stay married', or something to that effect. At media meeting at Number 10 PM v. quiet on the subject. At the end of the meeting she draws me to one side. 'What about you? Do you want to go into government?' 'Yes.' 'I very much want you to stay at Central Office for the time being. We need the continuity.' 'I will do what I'm told.' 'Had

you in mind Nick Ridley's job?' 'No.' 'You would have to start at the bottom.'
My face falls. This is rather different from what I thought I was lined up for.

I leave her in discussion with Wakeham and Gummer. (Previously she had
said that Gummer badly wants me to stay on). Downstairs I write a note,
'Could you delay decision until I have talked with Gummer this afternoon.'
Note goes into the meeting. Back in the office, talk to my Ann. She says, 'Try
to push yourself for office.' Later in the morning when meeting is over I get
a message in via Stephen Sherbourne:* 'I would like to go into government.'
Gummer comes back to Central Office in the afternoon. 'Job on offer not
very interesting.' It turns out to be in Defence, which I would have liked.

This is now the third time since the election that I have been asked to
remain out of government and carry on at CCO. Each time my future prospects look bleaker.

Reflections

Cecil Parkinson came back in 1987, initially as Secretary of State for Energy,
when he masterminded the remarkable privatisation of the electricity industry, for which I was the responsible minister. I shall suggest later that without
his hand on the tiller at that time, it is highly likely that the influence of the
formidable Walter Marshall, chairman of the Central Electricity Generating
Board, would have prevailed with the Prime Minister. In this case, the electricity industry would have been privatised, if at all, as a single monopoly.

Parkinson was also chairman of the party again, under the leadership of
William Hague, in the 2001–5 parliament. But after 1983 his career path lost
its momentum – as, indeed, did mine. He always said that the Sara Keays
affair brought not one, but two, careers to a halt: his and mine.

Up until his fall, he was a serious contender for the succession to Margaret
Thatcher. My own view is that he could have made a good Prime Minister.
He would have attracted around him an able team and he would have been
an effective promoter of Thatcherism with a kinder face. At his peak he was
a tremendous motivator of people around him. He had the capability of
making one feel good about oneself and so about the future.

---

* Political secretary to the Prime Minister.

Chapter 6

Margaret Thatcher, 1983–7:
second term

Still at Central Office

For the period between the general election in June 1983 and the early autumn of 1984, I remained at Conservative Central Office as deputy chairman under John Gummer.

Monday 30 January 1984
Media meeting with PM. Main topic of conversation is the incipient Mark Thatcher scandal (opposition saying he won a contract in Saudi Arabia using his mother's name when she was there two years ago). She takes it all very seriously – has clearly been thinking of very little else over the weekend.

Tuesday 6 March
Dinner with CP. He seems to have given up any thought of a return.

Monday 2 July
Media meeting at Number 10 with PM. Problem with local government legislation is largely one of presentation; also we do not have a clear idea of which powers of the GLC we wish to hand over to the boroughs. Jenkin* in trouble?

Later over lunch in his office with Norman Tebbit we discuss how to modernise his constituency; he feels local government problems temporary. Certainly he does not want to move his job; important things for him in the next two years include sale of British Petroleum, shipbuilders, and getting British Steel into profit by 1986. Would I like to join him? He thinks Ken Baker next in line for Cabinet if Jim Prior goes.

Alistair McAlpine has drinks with PM. They discuss my successor. He tells PM that we need a heavyweight; whoever does job will only be motivated to accept if I get good job. She apparently says, 'Point taken.'

---

* Patrick Jenkin, Secretary of State for the Environment 1983–5. Created 1987 Lord Jenkin of Roding.

Monday 9 July

Media meeting at Number 10 at 10.00 a.m. PM very concerned about fire at York Minster. She rings the dean. 'All our thoughts are with you. We heard about it on the radio, which is where *we* hear all these things.' I say to Bernard Ingham, 'She sounds as if she is under siege.' Also discuss Dikko's kidnapping by Nigerians.* She says we have too much at stake in Nigeria to withdraw diplomatic relations. She says to Robin Butler, her private secretary, 'Tell Peter Rees [Chief Secretary to the Treasury] to give them a million pounds and not to argue,' then, to us all, 'Is that enough?' Someone says, 'It sounds a good round number, but what about VAT? They will have to give a quarter of a million back in VAT.'

At a party in the evening at Number 10, Denis Thatcher is in a bad mood. I mutter something about 'We're getting on with modernising constituencies'. He says, 'Tell the buggers not to panic.' DT generally out of sorts, as it turned out, because the Prime Minister had left him no food in the fridge in the flat upstairs. She had told him to pick up a plate of canapés and take them up.† He considered (rightly) that this would be rather undignified.

Sunday 15 July

To lunch with Alistair McAlpine at West Green. Long walk in the garden with Norman Lamont. He feels it will be between Tebbit and Heseltine when the time comes.

---

* On 5 July 1984 Alhaji Umaru Dikko, an outspoken opponent of the Nigerian military government, was seized in London, anaesthetised and placed in a crate labelled 'Diplomatic baggage' on a Nigerian Airways flight from Stansted to Lagos. The Nigerian high commissioner and commission staff members were questioned about the attempted kidnap, as a result of which the federal military government demanded the recall of the British high commissioner. Three Israelis and a Nigerian security officer attached to the Nigerian high commission in London were arrested for the attempted kidnap of Dikko. The Nigerian government then arrested two British engineers in Nigeria for allegedly stealing Nigerian aircraft. When the three Israelis and the Nigerian security officer were sentenced to ten to fourteen years' imprisonment for the attempted kidnap of Dikko, the British engineers were given fourteen-year jail terms in retaliation.

† The modest flat on the top floor of Number 10 was an irritant to the PM, who compared unfavourably her living quarters (and the part-time cleaning she received) with those of ambassadors, military chiefs and some of her ministers. She also complained that, unlike her Cabinet inferiors, she did not have a 'proper office'. In later years a Prime Minister (Gordon Brown) was effectively fined £12,000 for charging the cleaning of his constituency home to the expense allowance; this at the time was completely within the parliamentary rules, which were then changed retrospectively.

Hanging on a hook by the back door is a flat cap which Alistair intends to put on his head 'when the Russians come'. He will respond to the question 'Where are the owners?' with 'The capitalist swine fled that way', pointing to the far horizon.

Monday 16 July
Media meeting. PM has had a terrible press. Miners' strike seems to stretch endlessly ahead. They have now been joined by the dockers.[*]

PM says, 'The time for "softly, softly" is over. We must fight back. Miners on television every day. What about Peter Walker joining in?' (Suddenly she is keen on Peter Walker.)

I say, 'Why don't you go on TV, Prime Minister?' 'What for?' she asks. 'To explain our stand.' 'No.'

Tuesday 24 July
Lunch with Carol Thatcher. She says she would love to come and stay with us in the country. Wish I got on as well with her mother as I do with her!

Tuesday 31 July
Lunch with Ian Gow. Agree CP will come back; Ian says he could make leader still 'if the revolution needs consolidating'. If we need more of it, 'Tebbit will be the man'. Gow thinks Walker and Heseltine will knock each other out. He would like Tebbit if Margaret ever leaves.

Minister at last
Then, out of the blue, there came a change.

Monday 10 September 1984
10.30 a.m. Annie Page rings me at Cropthorne to say that I have to be on standby for a call from the PM between 11.30 a.m. and 2.00 p.m. Take it in my bedroom. False alarm; could I be ready for PM in the afternoon or early evening? I explain that I have to take Antonia to school. When I come out of the room all the family, including Ma, lined up on the landing! Call from PM finally comes through at 3.00 p.m. 'I'm doing a mini-reshuffle. Nick Ridley has asked for you at Transport as parliamentary secretary.'

---

[*] This lasted for fifty-one weeks, ending on 3 March 1985. Thatcher's triumph over the National Union of Mineworkers, led by Arthur Scargill in a bitter and often violent struggle over pit closures, has rightly entered the folklore about her.

I say, 'Delighted,' which I am not, and that is the end of conversation and of a saga which began over two years ago with CP promising me the moon if we won the general election and with the Chief Whip promising 'a middle-grade' job if I stayed on as deputy chairman, and the PM last summer saying deputy chairmanship was more important than parliamentary secretary etc. Underneath I am pretty angry, but *c'est la vie.*

8.00 p.m. Nick Ridley, my new boss and Secretary of State for Transport, rings. We have a laugh and he says my job will be to do aviation (denationalise British Airways etc.), buses (denationalise the long-distance ones) and all roads to the left of a line drawn from Manchester to Southampton. Lynda Chalker does the ones to the right.

Wednesday 12 September

First day at Department of Transport. Annabel walks down Horseferry Road with me to the door. Everyone very friendly. Doorman well briefed. Day begins with a lot of laughter. Become more daunted as we go on. Big issue is the distribution of routes between British Airways and British Caledonian. BA fights very hard. I am still rushing backwards and forwards to CCO as I have one or two things to tidy up there, e.g. sacking of political correspondence secretary at Number 10. Impressed by Ridley's fire and mass of ideas.

Was asked by Charles Colville of *Berrow's Worcester Journal* what I had achieved at CCO. Replied: (1) ran the organisation which won the general election; (2) balanced the budgets and paid off our debts; (3) began the process of modernising constituencies. [The Conservatives when I left had a network of computers in the constituencies which technologically put the party well ahead of Labour until the rise of Tony Blair.]

Thursday 13 September

My temporary private secretary (Andrew Melville, whom Ridley for some reason calls 'Lord Melville') tells me:

We like red boxes completed every day;

We like all the stuff back every night. 'Last night, Minister, you kept three pages.'

By way of response – cheeky devil – I tell him not to give me more than ten inches every day! (Good lesson, this, for all new ministers. If you are going to be effective, you must get on top of your officials, especially your private office, in the first few days.)

Saturday 15 September
Three boxes at Cropthorne. Lamonts to stay. Take them over to the Lygon Arms. He is minister for tourism and Douglas Barrington* wants a K!

Monday 17 September
Dinner with Ridleys. Salmon caught by Judy. We discuss the issue of John King and Colin Marshall fighting like cats against Adam Thomson.† (I play tennis every Sunday with Colin Marshall.) Ridley talks of having spent the weekend dealing with a plague of birds, mainly pheasants, in his constituency.

Tuesday 18 September
Meeting with BA and Nicholas Ridley. Colin Marshall rings up later to offer a deal. Ridley wants, rather naturally, to play this himself.

Lunch with Jeffrey Archer. Archer is verbally supportive of my book, *Prime Minister Spy*; later tried to tie him down to writing a commendation. When he fails to come up with the goods I draft one for him: 'This is the book I should have written – Jeffrey Archer'. By return of post he writes 'A genuinely original plot which carries through to a thrilling climax'. Needless to say, this – and not my effort – is what is printed on the jacket.

Wednesday 19 September
Two-hour meeting on Bus Bill [to privatise long-distance buses]. Two hours with Michael Bishop of British Midland Airways. Two hours of Adam Thomson of BCal. I suppose I will get on top of it. Good talk with John King on the phone. Nicholas Ridley trying to bang all their heads together.

Wednesday 26 September
BA/BCal saga goes on. Over whisky with officials and Nicholas Ridley I press that we give way to British Caledonian. All that is now holding us up is a dispute over who goes into Atlanta. I think this is very important to British Caledonian. NR thinks they are bluffing. (He gave them increased short-term profits of £17 million by making BA switch out of Saudi Arabia.) I think BA would go further to get on with privatisation.

---

* A big figure in the hotel industry and at the time owner of the Lygon Arms Hotel, Broadway.
† John King was chairman of British Airways and Colin Marshall chief executive. Sir Adam Thomson was founder and chairman of British Caledonian.

Thursday 27 September
PM agrees with NR, as do Tebbit and Michael Allison.* Adam Thomson will be told it is all or nothing. However, I think they are under-estimating him. I believe him when he says that the US market is so crucial to them that they will trade it for almost anything else. We will see who is right: Ridley, PM, Tebbit or me!

4 p.m. Adam Thomson comes in and is told to take it or leave it. I personally sympathise with his case that he needs some of the US market. NR thinks his real needs are short-term profits and that he is now putting the government's entire competition policy at risk. The PM and Ridley clearly like King. I just hope that one day the arrangement we make does not come unstuck.† Thomson says he will put the deal to his board with a recommendation that they turn it down. After the meeting with him, NR asks for a sweepstake on whether the board will accept. Those who say yes are him, his private secretary and two middle-grade officials. Those who say no are me, the permanent secretary (Peter Lazarus) and David Knowles (deputy secretary for aviation and a very good man). I just wish we had a fallback position if BCal turn it down. We are so vulnerable to being accused of crushing the independents.

Monday 1 October
Visit DVLC Swansea. My first discussion with trade unions goes pretty well. On my return, a call from Peter Lazarus. Indications are that BCal is refusing. NR's judgement wrong. PL worried for SoS's position. Wonders whether anything can be done to retrieve the position. I say it is too late. Chance with BA was missed last week.

Tuesday 2 October
NR decides I should have a go at my friend and constituent Colin Marshall (with whom I still play tennis every Sunday) to see if I can get Atlanta off them. Colin and I have several meetings. I think it is all too late. They think they are home and dry. They also feel they gave us a deal which we are going back on. We will see what tomorrow brings.

Wednesday 3 October
Alistair McAlpine on the phone. Gordon Reece is coming back to CCO as a PR adviser.

---

* PPS to the Prime Minister.
† It did, some three years later.

Alistair seems to have taken my room at the party conference and has offered me a bedroom in his suite instead. I currently plan to go down informally for two days, as the ex-deputy chairman. My initiative to get BA to surrender Atlanta fails, as does my attempt to see John King.

Downing Street for meeting with PM about the future of the airlines. PM hints that she believes that the miners' strike will last for weeks, if not months.

Thursday 4 October
NR takes BA/BCal issue to Cabinet, who vote 10-7 in favour of BCal. Amongst those for BA: Allison, Rees, Tebbit, Biffen etc. For British Caledonian: Ridley, Brittan, King, Younger, Fowler etc.

Ring Colin Marshall, who is en route with King for a board meeting in Berlin. Marshall comes back. We all meet in Ridley's office at 3.00 p.m. to see what Colin's reaction is. Enormous relief that he comes to make peace. I wish all this had been done earlier.

Assassination attempt at Brighton
In his autobiography,[*] and writing about the events surrounding the bombing of the Grand Hotel, Brighton, Alistair McAlpine says: 'Michael Spicer showed a talent for leadership which I had never seen before.' My recollection and record of what happened is as follows.

Friday 12 October 1984
The day Margaret Thatcher is to describe as 'the one I was not meant to see' begins very early for me – at one minute past midnight. Having left my job as deputy chairman of the party only a few weeks earlier, I have no responsibilities and I am on friendly terms with most of the sixty or so key conference personalities crammed into the sitting room of Alistair McAlpine's three-bedroom suite in the Grand Hotel, Brighton. I am relaxed and enjoying myself. As is usual at Alistair's parties, champagne flows and the luxuriant supply of shellfish lies on mounds of ice on a table in the corner of the room.

By 1.30 a.m. the crowd has dispersed, happy and exhausted. Richard Ryder, Alistair and I finish a half-empty bottle of champagne, wish each other goodnight, and leave for our respective bedrooms, each of which is within the precinct of the suite. My room is on the other side of a small entrance hall.

The bomb explodes at 2.54, a few minutes after I have gone to sleep. Despite its proximity, the impact does not feel particularly traumatic. Maybe the

---

[*] Alistair McAlpine, *Once a Jolly Bagman*, Weidenfeld & Nicolson, 1997.

alcohol has dulled my senses. The shaking of the building is severe enough, however, for me to jump out of bed and leave my room instantly, covered only by a small towel; I hear the click of the latch to my bedroom behind me. The key to the room is locked on the other side of the door.

Alistair and Richard emerge from their rooms, sensibly wearing dressing gowns. My first words are to Alistair: 'Have you got a spare key? The catch on my door has fallen and I have locked myself out.' He shakes his head.

Richard Ryder is more sensitive than I am to the catastrophe that has occurred. 'Something terrible has happened,' he says. 'We must get out.' We all head for the door to the suite. When we force this open, we can just make out a black void through the thick smoke which belches into the room.

I say, 'There must be a fire escape.' There is – in the sitting room. We pull up the sash window and I climb out into the cold, dark night. On the street, three floors below, I hear voices and can just make out the shadows of a gathering crowd. With nothing but my small towel around me, I am, in effect, stark naked. I am suddenly aware of two women climbing up to meet me. They shout in what sounds like an Italian accent, 'OK? OK? Hotel, 'e blow up; we clean.' 'I'm just fine,' I say. 'But I need to get past you. I think you had better go back down. Cleaning the hotel can wait.'

As I approach the ground, the little crowd begins to clap. I touch down and someone (who I later discover is Michael Dobbs) thrusts a raincoat at me. Richard and Alistair both land safely.

I make my way to the Metropole Hotel next door. Someone says, 'The Prime Minister is safe. She has been taken away by the security services, as has the chairman of the party, John Gummer'. I get to the reception desk and ask for a phone. I dial 999 and say, 'My name is Michael Spicer MP. I am deputy chairman of the Conservative Party.' (I think it best to reinstate myself.) 'The Grand Hotel has been blown up and I need urgently to speak either to the Prime Minister or to the chairman of the party. I understand they are safely in the protection of the police.'

Within a few moments John Gummer comes on the line. He says, 'I must stay with the PM. There is some concern that there will be another attack. I think it best if you take charge on the ground for the time being. The PM's one instruction is that "the conference must go on". Find Tony Garner [the chief official] and work through him.'

I make my way to Tim Bell's room, which I use as a command post for the rest of the night. Someone gives me a shirt and a pair of trousers which are too large for me and are in constant danger of falling down. They are, however, an improvement on the towel, which I am now able to discard.

Tony Garner enters the room, as does Alistair McAlpine. I ask Tony to collect as many agents and party professionals as possible. Alistair suggests that he does what he can to get hold of warm clothing for all the former occupants of the Grand Hotel, who are wandering about dazed and in their nightclothes. I agree and he goes off to ask Marks & Spencer to open their shop and donate the necessary clothing. I ask Nigel Hawkins (i/c computers at CCO) to fix transport for those who need clothing. I learn that Anthony Berry MP and Roberta Wakeham have died* and that the Tebbits and John Wakeham have been seriously injured and are now in hospital.

Some twenty agents gather in a yard adjacent to the hotel. I pass on to them the Prime Minister's instructions and we plan the security arrangements for the skeleton conference to be opened at 9.00 a.m. (The main problem is that those delegates resident at the Grand Hotel have lost their security passes.) At this point my diary reads as follows:

> By 8.30 had got all agents into conference hall and waited for final instructions from PM, by now at Lewes Police College, via her private secretary, Robin Butler. These came at 8.40. We were in business. Doors open at 8.45. PM arrives at front door at 9.20. Conference begins at 9.30.
>
> She makes a defiant speech to a small group of us standing in front of the stage. The event is recorded by two television cameras. I clap so fiercely that my trousers do fall down. I decide there is nothing much more I can do and leave the hall. Outside it is a beautiful sunny day. I ring Ann for the third time since the explosion (one news bulletin has claimed that I am missing, but fortunately Ann knows otherwise). I tell her that I am heading for the beach. Two hours later my driver finds me fast asleep, curled up on the shingle. In the back of the car I struggle into a fresh set of clothes which Ann has sent me. We head for Worcestershire at 5.00 p.m., after I have attended a reception for the Conservative Board of Finance.

Monday 15 October
Drive with Alistair McAlpine to Brighton to see Margaret Tebbit, who is paralysed and on her back. She is remarkably cheerful, but John Wakeham is in a bad way.

---

* There were, in fact, five fatalities: Eric Taylor (north-western party chairman) and Jeanne Shattock (wife of western party chairman) also died that night; Muriel Maclean (wife of chairman of Scottish Conservatives) died later of her injuries.

Back to the Department of Transport

Thursday 25 October 1984

My first real blooding. The night before speak at Helicopter Advisory Board dinner at the Savoy. Am halfway through my speech when I tear it up. Say I am grateful to my officials but don't really understand what they have written and will instead 'speak from the heart'. Brings the roof down.

During the day I hold my first press conference to announce that we are in the midst of a colossal row with the Americans over transatlantic flights. Our companies are being threatened by US anti-trust laws which we do not accept; so for the time being I will not allow cheaper prices on the Atlantic routes. Very difficult to get the reasons for this over on TV later in the day, especially as all tickets so far sold by airlines must be made invalid. By midday am told that a large travel company has gone bust and have to answer a private notice question about this in the House of Commons (my first utterances there for about three years). In the event I am questioned for twenty minutes and survive, I think, with some credit. Suddenly I seem to be in every newspaper.

Not all my early life as a minister was spent on airline matters. On 28 October 1984 I wrote what I assumed to be a standard letter, no doubt signed late at night, to my colleague and friend Anthony Steen, Member of Parliament for South Hams.

> Dear Anthony
>
> Thank you for your letter of 3 October enclosing this one from Mr P. A. D. Murphy about the registration document for his recently acquired vehicle.
>
> I am sorry that Mr Murphy was inconvenienced in the way he describes …
> I understand that the new registration document was sent to Mr Murphy on 14 September. I hope that he received it safely and that his future dealings with the DVLC will be trouble-free.
>
> Yours sincerely,
> Michael

On or about 10 November Anthony sent me the following enclosure from Mr Murphy:

> Dear Anthony Steen
> Your size 10 boot has been
> Quite successful and effective.

Judging by the reply, which I have seen
Full of blarney, lacking only in invective.
Michael Spicer, dear chap, must have strok-ed his dimple
As he wrote, tongue in cheek, to one he thought simple.
Master of prose he might be, but, as you will see
He hasn't the foggiest of Form V5 Section 3...
[The letter goes on in similar vein for six more verses of rhyme.]
Many thanks,
Sincerely
P. A. D. Murphy

Much to the horror of my officials who, quite properly, had a very strict procedure for answering letters to ministers (and a large department for this purpose), I insisted on writing back to Anthony the following letter dated 15 November:

From: Parliamentary Under-Secretary of State
Department of Transport
2 Marsham Street
London SW1P 3EB

Dear Anthony
I am so sorry Mr Murphy's card was delayed,
He is clearly a man who calls a shovel a spade.
For the future I will do whatever I can,
To make sure things go better to plan!
Yours sincerely
Michael

To this Anthony replied as follows:

Dear Michael
Relating to Mr Murphy...
I am grateful to the Minister
And relieved there was nothing sinister.
But aviation is entirely another matter.
You'll be hearing more about that on... Wednesday!
Yours truly, Anthony

The interesting bit to me is his last paragraph, which foretold events I shall be describing shortly.

Tuesday 30 October
Fly to Belgium to negotiate with my Belgian opposite number for cheap air
fares in Europe. Get on pretty well with this at breakfast and then address
British Chamber of Commerce over lunch. On return trip launch first British
Airways 757 flight to London.

Sunday 2 December
BA issue reaching a crescendo. Apparently there is much more dirt to come
in the anti-trust case* in which BA involved in the US, brought by Freddie
Laker (who had been bankrupted) against BA. Billions of dollars are at
stake. We must surely now have a flaming public row with the Americans.
They have far more to lose than we have by a rethink on transatlantic travel.
Question is whether Nicholas Ridley can stand the strain; he was looking pretty grim this evening. He summoned Mr Parker, BA's international
lawyer, and my pal and constituent Colin Marshall. Nicholas thinks that
all the bad press he has been getting in papers like *The Times* is inspired
by Lord King. Luckily the PM, who is in Peking, has said that Ridley is
'very good, very good indeed' when asked whether she would sack him.
However, NR keen to impress on BA that they should shut up. He is pretty
rude about them, saying he won't take any more of their dirty tricks. Colin
Marshall is clearly shocked, but remains impassive. I like NR and wish him
well. I only hope he has the stamina.

Sittings motion

Tuesday 11 December 1984
Amongst the many crises in the department, we fail to get our sittings motion†
at the committee stage of the Civil Aviation Bill, essential for privatising
British Airways. The four Conservatives vote with the opposition parties and

---

*   Freddie Laker applied for licences for around 140 European routes, intending to open up
the European market to lower fares. Other airlines on the North Atlantic route undercut
Laker's fares in order to close him down. In February 1982 he was forced into receivership
but the public raised a £3.5 million 'Save Fredair' fund. The receiver sued the defendant
airlines in an anti-trust action and recovered £80 million to distribute to creditors. Laker
sued personally and recovered £8 million.

†   The motion, taken at the beginning of the first meeting of a standing committee, outlin-
ing the government's plan for the times/days of the week on which the committee will sit.
It is not itself a timetable motion (which restricts debate) and is usually uncontentious and
taken 'on the nod'.

defeat the motion. [These were the days when MPs who had outside interests were proud of them and represented them mercilessly.]

With a government majority on the committee of four (out of eighteen), this is as extraordinary as it is significant. The government's objective is to fix a maximum of 275,000 air traffic movements at Heathrow airport as part of the BA sales prospectus. This is opposed by four Conservative MPs: Patrick Thompson, John Wilkinson, Anthony Steen and Bill Walker. Steen's aim is to secure more slots at Heathrow for British Midland, with whom he has a consultancy relationship; Wilkinson, representing Ruislip-Northwood, is generally concerned about noise at Heathrow and wants less capacity there (the opposite of Steen); and Walker has been briefed by Alan Haselhurst (Saffron Walden), who is fighting to prevent a new airport being built at Stansted, and argues that the Bill is too restrictive of air traffic movements at Heathrow.

After the debacle in committee (without precedent for a government with as large a majority as ours) I tentatively mention to Nicholas Ridley that it might not be a bad idea if we were to improve our relations with the relevant backbench colleagues (in particular, perhaps with Alan Haselhurst, who, while not directly in the rebellion, is a hidden hand behind it).

Nicholas, who on the whole does not do PR, blinks at me and asks, 'How do we do that?' I say, 'I have no idea, but what about inviting Alan in for a drink and a chat?' 'I like a drink,' comes the immediate response, not quite the one I feel I have prompted. A date is duly fixed for Alan to come over to the Secretary of State's office in Marsham Street.

Alan arrives at the appointed hour and the three of us sit down in Ridley's armchairs. Nicholas opens his charm offensive with words to this effect: 'Alan, have a drink, and then let me tell you why you are a total shit for masterminding the block on our Airports Bill.' Understandably Alan, even then a senior backbencher, does not wait for more, saying 'I don't have to take this', and gets up to go.

When he reaches the door, Ridley asks him, 'Don't you want to hear why I think you are a shit? Nobody should put parochial arguments before the national interest. Where would we be, for instance, if I were to attack the Yanks for the nuclear base they run at Fairford, in my constituency?'

Needless to say, Alan never became a bosom pal of the department, though as it happens he and I got on well down the years, especially during his period as deputy speaker and mine as chairman of the 1922 Committee.

Nicholas Ridley was not at his best at the front of the shop. It is why Thatcher (very wrongly, in my view) did not make him Chancellor of the

Exchequer. Arguably one thing that you do not want in a Chancellor is that he should be a good talker, particularly in public.

Privatisation of British Airways

Thursday 13 December 1984
The biggest aviation issue of the day relates to the privatisation of British Airways. The problem is that we are beginning to fall foul of American anti-trust law. The very threat that this could involve British Airways paying up to $1 billion in damages (President Reagan having removed the threat of criminal prosecutions) could make it impossible to write a sales prospectus for the airline. By the time Nick Ridley, Lynda Chalker, David Mitchell and I sit down for supper in between votes in David Mitchell's house, the matter has become so fraught that the PM tells NR in one of the votes that we are to postpone privatisation of BA indefinitely. Apparently our lawyers have told NR that to do so would tacitly be to accept the validity of US law.

Friday 14 December
Went down to see Tebbits in Stoke Mandeville Hospital at around 11.00 a.m. Visited Norman first. At last he is coming back to his former self, having had at least three major operations. He has this idea that we should in effect allow British Airways Mark I to go out of business, and BA Mark II would take on all BA Mark I's liabilities except for the Laker suits. We would then face the Yanks with this. Norman due to come out of hospital any time now, although pathetically thin.

Wednesday 2 January 1985
To dinner with Judy and Nick Ridley at Naunton in Gloucestershire. Nick has managed to do some painting (unlike me, who still has a mound of paperwork from Christmas – also there seems to be an awful lot to do in the constituency). Two issues discussed over dinner in preparation for Nick's meeting with PM the next day:

The future of BA: the Laker threat. Are we or are we not to be tough with the Yanks? Nick and I all in favour of being tough. I guess the PM will also be but has she considered it may mean threatening air traffic over the Atlantic?

The future of airports, especially Stansted. The PM is reputed to have read the 2,600-page Stansted report over Christmas.

Other talk was of general matters, e.g. what will happen to Norman with Margaret [Tebbit] in such poor health and with his own health doubtful? (NT staying at Chequers for the time being – close to Stoke Mandeville.)

Saudi Arabia

Tuesday 2 April 1985
It is 4.30 p.m. local time. The British Caledonian DC10 from London
Gatwick touches down safely at Jeddah International airport. It is BCal's
inaugural flight to Saudi Arabia and the first visible result of the deal struck
between myself on behalf of the British government, British Airways and
British Caledonian.

I am on board to celebrate the opening of BCal's new route; not that there
is much joy about it amongst the Saudis. They would have preferred BA
to continue to own the rights to the Saudi routes; with BA comes access to
Heathrow Airport, close to central London and from which there is a mass of
flights going west to the Americas or south to Africa.

As the aircraft comes to a halt I am sitting on the port side and take in
from my window what is happening on the tarmac outside. A black Jaguar,
on whose bonnet flutters the Union Jack pennant, pulls up beneath the steps
which are already in place beside my aircraft. Out of the car steps the tall,
balding figure of Sir Patrick Wright,* our ambassador.

In the middle distance a convoy of buses draws up, filled with men in
white robes. 'Who are they?' I ask Patrick Wright when he and his private
secretary have come on board and have expressed their welcome. Patrick rolls
his eyes and says, 'VIPs.' He adds, 'They come to the embassy at any opportunity; my allowance of whisky and gin has completely evaporated and I am
left to entertain out of my own pocket.'

The ambassador changes the subject. 'By the way, Minister, I have a
message for you from Hisham Alireza, the next generation of one of the
great Parsi families and I believe a fag of yours at school.' The message reads:
'Michael, welcome to Saudi Arabia. It would give my father and me very
great pleasure if you would come to dinner at our palace tomorrow evening.'
I show the message to the ambassador, whose eyebrows shoot up in surprise.
'Gosh,' he says. 'Can I go?' I ask. 'Not only can you, Minister, but you must.
We have never before received an invitation like this from the Alirezas. They
are big here, very big. Before the days of oil they were the main source of
the King's funds; they remain large contributors but they keep to themselves
inside the walls of their various palaces. We would love to know a bit more
about what makes them tick.'

We descend from the aircraft to the ambassador's car and head for the

---

* Sir Patrick Wright, later Lord Wright of Richmond, became head of the Foreign Service
(1986–91) and ended up with me as a governor of Wellington College.

perimeter of the airport, followed by half a dozen buses. When we reach the embassy everyone files out and fights his way to one of the expectant waiters sporting silver salvers with the correct measures of whisky and soda and gin and tonic.

I am soon approached by a tall distinguished-looking Saudi in white robes lined with princely gold trimmings. His eyes are smiling as he holds out his right hand. 'Welcome, Minister. I have the honour to hold the British Caledonian franchise and am to that extent one of your hosts on this trip. Is this your first visit to my country?' 'It certainly is,' I say. 'A great adventure.' 'I am sure you will be well looked after,' he says. 'London is an important destination for us, and I know, despite the grumbles, that British Caledonian will do a great job.' 'I am sure you are right,' I agree. 'You will find Saudi Arabia full of paradoxes,' he continues. 'What a hospitable man Patrick is.'

Wednesday 3 April

I am driven through the portals of the Alireza palace. At the steps leading to the main entrance I am met not by Hisham, whom I have not seen for some twenty-five years, but by an old man who introduces himself as Hisham's father. 'You are most welcome,' he says. 'Please come this way.' He leads me into a large dining room which I later learn has one of the finest sets of Hepplewhite chairs in the world. 'Please do stay for a moment,' he says. 'Before you meet the rest of my family I want to ask a special favour of you.'

I cannot believe what I am hearing when he speaks next. 'Hisham, as you may or may not know, was a great admirer of yours when he was a young boy at Wellington College and you were head boy. Even now, I believe he will listen to your advice; sadly he no longer pays much attention to what I say. The problem is this. Hisham is developing some very modern – perhaps we should say western – ideas about the education of women. He wants to found what I believe you call a co-educational school in Jeddah. This is completely impossible. The King will not stand for it. I want you to tell that to Hisham. Possibly nobody else can.'

At first I am speechless; then I stammer, 'But I know virtually nothing about your country and I have not seen your son for twenty-five years, when we were both children.' He rises from the table and leads me by the arm to a large door. 'Try your best,' he pleads.

When I meet Hisham Alireza he embraces me. 'I bet my father has got to you already,' he laughs. 'The old man is probably right; I will tell him you persuaded me!'

The next time I meet my former schoolmate is when he brings his three brothers and their wives to lunch at the Manor in Cropthorne – together with forty brace of pheasants which he has shot the day before and which my wife Ann will have to pluck and store. She feels like prostrating herself on the mat we have laid down in the drawing room facing Mecca in case of need.

Aviation security

Clearly the whole issue of airline security troubled the American administration greatly. On 24 June 1985 President Reagan wrote to the PM about it.

Tuesday 25 June 1985
Last-minute decision (taken on the day) that I should fly to Montreal following an unexplained crash by an Air India 747 (everyone killed) south of Ireland, to discuss air security at ICAO,* having heard that US minister Elizabeth Dole was going.

Wednesday 26 June
9.30: Nicholas Ridley briefing meeting at which he floats the idea of breaking up British Airways and flogging it off in pieces to avoid US anti-trust law. Also tells me to tough it up with Mrs Dole, US Transport Minister, when I meet her in Montreal. Either they give immunity to our air service agreement from anti-trust law and we can consider a more liberal regime, or we will go for 50-50 capacity over the Atlantic.

3.30 p.m. local time: Arrive Montreal and drive to British delegation offices in ICAO building. Straight into writing my speech to council. Drafting session goes well. We can go to party given by the French. (Previously broke off from drafting speech to meet French, Belgians, Italians and Germans, to whom I trail my speech. Lots of intrigue and suspicion plus admiration between British and French.)

Thursday 27 June
Appear on Canadian breakfast TV. Just before I go on air I hear that there has been a deal to release US hostages in Beirut. Does this mean the US has given in?

At the morning council meeting Mrs Dole steals the show, mainly because she brings her own media with her. Her speech is typically American, with lots of gimmicks and magical solutions, but not much thought or insight and certainly no consultation with the other delegates.

---

* International Civil Aviation Organization.

The French manage to get a speech in, although supposed to be 'ministers only'. The Russians also intervene to say they have seen it all coming for weeks; the answer was to return all the hijackers to the countries of origin, i.e. all the poor sods who had pinched planes to escape from communism to be returned to the Soviet Union.

My speech is short, without many solutions but at least logical. Press attendance at the three press conferences after the formal session was incredible – seven or eight TV crews. (During the afternoon watch a little Canadian TV where I and the other ministers are second on the news on all channels.)

After the morning session, meet Mrs Dole for about twenty minutes. Give her Nicholas Ridley's message. I say, 'There are grave political problems of going on as we are, e.g. cost to the taxpayer of Laker settlement and the frustration at not being able to privatise BA – all because of laws we do not recognise. There is no way we can continue like this in the future. Unless we can get an agreement, we will insist on 50-50 capacity-sharing across the Atlantic, as opposed to the present 70-30 in favour of the US.'

Mrs Dole is very sweet but unfortunately has no officials with her. (It transpires subsequently that this does not matter. She tells her people, 'There will be hell to pay with the British unless we sort this out.') My firm position scares the pants off Foreign Office, who think I go far too far. Mrs Dole says she had relatives in the Vale of Evesham, so we hit it off. We agree to meet again.

Wednesday 17 July
Lunch with Michael Dobbs – rising star in the Norman Tebbit camp. Wants to take over from Selwyn Gummer as chairman of the party. Jeffrey Archer would become deputy chairman.

Friday 19 July
Jeffrey Archer speaks at South Worcestershire Gala Supper; enraptures his audience by speaking largely about himself. Over dinner indicates that he would like to be deputy chairman.

Negotiations around the world

Week of Monday 9 September 1985
Try to finish preparations for round-the-world trip (Singapore, Malaysia, Australia, New Zealand, USA). At one point everything seems to be falling apart. Australians don't want me to say anything in public. Malaysia doesn't want to sign an air service agreement while I'm there, despite the fact that we

are giving them everything they want. The talks between BA and SIA* will be over two hours before I reach Singapore. In America BCal start by being 'wet' about the publicity programme for my visit (they talk about a private lunch with the airport authority in Dallas). I say I have in mind to invite the entire staff of the TV show *Dallas* to strip in front of me to the tune of the BCal jingle! They come up with an open picnic lunch and a horse ride for me in a ten-gallon hat – which is fine. Final straw, Singapore want to change the timing of my visit to the minister, who is only prepared to see me for half an hour, at 9.30 a.m., as opposed to previous time of 11 a.m. I tell them to stuff it; unfortunately reason given for why I will be late is that 9.30 is too early for me. Singapore cancel meeting altogether. The whole trip looks as though it is going to be a complete shambles. I seriously consider cancelling. However, Malaysians decide I can sign even if they can't.

The truth is that none of these countries nor their national carriers really agree with British competition policy on civil aviation.

Saturday 14 September
In the end we set out for Singapore today. On arrival the high commissioner, Sir Hamilton White, is clearly none too pleased about the cancellation of the meeting with the Singapore minister. Trip is going from bad to worse. Finally he calms down when I tell him the circumstances of my decision about the proposed meeting (I have to admit I never anticipated that the meeting would be cancelled). The residence is quite remarkably beautiful in old-style Colonial surrounded by verandas, tropical greenery, swimming pool etc.

Sunday 15 September
Try to pick up the pieces. This is done with some success with a very good meeting with the chairman of civil aviation, Sim Boon, who says he will square things with the minister and expresses interest in open-skies policy. (I encourage our rather bolshie official, assistant sec., to pursue the issue in the context of the Hong Kong Treaty, which means we have to start negotiating new rights for all Hong Kong routes. We really could be on to something.) Meetings with SIA, Charter Consolidated Bank. Good press conference.

Tuesday 17 September
Leave Singapore residence 7.15 a.m. for Kuala Lumpur, where we duly sign new air service agreement. Local press indicate that we have been rather tough. (Our High Commissioner had previously driven me in from the

---

* Singapore International Airlines.

airport and we had worked out a line for meeting both with Mr Chong, Transport Minister, and press.) Problem is that Malaysians have ratted in a very unsavoury way on a deal to buy Rolls-Royce engines. We cannot pronounce our true feelings about this as there are other contracts in the pipeline; however we have to make known our displeasure while not going overboard in public as we are trying to win back a measure of goodwill. In the end I am probably too mild at the press conference.

Then ten-course Chinese lunch with Mr Chong. Back to Singapore to catch flight for Perth.

Wednesday 18 September
In Perth. Visited various local business (aviation) interests and local politicians. The state politicians are full of self-importance here. In the evening stayed at Alistair McAlpine's home, the Bishop's House (a restored nineteenth-century Colonial mansion in the middle of the city). A marvellous dinner party (Alistair himself not present).

Thursday 19 September
Fly up to Alastair's house in Broome in north-west Australia, where he is developing a wildlife park as well as buying up half the local, mainly aboriginal, property.

Sunday 22 September
Return to Perth. This is what I wrote in his visitors' book in Broome: 'Wonderful, wonderful, Alistair. The flight over the Kimberleys was especially sensational! The wildlife park is a tribute to your creative genius. To make a beautiful place out of a desert is to engage in the essence of art. Thank you for three happy and memorable days. Michael and Ann Spicer.'

Alistair's place is surrounded by iron ore and diamond mines, as well as cemeteries filled with headstones commemorating Japanese pearl divers killed by sea snakes or sea crocodiles. You name it, they've got it – except for people.

Monday 23 September
On to Sydney to stay with consul general. Reception for MPs, including Nick Budgen, Ivan Lawrence. Rolls very anxious about loss of aircraft engine order.

Tuesday 24 September
Visit various airline interests then on to Canberra – reception at high

commission. Next day see various ministers (officials to press for greater liberalisation of air traffic). Then back to Sydney for press conference.

Thursday 26 September
On to Wellington, New Zealand, stay with high commissioner at beautiful Homewood House. Dinner reception for Minister of Transport.

Friday 27 September
Various meetings at ministry during the day. Then on to Christchurch to stay with Ann's Aunt Myrcine.* Dinner at Christchurch Club with various members of Ann's New Zealand family.

Sunday 29 September
Fly via Auckland and Hawaii to Los Angeles. Arrive same day, having crossed international date line, and expected to be usual amusing self at dinner. At Hawaii ring Hawaiian Airways to check everything OK with the BAE 146 order.

Monday 30 September
Visit LA's John Wayne airport. John Wayne introducing noise restrictions which greatly benefit BAE 146. Speech at a dinner at Century Plaza. Given badge of Honorary Citizen of Orange County for the contribution made by BAE 146 to quieter airports.

Tuesday 1 October
Meet *LA Times* & record for Michael Jackson radio show and then on to Dallas. Dinner to celebrate British Caledonian's five years on the route.

Wednesday 2 October
Press conference over breakfast in Dallas to say warning words to American Airlines about their breaking the quota rules for flights to London (at expense of BCal). Then on to Washington for meeting with Elizabeth Dole. The fuss there has been in preparation for this visit is difficult to describe. Telegrams from Nicholas Ridley in China, letters from Industry Secretary and the Foreign Secretary – all taking a slightly different line about how I should tackle the meeting. DTI says they would like me to keep issue of the anti-trust laws (and our desire to see them removed for British companies acting outside the US) to the general level; Foreign Office want me to be specific

---

* Ann's great-grandfather was Sir Joseph Ward, twice Prime Minister of New Zealand.

but with no threats like tearing up air service agreement. Our department wants me to be as tough as possible. In the event meeting with Mrs Dole very agreeable but does not get very far.

Thursday 3 October
I toughen up quite considerably at a press conference and also at a lunch at the embassy for senior US officials and press. My speech at the lunch generally acclaimed by our diplomats. Afterwards visit head of FAA (Admiral Engen) to discuss airport matters – co-operation between CAA and PAA – then short meeting with chairman of Congressional aviation committee, Mr Mineta.

Friday 4 October
In New York for visits to Kennedy and LaGuardia airports and discussions with Port of New York authorities.

Saturday 5 October
Sleep all day!

Sunday 6 October
Home on Concorde at last.

Westland

Monday 9 December 1985
Had to stand in at a meeting of EA for Nick Ridley. Chaired by PM. Extraordinary meeting which lasted for 2½ hours. Leon Brittan v. Michael Heseltine. Brittan wanted to sell helicopters firm Westland to the Yanks (Sikorsky wanted to buy major stake). Heseltine wanted to work up a European option. PM tried to steamroller Brittan solution but rest of us, including self, resisted. Heseltine given chance to work up his alternative. Great personal clash between PM and Heseltine. Next meeting fixed for Friday 13th. (PM had tried to talk me down: 'You weren't here last time.' I had to keep going or sink. Said there was a case for looking at the alternatives.)

Cabinet committee EA (Economic Affairs) is usually chaired by the Prime Minister and takes place not, as with other important committees, halfway down Whitehall in the Cabinet Office, but in the Cabinet room itself. This is located at the far end of the corridor which leads straight from the front door at 10 Downing Street.
    The EA committee comprises all members of the Cabinet or their

representative ministers. A Cabinet minister has to have a very good excuse (and the PM's express permission) to send a surrogate. This convention applies whether or not a department has a direct interest in the matter to be discussed.

On 9 December 1985 the subject on the agenda was the sale of the British helicopter manufacturer Westland. This was really a matter for the Department of Trade & Industry (Leon Brittan) but the Department of Transport (as well as, of course, the Ministry of Defence) had its own interest in the matter and had therefore to be represented at the meeting.

The problem was that Nicholas Ridley, the Secretary of State for Transport, was on a long-planned visit to the Far East. Somewhat understandably, the decision was made that he should not abort this tour in order to be present at the EA meeting.

As minister for aviation I was deputed to go in his place. I was briefed to argue in favour of a competitive tender for Westland and to resist any move to accept a bid by Sikorsky without considering the merits of a bid from, say, a European consortium.

Michael Heseltine (Secretary of State for Defence) concurred with this view (no doubt for his own reasons) when he was invited to open the debate. Norman Tebbit, David Young and I supported this position (on grounds of competition). The Prime Minister became increasingly irritated; to her it was a simple matter of Europe versus the USA and there are no prizes for guessing whose side she was on.

The meeting was acrimonious and eventually broke up with the agreement to meet again later that week, on Friday 13th. On Thursday 12th a minute was circulated which left out the agreement to meet on Friday. For this date Michael Heseltine had been asked to produce a properly prepared case for the European bid.

On Monday 16th I bumped into Heseltine behind the Speaker's chair and agreed with him that the meeting the previous Tuesday had not been properly recorded. He was hopping mad about the cancellation of Friday's meeting and said the PM was acting like an autocrat, this was the end of Cabinet government and so on.

On Tuesday 24 December Michael Heseltine circulated to all members of EA a memorandum indicating that a European–GEC–BAe consortium would offer a better deal for Westland than the Sikorsky–Fiat one, which in any case would, he suggested, have Libyan involvement in it.

The rest is public knowledge. Heseltine stormed out of the Cabinet meeting on Thursday 9 January 1986 and resigned from the government. The row had now escalated into a challenge to the Prime Minister's authority.

Monday 3 February
NR calls me in. Political situation getting pretty miserable re Westland affair. He says PM will probably have to go and be replaced with Geoffrey Howe. He himself will not be a candidate. I said that although I personally owe this PM very little (ten years on back benches before she noticed me) she has been a great asset to the country; it would be sad if she should go under these circumstances.

Tuesday 1 April
Drove with NR to Heathrow (picking him up on the way) for opening of Terminal 4. NR in v. good form – just having bought himself a fishing lodge on the Scottish border.

Ron Williams turns left on M25 from the M40 and so we go round the motorway the wrong way. NR misses his smoking time when we finally get to Heathrow; Royals left waiting for a few minutes.

Meet Princess of Wales. She seems to be concerned about the numbers of aeroplanes over Windsor Castle. I say that sadly, there are no insulation grants available.

Friday 18 April
To Stansted to 'dig the first sod' of the new airport. Pictured with local MP Alan Haselhurst who, surprisingly, is smiling. He has been continuously and forcefully opposing the building of London's third airport. He has managed to squeeze out of us an annual fifteen million passenger limit.

Wednesday 25 June
Bump into Cecil Parkinson in the lobby. Agree to have dinner together in the Kundun restaurant, from which we finally leave at 11.30. CP seeing PM fairly regularly. Apparently I was discussed for returning to organise Central Office. CP claims to have talked her out of it and saved me from a future worse than death (on the grounds that it would not be fair to Norman Tebbit, chairman, and currently in disfavour for not organising CCO properly).

Other topic of conversation John Moore. He has tried to restrict part of a speech I am due to make in Amsterdam to being nice about the Dutch; I want to paint the wider European picture, e.g. our plans for liberalising air travel in Europe when we take on the presidency on 1 July. Having done the job for two years and been allowed a good measure of freedom by Nicholas Ridley I find this hard to take.[*]

Thursday 22 July 1986

Concorde to New York to speak in a conference organised by Rupert Murdoch to consider security and air travel over the Atlantic. Got on well with Murdoch – much more human person than I expected. Six channels devoted to the Royal Wedding from 6 a.m. on Wednesday. All New York seemed to be discussing Fergie's hairstyle etc. when I emerged downstairs and into 5th Avenue.

Friday 22 August

This is the last week in August, when everyone waits for the shuffle. I have been tipped by *Daily Mail* and *Daily Express* to become a minister of state. We shall see. The consolation prize for getting nothing will be another trip round the world.

Monday 1 September

To London by 7 p.m. train to attend a small group of ministers, chaired by the PM at 11.30 at Number 10. Present: Michael Havers, Geoffrey Howe, PM, Douglas Hurd, John MacGregor, David Waddington and self (representing John Moore, in hospital). Issue: imposing visas on Nigeria, Pakistan, India, Ghana and Sri Lanka. Group takes decision to go ahead – without reference to Cabinet. Geoffrey Howe v. upset with the manner in which decision taken. PM at her hectoring greatest/worst, depending on your taste. She tells GH he may have to go to Social Services if he goes on pussy-footing. (She apparently plans a minor reshuffle of mainly junior ministers when she gets back from staying with the Queen in Balmoral, with whom the press claimed she was on bad terms this summer.) GH in effect asks her not to hector him. I intervene to say that if we are to impose visas it should be sooner rather than later, otherwise the Nigerians in particular will rush in to beat the system. Also, if we are going to charge for the visas (there was an argument between her and GH about her proposal to charge – she said £20; he said not a penny more than £16), I say we should bear in mind the fares. She says, 'Everyone wants to be fair. I want to be fair to our citizens.'

---

[*] In later years I came to admire John Moore, particularly when I learnt of his fortitude in his infirmity and of his proposals in government at the Department of Health radically to reform the health service along the lines of the French system.

Douglas Hurd says, 'He means air fares, PM.' She calms down. At the end she tells GH to cheer up. On these occasions she sits opposite her ministers.

Monday 8–Tuesday 9 September
Visit Athens. Stay with ambassador, Jeremy Thomas.
   8th: Dinner in embassy gardens with Greek Minister of Transport to discuss airport security at Athens. Very heavy going. By the next day break him down a little. Talks overshadowed by impending government reshuffle.

Wednesday 10 September
Reshuffle finally announced on my return from Athens. No move for me – younger blood like David Mellor and John Major moving past me. Susan Rooke, my private secretary, very sad for me. Earl of Caithness in our department made MoS at Home Office; he came in one year after me! Still, it could all have been worse. Receive very warm telegram from British Caledonian: 'Hooray, you are still Minister for Aviation.'

Chinook disaster

Thursday 6 November 1986
A Chinook helicopter carrying workers back from the Piper Alpha oil rig in the North Sea crashes off the Shetland Islands. All forty-five passengers and crew are killed. It is the worst civilian helicopter accident ever recorded. As minister for aviation I am immediately despatched to Shetland; my instructions are to ensure that everything possible is done to retrieve the bodies and to enable friends and relatives to identify them with as much dignity as possible. I am also to do what I can to keep the domestic and international press in some sort of order.
   As I board the Royal Air Force HS-148 at RAF Northolt, the weather deteriorates badly. It soon becomes clear that the RAF does not have the appropriate insurance arrangements to fly me further than Aberdeen. The flight across to Shetland has therefore to be on a scheduled British Airways flight, for which I wait for several hours at Aberdeen.
   When I land with Susan Rooke at Sumburgh airport, the island is shrouded in thick fog; because of this our pilot is forced to make several attempts at landing before he finds a temporary gap in the mist.
   On the ground there is organised chaos. A large hangar has been comman-deered to house the corpses. What I find there is both horrifying and heroic. Neatly laid out on the stone floor are rows of naked bodies, some of them

mutilated by the force of one of the helicopter rotor blades which crashed through the roof of the aircraft. A team of doctors and medical assistants is quietly putting the bodies into some sort of order so that they can be viewed by the next of kin. I am told that this work will not be completed until the following day. I am also informed that on past experience some foreign magazines will attempt to photograph the scene; only the bad weather has prevented them from doing so already.

I make three decisions, which Susan Rooke transmits:

1. The hangar, which is hard to make physically secure, is to be surrounded by a military and/or police guard with orders to bar entry to the building to all visitors except for medical personnel for the next twelve hours.

2. This order should, in particular, apply to next of kin, who should be alerted to this before they leave Aberdeen. (I am told this is not well received by those concerned.)

3. The order should also apply with special force to the press and, in particular, to those foreign magazines which make a habit of publishing pictures of dead bodies (which the British press does not).

The only other action of substance I take is through the Ministry of Defence to order a Royal Navy vessel to break off its participation in a nearby NATO exercise and join the search for those who have perished but who have not yet been found.

Most of the two days that I am in Shetland are spent dealing with the press. Satellite technology is in its infancy and ITV is ahead of the BBC on this occasion with the news. My comment on this in front of Kate Adie, the BBC's correspondent on the scene, leads to an unseemly and publicised row with her. [Relations are only repaired some months later when I entertain her to lunch at the House of Commons.]

Sale of British Airways and airline competition

Wednesday 14 January 1987
6 p.m. First major clash at meeting with John Moore re our negotiating strategy with the Japanese. Issue whether we stick out for what BA want (and therefore do not embarrass the privatisation prospectus) or settle for terms which would give BCal preference on some routes in time for their summer schedule. Problem aggravated by the fact BCal not in good shape. I argued the latter strongly in front of Norman Lamont, who had stayed on from a previous meeting. John Moore defended BA; his view, supported by officials,

prevailed. My position based on protecting our multiple airline competition policy. I am very against privatising monopolies.

Thursday 15 January

Inevitably Sir Adam Thomson (BCal chairman) asks to see JM. Says he feels betrayed. I suggest compromise by which we set a deadline to the negotiations so that BCal will know where they stand.

Friday 16 January

Meeting with JM and officials who are v. against my proposals as it will seriously weaken their negotiating hand re BA sale. Finally we agree on a formula by which we tell BCal that in our estimate the Japanese will want to settle by the spring or early summer.

Monday 19 January

Lunch with David Coltman (chief executive of BCal) and David Holmes (deputy secretary for aviation) prior to vital BCal meeting with their shareholders. Just about persuade David Coltman that it is not in BCal's interest to go berserk (they still need us). Also if we don't get stable settlement in this round with Japan we will have to go back to them when they will wish ANA (All Nippon Airways) to come on the routes (ANA v. powerful).

Thursday 22 January (my birthday)

Peter Emery takes BCal issue to PM. We meet outside her office in House of Commons. Last time I remember being there was during the week leading up to the Falklands War (with Cecil Parkinson and Norman Tebbit – sitting in what was Ian Gow's room).

I go in first and brief her not to mention BA privatisation. Stick to 'negotiations must continue in our wider airline interests'. This she does rather impressively. Meeting all of ten minutes (seven minutes of Emery, three minutes PM) – tells BCal lobby: no dice. I go off with Emery for half-hour to pick up the pieces. Offer to meet Adam Thomson at any time with Emery.

Within the Department of Transport I was known to be sympathetic to BCal and the case it made for being able to compete with BA on fairer terms. An indication of tension within the department surrounding this issue is given by a memorandum I sent on 24 February to the permanent secretary, Sir Alan Bailey. (I have blanked out the name of the official referred to.)

I refer you to Mr X's minute to my Private Secretary of the 23 February and in particular the first paragraph which reads: 'Your minute of 19 February recorded a telephone conversation between Mr Coltman and Mr Spicer. All the points he raised are under discussion with IA, and there is a considerable risk that wires will get crossed, and BCal's management confused if they try to take up matters of this kind at Ministerial level. I hope you will do whatever you can to discourage such discussions for that very reason.'

I would have been very irritated indeed had Mr Coltman's telephone call not been put through to me. Relationships with BCal have become fraught and it has been extremely difficult to prevent them from rocking the boat during BA privatisation. I suspect Mr X underestimates these difficulties. The irony is that he himself asked me to convey to Mr Coltman the message that we were aiming for a total package deal in our negotiations with Tokyo and Seoul.

MICHAEL SPICER

Friday 23 January

Due to appear on *Any Questions* in Taunton. (V. nervous; luckily all goes well.) Ring Michael Allison, PM's PPS, to say I think all's well with Emery.

Sunday 25 January

4.30: Meet in John Moore's office in Marsham Street to discuss price at which British Airways is to be sold. Also present Norman Lamont (Financial Secretary to Treasury) and Treasury officials. Meeting starts with no advisers, Hill Samuel saying they could get sale underwritten at 130p. Ministerial team retires to consider this. We all agree that this is a fair price. When we return, Hill Samuel and brokers say that although they could underwrite at 130p, for the sale to be a success they think 125p essential. NL and JM wobble. NL rings Chancellor of the Exchequer (Nigel Lawson). The three of them agree to come down to 125p – £30 million off receipts (now £900 million). I and officials argue in favour of the original price.

Earlier I wrote a note to Moore: 'As long as we can sell the stock, which we have been told we can, I am sure you are right: we lose more votes by the fat cats making big money than by their losing it.' However, decision was 125p (partly paid 65p).

Wednesday 11 February

I have to defend a partly paid price on first day of trading of 105p, 38p above the partly paid price we received. The joys of politics!

A few months later a meeting took place between John King of BA and the Prime Minister. The following note of that meeting gives a flavour of BA's general approach to competition from BCal.

29 April 1987

The Prime Minister this morning met Lord King, Chairman of British Airways, at his request.

The Prime Minister congratulated Lord King most warmly on the successful privatisation of British Airways. Much of the discussion thereafter need not be recorded. However Lord King said that, whilst BA was firmly in favour of domestic airlines competing on domestic routes, BA was a little bit at cross-purposes with the Government on the matter of competition on international routes. There was a need for a single strong British international carrier to take on the four or five US mega-carriers and the many other international airlines. Air France in particular would become a fearsome competitor if it were ever to wake up. British Caledonian was an irritant. The result of giving it routes alongside BA was to increase the number of flights allocated to foreign airlines. British Caledonian were likely sooner or later to fail. They were, for example, only making small profits on the Saudi Arabian route, whereas BA had made profits of £17 million a year. Lord King said finally that Adam Thomson and people at the CAA were saying that the Prime Minister had decided personally that British Caledonian should be given the route to Seoul because they had to be given something.

The Prime Minister made no response to Lord King's comments, except to say that she was not even aware of any discussions about the route to Seoul and that in any case such decisions were matters for the Secretary of State for Transport acting in a quasi-judicial capacity.

Safe to say, PM favours a 'BA solution'.

Friday 13–Saturday 14 February

Fly to Sweden (Stockholm). Dinner with former leader of Swedish Conservatives. Raise with him and at lunch on Saturday with the chief executive of SAS, Per-Axel Bronnesson, the question of a more liberal, freer air regime between Britain and Scandinavia. I offered them rights to pick people up in UK in exchange. Dr Bronnesson seemed quite interested and said he would get back to us or ask his minister to do so. It could be quite exciting to get a breakthrough with the Swedes. Their joint ownership of SAS with the Danes and Norwegians is one of the factors holding up further agreement at the Council of Ministers in Brussels. Their worry is their vulnerability, being on the periphery of Europe. I said there were two ways of dealing with this, either retiring into a shell as they tended to do or, like the Irish or Portuguese were now considering, to demand more rights. After lunch went langlaufen skiing.

General election

Monday 18 May 1987
Date of general election announced, to be on 11 June.

Tuesday 2 June
Halfway through my election speeches (thirty-six in all). Average attendance 30–40. Back home at 9.30 to find a BBC poll showing a hung parliament. Talk about this to Chris Lawson and Cecil Parkinson, on tour in Cornwall.

The general election has appeared a tatty version of the last campaign – as if all the paraphernalia had been got out of an old children's acting box and dusted down to be used again. Especially sad that no greater thought had been given to getting the best ad agency rather than simply using the one which did us well before. Nothing as stale as last time's ad agency.

Friday 12 June
The Conservatives are returned with a majority of 102 at yesterday's general election. Margaret Thatcher is set for a third term in office.

Chapter 7

Margaret Thatcher, 1987–90: third term

Department of Energy

Monday 15 June 1987

Telephone message to the car from my private secretary, Susan Rooke, that Alastair Goodlad's office (PUSS* at Department of Energy) had been on to ask about me. This is a great shock as it suggests I am to go to Energy, where the newly reinstated Parkinson has asked for me – not as a minister of state as he had promised, but as a PUSS. Try to get on the phone to Parkinson to remonstrate but he is out.

Arrive at 3 p.m. at my parliamentary office in Dean's Yard. Annie Page, my secretary, says Downing Street on the phone. Weigh up whether to refuse the job if it is PUSS; decide it would be better to give myself time and the option to resign coolly if and when I have something better to do outside politics.

PM comes on. Congratulate her on election victory. She says wants to move me at CP's request to Energy (doesn't tell me that my old job of aviation to be amalgamated with shipping); rather apologetically says she cannot promote me (she almost sounds guilty). I say 'I must accept' but hope one day she will promote me, having served three years as the chairman and deputy chairman and three years as minister of aviation.

So I now have a PUSS job without any honorary title in a junior ministry where for a year or so there is no real parliamentary business. Ring CP to say I am furious and have accepted to give myself time to think about my future.

He says he tried his best to get me MoS† position. Clearly he is not powerful enough yet. [In his autobiography CP writes accurately: 'Michael was disappointed not to have been promoted and came reluctantly.']

---

* Parliamentary under-secretary of state (third level of minister).
† Minister of State.

Tuesday 16 June

Alistair McAlpine comes round for champagne with CP and me. Plotting for Norman Tebbit to go as chairman and Peter Morrison, the MoS, to succeed him; in which case presumably I would be MoS. Alistair pleased that the old team CP and MS together; sees it as part of a real long-term comeback for Parkinson. I realise that is still my best hope but some of my old enthusiasm has gone.

Thursday 18 June

Ascot – Ladies' Day – at invitation of Colin Marshall, just made a knight at my suggestion for services to British Airways. Last chat about aviation (have debriefed Ivan Brabazon, who takes over from me). Chairman of IATA, chairman of CAA (Christopher Tugendhat) both in the box with their wives.

What did I achieve at Aviation?

My job at the Department of Transport was not high level but it was high profile, especially when Nicholas Ridley was my Secretary of State. My almost weekly visits abroad – sometimes to faraway places – to seek greater competition in the skies, in a market where historically airline routes were carved up between national governments, provided the main thrust of my time in office. It was a clear strategy and well publicised as an attempt to bring down the price of air fares and to improve customer service.

I summed up the policy in what turned out to be a farewell speech to the Aerodrome Owners' Association on Wednesday 25 February 1987, when I said:

> Competition means choice, and greater choice means that the initiative is handed over to the customer. Competition is the means by which producers are made to serve the marketplace and not to rule it. In aviation terms this means that, in order to survive and to develop, airlines must provide services which are attractive to their passengers and available at the right price. To be specific, our competition policy has had four components: the privatisation of British Airways, the encouragement of a wide range of differing airlines, the promotion of competition on individual routes, and the provision of adequate safeguards against anti-competitive or predatory behaviour by any one airline.

The success of the policy was mixed, but it did set a direction and pace which to an extent was pursued in later years. Domestically, competition was assured not in the end by British Caledonian, which was bought out by

British Airways, but by British Midland, to whom were granted invaluable entrenched rights at Heathrow.

Pursuit of the policy for greater competition was punctuated at intervals by one-off big events – the privatisation of British Airways and of the main airports, the Chinook disaster, the launch of Stansted airport, the search nationally and internationally for greater airport security, which involved a major international speech at ICAO in Canada, and the deployment for the first time (1 January 1986) of armed police and soldiers at London airports.

There were constant smaller events which I have not covered. One of these that springs to mind is the day that I and my wife were feted in the Channel Islands for my decision to protect the rights of flights to and from Jersey and Heathrow. I also witnessed a slight thawing of relations on aviation matters between Spain and Gibraltar, to which I paid an official visit. I also put restrictions on the flight of modern-day 'Zeppelin' balloons over London after representations about their intrusiveness and, in particular, that they were giving people headaches.

Altogether it was an eventful, exciting and, as it turned out, enjoyable period in my life.

Electricity privatisation

Monday 22 June 1987
The big issue in the department is undoubtedly the privatisation of electricity. [In her autobiography,* Margaret Thatcher called it 'the most technically and politically difficult privatisation'.]

Determined for the moment to suppress my frustration – even bitterness – at not having had my past work recognised. CP introduced me to senior officials today as the man who did the work at CCO 'for which I got the glory'.

Electricity must be sold off in separate competing parts; we must resist the privatisation, à la gas, of a monopoly. If I don't get my way on this I shall leave the government.

Tuesday 8–Monday 14 September
Having been placed in charge of the privatisation of the electricity industry, I go on a tour of the United States to study the power industry there.

---

* Margaret Thatcher, *The Downing Street Years*, HarperCollins, 1993.

Tuesday 15 September
Meeting at Chequers. Present: PM, CP, NL, D. Young, Norman Lamont, me and officials. Options discussed:

1. Leave electricity industry as it is and privatise.
2. Take away a small chunk from CEGB.
3. Option 2 and take away grid from CEGB.
4. Split CEGB and take away grid.

PM concerned about her relationship with Marshall[*] but she does say industry has 90 per cent over-capacity. She seems rather in favour of postponement. Nigel Lawson and I make point: longer you postpone, longer unions and Marshall have to work up hostile public attacks.

Have lunch and break up 3 p.m. Nothing really decided.

Also worries about nuclear. I say that nuclear was no problem in US with small privatised companies except that the planning process made things difficult.

Tremendous security at Chequers. Armed police everywhere.

On coal, PM wants maximum liberalisation but *not* for UDM (our people) since they now run the inefficient pits – going to be difficult.

Spoke to David Young over lunch about CCO. He clearly wants the job of chairman, which he thinks he can combine with SoS DTI.

PM agonising about her friendship with Walter Marshall: one moment saying 'He's a great friend of mine – mustn't let him down'; next moment saying 'He has made some mistakes over investment; mustn't be over-influenced by my friendship'. Also he kept the lights on in the miners' strike.

Wednesday 7 October
Parkinson speaks at party conference. (I spent night before at Alistair McAlpine party and went up to CP's room to help with speech. He was ensconced with Ann P, Michael Fallon, his PPS, and John Derrick, his special assistant. I left after a while, saying, 'The speech is bound to be a success, whatever happens.') It is. That is, it is well received by the conference: long standing ovation etc.

At Alistair's party tonight CP in good spirits, which Alistair and I do not dampen – I say that the next leader will be chosen by the parliamentary party not by the conference. CP says, 'I know. I have spoken in 300 of their constituencies.'

---

[*] Walter Marshall, Lord Marshall of Goring, chairman of the CEGB.

Thursday 8 October
Newspaper headlines: 'Parkinson welcomed back'.

I visit open-cast mine in Lancashire, then to London by plane via Manchester. CP on the Robin Day *Question Time* show. TV is his metier.

Saturday 21 November
9 a.m. Drive down to Nuneham Court, near Oxford, for weekend discussion of future privatised structure of the electricity industry. Assortment of civil servants, financial and legal advisers. Chaired by CP.

7 p.m. Permanent secretary, CP and I meet in CP's room. PS says that Lord Marshall and entire board will resign if CEGB is broken up and real competition is introduced. Trade unions will back them. I say I will resign if it is not. Suggest CP works out what he wants himself and starts to sell it to PM before Marshall does.

CP startled by what officials tell him, and also by hearing that the Policy Unit in Number 10 has been shaping up to advise the PM to go slow on breaking up the CEGB and possibly kicking the whole subject into the long grass. CP says, 'I would resign at that point.'

I say it is outrageous that the government is being blackmailed in this way by a nationalised industry. I certainly cannot go along with a decision to bow to this, especially as during the day's conference it was agreed with all our technical advisers that it would be perfectly feasible (and desirable) to inject competition into the industry. I am absolutely against privatising a monopoly – especially if the reason for doing so is that the board wants it.

CP says he recollects that at our meeting at Chequers the PM said of Lord Marshall on a couple of occasions that 'he might be right'. He would need to test the PM's mind. Otherwise she may prefer his resignation to Lord Marshall's. I say this is totally improbable. She has only just invited him back into the Cabinet and clearly did not enjoy his absence. I say he must make up his own mind and sell it to her before she becomes boxed in with alternative advice. CP not convinced. We are balanced on a knife edge.

Sunday 22 November
CP distant, still very much in the mood to keep options open.

Monday 23 November
CP and I meet a group of new MPs. They have been lobbied by Lord Marshall. What about his views on obligation to supply and the grid? I say there are alternatives. CP says we are still looking at all options. (After Question Time

in the House, when we were able to fudge the issues, the backbench committee officers, led by John Hannam, meet us to stress we must take a firm line on competition; CP seems to agree with them.)

I see my PPS, Gerald Howarth, after Questions and fill him in a bit. I say I am getting into a corner but so be it. He says my judgement of the party's view is right.

Tuesday 24 November
Article in the *Telegraph* says: 'Electricity denationalisation, expected to yield £15 billion for tax cuts in the run-up to the next election, is the government's biggest privatisation so far. On the outcome hangs Mr Parkinson's real political re-entry.'

Go in to see CP. Suggest that it is beyond the realms of possibility that PM would accept his resignation instead of Lord Marshall's if it comes to the crunch. *But* he must make his mind up or be willing to argue it hard. If he leaves it too late, PM may get into a corner. He says Lord Marshall has already submitted a minute to PM implying threat of resignation. CP has fixed to see her after the summit conference on 14 December.

In the evening go to see Alistair McAlpine, whom I have been visiting every week since his heart bypass operation. He agreed CP needs to make up his mind and then sell it to PM. Marshall not so much of a threat.

Saturday 28 November
Find a minute in my box on the train to Evesham dated 25 November, headed 'Electricity Privatisation':

Dear Stephen*
    The Chancellor of the Exchequer had a bilateral meeting with your Secretary of State this morning. Chancellor said that he agreed that the only real choice was between Option C (take obligation to supply and grid from CEGB) and Option D: he favoured Option D (break CEGB into 5 parts). Under either option, steps should be taken to ensure that the grid becomes a passive common carrier. It was critical to separate grid from generation …
    Yours ever,
    J. M. G. Taylor
    Private Secretary to Chancellor

---

* Stephen Haddrill, Cecil Parkinson's private secretary. Later chief executive of the Association of British Insurers.

British Caledonian wiped out

Thursday 3 December 1987
David Coltman, MD BCal, rings me at 8 a.m. Have I seen the news that
the Spanish have removed their objection to more competition between
European airlines – because we now have an agreement about co-operation on
Gibraltar airport? Yes, I have. Does this mean Paul Channon (SoS Transport)
will look more favourably on SAS investment in BCal as opposed to BA
takeover? (Paul Channon asked my views on this on the bench on Monday
night). 'I imagine it might.'

In the afternoon John King, chairman of BA, comes to see CP and me.
(Cabinet has discussed BA/BCal issue), David Young having said he doesn't
want to intervene on competition grounds. Over the weekend he was quoted
as saying to King, 'Get your tanks off my lawn.' Apparently Young now
denies this. Tebbit has joined in, blazing in favour of BA and against Young,
whom he stopped becoming chairman of the party. CP indicates to King that
all will be well.

6.30: Weekly visit to Alistair McAlpine, still recovering from his heart
bypass operation. We agree that what is going on is part of a jockeying for
position for future leadership. Lord Young wants to be kingmaker. Tebbit
wants to be king. Interesting that both he and Heseltine are now on the back
benches. CP keeps in with both of them.

CP has first got to weather the storm of electricity privatisation. That
should break just after Christmas. He sees PM on 14th of this month; we will
probably all go to Chequers over Christmas.

Monday 7 December
PM meets Gorbachev at Brize Norton. That evening she approaches Douglas
Hogg, who is sitting on the front bench with a large packet on his lap. 'What
are you doing here?' she asks. 'Oh, I suppose voting, like me.' Hogg looks
startled. Norman Lamont says, 'Amazing what a good lunch can do for you'
– a reference to Mrs Thatcher's lunch with Gorbachev. (Apparently they only
ate one course.)

(Over the weekend shown paper on privatisation of electricity – argument
going my way (option C) – talk to CP on Tuesday 8th. I say it is v. good.)

Tuesday 22 December
BA finally takes over BCal without a whisper from the government. Tebbit
has won. There is to be no more competition between British long-haul
airlines.

The sad fact is that the 'saviour' took the form of SAS, one of the most restrictive airlines in the world. I tried to get a message through to Paul Channon suggesting that he at least expose SAS for what it is by setting out to negotiate a liberal bilateral with the Scandinavians but Paul did not return my call. I imagine he was simply resigned to BA taking over and determined to play as low a profile as possible. In the end the CAA gave the all clear to SAS but BA indicated it would object and that there would be long-drawn-out hearings which would kill BCal anyway – so they had to capitulate: not a very happy story for a government apparently committed to competition.

All my efforts earlier in the year and last year have come to nought. Such is politics.*

Tuesday 29 December

Dinner à quatre with the Ridleys at Naunton. He was very keen to persuade me not to leave the government.

Perfect evening: smoked salmon, pheasant, magnum of Château Latour, very jolly conversation. What will happen to Willie Whitelaw? – who will best replace him? George Younger? How to make the community charge more acceptable? I suggest switching education expenditure to the national budget and making the remaining items of local expenditure funded more locally.

Wednesday 13 January 1988

5 p.m. Call from Brian Griffiths, head of Number 10 Policy Unit. Can he come over and see me 'incognito'? Worried that our plans for privatising the electricity industry to be discussed with PM on Friday don't go far enough. I tell him that personally I rather sympathise with him but there are good reasons for not totally fragmenting the CEGB – in particular they are planning ten new power stations, six of them nuclear; if we keep a large rump CEGB these applications may be smoothly processed through the public inquiry system. Also persuade him that what we are doing – taking the obligation to supply from the generating side and giving it to the distributors, who will place contracts for new generation – very radical. After ten minutes I suggest that I fetch CP, who comes in – v. amicable conversation on the same lines.

---

* The one pro-competition action I was able to take was to give entrenched rights to British Midland, as mentioned above; this was of tremendous value to them and in particular to their major shareholder, Michael Bishop, created Baron Glendonbrook in 2011.

Later that evening CP and I, John Guinness (dep. sec.) and Willie Ricketts (asst sec. – brilliant) dine with CEGB. Eerie bonhomie about the evening.

Thursday 14 January

Dine with Michael Heseltine at Stafford Hotel. Very agreeable – so much so that I miss the vote at 10 p.m. Clearly thinks about nothing else but Thatcher's departure and how he is to replace her.

I tell him that I believe our defences would be safe in his hands, but that he has little chance of winning unless he can appeal to the right of the party. No candidate for leader has ever won from the left. He says that things could be very different in two years when Thatcher will be on the defensive because of new economic problems.

Friday 15 January

11 a.m. Meeting at Number 10 to discuss future privatised structure of electricity industry. Present: David Young, Cecil Parkinson, Nigel Lawson, PM (in chair), Francis Maude, Ian Lang, Malcolm Rifkind and several advisers, including Hans Liesner,* who was my economics tutor at Cambridge. PM typically robust. At one point I have to defend the proposal for two electricity-generating companies as against six on the grounds that current planning inquiries for nuclear power stations would be easier to sustain if the future nuclear company bore some resemblance to the CEGB. She says 'It's not essential' and pursues an argument about whether nuclear would need to be subsidised. A few minutes later she uses the point I have just made to attack another intervener. The whole discussion for two hours is conducted in a form of a confrontation between her and everyone else. CP has retained his way of dealing with her with a combination of firmness and smiles. She is still charmed by him. He stays on to talk to her at 1 p.m. after everyone else leaves. She is in for a frightful row with the present chairman of CEGB – her close friend for many years Lord Marshall, who does not want to be 'broken up' at all. Basically it has been left for CP to find a compromise with Lawson, who wants CEGB broken up even more. I am just about content with our proposal. Anything less competitive and I shall go. It will be interesting to see how the PM takes on Marshall. Just before the end I say (in response to her request for another paper, 'doing more on nuclear and reconciling ourselves with Lawson') that we had better move quickly as CEGB are to start giving

---

* Chief economic adviser, Department of Trade & Industry 1976–89; deputy chairman, Monopolies and Mergers Commission 1989–95.

evidence to the select committee on 25 January and that will certainly start the ball rolling in their direction.

Wednesday 20 January

Take Shirley Oxenbury up to see Cecil, with whom left at 8.45 for Goring Hotel to dine with Eric Hammond and John Lyons – electrical TU leaders. They are opposed to our plans to introduce competition into electricity. But v. civilised dinner at which CP reveals all our plans and asks them to keep them to themselves! Hope it works, and at least stops them striking. CP v. taken up with thoughts of Sara Keays and his daughter Flora in hospital. After dinner CP and I have a beer and return home around 1 a.m.

Monday 25 January

9 a.m. meeting at Number 11 with Nigel Lawson (CP late!).* NL still worried that our proposal does not introduce enough competition and wants to make CEGB smaller. CP argues against this as it will make change too disruptive. Also he is especially concerned about ensuring future investment in nuclear goes ahead smoothly. I suppress natural inclination to side with NL. At the very least NL's concerns will steel the PM when she faces Lord Marshall. CP becoming increasingly concerned about taking on Marshall, who has submitted very coherent case against his being broken up to the select committee on energy.

Tuesday 26 January

Meeting at 8.30 with CP and Kleinwort Benson (our financial advisers) prior to CP meeting with PM and NL to go through financial arguments for taking away only non-nuclear elements from CEGB.

Apparently meeting with PM went smoothly. NL still grumbling. This could be very useful in steeling her for her meeting with Lord Marshall.

Wednesday 27 January

Walter Marshall v. active around Commons. Apparently he was very persuasive. The quicker we start getting on with privatisation the better. My speech of the night before (pledging that the privatisation of the electricity industry would go ahead) receives quite good coverage in *Times* and *Standard*.

Thursday 28 January

CP understandably nervous at ministers' meeting. He doesn't like the thought of having to take on Walter Marshall, especially if PM's support is

---

* In her lighter moments Margaret Thatcher used to call him 'the late Mr Parkinson'.

uncertain. I make it plain again that I will leave the government if we do not stand firm.

Wednesday 3 February

CP sees Walter Marshall, who is predictably appalled by the idea of losing his monopoly.

Thursday 4 February

CP and Walter Marshall see PM at 6.30. PM apparently backing CP until half way through when she begins to falter in the face of Marshall's onslaught. No decision taken except that PM suggests that CP should go over to Chequers to have tea with her on Saturday.

At meetings with PM on 3 and 4 February, CP is apparently rather good once he gets in. Afterwards he says one advantage of all this is that 'I am getting more enthusiastic for our cause'. At the root of the problem is the fact that the PM is boxed in between CP and her friendship with Marshall (he who kept the lights on in the miners' strike of 1984). Put another way, it is Marshall's claim to know all about the technicalities and the dangers* of the industry against CP's commitment to competition. With CP there it is at least an even match in front of the PM, which would not be the case with any other of the current leading politicians.

Nigel Wicks, the PM's private secretary, feels Marshall's position is strengthening and thinks, as I do, that the quicker the decision is taken now the better. The whiff of a good row is beginning to waft around the House of Commons. If we do it now it will all be a great bore in Parliament. If we leave it, it could all become very sexy for the opposition.

Thursday 4 February

Shirley Oxenbury gives a small drinks party to celebrate her OBE. CP, Jeffrey Archer, Alistair McAlpine also present. Afterwards CP takes a group of us out to dinner. CP very bullish; all the press is forecasting that he will be promoted soon. Certainly he is very close to the PM again. He tells Ann that he will see me properly promoted this time.

---

* Marshall had a particular obsession with the reactive power necessary to maintain the stability of the system – and the need therefore, in his view, to keep the electricity industry as a single entity. 'It's all about megavars [reactive power], Secretary of State,' he would shout whenever he was in a corner.

Tuesday 23 February

Only two days out now from announcement of privatisation of electricity and still it has not broken in the press.

CP saw Philip Jones, chairman of Electricity Council, this afternoon and was uncharacteristically tough with him, banging his fist on a table at one point – in my view totally justifiably as Jones was treating him almost as if he were one of his staff: absurdly grudging about our proposals, accusing us of not consulting him enough. In fact we are always talking to him and he agrees with most of what we are doing, i.e. splitting up CEGB. He wants one holding company for the distributors with himself in charge; this we will not agree to.

Afterwards CP comes round to my office for a cup of tea to say he is still trying to get me to wind up the debate in Parliament. I don't think he will succeed because Scottish Office want to come in on our patch despite the fact that their proposals are roughly the opposite of ours. He wants me to have some of TV publicity; thanks me for all my support when he was wavering a bit – he is a very generous person in this way.

Tomorrow we see Marshall.

Thursday 25 February

CP announces privatisation of electricity to the House. I sit between him and PM, who is clearly pleased with his performance. His star is on the rise again.

Sunday 28 February

10 a.m. Ring Parkinson to congratulate him on publicity. He hasn't seen it but is increasingly irritated as I read it over to him. 'CP defeats Marshall and wallows in champagne afterwards', 'Lord Marshall may have access to Number 10, Parkinson has access to Chequers' etc. CP asks me whether I am the cause of the leak. I say on the contrary I feel rather aggrieved by it as I don't get a mention! 'If you hadn't rung me I would have thought that pointed the finger at you.'

Monday 29 February

CP still concerned about leaks to *Sunday Times* on his behalf. Colourful piece which talks of his ringing PM at Chequers when Denis is away. Still thinks could be me. Asks me in for a chat followed by his PPS, Michael Fallon. Later that evening Fallon comes up in a great state of concern. 'CP suspects us both of disloyalty and has told Richard Ryder, the whip.' I go to CP at 6.45. 'This really has got to stop; you're becoming obsessive and hurtful.' I remind him that I had had experience at Blackpool in 1984 of his irritation with friends who were 'over-active on his behalf'. He reminds me of the bad times he has been through and the pressures he has been under.

We leave in good spirits and I reassure Fallon and ask Ryder not to discuss all this with the rest of whips: to treat the conversation with CP as between friends, which we are.

Tuesday 1 March
CP still on about the article at ministers' meeting but it is dying down. What a storm in a teacup. My driver, Ron Williams, says, 'We will be on late in the coal debate tomorrow, sir'. He always acts as if my performance in Commons is to be a duet with him.

Selling nuclear to the Americans

Monday 28 March 1988
Due to address South Eastern Electricity Exchange in Boca Raton, Florida, on benefits to US of investing in British power industry. Have briefed Robin Oakley (political editor, *Times*) about this. Rung up by BBC on Sunday 27 March at midnight to say that the story is the lead in *The Times*, focusing on the point that US nuclear industry would be welcome. I said purpose was to encourage US investment generally to create jobs and set competition standards while maintaining our own very high safety rules.

Apparently CP in London in great state of fury as he has to answer questions in the House. My speech – yet to be delivered – needs changing. Take out investment in plant and put in more about need to comply with our safety standards.

Talked to CP at 6.00 a.m. (12.00 noon his time); on the surface very friendly but I could tell he was in a state of some excitement (had learnt this from my office in London) and indeed when I first came through on the phone I heard him refuse to take the call. A combination of Parliament and publicity (especially my publicity) makes him very nervous.

As it happens Question Time is very subdued. Some questions about my speech but nothing implying I am threatening safety. I understand CP deals with them quite adequately. I talk to him after this and he is much more friendly. Later that evening tells my PPS (Gerald Howarth), who had been kept out of the ministerial meetings that morning, that 'he had calmed me down'! In the meantime tremendous reaction in Boca Raton. People lining up to be able to invest in UK power.

Reflections

On 28 March I was involved in an event which was the lead story in all the major national newspapers – and from which my now fragile relationship with Cecil Parkinson never fully recovered. That day I made a speech in Florida. Under the front-page headline in *The Times* 'Britain invites US to invest in atom plants: £40 billion power contract to follow privatisation', Robin Oakley wrote:

> The government today launches an attempt to persuade American contractors, suppliers and builders of nuclear power plants to invest in the British electricity industry … In his speech to the Electricity Industry conference, Mr Michael Spicer says: 'The government would look with great interest to see whether new electricity producers will enter the field. It may well be, for instance, that there are generating companies in the US who will wish to invest in power stations in Britain. They will be welcome to do so.

The issue reached a political crescendo because it was the day that the department answered questions in Parliament. John Prescott for the opposition accused the government of 'begging for US capital to buy the electricity supply industry, even to the extent of allowing control to pass to foreign interests'. Cecil Parkinson did his best to defend the position but neither he nor, I suspect, the Prime Minister was best pleased. (I had been alerted to his anger during the night by my private office).

In my defence I make the following two points: first, my speech had, of course, been cleared word by word by the Secretary of State's office; secondly, for foreign investors to have the freedom to put their money into British power companies, nuclear or not, is a logical outcome of privatisation in a world whose economic well-being depends on the free flow of capital.

Ironically, exactly twenty years later – when, incidentally, I was president of the Association of Electricity Producers – it was a Labour government under Gordon Brown which successfully encouraged a French nationalised company, EDF, to buy Britain's nuclear plants.

Sunday 24 April

Proposing to go on another visit to USA. CP has not really been the same since the publicity I got on the last trip.

I have written a speech on the coal equipment industry – for Tuesday 26th in Chicago. Had planned to use this occasion to say something about the future of the British Coal subsidy. CP has vetoed this. Rang him yesterday at lunchtime, not so much about the speech but about our failing relationship. Ask him why, having agreed a line on coal (e.g. 'We have ambitions to privatise it but no plans', 'We are looking at ways to involve private capital'), he now won't let me use these phrases. He says Chicago not the place to make this speech. Fair enough, I reply, but do you not want me to speak at all? He says, 'I'm delighted for you to get publicity and indeed to make policy pronouncements. You made an excellent speech on nuclear power on Wednesday and I got a kick out of hearing people say so – but I don't want us making major policy speeches abroad.'

Friday 27 May
The recess has come not a day too early. CP and I have had very strained relations for the last few weeks, which came to a head on Thursday 19th when CP would not clear speeches I was due to make to Coal Industry Society (23 May) and to an IBM conference on regulation (25th). Finally had to agree to a speech from which all the newsy bits in the Coal speech had been obliterated; IBM speech not cleared until the day in question.

Thank God for some holiday (when I am revising *Cotswold Manners* for the New York publisher) and that CP off for two-week trip to Indonesia, China and Burma.

Wednesday 6–Friday 8 July
Official visit with Ann to Hungary on coal business. Stay at embassy with Len Appleyard (ambassador, v. pleasant). Hungary in political turmoil. They are still officially part of the eastern bloc but desperate to strengthen ties with west and becoming more sophisticated about how to do so. One minister said we used to think that all we had to do to attract capital was to allow it in. Now we know different. We have to reward capital. At one point Appleyard kicks out our beautiful 'interpreter' from the embassy car because she was becoming too friendly and is undoubtedly a spy.

Tuesday 27 September
Parkinson has meeting with PM while I am at informal Energy Council in Athens. Apparently they agree to do nothing about coal privatisation. I will hear details of this from CP next week.

Monday 3 October
Meet CP and receive his confirmation that he and PM have decided for the time being not to privatise coal. Tell him that I genuinely believe we are making a mistake.

CP is keen I should take over electricity decisions during the next few weeks while he worries about his role on Star Chamber.* (Shades of my role at CCO when he was on Falkland Islands War Cabinet).

Friday 7 October
Meet John Lyons, ESTUC, and other union leaders with CP. Discuss three issues:

1. They wish to see a draft of the Bill before Parliament does. (I intervene to caution against this).
2. A guarantee of all future pensions in the private sector. CP confirms this with an assurance that all existing pension liability will be transferred to private sector.
3. Joint (national) negotiating rights. CP said is willing to discuss this further.

(Fear of the unions is what is stopping him, and I suspect the PM, going further on coal privatisation.)

Monday 10 October
I send a memo re a *tête-à-tête* meeting CP has now planned with John Lyons:

> I imagine we will want to avoid getting ourselves into the position where the unions are able to claim at a later date that we have reneged on assurances. I fear this is now a possibility – with both Section 12[†] (which I believe we can strongly argue was never available for negotiation) and on pensions (where Friday's meeting may have led the unions to believe that we would give some absolute guarantee for all future pensions).

Wednesday 12 October
CP announces to party conference, 'We will privatise coal,' and gets a standing ovation. What he meant was that we won't privatise coal yet (i.e. until after the GE).

Friday 14 October
Go into the office briefly to digest Thursday's papers – full of CP's commitment to coal.

---

*   A small Cabinet committee assisting the Chief Secretary to the Treasury in his task of controlling/vetting departmental spending bids.
†   Bit of electricity legislation which provides for 'joint consultation'.

Apparently Peter Walker has telephoned in to ask at which Cabinet meeting the decision to include coal privatisation in the next manifesto was taken – answer, of course, 'none'! Decision not to privatise in this parliament taken between CP and PM. As with so much in this government, important decisions taken outside Cabinet by PM. (Similarly to the decision in principle to stick with nuclear.) It may make for strong government but we're moving away from collective government – except with the detail. On nuclear there are a number of specific problems – e.g. should all the costs be passed through to the consumer – and if not, which ones? These detailed questions are circulated to colleagues but *not* the big decisions of principle. A semblance of collective government is given – but it's not real.

Tuesday 29 November
Last night of the Queen's Speech debate. Ted Heath came up to me in the lobby, having made a particularly anti-government speech on the economy, to ask, 'When was your by-election?' I told him that I didn't have one because it was obliterated when he called the general election in 1974. He looked a little bewildered.

Chapter 8

Tony Blair

The Electricity Bill went into committee stage on 10 January 1989. Before it did so there was an extraordinary deal made between myself and the newly arrived but already rising star Tony Blair. In his auto-biography Cecil Parkinson described it as follows: 'Once published it [the Electricity Bill] had a relatively uneventful passage through the House due, in the main, to an informal agreement between Michael Spicer and Tony Blair who had replaced John Prescott as shadow Energy Secretary.'

Put like this, the 'informal agreement' would not seem to amount to very much. In fact it was a historical event which arguably contributed to the making of a future Prime Minister.

Blair put the proposal to me as we sat side by side on one of the thin benches which line the corridor outside the main committee rooms. In essence what he said to me was, 'I am a new brand of politician; I don't believe in wasting my time and that of my colleagues in opposition tactics which are mere gestures. There are several major points I want to make about this Bill, beginning next week with its effect on prices. Amongst other matters I want to highlight are energy conservation and the cost of nuclear power. I want these points to come up in time for the lunchtime news on dates of my choosing. In return you can have the completion of the committee stage of your Bill, whose passage with your majority I cannot prevent, by mid-March.'

His whip, schooled, as we all were, in the arts of maximum delay and of parliamentary guerrilla warfare, could not believe his ears. I, knowing how bogged down the Water Privatisation Bill, led by Michael Howard, had become in the room next door, could not believe my luck. Indeed, it felt too good to be true; I had no confidence that the deal could possibly hold. But it did; the Bill's last day in committee was 16 March. Blair climbed several feet up the greasy pole towards its top.

The future Prime Minister and I hit it off. Years later, when he was PM and I was chairman of the 1922 Committee, I wrote him a short letter of good wishes when he was ill. Within a few days he responded in his own handwriting.

In one sense our connection went back a long way further than the Electricity Bill committee. Tony Blair was twelve years old when I was first a parliamentary candidate in the north-east, where his father was an important figure in the Conservative Party. It is unlikely that we met then; certainly the story put about by one of Blair's biographers that I stayed with his parents is not true,* at least so far as I can recollect. I did fight Easington, which at that time included the village of Sedgefield, from which Blair's constituency later took its name.

Intriguingly (at least to me), Tony Blair persisted with what I believe is the myth of our early acquaintance in his autobiography. Very early in the book he wrote:

> I recall the very first time I met any politicians. Bizarrely, I think they were Michael Spicer, later a Tory MP, and even – but my memory may play me false – Patrick Jenkin, who went on to serve in Mrs Thatcher's Cabinet. They came to dinner in our house in High Shincliffe in Durham, the reason, I dimly recall, was because Michael – a young Tory prospect at the time – wanted to fight a hopeless seat to cut his teeth, and Dad had influence in Durham seats.†

The bizarre feature to me is that I recollect none of this; indeed, rather than touting myself round 'hopeless seats', as I describe in Chapter 2, the procedure was more the other way round.

I hope the rest of Blair's book is more accurate. He has, in my view, a good case on Iraq, in particular the importance of our intervention as a deterrent to Iran, which I agree with him is becoming a – if not *the* – major threat to the stability of the world. It would be a shame if all this were spoilt by sloppy research which indeed lay behind the justification for the invasion of Iraq in the first place.

On the Electricity Bill committee I had to be careful not to allow any bonhomie between Blair and me to blunt normal hostilities, especially when he and his colleagues made mischief between Cecil Parkinson and me.

As promised, Blair began the attack on the first day on the effect of privatisation on the price of electricity. The government argued that new competition would bring this down; the opposition said that the need for private companies to make profits would put it up.

On the occasion of the first sitting on 10 January 1989 Cecil Parkinson took the driving seat and became embroiled in a difficult argument with Blair about future inflation rates. Blair pursued the matter at the next meeting of

---

* Jon Sopel, Tony Blair: The Moderniser, Michael Joseph, 1995.
† Tony Blair, A Journey, Hutchinson, 2010, p. 8.

the committee, when Parkinson was not present. Here is part of an exchange as reported in Hansard at Column 69 of the committee proceedings on the morning of 12 January 1989:

Mr Tony Blair: We now know that the £40 billion (of future investment) on which the price increases were justified … was an invention of the Secretary of State.

Parliamentary Under-Secretary of State, Mr Michael Spicer: Rubbish.

Mr Tony Blair: I think the minister has been pretty hard done by. He has to carry the can for his Secretary of State. No matter how important the meeting, it is unfortunate the Secretary of State has not been here to justify his figure. [Parkinson can never make Thursday mornings in committee because he has to attend the Cabinet at that time.]

Mr Michael Spicer: I rise not to answer but to protest. The Honourable Gentleman may wish to reconsider the phrase that he used. He referred to the invention of a figure. That is utterly unfair …

Mr Tony Blair: Let me tell the minister that so far we have found this a very pleasant committee and after this morning's proceedings we shall find it increasingly pleasant.

This sniping at Parkinson was maintained over many sittings. On 21 February, for instance, Frank Haynes (MP for Ashfield), a Labour card, said:

Mr Frank Haynes: The Secretary of State was on his feet when we knocked off at 1 o'clock but knew damn well that he would not be here at 4.30 this afternoon. It is most discourteous to the committee.

Mr Michael Spicer: My Right Honourable Friend is at a meeting of Labour Party members of Parliament representing coal-mining interests, at their invitation. It is a long-standing engagement …

Mr Tony Blair: I want to reply briefly to the Secretary of State before the minister speaks again. I look forward to that as we always seem to get more from him than we do from the Secretary of State.

The banter was not all one way. Here am I speaking later in the same debate:

Mr Michael Spicer: We were watching the prospects of the 4.15 race at Sedgefield and were specially interested in a horse called Mind Your Back because of what the Honourable Member for Makerfield [Ian McCartney] was doing behind the back of the Honourable Member for Sedgefield [Tony Blair]. I must inform the committee breathlessly – I have just received the information that Mind Your

Back won the race. What should the Honourable Member for Sedgefield do about his Honourable Friends who sit behind him and watch – with increasing wonder – how he conducts the affairs of the Committee? …

The Honourable Member for Durham North [Giles Radice] rose to defend his Honourable Friend but there was no need. The Honourable Member for Sedgefield is proud of his record … If the Honourable Member for Sedgefield chooses to issue press releases rather than to talk about the Bill, that is reasonable, but it is also reasonable for us to comment on that fact, not necessarily out of malice or disparagement.

For good measure I took a swipe from time to time at the irrepressible Mr Haynes, who in the same debate asked me:

Mr Frank Haynes: Do I have the minister's permission to go public in my constituency … that the standard charge can be fixed at any figure?

Mr Michael Spicer: The Honourable Gentleman has my permission to go to his constituency and explain not only in his own words but to say that I told him, that that is the present system and that we are producing the proposals because we wish to change the system. He ought also to explain to his constituents why he has not been voting in favour of the changes … I grant the Honourable Gentleman my permission to go to his constituency and explain these matters but I insist that when he does so he also tells his constituents why he has not voted for the change.

Haynes was not to be outdone and we had the following short exchange:

Mr Michael Spicer: I shall not prolong the committee's proceedings.
Mr Frank Haynes: He wants to knock off.

The remarkable progress on what is a highly complex Bill may not have caught the eye of my senior colleagues, but it was noticed in certain quarters of the press. The following is a piece by Leith McGrandle, financial editor of the *Daily Express*. It cannot have endeared me to Michael Howard. Under the column heading of Viewpoint, McGrandle wrote:

What a contrast in the present fortunes of two ministerial Michaels charged with the tough jobs of ferrying the government's most controversial privatisation plans through Parliament.

Michael Howard is the Environment Minister piloting the Bill to privatise the water industry.

Michael Spicer is the Energy Minister in charge of privatising the electricity industry.

Both are immensely able, ambitious and high flyers marked for higher office.

There the similarity ends for the moment.

For Michael 'The Water' Howard is sunk deep in a watery bog in which the government's most unpopular privatisation proposals have become stuck.

While Michael 'Sparky' Spicer is sailing through the parliamentary obstacle course.

The Water Bill has been guillotined, large chunks passed on the nod, and has still been amended in a number of major ways.

The Electricity Bill, after three months of fierce argument in committee, has emerged with barely a comma changed. Unlike the Water Bill, it was not guillotined so every clause was debated.

There was throughout the proceedings an obsession with publicity and press releases which Tony Blair had developed into a fine art, recognising as he did that there was little for himself in the committee proceedings per se. This is illustrated on 16 March, the final session, at Column 1606:

Mr Michael Spicer: The Honourable Member for Sedgefield criticises the system that we seek to change and at the same time criticises us for changing it, so it is not surprising that his arguments should be increasingly discredited.

Mr Kevin Barron: Say that in a press release.

Mr Michael Spicer: I shall make sure that my remarks are heard outside and the opposition will not like that.

Mr Tony Blair: I am glad that we have at last managed to teach the minister that if he is going to say something he should make sure it is said in the form of a press release and I think that we have just heard his press release covering this morning's proceedings.

Sometimes I went onto the attack, as on 28 February (column 1268):

Mr Michael Spicer: Just for the record, as the Honourable Gentleman would say, does this imply that he intends to renationalise the companies?

Mr Tony Blair: I repeat … We shall reinstate electricity as a public service.

Mr Michael Spicer: What does that mean?

Mr Tony Blair: It means exactly what it says.*

All became sweet and reason at the very end of the proceedings when for instance, Malcolm Bruce, the Liberal Democrat spokesman, speaking for the last time in committee on the morning of 16 March, said:

Mr Malcolm Bruce: I thank the minister for his spirited response to the committee, although I would have liked to thank him more profusely for accepting the amendments that he resisted.

Mr Michael Spicer: I thank, quite genuinely, the opposition, not because of their arguments – as they have been wrong on the whole – but because it has been a courteous and good-humoured committee.

My next parry with Tony Blair was on the floor of the House at the report stage of the Electricity Bill on 10 April 1989, reported in Column 606:

Mr Michael Spicer: Speaking to amendment number 191, the Honourable Member for Sedgefield designated today as Consumer Day. I must tell the House that, after the passage of the Bill, every day will be Consumer Day ...

Mr Tony Blair: Perhaps the minister will care to confirm something that he was not prepared to commit himself to in committee. Under the contracts concluded by area boards and the duopoly structure – PowerGen and National Power – that the government are setting up, there will be no yardstick competition prevailing.

Mr Michael Spicer: The question of contracts is one that has yet to be settled ... There is no secret about the fact that the government intend that the contracts should not be agreed to in any way that will prevent future and further competition.

Mr Tony Blair: Will the Honourable Gentleman give way?

Mr Michael Spicer: I shall let the Honourable Gentleman intervene later. I want to develop an important argument. The Honourable Gentleman based his speech on the argument that we are doing nothing for the consumer. I have said already that that is manifestly untrue in respect of generation ... The Honourable Gentleman cannot get away from the fact that [at present] there

---

* The issue of whether or not to commit to renationalise was one of growing embarrassment to Tony Blair as he and the emerging group of 'new Labourites' wrestled with what to do about Clause IV in Labour's constitution, dealing with the public ownership of the means of production etc.

is one monopoly supplier. That supplier is to have its monopoly broken and from now on the industry will be geared up to encourage new entrants.

I had no further exchanges with Tony Blair until many, many years later, just after he had become Prime Minister. On 14 May 1997, as he was introducing his first Queen's Speech, I asked him with a straight face whether he would resign if he found himself having to transfer massive powers 'from this country to the government in Brussels'. He dealt with this adroitly and with humour: 'It is a little early to be talking of resignation.'

I was rather more effective in questioning the man who stood in for Blair in his absence, John Prescott, as well as the man who eventually succeeded him, Gordon Brown. In both cases I asked very short questions. I simply enquired of Prescott about a matter which normally would have been totally obscure but which that day was in the headlines of the nation's press. Here is the exchange, on 14 April 1999:

> **Sir Michael Spicer:** In view of the firm commitment given to the select committee on the Treasury by the Chancellor and economic secretary, will the deputy Prime Minister give an absolute guarantee that the withholding tax will not be introduced in this country?*
>
> **The Rt Hon. John Prescott (Deputy Prime Minister):** As Secretary of State for the Environment I constantly have to deal with the disastrous poll tax. The Honourable Gentleman should bear in mind that we have given local authorities the most generous settlement that they have ever received.
>
> **Honourable Members:** More, more.
>
> **Madam Speaker:** Order.

The next day Robert Shrimsley, chief political correspondent of the *Telegraph*, had this to say about the episode:

> After a confident start Mr Prescott was flummoxed when Sir Michael Spicer, a Tory backbencher, asked him to confirm that the government would block the EU's planned withholding tax – essentially a levy on an investor's overseas savings, designed to stop money flowing out of one country into another with a more competitive tax regime.

---

* A withholding tax is a tax on interest and dividends payable by a company to recipients in another country. As the domestic country cannot tax individuals in foreign countries, a withholding tax ensures the government gains at least some revenue from such payments.

However Mr Prescott was clearly bewildered by the question and turned anxiously to his Cabinet colleagues, Clare Short and George Robertson, who sat on either side of him. After a 10-second pause, Mr Prescott baffled MPs by ignoring the EU proposals and launching a stinging attack on the poll tax, which was abolished in 1991.

Afterwards Tories were amazed that he appeared to know nothing of the tax.

In *The Independent*, Michael Brown dealt with the same issue in the following way:

QUESTIONER OF THE WEEK award goes to Sir Michael Spicer (C West Worcestershire), who, having spent years giving John Major a hard time as a Maastricht rebel, put his skills to good use by flooring John Prescott when he stood in for Tony Blair at Prime Minister's Questions. Sir Michael used the infinitely more effective tactic of a one-sentence question: 'Will he give an absolute guarantee that the withholding tax will not be introduced in this country?' Unusually, the normally assured, combative and confident Mr Prescott lost the plot and stared in silence, open-mouthed at Sir Michael. To put it bluntly, Mr Prescott had no idea what this tax was (any more than 99 per cent of MPs) and burbled gibberish about the poll tax and local authorities. Luckily for Mr Prescott the Tory deputy leader, Peter Lilley, stood next and stuck to his scripted question on fuel duty. Mr Lilley's response highlighted the disadvantage of being tied to a pre-planned question. Sir Michael had created an opportunity for Mr Lilley to go for the kill. Instead, Mr Prescott continued to roar incoherently like a seriously injured elephant until the Speaker called time at the end of his worst half-hour since the general election … Like an elephant, he never forgets who causes him pain. He will recover quickly and retribution will surely follow.

Prescott was never fully confident at Prime Minister's Questions again. Almost ten years later, and after he had resigned as deputy Prime Minister, I bumped into him in the corridors (he had studiously avoided even eye contact in the intervening period). Even then, the matter was clearly still playing on his mind, perhaps because he was writing his autobiography at the time. On this occasion he looked directly at me, smiled and asked sheepishly, 'Remind me, Michael, what was the name of that tax?'

On 18 June 2008, I asked Gordon Brown the following question: 'Why are there always so many strikes at the end of a Labour government?' The Prime Minister mumbled something inaudible about Tory strikes being worse. I did not expect the force of the reaction and hilarious laughter this question received on both sides of the House. This was noted by the *Evening Standard* that night in the following terms: 'Sir Michael Spicer showed just why he is so popular on the Tory backbenches today, nearly bringing the House down.' Indeed, I became something of a specialist at short questions (on 14 October 2009 I asked Brown, 'Would he confirm that he will be soldiering on to the bitter end?'), to the extent that I wrote a brief piece about them for my monthly column in the *Worcester News*:

Two weeks ago I asked the Prime Minister in Parliament: 'Why are there always so many strikes at the end of a Labour government?'

Even I was surprised at the reaction: laughter and cheers from both sides of the House and much comment inside and outside Parliament thereafter.

How could fifteen words make such an impact? It is true that short questions can often unbalance the person answering. I once startled John Prescott by asking him 'What will he do about the Withholding Tax?' and even more unnerving was my question to a former Prime Minister simply asking 'Why?'.

Short questions in Parliament are not always effective. Frequently they take not only the Minister by surprise but also the person controlling the microphone. By the time he has worked out where you are and has focused the system on you, the question can be over and lost to the listener. It also provides little or no copy for the newspapers; its impact is therefore instant but invariably fails to linger on.

Furthermore to be effective it requires greater attention to detail than meets the eye. My recent question included for instance certain key words which were I think critical.

'Always' meant that the reference went further back than to the present spate of strikes, by implication to Callaghan's Winter of Discontent. 'End of a Labour government' took for granted that the Brown government is on its last legs and 'so many strikes' was to hit a socialist government where it hurts most; Labour after all is meant to be on the side of those who are prone to go on strike.

What the effective short question does do is to show how misplaced can be the modern habit of judging the worth of an MP purely by the *quantity* of what he says and does. Sometimes, not always, it is better to use the rapier than the blunderbuss.

Even a voting record can be a misleading measure of worth without some consideration being given to what the MP was actually voting for or against. My own highest voting rates were during the Maastricht Treaty in the early 1990s when I was voting consistently against my own government. Was that good or bad? I leave this for others to judge. What is clear is that the number of times I voted is totally irrelevant to answering the question.

I might have added that most questions, never mind the short ones, are best asked when you already know the answer.

My brief exchange with Tony Blair in 1987 did not prevent him from inviting me at the very outset of his premiership to bring a group of my schoolchildren for a tour of 10 Downing Street. When I did so, I could not have been received more courteously by Cherie and later by Blair himself. Cherie reminded me of the need to take photos for my local newspapers and pointed me to the best spot. She was very well briefed about me, saying at one point, 'No need to show you round this place after your time here as Margaret's PPS.'

My remaining involvement with Blair was through my captaincy of the House of Lords and Commons Tennis Club. I invited him to become president and in a letter dated 2 June 1997 he accepted.

Tony Blair is charming. His premiership was, however, a massive wasted opportunity. The enormous majorities that he gained gave him a wonderful chance, particularly in his first two parliaments, to introduce into the public sector the reforms he had promised.

Politics is often the art of doing the opposite to that which is expected of you: Nixon pulled out of Vietnam, Conservative administrations wound up the Empire, Thatcher increased public spending and put us more deeply into Europe. Blair could have made education, health and pensions responsive to consumer demand, for instance by putting money directly in the hands of patients to spend on doctors of their choice, and in the case of pensions, through properly funded and supported assurance schemes. He could have done all this in a way and at a time that it would have been virtually impossible for a Conservative administration to do. It was not to be. From the moment he sacked Frank Field,* he had pulled up the drawbridge behind him. He never again effectively emerged to take up his own challenge, although he used up a lot of political capital fiddling about at the edges.

The qualities which worked so well for him in opposition – especially his genius for self-promotion – turned out to be handicaps in government. On domestic matters certainly he was feeble and directionless. In foreign policy, by contrast, he was an adventurer; but his incursions in the Balkans, Iraq and Afghanistan were not thought through and were largely at the behest of the Americans.

---

* Member of Parliament for Birkenhead from 1979, minister for welfare reform 1997–8. He was an early champion of universal fully funded public–private sector top-up pensions.

Chapter 9

Margaret Thatcher: her downfall

Wednesday 22 February 1989

The last six weeks have been a strange experience. I am meant to be leading for the government on the standing committee on the Electricity Bill. We have a very effective opponent in Tony Blair, who issues press releases in the morning and then gives us the clauses/amendments in the afternoon. CP appears occasionally. The trouble is that secretaries of state can't be there all the time and they lose touch with the atmosphere. Yesterday was a case in point: CP arrived in a bad mood, still smarting from an attack on him in *The Times* by Peter Stothard. No doubt distracted by this, CP was not at his best when dealing with Blair.

Wednesday 1 March

While I am briefing for the committee on the Electricity Bill – in particular Clause 87, to do with security of power stations and the SoS's powers – a little middle-aged lady official called Hazel is introduced as our security expert. She starts to talk about our relationship with 'the box', otherwise known as Box 500, which is apparently a department contact point with MI5.

Tuesday 14 March

After the Budget speech, CP comes round to my office for a cup of tea. Tells me I am doing well with the Electricity Bill in the House and should be promoted in the next reshuffle – we'll see.

Wednesday 22 March

Last day of Parliament before Easter. Spend evening chasing Tony Blair, definitely the new rising star in Labour Party and new breed of designer socialist. Want to confirm the plan for report and 3rd reading where we are not on a guillotine. Early in the evening have a glass of champagne with CP. He is much more relaxed at present. Week ahead of writing *Cotswold Murders*.

Wednesday 5–Thursday 6 April

Interesting two days. I have had to take through the report stage of the Electricity Bill almost single-handedly without a guillotine. CP on Thursday at dinner for Gorbachev at Number 10. On Thursday I answer debate for seven hours non-stop 5–12.

Monday 10 April

CP in Russia opening a trade fair. I have to carry the department at Question Time and for report and 3rd reading of Electricity Bill. General consensus next day seems that I have done OK. 8½ hours solid!

At last things seem to be going my way.

Wednesday 12 April

Debate on *Newsnight* with Tony Blair on nuclear power went off well.

Thursday 20 April

CP comes back from Cabinet at 12 p.m.; they have been discussing football supporters' identity cards, about which, since the disaster in Sheffield, the party and, indeed, the Cabinet are rather divided. CP in expansive mood about PM's contribution to a previous discussion about nitrates and whether its use by farmers should be banned as it pollutes river water. Suddenly she asked, 'Does it fur the pipes?' looking at Nick Ridley, the SoS DoE. He looked down at the table and said, 'Under certain circumstances it might, PM.' CP apparently passed a note to the Cabinet secretary asking him whether 'any of us is qualified to say one word on this subject'. 'Certainly not,' came the reply.

I think CP broke into the story by way of explaining to me and a group of officials that the same was true of football ID cards on the basis that it is hardly likely that anyone round the Cabinet table has spent much of his or her life on the terraces!

Monday 24 April

Lunch at Downing Street with PM. Rather a relaxed atmosphere. Before lunch over drinks, the PM seems more friendly than usual to me; perhaps word has got to her that I took the Electricity Bill through Parliament without too much fuss (in contrast to Michael Howard's Water Bill). The real issue on her mind is Europe and the balance of payments. At one point she exclaims, 'Much to my horror I learnt from my hairdresser that all her sprays were foreign. I said I didn't want anything but an English spray on my hair.' She is in one of her most protectionist moods. CP and Peter Morrison take the opportunity to bring up the future of the Offshore Supplies Office, which the DTI (quite rightly) wants to close because it discriminates in favour of British and therefore more expensive products for the North Sea oil industry.

'You must keep it', she says, 'and if there are problems with the DTI, parade their officials before me.'

Over lunch the conversation is relaxed. She is dealing with ministers she likes. CP tells stories about the inefficiencies he found on a recent trip to Russia and Morrison tells a story which makes her laugh about how important he was made to feel by the Chinese as deputy chairman of the party. (I should have done better five years ago!)

One feels she is enjoying herself, though you can never lower your guard. At one point she says we must ensure that people living abroad can vote even though they have lived outside the country for more than five years. 'Most of them are Conservatives.' Wakeham says, 'We are doing our best.' 'You've got to do better than that. You've got to do it.' Wakeham is unwise enough to say, 'It's for the Home Office.' 'No it's not, it's for you.'

Tuesday 20 June

Bump into Nick Ridley after the 10 p.m. vote. Have a drink with him for an hour and a half. He expresses two views:

Nigel Lawson must go because (a) you cannot have a Chancellor quarrelling with the PM, and (b) he was wrong to go for further tax cuts and high interest rates. He should do the reverse in the interest of fairness and more efficient dampening of demand and less brutal effect on industry.

Europe has failed to keep Germany from discussing reunification seriously with the Russians.

He says he is keen to move to the FCO or the Treasury but will push for neither with the PM. He will resign if offered DTI. His job in DoE is basically done.

Monday 3 July

Lunch with *Independent* newspaper at Escargot, Greek Street. Thankfully take Pam Williams of the press department, whom I know well as she used to work with me in Aviation. Detailed discussion about the contracts to be struck between distribution companies and power companies and the future of nuclear. In answer to the question 'Do you have plans to keep nuclear within the public sector?' I say, 'Certainly not in our department. I know of none.'

I return to the House for a vote on the water privatisation Bill. Bump into Nigel Lawson. (Have previously been alerted by press office that *Independent* are doing a story about a row on nuclear privatisation between Treasury and Department of Energy). Mention news story to Nigel. He knows of it and says it has been caused by someone in DoE saying 'Certainly not in our department'. Rather nonplussed I ring Pam Williams, who says it is rubbish: the story of a row has been running for three or four days. The leak about the nuclear problem must have come from the Treasury. Tell all this to CP – not sure he believes me. Certainly Nigel doesn't when I see him again at a late vote.

Tuesday 4 July

Lead story in *Independent* embarrassing especially for Treasury: talk of Treasury rethinking whole of our nuclear programme. Ring CP to underline that I took Pam Williams with me to the *Independent* lunch and that I was not the source.

CP leaves office at 10 a.m. for meeting with PM and Lawson. Apparently according to CP, whom I see later in the afternoon on the Terrace (with five of his constituents who have won an auction to have tea with him), Lawson stomped into the meeting saying the *Independent* story must be my fault as I had had lunch with them the day before. CP said the story had circulated much earlier and that I had had a press officer as witness that I had not stirred up anything.

Apparently this was believed. It is certainly the truth. After the meeting, Lawson admits it had probably come from the Treasury.

Wednesday 5 July

Pursued all over the lobby by the press. Difficult to fob off. Walk into the House for a PM lunch reception. Bump into Dennis Skinner, the 'Beast of Bolsover', with whom I am always skirmishing across the floor. He is coming out of Victoria Tower Gardens, having been sitting there in the sun – looking a bit sheepish. We walk into the House together – itself unusual because he is known not to talk to Tories, let alone ministers! I say, 'I'm not sure whether the demise of the Liberals is good for you or good for us.' 'It's certainly not good for them buggers,' he replies.

Tuesday 11 July

Garden party. Glorious sunny day. Hot waiting in the hall to enter Buckingham Palace gardens at 3.15. Fumes blowing in through the ventilation system. David Hunt, deputy Chief Whip, arranges for Ann, Antonia and me to meet the Queen. Antonia very pretty in long cotton dress and very nervous. Queen talking at length to three people in front of us. Antonia says, 'How do we think of something to say for so long?' In the end our turn. HM seems to wait for us to speak. There is an awkward silence. Then she says, 'You've got the day off?' to me. We talk of traffic problems and of 'Philip' almost missing the garden party, of her car being stuck in the traffic last week. She says, 'It was so funny listening to the cab drivers; they really are cards, aren't they?'

I tell her that the Department of Energy will be moving into the block almost directly across the road from Buckingham Palace. She becomes really interested. 'Oh, so that's what's happening to the building. I wondered what they were doing with it when they thankfully decided not to turn it into a hotel.' Then she asks Antonia, 'What do you do?' She replies, 'Just finished secretarial college and planning to work for British Airways and perhaps to go into the Foreign Office'. Altogether about five minutes. Very relaxed after the opening gap.

Back home to change; on to Downing Street. As Antonia said, 'After that it was very ordinary meeting Mrs Thatcher', who virtually threw her into the room with one hand!

Decision not to privatise nuclear

Tuesday 18 July 1989
11 a.m. CP returns from a meeting with PM, Nigel Lawson, Malcolm Rifkind. They have decided not to privatise some of the nuclear power stations (old Magnox) because of the cost of decommissioning. We will announce this in Parliament on the last day of considering Lords amendments next Monday. It is very much a reversal of a previous position and will cause a row. The process by which this important decision is reached is another demonstration of the weakness of the Cabinet. We are really in a post-Cabinet government period. I actually asked at the meeting with CP whether the Cabinet had been told. 'No, but they will be.'

Wednesday 19 July
Meet Lamont, Financial Secretary, in the lobby; tell him, 'In case you become my boss, I want you to know that I was on your side about the Magnox decision.' (The Treasury are in favour of keeping the Magnox in the public sector; CP wants to bail out the privatised industry with money.)

Lamont asks what CP wants in government. I say to stay put because I don't think this is the real reshuffle. [Next year Howe and Lawson would go and the top jobs would become vacant.] Lamont says, 'He may be whistling in the dark; Nigel will probably want to go on to the next election.'

Thursday 20 July
What a strange summer this has been. The year that the 'greenhouse effect' became a political issue and the PM learnt that its primary cause was cows farting.

Visit to MI5

Monday 3 July 1989
Leave with CP for an address at Marylebone Road end of Gower Street. Turn into Gower Street from Marylebone Road and make a sharp left beside an anonymous building which apparently does not have a front door. Man with a two-way radio waves us into an underground car park full of unmarked cars and light blue unmarked vans. A lady by a lift takes CP and me to third floor and a man looking like Kim Philby introduces himself – Walker – turns out to be the director general of Box 500 (MI5). Introduces us to two others of his senior staff – a fair-haired man, slightly sinister, and a bespectacled chap. These two sit on DG's left and right opposite CP and me. DG apologises in advance that he will have to leave at 2 p.m. to catch a helicopter. Then he passes over a management structure chart defining the various activities of Box 500. Anti-terrorist, anti-subversion and anti-espionage. He explains purpose of new White Paper is for the first time to put the service on a statutory basis – up till now they seem to have depended for their existence on a letter from Maxwell Fyfe.[*]

DG says counter-terrorism (IRA) obviously key role at present but we shouldn't under-estimate 'counter-espionage' – clearly an attempt to bend the ear of an influential Cabinet Minister. Goes on to justify low overheads. 'Not relocated at the centre because we work through forty-five Branches.'

Over very good lunch joined by more junior and very impressive experts on energy matters, especially security on North Sea oil rigs. One of them explains that safety and security can have opposite implications, e.g. a ladder can be used for climbing down to a rescue craft or climbing up to blow up a rig.

I ask whether they find the quality of people they have to liaise with in the department up to scratch. (In our case it's a grey-haired lady who doubles up looking after stationery.) They answered diplomatically that relations with the department were good.

The reshuffle

Monday 24 July 1989
What a strange day. Come up on the 8.07 train and chat to Malcolm Caithness and Nicholas Ridley, about pending reshuffle. We joke about where to collect our pay cheques if we are sacked.

---

[*] David Maxwell Fyfe, 1st Earl of Kilmuir, Lord Chancellor 1954–62.

Halfway through the morning CP returns from Downing Street rather depressed to say he is going to Transport. I lunch with Irwin Stelzer – say I am not to be promoted and am now looking for a job outside. He says he will talk to Rupert Murdoch about a directorship and about publishing a book I want to write entitled *Defenceless Europe*.

4.30: CP announces in a statement that we will keep old Magnox nuclear stations in the public sector. During evening – hear we are to get Wakeham as SoS.

CP, Norman Lamont and my PPS, Gerald Howarth, meet for supper (after the passage of the Electricity Bill) in the restaurant L'Amicos. CP pretty upset about going to Transport. We try to console him: v. important to party, need to build it up etc. I say, 'There's a kiss of death about the reshuffle.' Lamont obviously v. pleased.* His time has come.

Tuesday 25 July

Leave by RAF 125 for Bonn in place of CP to sign contract for £1.6 billion of nuclear reprocessing on behalf of BNFL. Sign with Herr Töpfer, environment minister. Sixty or seventy press present. Then on to Brussels to see Leon Brittan about competition policy and protecting nuclear power. He is hopping mad about the way Geoffrey Howe has been treated.[†]

Wednesday 26 July

Parliamentary party very depressed about the reshuffle and the way that it has come out that Howe was offered Hurd's job and Lawson's official residence. By moving Howe PM has upset top three people in the government. End the evening defending nuclear policy on TV (*Newsnight*). Just as well holidays are upon us.

Thursday 27 July

12.15: One hundred or so officials involved in the Parliamentary Bill gather for a 'thank you' party. CP arrives from the Department of Transport at about 1 o'clock and makes a speech in which amongst other things he says what a wonderful job I did on the Electricity Bill and regrets that I was not promoted! 'I want to give a special thanks to Michael Spicer, who I think should have been promoted.'

---

* Norman Lamont was made Chief Secretary to the Treasury and promoted to the Cabinet.
† Sir Geoffrey Howe was moved from the position of Foreign Secretary to become deputy Prime Minister and Leader of the House. He was replaced as Foreign Secretary by John Major.

Despite all the tensions between us, in the circumstances of the time I doubt whether the electricity industry would have been privatised in the competitively dynamic shape that it was had Cecil Parkinson not been there to guide the process through.

Electricity is dangerous stuff. It is also intangible and impossible to store. When Walter Marshall talked of 'megavars' or 'reactive power', he was right to call into question the stability of electricity distribution systems. What he said – with its implications for the defence of a monopolistic supplier – was clearly understood by the scientist Prime Minister, especially as it came from her scientific mentor.

Only CP, or someone like him, with his caution and his charm could at the time have won out against these forces; but win he did, in a political minefield which no other country or government had trodden over so courageously. I am proud to have played my part in the process.

Sunday 13 August
CP thinks my problem has been the PM. He thinks it all goes back to 1984 when I went to see her at Chequers to discuss whether I should be next chairman of the party. Apparently this put her under unwanted pressure. I think it had more to do with the fall of Parkinson himself in 1983.

Sunday 20 August
The storm clouds may be gathering for Margaret Thatcher. There is talk in the press of a leadership challenge this autumn.

Tuesday 5 September
First day back in the office with new SoS, John Wakeham. 4.30 meeting with Bob Haslam, chairman of National Coal Board. Two issues:

1. Contract with the shortly-to-be-privatised electricity industry.
2. 'Liberalisation' of coal prior to privatisation, e.g. proposal to raise limit in private deep mines to 150 men (from 30) and open cast 250,000 tons a year from 25,000 tons.

Haslam v. steamed up about a letter I wrote to him on 31 July saying we wanted to do this after CP had left. He claims with some justification we were breaking faith on a previous commitment not to do anything controversial to coal.

PM and CP decided eighteen months ago not to touch coal privatisation till after the election. About six months ago this policy was modified v. much with the support of Cabinet, whose members had only just come into the picture – to allow for some increase in the private sector.

Thursday 7 September
First Cabinet committee meeting of the new term. New Foreign Secretary, John Major, in the chair, taking precedence over his former boss, Nigel Lawson. Subjects: Our response to EEC encroachment on merger policy; Leon Brittan, appropriate commissioner, features a lot. John Major's joke that he is beginning to be nostalgic about his previous job – Chief Secretary – goes down like a lead balloon. At least two people present (Nick Ridley and Parkinson) badly wanted and thought they might get the FCO. John Major looks v. lightweight – though he conducts the meeting competently enough.

CP whispers to me before we start that he has heard there are problems at his old department about privatisation of electricity. Apparently he has told the PM that it's not his fault.

Monday 25 September
John Wakeham calls a meeting of officials to settle immediately various outstanding issues: the old Chief Whip at work. I make a speech about the importance of competition in this privatisation which is not about better quality (as in water) but about lower prices, i.e. efficiency, i.e. competition. I seem to argue rather effectively because the meeting becomes one of how to stop the boards getting away with it.

In the afternoon Wakeham says to the industry finally that we are not prepared to buy their proposals. Suggests instead a form of protection (mix of contracts and limited franchise for the boards which fades out completely over eight years).

Thursday 28 September
Wakeham meets with PM to settle his package. He is a Mr Fixit who is uninterested in the finer points of policy. I, on the other hand, do hold to the view that the only real value of electricity privatisation comes through a demand pressure on prices through competition.

Monday 2 October
Willie Ricketts, a very bright assistant secretary, who has done most of the work on the Electricity privatisation, jokingly asks me whether I will go 'public' about my reservations on what is going on. I say, equally jokingly, my only option is to go 'private'.

Tuesday 3 October

11.30: Geoffrey Tucker, an old PR pro, comes in for a gossip before I go off to lunch at the Tower of London with my father's old regiment – Royal Fusiliers. He says how surprised he was to find me in my old job. Claims that 'Madame', as he calls the PM, did not consult anyone about the reshuffle except David Waddington (Chief Whip) about junior appointments and probably Charles Powell, her foreign affairs secretary and new guru. She was therefore shocked to find her moves were not universally welcomed. Apparently she saw Willie Whitelaw (Tucker's patron) after but not before the shuffle. According to Tucker she was visibly shaken when Whitelaw spoke to her.

Wednesday 4 October

My driver Ron comes to collect me for 9.30 Cabinet committee (EA, to be chaired by Nigel Lawson). Says he bumped into CP who asked him to get me to call him. CP confirms this at the Cabinet committee meeting. Later I fix to go and see him at 6.45, changed to go out to a Sudanese Defence Forces dinner (quite a week for my father's old regiments).

Over a glass of champagne in the Department of Transport, CP first points out the physical shambles of his office – which is being redecorated. CP reiterates his view that the PM blocked my promotion. He says he did his best. Says she is becoming increasingly isolated. She treated the Cabinet that morning as if they were the enemy. The issue was what to do about the 'safety net' for helping high-spending local authorities re the community charge. Present plan is to rob areas like mine to pay for it. Rumbling row about this could break out at next week's party conference. New idea is to rob various departmental budgets. She apparently told her Cabinet, 'You lot will have to pay.'

Monday 9 October

Drive up to Blackpool with Ron. Invited to dinner with *The Times*. I sit next to Robin Oakley (political editor) and opposite David Waddington. Robin says he was very disappointed that I had not been promoted. I say it seems that the PM and the gentleman opposite didn't like me. Robin wonders whether I once pressed myself too hard for Chairman. I say that's CP's story, which he has obviously fed to Robin. I then give Robin a potted history of my relationship with the PM as I see it – saying in my view I am the victim of having been too close to her in the 1983 election (like Janet Young in 1979 and Tebbit in 1987).

Tuesday 24 October

Dinner with Antonia in the Strangers' dining room. Parkinsons dining at the next-door table. A and I joined them for coffee. Ann Parkinson seems much more relaxed. CP says that PM gave him a belated choice to stay at Energy when he saw her at Downing Street. He said, 'How on earth could that be now that I have come in so publicly to see you, presumably about a new job?'

Wednesday 25 October

John Guinness (deputy secretary) comes to tell me he is about to send me a paper suggesting the nuclear industry stays in the public sector and the PWR programme is brought to a halt. Chickens are beginning to come home to roost. Apparently the price to the consumer of continuing with the nuclear programme as is will rise 25 per cent for some. I wonder what the PM is going to say about this. She has been personally committed and, indeed, has taken most of the decisions about nuclear herself and without recourse to Cabinet.

Thursday 26 October

Nigel Lawson resigns.* This is a serious crisis for the government and for the PM in particular.

Monday 30 October

11.30: Go with John Wakeham to Geoffrey Howe's office (Lord President in Cabinet Office). Present were Tim Renton, Murdo Maclean,† whips' PS, Wakeham, me and Geoffrey Howe.

Issue: The proposed Coal Bill, which will give more money to British Coal (a) to write off some of its debts, (b) to pay for further redundancies.

The third part is meant to be a measure of liberalisation (e.g. room for private capital to come into open-cast and deep mines). We have already indicated to the industry that we intended to raise the limits for private mines to 150 men underground and 250 men open cast. Geoffrey Howe says mood of Labour mining MPs makes this very difficult. It would be too provocative. Tim Renton, appointed Chief Whip over weekend, agrees with him. Wakeham says position of Department of Energy is to support the measure but as a former Chief Whip/leader of the House, he understands the reservations.

---

* Nigel Lawson resigned as Chancellor of the Exchequer over the role played by Sir Alan Walters as the Prime Minister's economic adviser.

† Later Sir Murdo Maclean.

I look around the room and say if they dropped it, I think it would be dishonourable. They then indicate that is what they propose to do. I say, 'I wish to register my objection in the strongest possible terms.'

At the end of the meeting I leave but they all stay on. Apparently they agree to approach the PM to get the measure withdrawn.

That afternoon I ask Gerald Howarth, my PPS, to see me. We agree that if the measure is dropped there will not be overwhelming objection on our side. Nevertheless I reserve my position.

Dinner with area board chairman, then back to the House to vote; mood v. ugly following weekend resignation of Lawson. Meet CP and NR in smoking room. We agree that it is potentially disastrous for the PM to have promoted her enemies and left her friends to one side. Apparently she rang CP over the weekend complaining that she had no friends around her!

Tuesday 31 October
Spend much of the day drafting a resignation speech in case coal liberalisation measure not accepted for Queen's Speech. This Opening of Parliament will be the first to be televised in full.

Monday 6 November
Meetings with Wakeham and Robert Haslam (chairman of British Coal), Robert Malpas (chairman of PowerGen) and Walter Marshall (chairman of National Power). Discussion with Marshall especially interesting as it is on the eve of Wakeham's meeting with PM to discuss end of the nuclear programme and keeping it in the public sector. Marshall, totally unsure of how imminent all this is, argues (a) that he has always said to the PM that our proposals would mean the end of nuclear, (b) if we keep nuclear in public sector he cannot guarantee to 'deliver' privatisation. (What he does not know is that we plan to sack him.)

Tuesday 7 November
11.30: John Wakeham comes back from PM to say he has been given green light on policy to keep nuclear in public sector and to stop building PWRs.

Ridleys come to dinner at Maunsel Street. We agonise over why PM promotes her enemies and keeps down her friends. After 10 o'clock votes, joined by Ian Gow, Nick Budgen and my PPS, Gerald Howarth. (General agreement – main thing is to fight off loony challenge to PM. Also agreement she is crazy not to have built up successor.) According to Nick Ridley, Nigel Lawson and Geoffrey Howe threatened to resign before over EMS so, in NR's view, they have got their 'comeuppance'.

Tuesday 14 November

'L' committee. Geoffrey Howe, Lord President, in the chair. Have to argue hard against both Howe and Renton for 'liberalisation' clause of the Coal Bill.* They say it is too controversial. I say in the end that we could accept the financial provisions of the Bill later than 31 March if necessary and they cave in. Just as well because on my return to the office I find a minute from the PM saying she wants it. [My private secretary, Chris Strutt, had scrawled over this, 'It appears you are on the side of the angels on this issue.']

Saturday 25 November

Anthony Meyer has announced he is standing against PM. I have now sent her the following:

> Dear Prime Minister
>
>   May I add my support to the many of others you will be receiving in the face of the unnecessary and potentially damaging election which now lies ahead.
>
>   I once worked closely with you as deputy chairman of the party and for a short while as your PPS. I believed in your leadership then and I believe in it now.
>
>   My position as a parliamentary secretary does not give me great weight in helping to steel the loyalty of others, but I will do my best.

Monday 27 November

Meet Ken Baker at McAlpine party. He asks me what I think will happen in leadership crisis. I say if whips are heavy handed, could well push the majority, who want to be loyal but who are also disappointed in some way, into voting against her. He is focused on how he is doing vis-à-vis Heseltine. I say the next leader will on past precedent have to have at least the tacit support of the centre right – which is at the moment going begging. He says, smiling, he will think seriously about that.

Leave party to watch PM on *Panorama*. One of questions which clearly irritates her is why Ken Baker told the press that he had advised her 'to get her act together'.

---

* Robert Haslam fought these proposals tooth and nail. I was probably the major counter-force to him and won the day when the measures were included in the 1990 Coal Industry Act.

Tim Bell tells me that he cannot even now persuade her of the importance of the parliamentary party; apparently Ken Baker tried to get her on the phone earlier in the afternoon and only managed to get through to one of her private secretaries called Turnbull.[*] As I said to Iain Sproat, she simply doesn't have any real politicians whom she can ring up and say, 'What shall we do now, old buddy?' All she has is Tim Bell, one or two paid officials, and possibly Alistair McAlpine. One wonders what next week's leadership election will bring. As Ken Baker said, 'There will be an awful lot of lying going on this week.'

Wednesday 29 November
Steens to supper. Anthony has been to a meeting of the left-wing Lollards Club. Apparently about sixty colleagues turned up. I wonder whether this is any indication that the anti-Thatcher vote may be stronger than originally thought on Tuesday. I will, of course, vote for her whatever happens.

Monday 1 January 1990
For the first and only time in my life, I write to PM asking to be promoted.

Wednesday 3 January
Get up for a bath at around 8 a.m. Ann comes in: call from Number 10. Turns out to be Andrew Turnbull, PM's PS. The PM would like me to come to London: 'She has a proposition to make to you.' 'Good or bad?' 'Good – promotion.' 'To minister of state?' 'Yes.' 'I'll come!'

Have to postpone a lunch with Pershore Rotary and catch train. Arrange for sandwiches with my PS, Chris Strutt, at Department of Energy. Then round to Number 10 at 2.30 for 2.45. When I enter her study at exactly 2.48 she is looking very fit. I stand while she talks to her PS. 'Do sit down, dear,' she says. Then, 'There has been a Cabinet resignation. I'd better not tell you who because it's not due out till 4.30 and then no one can think you said it.[†] I am moving Michael Howard into the Cabinet and I want you to take his job as MoS at Environment. Tony Baldry, John Wakeham's PPS and who has also fallen a little behind [he came into the House in 1983], will take your job.' It is as close to an apology as she can give. Later back in my office Tim Renton rings to congratulate me. I thank him for the part he presumably played.

'There were three of us. [I guess him, PM and Geoffrey Howe.] We were unanimous. I had been especially impressed by your steadfastness on the coal

---

[*]   Andrew Turnbull, economic private secretary to Margaret Thatcher. Cabinet secretary and head of Home Civil Service 2002–5. Created 2005 Baron Turnbull of Enfield.
[†]   The Rt Hon Norman Fowler MP resigned as Secretary of State for Employment.

liberalisation issue; we may still want you to take the Bill through the last stages of committee. [This has since been confirmed.] You obviously had rows with David Waddington.' I didn't, but clearly Waddington didn't like me.

With the promotion comes a return to the swaying Marsham Street Towers (this time the middle one) but not to Nicholas Ridley as Secretary of State. (Sadly for me, Ridley had been moved to the Department of Trade and Industry some months earlier* when he was replaced at Environment by Chris Patten.)

Also with the new job comes a 'silver card' for my driver, Ron Williams; this apparently enables him to take a short cut when he wishes to do so across Horseguards Parade. And once a year, for reasons going back into the mists of time, a shoulder of venison arrives at the minister of housing's local railway station, a gift from the monarch via British Rail.

With housing comes planning, which essentially means acting as judge and jury on almost every important planning dispute throughout the land which has been 'called in' by the Secretary of State.

I am determined when I arrive in this department to make some sort of mark on policy. The excellent briefing I receive from my predecessor, now newly promoted to the Cabinet, Michael Howard, reveals that the right to buy/sale of council houses is well advanced (some 120,000 houses are sold during 1990); coming up to the start line is the policy of transferring councils' remaining housing stock to housing associations with the incentive that if they make the transfer, local authorities can keep the capital receipts.

Waiting to make an entrance is the funding of more hostel places for those sleeping rough. I personally am equivocal about this. On the one hand I helped to found Crisis at Christmas in my PEST days in the 1960s and am well aware of the issue. On the other I know that there are already sufficient hostel places which, for one reason or another, are not taken up, especially by women. There is also the problem, which I witness for myself in cities such as Hamburg† and Copenhagen, of setting up a honeypot in the city centre which actually attracts young people to its streets.

---

* On 14 July Ridley was forced to resign from the government altogether, having been shopped by Dominic Lawson, in the Spectator, who 'quoted' some rude remarks Ridley made about the Germans over a private lunch at Naunton after it had been understood that Lawson had switched off his tape recorder following a formal interview beforehand.

† I was visiting rough sleepers around the central station in Hamburg on the night of 4 July 1990, when England lost the semi-final penalty shoot-out in the World Cup. Hamburg erupted so suddenly and traumatically that a prominent Ausländer like me had to be swept up by the police and, in my case, locked inside the Four Seasons hotel for my own protection against a baying mob.

It is the old who refuse to accept organised shelter (as much as the young) who are my chief concern. Few of these provide the merriment of one old boy who pops out of the top of a cardboard box when I am visiting a rough sleeper group (with their dogs and inevitable dangerous fire) under the roundabout at Waterloo Bridge. He is dressed in a dinner jacket with a large hole at the back and in an impeccable public school accent says, 'Good evening, Minister. This is indeed a very great honour you do us. You find me in my winter quarters, having just arrived from the seaside.'

Whatever the arguments for and against, I prepare to announce the first grant ever, of £15 million, for those sleeping rough in London and in other big cities.

Monday 29 January

My first real Cabinet committee where I have to fight for a policy re the homeless. Papers not brilliantly written by officials. I will need to strengthen the team here if this policy is to have legs. My proposition broadly accepted, that we need to attack the problem at three levels:

1. basic shelter;
2. more hostels;
3. easier access to flats, with counselling at all levels.

Friday 23 February

Write following letter to John Major, Chancellor of Exchequer, on Minister for Housing paper:

Dear John

I am very sorry that a long-standing engagement prevents me from coming to the meeting next Thursday [meeting of Ministers of State to discuss Budget]. There are three short points I would have made if I had had the opportunity of doing so.

There must be a danger now of a demand squeeze turning into a real threat to supply side confidence. There seems now to be a lag of about 3 years between a major change in interest levels and investment rates. This would lead us straight into the election period. It could be serious, I suppose, if there is any downturn in the world economy.

The recent history of the economic management of this country has been one of over-compensation within the business cycle.

If inflation is inevitable, it might be as well to make a virtue of it and to turn
it to good use, like the Japanese used to do, in terms of real economic growth.
   Yours sincerely
   Michael Spicer
   PS Good luck and no reply needed.

The implication of this is: don't worry about the value of the pound, in
particular not against European currencies. It was the first of many shots
across Major's bow on this issue.

Thursday 8 March
11.30 Cabinet committee meeting at Downing Street, to discuss unification
of East and West Germany and its repercussions. PM in very robust form
– amazing considering the pressure she is under. She tells Douglas Hurd
(Foreign Secretary) there must be three conditions for our support: (1) internal
trade border within Germany to prevent unfair trading from East Germany
through the West, (2) West Germans pay for all East German reconstruction,
(3) we are protected from effects of subsidised over-producing East German
agriculture.

   Ridley says whole thing is pretty hopeless. Rising interest rates/infla-
tion within Germany means we must steer well clear of joining common
currency. (His actual views are that we should not touch Europe with
a bargepole.)

   I say that clearing up East Germany should give our construction industry
opportunities, especially since West Germany will be so stretched. PM says
our industry is also stretched. I say it was six months ago – not now. Geoffrey
Howe and I think John Major agree with me. Cecil Parkinson does not – he
says he can't even get his roads built to time and cost.

Wednesday 14 March
Present a paper on homelessness to Cabinet committee: idea is to set up emergency shelters for young rough sleepers. The government lost a vote during
the night so whips this morning said I could not go to Mid Staffordshire
by-election. However, Ken Baker steps in and I leave on 5.25 train. Speak
with Michael Heseltine on the two alternatives, socialism (central direction)
v. personal initiative. Heseltine has third – middle way. I have to warm up
audience before Heseltine and Charles Prior* arrived. Afterwards approached
by ITV: What do I think about Labour's 20-point lead in polls? Ever since I

---

*   The Conservative candidate at the by-election.

was deputy chairman I have never commented on polls. 'What matters is the cross in the ballot box' etc.

Wednesday 18 April

Return from Easter break on a train which reaches Paddington at 3.30. 5 p.m. meeting at Number 10 with PM, Cecil Parkinson and Norman Lamont on two proposed new lines for tubes in London. PM seemed to be almost on a 'high'; surprising with things going so badly in the country. 'At least this is capital expenditure,' she said.

Parkinson presents the case for and Norman argues against. I intervene to give DoE position. She says DoE don't realise the commuter crush problems. I say I'm in favour. 'Oh,' she smiles. 'In that case go on.' I say, 'We are in favour because we approve of development in central London as opposed to green belt.' 'Why don't we make business pay by adding to the business rate?' she asks. 'Because we've put the business rate up by rather a lot in the south,' I say. In the end she says to Parkinson, 'Go ahead and do it but don't ask for more money! You're an accountant, be creative. Norman Lamont hasn't got any money! You must use your own.'

Thursday 19 April

Cecil Parkinson came up to me in the voting lobby to congratulate me on 'your stand against PM yesterday'. (At one point she said, 'Put them all on buses.' CP: 'The journeys take too long.' MT: 'Then why go on paying subsidies to buses?') CP seemed rather worried about her. I said, 'Yes, she seemed to be on a high!'

Monday 23 April

Lunch with PM and others. PM turns to me at end of lunch and says, 'How's Environment?' I say, 'Fine.' She smiles. 'Good.' I say we plan to build more houses. 'I hope you don't want any more money!' 'No,' I say. 'Did everyone hear that? Chief Whip, Deputy Prime Minister?' 'As long as you allow us to keep ours,' I say. Then I turn to single homeless issue. 'PM, I agree completely about cleaning up the problem but we must have somewhere to move them on to.' She says, 'Move them on to somewhere with discipline, e.g. Salvation Army hostels.' 'I agree, but you must modify the minute you sent saying no more resources. We must have somewhere to place them.'

Her PPS nods, as does Selwyn Gummer, who says he liked the letter I sent out pointing out that much of the problem was to do with break-up of families. As table rises, Colin Moynihan and Mark Lennox-Boyd say jokingly, 'What a naked bid for power, Spicer!'

Later I see Lennox-Boyd in the voting lobby. I say, 'PM is in rather good form these days.' (Her position in the polls, and that of the party, is at record low levels.)

He says, 'She's enjoying herself. She's trying to do her best.'

Wednesday 25 April

In the middle of an important briefing on homeless, Annabel comes through on the phone from Cropthorne, where she is still on holiday with Ann (swotting up for her GCSEs) and asks me to help her with an essay on 'the pressure of relationships'. 'I've got a blockage, Daddy'. I break away from meeting and do my best to help.

Tuesday 8 May

Invited to US Residence by Ambassador Henry Catto to meet Dan Quayle, US Vice-President. About thirty others there, including Ken Baker, Geoffrey Howe, Neil Kinnock. Mention to Quayle that I had a house in Sarasota. 'That's where Denis Thatcher is,' he says, 'playing golf. I know because he wasn't at Chequers last night.' Quayle very affable but a very lightweight speech in honour of the Eisenhowers before lunch.*

Thursday 10 May

Meeting at Number 10 with PM at 9.30 to discuss our attempts to seduce MCA to build a massive theme park at Rainham Marshes on the north bank of Thames. PM very keen on this. 'Surely you can get some derelict land grant,' she says to me. To Robert Atkins, representing Transport, she says, 'Private industry is roaring ahead but they are being held up by the public infrastructure, trains and roads. We must do more.' She was in pretty good spirits given the pressure she must be under due to our position in the polls.

Thursday 24 May

5.30 meeting at Number 10 to discuss future of the rail link for the Channel Tunnel terminal. Arrived at 5.25. PM standing in the ante-room outside the Cabinet room. She was looking very attractive in a smart pink jacket and black skirt. In a very good mood. Parliament had broken up for Whitsun recess. 'Some of us have to go on working,' she said. Norman Lamont also present. 'Who are we waiting for?' she asks. 'Cecil Parkinson,' someone says. She smiles. The door opens at the end of the passage. Cecil sees us waiting

---

* In 1990 the centenary of the birth of Dwight D. Eisenhower was celebrated.

at the other end – horrified. 'Let's go up to the study.' Decision taken at the
meeting to shelve the link as it will not stand up in the private sector and
we are unwilling to put public money behind it. My intervention is that
if we want to keep the proposed route from Folkestone to King's Cross as an
option, we will have to 'secure' it for planning and compensation purposes.
This is agreed.

This vital decision is taken by four people: CP, me, PM and NL. At the
very end the PM suddenly says, 'This is such an important decision, perhaps
we had better put it to a Cabinet committee'. Power of PM is enormous,
as is her resilience. As we leave the room we briefly discuss Labour's new
policy document. I say, 'If they get in they are dedicated to reintroducing
rent controls and security of tenure and will thus kill off the private rented
sector.' 'They're not going to get in,' she says. There is great bounce in her.
Truly remarkable.

Tuesday 19 June
Dinner with the trade association of the aggregates industry at the Savoy.
They tell me that they are now planning for a major recession next year. I say
I will pass this on to John Major. I do at the 10 o'clock vote. I say, 'Shoot the
messenger if you wish.'

He says, 'I don't think I should.'

Tuesday 26 June
Ridleys to dinner. He comes out with the surprising idea (for him) that we
should reduce interest rates and put up taxes. He agrees with me that one
of the major problems with interest rates is their lagged effect on economic
activity. This is exactly my view. If interest rates remain high for much longer
we really will be in trouble next year.

Wednesday 27 June
Cecil Parkinson understandably irritated because Energy select committee
has gone for him for 'bungling' nuclear power in privatisation of electricity.
This is hitting the headlines but very unfair. Privatisation brought out the
costs of nuclear.

Thursday 28 June
Gerald Howarth and Bob Dunn organise a pro-Parkinson rally at '22
Committee. Bump into Sheila Gunn of *The Times*. Apparently they are writ-
ing a story about this which includes me. It will say that it's unfair that CP

and I should be blamed without having given our side of the story to the select committee.

Monday 16 July

Ring Nicholas Ridley, who was forced to resign from the government two days earlier on account of an interview with Dominic Lawson of the *Spectator* when he likened the European commissioners to Hitler etc. I admire Ridley and had certainly hoped he would not have to resign. When I call him in Naunton he seems quite bullish. Fed up with all the 'dirty unwashed' press who are staking out his home. 'They want to go home if I will give them some statement, which I won't!' He seems inclined to continue the debate about Europe from the sidelines, 'unless I get bored'.

The 'Right' were pretty miserable when I went down to the House.

Thursday 19 July

Garden party with Antonia and Ann. Then on to Number 10 for drink. PM says in front of Ann and Antonia, 'Nicholas Ridley is one of the most original politicians of our time. I gave him the opportunity to stay – as I did with Cecil and Leon – but I told him it would be miserable for him and Judy.' He deserved better.

Sunday 29 July

Get up at 5.30 to minute following:

> The housing and construction sectors are heading, probably now unavoidably, for a major slump next year. (One of the problems of a high-interest-rate policy is its long lag effect; the real 'pain' is felt many months after you have decided to let up.) Orders for next year in the construction industry have apparently collapsed. With mortgage arrears and repossessions already at an all-time high, and no doubt growing rapidly, speculative house-building must also be set to grind to a virtual halt. New subsidised rented housing is running at its lowest levels since the 1920s.
>
> In view of the electoral implications of all of this, we are bound to press for fiscal measures to maintain some sort of housing investment programme.

Sunday 5 August

Lunch party at Cropthorne. Middle Eastern crisis breaking. Colin Marshall keeps on having to leave the room to take calls from BA operational centre about 747 stranded at Kuwait. Apparently it landed two hours after the Iraqis had invaded, which does not say much for our intelligence services. Colin faced with decisions as to whether to permit his pilot to fly the plane voluntarily to Baghdad. Rightly he says, 'No.' If the Iraqis force his hand, a rather different matter.

Friday 17 August
Article by Tim Congdon in *The Times*. Shows lags between high interest rates and their effect. I have been saying this privately for months. If we keep interest rates at their present level (with high value of pound) we will have a slump next year and lose the election. Congdon also says that inflation often goes up after the boom, i.e. *now*, when earnings rises are no longer matched by investment or productivity rises.

Wednesday 22 August
Pressed by my friend Anthony Steen,* I manage to include special arrangements for the rehabilitation of derelict and contaminated land in our cities. For this I have the backing of Number 10, as is indicated by the following letter.

> From the Private Secretary
> 10 Downing Street
> 20 August 1990
>   … The Prime Minister has noted that the Lord President and Mr Patten consider that the Planning Bill is worth proceeding with and agrees that the Bill should not be streamlined further. She notes that further work is being carried out on charging for appeals and that H Committee is to discuss Mr Spicer's proposals on public sector land. On both these points she would like to see positive consideration being given …

Wednesday 5 September
In London for the special debate (Thursday/Friday) on the Gulf crisis. Meeting of H committee at 10.45 to discuss my plan for new legislation to facilitate sale of vacant public-sector land. Geoffrey Howe in the chair. He has been pretty unhelpful all along about this. On this occasion the real opponent is David Hunt (SoS for Wales). Attacks my proposals until the meeting begins to go against him (Ken Clarke, SoS Health, and Angela Rumbold,

---

* Member for South Hams, later Totnes, and founder and first director of Task Force 1964–8, raising millions of pounds to tackle urban problems.

MoS at Education, very helpful). Then Hunt comes in saying he would do it in Wales!!

Wednesday 12 September
Return from spending two nights at our embassy in Paris looking at the French homeless problem. With a collapsing private rented sector – much more important to them than us – and with 100,000 immigrants they have a rapidly growing problem.

3 p.m. meeting in the Cabinet room with PM and Chris Patten to discuss our long-term ideas on housing. PM remarkably bouncy considering what must be on her mind re the Middle East. She explains that council housing has been the bane of this country and we must get rid of it. Patten clearly doesn't agree but keeps his peace. I do agree with her. (As always, it's her enemies she has promoted so I am in a weak position to support.) However, I get her agreement to look at ways we can support private-sector renting, which has now declined to 7 per cent of the stock. What she is really interested in is rent-to-mortgage and homesteading. I say we are already at 68 per cent for home ownership. Not much further to go. At one point I remind her that mortgage relief costs us £8 billion at current rates of interest. She glares at me and says, 'It doesn't cost anything; it's their money.' On the whole, however she is in a good mood and willing to listen – although a ball of fire. At the end Chris Patten has to leave meeting to catch a train to his constituency (the meeting had over-run by half an hour; went on for 1½ hours). I found myself almost alone with her and said, 'We mustn't be despondent. Housing is basically a great success. The French are very envious about what we have done for home ownership.'

She said almost quietly, 'I know, but it still depresses me that we have not done more to throw off the dependency culture.'

I said, 'We're getting there.'

She repeated this and smiled. She is an extraordinary woman, at sixty-something looking more dynamic and attractive than ever. All this in the midst of the Gulf crisis.

Reflections
Such was the emphasis at the time on the right to buy that it was not easy to get permission to make a speech about letting. Indeed, it required a meeting with the Prime Minister in the Cabinet room a week before the conference together with my Secretary of State, Chris Patten.

This is what Margaret Thatcher says about this meeting in her autobiography:*

> The September 1990 discussion with Chris Patten and Michael Spicer was not an inspiring one. Michael was keen to concentrate on new measures to revive the private rented sector. I agreed with him on this, but I thought that in the short term it was more important to tackle the problems of public sector housing. Chris, I suspect, thought that the best way of doing this was simply to build more public sector houses. In any case, he seemed content to work within the present local authority-dominated framework. After the meeting I had a discussion with my advisers and penned a personal minute to Chris Patten in which I noted my disappointment. I added: 'I am not persuaded that we are yet being sufficiently bold in carrying forward promising and practical policy initiatives in the short term; nor have we yet explored with the necessary thoroughness and vision the full range of policy options for the longer term.'

This is a perfect example of the Prime Minister who, having promoted those who fundamentally disagree with her policies (in this case, Chris Patten), is surprised by the predictable effect. It also well illustrates the fact that Margaret Thatcher had her own priorities within a set of policies which could all broadly be called Thatcherite. In this case, the sale of council houses was 'good'; improving the private rented sector was, if not 'bad', unimportant.

It is the last time I speak directly to her as Prime Minister.

Saturday 29 September
Write to John Major in own handwriting to plead for interest rates to come down.

Friday 5 October
On the drive back from the airport to Cropthorne learn from Ann that we are to go into the ERM and that interest rates are to 'come down' to 14 per cent! I would have hoped at the least that we would have brought down interest rates (and the pound) before we entered ERM. Now we are locked into it.

Do final draft for my speech to party conference.

Monday 8 October
Travel with Ann by car to have lunch with Ma at her club in Lymington. Then on to Bournemouth for the party conference.

---

* Margaret Thatcher, *The Downing Street Years*, HarperCollins, 1993.

4.30: Go for practice with the dreaded Autocue machine and give my speech to some poor Australian girl who seems to be responsible for typing out all conference speeches. Very helpful practice session with Harvey Thomas, the electronics and presentational guru.

Dinner in the evening with Robin Oakley and *The Times*. Tip him off that I am going to make an announcement the next day about rent-to-mortgage.

Tuesday 9 October

Much running around with Ann making sure my speech ready and practised. In the end it goes down rather well, though delivered to a half empty house.

I make the issue of private renting a central one when at 5.00, for the first and last time in my life, I wind up the debate at the party conference at Bournemouth. This is how I end my speech:

The main concern for our housing stock goes wider than the issue of empty council houses. There are in this country around 600,000 empty private houses. The question is: why are they left empty? Why are they allowed to go to ruin? The main answer, in my view, lies in the almost total collapse in this country of the motivation to let. People, especially elderly people, are often terrified to rent out their property. They would rather see them falling to bits and empty than risk filling them with tenants who they fear may not pay a proper rent and may never leave.

The 1988 Housing Act has provided the basis for putting this right. On the one hand it is very tough on landlords who harass tenants – including stronger provision for prison sentences. On the other hand the Act re-establishes a market-based and contractual system for renting.

The problem is that these new rights and opportunities for landlords are not sufficiently widely known. And so today I am launching a nationwide publicity campaign aimed at putting this right. In particular, I have published today a charter of landlords' rights.

… On behalf of the government I want to make it absolutely clear that we view a good landlord as a vital source of accommodation, especially for single people. At the turn of the century he provided some 90 per cent of the nation's accommodation; even after the Second World War the figure was over 50 per cent. Now it is down to around 7 per cent.

Wednesday 10 October

The fact that the Autocue went backwards during part of my speech yesterday does not prevent the chairman of the party, Ken Baker, scribbling me a note today: 'You were *very* good yesterday. I watched from the back of the hall. Sorry about the Autocue!'

Tuesday 6 November

Drinks at Number 10 on eve of opening of Parliament. Robin Butler reads out Queen's Speech. PM is in good form despite ghastly press and resignation of Geoffrey Howe. At one point am saying to John MacGregor, just promoted from Education Secretary to Leader of the House, 'We must not wobble about our education reforms.' PM comes up. 'I'm not a wobbler,' she says.

I say, 'It's going to be all right' (we're 21 points behind Labour in the opinion polls) 'so long as we don't have an incomes policy. Then inflation will come down, wages will go up and we'll win!'

She laughs and says, 'You cynic.'

Wednesday 7 November

Dinner with the Ridleys after the Queen's Speech. Discussed his resignation, then Geoffrey Howe's. On the surface he is happy being chased by the press and media (*Panorama* are doing a complete programme on him on December 10). We agree the PM's major problem is that she tries to do everything herself. She can't, especially now that she has surrounded herself with all her enemies. He repeats his view that we should have tighter expenditure and lower interest rates. He says that we have entered ERM at a disastrously high exchange rate for the pound (I felt this at the time) against the Deutschmark.

NR thinks Major a disaster and that there will be a run on the pound at some time. On present policies he feels we could lose the election. If there is a serious threat to leadership he may stand himself. If PM is a captive of Major on the economy, she is a prisoner of Hurd on Europe. Each is a disaster.

Meeting with Prince Charles and Princess Diana

Thursday 8 November 1990

Attend a conference* on homelessness in Threadneedle Street chaired by Prince of Wales; sat next to the Princess. Prince getting more and more involved in what he thinks is a non-political subject. He's quite wrong about

---

* Chris Patten gave his approval to this event when he took over from Nicholas Ridley, who resisted it. Relations between the heir to the throne and Ridley were invariably strained; this got Nicholas Soames, Ridley's PPS and great friend of the Prince, into an impossible position, which ultimately he could not hold onto.

this. Homelessness could not be more political, as is shown by some of the presentations. They blame the government for not building enough houses. I say we had built considerably more houses per head of population. The problem is the break-up of families, which is going on around Europe. HRH at one point says that he had wanted to form a housing association in the Duchy of Cornwall but there was no money from the Housing Corporation. I say that we have doubled money for the corporation (£1.2 billion) and we will double it again in the next three years.

Before the meeting HRH suggested that housing action trusts could be made to work if we gave control to the tenants. He wrote me a note related to this and the precedent that he sees for this at Thamesmead.* The note was passed to me during the meeting.

As we sat down I asked the Princess whether she was going to make a speech. She said, 'You must be joking.' Then she offered me some water. (This is the first time for some weeks that the two HRHs have been seen together).

Reflections

What really was my personal initiative is the renewed emphasis I gave to the private rented sector. This arose from a concern that our private lettings market is so small compared to other countries (e.g. Germany 70 per cent, against our 7 per cent) and the effect this has on the mobility of labour and thus of industry. It also sprang from my realisation very early on that a large part of the 'housing problem' is not just that we need to build new houses, but that we also have to make better use of those which are already there. Nowhere is this more apparent than in the private sector, where there are 600,000 empty homes.

On the morning of 8 November I had this issue out with the Prince of Wales in front of all the major housing lobby organisations, such as SHAC, Shelter and Crisis. The Prince had invited them, together with myself as minister for housing, to join him and his wife to thrash out the issue of homelessness under his chairmanship.

I was placed on the Princess's left; Prince Charles sat on her right, with an official from the department on his other side. The four of us faced an audience of some twenty representatives of the interest groups.

---

* Thamesmead is a vast housing estate, with some peripheral industry, situated on former marshland in south-east London between Woolwich and Erith. After the land was vacated by the military, the Greater London Council developed the estate from the mid-1960s to the early 1980s. After the abolition of the GLC in 1986, the estate's ownership transferred to a trust company, run by the residents and independent of any public control, under the chairmanship of Clive Thornton.

The heir to the throne opened the proceedings by asking, 'Minister, perhaps you would be kind enough to lead on this one. What are we to do about homelessness?' I responded, 'For a start, Sir, we have to do something about the million and a half empty homes, 600,000 of which are in the private sector – and of which a considerable proportion are owned and managed by the Duchy of Cornwall.' The room fell silent. The Prince smiled and said, 'Touché.'

The official coughed and said, 'I know the minister will wish to add that the government have launched a number of schemes for home improvement and for low-cost house build.'

The ice was broken and a lively discussion followed. During this the Prince scribbled a note which the Princess hands to me, digging her elbow into my ribs as she did so. It read:

Mr Spicer,

According to Clive Thornton, who has only just given up as Chairman of Thamesmead, the capital value of the former 'estate' has increased from –£15 million when he took over as Chairman to +£400 million *now*!

Friday 9 November
The Times has a leader today on the autumn statement saying we have ceased to be a radical government. I think Simon Jenkins (the editor) is right. And now we hear that there will probably be a challenge to the PM. It's all falling apart, with not much hope of redemption because Major (a) has got us into the ERM at too high an exchange rate, (b) has not cut public expenditure, (c) is keeping interest rates too high.

I am copied in to one last letter the Prime Minister writes about me to a Mr W. Hogbin.[*] Mr Hogbin wrote to the PM on 7 November in the following terms:

Dear Prime Minister,

I am sure that you would wish to know that members of the Export Group are extremely grateful to Mr Michael Spicer for the time and energy he has devoted during the past month to leading construction industry missions to Hungary, Poland and Czechoslovakia.

At the present state of change in these countries the assessment of business possibilities will rest heavily upon our feeling for the direction and pace of the

---

[*] Chairman of Taylor Woodrow International Limited.

changes, and the access to ministers and officials which his leadership was able to secure was invaluable.

W. Hogbin, CBE

In her reply the Prime Minister says:

Dear Mr Hogbin
Thank you for your very nice letter about Michael Spicer. I was very pleased to hear that the construction industry missions were a success.
Yours,
Margaret Thatcher

Monday 19 November
9.45: Bump into Michael Heseltine in the 'No' lobby on the night before the leadership election. Tell him, 'I'm sorry, Michael, but I cannot vote for you. It's my army upbringing not to desert the CO. I would no doubt feel the same about you. You will probably sack me on Thursday, but that's the way life is!'

He smiles and says, 'It's good of you to tell me.'

I say, 'The one thing we must do is to unite when this is all over.'

He looks very confident.

Afterwards walk through the lobby with Michael Portillo, who says he is feeling better about it all.

(My guess in the voting: Thatcher 190, Heseltine 120, abstain 57. Actual: Thatcher 204, Heseltine 152, abstain 11.)

Wednesday 21 November
PM back from France. 7.00: Come out of my room beside the ministerial conference room and go up back stairs. At end of corridor outside PM's room is Norman Lamont, white and with dark glasses. I ask him if he is going in to see her. 'Yes,' he says, 'it's all over and I am going to tell her.' (Norman was previously very supportive of her – calling Heseltine 'selfish' and 'dishonourable'.)

Bump into Ian Twinn, a Thatcher supporter, in corridor outside, behind the Speaker's chair; watch Chris Patten and Selwyn Gummer heading for PM's office. 'The rats are at her,' he says. Then see Wakeham, who is meant to have taken over from George Younger as her campaign manager. 'Is all OK?' I ask. 'No,' he says. I assume from this she is not going to stand for second ballot. Go over to CCO to talk to Ken Baker to ask him if all fell apart whether he would stand. 'No,' he says. 'There isn't time. I would only get a handful of votes.' I say, 'If that's your judgement, so be it.'

Reflections

I was not involved, one way or the other, in Thatcher's downfall. Of course I voted for her to continue. I am a Thatcherite. If having been a PPS and vice-chairman/deputy chairman of the party are assumed as having been part of Thatcher's administration in its broadest sense, I think I am the only person to have joined it on the first day, served throughout, and then to have left on the day that she departed.

Mine, however, was not an emotional commitment. My personal relationship with her was a difficult one for years. She did not bring me into a position from which I could effectively help to protect her. At the moment of her fall I was simply one of her footsoldiers who marched to the sound of her drum when she beat it. I badly wanted her to stay but accepted her departure as a matter of fact when it was brought about.

When I discovered late on the evening of 21 November that a plot* was afoot to topple her I did make for Central Office and spent some time with the chairman, Ken Baker. He and I agreed that it was too late to save her. My own thoughts were about the future: what was to be done to protect her legacy?

Meanwhile each member of the Cabinet was summoned to parade individually before her. With three exceptions each muttered (in one case blubbed) the identical formula: 'I will vote for you but you haven't a chance.' The die was cast. The three exceptions are Ken Baker and Cecil Parkinson, who supported her, and Ken Clarke, who didn't.

Dated 22 November 1990, and addressed '10 Downing Street, from the Principal Private Secretary', the following letter reached me in the internal mail:

Dear Mr Spicer

Mrs Thatcher has today submitted her formal resignation to the Queen.

In accordance with constitutional practice, Mrs Thatcher invites her colleagues to place their offices at the disposal of the new Prime Minister. Until a new government is formed, Mrs Thatcher trusts that Ministers will continue to discharge their present duties and responsibilities.

Yours sincerely,

Andrew Turnbull

---

* The first to decide collectively that her time is up and that something needs to be done about it are apparently John Gummer, John Wakeham and Kenneth Clarke. Wakeham also becomes the manager of her abortive 'campaign' to win the second leadership ballot. It is not surprising that Wakeham is a bit mixed up; he is at the same time sceptical of her policies and married to Alison, who had been her personal assistant and confidante.

Margaret Thatcher's fall, both in its timing and in the way it had occurred, was a tragedy in the Shakespearean sense: that is to say, it was heroic and largely of her own making. It was not just that she carelessly appointed her enemies (or those who were lukewarm about her) to key positions; she actually fell out with, or sidelined, those who wished to serve her cause. As at the court of Queen Elizabeth I, and as a front-line politician, the closer you were to her the more brittle became the relationship.

When the final crisis came, the only real friend at hand was Peter Morrison, who proved not to be up to the job of organising her defence – though whether any one person could have saved her in the end is another matter. As the ballot was for her such a near miss it is arguable that Ian Gow might have pulled it off had he not been assassinated by the IRA.

The question as to why my own promotion was so limited and belated, given the closeness for a time of my association with Margaret Thatcher, is a minor footnote to all this. It may, as Cecil Parkinson suggests, have had to do with the fact that I was the founder of PEST (though I maintain that as the backer of Heath versus Maudling and as one who publicly attacked the notion of an incomes policy,[*] I and PEST were embryonic Thatcherites in the context of the age). What I think was a factor in the slowness of my progress under Thatcher was that after Parkinson's fall she felt the need to distance herself for a period from the entire Parkinson set, of which I was undoubtedly a part.

I thus added to the unqualified rule that under Margaret Thatcher, sometimes by accident, sometimes by design, no close political associate of hers (with one exception) was with her at the end. She carried to a disastrous fault the Lyndon Johnson maxim about ensuring that your enemies relieve themselves inside the tent rather than outside. In Margaret Thatcher's case the tent fell in because there was no one left who felt strongly enough about it to hold up the poles.

It may be, to adapt the phrase that Clement Attlee is supposed to have used when sacking one of his ministers, that the Thatcherites were all 'no bloody good'. It is for others to judge whether this applied to me. In this context, one interesting (at least to me) view was recently expressed to me by Anastasia Pollard as she painted the portrait on the jacket of this book

---

[*] Writing in *The Statist* on 8 April 1965 I said, 'If it is true that it is undesirable or impossible to control profits, then it is unlikely that wages can be controlled.'

in 2010.* 'I suspect your problem', she said, 'is that you may not be a good follower.' I think she may be right. I am not a good courtier. I am at the same time too nervous and too clear in my own views to be the perfect servant.

I will add this: one of the joys and one of the tribulations of serving in politics is that it is virtually impossible to create a general set of rules as to what makes a 'good' politician. Put another way: there is no such thing as a perfect politician. The reason is that political merit is as much a function of time and of the configuration of politicians as it is of applying an objective set of standards. Sometimes you need a person of the right, sometimes of the left, and sometimes of no faction at all; there are moments when it may be better to be a woman than to be a man; at others the reverse may be true. There may be a dearth of those with powers of oratory or there may be a surplus of them, and so on.

The element of sheer chance that goes with political preferment carries with it the enormous benefit of preventing ambitious politicians who fail to make it, from becoming unbalanced and even going mad. It is a feature of political life that those who wish to standardise the candidate selection procedures in the political parties would do well to keep in mind.

In the end Margaret Thatcher came to appreciate that she had been wrong (disastrously so) in her carelessness for her political friends and in her disdain for the parliamentary party in general. Writing at the end of her autobiography about her effort to stem the tide ebbing away from her, she says rather poignantly, 'Norman [Tebbit] and I began to go round the tea rooms. I had never experienced such an atmosphere before. Repeatedly I heard, "…This is the first time we have seen you."'

It was not the general electorate who threw her out. It was the people who had the power to do so – her own parliamentary party, led by the enemies with whom she had surrounded herself. The same people now prepared to install her successor. Turbulent times lay ahead, certainly for me.

---

* Winner of the 2009 Ondaatje Prize for portraiture (in association with the Royal Society of Portrait Painters).

Part II

Rebellion: the Maastricht Treaty

Chapter 10

John Major, 1990–92: his first term of office

1990

O n 28 September 1990 (at the start of what was then the worst economic recession in modern times), I wrote in my own hand to the Chancellor of the Exchequer, John Major, the following letter on House of Commons paper. I had written in similar terms on 23 February.

Private
Dear John

I fear you must be receiving many representations about the future of economic policy.

My credentials for writing to you are first of all that in the 1970s I founded, owned and managed an economic forecasting company called Economic Models, which is now part of DRI, the largest econometric company in the world. In my present government job I keep in touch with the building and construction industry, which is I suppose as sensitive as any to changes in economic conditions and policies.

I have been asking myself again why it is that the UK continues to suffer worse swings of 'stop–go' economic cycles than any of our competitors with more serious effects, in particular on business confidence.

The answer, I believe, continues to be that our economic and monetary authorities have less of an appreciation than others of the lags in the economy, in particular between changes in interest policy and business investment. They tend, as they have done for the past fifty years, to respond to the events of the day without projecting forward the effects of their policies for the necessary 18 to 24 months. These policies are therefore alternately more severe and more lax than is required.

Thus, for instance, high interest rates introduced when the economy was already entering a downswing (and when inflationary forces were mostly caused by a slowdown of productivity increases) will begin seriously to bite as the economy enters major recession next year. (As I am sure you know, orders next year for the construction industry are virtually non-existent and the current estimate is for 100,000 redundancies.)

The question now is whether we have the time to operate interest policy so as to restore some confidence before an election in 1992. I think the answer must be 'only just' if the election were in May or June 1992.

The two arguments against reducing interest rates are (i) inflation, (ii) the pound. Inflation will be brought under control by the emerging slump/recession. The pound, given the oil position, is likely to be seriously threatened only by a growing fear that we might lose the next election. This fear, one hopes, will abate with restored economic confidence. <u>In any case, a pound related to genuine market conditions is surely what is required for our balance of payments.</u>

None of this is to deny the soundness of your policies to deal with the supply side of the economy; it is to presume that there is a closer relationship than perhaps we have recently allowed for between demand affecting policies and supply conditions.

For this reason I have been convinced for some months that interest rates are too high for our political good; that they should start to be reduced at once. The time to raise them again may well be after we have won an election in 1992.

Yours ever,
Michael Spicer

This letter received a response dated 26 October defending the government's anti-inflation stance. John Major would have understood completely that the key sentence in my letter is the one I underlined. It totally undermined his enthusiastic commitment to being in the European Exchange Rate Mechanism, which was his single proud achievement at the Treasury.[*]

With this in mind I voted for John Major when the time came with a heavy heart. In the end he is all that stood between Michael Heseltine and the premiership.

The weekend before Major's election, on 24 and 25 November 1990, I stayed at the Lantern Lodge Hotel in Hope Cove, Devon, with my mother and Ann. I was impervious to the foul weather raging across the cliffs outside as I was semi-permanently on the telephone taking frantic calls from Major's campaign team, notably from Norman Lamont, who, being a friend of mine,

---

[*] John Major's later recollections of his position at the time are rather different from mine. Writing in the *Daily Telegraph* on 27 November 2010 he said, 'As we returned to growth I wished to exit the ERM – I had never thought of it as a stepping stone to economic and monetary union.' If I had known this at the time it might have saved us all a good deal of bother.

was sensibly deputed to tie down my vote for his new boss. 'You, Michael, are now almost the last Thatcherite to hold back from endorsing John; she herself, as you know, did so many days ago. I can't understand what is holding you back.'

What I did not reveal is that I was in very close contact at the time with Nicholas Ridley, the great Thatcher supporter and defender of her faith. Nicholas was talking to both Thatcher and Major. 'It's no good,' he said to me towards the end of one of the many telephone conversations we held that weekend. 'She can't accept that Major doesn't support her beliefs or even, for that matter, admire the legacy she leaves behind.' In a final call he said, 'It's between Major and abstaining; and I think it would look absurd to abstain.'

Late that evening I picked up the phone and dialled Major's campaign headquarters, conscious that I was one of the last to do so. When I got through I asked for Lamont. I got someone else, whose name was not known to me and which I was quick to forget. 'I am going to vote for your man,' I said, 'but in view of our respective different positions on the ERM, I do so reluctantly.'

'We know.' The voice at the other end sounded weary.

I added, 'In the context of my letters to John and of my views on the disastrous nature of managed exchange rates, I would not expect to be a member of Mr Major's administration if he forms one.'

'I will ensure that this is passed on.' The voice had become clinical. For him all that counted was that my position made my pledge more plausible.

The next day, Monday 26 November, a police outrider arrived to escort me to the north of the county where I visited a new housing estate in Emma Nicholson's constituency of Torridge & West Devon. It was the last major duty I undertook as minister for housing. It was no surprise to me that I was not part of Major's ministerial team when it was formed on 28 November 1990. I was about to learn that the path of a backbench former minister can be a rough one.

The only person I genuinely missed when I left government was my driver, Ron Williams, and I think the feeling was mutual. I certainly did not miss the car, but the man. He had become part of the family. For his part, Ron never really settled down with any one minister after my departure. We kept in touch, especially after he retired from the Government Car Service. He drove both my son Edward to his wedding on 3 October 1998 to Lulu Pederson and my younger daughter Annabel when she married Jon Bush on 8 April 2000. In each case, he also drove the bride and groom away at the end.

1991

The year 1991 provided a lull before the Maastricht storm which raged throughout most of the next parliament (1992–7). It is of some historical interest as it was John Major's first full year as Prime Minister.

It was also Margaret Thatcher's last full year as a member of the House of Commons. It was probably her unhappiest time in politics. She desperately wanted to avoid 'doing a Ted Heath' against Major; and yet she bitterly resented having lost power to him and it began to dawn on her that, contrary to her early hopes, he was not 'one of us'. Her distress focused on two issues: Europe and the Maastricht Treaty, and the threatened abolition of the community charge. A large part of her angst was due without doubt to the amount of sovereignty she had herself given away in Europe, most notably in the Single European Act.*

In her psychological exile she was surrounded by a small gang of MPs, of whom I was one. The person with the greatest influence on us all, but frustrated by loss of power and rapidly failing health, was Nicholas Ridley. For him the wheel had gone full circle; he had returned to the position he held in the days of opposition in the 1960s and 1970s, that of guru of the right.†

Sadly, it was now late – too late – in his life for him to have much effect. The tragedy, of course, is that Margaret Thatcher did not make him Chancellor of the Exchequer when she was in a position to do so. Had she appointed him to run the Treasury, there would probably have been no ERM crisis, no Black/White Wednesday and probably no long-running Conservative debacle, even if there had been a one-off electoral defeat along the line.

By 1991 Margaret Thatcher was an outsider and destined to remain so. Gordon Brown made a histrionic attempt to relate to her by very publicly inviting her to tea at 10 Downing Street – almost twenty years after her political demise – but that was a rare example of one of her successors, in this case a political opponent, making a bit of a fuss of her. By the time David Cameron

---

* The Single European Act (SEA) was the first major attempt made by member states to amend the arrangements made under the Treaty of Rome (1957). Although the European Community had been in operation for nearly thirty years, it had not achieved its aim of a genuine common market. The SEA's main effect was to set a deadline for the creation of a full single market by 1992. It also created deeper integration by making it easier to pass laws, strengthening the EU Parliament and laying the basis for a European foreign policy. In these ways it took the process of European integration to a new level, laying the groundwork for the rapid changes of the 1990s and 2000s.

† In my view, Nicholas Ridley was the real inventor of 'Thatcherism'. He was l'uomo universale: painter, engineer, politician, architect, and always immensely admired by those who worked immediately under him – politicians and officials alike.

arrived on the scene, it was all really too late. He organised a reception for her at Number 10 soon after he became Prime Minister but sadly she was at the time too ill to attend.

I report the events almost entirely through the eyes of my diary, in which I made increasingly full notes. Where these expose the weaknesses of Margaret Thatcher's position, I have not deleted or edited my original words.

It was a difficult time for me too. Like Thatcher, I was not prepared for the role of rebel. Nevertheless it became my aim to do what I could to help preserve what has come to be called Thatcherism, but which might well have been labelled Ridleyism: the antithesis of socialism, the diversification of power, the recognition that society is the sum of the individuals that make it up and that a dynamic society is one in which individuals are well motivated (a notion to which David Cameron has added the idea of the selfless society being driven by individuals working at least in part on behalf of each other).

During 1992, holding the view that the most appropriate society for accountable government is the nation state, I gradually became the chief organiser of the parliamentary end of the anti-Maastricht campaign.

My letter of 28 September 1990 to John Major, with which I opened this chapter, is the key to my position on Europe. As an economist my face is set irreversibly against any arrangement which looks like a fixed or managed exchange rate. As a politician I cannot contemplate the loss of sovereignty with the abolition of the nation's currency in favour of the Euro. I am certainly one of those who feel that the greatest achievement of the Thatcher government was to abolish exchange controls. For me at this time the fight to maintain sovereign control of our currency and thus of fiscal policy was the essence of what lies ahead.

I tried to summarise my position in two letters to the national press. On 18 December 1990 *The Times* led with my letter headed 'Drawbacks for Britain in ERM':

Sir,

You said in your Leader of December 14 'The highly political decision to enter the European Exchange Rate Mechanism last October and at an exchange rate of DM2.95 to the pound looked like a mistake at the time. Today this can no longer be doubted...'

I agree, and said as much in the House of Commons two weeks ago. The crucial point for this country is the link between the present ERM bands and British interest rates.

Treasury Ministers argue that the present levels of interest rates are part of a policy of reducing inflation. This position is now indefensible. Inflation was caused by excess money supply and too low interest rates in 1987/88. Inflation is now crumbling, as it was bound to do because of the recession.

Just as low interest rates some three years ago caused inflationary pressure last year, so continued high interest rates now could turn the recession into a full-blown slump next year or the year after. The true purpose of high interest rates now is not to reduce inflation but to maintain the position negotiated for sterling within the ERM.

The grave prospect is that as German interest rates rise to pay for the reconstruction of the east, so our interest rates will be dragged up further. The government cannot allow this to take place. Sterling must be uncoupled from its present relationship with the DMark. We must renegotiate the ERM bands and cut our interest rates at once.

The effect of not doing so is the likelihood that the Conservative Party would lose the next general election on the back of a gravely wounded economy.

Yours faithfully

MICHAEL SPICER

On 8 January 1991 the *Daily Telegraph* also led with the following letter from me, headed 'High interest rates could lead to overkill':

Sir,

Your editorial (January 7) argues that a realignment of sterling within the ERM would necessarily be inflationary. Not true.

The question is, if the pound fell in value against the DMark, would we spend more on more foreign goods? The answer depends on the level of our purchasing power and what economists call elasticities of demand. In the present recession a fall in the value of the pound would not mean a rise in expenditures abroad. It would probably result in a switch to cheaper British goods. It would therefore be anti-inflationary.

Furthermore, if a fall in the pound coincided with a fall in interest rates leading to a rise in investment and productivity to match current wage demands, this too would be anti-inflationary. Low interest rates are inflationary only when they coincide with an overheating economy as they did in 1987/88.

The more fundamental point about exchange rates is that they should not be maintained at artificial levels, as is certainly the case at present, when sterling has to be supported by 14 per cent interest rates.

Of course you are absolutely right to emphasise the crucial importance of bringing down inflation; the current deep recession will achieve this. With continued high interest rates and sterling exchange rates we are going for overkill, with grave potential consequences for the economy of this country.

Yours faithfully
MICHAEL SPICER

History vindicates the argument that I put forward. Britain was headed for a major economic recession. Let the diary notes now pick up the story again.

These will take us through the great rebellion over the Treaty of Maastricht, in which I played a leading part, to the fatal 'Fresh Start' meeting which I chaired and which prompted John Major to resign as leader of the party, to the removal of the whip from eight MPs and to my role as a go-between in the process of restoring their membership of the party.

As I reread my diary notes, I am conscious of the unstable nature of Major's administration. Although Thatcher's demise, as my notes also show, did not come totally out of the blue, Major's ultimate departure had much deeper roots than Thatcher's and was much more predictable: indeed, the imminence of Major's fall was the working assumption every time two or three Conservative MPs gathered together. I was party to many such meetings.

Fresh Start, NAAFI, European Research Group, European Monitoring Group* – I was at the heart of all of them. Each comprised people of varying degrees of eminence and each was appropriate to people from different levels within the Conservative Party. There was not much overlapping. Together the groups added up to a movement greater than the simple sum of its parts, if only because their multiplicity sometimes confused our European federalist opponents.

For me it was in many ways an exciting period of my life: it could also be deeply depressing. I am not a natural poacher. I found being gamekeeper for the last nine years of my political life much happier, though whether they were as rewarding is another matter.

Thatcher's final period as an MP

Tuesday 8 January 1991
Ridleys come to stay the night. Over dinner we discuss the past and future. We come to the conclusion there are four immediate objectives:

---

* Not its real name, which for reasons of confidentiality I have withheld, as I have the story of how it was formed. I have restricted the report of conversations to utterings reflective of the public views of the individuals concerned – and only on matters which were significant at the time. I eschew tittle-tattle or small talk. In this way I try to reflect any historical significance of the meetings without totally breaking all confidentiality.

1. Lay down some markers in public about our position. Not to be too heavy handed about this, in order not to lose support by seeming to be carping and disloyal.
2. Write our history. You can say quite a bit about the future by talking about the past.
3. Keep Margaret Thatcher as much 'under control' as possible (meeting her for lunch on the 21st).
4. Build up slowly a policy thinking team for the future.

Thursday 10 January
Letter in from Richard Ryder, Chief Whip, offering to keep in touch. (Written in his own handwriting.) Also card from my association chairman, Vanessa Chesterton, saying the mumblings of discontent with my apparent attacks on the government are growing. This will need watching. I shall have to devise a positive speech for the AGM. Discuss this at length with Vanessa – I think she will be supportive if the going gets choppy, as it might.

Wednesday 16 January
Lunch with Cecil Parkinson. He tells me that Norman Lamont contacted him early on the Wednesday (21 November) of the anti-Thatcher coup. When CP called on him Lamont said. 'It's all over for Thatcher – join us.' CP said, 'I want to persuade her to stay on; if she goes I would probably vote Major but that's all.'

After lunch, CP and I meet up with Alan Watkins (*Observer*) (writing a book about the Thatcher fall) and Ian Aitken (*Guardian*). Neither, of course, is a friend of the Conservative Party. Watkins out to assess the role of Wakeham – who advised her to see her Cabinet individually.

Monday 21 January
Lunch at the Savoy with Thatcher, Tebbit, Ridley, Gordon Reece and Peter Morrison. Ridley leads discussion: government doomed because of its economic policy.

We decide to meet again as a group, perhaps eventually pulling in some younger ones. We would start with inner circle and work out. Plates are used to demonstrate this. Ultimately run out of plates so I have to toss in my coffee saucer. Margaret Thatcher collects them and stacks them, which is not really the idea.

Ridley says he asked Norman Lamont how he was going to meet war costs[*]

---

[*]   First Iraq War, 1990–91.

(Tornados cost £20 million apiece) and run a controlled budget. Lamont said we simply won't replace the equipment.

Thatcher says that re ERM she would have supported the higher and lower levels for two days and then let it go – that was her plan. Re her talks with Bush before the war 'we were able to help steel him'.

It is agreed that I will act as co-ordinator.

Wednesday 13 February

7.00 p.m. Drink with Margaret Thatcher in her 'new' room in the lower ministerial floor. Apparently Nick Scott moved to accommodate her. 'I hope I've made it cosy enough,' she says. Nick Ridley present. Discuss the formation of a series of groups to keep the 'fire of Thatcherism burning'. In particular talk about the YC conference of the previous weekend. Patten and Major have started to develop the idea of the 'social market', whatever that is.

After dinner we reconvene at 8.45, this time joined by Gerald Howarth, my former PPS, taking time off from George Young to work for Margaret for one week while Peter Morrison in USA. We discuss Margaret Thatcher's future as an MP. I say it's selfish but we need her as a rallying point. She repeats 'rallying point'! Then she says, 'The only problem is I hate coming into this place now', meaning the Commons. We are to meet again in my house for supper on 26 February. I still find it hard not to call her PM.

At one point we briefly discuss Peter Lilley, whom she promoted to the Cabinet on Nick Ridley's departure. MT says that when she failed to get the necessary votes for the leadership, her office rang from Paris to ask DTI to help with briefing for an upbeat speech on the economic record. Apparently Lilley said that her day was over and that there was not much he could do to help.

Tuesday 26 February

Dinner at Maunsel Street with Ridley, Portillo and Thatcher. Decide to set up a 'high command' to mastermind all the Thatcherite network of journalists, MPs, academics etc. Portillo stands slightly to one side as minister responsible for the community charge.

Wednesday 6 March

Dinner at Maunsel Street with Nick Ridley, Tony Favell,* Bill Cash, George Gardiner. Favell to be i/c parliamentary support. Looking for 150 signatures

---

* Member of Parliament for Stockport 1983–92. PPS to John Major 1986–90.

to an anti-federalist early day motion.* Bill Cash to build up European politicians' network. George running a movement outside Parliament. I will act as general co-ordinator. General view, which I do not share, that there will be an election in late summer.

Wednesday 13 March

Invited by Neil Hamilton (whip) to join his table for dinner. Also there is Chris Chope (DTI PUSS). We are joined later by Michael Portillo (MoS, DoE). Conversation led by Neil fairly rebellious. Neil at one point says we might do well to prepare for a period of refurbishment and recharging our philosophical credentials in opposition. Portillo has a problem: having been the minister responsible for community charge, he looks like having to defend dropping it. He admits he is bobbing about like a cork. Talk to Chris Chope about his present inclination to resign if we drop the community charge. I say the big one is Europe. He might do well to hold fire until then. Before dinner meet Robert Jones, who is leading the poll tax rebellion. He says Ridley's or Thatcher's intervention would not be helpful.

Tuesday 26 March

11 a.m. Go round to 93 Eaton Square† with Nick Ridley to finalise arrangements for forming MT's steering group. We agree this should comprise MT, NR, me (secretary), George Gardiner, Robert Jones, Bill Cash and Alexander Hesketh.

After the meeting (where we also agree the two big issues are the future of the community charge and Europe) I go back to College Street, where MT has her temporary offices, and discuss dates with her retiring diary secretary, Amanda Ponsonby. We discuss MT's future; apparently there is pressure from the constituency (which she is resisting) to do more there. This may turn out to be an important determinant of her future. My current feeling is that she will go, in which case we will have to think out very carefully how we play the steering group. We cannot be dominated by 'bolshie' ex-ministers. The mood is turning against us.

---

* An early day motion is a procedural device for MPs to register a point of view. It does not come up for debate on the floor of the House of Commons. It can, however, be a very significant way of expressing a collective opinion on a topical matter.
† Thatcher's newly rented house.

Wednesday 27 March

John Major comes up to my table in the members' dining room. (I am sitting with Robert Rhodes James.) I offer him a glass of port; he declines this politely, saying he has to get back into the wind-ups of the no-confidence debate, which I congratulate him on having opened very well.

I then say that I understand he had a good meeting earlier with Nick Ridley where he (Major) said he didn't wish to introduce further measures which would upset Thatcher; Ridley also said he was fed up with Patten et al. being publicly rude about him. Major apparently appeared rather shocked by this. John is now further surprised that I know about this meeting with NR, which has only taken place a few hours earlier. I say I am a friend of NR, with whom I keep in close touch (but he would not have broken any confidences). All rather sobering for JM.

At 9.45 go down to see Thatcher. Tell some of this to her but she is in a bate over what she calls Major's deception about the money being spent on the community charge, which has not so far been revealed.

Monday 15 April

4 p.m. First meeting of what Ridley calls the 'Steering Wheel Group'. Present: Alexander Hesketh (shortly to be Chief Whip in the Lords) Ridley, me, Thatcher, Bill Cash. Conversation centres on what sort of organisation we need. Bruges Group has recently launched a personal attack on PM and view is that this was very stupid. Question is whether the secretary of Bruges Group should be sacked.

Thatcher very keen to attack on community charge. We remind her that Europe is the big issue.

Tuesday 16 April

Have a chat with Norman Tebbit, who has a strong piece in the *Evening Standard* attacking enemies of PM who want to lose the next election. He tells me that he is playing a bridging role. Also bump into Dennis Skinner, who is as fiercely anti-federalist as ever. There may be some funny alliances in the next parliament.

Wednesday 17 April

Lunch party at Eaton Square in a house which Thatcher has borrowed from some Americans. Conversation flows freely. Ranges from whether M0 or M3 (fixed money supply) is best measure to the pressure being exerted by editors on people like Frank Johnson – writing anti-Major copy. Thatcher judges lunch a great success despite initial reservations.

She is very up and down. Great issue is whether she will stay in Parliament. Her mind is still very active and she is determined to fight to preserve what she started. She is finding it difficult to adjust to not having the power to affect decisions. She says she would never have done a deal with Saddam Hussein so the Kurd issue would not have arisen as it has.

Friday 26–Sunday 28 April
Conference on energy in Jackson Hole, Wyoming hosted by Senator Malcolm Wallop and his wife French. Verbal battle between me and the German delegation about the future of Europe. They admit to doing deals with the Russians and to being slightly alarmed by trends in the Soviet Union.

Ann and I are entertained very generously. Last night the party was taken out to what they call a 'dude ranch'; 'dudes' are stupid tourists, greenhorns!

Friday 3 May
Nick Ridley rings me at Cropthorne today to say he has missed having me around (we have been in the USA for past two weeks). 'Life has been ghastly,' he says. 'The thought police, i.e. the whips, have been very active. They now forbid ministers to talk to the Bruges Group.' Also, 'the frightful local election results' (we lost 850 seats – twice as many as expected at worst) 'show that the community charge was not to blame'. (The local elections were fought after the announcement that CC was to be abolished.)

Wednesday 8 May
Meeting with MT, NR, George Gardiner and Bill Cash at MT's College Street offices. Discussion focussed on European Union and 'union citizenship'. Decide to work up an EDM supporting PM's apparent hostility to this.

MT rather demoralised and rambling, also looking older. Today's *Evening Standard* carries front-page report of an interview in *Vogue* which presents her as 'disorientated'. NR (with whom I have lunch) also confesses to feeling old and demoralised. He has put his house in Naunton on the market. I dread reaching this point in life. I suspect it comes quicker than one expects.

Tuesday 21 May
Richard Ryder, Chief Whip, comes up to me while I am sitting in the members' lobby. It is the night after 105 members of the Conservative parliamentary party signed a motion against federation in Europe (organised in part by me). Richard says something to the effect that the party is much more at peace with itself these days. I say it is more like two warring armies looking at each other across the trenches.

Late that evening bump into John Cope (deputy chairman of the party). We have a couple of whiskies together on the Terrace. I say in effect his job is an impossible one with the economy going the way it is. He says, 'You have become very right wing. Whatever happened to the PEST days?' I say PEST has been hijacked by the Tory Reform Group. In my day it was anti-planning – more concerned with liberal free-market issues.

Friday 24 May
Bill Cash rings me at Cropthorne. Denis Thatcher is running around saying we did wrong on the anti-federalist motion. I say MT has got to come off the fence, otherwise in effect we must go it alone. We agree to bring up the story behind the motion with her when we meet on Monday 10 June. The fact is that the Chief Whip said that he had got the PM's tacit support for the motion. Whips then backed off from this position when they realised that they were taking sides and, indeed, because of a letter Bill Cash sent out to catch tail-enders saying motion had been 'passed' by PM; several colleagues signed who might not have done so otherwise.

Talk to Nick Ridley on the phone about all this. He feels DT out of touch with MPs' views.

Tuesday 4 June
Jonathan Aitken, Tony Favell, Bill Cash, Nick Ridley to supper. Discuss NR's speech for the next day quoting back much of John Major's speech against EMU at him. NR worried whether this may be antagonising people. We steel him up. Then decide we must stand firm against Delors compromise, increase EDM campaign and keep pressure on government. Decide to find ourselves a professional PR bloke. (This is left to me.)

Wednesday 5 June
NR's speech quite a media sensation. Talk late into the night with Bill Cash about tactics, especially what to say to Margaret Thatcher on Monday when NR will not be there. Agree this is a very testing time for her. Has to stick to what she believes, especially on Europe, but not to do a 'Ted Heath'.

Previous night I saw Ken Baker in the voting lobby. Told him again he must come off the fence if he wants support of the right. He repeated that his firm stance on immigration policy in July would achieve this.

Monday 10 June
Meeting with Nick Ridley, Robert Jones, Margaret Thatcher, George Gardiner and Bill Cash. Discuss Europe. MT firm in her opposition to a

single currency. I tell her of what I am doing with Christopher Story* on the secret treaties between European countries and Russia. She says she would like to discuss the details of this with Christopher and me later that day.

We duly meet in her office in the House of Commons at 9 p.m. Christopher begins by discussing the text of the treaties. These interest her very much (as they interest me) because of the implications for NATO and federal Europe. When after an hour he develops his theories of a communist plot involving Gorbachev – as I warned would be the case – she becomes argumentative, having just returned from endorsing what Gorbachev is doing. 'We must back him and the pluralist society he is trying to build up.' Christopher leaves disappointed.

Thursday 13 June

Cocktail party at Number 11 (Norman and Rosemary Lamont). Meet Sir Terence Burns, new PS at Treasury, who used to work for me years ago as young assistant to Jim Ball and as a consultant to Economic Models. He says that my letters to John Major forecasting an economic slump were 'rubbish'. This is an indication that Major has taken them seriously. I say this is the first democratic government in history to commit hara-kiri, but he (Burns) will be OK because his job goes on. Shows how out of touch economically and politically Treasury officials are.

Sam Brittan is listening to this and asks me why I take the view I do on floating exchange rates. I say because I once read a book by him called *Left or Right: the Bogus Dilemma*† and still believe in it!

Norman Lamont comes up to complain about an article Nicholas Ridley wrote the day before in the *Evening Standard* – arguing that in certain cases loyalty to issue was more important than loyalty to party. Then the PM comes up. Sam Brittan says he hopes we would not use the veto in Europe. The PM looks at me for my reaction. This is to ask to have a word with him in private. He says, 'Of course.' I say that I hope he realises that the side of the party I am on represents his natural allies (we had voted for him and would probably do so again), whereas the Heseltinites are his natural enemies who are on the move again. He makes no comment.

Friday 14 June

PM makes a speech on Europe in Cardiff which is heavily applauded by David Hunt and Chris Patten.

---

* Owner and editor of *International Currency Review*.

† Samuel Brittan, *Left or Right: The Bogus Dilemma*, Secker & Warburg, 1968.

Saturday 15 June

John Major's speech interpreted by *The Times* as pro-European federalism and criticised as such. Ann and I go to semi-finals of the Stella Artois tennis tournament as guests of Frank Lowe.* Talk to Professor Brian Griffiths, former head of MT's policy unit and now chairman of the Centre for Policy Studies. In presence of Mark Thatcher he says he wants close ties with Thatcher Foundation. Mark Thatcher and I have a discussion after lunch while the others go off to watch the tennis threatened by rain. He confirms that there is enormous press interest in his mother's speech due next week in Chicago. He says it is possible she has toned it down to make sure it is not too anti-Europe. I have the feeling from him she may have decided to leave the Commons. He says she may do this without necessarily going into the Lords. He seems to have a rather strange idea that even when she has left the Commons she should keep in touch with one or two PPSs! People who are not MPs have a false idea of what can be done outside Commons.

Sunday 16 June

Press very clear that Major's speech is federalist. (I think it is a watershed. We now know he is not on our side.) Tony Favell rings in some distress. Says he may have to resign the whip. He is sure that John Major has decided to agree to a single currency and certainly not to veto the new draft Treaty of Rome. All this is very worrying and is going to put me in a difficult position. Tony Favell is a very honourable man, one of the very few people to have resigned from a political job (PPS to PM) on an issue of principle.

Monday 17 June

Jacques Delors talks in Luxembourg of a federal Europe for the first time and our Foreign Secretary has to reject this. Everyone waits for Margaret Thatcher's speech in Chicago.

Talk to Sam Brittan about previous Thursday night at Downing Street. Both he and Robin Oakley say that Nicholas Ridley's book is going to open up old sores. The question Ridley is going to have to answer is why, when Nigel Lawson is delaying his book till after the election, he is not. Thankfully the book comes out just as Parliament is leaving for the summer.

---

*   Founder of Lowe Howard-Spink advertising agency and sponsor of the Stella Artois tournament. Knighted 2001.

Tuesday 2 July
In House of Commons bump into Tristan Garel-Jones. TGJ is in charge of European policy. We argue about this and about the strength of our support for some time behind the Speaker's chair and in the smoking room. TGJ takes especial exception when I talk of defending our birthright.

Friday 5 July
Am told by Special Branch in Worcestershire that my name has appeared on IRA death list, probably because I am thought to be a friend of Margaret Thatcher.

Wednesday 17 July
Lunch with Robert Cranborne. On Europe we agree to approach Conrad Black, owner of the *Daily Telegraph*, Michael Howard, Employment Secretary, and Alexander Hesketh, Chief Whip in the Lords.

Saturday 20 July
Jeffrey and Mary Archer's twenty-fifth wedding anniversary party in Grantchester. Major and Thatcher there, also Howard, Lamont. Stay with Robert Rhodes James (recently knighted and part of the new Major establishment). Notice a paste-up picture on his stairway wall, done in early '80s, with caption 'The wets'. Includes Chris Patten, Tony Grant, Peter Bottomley, Peter Tapsell,* Robert Rhodes James, Tristan Garel-Jones, Stephen Dorrell. Confirms Thatcher hadn't a clue who was for her and who was against. Or perhaps she simply didn't care.

Thursday 25 July
Lunch with Frank Johnson and Perry Worsthorne (editor) at *Sunday Telegraph*. We agree on most things: need to preserve the Atlantic alliance, inadvisability of trying to ape the socialists through the Citizens' Charter etc. I say there is one specific danger – too much regulation which will have an anti-competitive effect on former nationalised utilities.

Sunday 28 July
Staying in Antibes. Anchored off the coast is a five-decker owned by Budge[†] –

---

* Sir Peter Tapsell, Member of Parliament for Louth & Horncastle. Became Father of the House of Commons in May 2010. He first entered Parliament in 1959. Before that he had been personal assistant to Sir Anthony Eden.
† Richard Budge, owner of RJB Mining.

which we visit. Sunday papers full of the CBI report (came out last Thursday) saying recession getting deeper. Interest rates at 11 per cent; gap between inflation (4.8 per cent) and interest rates now very wide. Lamont gets a slating. *Sunday Times* calls for his removal and replacement by Heseltine.

Thursday 5 September

Henry Porter, formerly deputy editor of *The Independent* and son of constituent Harry Porter, rings. Met him before over dinner at MEP's house (Edward McMillan-Scott – with whom I had been arguing the toss over Europe). I had expressed the view that elections won or lost on the economy alone. Henry rings to ask whether I am planning to write an article in response to new Conservative lead in Sunday MORI poll of 3 per cent – to be confirmed apparently in tomorrow's Gallup in the *Telegraph*. I tell him I stick to my view that whatever the polls are saying, we are unlikely to be winning in the middle of a deep recession. It all smells like Wilson's election of 1970. But I'm certainly not going to write an article saying 'We're losing really'!

Friday 6 September

Norman Lamont speaks at South Worcestershire Conservative Association dinner at Prince Henry's School, Evesham. Competent performance, although he is surprisingly nervous.

When we get home Norman and I talk till 3 a.m. about Europe. He says we could probably engineer things so that we would not sign a new treaty which in effect accepted the principle of a single currency, not at least until the convergence of all countries. I say the one thing which could split the party would be the so-called Delors compromise, whereby we would sign a treaty permitting all other countries to go ahead with a single currency while we opted out. This would legitimise it all in a way which I certainly would find unacceptable.* It would also hasten the pace towards the creation of fiscal co-ordination and ultimately a federal state: the pressure for us to join this would be immense.

Sunday 8 September

Lamonts staying with us for the weekend. Norman seems to be a bit off colour having read a long piece in the *Financial Times* giving lists of people close to Major who go to breakfast with him. NL was not included amongst

---

* This is precisely what was agreed at Maastricht; my comments may have been the first early warning of what was to come to be received by a senior member of the government.

them. At one point he turns to me and says, 'You're not a real Thatcherite because you don't give absolute priority to reducing inflation.'

I reply, 'Your policies have put up inflation because of the effect of high interest rates on investment and productivity.'

Monday 9 September
News of Lamont accepting as a basis for negotiation a Dutch plan in the Hague at meeting of EEC finance ministers for a two-track move to a single currency; we would accept: (1) ERM, (2) Economic Institute (not bank), (3) single currency for those where economic convergence was proven. Delors furious about this.

Rosemary Lamont rings to say Norman has left his suit behind. I say we will get it to him.

Sunday 22 September
Papers full of a proposal by Lamont to set up a two-tier Europe, with a club of eight to work towards a single currency.* This seems to fly in the face of previous government assurances. Ring Robert Cranborne about this as I know he is going to Chequers for lunch.

Cranborne rings me later to say he has had 45-minute talk with PM, who poured out his heart to him. Apparently the game plan is still to stop a single currency and a federal Europe.

PM gave Cranborne permission to talk to me. I ring Bill Cash. Lamont has been onto him with reassurances. What is going on? It looks as though they are trying to ride two horses. Apparently the press briefing has all been in terms of a change in policy.

Cranborne's position is very curious. On the one hand he is friendly with Major, Patten, Garel-Jones, and seems to want to keep their friendship. On the other, he wants to monitor with a cold eye HMG's position on Europe.

Wednesday 25 September
Hannah and Robert Cranborne to supper in Maunsel Street. Agree to prepare a positive statement of what we think Europe is all about. Also decide to

---

* This curious policy of a two-speed EU, with Britain encouraging those in the faster lane to introduce central fiscal controls while herself remaining in the slower one, has been revived and given more emphasis by the Cameron government. I raised this issue with the Chancellor, George Osborne, publicly asking him what his fellow European ministers thought of this British position. On 23 October 2011 President Sarkozy of France said he was sick and tired of Britain pontificating about the Euro from the outside.

plough on with trying to get Michael Howard to join us. Robert is very keen to support Major's line in Europe. This today looks as if it is going well. Dutch have come up with a proposal for political union which is so uncompromising (foreign and security policy to be subject to majority voting) that we will have to vote against it. The Germans will not agree to monetary union. Helmut Kohl may come over and stay at Cranbornes' home with PM. Garel-Jones apparently very fed up with Dutch, who threaten to spoil his plans.

Thursday 26 September

Seven European states vote down Dutch proposal. Sadly I fear Dutch will come up with what will be claimed as a compromise at Maastricht in two months' time.

Monday 21 October

Dine in members' dining room. William Waldegrave sits opposite me the day after he has said on *Walden* that he wishes to withdraw tax benefits on health insurance for the elderly. People around the table congratulate him on speech he has just made in the House saying that in no way will we privatise anything in Health Service. I bide my time then say to him, 'Unless you can promise people immortality you will never win the argument on Labour's ground by bidding up on health spending. We must have distinctive policies of choice to accompany promises of extra resources. That is why your tax exemption position is so sad.' He looks rather shocked. Later that night discuss with Neil Hamilton whether Bill Cash can win chairmanship of parliamentary party's European committee. Would Tebbit be better?

Tuesday 22 October

Bill Cash is in a state about what he has heard about my discussion with Neil Hamilton. The Whips' Office want to get him off the chairmanship of the European committee and are thinking of running someone like Fowler or Jopling. We do need a good anti-federalist candidate to send right signals to Major as he goes off to Maastricht. However, I tell Bill if he is going to stand, there is no way that another anti-federalist should stand against him.

See George Gardiner after this; he is very keen to run. Tebbit doesn't think he can deliver the 92 Group vote to Cash.

6.30: Go up to Carlisle Place for drink with Nick and Judy Ridley. He is still not fully recovered from his summer lung operation. (His right eyelid droops and he gets very tired; I hope he is OK.) We agree to fight any compromise on monetary union and to find out precisely what is Thatcher's bottom line. I am seeing her the week after next. Also agree to back Cash.

Then on for a small dinner party with Peter Morrison (he was her PPS and is now leaving Parliament). Peter tells of last Cabinet when he, Charles Powell and Thatcher entered Cabinet room alone. (Rest of Cabinet outside waiting for John MacGregor, who was late.) Peter says she put her resignation speech at bottom of agenda although Palace had already been told of her decision. He told her 'No way'. According to him, she half-changed her mind up to the last minute.

Wednesday 30 October
Dinner at Cranborne's London home with RC and Michael Howard. My view is that the EMU treaty is potentially the real cut-off point. Howard thinks there is no alternative but to try to water it down and sign. Robert agrees with MH and offers to find an audience/place in Europe for him.

Wednesday 6 November
Following to supper at Maunsel Street: Tony Favell, Bill Cash, Chris Gill, John Townend, Bill Walker, Chris Butler, James Cran. We agree to canvass the people who signed the anti-federal EDM, and on my advice to put Bill Cash up for re-election as chairman of the European committee next week. This will be hotly contested (probably by Norman Fowler sponsored by the federalists).

Thursday 7 November
Meet the same crowd in my room at 11.45 to complete canvassing plans, joined by Toby Jessel.

4 p.m. Meet Thatcher, Ridley and Cash (also present John Whittingdale). Discuss the limits on the EMU opt-out clause. Ridley stresses need to be supporting Major. Thatcher very unsettled. She is very unhappy about Lamont's autumn statement the day before when he announced increased spending plans of £5–£11 billion. 'Everything we did is slipping away.' She feels powerless.

That evening dine with Ridleys; agree that he not I should write a piece for the *Evening Standard* pointing out limits on opt-out.

Saturday 9 November
Piece in *Times* saying Ridley has advised people to weigh up candidates; if they are federalist should not vote for them even if Conservative. (Very odd given what he said about supporting Major. I wonder how well he is.) This

breaks into a major news story on the TV bulletins. I issue a statement to PA at 6 p.m. saying he is wrong. Michael Howard did so earlier in the day, as did Bill Cash. Ring Ridley and tell him.

Sunday 10 November
Papers not quite so full of Ridley story as I expected. Talk to him again. He says he will go ahead with *Evening Standard* piece on the opt-out from the EMU treaty. I plan to abstain next Tuesday on council tax vote. Michael Portillo came up to me in the lobby about this last Wednesday 'just for form' as he is minister in charge. I told him that if I get too excited I will vote against him. There are at least ten reasons for this. How many does he want? He smiled, 'None.' Last week my whip, John Taylor, rang me about all this and got the same answer only I had started to list the reasons, e.g. community charge was the first real attempt to get accountability into local government etc. 'Stop, stop,' he cried. 'Not for the first time I agree with you!' That from my whip.

I write to Sydney Chapman, the pairing whip and a bit of a friend, on Tuesday in similar fashion – he thanks me for being so courteous.

Back to Ridley. I advise him to be rude about Labour in the *Evening Standard* article. 'I will try', he says, 'but there is a lot to say.' 'It would be a good antidote to what you said yesterday.' 'Understood,' he answers, not very convincingly.

Tuesday 12 November
5 p.m. Meeting with Cash, Favell, Gill, Cran, to try to organise Cash's re-election to European committee – hopeless. Abstain at the end of the Council Tax Bill second reading.* Ridley brings round an article which he has drafted for *Evening Standard* suggesting that his outburst was directed against possibility that people might vote for fourth parties – not a drive to vote Labour. I suggest he highlights this a bit.

Wednesday 13 November
Cash goes down to Fowler at European committee. Fowler people try to make out this was a landslide. I suspect Cash got somewhere around 100; since he was the anti-establishment candidate and whips have worked very hard, it must have given them a bit of a shock.

---

* Thatcher and Ridley also abstained.

Thursday 14 November
Lunch with Robin Oakley. Agree to send him my speech for Monday saying no compromise on single currency.

Evening up to see Annabel in school play at Rugby. She has a non-speaking part as a madwoman in *The Changeling* by Middleton and is *very* good.

Friday 15 November
Newsnight camera crew down to Cropthorne. I say will vote for government, having discussed this with Ridley, in forthcoming debate on Europe but am deeply concerned about single currency.

Saturday 16 November
Cash, Favell, Gill all ring. Persuade them of my view. Agree about possibility of letter to *Times* making points clear.

Sunday 17 November
Bill Cash on the phone. On *Walden* programme, Cecil Parkinson said he would be very tough on Major but then said if he came up with wrong answer at Maastricht would not vote against him. Really is time the grandees gave way.

Monday 18 November
Speech against single Euro currency at Royal Over-Seas League. Audience very sympathetic. *Times* gives some prominence to a trail of the speech. I talked to Robin Oakley yesterday.

Wednesday 20–Thursday 21 November
Sit through fifty or so speeches in the Euro debate in order to get in as the last speaker before the wind-ups on Thursday. Clearly the Speaker,* who does not seem to care much for me, is intent on keeping me out.

On Wednesday meet Sydney Chapman, to whom I say I will only vote for the government if I am able to say why. Apparently this is taken seriously. The entire Whips' Office has a meeting about it the next day (especially as I have told Chief Whip Richard Ryder that I think his office is doing a good job in these difficult times in representing all shades of view). Richard comes up to me on Thursday and says whips are doing their best to get me in. I do by the skin of my teeth. Afterwards in the division lobby Colin Moynihan, currently a minister in the Department of Energy and a friend of Antonia's

---

* Bernard Weatherill MP; created 1992 Lord Weatherill.

(and mine), comes up and says, 'By gum, you seem to terrify the whips. You were speaking three minutes after 9 p.m.' (I had only started at 8.54) 'and someone on the front bench says, "Shut him up." A whip steps in to say, "No, let him finish."'

I end my speech with the following: 'I will support the government tonight. I wish them well in the defence of British interests at Maastricht. However, that will not be the final say. That will come when we know what has been achieved at Maastricht ... On the issue of the single currency there can be no compromise. If Parliament were asked to ratify a treaty which I believed made British accession to a single currency inevitable, I would not vote for it."

Monday 25 November

I go on the *PM* radio programme to make the point (agreeing with Tebbit) that elections are won or lost not on debate about Europe but on the economy. I am asked if it will come right in time. I say, 'I sincerely hope so, otherwise we will return to industrial chaos, which invariably accompanies a socialist regime.'

Later in Parliament hear from Tony Favell that John Major approached Christopher Hawkins, who used to be a federalist but has now changed. Thinking he was still a federalist, Major said, 'Don't worry, Chris, we will settle at Maastricht.' If true, very revealing. Also hear that Tebbit was removed from proposing the debate on the Queen's Speech at the last minute in favour of Peter Walker. Perhaps explains why Tebbit is now hopping mad.

Wednesday 4 December

Private lunch at Reform Club given by Dick Body, long-standing anti-Marketeer. Austrian ambassador says real reason his country wants to enter EC is political, not economic. 'Worried for our democracy.'

ARCO[†] dinner at Claridge's. Sit next to Peter Shore, Labour anti-Marketeer. He agrees he would like to join some cross-party movement. Suggests a triumvirate: himself, David Owen and John Biffen. I agree to do what I can to set it up.

Former President Jimmy Carter gives an extremely boring off-the-cuff speech on foreign aid. Margaret Thatcher says it's the only time in her career she's ever woken up in the pauses to a speech.

---

*   Hansard, HC Deb, 21 November 1991, vol. 199, cols 504–5.
†   Major US oil company, now subsidiary of BP.

MT says she thinks Maastricht will break up in disarray. I say I wish I was as optimistic as her.

Find a lot of worried support around the room. New US ambassador Raymond Seitz makes a point of coming up to me after dinner. It would seem the Yanks haven't written me off totally yet.

Tuesday 10 December
Dine with Thatcher at her new home in Chester Square. Also present: Ridley, Gerald Howarth (her new 'PPS'), Tebbit, Edward Leigh (PUSS), Michael Forsyth (MoS, Scotland), Christopher Gill, Tony Favell, Bill Cash. Results of the Maastricht agreement come through; evening deteriorates into a verbal brawl between ministers and the rest about what our position should be. Ridley and Tebbit try to persuade ministers to resign. They in turn argue that it would be very irresponsible for Thatcher to vote against the government. She expostulates, 'But it's a matter of principle; the country is being sold down the river.' Denis Thatcher argues for unity and for the need to win the next election. It all becomes quite nasty, with Howarth, my former PPS, telling me to call off my friends.

At one point Michael Forsyth looks as if he might have certain reservations about Maastricht (the dinner takes place before we know what is actually happening). Edward Leigh says to him in an audible whisper, 'Don't do anything rash, Michael, for God's sake.'

Wednesday 11 December
Michael Howard and Robert Cranborne to dinner. Michael wants us to concentrate on European countries, building up cells of free marketeers. We agree.

I am reeling a bit from the triumphalist arrival of John Major in the Commons that afternoon. He claims 'game, set and match' at Maastricht. I wonder. I refuse to sign an adulatory EDM when I vote on some fisheries motion at 10.30.

Thursday 12 December
Lunch with John O'Sullivan. He feels we should build up an Atlantic operation. I agree.

In evening to Thatcher fortieth wedding party at Claridge's. John Major turns up despite press speculation to the contrary. The effect is that MT announces to the press outside that the deal at Maastricht was wonderful. God knows where that leaves us – her as a figure of history – us on our own.

Lamont is a bit surly about my position. I tell him, 'Wait till you need me when your back needs guarding.'

To Ken Baker (Home Secretary) I say Major's efforts are a triumph by the standards he set himself. Despite entreaty from Michael Howard am shaping up to abstain (reasons to be given in a letter to the whips which I begin to draft).

Saturday 14 December
Reports in *The Times* diary that the PM turned up at MT's party only when she agreed to praise him for his efforts at Maastricht. It may explain why she said it was all 'very painful' when she returned from the doorstep at Claridge's.

Monday 16 December
Nicholas Ridley rings from Cumberland to ask how I am going to vote on Thursday – answer, I will abstain. He is very depressed and uncertain. Has just talked to MT. She says she is under strong pressure to vote for Major. I say that will be her problem, not mine. The people who have got to her are the right-wing ministers, who want to use her to square their consciences for not resigning.

Tuesday 17 December
Jeffrey Archer supper party. Accost Frank Johnson about his pro-Euro article in last Sunday's *Telegraph*. Ann says, 'Mike commented that you must have been got at, when he read it.' Frank is a little shaken. Also his article apparently doesn't appease Norman Lamont, who objects to its tone, although it is friendly. I have a feeling Lamont is being both cocky (after Maastricht) but very defensive re the economy and his relationship with John Major. (This is highlighted in a rather poor leading article in the *Evening Standard*.)

Bump into John Moore, who is drinking champagne. I tell him if he'd had the occasional glass of champagne two years ago he would probably still be in office and an aspirant for PMship, if not there already. He laughs, which is good to see.

Towards the end Mary Archer comes up to me to say that MT wants a private word with me. (Would that had been the case when she was PM.) Sit on a sofa with her for half an hour or so. (Ann goes home with the Tebbits.) She is all over the place but seems now decided upon abstaining, although she says, 'Don't tell the press.' I say I never tell them anything these days and that I am going to abstain myself. There will probably be about twenty of us altogether.

When I ask MT what she thinks we should do if John Major loses the general election, she says, 'Skip a generation: go for Portillo.' I wonder. I think the party will want a heavyweight bruiser. That is why Heseltine is so dynamic. I am not sure we can build up Michael Howard in time.

Thursday 19 December
Thatcher, Ridley and I and several others abstain on the Maastricht vote.

Friday 3 January 1992
Dinner at Temple-Morris, Hereford. Peter TM very agreeable but on the opposite side of the party to me. He thinks we will lose the next GE and that Michael Heseltine will receive the summons from the party. God forbid, but I think he may be right. We have got to get our act together with Michael Howard and Michael Portillo.

Tuesday 7 January
Prime Minister makes speech in Scotland where he characterises those of us who dispute his economic policies as 'dismal johnnies',* shades of Lamont's 'faint hearts' last year. (Lamont acknowledged last week that he got his forecasts wrong.)

Monday 20 January
Have a beer with Norman Tebbit, Peter Morrison and Tony Favell after 10 p.m. vote. Norman Tebbit says trick is to have a weak dollar (in which our commodity imports are priced) and a strong Deutschmark, to keep out German imports, i.e. what we could have if we weren't in the ERM.

Tuesday 4 February
Play bridge between 10 p.m. and 12 midnight with Nick Ridley, Fergus Montgomery, Ray Whitney. So carried away are Nick and I that we vote with the government and against twenty-seven of our colleagues who wish to deny extra resources to the EC. My excuse is that with an election two months off, I am very keen not to be seen to be the cause of any loss at the polls.

Thursday 6 February
After 10 p.m. vote walk home with Bill Cash. Agree the Portillo–Howard axis is the best we can hope for. Discuss what kind of an organisation we need.

---

* To be added later to a fuller repertoire of abuse, e.g. 'one sandwich short of a picnic', 'bring on the men in white coats' and, of course, 'the bastards'.

I say too early for mass movement. Need club arrangement with press and MPs, also small informal network of like-minded people.

Thursday 20 February

Stay in to dine in members' dining room because I want to speak in the referendum debate tomorrow. At my table Bowen Wells (on the left of party) expresses the view that Britain funded an empire in the last century because she could not make common cause with Germans in Europe. This was a much better dinner than the one I had on Tuesday when there were a bunch of arrogant young anti-Thatcherites (e.g. Jerry Hayes). I felt I was amongst socialists. I bump into Thatcher at 10 p.m. vote and tell her so. 'Come down and have a whisky,' she says. After two whiskies and having been joined by Neil Hamilton, Bill Cash and Edward Leigh as well as her PPS, Gerald Howarth, we are able to discuss how we would treat a deal on PR if there were a hung parliament.

Tuesday 25 February

Brief encounter with Norman Tebbit in the lobby. Ask him why he had came out on TV in favour of Kenneth Clarke. Tebbit says, 'To warn off Michael Heseltine.'

Wednesday 4 March

11 a.m. To see Robert Cranborne to go over lists of 'sympathetic' MPs. Also to plan dinner next week when we hope Conrad Black will join in. Give lunch in Commons to Anatole Kaletsky. We are in agreement about ERM etc. Discuss prospects for general election, which are gloomy. He thinks Terry Burns at the bottom of disastrous economic policy.

Later in corridors of Commons chat to Nicholas Ridley, who thinks Major's days are numbered. Bill Cash over tea thinks we should go for Portillo. I say this is premature. Stick with Howard. I am aware, however, that this will not be easy. Howard not very user friendly. Not around the House much. But he is a man. Portillo still a boy. What we need is to keep them both very close together.

Friday 6 March

Nick Ridley stays the night at Cropthorne. He is very tired and not very well, although he arrives in his pick-up truck to collect some stones from a quarry in Gloucestershire for his house in Cumberland. His main piece of information is that Ken Clarke has made an overture to John Biffen with a view possibly to courting the centre-right vote in the party.

Tuesday 10 March
Budget Day. Supper with Margaret Thatcher at Chester Square. General agreement that Budget OK on tactics but strategy all wrong: very high public borrowing and high interest.

Wednesday 11 March
Annie Page rings me at Park Lane Hotel where lunching with Neil Bryson, David Porter and John Harris, all from AIEP.* Annie says Major has called election for 9 April. By the evening quick polls show Budget has not worked. Fifty-point fall in stock market.

Thursday 12 March
Chris Patten (party chairman) addresses '22 Committee and says we are going to win with a large majority because we are more competent – in the midst of a ghastly recession which we have created. On to Swan Walk where meet Robert Cranborne's father, Lord Salisbury. Portillo in excellent and thoughtful form. After 10 o'clock vote meet up with Hamilton and Howarth in Thatcher's room. Chat about what will happen after election.

Friday 13 March
Breakfast with Michael Howard and Robert Cranborne. Discuss possibility of Conservative defeat and consequences. Main point: Howard would not serve in a coalition government with Liberals and advises we should keep Major in place.

The No Turning Back (NTB) Group is meeting on Friday after polling day – in case Major tempted by coalition. Group comprises: Portillo, Howarth, Chope, Michael Brown, Forsyth, Hamilton, Leigh, Forth (all PPSs and Ministers). Nick Budgen, usually very much a loner, comes up to me and says we must team up in the next Parliament. At present this means Budgen, me, Chris Gill, James Cran, Favell, Cash.

The mood on the last day in Parliament is strange. For a start it is a Friday and yet the place is full. Rumours flying around about collapse of stock market and sterling linked to very bad opinion polls. Somehow the government had thought that the Budget would overcome the effect of the recession.

---

* Association of Independent Electricity Producers. I had chaired the AIEP since 1990. Later it became the Association of Electricity Producers (AEP), representing all power companies. I became its president, which, at the time of writing, I still am.

General election campaign in the constituency

Saturday 14 March 1992
Interviews in the constituency – very quiet. Only people who seem to be edgy are some of the district councillors. Long session with Susan Burlingham, my agent, over lunch signing election papers and finalising election address. Then go to cinema and dinner at Alexiou's in Chipping Campden with Ann.

Sunday 15 March
Polls still show the two major parties neck and neck. Lamont puts up a defence of his previous 'it's going to be all right for the economy' position. Apparently it's still going to be all right. Last-minute panic with the copy for the election address. Have decided to cut out first paragraph which admits there is a bit of an economic problem and go straight into the difference between socialists and us. Ring Tony Favell to offer to canvass for him next Wednesday. I fear it may be a bit of a wasted cause given the present polls but I am very fond of Tony. I hope he swims against the tide.

Monday 16 March
Day of finalising election address. Open a water purification plant (apparently Labour have said they could nationalise water). Sign letters for the last time on Commons paper (Parliament dissolves today). Labour produce their 'budget' ignoring interest rates/ERM issue. Despite everything Harris has a poll showing Conservatives 7 per cent in the lead. Average polling – 40 per cent not enough to give us an overall majority.

Tuesday 17 March
8.10 on BBC Radio Worcester with a Liberal and Labour. Subject is Labour's shadow Budget. Anatole Kaletsky on the radio as I drive into Worcester, saying this is one of the most swingeing proposals – to increase tax on the middle rich (£21,000 and up; £5 billion to be collected from them) – ever. This supports an article he has written for today in *The Times*. Will this be Labour's Achilles heel? Were they mad to produce a detailed Budget which we could attack? Surely one of the luxuries of opposition is not to do this. However, I run straight into the question at the radio station of why we have let the economy down. Presumably we're going to get this the whole time. Spend rest of the day tidying up at home and preparing some press statements.

Sunday 22 March

Major answers questions on *Walden* programme implying that we are 'more caring' than Labour on health and education. Leaving aside the meaninglessness of it, it seems rather foolish to play on Labour's ground. We should be putting the fear of God into everyone about the potential financial crisis which could follow a Labour government. Certainly we have got to do something to stop the slide in the polls. Talk to Ridley to ask him what he makes of the slow fall in inflation with tight monetary policy. My own view is that interest rates are actually inflationary. High cost of capital and low productivity etc. Michael Howard comes on the phone while I am talking to Ridley. He still thinks something will turn up in the last week and we will win.

Tuesday 24 March

Difficult day. *Newsnight* ring to say they want to film me and someone with his own radical views about ERM. Phone Nick Budgen to see what he is doing (he was the other invited). We decide to go on to say whatever the present problems it would be worse under Labour. Within ERM interest rates would have to go up and there would be a financial crisis. In the event it all works out rather worse than anticipated. They were clearly out to paint me as a rebel (though they were given no quotes to support this). At a meeting in Honeybourne a lady gets up to say I was not positive enough on Europe. They zoom in on her like vultures. I do not think it will look very good on Friday night. Luckily the association chairman, David Finch, is around and I am able to warn him that it was all a bit of a set-up. At the end of the meeting at Honeybourne, Finch hangs around in front of the TV people, then announces that he is chairing the next meeting at the Littletons and that he is the one with the key to the village hall. When we arrive there, following him, the hall is pitch dark. We have to use a torch to enter. Several figures emerge from the shadows, one from a pub across the road, and some sort of a meeting gets under way in front of the TV crew!

Wednesday 25 March

Canvassing in new up-market estate in Evesham full of pretty young mums saying wouldn't it be exciting 'to have a change', until I point out that that would mean a financial crisis, which turns them rather gloomy.

Saturday 28 March

Cavalcade in Malvern. People in the shopping arcades seem quite friendly. Then to a briefing meeting at Pershore, chaired by David Finch, which is friendly and efficient. After this I drive up to Cannock to canvass for Gerald

Howarth. Somehow we miss each other but I do two hours for him. Opinion polls on the radio continue to show Labour with a lead of two points, pointing to a hung parliament.

Sunday 29 March
Tony Favell on the phone. His spirits seem to be up. He has had Heseltine, Tebbit and also, amusingly, the hard market economist Patrick Minford canvassing three times for him, apparently answering questions about the recession on the doorstep (which he forecast like me because of high interest rates) with standard response (Don't worry, we'll get over it, it's all the world recession etc.!). Kinnock on *Walden* programme pretty hopeless but gets away with the last word that Tory tax attack is all for the 10 per cent richest.

Anthony Steen rings at 10.30; he is finding (as I am) that the drift away is from ladies between twenty-five and forty. He also says – again like me – that the Liberals were very low profile this time. In his case all the workers had gone to North Cornwall, North Devon and Plymouth; in mine to Cheltenham and Hereford.

Tuesday 31 March
Annie Page down by train to deal with post. Good, well attended meetings at Corse Lawn (45), Upton (35) and Ripple. Severe fall in morale of Conservative supporters caused by three opinion polls showing support moving rapidly to Liberals and leaving Conservatives 4–7 points behind Labour. This is what Ridley forecast before the election and what one has felt on the doorstep.

Wednesday 1 April
Canvassing in Malvern. 'Don't knows' in the lead on the estates. Meetings in Severn Stoke, Kempsey and Callow End. Last one well attended by gypsies protesting against threatened eviction. Polls that evening point (with others) to a Labour lead of 3 per cent. I am filmed fleetingly on BBC *Newsnight* being tough on Europe. More lengthy interviews with John Biffen and Nick Budgen, who told the *Newsnight* people that Major was greatly over-promoted.

Wednesday 8 April
Eve of poll. 'Cavalcade +' stopping in shopping centres in Evesham, Pershore, Upton and Malvern. Much friendlier reception: there is a tangible change in mood. Perhaps it is just that this is the first sunny day. Edward arrived from London and came out with us, which was nice, as did Annabel (taking a break

from her work for A-levels). Also our twenty-fifth wedding anniversary; Ann gave me a lovely McCall drawing (one I had long admired in his notebooks). I gave her a beautiful orchid but plan to choose a piece of furniture for her after the election. Susan Burlingham (my agent) armed with flowers; she has been very supportive and very efficient. Also masses of cards from supporters in the constituency.

Eve-of-poll meeting in Malvern takes on the nature of a revivalist rally. Cake appears for silver wedding; everyone seems very pleased with the speech.

Thursday 9 April – polling day

To polling station around 8.45 (Cropthorne). Annabel votes for the first time; give Edward's and Antonia's proxy votes. Beautiful hot day, could favour disaffected Tory vote; ultimate feel-good factor. People very friendly; something is going on. Only real desert in Broadway, where there are no tellers and no posters.

Exit polls show a hung parliament in Labour's favour. They are wrong. (In South Worcestershire my majority over the Liberal Democrats was 13,645. Nationally the Conservatives were back with an overall majority of twenty-one.)

Friday 10 April

'Thank yous' on all my posters. Talk to Ridley, McAlpine, Cash, Favell (lost), Howarth (lost). Michael Howard rings in the evening. He is waiting for the call.

Colin Marshall rings to congratulate. The Conservative victory means that John King will stay on as he thinks (wrongly) that he gets on well with Major. (In fact Tory high command will not forgive him for cancelling BA's donation.)

Reflections

On rereading these notes, I am struck by just how directionless we Thatcherites were at this time. We were in shock and, more important, so was she. We were, above all, confused about what we wanted to achieve, especially in the short term. A determination to protect her achievements and what she had stood for was matched by a strong disinclination to 'do a Ted Heath' and to resort to sulking disloyalty or, indeed, to any form of disloyalty, let alone to organise any form of putsch against John Major. Early attempts to resolve the dilemma were made by inflating those utterances of the new Prime Minister which gave even the faintest signal that he was 'one of us'; but these signs were dim and increasingly spaced out.

The immediate embarrassment was resolved by the general election on 9 April 1992. After this Margaret Thatcher left the main political arena and took her place in the House of Lords. The focus in the House of Commons immediately shifted from being on one personality to being on one issue; it is to the European matter that I now turn.

Chapter 11

John Major: the Maastricht rebellion

At this point and for a short while the diary notes become pretty thin. This is ironic because it was also a time for me of great activity. Quite simply, for a brief period I became a central – if not the central – figure (on the rebel side) in what was arguably the biggest crisis within the Conservative Party since the split on the Corn Laws in 1846.

It is hard to describe the enmity which built up at the time between Conservative MP and Conservative MP. In the dining room Eurosceptics would not sit at the same table as Europhiles and vice versa. In the voting lobbies it was not unknown for one Conservative MP to spit at another. Physical violence occurred during the course of one or two crucial votes.

Why I did not record these events as copiously as I did other less significant occasions is not totally clear to me. Perhaps it was because the intensity of what was taking place was for me so great that I became emotionally and physically drained – at least to the extent that I had no energy to prolong the days by writing a diary by night.

What I did do in 1992 was to write a book, *A Treaty Too Far*,[*] which was published on the day of the crucial 'paving' vote. This does give a graphic account of certain key moments at the start of the rebellion. Another contemporary description of what took place on the rebel side, impressionistic but in my view very accurate, is Teresa Gorman's *The Bastards*.[†]

At the very beginning there were four key players on the Eurosceptic side: James Cran, Christopher Gill, Bill Cash and myself. At the parliamentary level, which, with the impending passage of the Bill ratifying the Treaty of Maastricht, was all that really mattered in the early stages, Cran, Gill and I made the early running. Cash manned the research engine room, from which he emerged to become a major figure in the projection of our case to the public. Throughout there was tension between Cash and me, though, at least for my part, each always had considerable admiration for what the other was up to.

---

[*] Michael Spicer, *A Treaty Too Far*, Fourth Estate, 1992.
[†] Teresa Gorman, *The Bastards*, Sidgwick & Jackson, 1993.

No such tension existed between me and Gill – at least in the critical formative stages. It was different later, though it was not until I read Gill's autobiography* that I learnt just how great was his antipathy towards me; he even implied that I was some sort of double agent. I think there was a whips' spy in our group, but it was not me. I believed at the time, and still believe, that the spy was someone who later became a whip himself and later still a very senior figure in the movement to get Britain out of Europe. We suspected his duplicity all along and from time to time fed him information we wished to reach the government.

My aim – easily misunderstood – was to do what I could to block the ratification of the Treaty of Maastricht, while at the same time maintaining the credibility of my point of view on Europe within the mainstream of the party. In so far as the enshrinement of the treaty in British law was the objective of the government, this did mean that I was on a rebellious collision course with those at the time leading my party. However, and this was the difficult bit, I was also intent on winning the party and the future leadership back to the path on Europe from which I believed it had strayed with the fall of Thatcher. I wanted, in other words, to create a rebellion which would reorientate and redefine the core of the party. It was a high-wire balancing act, which arguably had some success when we went into opposition; how permanent this was only history will tell.

There were three distinct phases to the genesis of the rebellion: the assessment beginning in 1991 of what was wrong with the Treaty of Maastricht, a parliamentary manoeuvre called an Early Day Motion in response to the referendum vote against the treaty in Denmark in the summer of 1992, and a reaction to the 'paving' vote in the House of Commons in the autumn of 1992.

The Treaty of Maastricht, initialled by the new Prime Minister, John Major, on 9 December 1991, was an amendment to the Treaty of Rome, to which the United Kingdom had become a signatory by terms of the Treaty of Accession of 1972. Maastricht required to be ratified by Parliament. Its major deficiency, in the eyes of its critics, was that it removed the power of sovereign states to manage their own economies. It did this in a number of ways, in particular by giving the European Central Bank the power to set and police monetary policy including interest rates, by making provision for federal controls of public spending through deficit constraints and, crucially, by merging the currencies of the member states into a single Euro. The latter was to be done 'irrevocably', which would, for instance, have totally destroyed the British

---

* Christopher Gill, *Whips' Nightmare*, Memoir Club, 2003.

constitutional principle that each parliament is sovereign in its own time and cannot therefore bind a future parliament.

Britain secured an opt-out from the single currency and one demand of the rebels was that there should be a commitment by the Conservative government to protect and preserve the independence of sterling into the future. One reason why the government refused to make such a deal with us – and it would have defused the rebellion – was that the belief existed, and still exists, that the European Court of Justice would ultimately find Britain's position outside the Euro to be illegal.

My own objection to a single currency, expressed at the time in various letters to *The Times*, in Parliament and in *A Treaty Too Far*, was part political and part economic. I do believe that control over one's money is the essence of independence and of nationhood; and I do believe that a permanently fixed exchange rate – which is the characteristic of a currency merged with others – is distortive and debilitating for an economy.

Fresh Start motion

In the early morning of Wednesday 3 June 1992, the news broke that in a referendum on the Treaty of Maastricht the day before, the Danish people had voted 'No', knowing that ratification of the treaty required a unanimous vote by all member countries. I immediately put my name at the top of Early Day Motion[*] number 174. I had previously agreed the wording of this Motion with James Cran and Christopher Gill. It read as follows:

> That this House urges Her Majesty's Government to use the decision to postpone the passage of the European Communities (Amendment) Bill as an opportunity to make a fresh start with the future development of the EEC and in particular to concentrate its efforts on the chosen agenda of the British presidency which is to extend the borders of the EEC and to create a fully competitive common market.

This came to be known as the Fresh Start motion.[†]

---

[*] EDM 174 was arguably one of the most important (certainly most famous/notorious) motions ever tabled.

[†] In his autobiography John Major puts it like this: 'Early Day Motions are often the parliamentary equivalent of graffiti ... But not this one. They [the Eurosceptics] knew its capacity for damage the moment they saw it.'

Cran, Gill and I then proceeded to scour the House of Commons for the names of other supporters. Within a few hours, ninety-one Conservative backbenchers had signed. But this turned out to be a high point. I tried to describe in *A Treaty Too Far* the mood of my colleagues on the afternoon of Wednesday 3 June:

> The sense of relief that the Danes had let us all painlessly off the Maastricht hook was immediately replaced by despondence at the government's response … Government Whips began to huddle together in the Members' Lobby and elsewhere, like American football players in a scrimmage, to plan the retrieval process … I and a few others, who only that morning had begun to look forward to a peaceful summer ahead, swiftly concluded that we must make some gesture of our own.

Rather generously, in *The Bastards* Teresa Gorman put what followed like this:

> Michael's EDM appeared on the Order Paper the next day. Its long list of supporters was the number one topic at the Whips' meeting held at 12 Downing Street, the official residence of the Chief Whip, Richard Ryder. 'We have a serious problem on our hands', said Richard, 'and I want action.' … Michael Spicer's triumph, his inside knowledge of government and his pleasant nature, marked him out as an acceptable leader of our dissident group, which took its name from the 'fresh start' mentioned in his EDM. Initially regarded by the Whips as a sort of Dad's Army of misfits, we soon formed as disciplined a task force as any SAS brigade … During the passage of the Maastricht Bill, the group hovered at around 26 stalwarts … We soon had too many members to fit comfortably into the small committee room in Westminster Hall and now met regularly in Room J on the lower ministerial corridor inside the House of Commons … The genial Michael Spicer chaired the meetings with a relaxed and amiable manner but with all the skills necessary to silence a windbag.

John Major in his autobiography[*] has a rather different take on me:

> Michael Spicer, the originator of the Early Day Motion the day after the Danish referendum vote, remained one of the guiding spirits behind the rebels – although he kept cordial contacts with the Government Whips throughout … Michael was amiable whenever we met but rumour in the parliamentary ether was that he was among the most hardline of the rebels.

---

[*] John Major, *The Autobiography*, HarperCollins, 1999.

For reasons which have never been entirely clear to me, Major's main response to the Danish vote – besides claiming (accurately) that it would be reversed, was to commit himself to an hors d'oeuvre vote on the treaty, to be debated in advance of the proper ratification Bill.* This was termed a 'paving' vote and served merely to put the Bill at risk before it had even reached Parliament. The paving vote was scheduled for 5 November and became the focal point for the members of the Fresh Start Group, for the government itself and for the media.

The build-up to this vote on all sides was feverish. Everyone knew that it was critical. John Major has confirmed in his autobiography that, had he lost the vote, he would have immediately resigned.

A foretaste of all this came a few weeks before Parliament returned for the autumn at the Conservative Party conference in Brighton, where young people everywhere paraded in Fresh Start T-shirts with which I had provided them. On the floor of the conference itself on Tuesday 6 October, Norman Tebbit made a powerful speech attacking the Maastricht Treaty. In the afternoon, Douglas Hurd, Foreign Secretary, made an equally powerful one defending it. The conference cheered both speeches.

On Monday 3 November, the night before the crucial paving debate, I chaired a meeting attended by over thirty colleagues, more than enough to overturn the government's majority, given that Labour would vote with us. We were joined by Willie Ross from the Ulster Unionists, who made the point that whoever attended the meeting was a 'dead man' politically while the present leadership was in charge. They might just as well, therefore, 'go through' with their vote against the government the following day. The inimitable Teresa describes the occasion in this way:

> Our meeting was scheduled for six o'clock … Each time the door opened and a new face appeared a small cheer went up. 'Welcome,' said Michael Spicer, 'come in and join the club' … Someone in the room may have been sent by the Whips, but who was the Judas? … John Biffen arrived, quietly spoken, unassuming, but a heavyweight nonetheless, ex-Cabinet Minister and former Leader of the House … Next came Peter Tapsell, historian and banker … Another of the new intake was Iain Duncan Smith … The room was getting crowded … At the end of the table Michael sat, pen in hand, jotting down notes, ticking off names. He was a good chairman, neither charismatic nor dominating, his natural good humour had kept us all going, so far. 'It's three minutes past starting time,' he said … 'It's time for us to commit ourselves. The Prime Minister has given us the best chance we will ever get to kill this

---

*   The European Communities (Amendment) Bill.

Bill before it kills us … Now, will anyone who has decided to vote with the government please leave the room'. We waited, tense, eyes moving around the gathering. I counted forty people now. A chair scraped. Someone got up and moved to the door, then someone else and another. They left silently, without resentment on our part. At least they were being honest. 'Now I want to go round the table to find out who will be voting No and who will be abstaining.' As each Member stated his or her position, Christopher (Gill) marked the names off on his list. So did Michael … 'I think we are home and dry, so long as everyone remains committed. I ask you again, if you don't think you will go through with it, please say so now. We don't want to be over-optimistic but the numbers look satisfactory.' … Elsewhere in the building Government Whips were having their own meeting. They too were ticking off names on a list. Later that evening one of the new Members who attended our meeting was frogmarched by a Whip to a dressing down on the chilly Terrace. 'Those rebels will bring you ten minutes of fame and a lifetime in the political wilderness,' he was told. He caved in.

And so it went on. As the crucial vote approached, the actions became more brutal. One senior colleague, having been caught in the men's cloakroom, was pulled by his hair into the government voting lobby.

The net effect of all this was that when the result of the vote was announced at 10.15, the figures were 319 for the motion, 316 against, a government majority of three. We had had thirty-two pledges the night before. This had dwindled to twenty-six, with six abstentions.

In my view, this was the single most decisive event in a rebellion which stretched many months ahead. Had we won this vote, as the night before it looked as if we would, history would have moved in a different direction. John Major would have resigned and the process of ratifying the Maastricht Treaty would have ground to a halt.

On the only other occasion when theoretically the opportunity re-presented itself, the government did lose but immediately (and with questionable legality) brought forward almost the same motion with a vote of confidence attached to it. This time, knowing that, were the government to lose the repeated motion, there would be a general election, I led the rebels back into the government's lobby.

The fate of Maastricht was indeed sealed almost a year before the ratification Bill became law. In his autobiography John Major takes the same view:

As I took my place on the Treasury bench, I still did not know whether we were about to win or lose the division. I did know that defeat could not be brushed aside. If we had lost I would have risen in my place and announced my resignation; the combination of Black Wednesday and the inability to proceed with the Maastricht Bill would have made my position untenable. I would not have gone on.

From my point of view what Major wrote next was even more relevant: 'The second – more crucial – vote was on the government's Paving Motion to resume consideration of the Bill immediately. It seemed innocuous, but if we lost it would have been very difficult and may have proved impossible to reintroduce the Bill at all without splitting the party irrevocably.'

Let me now wind back a little and pick up the few diary notes I did make. They give some feel for the build-up.

Thursday 30 April 1992
Travelling to US to see my publisher about a new project. Preparing for the anti-Maastricht dinner in two weeks' time. I am apprehensive about this as I will take the chair. It's going to be hard struggle taking on the weight and majesty of government.

Saturday 2 May
Dinner in New York with John O'Sullivan. He is planning a speech for Mrs T. and wonders what to put in. My advice: as little as possible. He also says she may not want a place in the House of Lords for the time being. I find this a little implausible. JO'S doesn't want her to go there because it will look as if she is retiring. Sadly she has.

Tuesday 5 May
Lunch at White's with Robert Cranborne, recently made PUSS at MoD. Apparently PM has told him if he behaves himself (i.e. is loyal on Europe) he will be leader of the Lords. The Blue Chips are closing ranks. Cranborne tells me that the BCs are as anti-Heseltine* as we Thatcherites. He is a close ally of Patten and Garel-Jones but he wants to keep the Eurosceptics going. Wants me to take over his continental Eurosceptic friends. All very Cecilish!

Monday 18 May
10 p.m. Norman Lamont invites me to his room in the Commons for a drink, 'not to talk about Maastricht,' he says. Actually that is exactly what he

---

* No doubt true, as their champion, until he lost his seat, was Chris Patten.

does want to talk about. Sit with him reluctantly drinking whisky (my diet only allowing wine these days) for almost two hours.

Thursday 21 May

11 a.m. Drop in on Margaret Thatcher at Chesham Place. She has a vast suite of offices where apparently her biography is being researched. She has a bad cold and is uptight about the debate in the second reading of the Maastricht Bill. I speak that night in what the BBC calls a passionate speech. I imagine they meant 'impassioned'. MT excited about an article she has written in the *European*. She sends her driver off to fetch an IEA pamphlet purporting to show that the Commission is gaining in powers. I have to excuse myself from waiting for his return as I want to think about my speech. In the end I deliver this without notes and it seems to go down OK, at least with supporters.

Reflections

I was very nearly not called by Michael Morris, the new deputy Speaker, and had a row in his office with him. He had told me I would be called on the second day of the debate and therefore had no need to stay up on the first. He eventually relented and pushed me up the list.

I dealt in this speech with the central question of the opt-out from the European currency, which the government argued was the main reason for people with views like mine to vote with them. Here is how I addressed the issue:

> I can imagine, when we have set up the institutions and signed in principle to the treaty, the whips coming up to me and saying 'Look here, Spicer, you are talking about the opt-out as if it were a real option. Have you gone completely out of your mind? ... The whole thing is in place ... You have to go along with us ... We signed it all in 1992 ... weren't you there?"

It was my way of saying that, once the treaty went through, the pressure for conformity, particularly from the European Court, would be so strong that no single country would be able or allowed to hold out against it. Twenty years later I remain convinced that this is the probability unless the currency collapses through its own internal tensions.

25 June

10.30: Meeting with Ken Baker. He is coming round to the cause;

---

*   Hansard, HC Deb, 21 May 1992, vol. 208, col. 570.

would rather like to lead us but not ready yet to make the jump. The guillotine vote in the Maastricht Bill will sort him out one way or the other.

2.00: Meet the Fresh Start Group. Brilliant meeting. Plan a petition at party conference and a meeting in the summer in my home and a mass rally with Thatcher. Agree we will fight Maastricht all the way.

4.30: Meeting with Thatcher. She is in good shape and ready to do battle in the Lords. Willie Whitelaw cannot introduce her because she made him a more senior rank! As I went in, Cranborne was coming out. People are saying that Cranborne has been meeting with Patten and Garel-Jones in support of Maastricht while he and I were meeting against it.

Friday 10 July
Party in the Tower of London for Annabel (18) and Antonia (21). Great success and enormously enjoyed all round. Each girl looked beautiful in her different way. They each made a sweet speech of thanks. Afterwards took two of their friends to dinner at the Kundun restaurant in Horseferry Road. In the morning rang Margaret Thatcher. She was vexed about being misquoted in the *Evening Standard* attacking Major's economic policy. I suggested we try to keep a slot for her at the party conference. Bill Cash rang earlier to say that he had met Philippe de Villiers, the up-and-coming Chirac party deputy who is going to rival Chirac and in particular to attack the federalist onrush in the EC. We plan to meet soon.

Wednesday 22 July 1992
10.30: Meet at Thatcher's office, 22 Chesham Place, with Bill Cash and de Villiers. Thatcher agrees to write a piece for *Figaro* just before the French referendum on 23 September. Bill, de Villiers and I leave at 11.45 for half hour meeting in the Carlton Club where we agree to hold a meeting of like-minded European MPs in France on 5–6 September and hopefully issue a declaration then.

Thursday 10 September
Phone call to Thatcher. She comes out of a meeting at 10 a.m. to talk to me. Three points I make:

1.   Have organised dinner for her at the party conference.
2.   My book (*A Treaty Too Far*) finished ready for her foreword.
3.   Have written to Danes to set up international Marketeer but anti-political union organisation.

We discuss whether PM would move on ratification before the Danish problem had been sorted out.

Wednesday 23 September

Parliament recalled to discuss sterling crisis. We left the ERM the Wednesday before while Ann and I were in a château outside Bordeaux. In my absence Christopher Gill called a meeting for today with the hard core Fresh Start Group and for 12 noon tomorrow for all those who had signed the Fresh Start EDM. Seventeen turn up today, including Teddy Taylor, Nick Budgen and Richard Shepherd, who tries to make us formally vote against the government in the quasi vote of confidence tomorrow. James Cran walks out. I say I will vote for the government. Bill Cash peeved by in his view being upstaged by me especially on Sunday night on BBC *Newsnight* when I commented on the result of the French referendum and was called leader of the Eurosceptics. Bill in a huff and determined to vote against HMG or at least abstain.

Thursday 24 September

Overnight I devise a Fresh Start EDM Mark II which I put to the meeting of fortyish colleagues.[*] They accept it with minor amendments. (By the evening it attracted over seventy signatures, including Peter Tapsell's, and by Friday it was headline news.) See Richard Ryder at 1.30; he has warned the Cabinet I am coming. There is to be no bargaining with me. However, I explain I will be voting with the government anyway. I have come to advise PM against making it 'inevitable' that we will rejoin ERM. In the debate Major is unnecessarily rude about Tebbit; he is also pretty curt with me when I ask him in Parliament whether there will be a free vote on the Maastricht Bill.

[In his biography of John Major,[†] Anthony Seldon puts it like this: 'Major was particularly unsettled by Spicer's question asking whether a free vote would be permitted on the Maastricht Bill'.]

Lamont makes a better speech in the wind-up. (Lamont also did well at a meeting of the finance committee on Friday which I could not attend as Gill, Cran and I met at Gill's home to consider how to downscale our activities at the party conference so as not to destabilise a bandwagon which was rolling

---

[*] 'That this House welcomes the Government's decision to leave the ERM, and urges a fresh start to economic policy, in particular the abandonment of fixed exchange rates and a commitment to sound finance, stable money and the right climate for steady growth.'

[†] Anthony Seldon, *Major: A Political Life*, Weidenfeld & Nicolson, 1997.

well in Parliament.) Also talk to Gerald Howarth about inviting Thatcher to our dinner at party conference.

Monday 5 October
Arrive in Brighton for the party conference. Check in at Metropole Hotel and go down to suite Kent 3 to see how preparations are going for the petition by organisations in support of the two EDMs which I led in the summer in the House on Maastricht and the ERM. Press have begun to rumble what was going on in my name, and the room number was been advertised this morning in the lobby of the hotel. When I arrive at the suite there are already signs of potential 'door-stepping' – a TV crew is lurking. I decide that the MPs should distance themselves so as not to be seen to be joining in the plotting; others take on the operation for the week (not wholly successfully: collecting about 1,000 names).

I leave to prepare for a *Newsnight* debate with Edwina Currie. Did not sleep the night before because of a faulty alarm switch across the road. I do not think I was at my sharpest but the audience was supportive.

Thursday 8 October
The European debate: Tebbit cheered but goes over the top and attacks Major. Hurd manages to exploit the reaction against this and gives speech to win the day. This definitely has an effect on signing of the petition. For the rest of the conference, opposition goes underground to fringe meetings. These (including two that I do) are well attended.

Tuesday 13 October
Having spent the night in Durham seeing Annabel, drive down to the news that thirty pits to be closed. This really has brought out all the lefties in our party. There are the makings of an unholy alliance between them and us Marketeers. Each from his different perspective is now banging on about the recession.

Tuesday 4th November 1992
The big paving vote. On the previous evening I chaired a meeting of thirty-four colleagues and William Ross (Ulster Unionist). We developed a policy of voting with a Labour amendment to delay Maastricht and voting against the substantive motion. Had everyone voted the way they said they would I would not have ended up with a few colleagues in Teresa Gorman's house at 11 p.m. miserably wondering why we lost by three votes. At about 9 p.m. I warned the opposition deputy Chief Whip that Smith's belligerent speech would make it easier for waverers to support the government. It was also

portrayed as an anti-Major plot (encouraged by an article in the weekend's *Sunday Telegraph*[*] claiming that I was out to get Major).

Saturday 8 November

Downing Street denies that the PM offered Michael Carttiss a deal in the voting lobby not to ratify Maastricht until Danes made their final decision.[†]

Thursday 19 November

A bizarre event after the 10 p.m. vote, in the smoking room. Heath castigates Leigh and Hamilton for being 'traitors' to the government. They should get out because they have been 'running down the government at every point'. Nick Scott joins in: 'You didn't have the guts to resign.' Hamilton says, 'Far from running down the government, we suggested a way of winning over the waverers by delaying the third reading until after the Danish referendum.'

Monday 7 December

Meet with Cranborne, Howard, Portillo at Conrad Black's home. Howard and Cranborne take view that now we are out of ERM (for which I say there is no credit due to the government) all will be well. Maastricht is price for party 'unity' and being at the centre of Europe. Portillo more sceptical. He says if we go further than Maastricht the party will fall apart. MP impressive.

My present view is that John Major will have to stay at least until the next election. Then MP can take over. He will be in his mid-forties; but all this may change.

Tuesday 15 December

Coffee with Cran and Gill in Rodin's restaurant after the 10 p.m. vote. Agree that we will not have regular discussions with Labour re the Maastricht Bill.

Earlier in the evening Teresa Gorman invited all our group (some twenty MPs) for a drink. I was asked to address them. Said the battle in Parliament for the moment is all about keeping the ball in play for the Danes. Report on my visit to Denmark and the hope that all is not lost there.

---

[*] I pleaded with the editor, Charles Moore, not to print this, but to no avail despite his apparent support for our cause. From the perspective of time, I do now appreciate that his first loyalty and interest was bound to be for his newspaper.

[†] In his autobiography, Major accepts that a deal was struck with Carttiss. 'The next morning Michael Carttiss revealed our pre-vote exchange in which I told him that we wouldn't complete the Bill until the position of the Danes was certain … my action reflected reality.'

Thursday 17 December
Pia Kjærsgaard, whom I visited in Copenhagen the previous weekend, rings to ask for an article for her party's magazine.

Thursday 21 January 1993
Eve of my fiftieth birthday. Meet Ted Heath in the smoking room. He and I get on quite well despite our differences over Maastricht. He asks me whether I feel guilty 'as a Thatcherite' for the failings of the economy. 'On the contrary,' I say, 'it was only when Thatcher went off course in the mid-'80s and began to engage in managed exchange rates that things began to go wrong.' He says it is time for Keynesianism again, by which he means more public spending. I say, 'Keynes today would be very difficult to predict. He was also against managed exchange rates, e.g. the Gold Standard.'

At dinner in the House joined by the Chief Whip, Richard Ryder. We discuss the two strands in the Tory Party, the Patrons/Wets v. the liberal marketeers. Disraeli v. Peel. I said very dangerous if the one who gets into temporary ascendancy kicks the other in the teeth. Ryder certainly accepts the historical analysis. His quick intellect may be right for the moment. After dinner, where I buy the port, talk for 2½ hours with Garel-Jones about the Maastricht Bill. I tell him if he hypes this up to expect the worst. He tells me of his reason for announcing his departure from government: cannot lead his Spanish second life. Strangest possible occurrence that I should see in my fiftieth birthday with Garel-Jones.

Friday 22 January
Sadly my heavy work and, I'm afraid, boozing the night before have taken their toll. I feel pretty tired and terrible – and anxious about my party in the Tower of London. But all goes pretty well. Thatchers come as well as Tebbits and Lamonts. But Colin Marshall, chief executive of British Airways and under a cloud because of the Virgin business, does not show up. I tell Lamont that Heath plans to call for more public expenditure during the Budget debate. Thatcher tells my chairman (David Finch) I need every support on Maastricht. Finch says the support is 50/50.

Monday 22 February
Government backs off from a procedural vote on the Maastricht Bill for the tenth time – believing they cannot win. (The pressure of the Irish puts the fear of God into them.) I still feel I will abstain on Amendment 27 on the following argument:

The Social Protocol (removed by Amendment 27) would give justification under the British opt-out for Britain to argue against having to comply with social provisions promoted elsewhere in the Bill if the matter comes to the European Court; so the court will be the ultimate arbiter.

Cannot vote with the government because they have said will ride rough-shod over what Parliament determines, whatever the result of the vote. Whatever the *legal* position I am not willing to be party to a position which is perceived to overrule Parliament.

Tuesday 23 February

Headlines in the papers about 1922 Committee 'punch-up'. Jopling, Churchill attacking Eurosceptics for disloyalty (WC having threatened to defeat government on pit closures and Jopling having attacked them on leasehold reform).

I ring James Cran at about 8 a.m. to suggest that I should see the Chief Whip and point out to him that he is almost inevitably heading for a defeat on Amendment 27. He may claim that because this does not prevent ratification he does not care about this but:

Other amendments related to 27 are going down, which may kill off the treaty.

If he is thought to ride roughshod over Parliament, victory may be a pyrrhic one.

Bitterness on both sides of the party may be lasting.

Monday 8 March

Government defeated by twenty-two votes on an amendment giving local government representation on the Committee of Regions provided for by the Maastricht Bill.

Tuesday 9 March

I met chairman of the 1922 Committee, Marcus Fox (following a very well-attended meeting of my anti-Maastricht committee), to see whether we can cool down tempers on both sides.

Wednesday 10 March

11 p.m. Long chat (and very amicable) with Chief Whip to probe as to whether there is any accommodation possible between us, especially on the forthcoming Amendment 27, which could wreck the treaty. I float the idea of our giving him the amendment in return for an absolute commitment not to have ERM or single currency in this parliament. He is interested and says he would like to meet again on neutral territory with John Biffen and myself.

Only PM and Foreign Secretary would know. I say Cran would have to know on our side. (Meeting fixed subsequently for following Monday.)

He also shows me a draft of what he wants Marcus Fox to say at 1922 Committee the next day – to dampen down tempers, much of which on the other side is frankly synthetic.

Prior to this meeting drinks with *The Guardian* at Reform Club. Guest of Fourth Estate. Talk to Victoria about doing a book on Nicholas Ridley. Also meet Neil Kinnock. He says I am far too nice to be an effective leader of the rebels – we'll see! Geoffrey Parkhouse of the *Glasgow Echo* says he has been talking to John Biffen who has floated the idea of a deal around ERM/single currency. I must try to stop John gossiping if this is all to become serious.

Still earlier that day talked to David Finch about his quotes in the *Telegraph* where he appeared menacing about future deselection. He is basically friendly and he tries to present a balanced case; the trouble is that the press only pick up the bits that are hostile to me.

Monday 15 March

Meet John Biffen at the Park Lane Hotel at 5.30. He seems to want to pack in our opposition to the Treaty of Maastricht. I say we can only trade off Amendment 27 against something pretty big, e.g. commitment not to do ERM and single currency in this parliament.

6.30: Put this to Richard Ryder, who arrives for this purpose. We agree to keep it all secret. Richard says he will come back in a few days' time. The only people he will discuss it with are the Foreign Secretary and the Prime Minister (NB not the Chancellor of the Exchequer). He tries to suggest we should give up on all further delaying tactics. I say I would not be able to sell this. Our people already feel we have given enough, assuming Amendment 27 is the only thing that could possibly wreck the Bill. We need a few victories to encourage the Danes.

(I do not mention that if we capitulated – which we have no intention of doing, having won a substantial vote the previous Monday and with the lads and lasses in a pretty gung-ho mood – there would be no possibility of keeping the deal a secret. It would be all too obvious.)

In debriefing with John Biffen afterwards I suggest that we win each way. If we do not deliver the vote the treaty will be disorientated; if we do deliver we will block the single currency.

Thursday 18 March

Talk on phone to John Biffen. Neither of us has heard from Ryder. But Bernard Jenkin and Iain Duncan Smith want to deal on ERM and single currency.

Biffen apparently advised them to talk to Michael Howard. I say it would be slightly unfortunate if government form the view we are cracking up. We may need to steel things next week. Ring James Cran to pass all this on. He agrees.

Friday 19 March
RR on the phone to Cropthorne. He has talked to PM and Foreign Secretary. Wants to talk to Chancellor of Exchequer (Lamont): is that OK? I say, 'Yes, of course.' He agrees to come back with detailed proposals over the weekend. I then ring James Cran to keep him in the picture.

Saturday 20 March
Interviews in Evesham, Pershore, Upton and Malvern. People who come to see me very supportive on Maastricht. Also a number of branch chairmen now ringing or writing in to give support. Against them apparently the divisional treasurer, Richard Williams, threatened to resign over my last vote. The nearer the top you get, the more tricky it is. The same I suppose is true nationally. Cabinet pro Maastricht: parliamentary party if left to itself full of reservations. Party in the country even more so once you get past divisional officers.

Wednesday 24 March
11.20 p.m. Another talk with RR in his room. He says he is getting heavy complaints about our people conversing in public with Labour whips. I tell him 'Point taken', and then raise question of the mass purge of POST* people including myself. I say, genuinely, I am not concerned about myself – on the whole I prefer to be paid for jobs like that! – but Gerry Vaughan most miffed as he was one of the founding fathers. If he is kicked off, it would not help matters later to settle down. RR claims not to know anything about this and will look into it.

We discuss the so-called deal. Lamont is considering a statement on the opt-out. I say there must be no formal coupling of this to anything we do. It will be tight; the name of the game at our end will be abstention, but the Irish are in effect taking our whip and their abstention may be decisive. We agree to meet again.

Thursday 25 March
Heath and I find ourselves pretty well alone in the members' dining room, he with Peter Luff, I with Neil Hamilton. I go over to Heath, who is looking very blotchy. He asks me rather ungraciously what I intend to do after the

---

* Parliamentary Office for Science & Technology.

election – by which I infer afterwards he is assuming I will be deselected. Not quite appreciating this at the time, I say something bland – like 'As you yourself well know, the tide swirls around those who stand fast'. He glares back and leaves the table.

Friday 2–Sunday 4 April 1993

Weekend in Copenhagen with Pia Kjærsgaard of the Progress Party. Give a good press conference on Friday which is well reported and covered on TV. Main point is to assure the Danes that if they say 'No' in their referendum on 18 May, they will not be alone. Britain certainly will not ratify and Article 236 of Treaty of Rome says that there must be unanimous agreement for the treaty to go ahead. Danes really do have a sense of independence and a great pride in their democracy. I put out a statement in London that Danish 'No' a virtual 'certainty'. The bandwagon is rolling. They are being reassured that they are not on their own. Becoming respectable again to vote 'No'. I agree to try to supply some more money in addition to the £2,000 already sent. Also will try to get editors of *Times* and *Sunday Telegraph* to come and speak and Alan Walters to make point that (a) Danes not on their own, (b) free enterprise can exist without political union.

Back at home in England Labour rat on Amendment 27 and substitute it with an anodyne motion on Social Chapter which has little effect on the Bill. Michael Morris, the deputy Speaker, has been the instrument of this, claiming presumably that it's his job to get the Bill through given the second reading vote. Labour huff and puff but find this a convenient smokescreen.

Thursday 8–Tuesday 13 April

Easter weekend. Manage to organise for editors of *Times* and *Sunday Telegraph* to go over to Denmark to speak in the Parliament. Main points they need to make: (a) Denmark not going to be on her own, (b) jobs not at stake without political union, (c) 'No' vote does not mean leaving the Common Market.

I write to David Finch to tell him constituency association support for me 'over Maastricht is running at 3:1 in my favour'.

Tuesday 27 April

Ring Margaret Thatcher at 8.45. Things have not been going well on Maastricht. Major made rude references over the weekend indicating he wants war not peace. Hurd said in Denmark words which were aimed at implying that if they said 'No', Denmark would be on her own. I tell Danish press (on the phone) that, under Article 236 of Treaty of Rome, substantial change as proposed at Maastricht requires unanimity.

Tell Thatcher we should quiz Major on this in the House. (In the event Bill Cash gets in a good question.) Ask Thatcher whether she intends to join in. She says 'No', except that she will talk to Danish TV if necessary next week ('Too busy writing my book').

Tuesday 4 May

Start day in Cropthorne rather gloomily. The problem is the forthcoming amendment to the Maastricht Bill which would have the effect of removing Major's opt-out from the Social Agreement. To vote for it might wreck the Bill. A combination of ourselves, the Liberals and Labour would certainly win – but in such a way on such an issue as to infuriate the party.

Chair the regular meeting of the Fresh Start Group at 3 p.m. Agree to press on. Hold further meetings during the day after the Speaker* has in effect said she will allow a vote on the crucial amendment (which was in draft and which had been cleared by the deputy Speaker, Michael Morris).

When victory seems certain go to see Richard Ryder. Put to him the point that a concession by the government (rather than a defeat) would be better all round for party unity. I tell him that since the PM's rude remarks about us the week before, our lot are almost out of control – I even hint that we might vote against the Budget. He is very polite – as he always is to me; luckily we do get on well – he seems to agree with my point on party unity. He wants my help with the European Boundaries Reform Bill and a vote on the Social Chapter under Amendment 74 (which the government conceded).

I say unity could break out as long as the policy was right. I would certainly want to stand down the army, although we would wish to leave behind a rear party with a command-and-signals system in place. The PM would also have to join in on the moves for unity.

Altogether a most satisfactory chat. (He even recognises that although we are between thirty and fifty, we have another 100 sympathisers.)

Wednesday 5 May

Day of enormous tension. James Cran much on radio – talking of 'see each other in court'. Meet Fresh Start Group and decide must not vote in a way which will be interpreted as voting against the social opt-out. I report that at lobby briefing government did not say whether or not they

---

* The Rt Hon. Betty Boothroyd MP, created 2001 Baroness Boothroyd.

intend to press this to a vote. Very reluctantly I decide I will, if necessary, have to vote against the government, although it will cause a riot in my constituency on the day that the boundary changes are to be announced. (These came in the afternoon and are dramatic though not cataclysmic or disastrous.)

Two whips approach me: will we vote against HMG? Yes. If government concedes without a vote will we co-operate for the rest of the evening? Yes.

Much tension and nail-biting as Douglas Hurd gets up to speak. A vote will be a serious embarrassment to some of us, e.g. me. I have very limited support amongst the officers of the association.

In the event it is all OK. We win without a vote. The Treaty Bill moves to the House of Lords with question marks attached to it – as I say on TV. Out to dinner with Richard Shepherd and Nick Bonsor. They propose I join a lunch club of which they are members. It is called NAAFI (No Ambition and F***ing Interests). I humbly accept.

Friday 7 May

Wake up to news of debacle at Newbury by-election and rout at county council elections.

Everybody saying the answer is to sack Lamont – rubbish. The answer is to establish policy in the right direction, e.g. away from ERM and a single European currency. Talk to James Cran on phone. He feels I was too conciliatory to the government after the vote on Amendment 27; but my view is that it is important to change pace to surprise and to be able to deliver. What we must now do is to treat with the PM to ensure we do not go into the single currency or ERM within this parliament. Can we deliver anything in return? To abstain on the Boundary Bill will not be enough. Whips will want us to vote with it. We can vote with government on Social Chapter.

Saturday 8 May

Two interesting phone calls:

From James Cran. Apparently the press are trying to run a story suggesting that I am going to be a stalking horse to unseat Major – rubbish; but it may do no harm to be thought such – constituency association will have to take this on the chin.

Michael Shrimpton – a Labour barrister retained by Bill Cash to challenge Maastricht Treaty following Amendment 2 – rings to say the plaintiffs need to be more heavyweight. Bill Cash alone will not do. I say I have been told any plaintiff will do and the courts will then take over. I am also reluctant to interfere with Bill Cash. He says, 'Not so'; it needs heavy-weights otherwise the judiciary could throw it out, however good the arguments. I suggest he bring it to a head with Cash and then come back to me.

Tuesday 11 May

5.00 p.m. Fresh Start meeting. Gung-ho air about the place. Several want to vote en bloc against the government on a fisheries order; others, e.g. Tapsell, counsel caution and advise to keep our eye on the ball. I am of this camp. We agree to meet behind the Speaker's chair at about 11 p.m. after the frontbench speakers have sat down.

6.15: Meet Richard Ryder. Tell him unless we can set up a framework for peace involving a discussion of policy etc., things might get out of hand at our end. He is clearly shaken when I tell him he might lose his majority on the fisheries order – I say that if cooler heads had not prevailed, he might have lost last night on VAT on fuel in the Finance Bill. I suggest I should have a chat with PM and see where we go. He agrees to approach PM.

11 p.m. Some twelve of us meet in the ministerial conference room behind the Speaker's chair. We must be the only non-ministerial group to do so. Decide on a policy, this time to vote with the government, which most of us do.

Wednesday 12 May

Bump into William Rees-Mogg on the way to dinner with Teresa Gorman at Rodin's. Teresa has much more to her than meets the eye. She has both a sense of philosophy and practicality. WR-M reckons that if Major loses another by-election like Newbury he's a goner.

Peter Tapsell says I must place a story about how clean our campaigning has been. I think it's premature. The party won't enjoy hearing us boast; additionally, if we are to put the fear of God into federalists, we had better be seen for what we are – efficient and fearsome.

Thursday 13 May

To Denmark (for the third time) with Ivan Lawrence and Patrick Minford. Press conference organised by Pia Kjærsgaard's Progress Party. Sadly all the opinion polls against the 'No' vote. It looks as though the game's up in Denmark. Dinner with Pia in Tivoli. BBC man comes up – am I coming back to Denmark next Tuesday for the vote? At that moment I plan to do so but decide later in the evening to change my mind.

Tuesday 18 May
Danish referendum results in a majority in favour of ratification of the Maastricht Treaty.

Wednesday 19 May
Have highly bullish meeting of Fresh Start Group. Twenty-three present. Agree to keep together when Bill through Commons.

Adrian Lithgow, political editor of the *Daily Mail*, bumps into me on the Terrace. Offers to buy me a G&T and I know something is up. He furtively asks me to sit with him at the far (Big Ben) end of the Terrace. Then he proceeds to tell me he hears that Lamont blocked a deal on ERM with Eurosceptics. I try to bluff him out but he reveals he knows the date of the meeting (15 March) with Ryder and Biffen. I say we and the whips are always 'sniffing around each other' and Lamont did not block us off. I don't think it washed. Later warn Lamont in the Aye lobby. He says he knew nothing about a deal. Drop a line to Ryder to warn him.

(Earlier Biffen confessed it was he who had spilt the beans. It doesn't do us much harm since the deal on the social agreement never came off. Shows we were being taken seriously by HMG.)

Thursday 20 May
Meet Ryder. He seems grateful to have been warned. I say I have poured a bucket of water over it all – or tried to – but no doubt *Mail* will do what they want. Apparently Ryder still agrees with idea of meeting PM.

Speak for five minutes in third reading debate – not very inspiringly. Problem is that the subject is beginning to pall a bit.

Friday 21 May
Bump into Bill Cash and lunch with him on the Terrace. Discuss the previous night's vote, when Eurosceptics polled our maximum – forty-one with six abstentions.

Speak to Pia. She sounds rather tired and depressed. Plans to come over to UK. Her one ambition in life is to meet MT. I wonder if I am capable of organising this these days.

Monday 24 May
Chair a dinner of Fresh Start Group and fourteen Lords under Malcolm Pearson at St Ermin's Hotel. Each of our chaps (twenty of them) gets up and makes a protestation of faith, rather like what I imagine happens at a religious revivalist gathering.

Norman Lamont

Wednesday 26 May 1993

Portillo fortieth birthday party. Thatcher makes the speech. Everyone there from the centre right (except, strangely, Norman and Margaret Tebbit, with whom we had dinner at Rules later). Talk to Denis and Margaret Thatcher, Charles Moore, Simon Heffer; David Willetts suggests that I should change the subject from Maastricht.

Cecil Parkinson comes up while I am talking to Lamont and denies that he has been calling for Lamont's resignation. Lamont himself seems determined to stay.

Lamont and I discuss the Eurosceptic position. I say there are three flashpoints ahead (he agrees):

1. Labour's amendment on the social agreement;
2. The European political boundary changes;
3. The Budget.

I say that in order to avoid tears on these matters, I would need to talk to the PM. Lamont says he will try to fix this as 'I am very close to the PM'. He goes on to say he is violently anti the European Parliament. Finally he says that 'people in the press' have left him with the impression that I am undermining him. I say this is not correct either of my public or of my private pronouncements.

Thursday 27 May

Lamont sacked without writing the normal letter.

In view of what he said last night, he must be shattered. Parkinson on the radio saying it is a good thing he has gone! All very ironic in view of what was said at Portillo's party.

Sunday 30 May

Lunch with Gerald and Lizzie Howarth – also there the Hamiltons: still cursing at Major, still in the government. Norman Lamont rings up when I get home, mainly to thank me for having offered to put him and Rosemary up when he was sacked. Says that the true story of what happened over the so-called deal with Ryder is that Ryder asked him what he thought; Lamont said to PM that his advice was to leave a deal till later. PM and Hurd accepted this. The whole matter was dropped. Lamont seems pretty cheerful on the telephone. He is staying for one week at Dorneywood, allowing Hilaire to study for his A-levels. Lamont asks me where to apply for offices. I say, 'The whips.' 'Oh God, I don't want to have anything to do with them for months. It will be rather fun finding out what the 1922 Committee is all about again after fourteen years. What sort of a speech should I make to the House?' 'Depends whether you want someone to employ you afterwards,' I reply. 'The going is pretty rough for rebels. People pay to have the ear of the government.'

[In his autobiography,* Lamont wrote of this period, 'Michael Spicer had said to me, "You will find you get the 'bitterness' label. We have all had that!" … I soon saw what he meant. From now on, whatever my arguments … no report could appear in the newspapers without the words, "embittered former Chancellor".']

Sunday 6 June 1993
In Wyoming for conference on free trade. Usual arguments between Europeans and US v. Japan on the latter's trade surpluses. Conference dominated by an amazing Russian or Ukrainian woman who wears tight miniskirts and high boots, has long peroxide hair like a lion, claims to be a rocket scientist. Also there, Senator Watson (Wyoming) and Dick Gephardt, deputy leader in the House and former Democratic presidential candidate. Also Secretary for Trade.

Phillip Oppenheim, PPS to newly appointed Chancellor of Exchequer, Ken Clarke, is on the trip. He gives the impression that Clarke sees his job as a potential poisoned chalice. All options in the Budget have their grave risks for him personally – cut expenditure, raise taxes or do nothing. This is why he thought Lamont would stay – to take the flak up to the point where things were getting better.

Meeting with PM

Wednesday 9 June 1993
Go to Queen's Club to watch the tennis with Ann. Back to the House to find the place in a turmoil. Major has made a bad speech and Lamont proclaimed by the press to have stabbed him in the back. Very dangerous for us. (1922 Committee turn on us.)

Meeting of Fresh Start Group at 6 p.m. Main issue: do we invite in Edward Leigh, who has just been sacked by Major? Consensus that we should wait a bit. (People feel he voted for Maastricht and should now earn his spurs.) Second issue: who will be in a painting of the rebels and who

---

* Norman Lamont, *In Office*, Little, Brown, 1999.

will paint it? Finally we get back to how we shall vote on Social Contract and on European Parliament's reform of boundaries. Everyone seems to find this rather boring!!

After 10 p.m. vote Graham Bright comes up to me. PM would like to see me in response to my letter to Ryder. Go straight to PM's room. I say that things are in danger of getting out of hand. PM has my blessing if he balances left and right in the government. At the moment the composition and balance of the Cabinet is all to the left as are the policies and rhetoric.

PM says 'party in danger of falling apart and Europe has brought it about'. He has inherited the European problem and has done his best to find a middle way. Indeed his political leaning is straight down the middle, 'liberal' on economic policy and left on social policy, especially keen to bring inflation down. 'Problem is', I say, 'that the two positions may be in conflict over the Budget.' Need to be more positive and assured on privatisation measures, e.g. railways, and why abandon privatisation of Post Office? 'I didn't want to,' he says, 'but it's very difficult when we have such a small majority.' 'Having just run a rebellion,' I say, 'it looks rather different on the other side of the parapet; Labour is so undisciplined.' Then I suggest, 'Why not come and have dinner with us?' 'That might be good for the party but could be bad for me,' he says. 'I will think about it; my door is always open.' I say, 'Not quite the point.' 'I will think about it; let's talk again.' Very man-to-man conversation and friendly. I am rather impressed how calm he is. 'I am very unpopular but so are all other leaders of the seven top industrial countries.'

Whole meeting lasts about half and hour from 10.30 to 11 p.m. and is very amicable. Problem is that as I come out Richard Needham and Tristan Garel-Jones are going in. What will they make of it? Will they bend ear of PM against me? Will he listen to them? Danger now is that we all become too cocky.

Thursday 10 June

Atmosphere in House still foetid. Norman Fowler, party chairman, has called Norman Lamont's resignation speech dead silly and nasty and raised again the fact that funds were used to bail NL out.

Bump into NL as he comes from the 1922 Committee. He says, 'I rang Downing Street and told them to lay off, otherwise I will stick some dynamite up their arse.' I recognise the syndrome – he is being forced into opposition but that opposition will inevitably become less and less effective.

NL's old Cabinet colleagues are mad to stir him up on TV. Michael Howard, his old friend, is especially prominent. Clearly he feels the need for exposure vis-à-vis Clarke, who made a very successful wind-up speech on

Tuesday. As I come into the House at about 8 p.m., Howard is lining up to speak to TV on the Green – of all places – I wave to him and he waves back. The other chap before him on the Green was John Smith.

Pete, the doorman at Dean's Yard, says, 'Your sceptics have been the only decent opposition in this parliament.'

Friday 11 June
I am represented in the *Telegraph* as one of Mr Major's enemies. The letter I draft in anticipation of the inevitable barrage I will receive on this is:

> Not everything that appears in the newspapers is accurate, especially in the tone of the headlines and captions. My position on the signing of the Treaty of Maastricht is well known. I am against it. My views are fully documented in my book *A Treaty Too Far.*
>
> My personal relations with PM are good.

Sunday 13 June
Ring Michael Howard. He says all is midsummer madness; must back Major. Agree to meet privately. My views are that (1) Portillo is the key, (2) Howard must take a firmer position on main issues – but at the same time not be front-runner. Must be supportive but with a point of view. Strength of Clarke is that he seems to be a man of character.

In the evening ring Norman Lamont; he appears to be pretty furious still. Seems to be egging me on to vote on Social Chapter, which he says would bring the government down. He says Major trying to look right wing now – tough on public expenditure – exactly what he did during the leadership challenge.

I say I don't think the time is right to change leaders. There is no response at the other end of the line. We both, however, note that Major has said, 'Perhaps we went too far with *laissez-faire* in the '80s'. Agree to meet for lunch the week after next. Ring Judy Ridley in Cumberland to tell her that Norman will be an usher at Nick's memorial, to which at late notice the PM is now coming.* We want someone who is *really* on our side next time.

Michael Howard

Monday 14 June 1993
9.45: Visit Michael Howard at his government safe house. Tell him that

---

* Nicholas Ridley, created Baron Ridley of Liddesdale in 1992, died 4 March 1993.

Ridley had been in favour of him taking over the leadership of the party. Also warn him that a Social Contract crisis lies ahead. He must keep out even though he feels social opt-out is his own contribution. Important thing for him is not to upset his potential base.

Main points I make to him are:

1. Must get Portillo on side: he is the pivot between himself and Clarke.
2. Although Clarke ahead in polls, he has a tough job.

Emphasise importance of warlords – George Gardiner (92 Group), me (Eurosceptics), Portillo (No Turning Back).

Tuesday 15 June

Meet Richard Ryder 5 p.m. He has to go in ten minutes to a meeting with Speaker but we talk till 6.30. Agree that it would be desirable for PM to have dinner with us with three ingredients to his speech:

1. Effective apology for rude words about us.
2. No ERM or single currency in our 'lifetime'.
3. We deliver vote on Social Chapter opt-out and vote on European Parliamentary Bill.

Have dinner with Edward Leigh. Agree he will speak to the guys about experiences in government.

Bump into Ken Baker. Rumours flying around that he may stand as a candidate against Major. Seems very unlikely to me but he has nothing to lose by doing so.

Wednesday 16 June

Ryder rings to say that he is trying to put off Boundary Commission Bill till week after next for us to be able to work out formula with PM. I say if PM does the deal I can deliver the vote.

Michael Howard in a state in the division lobby. His Bill on boundary changes for European Parliament will be subject to a parliamentary committee rather than to the Boundary Commission. He is worried about having heard that we may vote against. This would mean that he would have to do a deal with Labour to give them a seat for Scotland. I tell him that hopefully we will be able to do a deal with PM. Teddy Taylor in meantime stirring up Labour against the Bill.

Thursday 17 June

Louise, my secretary, tells me that she went to a cocktail party at Number 10 for House of Commons secretaries last night. The PM said, 'If I am here next year we must do it again.' She was amazed how negative he was. Also he asked her who she worked for. When she said me, he responded, 'I had a very good meeting with Michael last week.'

Lunch at Savoy with Andrew Alexander (deputy editor, *Daily Mail*, and a strong Eurosceptic). Jak* comes up (I think he was lunching with Heseltine) and is very jolly; haven't seen him for years.

Tuesday 22 June

Talk to Ryder before Fresh Start meeting. PM not willing to decide to come to meet us till after summit in Copenhagen. RR's tone different from erstwhile. PM probably being got at by those who feel our noses should be rubbed in the mud.

See RR later in the evening; he confirms there are views (a) that we should be crushed (b) that we will disintegrate. He claims to believe neither. I say if the gesture is not forthcoming soon, I will begin to lose control and the wild boys will take over. Choice is between peace and war. It's not looking too good.

Teddy Taylor goes around accusing us of being wimps. He it was who sold out at the time of the signing of the Treaty of Maastricht.

At meeting of Fresh Start at 5 p.m., I am asked to meet George Robertson, Labour spokesman, to see what they are doing on Euro boundary Bill. As expected, when I see him Labour is voting for Suffolk seat but will allow the Bill to go through on abstention.

Wednesday 23 June

Nicholas Ridley's memorial service. I am an usher. St Margaret's pretty full. PM there. Thatcher delivers the address: NR a man of vision.

Baker (still in the game, as are Clarke and Howard), Alexander Hesketh and Malcolm Caithness all present. Hesketh on our side (though Chief Whip) and Caithness also with us, though he is main spokesman against us. Before service Tebbit rings to say cannot make it as preparing a speech against EMU and timing difficult – strange. Lamont a fellow usher; looks very miserable.

Afterwards off to Windsor for polo. NR would have approved. Talk to Martyn Lewis, BBC newscaster. Late at night talk to Ken Baker; he claims to be shocked that HMG may accept Social Chapter and if we vote them down will split the party (I doubt it). Talk to Richard Body re vote on Euro

---

* Raymond Jackson, cartoonist, *Evening Standard*, 1952–97.

boundaries. We decide that it is only about extra vote for Scotland. Cannot vote against HMG. But George Robertson comes up to see me in the members' lobby. 'What if we vote against the Bill?'

I say, 'I don't believe you will but if you persuade us you will it could be different.'

He goes off to think about this.

Thursday 24 June
Lunch with Norman Lamont at Gran Paradiso. On the surface he seems very calm; has lost none of his humour. He is very angry with Major. Says we have the power to wreck the treaty by voting with Labour for the Social Chapter, which he claims Major could not accept. I say I think PM will accept it or go ahead without parliamentary approval. Lamont responds (as did Baker), that in that case there will be a major crisis. At PM's Questions, PM announces that Michael Mates has resigned. Who will take his place at Northern Ireland? What about Bill Cash? He is Catholic, a friend of the Unionists, I think with Irish blood. It would reduce our numbers by one and could be presented as a peace gesture. I think he would accept it.

Wednesday 30 June
Drinks party at Michael Howard's house. This followed his opening of second reading of European Boundaries Bill on which Fresh Start group had put down an amendment to second reading motion. Michael Howard's speech good humoured, as were interventions by Bill Cash, Teddy Taylor and others. But, as I say to MH at his party, he will have to concede at committee stage on the floor; the main objection is the removal of the Boundary Commission and public inquiries. He says he may ask his officials to look into whether Blair's view that inquiries could be done in time is correct.

Prior to the party, talked to Ryder at edge of the chamber; told him I had not put his message (that PM was not prepared to have dinner with us but was available to see us) as we had been rather taken up with discussing what to do in the Boundaries Bill, and there was nothing to discuss unless the PM had something to offer.

Tuesday 6 July
See Ryder again at 9.30 p.m. He is heading for a defeat, I say (he seems to agree), on the Social Chapter unless the PM makes some sort of gesture. His view is that this was what should happen; but PM advised by Hurd that no deals should be made. (Previously we had a Fresh Start meeting where we had effectively agreed to dig in our heels.)

Monday 12 July
Chat to George Gardiner late at night on the Terrace; beautiful clear crystal summer evening. He is worried about being re-elected to 1922 Executive committee in the autumn. Apparently his own 92 Group can't be relied to vote for him en bloc! What about our group? Conversation moves to leadership. He is not averse to MH. We both agree KC will not do. We also agree PM running out of assets.

Pace quickens. Message for me to visit Ryder. Fresh Start getting more hyped up, especially Tony Marlow and Peter Tapsell, both of whom are at the Downing Street reception for MPs. After dinner talk to Ken Baker on the Terrace. He will not make a move himself but encourages us to go over the top so he can pick up some pieces in the ensuing debacle. The other bird of prey is Lamont, who also says he wants to see me. I agree to meet him at 3.30 the next day.

11 p.m. Meet Ryder. He says HMG will commit to not going back into ERM if we do not vote with Labour on Social Chapter coming up next Thursday. We agree that I will put this proposition to Fresh Start in meeting the next day. Things are moving to some sort of a climax. I say it may be difficult to carry along the lads and lasses but I will try.

Wednesday 14 July
Day of ups and downs. RR and I exchange correspondence by fax re a possible 'deal' on the Social Chapter. Meet him in the afternoon. He has been frightened off by the papers; his reply to mine is a brush-off. Nothing to put to the twenty-four Fresh Starters, who are in a jittery mood – divided between those who want open war (Taylor, Wintertons, Cash) and those who want to consolidate (Jessel, Biffen, Michael Lord). Ryder suggests meeting with Clarke.

See Lamont at 3.30 after I come back from speaking to Minet, insurance brokers, where Edward works. Lamont, with nothing to lose, tries to egg us on to rebellion (like Ken Baker, with whom he clearly is in close contact). In the evening, dinner with Conrad Black, Michael Portillo, Michael Howard, Robert Cranborne. Michael P. advocates abolition of Common Agricultural Policy. I say, 'Wonderful, but after Maastricht the law won't allow it.'

Thursday 15 July
RR asks me to see him at 3.30. We agree that I should try to sell a deal on the Labour amendment on the basis that HMG commits itself not to re-enter ERM. Later it emerges HMG proposes a very anodyne motion.

Going to be hard to stop people voting against this, especially as to do so would delay the treaty.

Later chat with Bernard Jenkin and Norman Lamont in smoking room. The key issue emerging is the vote on the main motion, not the Labour amendment. NL has lost none of his fun; it's even better for being venomous.

The final vote

Monday 19 July 1993
Meeting with our twenty-three members of Fresh Start. Put to them the RR deal: government commits to no ERM in this parliament, we do not vote with Labour on Social Chapter. Majority against this. They want to press on.

Tell this to RR at about 12 noon. The ground is now prepared for open war. Government trying to get the Irish. RR seems to feel we are into a period of stalemate which could destroy PM. I tell him that I will probably abstain on the first vote (Social Chapter); neither can I vote against colleagues who feel this is the only way of stopping the treaty.

RR looks stunned and says it 'could be end of the government'. We sit in silence for a while, sipping whisky. I ask him whether he has anything more up his sleeve; he says 'No'. I agree I have nothing up mine except, off the top of my head, to suggest he puts off the vote on the Social Chapter until the law case is through – some of the point for voting with Labour being to improve the case in court. He says, probably rightly, it would only prolong the agony. Told RR one major problem is that the offer has been left so late. There is no trust as to real intentions of HMG. That is why I offered a dinner.

Tuesday 20 July
Commons febrile. Gossip blows one way and another. Some of the people who had been very gung-ho on Monday (e.g. John Carlisle) backing down. Dinner with James Cran at Rodin's; he is also thinking of voting with government. Get back home late at night. Ann has been to party given by Anne Jenkin. HMG thinking of making the Thursday vote a vote of confidence in Major.

Wednesday 21 July
Last full meeting of Fresh Start before the Social Chapter vote. Strong feelings expressed for and against voting with Labour. I am against it and would prefer to concentrate on main motion, which is related to the activation of the Bill. I will therefore abstain on Labour's motion and vote against the main motion. This position has the merit that it enables me to hold the two sides of the meeting together at least to the point that they remain in the same

room. Biffen says will vote with HMG come what may. He says it's all over. I surmise that he is tired and getting old. He keeps very much to himself these days; however, he does provide a cloak of respectability for the new members.

Jenkin (a prisoner of his rhetoric during first days in Parliament and last days of Thatcher while he was a candidate) is uncertain about what to do; he has abstained for many of the votes in the past. Barry Legg and Iain Duncan Smith will stick with it. Cran announces he will not be with us and Winterton, back from Number 10, asks, 'What's the point?' John Carlisle is on TV in effect saying that those of us who stay with it are mad. I don't mind those who change their mind – we all do that – but I'm not keen on those who moralise about it. Tapsell now the strongest. Cash more interested in appearing on TV than in our meeting. Anyway it still looks as though government will lose.

Thursday 22 July
Times sticks with us to the end – wonderful leader; will be able to use this when writing to constituents.

> 'Reason and Conscience'
> The Tory rebels should not be swayed by threats.
>   … Those who are not persuaded by their own powers of reason should not be cowed by threats. Still less should they be swayed by other charges, such as that they are being boring and wearisome. According to the *Daily Telegraph* on Tuesday, Mr Major should ignore a losing vote … This government will be harried and wearied to its end if it tries to make that wishful thinking into reality. The British people will not bear it …
>   There are few certainties ahead tonight – and fewer still thereafter. As the conflicts with authority continue, the best compass for a rebel Conservative MP will remain one constructed from his own reason and conscience.

Tennis for Commons at Wimbledon. Malcolm Moss my partner at tennis. He has just been made PPS to Patrick Mayhew (SoS, Northern Ireland). He left early to involve himself with the deal with Irish – eventually successful in winning over nine Ulster Unionists. Malcolm and I arguing with each other between gritted teeth, while we try to get the odd point off the AELTC veterans, e.g. Basil Hutchings, who is becoming a bit of friend (and hope-fully my entrée to Wimbledon membership).* Back to London with John Hannam, the captain.

---

* Sadly he dies before he can bring this into effect.

Hannam drops me off at the roundabout by Lambeth Bridge. Walking up Horseferry Road, spotted in his car by Andrew Robathan, a new Member – honest former army officer and a patriot. Take him back to Maunsel Street for a cup of tea. He voted with us in third reading of Maastricht Bill – brave of him. Clearly wants to do so tonight in the Social Chapter vote. Meet Michael Prescott of *Sunday Times* at Rodin. Can't imagine what sort of piece he will do on Sunday. Give him all the gen about Fresh Start. But he trivialises us. Masses of bids from the media, which no doubt Bill Cash is piling up. I turn them down.

8.30: Meeting of the group. Agree to go for the jugular. I say the figures look good. Then go up to Ivan Lawrence's room, having bought a bottle of white wine in the Strangers' bar. Sit with him and his personal assistant until the vote in which we are abstaining (Labour's amendment including the Social Chapter). This is a tie. Speaker votes for HMG. Ivan and I leave to vote against the government in the main motion and return to his room. Government defeated by eight votes, even though nine Ulster Unionists vote with them on the basis of God knows what deal. This means treaty can't come into effect and Major goes for a vote of confidence. I leave for home through the House of Lords. Expecting great recriminations tomorrow.

Friday 23 July

11 a.m. Meet group. There is no mood to fight on but we agree to pretend to do so. The government thinks we are sufficiently mad to believe us. It is agreed I should see Chief Whip and through him get friendly allusion to us in Hurd's wind-up speech. Hurd agrees to do so. Also I say that I want friendly letter from party chairman, whom I also see. On basis of this we agree to vote for HMG on a vote of confidence! Tebbit joins Fresh Start meeting to thank us.

Rupert Allason to get a bollocking from the whips for pushing off to his home in Bermuda in the middle of a confidence vote! I agree this is a bit eccentric and do not press that we should come to his rescue. Tony Newton comes into RR's office at one point and seems incredibly relieved when told peace is breaking out, as is Fowler. Hurd's speech does not say much but mood of party one of relief, not of recrimination. Good thing; means we live to fight another day. Must say this to Teresa Gorman, who at lunch fires most questions at me as to what it was all about. I say it's about the future. They will never dare tangle with us again. Lunch on Terrace with Peter Tapsell, Teresa Gorman, Christopher Gill, Walter Sweeney and Toby Jessel – all heroes in their own way. Even the sun is shining on them.

End of term, end of epoch, end of war atmosphere. We still carry our arms. This is the view I develop in the media – who I think are beginning to portray us as the victims, much to the irritation of Ted Heath, who stands behind me during one of the TV interviews.

As I go through lobby on the vote of confidence, Hurd thanks me.

I say, 'You didn't give us much; it will need a gloss from party chairman if things are to settle down.'

He says, 'Others got at me.'

Reflections

On 22 July 1993, the government lost a crucial vote which, had it been allowed to stand, would have wrecked the ratification process. As it was, the next day Major, backed in particular by Ken Clarke and Douglas Hurd, brought back virtually the same motion as a vote of confidence in the government.

The Fresh Start Group met in Room J early on the morning of 23 July. Some of its members suggested taking the whole matter to the High Court since it apparently broke one of the rules of Parliament – namely, that once a vote has been taken it is decisive. Together with Peter Tapsell, an influential member of our group, I took the view that enough was enough. We had done our very best to stop the Maastricht ratification process. We could not, in my view, now pull down our own government. I spoke strongly in favour of trying once again to do a deal with the government over the permanency of the single currency opt-out. I knew we were in a strong position early in the morning as senior members of the government were now terrified that we might bring about their political collapse. By the time I saw Hurd in the late morning before his wind-up speech, word had got to him that we were disinclined now to push matters over the cliff face and his mood had become uncompromising. I did my best to ensure that he would guarantee in his speech that there would be no recriminations, particularly against the newer and younger members of the group. He agreed, but later reneged on even this commitment.

My view is that this really marks the end of the debate as to whether Europe can be changed from within. One day there will be a referendum on whether or not Britain should remain a full member of the European Union. Until then the rhetoric and the fury will be synthetic and not very meaningful.

Friday 20 August 1993

I receive the following letter from Sir Peter Tapsell, written in his own hand:

Dear Michael

Amid all the excitement over the final votes on the Social Chapter and the Vote of Confidence, I only found the opportunity to express to you, in the briefest manner, the sense of gratitude I feel towards you for the role you played in helping to organise Conservative opposition to the Maastricht Treaty.

Your chairmanship of all the meetings of our strange little group of anti-Maastricht patriot guerrillas was at all times masterly. The charm and tact and wisdom, combined with firmness, with which you guided so disparate an assembly towards clear and sensible courses of action was remarkable.

Clearly, too, your negotiations on our behalf with a wide range of colleagues on both sides of the House was conducted with equal success and finesse.

Your judgment of the changing mood of the House was always impeccable and your predictions of the outcome of divisions were uncannily accurate throughout.

Above all, I have respected and admired the tireless energy and dedication with which you have thrown yourself into this great parliamentary struggle of the British people to continue to govern themselves in their traditional way and to continue to exercise their liberties under the Laws of England and Scotland.

Whatever the decisions of the German Constitutional Court, one thing is certain. After such a parliamentary battle, no Conservative government in our political lifetime will attempt to venture any further down the path towards a European union or a single European currency.

In that vital sense, our anti-Maastricht group are the victors. I have been proud to have been one of its members ...

I may say I have a similar admiration for Peter Tapsell. He is one of the unsung heroes of British politics. He is certainly one of the longest-serving MPs in modern times, entering Parliament in 1959, becoming Father of the House in 2010. His political integrity is second to none. He refused to join Thatcher's shadow government because he disagreed with her economic policy; at an already mature age he threw himself with gusto into the anti-Maastricht campaign. His constant and steadfast presence, both in the chamber and at our planning meetings, gave immensely greater dignity and backbone to the whole operation.

Chapter 12

John Major: resignation

Monday 26 July 1993

The House of Commons, which I enter at about 5.30 p.m., has very much the feel of the day after a party. It is the day of the summer adjournment debates. Those who are there (not many) John Biffen says are regulars of the Adjournment Club (Fergus Montgomery on Manchester airport etc.).

Meet Biffen while reading about the impending Christchurch disaster in the *Standard* in the smoking room (apparently we have given up and are not sending any ministers). Biffen says the mid-term blues will go on beyond the economic recovery. Major, he adds, has neither the confidence nor the experience to enable him to ride out the present crisis. He has called three of his Cabinet colleagues 'bastards' and he will go some time next year.

Tuesday 27 July

Government (Douglas Hurd) has written publicly to Bill Cash to ask him for his input to policy on Europe. I ring RR and subsequently Douglas Hurd comes on the phone. I tell them they have done three things: (1) annoyed/given ammo to Ted Heath et al., (2) built up Bill Cash's personal bandwagon, (3) undermined relations with our group. Hurd very apologetic. 'Shall I write you a letter?' I say I will consult colleagues.

Monday 2 August

Michael Howard calls to remind me (on the day ERM collapses and we sign Maastricht) that he has always been against re-entry to ERM – whereas Clarke has always been in favour. We agree to meet and assess developments in the autumn. His call reminds me that David Heathcoat-Amory, who is meant to be in charge of European policy – and whom Ryder claims to have told to be in touch with me – has not been. It may be just as well. I am not sure how close we want to get to them. Better perhaps, as Tapsell has advised, just to put our case on the table and leave it there, rather than to be seduced into compromising with what they want.

Wednesday 4 August
Bill Cash rings. We talk for about half an hour. He begins by congratulat-
ing me on a radio broadcast I did on Monday re ERM collapse and Britain's
signing up to Maastricht. He wants co-operation between us. Although
he has become a national character, he is clearly worried by my seeming
pre-eminence in the parliamentary party re our group. I say, 'It's all very
well but you're not a team player. I once asked you to contribute £200
of the millions you have collected for Teresa Gorman to go to Denmark in
the referendum. You refused, I guess because it was not directly organised
by your empire. I now plan to collect some resources and others agree. I
think we should go our different ways. We can meet at the crossroads every
so often.' Bill I think is a little chastened by all this. His call was prompted
by a meeting with Douglas Hurd, who told him that 'not all your group
approve of us meeting like this'. Bill thinks they are trying to divide and
rule. I doubt it – they need to be able to treat with an organised force.
Anarchy in our ranks does not suit them.

Wednesday 1 September
Ring Teresa Gorman's office – with whom I have been in some contact
about her book, due out for the party conference. Discover she has made
no mention of the government's offer re ERM during the Maastricht affair.
Hope I have succeeded in getting something in. Talk to Dan Hannan, who is
going to join me as my research assistant on 13 September. Inevitably he got a
double first and is in good form, newly back from the Middle East. Also talk
to James Cran. As usual we agree – waiting game is what is required; keep a
power base but not a party within party.

Friday 17–Saturday 18 September
Major's future now becoming the subject of febrile press speculation. At least
four MPs have come out calling for his resignation.

Sunday 19 September
Major on a trip to Tokyo makes another of his name-calling press briefings.
This time we are 'devils on the fringe'. The effect is predictable – press speculation as to whether he has become paranoid.
    I call Michael Howard, mainly to say we cannot allow the Portillo–Clarke
dream ticket idea to gather momentum. Howard understandably cagey about
giving any response.

Tuesday 21 September
Lunch Ken Baker. Agree that PM seems to have gone off his trolley in attacking us all from Tokyo and that it all looks pretty bad for him.

Wednesday 22 September
At his request meet Tom Arnold in the pub on corner of Whitehall and gate into Norman Shaw. We sit on a bench outside as, symbolically, black storm clouds gather over Parliament building. Tom says he cannot believe what PM is doing – especially bizarre is news today that PM angry that his 'barmy MPs' slur (added to 'fringe devils') was leaked; it was apparently meant for party conference where he would really hurt Gorman etc.

Saturday 25 September
Long talk on phone to Norman Lamont, who had previously rung me. He is not enjoying the sweat of the back benches. 'I remember you saying how unpleasant it is being an ex-minister out of tune with the government; I didn't believe you at the time but I see what you mean now. If you continue to play you can do nothing right.' We agree that if Major goes the important thing is that Clarke should not succeed – nor, for that matter, Hurd. Lamont is not so certain about Howard.

Sunday 3 October
Sunday papers full of Margaret Thatcher saying the leadership rules must be changed to protect Major. Clearly she's fearful of Clarke getting it. What we must do is to invent a successor to Major. I suspect it has to be Howard.

Friday 8 October
Michael Howard makes triumphant speech on law and order on Wednesday at the party conference. The trouble with Michael is that he has no following except for me and I am not sure my support is fully appreciated! He must somehow set up his stall – especially on economic policy – without appearing too grasping or disloyal.

Thursday 14 October
On holiday in south of France. Talk Maastricht with an intelligent German business consultant. He is very worried by the implications for democracy of the present European set-up, but says that both the federalists and the anti-federalists seem to have no real care about a united Europe which is also democratic. I say you must evolve the democratic institutions. They cannot be superimposed. Above all, accountability requires a sense of allegiance – a

legitimacy. This in my view could only be achieved – at least into the fore-seeable future – at the level of the nation state; it is what is lacking in the European government as presently conceived. In its absence, the democratic institutions such as the Parliament will be artificial and no balance for the undemocratic Commission/Law Court/Bank. The strength of the British Parliament grew out of a real need to protect the people against autocracy and dictatorship. There is no such common purpose with respect to the European Parliament.

Tuesday 19 October

Second day of the defence debate and first day of voting. First real day back for Parliament. Mood is sombre. Defence cuts are upsetting a wide section of the party. Poll amongst Fresh Starters of whether to form up again. Marlow and Cash want to do so. Cran et al. want to let things rest while preparing policy for the long term. We'll form a dining club – for which Dan Hannan will prepare papers – and with links to other parliamentarians on a network-ing basis. It's all going to take time and hopefully not be too high profile.

In the meantime Teddy Taylor, Richard Body etc. plan to attack every European thing that moves, including a motion this week for a free trade area.

The real test of nerve will be next year with the European tax increase Bill. We shall have to be sensible without seeming to run away.

Wednesday 20 October

Chat to Biffen in his room. He wants to resuscitate Fresh Start but on the basis that it is not too hostile. He thinks Major is bound to survive till the next election.

Dinner with Nick Bonsor. He is very supportive of John Major and will only join if Whips 'give permission'.

Thursday 21 October

James Cran and I agree to move slowly.

Meet Marlow in the House. He wants to join in; the problem is his call in the summer for resignation of John Major – we don't want to continue to look like rebels.

Meet Richard Ryder in the lobby. We agree to have dinner together

A surprising number want Fresh Start to continue: Iain Duncan Smith, Marlow, Tapsell, Cash etc. Cran and I are very reluctant; we don't want to be steamrollered into something silly next year. That is why we want our small (dinner or breakfast) policy group.

Thursday 28 October

8.30: Dinner with Richard Ryder in the Strangers' dining room. He is ten minutes late, very apologetic. Just before the 10 o'clock vote, for which I am paired, his charming PA, Shona, who used to work for Alistair McAlpine, comes to say there are problems with getting someone for *Any Questions*. Ryder would be away for half an hour at 10. Nevertheless we have had a very friendly dinner. I make the point that I think PM is 'safe' on everything except if there were a debacle over the European elections or a major row (with the government not getting its legislation) over the European Finance Bill. My main position is if possible to keep out of it – to focus on 1996 Inter-Governmental Conference (IGC) and on how we could change the Treaty of Rome then with the help of other European parliamentarians.

Ryder says PM's view, probably, is that he has gone far enough with his article in *The Economist* etc. I say if I were to play any part in all of this, he would have to come back to me within the next three weeks. If I do not take the helm I doubt whether there would be anything to negotiate because the boys and girls would push ahead to destroy the Euro finance Bill next year. My preferred intent is to set up a policy group/dining club to look at policy for the IGC and to link this with parliamentarians from other European countries.

RR says there are three dangers ahead: Euro elections, Euro finance Bill, definition of federalism. I am not sure how the latter could be a flashpoint – but still. He asks me what we think of Douglas Hurd – I say not much following the way he treated us after the Maastricht votes. Then he says Heathcoat-Amory is on our side. I say, 'I'm glad to hear it; he was pretty vicious against us as a whip.'

RR's main interests are what I could deliver and what the price would be. On the latter I say genuine support of anti-federalist position by PM. RR says Euro-enthusiasts might say 'We will back a new leader who is unashamedly pro-Europe', e.g. Clarke. I say the real threat comes from the Eurosceptics. They are also the PM's natural constituency in view of the Clarke threat. RR expresses doubts that he will be able to get the European Bill upstairs into committee or through a timetable motion.

Monday 1 November

Have supper at Rodin's with Bernard Jenkin, one of the brightest of the new intake Maastricht rebels. He is caught up in his own rhetoric before he came into the House – when it was fashionable to be a Thatcherite. However, by and large he stuck it out, abstaining most of the time. Now he's trying to find a way back into favour. He may be being a bit hasty; his gang (Iain Duncan Smith and Barry Legg) will join a non-kamikaze group, probably including Lamont and Baker. (However, the kamikazes do give the whole thing some bite!)

Tuesday 2 November

Lunch with Lamont who is delightfully full of bile. Intends to ask questions of the PM on a regular basis. Claims that it was he who insisted – against the will of the PM – to reduce drink taxes. Dine with Cran. Agree to reform Fresh Start.

Gerry Vaughan says there are rumours that the manifesto is going to be very federalist – perhaps that explains RR's comment about the word 'federalist' being a flashpoint. See John Biffen. He wants Fresh Start to be reformed but after the elections to committees. This is what we will do.

Tuesday 23 November

Dinner at Maunsel Street, which we have just finished refurbishing, with Portillo and Howard. Portillo indicates it is going to be a tough Budget so far as expenditure is concerned. Michael Howard has to leave early to be on the bench at 9 p.m. for the closure of the Home Office debate on the Queen's Speech. When he leaves Portillo indicates, in response to Clarke's comment a few days earlier at the CBI conference, that he is personally in favour of going back into ERM. Howard is in favour of an 'academic'-type conference about future of Europe.

Thursday 25 November

Give dinner in Strangers' to French Wallop and her son, Scott, by a previous marriage. Apparently Malcolm Wallop has announced that he will resign as a Senator. He plans to stand for governor of Wyoming and then possibly for President. He would make a good one: the first witty man with real belief we will have had as leader of the west for some time.

Monday 29 November

Drive back with Ken Baker from Alistair McAlpine's company's annual do at the Intercontinental Hotel. Ken is just as angry as Lamont about the government but he is more restrained. After a wonderful concert at St John's, Smith Square, in which Toby Jessel is the soloist, meet up with Lamont in the members' lobby. We have a quick drink in the smoking room. He plans to stay in politics, which means looking for a new seat – 'even if I have to go before thirty selection committees!' He could just become a man with a future. I say I was angry with him some months ago over ERM etc. (and he would not have changed his spots of his own will); nevertheless I rather admire what he is up to now – and in politics you learn to take matters as they crop up – no point in living in the past.

Friday 10 December
5.30: Interview Dudley Fishburn* on *Target*† about future of Major and then on to Conservative graduates' party at Central Office. My book *A Treaty Too Far* was raffled amidst cheering. Michael Howard, Alan Duncan and Peter Lilley were there. Introduce Michael Howard to Dan Hannan. Dan is engaged in preparing the academic conference which Howard suggested at one of our dinners. Howard is, however, very wary of any overt involvement. Howard very cagey in the lobby later on. He seems to be more worried about being seen with me than before, which is odd as our lot has begun to win back places in the backbench committees. James Cran got Irish committee VP and Peter Temple-Morris was beaten for chairman-ship – by Andrew Hunter.

Clarke winds up a debate on Europe by joining with Labour, who want more expenditure for the Commission and more centralisation, enabling him to ignore the fire from behind him from the Eurosceptics, who have not gone away.

Dinner in members' dining room. At my table Ian Taylor and Robert Atkins. Tell them of the interview I have done with Dudley Fishburn where he defended the view in his newspaper that Major might have to go next year. Ian Taylor, to my surprise, says he defends Major in public but finds it hard to do so in private. There is no direction or authority to his government. Taylor is a European federalist and pretty left. Interesting that he is disillusioned with Major. No doubt he feels he has a strong candidate in Ken Clarke. Later Clarke comes into the smoking room while I am having a glass of champagne with Austin Mitchell (who turns out to be married to a New Zealander and to know all about Ann's great-grandfather). Clarke is very jolly and joins in with the champagne. He certainly is what they call charismatic, full of good cheer and general bonhomie.

Thursday 13 January 1994
Labour Party is doing a bolsh and forcing us all to vote every fifteen minutes. This gives us a chance to rub shoulders in the lobbies and vent our spleen

---

* MP for Kensington 1988–97.
† Sky TV political discussion programme on which I stood in from time to time for Norman Tebbit as one of two paid questioners, the other being Austin Mitchell MP.

on each other. Tension lightened by the fact that the right is winning all the by-elections for officers of party groups, e.g. Townend chairman of Finance.

Sunday 16 January
Yesterday Major was reported as saying he will crucify his 'f***ing right-wing' ministers who have tripped up on Back to Basics. Back to Basics, which he invented, is a fiasco; no one knows what it means. Moral crusade? Reform of government to abolish 'dependency culture?' Or just decency? For me Back to Basics means tackling the 'dependency culture', low taxes, high growth.

Monday 17 January
Dinner with Temple-Morris in the House (he is still chairman of the left-wing Lollards). He and Ian Taylor are pretty fed up with Major and in a hurry to get rid of him. They did not vote for him and want him to go. TM is not averse to Howard, though he would vote at present for Clarke. There are the makings of a deal here.

Thursday 20 January
Bonsor, Cran, Gill, Townend, Jenkin, Duncan to supper. European Research Group (ERG) off the ground (Dan Hannan has prepared some brilliant papers). Discussion soon moves off Europe to the leadership. Everyone beginning to take it as a foregone conclusion that Major will go. We agree to go for a conference of European politicians; also to keep the Chief Whip in the picture.

The Hamilton–Leigh plan is to run Portillo and lose and then run Heseltine. It could come off unless we can find a unity candidate in the first round. It means Portillo backing Howard. Howard as yet has very few takers but he, unlike Portillo, could unite the party. Strangely enough he could do badly in the first round but win in the second – if he survives to. The key is Portillo. He will not be in the mood at present to back off as he is getting a lot of push. However, he is also at the receiving end of some very hostile press, such as last Tuesday's *Standard*.

Tuesday 25 January
Fresh Start in Room J at 5 p.m. Great debate about whether we should (a) participate in the manifesto writing, (b) be supportive with high profile in the Euro campaign. Majority view is that we should be cautious; very important not to get blamed for being disruptive. Peter Tapsell suggests a 'supportive' letter to *The Times*! I say the last thing it will be seen as is supportive – whatever it says. Peter, who is a great man, brave and steadfast, is on this occasion

all over the shop. Having last summer advised against being associated with the manifesto, he is now arguing for doing so.

Wednesday 26 January
Dinner with Cran and Gill to work out our position re leadership if it becomes vacant. We want someone of our views – not a 'compromise' who believes the opposite to us, e.g. Clarke, Heseltine or Hurd. Trouble is that Portillo not yet quite ripe. Leigh and Hamilton running him as a stalking horse for Heseltine. Problem with Howard is that he has no following because he doesn't seem to stand for much. I agree to talk to him and report back. By chance I meet Howard in 10 o'clock vote and we go to his room for half an hour. Over whisky I sketch out how I see position. Paradox: right has no candidates although they are in majority in parliamentary party – witness backbench elections where we had a clean sweep. MH and I agree to meet again soon.

Tuesday 1 February
4 p.m. Meeting of ERG. Bernard Jenkin questions why we need something different from Bill Cash's operation and the answer given by Ivan Lawrence was 'Bill Cash'. Try unsuccessfully to establish a view on MH. Decide that I should see MH to try to take things further.

Invited to *Newsnight* to give our view on Europe. Am intent on going on and saying that we can all co-operate in an anti-federalist platform, then after talking to Cran decide not to be accused of making waves. Tell this to Graham Bright (PM's PPS) who says he will take soundings. Comes back while I am dining with Bonsor in members' dining room to say powers that be think it would be a good idea if I go on. Go back to BBC to reoffer services. Then to Nick Baker (pairing whip) to get paired. Garel-Jones comes in to say PM's rebuff of George Gardiner is an attack on right wing as a whole. (I am going on TV to say it is not). For some strange reason Garel-Jones allowed to stay in Whips' Office while all this going on. He must still carry a good deal of clout with PM or be thought to do so by whips.

In the event programme OK. I am supportive but I don't think sycophantic.

Thursday 3 February
Lunch in members' dining room with Richard Ryder and Ken Baker. RR tells an amusing and semi-obscene story about my whip, David Lightbown. When RR leaves the table Ken wants to talk about the leadership problem; sparkles when conversation leads to the possibility of his still being in frame. I say he let himself down at paving debate (when he promised in 6 o'clock news to abstain and then capitulated).

Major speaks to 1922 blaming all the problems of the government on divisions in the party, thus deflecting from his own leadership. What he is doing is what he has attempted twice already, at the party conference of 1993 and through his summer tour of area councils – to appeal over the heads of the parliamentary party to the party in the country. In the short term they will like the idea of MPs having their heads banged together. In the longer term they too will want results and a set of policies which add up to some defensible objective. He misses the point too that the people who voted for him were the MPs.

Supper with Bill Cash., He's worried that if we win he may be left out of the spoils. The answer, I say, is for us all to stick together and to stick it out.

Tuesday 8 February
See Michael Howard in his room after 10 p.m. vote; tell him the newly formed European Research Group is growing. Angela Rumbold and John Watts want to join in. Also Fresh Start in good shape, debating at enormous length as to whether or not we should join in with the manifesto. General view is that we should be supportive but not party to its creation.

MH still believes (probably rightly) that Major will survive but is prepared to contingency-plan against it – especially against the possibility of a stalking horse doing well. Will see Cran and Gill and 'see how we get on'. Says they are *parti pris*. I say, 'Yes, but they could lead you to an army which at present you haven't got; indeed, your support is zero at present but we might be able to change that.'

Wednesday 9 February
Meet Emma Nicholson in the street when I am returning with the morning papers; she lives two doors along and we had been on opposite sides in a friendly way on *Newsnight* last Thursday. She went on telly yesterday to say that Back to Basics was dead. For this she received a telephone call from Richard Ryder ordering her not to go on telly again – for some reason for three weeks – except on constituency matters and about Marsh Arabs. Apparently he was very abusive – kept on saying 'I am the Chief Whip'. She is frightfully upset.

Thursday 10 February
10 p.m. Sit next to Ted Heath. 'What do you do with yourself now you can't make trouble?' I ignore the insult. 'I agree with you on Bosnia. Where is the pressure for us to become involved in the war coming from – the Yanks?' 'Yes.'

Portillo comes up. 'You and Bill Cash mustn't quarrel.' I say, 'You're right, of course.' We agree to meet next week.

Friday 11 February

Meet Peter Temple-Morris before 11.30 vote. He is in a terrible bate. Whips leaked the bollocking meeting he had at which he was told to belt up re piece in today's *Times*. Amazing how they have now upset both wings of the party.

Bill Cash has been holding meetings of MPs who want to create trouble for the party now.

Wednesday 16 February

10 a.m. See Portillo in the Treasury. I sit in one of his armchairs. He says, 'Come and sit at the long table; it's more businesslike.' He won't be an easy PM.

We discuss Europe; he agrees that we must capture the consensus – draw lines in the sand. Seems interested in what I am up to. I tell him that I had seen Jim Miller the day before – who had given us money. Talk about public expenditure. Portillo brings out charts to show me it is coming down under him. I say, 'I sincerely hope that's the way it turns out.'

Lunch in members' dining room with Michael Heseltine and Tom King reminiscing about the time Michael waved the mace and I got into a punch-up in 1976. Michael in rude health after his heart attack.

Thursday 17 February

Five minutes late for meeting with Angela Rumbold (deputy chairman of the party) because I have been struggling in Chelsea Town Hall at a bargain sale of curtain material run by Osborne & Little. Beard Angela in her room, having missed her in central lobby. Persuade her to join the ERG – quite a coup in the circumstances. May go for David Howell now – having remet him in his car yesterday.

Lunch at Rodin's with Clive Sinclair, the inventor and an old friend. He reminds me of the forecasts that the Chinese will overtake America in ten years' time in absolute GDP.

Wednesday 23 February

Tom Arnold says he wants to meet up to discuss a government more unpopular than any in recent memory. We agree to have breakfast next week. This seems to belie Michael Howard's view when I meet him with James Cran and Christopher Gill that we have 'passed the worst'. General chat with Howard about policy. Everyone sniffing around each other.

Nothing conclusive nor is anything planned to be. Gill goes at MH like a terrier, asking why he thinks ministers are so weak. Cran very sophisticated; indicates his disapproval of NTB's backing for Portillo. I have at one moment to say to Gill, 'We haven't come for a general moaning session.'

Thursday 24 February

Bernard Jenkin decides to throw in his lot with Cash. Have a drink with Lamont after 10 o'clock vote. He's still hopping mad and threatening to stand against Major in the future. He seems to feel he has really messed up his life. Thrown away the chance of the DoE and now of going into the House of Lords; he mopes about his mistakes in government – which he blames on Major. He claims the Treasury had little to do with going into the ERM. It was very much a personal 'success' of Major, with the help of the FCO.

Thursday 3 March

Dinner at Portillo's flat in Ashley Gardens. I arrive there at 7.30, chat to Michael about the persistent leadership issue. He accepts that he is only real candidate of the right – given that Michael Howard in his view has no following and no hope of attracting one. Portillo's view is that the rise of Heseltine has strengthened Major's hand – as being seen by the right still as the only saviour against Heseltine.

Qualified majority voting

Thursday 10 March 1994

After PMQs, bump into Douglas Hurd, who is clearly going to give way on qualified majority voting (QMV). Toby Jessel and John Whittingdale come up to me in 10 o'clock vote with similar view; we all go in to the Chief Whip to warn him of rows ahead if HMG give way. RR sympathetic but says to talk to Hurd. Later Tony Marlow confirms his worst fears after talk to Hurd.

Evening meeting of Fresh Start at 5 p.m. – not a success. A real divide exists between Cash/Tapsell and Spicer/Cran. They want to kick over the traces every time we meet. Whole thing becoming personalised between Bill and me, as pointed out by Teresa Gorman. I say this a matter of tactics, not of personalities. Have one of my agonising sessions for half an hour with Cash at 6.30 in the smoking room until we move into the card room.

Tuesday 15 March

Euroscepticism in ferment about the proposed changes to the blocking minority vote.

Lunch with Progress Party from Norway, Christian social parties of Portugal and Spain and Cran, Gill, Lawrence and Daniel – in Wassall's office.*

Dine with Richard Ryder à deux in Strangers' dining room. He seems rather shocked when I say some colleagues might resign whip if the QMV issue goes the wrong way. He says that European legislation probably postponed to next year (both VAT and accession). I say Major really ought to work out where his real support comes from, i.e. centre right. Also tell him about the ERG. He accepts an invitation to lunch.

Wednesday 16 March

Bill Cash calls a meeting of Fresh Start in my name. Everybody thinks it's my meeting and is fed up I'm not there. Meeting with Douglas Hurd and European Affairs committee. (Prior to this Ulster Unionist and my neighbour John Taylor says John Major has told Jim Molyneaux† that it's all sewn up on QMV.) Douglas Hurd pretends he is fighting hard. Cash and I agree not to speak on this matter in the chamber – let it come from the body of the church. Very effective, especially Terence Higgins: 'Who doesn't want expansion of Europe? Why give them anything in return?'

Wednesday 23 March

Lunch with George Gardiner at Gran Paradiso. He thinks Portillo can make it.

Thursday 24 March

Lunch with Ken Baker. He thinks Portillo is flawed. Seems Heseltine now has field to himself, so we should back Major.

Dine in Strangers' with French deputy Griotteray, Cran and Hunter. We have the makings of twelve Ulster MPs to join our lot. Griotteray suggests twelve from each country – very symmetrical. We will need French translators at Oxford.

Monday 28 March

All the gossip in the morning that Major is due to back off from his 'brave' stand on QMV.

During the day meet most of the key players. During Parliamentary Questions Douglas Hurd in effect says we are going to give way. Those who were anti-Maastricht but who did not vote against it make the running.

---

* Wassall is an investment company which allowed the ERG to use its dining room in its offices in Victoria Street for periodic lunches with Cabinet ministers etc. as guests.

† Leader of the Ulster Unionists 1979–95.

Find myself dining with Michael Heseltine. We leave the dining room alone for a vote at about 10.30. He is very friendly, clearly playing for the right-wing vote. 'I suppose for the moment you will stick with Major?' he says. 'Yes,' I reply.

Michael Howard comes up in one of the votes to say he wants to see me, Gill and Cran tomorrow. He may be leaving things a bit late. Have a brief word with Portillo in the smoking room. He's not going to resign when Cabinet does its climbdown tomorrow but he is getting pretty restless and is waiting for his opportunity. In the smoking room much of the evening. Leave at around 1 a.m., bump into Richard Ryder; tell him PM will capture support of two-thirds of the party and the country if he says 'Non'.

Tuesday 29 March

The day the PM caves in on QMV. Westminster in an uproar of sullen silence. For the first time in my life in Parliament, nobody wants to ask questions to PM – waiting for his climbdown statement, which comes in spades. Marlow calls for his resignation.

Fresh Start meet at 5 p.m. Some 25 present – almost a full house, with the exception of Marlow and Biffen. Tebbit comes in at one point and warns us not to go over the top now; let it all stir. Others want to plan for a great rebellion on uprating of VAT. I say we should focus on 1996 – not especially well received. I don't know how much longer I can go on chairing these meetings.

Portillo comes up to me in lobby at one point and says he has 'thought hard', by which he means about resigning from the Cabinet, and then considers it would be ill judged and look a bit immature. Marlow rushes past on the way to a TV studio. 'I'm not going to resign the whip – why should I?' Baker looking serenely happy.

Times (Nick Wood) approaches me to say, 'I hear you had dinner with Heseltine last night.' 'Nothing in it, old boy; it's what we do in the members' dining room.' No doubt they will still try to say it's all part of Heseltine's bid for the right.

BBC sit outside Fresh Start meeting. I tell them after the meeting that we talked about 1996 and not about the leadership – at least this was half the truth and they knew it.

Later in the evening (10 p.m.) see Howard with Cran and Gill. Howard's main aim is to keep Major alive (politically). Cran (and I) very forceful about the need for Howard to do more to promote himself if he's in the running. I have a growing feeling he's not. But you never know who will fit the mood at the time and his support could still be important to Portillo.

Wednesday 30 March

Lunch in members' with Richard Shepherd. 'I agree with you, Michael, that it's about 1996 but some of us will hound the government at every turn until they have agreed on a referendum on the nature of 1996. To this effect we don't mind whether it's Heseltine or Major in power. In some respects Heseltine may be easier to deal with because he is stronger.'

Talk to Thatcher on the phone. She doesn't say much but implicitly seems to agree that if possible things needed to steady down with Major. If the quarrelling goes on his position will become untenable. The field will be more open than people imagine.

Toby Jessel comes up worried about report in *The Times* that I had been having dinner with Heseltine!

Carlisle and Gorman have now come out saying Major must go. Talk to Cran in a pub on the way home. Agree for the time being to go with Howard and Portillo, though not sanguine as to the result – nor of the ability to save Major, which for the time being I will try to do.

Thursday 31 March

Telephone Graham Bright to suggest I talk to PM over Easter about threat of autumn challenge to the PM that will come from certain members of the right who no longer care whether Major or Heseltine PM so long as able to force a referendum on Europe in 1996 or 1997, and need to involve a representative number of right (and arguably from left) in government.

Saturday 2 April

Lamont rings to ask what's going on.

Tuesday 5 April

Baker rings from Burgundy – like Lamont to find out what's happening. Lamont especially interested in press reports that I have been speaking to Heseltine. I don't know why Baker rings. I tell him that the weekend press has fanned the flames of the leadership crisis with reports of only forty out of 100 MPs backing Major. No doubt that figure will rise until the next crisis, with the results of local and Euro elections (not to mention a string of by-elections, the last of which will be the formerly Conservative seat of Eastleigh).

Monday 11 April

Teresa Gorman rings to say we must build up a right-wing candidate against Major. I don't know whether she has herself in mind after a spoof article in *The Times* last week by Matthew Parris naming her as the Duchess of Billericay. Perhaps she really does think she can do it. She would certainly have PMT licked and takes all the right kind of hormone treatment, on which she recently lectured in Scandinavia. Actually she is much better and brighter than her reputation.

In afternoon pay my annual pilgrimage to Long Lartin high security prison. Amongst others meet a Libyan terrorist who will be moved at dawn tomorrow (although he has only six months to go) because there is information that he will be sprung by Libyan government using helicopters. Also overhear one notorious inmate with a 38-year sentence saying he is moving cells because the snooker players are making too much noise on the landing outside his present cell.

To back PM or not?

Tuesday 12 April 1994
House back. PM very quiet and white at PM's questions. Graham Bright, his PPS, says in one of the votes that he would like to see me 4.20 Thursday in the House, secretly.

Move over to Tapsell's table in dining room to finish coffee. If Heseltine gets in, Tapsell should be due for a Cabinet post. He would be good.

Thursday 14 April
4.20: Meeting with PM in his room in Commons. Offers me a cup of tea, which I accept. Also present Graham Bright. PM looks washed out. Speaks very quietly; has just finished PM's Questions where he accuses Margaret Beckett* of 'peddling untruths'. Speaker asks him to withdraw; he doesn't. Trouble may lie ahead on this.

I make the following points:

1. His support is haemorrhaging from left and right, especially from right.
2. He remains the best the right has for the time being and therefore the question is what to do.

I suggest:

---

* Shadow leader of the Commons and deputy Labour leader 1992–4, president of Board of Trade 1997–8, leader of Commons 1998–2001, SoS Environment, Food and Rural Affairs 2001–6, Foreign Secretary 2006–7.

1. Referendum on 1996 IGC. He says he is considering it but would have to eat a lot of words about referendums. I say it would take the issue out of Conservative politics for the present. He asks what would the left think. I say they would probably buy it – quote Ray Whitney as a 'Gaullist'; presumably he wouldn't like to be faced with a federalist constitution in 1996. Major says I won't split the party in 1996.
2. I suggest he makes up his mind which side of party he is on. Three reasons for being on the right:
   a. They voted for him originally.
   b. They are in a majority.
   c. No real candidate to threaten him.

I say I know one of his problems is that some of his best friends are on the left; he smiles wanly and agrees.

We agree the local and Euro elections look pretty grim. I say if the results are bad he should draw a line and start again – not try more of the same 'Crisis – what crisis?' He says that a lot of bad press is fed from colleagues. I say – with one or two possible exceptions – not from Eurosceptics.

He says we may have to go into opposition to save the party. He is muddled on this point because he also says, 'Unlike you, Michael, people in the party do not realise how awful it is to be in opposition.' Is this a threat that he might call an election?

On the question of Back to Basics, we agree he has been unlucky but that it was a good idea. He says it has now attached to it a 'hoot factor', by which I think he means ridicule. He says that if he revived it, to his certain knowledge two further Conservative scandals and three Labour ones would pop out.

At the start of our talk he says he has failed to achieve unity in the party. When he took over he had real handicaps:

1. His famous predecessor;
2. The European faultline;
3. A small majority;
4. The pain of the aftermath of the leadership battle.

Also 'lack of experience' and, he says, lack of firm views on either the economy or Europe. 'I am dead centre on both of these – although I will never agree to further federalisation. If I had had stronger views perhaps it would have been easier for me to impose these.' Nothing if not frank and honest.

Frankly, it is rather a sad litany of excuses of a battered and very demoralised

man. I leave saying words to the effect of 'If you can't bridge the European
fault line there is not much hope'.

Monday 18 April

Still reflecting on the meeting with PM on 14th. Effectively I gave him the
choice of coming over to the right and regaining our support. On past form
he won't; still thinks in terms of 'balancing' the various interests or of out-
and-out lurch to the left. Strangely enough Alistair McAlpine came out in the
Sunday Express this weekend with precisely the same package that I offered
the PM. I haven't seen Alistair for months.

Summing up: Major is a man without any real political perspective. He
does have a few cronies who will not allow him to do the sensible thing,
which is to make a comprehensive play for where his natural majority lies –
on the right.

Heseltine assumes that the tactics of the right will be to keep Major in play
but if my analysis of Major is correct, the right has nothing with which to
trade with him.

Tuesday 26 April

Dinner at White's with Nick Bonsor. He wants to be the next leader of the
party. We could do worse. Back in the House for 10 o'clock vote. Toby Jessel
takes me up a rickety staircase in the library to look for the Michelin guide
to France in search of the address of his favourite Normandy restaurant, Le
Cochon d'Or at Beuzeville, south of Honfleur.

Wednesday 27 April

Meet Portillo in the Treasury and travel with him to Conrad Black, who
repeats that he will back Portillo and will get Murdoch alongside. One embar-
rassment: when Black asks Portillo who are his organisers in Commons,
Portillo says he would rather not say. Black presses him. When he says Neil
Hamilton, it is clear his embarrassment is that this should have been said
in front of me, who believes that Hamilton is also working for Heseltine.
I say in the car, 'I hope it is not becoming too complicated. Don't forget,
Hamilton's close friend Leigh is firmly for Heseltine.'

Portillo indicates on Europe that we may need to pull out or float ideas
for doing so. This is in response to a comment from me that people do not
know his views.

Thursday 28 April

Splash story in *The Sun* that PM thinking of pulling out of Europe if necessary. I think this story may have been encouraged by Portillo in view of what he said to me the night before.

Talk on phone to one of my constituency supporters – Alex Stuart Cleary, who is worried that I may be deselected. Tell him highly unlikely. New association would have to have a motion to reselect me; if that failed, there would be a motion to have open selection. I would try to pack that meeting with my many supporters.

Saturday 30 April
Portillo reported to have said we will go into single currency over his dead body. He seems to have taken rather seriously what I said to him about his views on Europe not being known.

Sunday 1 May
Frightful row in the press about Portillo. Michael Howard rings, ostensibly to say that he would like to take part in the Oxford conference but in reality to say that the attacks on the PM getting out of hand (ref David Evans's call for sacking of six ministers); he liked my TV performance last Thursday. He says Portillo not ready, 'nor am I', so Heseltine would be a certainty if Major goes. I say the matter may not be containable unless Major comes to meet us on policy and in the government reshuffle. Michael sort of concurs. Reminds me that we had agreed that the Oxford conference would largely comprise academics. I say OK but some of its suggestions are likely to be pretty sharp.

Monday 2 May
Press suggesting that reshuffle might promote Bonsor, Lawrence and Watts. In the lobby Temple-Morris on a high about Heseltine. Says that a deal will be done with Portillo once he has been beaten. From Portillo's point of view all to play for – if he wins he is PM, if he loses he does a deal with Heseltine. Hamilton and Leigh are his go-betweens and will do the deals.

My problem: only worth backing Portillo if he means to win; no point – as I said to him – if it's all a façade orchestrated by Hamilton et al. There is collusion emerging between Heseltine and Portillo. Do we have to save Major? Apparently in the members' dining room tonight Temple-Morris, Jenkin, Hamilton, Shepherd and Marlow were getting on like a house on fire – all over each other. Portillo plan seems to be: to help to destabilise Major, then to stand against Heseltine, do well and remain in a senior post until next time. Portillo certainly thinks Major will go – he told me so. The question is: can Portillo win? If not, we must back Major. I'm not willing to play games with Heseltine/Hamilton.

Temple-Morris thinks that having got rid of Thatcher – and with help of right – can put in Heseltine. T-M wants to finish the job off he started with the overthrow of Thatcher.

Tuesday 3 May
Decide finally to back Major. This is the view of Bonsor and Archie Hamilton but not, as I discovered at a BAA reception, of George Gardiner, who is out and out going for Portillo with a deal with Heseltine. Toby Jessel says trouble is he isn't a very good Prime Minister. Sydney Chapman, a whip and a friend, says, 'I hope you will not feel your destiny is presently to write the odd book and paint the odd picture.' (He's coming to stay in the autumn.)

Friday 6 May
Day after disastrous local government election results. Conservatives third to Labour and Liberals. On the radio Norman Fowler blames it all on disunity. I tell him in the tea room that the electors think it has more to do with disastrous economic policies. (John Carlisle offers himself up in the *Today* programme as a stalking horse.) I write supportive letter to PM.

John Smith dies

Thursday 12 May 1994
John Smith died.
Last night I was on *Newsnight* arguing against a Liberal and a Labour councillor, who as far as I could see wanted all regional funds to be channelled through Brussels. Politics has seemed to settle into a groove where all that really seemed to matter was the Tory leadership. Indeed, Tony Benn has written a letter to *The Times* complaining about this, for which I congratulated him. Today John Major looks much safer, because the spotlight will be off him for a bit. He has asked to see me next Tuesday.

Tuesday 17 May
4.30: Meeting with PM. When I enter Major's room in the House of Commons, a group of Tory MPs who had rebelled on a disability matter (John Hannam and Alan Howarth) are leaving. I say to Major as I go in, 'Dealing with a bunch of rebels?'
   He replies, 'I wouldn't know a rebel if I saw one'.
   He clearly feels that John Smith's death has taken the heat off him. The Prime Minister also feels that 'Europe' is going 'our way' and that he doesn't

have to give much on it other than a reasonably 'robust' manifesto. To that extent it is a bad time to see him. The German presidency is going to press for enlargement (to satisfy German objectives in central Europe), and for more centralisation and regulation. Euro election results could be presented as mid-term blues and there is no need to trade further with us – all slightly depressing. I argue that European federalism now has a momentum of its own which we would need to reverse. He says he really couldn't see his way to do this – certainly not with Britain leading with its chin.

I mention that I had been at a conference in Prague over the weekend where the nation state was alive and kicking and protecting democracy.

Sunday 22 May

Thinking back on visit to PM, I don't think I got through to him that there has to be a deal. He said there were twenty-five trouble-makers on each side – 'irreconcilables', I think he called them. In that case, with a majority of sixteen he's had it. What he needs to do is to pull the key figures into his administration. Somehow I have got to get this over. Today's onslaught by Gardiner in *Forward** may help to remove the impression that all is now well with the demise of John Smith.

Tuesday 24 May

ERG lunch in Wassall's office with Chief Whip. Present: me, Rumbold, Bonsor, Cran, Gill, Lawrence, Hannan. First discussion: in answer to Gill that government is out of touch with mainstream of the party, Ryder says government represents the best talent; however, he concedes the difficulty of his task of representing the party to a sometimes not very sympathetic government. Warns us against attacking the government on the 'Own Resources' and Accession Bills. Also says that will advise Foreign Secretary to lunch with us and use his good offices to that effect.

Mood amongst the whips is starting to turn nasty in anticipation of losses at the European elections. They are lining us up as scapegoats. The message that their best tactic is to ally themselves with us has not got through.

Later at meeting of Fresh Start the mood is gung-ho. As always some twenty people show up, each with his or her own agenda. Not sure how much longer will go along with it. Teresa says we must pull out of the European Union. Barry Legg and John Biffen say we must cleanse ourselves first.

Drive back to Maunsel Street with Ken Baker. We agree that since Smith's

---

* Magazine of the Conservative Way Forward pressure group.

death there has been a change. Heseltine no longer quite the threat to Major. All still hangs a bit on Euro elections.

Wednesday 1 June
Newsnight onto me. 'What's going on? Your side seems to have won the day with PM.' I say if so, it's a return to normality.

Friday 3 June
Canvassing in villages where branches have broken down. Elmley Castle, Ripple, Severn Stoke, Powick, Eckington, Combertons. General response – Major no good, 'can't make his mind up', 'sings two tunes' etc. If this is going on throughout the country he's in some trouble.

Wednesday 8 June
Eve of European elections. Talk to Lamont on the phone. He believes we will still do appallingly badly despite what I feel is a change in the mood largely reflective of the D-Day landing remembrances – also due to Major's tougher rhetoric on Europe. The main question is whether after all his chopping and changing, people will believe him this time. Lamont looks intent on standing for leadership this autumn.

Friday 10 June
We come third in the by-election for the 'safe' Conservative seat of Eastleigh. I do a bit of TV from Eastleigh to which Ma drives me from Haven Hotel in Poole where we are meant to be having a quiet lunch! My main point (reflected in an unpublished letter to *Times*) is that the appalling result was caused by memory of the recession caused by ERM. Must never play again with fixed exchange rates.

Saturday 11 June
Before driving up to Annabel in Durham, receive a strangely warm letter from Major. Was my letter to him too accommodating?

Tuesday 14 June
ERG and Fresh Start. John Biffen says government is brain dead and will never recover. Usually wrong on psephological matters; in 1983 he said Liberals would wipe the floor with us.

Wednesday 15 June
Arrange to meet Peter Temple-Morris, chairman of Lollards. We sit at 6 p.m.

on the Terrace – warm evening. Trouble is everyone comes up to find out what is going on. I think there are the makings of a truce with him so long as he gets a job in government. The reason for this from our point of view is to stave off a Heseltine challenge for a year, until (a) Major even firmer with his policy, or (b) Portillo or Howard coming along more. Meet Heseltine (by mistake) on the stairs going to a vote. He says he is keeping his head down in his departmental work – which means he is still in the game, as confirmed by T-M and a friend of Heseltine's called Simon Day, whom I met at dinner the night before.

Thursday 16 June
Late-night dinner at the Garrick after seeing Tom Stoppard's excellent *Arcadia*. Glass of white wine with Frank Johnson (lots of jokes about how we are the loyalists now. Also he says that Lamont has been wining and dining with Heseltine!) and Mrs Woodrow Wyatt.*

Monday 20 June
Meet Graham Bright. I say that there is possibility of peace between warring factions on Europe if key figures are more involved. He says PM might rather agree with this. Will fix a meeting with him next week.

Tuesday 28 June
Meeting with PM, 3.40 in his room behind Speaker's chair. I congratulate him on rallying the party on Delors veto. He is clearly pleased. I say, however, it's all very brittle. Two flash points: Accession Bill and, most importantly, Euro budget.

On the powers of the Commission and powers of law court, he is much on our side. He seems a genuine convert. Talk of there having been an excess of 'Eurocrap' at the Corfu IGC. I think he has enjoyed the adulation of the party and did not like the bitterness of the IGC. There is everything to play for. I then chair a very bullish meeting of Fresh Start.

Chat to Bill Cash on the Terrace. He still wants to get rid of Major, even if it means Heseltine.

Thursday 14 July
ERG meets Hurd. Several points arise from a presentation by me of our proposed paper for Oxford:

---

* Lord Wyatt of Weeford, journalist and chairman of the Tote.

1. Hurd doesn't like the proposals, especially for 'variable geometry'.
2. He is unwilling to see change in the role of the Commission.
3. He argues that the 1996 IGC would go on for some time, particularly post our general election.
4. He rests his case for the multi-speed Europe on the opt-out.

He asks us whether we are in favour of free trade or Mr Goldsmith's protectionism. I say, unashamedly, free trade. In general he is rather shaken (a) by the specifics of our programme (generalities were OK but not specifics) and (b) by the contact system we are building up in Europe. The view of the group after he leaves is that nothing will go right for us until he leaves the government.

Late that night I bump into the minister for Europe (David Heathcoat-Amory), an establishment figure building his reputation on being vaguely sceptical on Europe.* He says Major really doesn't like 'abroad'; he doesn't like the food or the weather or the people. He does like coming home and being cheered when he stands up to the EU on such matters as whether one federalist as against another federalist should be president of the Commission.

Friday 15 July
In Oxford with Dan Hannan to look over Brasenose, where we will hold the conference and to meet Sir Patrick Neill, warden of All Souls, who will welcome the conference to Oxford. (I will chair it.) A rather good idea for a novel/book emerged in my mind – What happens when the two legal systems clash?

1. Attempt to override Act of Accession
2. Taken to Euro court
3. Euro court rules against House of Lords = chaos
4. Two legal authorities
5. Civil war? – arrests made by each side.

Monday 18 July
Dinner in Strangers' with Annabel, Malcolm Rifkind and his daughter. Lovely father and daughter occasion. After dinner talk to Rifkind about Europe. Much to my astonishment he is against a single currency and

---

* David Heathcoat-Amory succeeded me as chairman of the ERG and became a highly effective opponent of a federal state of Europe.

highly supportive of NATO. However, believes EU fills the role of stopping Germany going nuclear.

Wednesday 20 July

Reshuffle day. No one who voted against Maastricht promoted. Maybe from Major's point of view it's the right thing to do – to punish or at least not to reward rebellion. But it means that more than fifty battle-hardened warriors now believe they have no life and hope under Major.

Monday 25 July

James Cran rings for a debrief chat before leaving for his hols. I have made two vain attempts to deal with the PM. At the end of the day his friends are Mellor, Garel-Jones, Atkins – and when we forget it we misunderstand him.

Wednesday 27 July

Hilarious evening re-forming the Severn Stoke branch. In addition to the Constituency chairman (David Finch), Ann, Susan Burlingham (agent) and myself, five people show up. Three have arrived (including 92-year-old lady whose birthday it is) by mistake. A man is chosen as chairman of the branch. A lady aged eighty asks why she has been thanked – agent had said she should be on the committee. Thus was the new branch formed, vigorously to bang the drums for the Conservative message and to take it into the future.

Friday 29 July

Arrive at a constituency function at Conderton Manor (the beautiful Cotswold stone home of Jane and William Carr)*. Meet a barrage of questions about an article by Boris Johnson in the *Spectator* in which Cran and I are in effect accused of selling out on Europe. Cash comes over as the big hero/leader whom we are meant to be letting down.

Must ring Johnson to point out three fallacies:

1. If there is any 'leader' – which there isn't – I have chaired all Fresh Start meetings.
2. Our position is not one of 'giving up' the European issue for fear of Blair but of trying to find ways of uniting party behind our view: Cash thinks the best way is just to snap at government's heels on everything that comes up.
3. Not true that we have stopped activities.

---

* William Carr's family once owned and sold to Rupert Murdoch the *News of the World*.

Wednesday 3 August
Much toing and froing on the phone from Cropthorne with Nick Wood, senior lobby correspondent of *The Times*. He wants to 'splash' the story about our Oxford conference – clearly short of copy at the moment. I am cautious. I don't want this all to take off in the wrong way – on the other hand have promised him an exclusive.

One way of interpreting Major at the moment is that he has traded off keeping the fifty Maastrichtites out of government in return for adopting our position.

Friday 26–Sunday 28 August
Stay with Gail and Peter Lilley at their home at Ablemand, in Normandy. Guests include Alan Howarth. Lilley very discreet but Howarth surprisingly frank about Major, who he thinks is ghastly. [Soon after this Alan Howarth deserts Conservatives for Labour. I had no inkling this would happen – always took Howarth as being on the right, certainly of Major.] General view, however, (including mine) is that Major will probably survive because the right has no clear candidate with whom to replace him. Over dinner on the Saturday in a local restaurant joined by Nigel Evans, PPS to David Hunt and a pleasant new MP (Ribble Valley), who seems to think along our lines.

Tuesday 13 September
Speak at lunch at American Enterprise Institute, organised by Irwin Stelzer. Andrew Neil, formerly editor of the *Sunday Times*, gives a response. It all goes down rather well. At dinner that night in the home of Irwin and Cita Stelzer guests are Richard Perle (formerly assistant Defence Secretary), Jeane Kirkpatrick (Reagan's ambassador to the UN) and Andrew Neil, who now has a sixty-minute talk show. Conversation mocks Clinton's 'invasion' of Haiti. Jeane says, 'You should never invade somewhere you have not visited.' Weakness of British government faced by Blair. I say Major should have gone out of his way to unify the party after Maastricht – instead of punishing the rebels.

Friday 16 September
Travel to Brasenose College, Oxford. Various members of centre-right parties from fifteen countries gathered. Michael Howard and Patrick Neill speak at dinner in Hall. Michael general but supportive. Patrick very interesting about the European Court.

Saturday 17 September
I chair the conference. A good deal of agreement about single currency, the

law court and the Commission, but big argument looming with French about free trade. We may just have to bypass this. Agree to meet again in Paris on 9–10 December with British (i.e. me) organisation.

Monday 19 September
Nick Wood's piece in *The Times* just right. At last we are being treated with some gravitas. Low-key approach seems to be paying off.

Politics are in a state of suspense. Nothing much is happening. Liberals making idiots of themselves at their conference. Everyone waits to see how Blair and Major perform at their party conferences.

Tuesday 11 October
Party conference in Bournemouth.

End up at private do given by Alexander Hesketh (a kindred spirit) who has taken over from McAlpine and Archer as the entertainer; so I am half back in vogue again. (George Jones of the *Telegraph* kindly points this out.)

Wednesday 12 October
Bump into Boris Johnson of the *Sunday Telegraph*, who says, despite his recent attack on me for 'compromising with Major', he at least would like to hear my side of the story.

Portillo makes an outspoken speech, which is well received by the conference, but I have a feeling he is looking too factionalist for his own good with MPs. Aitken nowhere to be seen.

Friday 14 October
Watch Major on telly from the safety of Cropthorne, to which returned on Thursday. He really is very weak and tinny. The reception is not ecstatic – just polite – very unusual for a party conference. One wonders if he believes in anything. Aitken still nowhere to be seen – in fact uniquely so. Presumably he's doing his public expenditure round (as Chief Secretary) but one would have thought he could have put in a brief appearance on the platform; he's doing the 'low profile' to a fault.

Monday 17 October
Finally back to London by train. Two women sitting in next seats chatting – surrounded by rucksacks, possibly back from a course with SAS at Hereford as the conversation indicates they are service people. Pretty Asian girl tells of the days when she was duty clerk at MoD. What she dreaded was Alan Clark arriving at the weekend to collect his red boxes. Other ministers sent their

drivers. Alan came himself. One weekend he came when she was in the bath. He rang duty clerk's flat. She said wait at front door. 'I didn't want him up to the flat because he would never go and I wasn't properly dressed. When I arrived at the front door Clark had gone and was lost in MoD building; reception people said they couldn't stop him. Then he kept ringing up from different parts of the building – swearing and asking where was I. I said don't come to the flat, go to your office, whose whereabouts he didn't seem to know. At last I met him there.' Girls were travelling first class.

Wednesday 19 October

An unusually tetchy and rather unpleasant meeting with Richard Ryder. He starts by saying in effect that he doesn't want any more nonsense from the Fresh Start people over the Euro budget Bill. I say he hasn't helped himself by turning everyone into pariahs at the reshuffle. He almost has an apoplexy at this and starts to raise his voice, in effect accusing me of breaking up the party. I say that I happen to agree with him that the Euro budget should be let through. He calms down and we agree to meet again – though afterwards I begin to develop reservations about doing so. He has revealed his hand as being pretty hostile to us. The question is whether there is anything to be gained by the cause from keeping lines open to him. We are civil to each other in the loo during a vote and are currently due to meet again next Thursday.

Good meeting of ERG – present: Rumbold, Bonsor, Cran, Gill, Malcolm Pearson. Agree to ask Marion Roe and Archie Hamilton to join us.

Dinner with Bonsor and our ambassador to Ukraine in the Churchill room. Ukraine at last struggling to become a democracy – handing back its nuclear weapons to Russia.

Bridge with Mates, Baker and Witney. I partner Baker and make £10!

Monday 24 October

Bump into Lamont in members' lobby, 5.30 p.m. Over a cup of tea in the smoking room tells me he still thinks Major is on the skids. He wants to join the Fresh Start Group.

Tuesday 25 October

3.30: Major announces that Hamilton has been sacked.

4.15: Meeting of Foreign Affairs committee. Present: Jenkin, Duncan Smith, Gardiner, Cash and me. Speaker David Davis – who admits under cross-questioning that all flowers may bloom on the way to the intergovernmental conference in 1996.

5.30: Fresh Start meeting. Attempt led by Cash, Duncan Smith and Jenkin to oust me from the chair. Undercurrent of resentment about my other group (ERG) but majority desire to leave things where they are. I will stay for the time being. Chat to Cash and Teresa Gorman afterwards. Temporary truce has broken out.

8.30: Dinner with Richard Ryder in Strangers' dining room. Try to impress upon him that (1) we have the majority, (2) I hope that David Davis's 'let all flowers bloom' means what it says because there are some very significant flowers we will wish to cultivate, (3) we will invite PM to our next ERG meeting.

Thursday 27 October

Prime Minister comes to the table I was sitting at in tea room. Clearly feels he has come off well in a row with Blair. Everyone round the table goes very wooden. PM moves off after a bit. Before he does so he says, 'I will not accept open procedure on the privileges committee. I will let it start without Labour.' (Labour members have withdrawn until it is open to TV etc.) I wonder whether this will be another example of Major's firmness in the face of future climbdowns. Everyone is getting pretty fed up with the way he treats – or gets Ryder to treat – Hamilton.

Thursday 3 November

Chair Association of Independent Electricity Producers AGM. Theme of my speech: progress towards a competitive electricity market. Very good mood at the meeting. Charles Wardle, junior minister at Energy, the government speaker. At lunch he gives me an earful against Michael Howard, under whom he has served at the Home Office.

Friday 4 November

Write the following letter to Michael Heseltine about his failed attempt to privatise the Post Office.

> Dear Michael
>   It is tragic that you did not win on the Post Office both because of the intrinsic merit of your case (though I would have done Post Office Counters as well) and because of the loss of identity which the party now suffers.
>   If only we were closer on Europe…
>   Yours,
>   Michael

Monday 7 November
Rush back from the Haven Hotel, Poole, where we have spent an idyllic weekend with Ma. Lunch at the Auberge de Provence with Michael Howard, booked under the name of Mr Barnes. Talk about Charles Wardle, who seems to be out to get Howard. Re Michael Portillo, Howard tells of a meeting he had with Toby Aldington,* who said leaders were never chosen from people whom one section of the party particularly did not want, Thatcher the exception. At the time her potential enemies were dozing. Howard says he is still in the game and hopes the Criminal Justice Act will in the end stand him in good stead. We are becoming closer politically. I suggest that if Portillo was leader – even though I might vote for him – we would both be swept away. On reflection Howard would survive as he is part of the furniture.

The Euro budget

Friday 11 November 1994
A good annual meeting of supper club in Wychavon Hall in Pershore. Commit myself to vote with government on Euro budget. Audible sigh of relief around the hall, which is full of my supporters whom I may still have to call on in the event of a challenge to me at the next election.

Sunday 13 November
Remembrance Sunday. Lay wreath at Pershore Abbey. Sunday newspapers full of the impending revolt on the Euro budget. Michael Howard rings at about 6.30 to ask whether a second chamber for European Parliament 'would help'. I say no – the idea is to reduce the power of the European Parliament, not make it more respectable.

7 p.m. Robert Cranborne rings. Wants to meet next week. Indicates that government is going to make a vote of confidence of the first vote on the Euro budget. A major rebellion would not look good for the government. It might even put Major's position under pressure.

Tuesday 15 November
Richard Ryder rings to confirm government is planning to make the Euro budget vote a vote of confidence. I say I do not want to comment on the phone and will come in to see him at Number 12 at 5 p.m.

---

* Toby Low, 1st Baron Aldington.

When we meet I confirm I do not plan to vote against the Bill. Ryder says he probably will not stand again after the next election. Will not say whether there will be a withdrawal of the whip from those who do not vote with government. I say that the government is in peril because some ten may still vote against in vote of confidence. I cannot help much if there is nothing on offer. We agree to keep in touch. PM will say in his speech tomorrow that votes will be votes of confidence. All very big stuff.

Ryder feels referendum on single currency may have to come. Also accepts Maastricht was more important than government conceded at the time.

I ask why hype up the vote so much. He says government credibility on the line having signed the agreement. I say it's because we have a left-wing government which threw out the Post Office privatisation. He says it wasn't like that. Heseltine said he could sell it 'to his friends' but failed. I say it was Major's strategic mistake to fall out with right wing. I tried for several years to make peace but overtures shunned.

In some ways my life will be easier with the vote being made one of confidence. I am less involved. But government is in peril.

Friday 18 November
Tony Marlow rings suggesting we should put up Bonsor against Fox for the chairmanship of the 1922 Committee. I agree to talk to George Gardiner about this.

Wednesday 23 November
Last day of Queen's Speech debate. Interesting conversations.

Ken Baker: 'Why don't government do a deal with you?' 'Because they can't. We could come up with something; but they are so disorganised that they cannot offer anything.'

Dykes/Madel in the smoking room. They will not vote for Bonsor despite his 'one nation' credentials or sound policy, because of his views on Europe. Europe is *the* faultline. Peter Temple-Morris has lost his troops.

Ted Heath especially morose in the lobby. I say, 'Cheer up, Ted. I fear you're wining in Europe'. 'At a ghastly price,' he says. 'What do you mean?' 'Industry is fed up.' 'You mean big industry. They are always wrong. Look at the 1930s.' 'Rubbish,' he says, 'that was Montagu Norman.' 'All the same thing,' I say, 'distorting the exchange rates.' 'Thatcher did that by keeping the pound up above its proper level.' 'What's that?' I ask. 'Proper level,' he grunts. Then sees Major and scowls. He allows Major to go through the voting doors before him and glares at him. Not a word is passed between the PM and former PM. They obviously don't like each other. That's a good sign.

Thursday 24 November

Dinner with Nick Bonsor in the Harcourt room after he was narrowly defeated for chairmanship of the 1922 Committee. Also (Archie) Hamiltons. Conversation light and about Europe. Archie – who has joined the ERG – says we must impress the importance of stopping monetary union when we meet PM.

Saturday 26 November

Talk on phone to Cran and Gill. The latter is going over the top on Monday. Apparently he had an hour with the PM last week and came out even more distrustful of him. Gill also says someone has been approaching him about a leadership challenge.

Sunday 27 November

Talk to 'Biffo' and Tapsell, Cran, Lawrence. They all agree that the Fresh Start meeting billed for Monday has been hijacked by Leigh apparently to further his plan to unseat Major. His main object seems to be to persuade people not to go over the top on the Euro budget Bill and thus be removed from the whip, whereby they could not vote against Major. Newspaper reports that Leigh has the necessary thirty-four with which to challenge Major. We shall know on Wednesday.

Return to London and to the office to sign letters late at night. Call from Teresa Gorman to say others want the Fresh Start meeting to go ahead in my absence. I think I have been consistent throughout in my aims: to try to stop Maastricht and now to rally the Conservative Party behind radical changes for 1996.

Monday 28 November

Leave home, after doing radio interview, to catch a bus to Waterloo – off to see Ma, who has been burgled in Milford-on-Sea for the seventh time.

Eight abstentions in the vote,* Bill Cash not one of them. See him in the smoking room – he is miserable, even contrite. Right to the last his line has been that it's the vote that counts and he didn't come up with it.

Richard Ryder rings in the afternoon. We agree to meet late in the week to see how we could sort things out. I say what matters now is the government's commitment to an anti-federalist stance. Say same thing to Jeremy Hanley

---

* The European Community (Finance) Bill raised Britain's contribution to the community's budget. The vote was turned into a 'vote of confidence' which the government won by twenty-seven votes. The eight Conservative MPs who abstained lost the whip.

(chairman of party) at Alistair McAlpine's annual party at Intercontinental. He says, 'You, Michael are the key pivotal point.'

I say, 'I enjoyed your party conference speech. If you mean we are all anti-federalist we can do business.'

Thatcher there. Sit with her for a while filling her in. 'What can we do to stop Major taking away the whip?' she asks. 'Nothing,' I say. 'They decided on it ages ago. We will have to find a way of picking up the pieces on our terms.'

The Independent characterises the Conservative Eurosceptic movement in Parliament thus:

> A meeting last week of the Fresh Start group of Eurosceptics illustrates how far the potential rebels are from being a monolithic group.
>
> Indeed, there are broadly three sections: the head-bangers, as they are known, even by some of their fellow right-wingers, bent on opposing virtually any piece of legislation connected with Europe. There is a group in the middle which has been unsure how to vote tonight. And there is a group, almost certainly the largest, which includes Michael Spicer and James Cran, probably the most thoughtful and tactically astute of the Maastricht rebels, who have consistently argued that the 1996 Intergovernmental Conference is a vastly more important issue and that it has never made any sense to go over the top on the European Finance Bill, irritant though it may be. This group was always going to support the government.

Monday 5 December
Meet Chief Whip, 5.15, in his room. The head of his office is on the phone saying, 'The Treasury do not have contingency money if we lose the vote on VAT in tomorrow's Budget vote.' (Some de-whipped rebels are threatening to vote against the government.)

Ryder reads me out the kinds of position which HMG thinking of adopting at the IGC. Most of it not very exciting or – in so far as it makes the EU work better – not very acceptable. Wider expansion to the east – OK but no mention of its effect on CAP. Rest of it is of the type which says 'stamp out fraud'.

One point does make me prick up my ears – 'Protect/change the role of national parliaments'. What I think this means is make Commission report to national parliaments. But it may prove a good rallying point, especially as our information is that the Germans (not Kohl) like it and so do the French.

Tuesday 6 December
Government loses VAT vote. Labour in uproar. Bump into Michael

Heseltine. 'All that's missing is your picking up the mace,' I say. 'I was thinking the same thing myself,' he replies.

Friday 9–Saturday 10 December 1994
Travel to Paris by air with Cran, Lawrence, Bonsor, Pearson. Chair meetings of ERG in the National Assembly. Despite reservations of Peter Rosenbaum from Germany, manage to secure agreement for some pretty radical conclusion, as outlined in the ERG pamphlet published at the Oxford conference.* Camera team from *Newsnight* interview Bonsor, Lawrence and me in a café on Saturday morning. They try to confuse the European issue with general restlessness in the Conservative Party. Indeed, press interest focuses more exclusively than ever on our rows.

Monday 12 December
Patrons' Club lunch in House addressed by party chairman, Jeremy Hanley, who says, in effect, Michael Spicer is not too bad a chap and you should back him. I say to Hanley that he's not too bad a chap but he must treat with the rebels, otherwise we could lose a general election in the new year.

The lunch guests go up and hear PM say words to the effect that 'single currency will not come about before the end of the century'. He says 'the economic circumstances will not be right' by then.

I ask, 'How does this square with the fact that the Treaty of Rome amended at Maastricht means it *must* come about by 1 January 1999?'

He says that suits some but not us. We are being dragged to a federal state with mirrors.

Wednesday 14 December
Chair meeting of Fresh Start (eighteen present). Main discussion – whether to let in the whipless. Agreement to come back to the issue in January. Bump into Michael Howard at the bar of the House. Tell him he has been party to a terrible blunder in forcing the whip off the rebels. They will make their demands as to how they could come back. Next flashpoint might be vote on committee memberships in view of the fact that government has lost its majority. He looks

---

* *A Europe of Nations: Conclusions of the European Research Group*, with a Foreword by John Major and Introduction by Michael Spicer. The most significant concept produced in this was that of 'variable geometry', which in effect allowed different countries to centralise on Brussels at their own pace: 'Consent and flexibility must underpin European integration, with different groups of states able to co-operate in different areas of policy within the nexus of a free market.'

a bit white and says we must meet next week. As if to confirm all this, Tony Marlow comes up to say he is feeling disorientated without a whip. MH says, 'You know how to get back.' 'Yes,' says Marlow, 'on our terms.'

Thursday 15 December

Meeting at FCO with David Davis, minister responsible for Europe. Read list of 'demands' from Paris and say we are meeting PM on 18 January. 'Just in time,' he says, 'because positions will start to be finalised in February for submission to the review committee, which is going to be a highly political operation.'

Tuesday 20 December

The PM has announced in the *Financial Times* that the rebels will stay out of the party whip for months rather than days. From my point of view this is bad in that I am associated with the rebels and it confuses the arguments in Europe with rebellion against Major. Much worse is the effect on the party. This guarantees rifts for months. I cannot see any rationale behind this unless (a) Major does not really care about the party, (b) he is secretly in favour of a federal state of Europe, (c) he judges that by approaching the rebels now he would not get them back at the moment – and therefore he plans to 'freeze' them back in.

Wednesday 21 December

Tony Marlow on to me. There is still scope for a 'truce', but not if the rebellion is left to fester; could get worse; could feed on itself. No demands for a return to the whip will be made at this stage but they may be later. Talk on the phone to Ryder, who says the government's position is clear: the rebels must earn their way back. 'But', I say, 'this is not how they see it; if they don't come back so be it – but don't count on their support.' Things could get worse, e.g. the vote on committee structures on 10 January. Tragedies happen often not by design but by default. This could be one of them.

Talk to Tony Newton, leader of the House. He asks what will be the first flashpoint. I say the vote on committees on 10 January. He merely takes note of what I say. Michael Howard completely agrees with my analysis but says he is unlikely to see PM before Christmas. The plan apparently is to assume there will be no tricky votes in the next few months and then to announce everybody has been good and to have them back.

Thursday 22 December

Ring Marlow to say 'No deal'. Meanwhile Major bangs on about the need for unity.

Thursday 29 December
Major writes a letter to constituency chairmen extolling the virtues of unity. Europe is the problem. We must all shut up about this. What can be his motive for stirring things up in the name of unity? Answer: to use disunity as an excuse for the inadequacies of his administration. He wants the Euro rebels as the scapegoats. It suits him to keep the whole issue boiling.

Friday 30 December
Give lunch at Dormy House to my chairman to be, Richard Williams. Tries out the argument that an open selection would be 'good for me'; would establish my position. I disabuse him of this: 'It would be divisive beyond belief. I would not forgive those who allowed it.' Also says Susan Burlingham has heard there would need to be unanimous vote to prevent reselection. I say this is unimaginable. Would mean reselection in every constituency in the land. I suspect someone at area office is up to mischief. I have asked to see this advice in writing.

My impression is growing that I will 'lose' at Finance and General Purposes Committee level and will have to make a stand at 'executive' level; I need to work up my friends on this.

Wednesday 11 January 1995
Wander into members' dining room to find PM sitting on the large table over on the left almost alone with his PPS, John Ward and Michael Howard. Rather reluctantly I go over to sit with him; it would be discourteous to have done otherwise – the dining room is pretty empty. 'Is this going to embarrass you?' I ask.

He laughs. 'Not at all.'

We are joined by Paul Marland, Jill Knight and Hector Monroe. Conversation rather stilted and mainly about Christmas holidays and the disastrous MCC effort in Australia.

At one point Tony Marlow comes up behind the PM and me (sitting next to each other). Marlow says something to the effect that 'our letters will be published in tomorrow's *Daily Telegraph*'.

PM says, 'Don't forget who the real enemy is, Tony. I have cleared the air on Europe in my Sunday broadcast.' Major made some Eurosceptical noises on *The Frost Programme*, saying 'Thus far and no further in Europe'. Tony Marlow says, 'One swallow doesn't make a summer.' PM: 'I'm going to do it again.' I say to Paul Marland on my left, 'The point is that what is going on in Europe will need reversing; it's not good enough to stop any more federalising.' Tony Marlow gives a rather cynical look as he leaves PM.

Later I spend half an hour with John Ward, preparing for Wednesday's lunch with PM. I do my speech about 'He mustn't think we are against him – unlike the left, we don't have another candidate'. But he must do something about his Cabinet when Hurd goes, to reverse the pro-federalist weighting (Clarke, Hurd, Heseltine) – e.g. put Howard in FCO. Also he must take the initiative to reverse the trends towards a federalist Europe at the IGC. Ward agrees that although his rhetoric is on the right track he still has friends – such as Garel-Jones – advising the opposite. Ward sees it as his job to be an antidote for this. Going through the lobby bump into (a) Michael Howard ('We must meet'; he wants to be Foreign Secretary) and (b) Portillo, who agrees we must reverse things at IGC but French/Germans may go bolshie after Major's statement.

Wednesday 18 January
PM visits ERG at Wassall [an investment company in Victoria Street]. I open by saying who we are – stressing the Euro dimension of our activities and saying we need to reverse present momentum – ringfence parliamentary rights, reform Commission and law courts and avoid monetary union.

PM, prompted by Cran, gives a forthright attack on single currency. I ask, 'Why don't you make those views public?' He says, 'I might.' Townend asks, 'What about your Cabinet colleagues – are they with you?' 'They will be.' I ask, 'Will you write the foreword to our pamphlet?' He says, 'Yes.' (That means we should be able to get 200 names on it.)

When I am taking him down to his car in the lift I say, 'The real issue is whether you will stick to this policy.' (Ivan Lawrence has made the same point publicly.) Major says, 'Yes. It is just a question of how I do it; I have to worry about the big beasts in the jungle.' 'Do you mean Clarke and Hurd?' 'Yes.' 'But you're in charge.' He smiles wanly.

Thursday 19 January
I bump into Richard Ryder in the lobby. He says, 'PM was very enthusiastic about your meeting.' Ryder knows both about the PM's commitment to come again and to write a foreword to *A Europe of Nations* after he has made his big speech. Ryder says he is really pleased about this: 'You should press the PM for a date for the next meeting. Also I want to have another dinner with you; there is so much to discuss.'

---

* *A Europe of Nations: Conclusions of the European Research Group*, published by the ERG in 1995, arose out of the meeting at Brasenose College, Oxford on 16–17 September 1994. Some twenty European countries were represented.

Monday 23 January
Meeting of Fresh Start in Room J. Norman Lamont present for the first time.
Bill Cash clearly knows about our meeting with the PM and pushes me to
say what happened.

Thursday 26 January
Drinks party for Geoffrey Tucker's seventieth birthday at Brooks's club. Ted
Heath there looking very rotund. He does his usual 'I don't know what has
happened to you' bit – so I remind him that I had joined his cause when he
was a free-market anti-corporatist fighting Maudling. He says, 'I still am.
That's what Europe is all about.'

I say, 'No, it's not. It's a protectionist racket.'

All this is done, supposedly, with some good humour on each side – to the
extent that I push my luck and ask him whether he thinks policy on Europe
is going rather well at the moment (I want to find out how much he knows
of developments in Major's mind). He grunts and moves off and I have my
answer. This is confirmed in a ride back home with Michael Portillo, who
says the Cabinet meeting was a rout of the Hurdites (reported in *The Times*
the next day). The problem is that the government is still thinking of vetoing
any change rather than rolling the carpet back as we want.

Tuesday 31 January
Everyone is becoming a Eurosceptic now – at least while Major toys with
it. Malcolm Rifkind has made a speech supporting the nation state. Charles
Wardle comes up to me in the lobby and expresses the view that Major should
stand firm. Wardle is a great friend of Clarke. I say, 'Well, it would help
if Clarke suggested this. 'Clarke is much maligned,' says Wardle. I raise an
eyebrow. He says, 'For instance, he was not behind the decision to remove the
whip from the nine.' 'What about the single currency? He is publicly pretty
firm on that.' 'It's all a question of timing.' 'It's a matter of principle,' I say.

At dinner in members' dining room, Edwina Currie says surely we can
get together. 'I believe', she says, 'in free trade and in abolishing the CAP'
– whatever next? (Edwina and I are old TV sparring partners on EU.) Then
off to the smoking room, where Bernard Jenkin, Iain Duncan Smith and
Nick Bonsor joined by Portillo. Re Wardle's defence of Clarke, Portillo says,
'Clarke and Major divided the Cabinet between them when they interviewed
each member to ask his views about the whip.' It is a travesty to say Clarke
was not involved.

Brief chat with Michael Howard. He seems to believe there are a limited
number of items which could be pressed for in 1996 and 'delivered', e.g.

greater strength for the Council of Ministers re the law court. Iain Duncan Smith says the law court is now working *sui generis*.

Wednesday 1 February

Dinner with Richard Ryder in Strangers' dining room. I arrive early and tell the waitress who is joining me. She says, 'Good, it's Sexy Legs!' Richard is cheered up when he hears this. It has been a difficult day for him (possible revolts on Rate Support Grant e.g. Alan Howarth).

Inevitably the subject moves to Europe. Ryder says 'the other side' are coming out with a pamphlet (apparently they are split on the single currency issue). He also says that there is no intention of returning the whip to the whipless until they start voting with the government. I say in that case the PM's speech on Europe is going to be crucial. Ryder then says there will be a vote on the progress of Maastricht. He promises to show me the motion. This sounds like another flashpoint. Ryder confirms he is leaving after next election.

Later in the evening PM approaches me to apologise for not having signed the foreword for *Europe of Nations*. He says he would like to look at the text first; I say he has one but we will have another in his office the next day. I ask him when the speech is coming. He says it is almost written but they have not yet found a platform for it.

Tuesday 14 February

Lunch with ERG at Wassall. Meeting first to discuss PM's new reservations (which I gleaned on Friday from a phone conversation with his private office). We decide that I will see him (as invited by him); if he refuses to sign the foreword I will ask him to meet the whole group.

Lunch with David Davis, minister for Europe, and an apparent sceptic but in reality a hard-nosed career politician (as a former whip he was very tough on the sceptics). He says that he will do his best 'to stop the rot'. We say, 'You've got to turn the clock back – especially re the law courts.' I think he is a bit surprised by the toughness of our position.

4.50: See PM in his office behind the Speaker's chair. He has had quite a good run at PM's Questions except for an apparently helpful question from Michael Brown: 'Is it true that under his premiership we would not join the single currency and under Blair we would?' Major says something like 'Rhubarb'. He says to me, 'I have told my warring government – who are now the real problem (not the party) – to shut up.' I say that there is a vacuum of leadership à la Balfour period. 'We don't expect a final position but we do need a point of view – then the dissidents can be told to shut up.'

We discuss the foreword to the ERG Oxford pamphlet. He clearly does not want to sign. 'What about a question to me in the House and I will give a friendly answer?' I politely duck this! I suggest that the real problem of the 'other side' in the party is not the federalist debate but that they are worried that we are anti-European. This pamphlet is a European project – Britain not mentioned once – and signed by seventy or so European MPs. That is the point to play on. He says that is an excellent idea and he will go ahead by Monday. In relief I ask whether it would be against his wishes to get others in the parliamentary party to 'sign up'. He says, 'Yes, it would prompt a counter-action.' I agree not to do it.

We part on the best of terms. He says at one point that he 'would want' a referendum before going into a single currency.

I see Richard Ryder at about 10.45 on my way home to suggest he delay Euro vote on Maastricht until after pamphlet published. Would help Euro rebels come along. He agrees.

Walk home with Chris Gill. He is enjoying himself and shows no signs of coming back – may even be his intention to stand as an independent.

Monday 20 February

The foreword arrives from PM. Dan Hannan goes to collect it; it's perfect. See PM's PPS in the lobby. 'My God, there's been a lot of nail-biting about this one.' I agree to clear a line about it with Number 10. It's lucky for us the PM's mind is on Ireland this week. The document is due to be published on Wednesday.

Peter Temple-Morris comes up to me in the lobby to say he is very worried that they are getting marginalised now.

Go down for lunch with Ma at Lymington Club as I do every month now. Good gossip. Tell her that part of the fun of all this is that I want nothing from Major – nor will he give me anything.* (He will never really forget Maastricht.)

Tuesday 21 February

Dinner at Maunsel Street. Present: Conrad Black, Michael Howard, Michael Portillo, Robert Cranborne and me. Except for me and Cranborne no one knows that there was to be a vote on Maastricht on Monday – so much for Cabinet trust.

Portillo only one who does not seem surprised when I show them PM's foreword to *A Europe of Nations*. He says Bonsor was keeping him in the picture.

---

* I was wrong about this; he 'gave' me a knighthood in 1996.

Monday 27 February

7.30 a.m. At BBC to do *Today*, then round of various TV studios. Story of *Europe of Nations* – excitement at Major's foreword – knocked off front page by collapse of Barings Bank. Speak to about sixty people at the Faculty of Politics, Reading University. Professor Chris Davies (with whom I was at Emmanuel College) in the audience.

10.15 p.m. Up to *Newsnight* to discuss future of the European Court.

Tuesday 28 February

Fresh Start decides I should see the Chief Whip to try to get PM to say 'no single currency without referendum' on Wednesday. See him after dinner in Churchill room with David Porter.* I assume he already has enough votes for Wednesday and say, Let's talk about it in terms of helping the party to settle down in the medium term.' He agrees we should talk further and that PM very close to saying what we want to hear.

Wednesday 1 March

After PM's speech David Davis comes up to me in excitement, hoping I will share his optimism. Trouble is the PM never gives any idea where he stands on the matter of principle, i.e. its political effect. This is what irritates a very dyspeptic Lamont, who jumps up and down all day in the chamber and finally votes with Labour, having had a put-down from Hurd in the wind-up.

Friday 3 March

Matthew Parris in *The Times* says Major has restored the ancient British art of making a virtue out of indecision or 'wait and see'.

Saturday 4–Monday 6 March

In Durham for Annabel's twenty-first. Fifty students to champagne and shepherd's pie. Wonderful people. Sunday evening chapel at Hatfield College, preacher Bishop of Durham.

Tuesday 7 March

Chair a meeting of Fresh Start. Present: Lamont, Cash, Tapsell, Biffen, Jenkin, Duncan Smith, Carlisle. Almost open insurrection against Major. Not whether he has to go but when and what we extract in the process. His policy of playing one side of the party against the other is not working. (We are now 40 points behind in the polls). My speech at York, made on the way

---

* Chief executive of Association of Electricity Producers, of which I am President.

down from Durham yesterday, quite well reported in *Times* and *Telegraph*. Lunch at Garrick with Robin Day and Judge Stephen Tumim, chief inspector of prisons.

After 10 o'clock vote: briefly talk to Neil Hamilton, Iain Duncan Smith, Bernard Jenkin. Relieved to hear that No Turning Back apparently no longer backing Heseltine.

Tuesday 14 March

Richard Ryder comes up to me in the members' lobby. Says there is a vote coming up on CAP. Clearly he is worried about it. I say there is nothing much I can do to help – real problem is that the government cannot make its mind up on Europe. He says, 'Neither side must be allowed to win.' That is a recipe for disaster. It means the absurd balancing act between Clarke/Hurd/Heseltine and the rest of the party will be allowed to go on. He stresses rebels can only come back if they behave themselves consistently over a period of time. It appears he doesn't want them back.

Dinner with Cran and Gill. Talk about the future of the rebels. I say the position is like this in my view: PM/Chief Whip are worried about a leadership challenge. Do not therefore really want the rebels (extra voters against Major) back but must not be seen in this mode. Rebels don't want to be seen to surrender – all the makings of a tragedy ending with the rebels leaving the party. I suggest rebels may up their threats at next opportunity, including voting against HMG on a confidence vote, and then do a deal which involves their return. Trouble is some of them are enjoying themselves too much.

Friday 17 March

Drive to Malvern from London for association lunch with Patrick Mayhew. Given our different views on Europe, obvious coolness between us. No reaction when he extols the virtues of the PM. People just look at the floor – very unusual for party workers.

Sunday 19 March

Peter Morrison rings to say he has been to see the PM to suggest he resigns. Peter says PM has wholly lost the respect of the party and Aitken should replace him. I do not think either will be easy to effect. Peter out of things now – he was Margaret Thatcher's last, and some say disastrous, PPS.

Tuesday 21 March

Do *Live at Westminster* attacking CAP but saying why I will vote with the government. Tebbit (who successfully addressed a mass rally in Yeovil last night) puts his head round the door of Room J, where Fresh Start always meets on Tuesday afternoons. About twenty-four present including Lamont and Tapsell – half of them only come to disrupt Major's life/existence. Agree to send Tapsell off to see Major to tell him it is between his future and the party's and the country's and his determination not to quarrel with Clarke/Heseltine. Tapsell thought a good emissary because he is a friend of Heseltine. After meeting, Bill Cash and I brief him a bit on detail. My job to see Ryder to get Tapsell an interview with PM. This I do – at 9.40 in Ryder's room.

Wednesday 22 March
Meet Cran after we have both done telly in Millbank (he on Northern Ireland, me on Clarke's speech about reducing taxes, with which I agree). Then on to a very friendly lunch with Paul Goodman of the *Sunday Telegraph*, with whom I once had dealings when he was a rebellious student and I was deputy chairman of the party.

Thursday 23 March
Charles Moore, editor of *Sunday Telegraph*, to lunch with ERG. I am suffering from food poisoning (as is Ann) following a dinner at the Speaker's House the night before. However, we get through. Main point of interest is the fear of Heseltine, which still lurks and inhibits all of us from seeking a change in the leadership.

Sunday 26 March
Charles Moore runs a very anti-Heseltine leader in *Sunday Telegraph*, perhaps prompted by my encouragement to this effect as I showed him down in the lift on Thursday. I am on a TV lunchtime show live from Cropthorne – making 'we must all rally round the cause' noises.

Monday 27 March
Brief chat in members' lobby with Cran. Gill apparently wants out of ERG because he needs cash to finance whipless operation. The tragedy proceeds. Between seven and nine of rebels now don't want to come back. Government thinks it doesn't want them – I suspect this is what I will find out from Ryder tomorrow (cf. Major's remark to me – 'It may be good for the party but is it good for me?'). If he brings them back they could be 7–9 votes against him. Meanwhile government's majority this evening thirteen. The government and the party could be destroying itself. Only possible solution:

Rebels to realise (a) they have no role outside other than as TV personalities – no role to influence party, (b) they are destroying themselves politically.

Government realises it is destroying itself and the party.

Eurosceptics are being undermined as being disruptive/associated with rebels. This must stop.

The government must be told that it must restore the whip unconditionally – except that acceptance of the whip would presume it would be obeyed. At present there is no pressure/reason for rebels to return.

Tuesday 28 March
Dinner in Strangers' with Ryder – overlooked by a very suspicious Bill Cash. Go through my views on the whipless – trouble is that Clarke refused to see them today (much to the apparent irritation of Ryder) so relations between them and the government are bad again. I still feel government mixed-minded about taking them back, which is silly and possibly disastrous.

Wednesday 29 March
Bump into Robin Day in the reading room at Garrick. He thinks Major will bow out in the autumn. I say, 'It doesn't sound very plausible.'

Tuesday 4 April
Lunch meeting of ERG at Wassall. I open by saying who we are and stressing the point that the move towards a federal Europe now has its own dynamic through the Court and Maastricht. To say 'thus far and no further' is not of itself good enough. We need (1) to realise the strength of the British position, (2) to have a clear objective and (3) to trade what we want (protection of sovereign right of Parliament) against what they want: closer federalism. Variable geometry (everyone doing their 'own thing') is the solution. Portillo almost says the 'game's up' – outflanking us but not really proposing to do anything about it. Lilley seems to agree with us, as does Aitken. It is a good airing of views but probably does not achieve much. Although we say we will try to meet the softer Cabinet members, e.g. Rifkind, Lang, Newton, Shephard.

Wednesday 5 April
Lunch with Michael Prescott and Andy Grice of *Sunday Times*. They seem reasonably well disposed. I agree to try to give them something in advance of the Brussels conference.

Tuesday 18 April
Dinner with Malcolm Pearson, Tim Melville-Ross (Director-General of the Institute of Directors) and Anne Robinson. Agree must do something

comprehensive about businessmen and single currency. Decide to try to work towards a conference, perhaps at Oxford. Pearson says Thatcher was in a terrible bate – initially stirred up by my son Edward. (Thatcher and Pearson staying with Archie Hamilton; they had all gone to dinner with Onslows. Edward had got into discussion with MT about Bosnia.)

Wednesday 19 April
Met Archie Hamilton in members' lobby. He confirmed that Thatcher had not been pleased with the discussion on Bosnia – but that Edward had withdrawn 'in time'. Some other young man had really taken the flak. It really is extraordinary that she should have bothered to engage with them at all.

Negotiating with the whipless

Thursday 20 April 1995
Strange day. Begins with my letter demanding the return of the whipless being printed in *The Times*:

> Sir,
> I am appalled that another Bank Holiday has gone by without there being a restoration of the whip to the nine Conservative whipless MPs. Their continued absence from the Conservative parliamentary party is a gift to those who wish to undermine the general unity and purpose of the mass of our party. Both the government and the whipless have a clear interest in the immediate resolution of this matter. The government needs the nine votes in the Commons; the whipless need to re-establish their influence within the mainstream of the Conservative Party and to avoid the danger that they and the cause they represent will be marginalised.
> It is crucial that there is now a closing of the ranks.
> Yours faithfully,
> Michael Spicer, House of Commons

Summoned to see the Chief Whip and PM in the PM's office at 4.00 p.m. PM says he does want them back – has changed his mind on this but does not want the embarrassment of (a) giving them any concessions, (b) having them chew over in public whether they will accept his offer. (I think RR has painted the whole thing as being more difficult than I hope it will be.) I say I agree with him and will offer my good services to get them to accept the situation as long as the offer is made without strings and to them collectively. PM agrees to this and says if I need to do so I can say am operating with his agreement – though he accepts that this has risks. He then says he thinks things are going better despite the impending disaster at the local elections. I agree and say could go even better if we were firm on Europe. He smiles wanly. Somehow he doesn't seem to make the connection between the two. We part on good terms with my accepting the assignment.

On to see Thatcher at 5.30 in her grand offices off the King's Road. She is all gung-ho about attacking the moves towards a federal Europe – very supportive of my evidence to the House of Lords until (a) Mark Thatcher rings, (b) I ask her to take part in a conference in Lisbon at which she would be the star. She says, 'I couldn't interfere with Portuguese election.' Mark rings and I leave the room to ring Dan Hannan, who had had a meeting some weeks before with Portuguese. He says new friends the Partido Popular would be happy to welcome Lady Thatcher even if it were after the election.

When I go back into the room, Thatcher seems to be totally distracted. I say, 'OK to do Lisbon after the election?'

She says, 'I can't do it anyway this year because I'm too busy, e.g. going to India, Japan and South Africa.'

I say that we would need to get Major's blessing so she need have no concern about upsetting Major or doing a Heath (earlier we had agreed there was no currently viable, credible alternative to Major). She says she doesn't want to make a speech about Europe at all this year. Then as I get up to leave she says, 'If I had my time again, I wouldn't go into politics because of what it does to your family.' When Denis comes in to check something with her, as usual he is very friendly to me; 'Liked your son' re last weekend. Then he says 'Do you want a drink?'

Lady Thatcher asks, 'What about me?'

Two PMs in one day and all I have done is write a letter to *The Times*!

Saturday 22 April

Talk on the phone to Tony Marlow. What does he think of my letter to *The Times*? He hasn't seen it. I summarise it. He says, 'That's not totally unhelpful but I am quite content with the way things are; one day we might come back – we will wait on events.' I ask, 'What if there were an offer from the government?' 'Are you acting for the government?' he replies. 'Let's put it this way: I believe strongly you should come back.' 'Do you think the government might make an offer?' 'I have a gut feeling they might.' 'It would need a firm offer made to us collectively.' 'Let me try.'

I repeat this conversation to Chief Whip. 'Can I have the authority to act for the government at a full meeting of the whipless?' Ryder says, 'I will check with the boss.' A few minutes later he comes back. 'The boss would prefer it if you could say to them you are acting for yourself but have a feeling the government will buy it.' I say, 'I don't think that will wash.' He says, 'Could you talk to PM direct?'

I do this. PM agrees I can go ahead on the basis I have suggested as long as the whipless will become team players if they come back.

Sunday 23 April

Ring Marlow to say it's all 'on' and that the government want to restore the whip to them: it's just a question of how to do it. He will go along with it if the offer comes. To varying degrees Gorman, Gill (rather hostile), Shepherd (also rather hostile) take same line. Teddy Taylor says he will act as go-between with HMG. I report this to Ryder who says he does not want this. During the day Ryder and I agree that an offer of the return of the whip will be sent out anyway. (Government's position is therefore hardening in favour of giving the whip.) Arrangements finally made with Taylor that he will convene meeting tomorrow in the House for 4.30. I will be available to go in at 5.00. Assume all is settled; whip would be restored immediately.

9.30 p.m. Nick Wood of *Times* rings. Has been tipped off that the whip is to be returned and to ring me. I say I cannot help. Ring Ryder, who is furious – will wreck tomorrow's press conference at CCO.

10.00 p.m. Major comes on the phone – 'only to be expected; but let's go ahead hoping for the best'.

10.05 p.m. Teddy Taylor, whom I had previously rung, says he has talked to everyone. Looks like a Budgen job. They have all been asked not to say anything more. We will see what the morning holds.

Monday 24 April

Further telephone calls to Richard Ryder. Agree that a letter restoring the whip will go out anyway by 6.00 p.m. Meeting of Euro rebels called for 4.30. Agree with Teddy Taylor that I should be available for 5.00 and go in at 5.15. Ask Dan Hannan to collect a mobile telephone from the Chief Whip's secretary, Shana. At 4.50 go in to see Ryder, who says he plans to send out the 'tough letter' to all. There are signs that they are playing up – making demands etc.

The two letters agreed are:

I am writing to confirm that as from today, the whip has been restored to you, and I am pleased to enclose this week's copy. (If you do not want to receive the whip in future, then you should let me have your formal resignation of it in writing.)

The bracketed sentence would be left out if all was well with everyone.

In the event I arrive at the meeting at 5.15. Asked to stay outside.

5.20: Christopher Gill comes out – takes me by the hand and says, 'We are going home, Michael.' I say, 'You must be joking'. When I arrive in the room, two (Budgen and Shepherd) have left by another door. Taylor, Gorman, Taylor's PA and John Wilkinson are left in the room. I say, 'You shits,' which prompts the return into the room of Shepherd, Gill and Budgen. I go on, 'We had an agreement to meet here.' They say, 'What's the point? There's nothing to discuss. The whip's going out anyway.' I say, 'I have talked this over with each of you. You have indicated that if the whip is given to you, you will accept it. We could have discussed the way it was done. I had assumed the meeting was to formalise that view.'

They say they want to think about things overnight and to respond the next day – thus giving the impression that the choice to return is theirs.

I go back to Ryder rather dejected. He immediately orders the tough letter to be sent out.

Later I see Budgen, who is friendly and says he hopes the letter has gone out straightaway. I say it has. (Budgen wants the whip back but did nothing to help.)

My view, I suppose, is that at the end of the day if I hadn't taken a grip on things, nothing would have happened. Each side was mesmerised by the other; the government was especially indecisive. I was over-optimistic about being able to do it cleanly.

I certainly felt the rebels were not doing much good outside; I'm not sure they will now do much good to our cause inside. They are individualists – for good or bad. I certainly don't think they will settle down in Fresh Start. I'm not even certain I should carry on as chairman of Fresh Start.

Just before 10 p.m. vote, ring home; PM wants me – contact him through Downing Street on his car phone. He is, understandably, concerned about a planned press conference by the rebels for tomorrow. I say, 'I'm afraid they are nothing if not unpredictable.' We are then cut off.

Tuesday 25 April

10 a.m. Appointment in Camberley with the dentist, where Ann rings me to say PM rang to thank me. Ann has had very friendly chat with Major! She says to him, 'At least Michael tried his best.' PM agreed and called the rebels mercurial. Apparently he was very charming to Ann.

I will write him the following letter.

My wife, Ann, enormously appreciated your very kind telephone conversation with her today. Whatever the difficulties, I'm sure you were right to lance the boil now.

Return to office in Dean's Yard at 12 noon, vote 12.30. News – all the whipless are back. I go on the *PM* programme. See Robin Oakley, now with BBC as chief correspondent – very apologetic that due to a technical fault they had had to drop reference to me yesterday. This was a weakness in the story. People in Parliament coming up to me to congratulate me; it's worked! At a dinner for the parliamentary energy group Dickson Mabon (Labour) congratulates me as one politician to another: 'Get all your colleagues' congratulations in writing. They will turn against you if things go wrong!' Even Bill Cash is pleasant. At Fresh Start meeting everyone welcomes back Teresa Gorman with a birthday cake supplied by Peter Tapsell. Lamont, Lawrence, Tapsell, urge us to see PM next week before local elections. I urge caution because will be leaked to press/seen as disruptive.

6 p.m. Budgen in smoking room in effect accepts that he leaked story to *Times* because he did not trust HMG to go ahead with it – having sworn he did not do it. Also present Christopher Gill – says he has 'a short memory' – i.e. from last night when I swore at him and others. I must say I would not go into a jungle with him. Budgen says Gill is sensible but politically stupid. I ask Budgen what he says about me. 'You were masterly yesterday – combination of suave elegance with bruising toughness.' I doubt if he meant it.

At 10 o'clock vote see Marlow, who has just returned from Europe. Am coming to really like him; he is effective in a way that is not publicly recognised. If ever I was in a position of power, I would use him. Wish he had been there yesterday. Still, it's all over and rather a success.

Major did not see it in quite the same light. In his autobiography,[*] he concluded the matter with the following:

Michael Spicer, the leader of the sceptics throughout the Maastricht rebellion, came as an intermediary to discuss the return of the whip ... Michael was persuasive. He supported the views of the whipless rebels, but spoke disparagingly of their behaviour ... Michael had held the sceptics together in opposition to the Maastricht Bill and it seemed likely he could hold them together in support of the government in the future. I gambled that he could ... I should have pressed for detailed promises of good behaviour, but had not done so

---

* John Major, *The Autobiography*, HarperCollins, 1999.

because I believed that ... they would both behave and be conciliatory. They did neither.

This gives the impression that I was acting on behalf of the whipless. The detailed diary notes very clearly show this to have been far from the case.

Wednesday 26 April

Meet Peter Tapsell and Bill Cash at 4 p.m. Bill very anti the former whipless – saying they are mixing with strange people outside. We consider (a) whether to go ahead with the much-publicised meeting with PM, (b) whether to invite back the whipless to Fresh Start. 'No' on first and 'Maybe' on second.

Talk to Ryder for one hour. Chew over how to honour PM's agreement to meet Fresh Start. He suggests announcing a June date at the meeting next Tuesday. We also discuss leadership and neutral role of Whips' Office. He thinks he may well have thirty-four names on his desk after the 4 May elections and we may be into a full-blown leadership election.

Tuesday 2 May

Chair a meeting of Fresh Start in Room J at 5 p.m. About twenty-five people there, including Marlow, Budgen and Gill from the former whipless. We discuss meeting with the PM, which he has offered in June, and a policy paper prepared by Iain Duncan Smith. Amongst other things this presents two tactical options for the IGC: (1) 'veto the entire discussion' until we get what we want; (2) present the ERG variable geometry policy and use the threat of a veto to get our way. Inevitably the blusterers, which is the majority of talkers, opt for (1) until I point out that we don't have the power to 'veto the discussion'. The blusterers are the least reliable when we actually take some collective action, e.g. in the closing debates of Maastricht.

Friday 5 May

Westminster Hall for VE celebrations with the Queen. Very moving service. Ann and Edward with me. After service go over for a buffet/cocktails at Queen Elizabeth II Conference Centre, opposite Westminster Abbey. Very hot day; masses of TV cameras everywhere looking for soundbites on our catastrophic defeat at local government polls the night before. Major enters the cocktail party. I see him on my way out and say, 'Stick with it.' I introduce him to Edward and Ann. He hugs Ann, saying, 'You were wonderful when I talked to you on the phone the other day. I shall always ring you for comfort in an hour of crisis.' He says to me, 'I am on the point of writing to thank you.' 'Please don't. It really isn't necessary,' I reply. The warmth between us is bizarre. Edward says afterwards, 'Don't get too close to him just as he collapses.' I say, 'That's what I always do to leaders.'

Newsnight are waiting for me on the steps outside. I tell them something sufficiently banal for it not to be used.

Tuesday 9 May
Take David Porter, chief executive of the Association of Electricity Producers and a good friend, to lunch at the Garrick. Meet Lamont and Peter Jay in the bar. Discuss the possibility of the president-elect of France, Jacques Chirac, doing a secret deal with the Germans. Meet Denis and Margaret Thatcher on the way out. They have been to a private lunch for Denis's eightieth birthday. He still looks amazingly spry. Also coming out Richard Ryder, with whom I get a lift back to the House.

Thursday 11 May
Breakfast at Connaught Hotel with Tom Arnold. He wants to move actively towards getting rid of Major. Sit trying to draft a letter to the PM at the central desk in the 'Aye' lobby. If one sits with one's back against the window one has a good view of all the passers by. One of these is Michael Heseltine, who has just announced extra 'liberalisation' measures for the not-to-be-privatised Post Office Services. I say to him, 'At least you haven't given them a carte blanche in the public sector.'

He stops and comes up to me. 'I'm furious to have been let down by our own side' – i.e. his own friends Dykes, Madel et al. Wonderful irony. Supper at Pratt's with Daniel Hannan.

Monday 15 May
Bump into Marcus Fox just after his return from a visit to the PM. He claims that he told the PM a reshuffle had to mean a new government, backed up by a new initiative on policy, not an exercise in musical chairs; this squares with the letter I send to PM today. Not many of us have much confidence he will do what is necessary.

Wednesday 17 May
Talk to David Heathcoat-Amory in the voting lobby. He makes the point that if we were to make demands à la our pamphlet, there would be demands 'on the other side'. I say, 'It might be that the European federalists would let the IGC go without asking for very much. That would certainly be the smart thing for them to do since they virtually have everything they want already.'

Tuesday 23 May

Dinner with Nick Bonsor. He is in a mood for 'busting up' the party if Heseltine takes over. 'I will refuse to co-operate and I will say so in advance.' He is strangely assertive about this.

Bump into Michael Howard in the division lobby; we go to his room for a drink. Agree that Major is in grave danger – certainly of being challenged in the autumn. Question is whether he will go on if he 'wins' but 80–100 abstain or vote against him. We both agree that there must be seen to be a new sense of direction. Michael and I debate the finer points of how we should negotiate in Europe, whether indeed the other countries will join in a negotiation, whether they will make demands for more federalisation, which we can trade against our demands for protection of the parliament. I am impressed by Michael Howard's grasp of the point, especially of the implications of variable geometry. I ask him whether he wants to be Foreign Secretary if Hurd goes. He says 'Yes'. I say I will try to bring pressure.

Wednesday 24 May

Put the idea of Howard as Foreign Secretary to a meeting of ERG which includes Townend, Gill, Archie Hamilton, Lennox-Boyd. They all rather like the idea.

Monday 29 May

Bank holiday. All the news full of the taking of British hostages in Bosnia and of Parliament being recalled – causes us a problem because we are meant to be going on holiday tomorrow to Spain, all having been paid for.

Michael Howard rings to say he has talked to PM, who intends to fight off any challenge. He does not think Hurd will go but if he does it's important not to be seen to be forcing Major's hand.

Fateful 'Fresh-Start' Meeting with PM

Tuesday 6 June 1995

Return by boat from holiday in Spain – straight up to the House of Commons for 10 p.m. vote. Nick Wood, political correspondent of *The Times*, looking for me, as are George Gardiner and Norman Lamont. Turns out that Wood is doing a piece for the next day's *Times* which reveals that Fresh Start is due to meet the PM next week and that this will be a face-to-face confrontation between the PM and Lamont. Lamont denies that he is responsible for the piece – he probably isn't and Nick Budgen probably is. It really doesn't matter. Some exposure for us is probably a good thing.

Wednesday 7

Fresh Start meeting. Some thirty-seven present – we have extended the membership. A bit of argy-bargy, especially from Peter Tapsell, about *The Times* article – also about how engineered should be the meeting with PM. My feeling (and that of John Biffen) is that by and large we should let it run – it will have a life of its own. Large and good-natured meeting – standing room only. I stress the point that there is no spokesman – we are all equals. This pleases them. The truth is I have now chaired every meeting (bar one) since we started in 1991. The next move may be to widen even further and take on board 100 or so MPs. Meet Graham Mather MEP for a drink. He tells me that there is a great split amongst British MEPs: federalists v. go-slows.

Dinner with Peter Oborne of the *Standard*.

Thursday 8 June

Edward McMillan-Scott (MEP and a constituent) comes to the Pugin room for tea. He has asked to see me. (I have a tape recording of a message he left with a Party official during the Maastricht crisis saying he would be happy to join in the political fight against me.) I let him know I know about his activities during Maastricht though I do not give him details. I say I do not bear grudges. He says that although we disagree on a lot of things, we can at least be friendly. I say 'Yes'. He personally is in favour of a single currency.

Later have a drink with Michael Dobbs. He is writing a new book and wants help with the character of an MP who plays tough with the whip in the interest of his constituency. I suggest a few names, e.g. Nick Winterton.

Tuesday 13 June

Chair lunch of ERG with Tony Newton and Ian Lang. Both very agreeable, invited along because they are soft centre of the Cabinet and Major confidants. Neither is apparently hostile, though Lang took the classic government line – 'Trust us'. Newton more thoughtful.

5 p.m. PM to Fresh Start in the large ministerial room under the chamber. I take the chair. PM late after a duffing up from Blair at Question Time: 'Thatcher says "No, no, no" – he says "Don't know, don't know, don't know"'. I take the chair, say there are sixty present – could have invited twice that number. Meet exclusively on Europe; think we are in tune with his thinking. He then does 25-minute speech – far too long; everyone begins to get edgy. This boils over in question time. Goes along quite nicely until Bernard Jenkin blasts out 'Rubbish' to something the PM says. Iain Duncan Smith interrupts him later and Bill Cash also shouts 'Wrong'. Speeches by Lawrence, Lamont

and Bonsor. They speak in terms of what is good for the PM. Afterwards Carlisle and Budgen rush out to the press and say PM was 'mauled'. I go up to his room to see whether we can agree a common line. He says the bovver boys will have got there first, and he is right.

I go on BBC TV and try to calm things down, but I am only one of many they interview.

Meet PM in voting lobby. He looks pretty depressed. I say, ' At least it wasn't a bland meeting.' 'You can say that again.' 'The TV coverage is not too bad.' 'The tapes are pretty awful.'

This is Anthony Seldon's take on the meeting.* It supplements mine. Both descriptions are, in my view, pretty accurate.

The final blow came on Tuesday 13 June at a meeting Major attended of the Eurosceptic Fresh Start Group ... Major arrived flustered, fifteen minutes late, and in a 'chippy' confrontational mood at a windowless conference room in the Commons and was surprised that the meeting had attracted between 55 and 60 MPs. The meeting was convened by Michael Spicer, Chairman of the Group, and a right wing conciliator who believed Major's views should be listened to respectfully, not least because of his growing Euroscepticism.

The meeting began amicably enough, with attenders banging desks, albeit perfunctorily. Spicer welcomed Major, and said that the Group wanted to discuss two issues, the single currency and how to reclaim powers from Brussels. Major was invited to open the discussion. Speaking for a little over ten minutes he talked of his determination to maintain the veto obtained at Maastricht ... Attenders sat there stony-faced, resenting Major for lecturing them ...

The meeting came to life when John Townend, Chairman of the party's backbench Finance Committee, asked whether it was not time for the Prime Minister to come off the fence ... The cheers that echoed around the room were the first indication that Major was losing control of the meeting.

Known enemies of Major then joined in, including Lamont ... George Gardiner ... Bill Cash, Iain Duncan Smith and Bernard Jenkin. All spoke bluntly and dismissively of Major's stance. Major, losing his patience, angered his audience by saying that he did not believe the public cared that much about Europe and before long MPs were shouting out their disapproval of points being made ... In an increasingly undignified meeting it was Sir Ivan Lawrence, Chairman of the Home Affairs Select Committee ... who delivered

---

*   Anthony Seldon, *Major: A Political Life*, Weidenfeld & Nicolson, 1997.

the most damaging blow when he stated that if Major did not change his line on the single currency, the party would not be around to decide in 1999 because it would have already been voted out of office.

Major had had enough. After an hour he walked out of the room to the sound of half-hearted applause looking, according to several reports, shattered by the most unruly and disrespectful meeting he was to attend as Premier.

Major himself summed up the event thus:* 'The meeting was a disaster … That meeting more or less made up my mind. We had to stop the rot and now I felt I knew how to … I decided to give the parliamentary party the opportunity to replace me.' Nine days later, on 22 June, Major resigned the leadership of the Conservative Party.

---

* John Major, *The Autobiography*, HarperCollins, 1999.

Chapter 13

John Major: planning his succession

Wednesday 14 June 1995
*D*aily Mail headline, 'Eurosceptics savage Major'. *Daily Express*, 'Major
mauled'.

Report of his being in despair. I talk to Peter Tapsell. We agree it's
a major setback in terms of winning the hearts and minds of the centre of
the party. This confirmed in the canteen at lunch when Terence Higgins and
Michael Neubert have a go at me about splitting the party, killing off the PM
and losing the election.

With all this ringing in my ears, I collect Ann and drive for three hours
to Upton-on-Severn for the first executive meeting of the new constituency.*
This goes very well; I make what everyone seems to think is a popular speech
and (hopefully) consolidate the new seat for myself.

Leadership vote

Saturday 17 June
Michael Howard rings. I tell him that his advice may be last hope for Major.
That is to say unity can only come if Major is seen to side with the majority of
the party instead of trying to balance 10 per cent against the 90 per cent. The
problem is a large number of the 10 per cent is in the Cabinet – Heseltine,
Hurd, Clarke, Dorrell, Bottomley, Gummer, Hunt.

Sunday 18 June
Try to defend my position on early morning telly, e.g. PM must firm up on
Europe, if only for his own good.

Then drive with Ann to Andrew Alexander's home near Hastings. Lots
of people there including Lamonts, David Davis, John Wells (satirist),
Gormans. Walk around Andrew's lake with Lamont, who thinks Major is a
certain goner.

---

* Boundary changes mean my present constituency – South Worcestershire – disappears
and the new constituency of West Worcestershire is created.

Monday 19 June

Drop in to see Richard Ryder, who suggests a walk in St James's Park. Establish that he is leaving the government. I say the only way for Major to save himself and the government is to give a clear direction, not to write forewords to leaflets attacking the Eurosceptics, which he has done today. He will need completely to restructure his government and to produce European policies for the IGC which are credible, in other words he must realign his government with his parliamentary party – even if this means losing Clarke and Heseltine. (The Ulster Unionists would back him in a vote of confidence.) Instead the fear must be that after the Fresh Start meeting the PM will go back into his shell. His intention to do this is confirmed in the 10 o'clock vote when he blows off at Peter Tapsell, who apologises for the Fresh Start meeting. PM says that he will 'give' nothing further to us for the foreseeable future. He is furious. Richard Ryder had agreed to fix up a meeting between me and PM. This is unlikely to come off; if it does and he gives me the Tapsell treatment, I shall fire back. It is he who is running a two-stream policy – trying to appease the right and left and falling flat on his face, bringing the party down with him.

The whole thing is ghastly. The Prime Minister shouldn't be 'trading' with us at all; he should be doing what he considers right for the country and the party. I am reminded of his phrase 'It may be good for the party but is it good for me?' He sees everything in terms of trading between different sections of the party. 'I will give you something in return for something I give them (if you're good).'

My aim even in the dark hours of Maastricht was behind the scenes to bring him and the right together. It looks as though I have failed. Talk to Howard during one of the votes – he thinks Major still saveable.

Tuesday 20 June

Richard Ryder comes up to me in the lobby at the vote on second reading of a mental health Bill (in which I spoke). Despite his entreaties, PM will not see me. What this means is that trust has broken down between PM and a large section of his party. The end must be nigh for him; things can't go on much longer like this – and it may be for the best now if he goes quickly. He may have decided to go already.

Thursday 22 June

Major's letter of resignation* read out by Marcus Fox at the 1922 Committee; stand by for a week in which everyone lies through his teeth.

---

* John Major announced his resignation as leader of the Conservative Party to contest the position again and called on his opponents to 'put up or shut up'.

Friday 23 June
Lead ERG delegation to Brussels, pursued by BBC TV.

Saturday 24 June
Meet Ian Lang, who is part of Major's campaign. Tell him that Major refused to see me earlier in the week. This shakes him a bit, especially as he had seen the ERG group on TV (*Newsnight*) the night before. I thank Ian for his handwritten note following the ERG lunch. All talk on telly is about Norman Lamont standing against Major. The really interesting thing is that the enigmatic John Redwood has not declared his support for Major. If Major wins, Redwood will be a goner so he may as well stand against him anyway. He would be a serious threat.

6 p.m. Arrive back from a bitterly cold day at Tidworth watching Princess Anne give new colours to the Worcestershire and Sherwood Foresters. Still no news of Redwood, though lots of pictures on TV of Norman Lamont buying newspapers.

Cranborne rings. (He is running Major's campaign.) Without being asked I say, 'Yes, I intend to back Major because I don't want Heseltine.' When prompted, I continue, 'Nevertheless Major has lost the trust of a vast number of his backbenchers. He didn't call Clarke a bastard.' Cranborne says, 'We must try and patch things up when all this is over.' I agree. 'What about meeting later in the week?' he suggests. 'No point.' 'Bear in mind I will probably be pretty close to the PM after this.' 'I will,' I say.

6.25 p.m. John Sergeant of the BBC rings. 'Would it make any difference if Redwood stood?' 'Let's take each day by day,' I say.

Sunday 25 June
Michael Howard rings in the morning to do his bit for Major (he is on his team). I give him much the same treatment as Cranborne, i.e. 'Major doesn't deserve my support; there is no trust between us but his departure would let in Heseltine so I favour his staying'. I do add, 'If Redwood enters the lists things might change. The cause is not Major's cause but that of Britain and the party. I will do what I think is right for each.'

Never-ending stream of telephone calls, including Howard and Cranborne from Major's office, Woodrow Wyatt (I'm sure acting for them) and Archie Hamilton, who pretends to ring to apologise for not coming to Brussels. They are all told the same thing. I will vote for Major solely because he is the main bastion against Heseltine. Archie tries to get me to go further: 'Would I in effect campaign for him?' No.

Meanwhile two calls from someone I met last Sunday at Andrew

Alexander's party called David Lord, acting in some way for John Redwood, who has not announced his support for Major. I tell him exactly what I was saying to Major. Various journalists, including Robin Oakley of the BBC, ring to find out what is going on. Big issue is what will Redwood do. If he stands it really will put the leadership stakes up a notch. Bonsor and I agree to take the line we have developed.

10.45: ITV news seems to confirm that Redwood will be standing.

Monday 26 June
Redwood announces his candidature. I have already decided to stick with Major on this round. This puts me in an awkward position with all those – mainly the avid rebels – who have gone across to Redwood (especially my gung-ho and brilliant research assistant, Daniel Hannan). My view is that the departure of Major is all about the arrival of Heseltine. Lunch with Patrick Cormack at the Athenaeum – gorgeous hot day. We have lunch on the terrace. Patrick has now changed from Heseltine, (a) because Hezza tried to do too many right-wing things, such as privatise the Post Office and the coal mines, and (b) because he never talks to his supporters. Anthony Steen, who has an office downstairs in Dean's Yard, thinks the same.

Back to the House, where everyone is moving around like sleuths in search of a plot. Bonsor invites me to go up to see Malcolm Rifkind to discuss the haemorrhaging which is going on from Major. I say Major has handled it so badly – treating the right as his enemies when the real threat is coming from the left, and the centre right are his only possible allies.

When we come out of Rifkind's office we bump into Redwood, who tries to avoid us.

Tuesday 27 June
After a sleepless night decide to take a delegation of Bonsor, Ivan Lawrence, Mark Lennox-Boyd, to see Major, (a) to get him to agree to a more sympathetic Cabinet and (b) to be tough in IGC and to insist on repatriation of powers. (Ring Ian Lang about this, who seems sympathetic.) Also decide to see Portillo.

I ring Portillo when I get into the office after meeting Tom Arnold for breakfast. (Tom is to be one of Redwood's backers. He sees it purely as a question of who will save his seat.) Portillo says the press are outside his office in Tothill Street, so we agree to meet ten minutes later in his office in the House. We both walk over separately. Meeting is very businesslike and friendly. He is going to stand in a second round – if there is one, and we both think there will be – whatever Redwood does. We start to think about names of supporters. In the meantime we agree not to say much to the press.

Wednesday 28 June

More febrile activity in the corridors and terraces of the House. The very hot weather is not helping. Long chat with Nicholas Bonsor. He is currently running with Major, saying nice things of Redwood and asking me to arrange for him to see Portillo. Apparently he talked to Major about me. Major said, 'Michael is voting for me but not proselytising my cause.' Bonsor replied, 'You must see him. He is upset about your refusing to see him some days ago.' Major said, 'I didn't refuse to see him. Ryder said he [Michael] was available if there was anything to talk about. I didn't think there was. I don't blame Michael for the Fresh Start fiasco – though he may think I do.' And then he apparently told his PPS to fix up a meeting with me – all rather unsatisfactory. All I want to tell him is that I'm rather put off by the fact that for many years I have tried to build bridges between the Eurosceptics and himself and he keeps burning them down. Meet up with Neil Hamilton, who has been PPS to Portillo – seems to be going across to Redwood.

Spend some time with Jonathan Aitken preparing him for his speech in my constituency on Friday.

Thursday 29 June

Phone rings in my pocket at lunch at Wimbledon with Basil Hutchings: PM wants to see me at 6.15 (fifteen minutes after introducing Portillo to Bonsor).

6.00: Meet in Portillo's room with Bonsor. Discuss possibilities of a campaign. Bonsor agrees to sign Portillo's nomination papers (for the second round if this takes place).

6.15: See PM. Tell him if he wins he must reconcile himself with the centre right. He says, 'OK, but I've had it up to here [lifts his hand to his neck] with all of them'. Says he remembers the day I was adopted for South Worcestershire in December 1973. He was reading the *Evening Standard* in the City. Read that I was thirty (same age as him) and he began to have aspirations to become an MP! Very amicable meeting; neither of us knows whether it will be the last time we will meet with him as PM.

The truth is – as I tell him – the leadership of the party is out of tune with the party itself. If he stays on he must alter his Cabinet to put it right. Before the meeting starts I ask his PPS, John Ward, to leave – which he does with much grumbling (I certainly will have an enemy there if Major survives).

Friday 30 June

Over to Worcester for lunch and to watch Worcestershire play Leicestershire on a boiling hot day. Then to Hereford to collect Jonathan Aitken at 5 p.m., to bring him over to Cropthorne. He takes various phone calls from Downing Street and pronounces Major a 'goner'. The 6 o'clock news, however, says Major doing a comeback with Redwood's campaign stalling despite his becoming more shrill against the PM.

Jonathan Aitken is the speaker at a constituency dinner to commemorate the twenty-first year of my being the MP. Takes place in the lovely home of Rosalie and Nigel Dawes at Birtsmorton Court, best described as a mini-Hampton Court, once owned by Thomas Cromwell, with its moat and sixteenth-century council chamber. Wonderful baking midsummer's night. Everyone in a good mood; I commit myself to voting for the PM. Jonathan rather distracted (presumably by his court case for libel).* On the way to the meeting Jonathan talking to Number 10. 'Spicer is sound here,' he says to Robert Cranborne. I make a supportive statement in my speech of thanks.

Monday 3 July

Eve of poll for leadership vote. Peter Temple-Morris (Heseltine group) surprises me by saying that he thought 110 would vote against Major – he seems to be genuine when he claims he will be voting for Major.

Tuesday 4 July

Day of leadership election.

Michael Howard rings to make sure I am still on side. I say yes, because of my fear of Hezza, but I have no illusions about Major.

Meet Archie Hamilton – part of Major's team. I ask what the Hezza people are doing. He says, 'I think they are voting with us but if they don't we've probably had it.' I vote Major at about 4.30: (1) fear of Hezza, (2) fear of chaos in a second round, (3) views of the officers of my association.

Ring my chairman, Richard Williams, at 8 a.m. He remains firm for Major. But previous chairman, David Finch, rings at about 3 p.m. to express his reservations. I tell him to thrash it out with Williams.

[John Major received the backing of 218 of the party's MPs in the leadership election, with John Redwood getting 89 votes. This majority was sufficient to avoid a second ballot.]

---

* Jonathan Aitken resigned as Treasury Secretary on Wednesday 5 July to fight his corner.

Thursday 6 July
Lunch with Daniel Hannan. Later Peter Stothard (editor of *The Times*)
comes up and says, 'You did the wrong thing'. (Reference to my not voting
for Redwood.)

My reasoning has been that if the vote had gone to a second ballot, (a)
the party would have torn itself to shreds (my association have already called
an Executive for today to discuss the leadership had it proved necessary), (b)
Heseltine would have won (though clearly he did not think so, otherwise he
would not have done his deal). He would have won because he would have
attracted the main core of the party in search of a general election winner –
certainly he would have been the choice of most of the constituencies. The
net result of all this is that the right is now on the back foot. Clearly the PM
believes it because he is now shaping up to the right. The *Evening Standard*
tonight talks of a hardening against Eurosceptics. All we can do is to re-form
through the ERG etc. Final point – I and Tapsell and Biffen have always
tried to distinguish the European cause and the leadership issue. Sadly, the
two have become entwined. They did so at the Fresh Start meeting – much
against my wishes.

Cocktail party with Tom Sackville – full of MPs of all sizes and factions.
Talk to Sandra Howard. Apparently MH is hopping mad about having been
frustrated in one matter of policy that morning by the new deputy PM,
Hezza. A number of questions arise about Hezza. Did he do a deal with
PM before the latter threw his towel in the ring? What made him in effect
pull out? Doctor's orders? Or fear he would lose?

Friday 7 July
Someone from the *Sunday Mirror* rings me. I say that Hezza is the loser.
Although he may be making the running at the moment, Downing Street is
always in charge; it has the patronage and the telephone operator.

Sunday 9 July
Michael Howard rings. I say the right are furious with the likes of him
and me for keeping Major in place. If eleven or so more of us had voted
with Redwood, Major might have been a goner. Then we would have torn
ourselves apart and whoever won – probably Hezza – would have had a very
hard time of it. The party might even have split.

Monday 10 July
10 p.m. vote. Tapsell comes up – 'We must re-form in a sensible way. We
cannot leave it to the loony right.' Angela Rumbold says the same thing.

This theme pursued earlier at a meeting at Mark's Club, attended by Michael Howard, Michael Portillo, Robert Cranborne and Conrad Black. Cranborne and Howard ran Major's campaign and are somewhat bemused by the consequence, i.e. Major's revenge on the right. I say he is splitting the party, probably beyond repair.

Driving back to vote in the House, Portillo says he assumed I was a Major spy [remember on 27 June I had left his office to visit the PM]. I attempt to disabuse him of this.

Cranborne says the campaign arose by default rather than design. He became campaign manager because when Major decided on around the Wednesday (the day before his resignation to the 1922 Committee) to 'go for it', he had no one organising anything – he had thought no further than the resignation press conference. Cranborne filled the vacuum.

Tuesday 11 July
Write Portillo the following letter:

Dear Michael
    Further to our chat last night, my soundings led me to believe that the voting figures on a second ballot would have looked something like this:
    MH: around 190
    JR: 60–80
    MP: 50–60
    I do not believe the combined right-wing candidates would have attracted more than around 130. The 'save my seat' vote would on this occasion have gone all the other way in part because of the perceived extremist/disruptive nature of the right. It is clear also that Major would have backed Heseltine.
    A fourth candidate might have reduced the Heseltine vote marginally but at best this would merely have forced a third ballot, which could itself have further bruised the Eurosceptic cause. Arguably, if the figures I have suggested had gained credence, as I think they would have, before the second vote, a pre-emptive deal might have had to be struck on not very favourable terms from our point of view. You personally, I believe, would have been rather vulnerable.
    As it is Heseltine is not Prime Minister and in my view will begin to fade away. The right's task is to make itself electorally appealing again. You have a great potential role there.
    All this is by way of explaining my recent position and my determination to do what I can to build for the future.
    Yours,
    Michael

Thursday 13 July
PM speaks to the 1922 Committee. Pretty lacklustre performance. Sombre reception; the programme looks fairly 'left and right' as he terms it.

Better evening at Number 10: party in the garden, which is rather pleasant on a warm night.

Bump into Major on the way out. Ever since the whipless business, he seems to have taken a bit of a liking to Ann. Directs her to the Cabinet room. I tell the story about Harold Wilson and Alistair McAlpine.* PM seems to like it, even though McAlpine has been outrageously rude about him.

Sunday 16 July
Perry Worsthorne and Frank Johnson (*Telegraph*) in their different ways begin to set the balance right in favour of the position I have taken lately.

This is a good day on which to try to summarise what I think happened over the last four months:

After the ERG meeting there was a chance of getting the PM on side – especially once I had got the whipless back. The party could have largely united behind a 'Eurosceptical' position.

With some hesitation I went along with the Fresh Start meeting on the grounds that it might consolidate this position.

In the event the Fresh Start meeting was a bust-up between the PM and the Eurosceptic right.

The PM took them on (when Redwood unexpectedly came in) with some kind of a deal with Hezza. There was in my judgement no way Redwood would beat Major. I tried to salvage what I could at my meeting with Major. Accumulation of (a) distaste for Hezza, (b) realisation that Major would win, (c) need to protect 'right' from being seen to be totally barking and disloyal and (d) constituency considerations made me vote for Major but – given the anti-right nature of his campaign – denying myself a 'proselytising' role. You could say mine was the worst of both worlds – but it was the only one possible for me.

---

* Alistair McAlpine found himself discussing the nature of power with Harold Wilson when the latter was Prime Minister. During this discussion, Wilson asked McAlpine to go to the window overlooking St James's Park. 'Do you hear a band playing, Mr McAlpine?'
'I do.'
'Are they playing the march from Aida?'
'Yes.'
'I know that to be the case because I tell that band what to play. That's power.'
'I see', said McAlpine, totally bewildered.

Michael Howard rings at 12 noon. He is still concerned with what he considers to be Heseltine's triumph. Plans to be more assertive himself – with a speech at party conference and buttering up of MPs.

Monday 24 July
Drop in on Robert Cranborne at his request at the Privy Council Office. Robert has apparently persuaded the PM that he ought to make some effort with the 'soft' Eurosceptics (like me?). I say, 'But I have had a lot of meetings with the PM over the past four years' – give him details. These have not come to much. Indeed, he has let me down personally at every turn. Clearly I would never say 'No' to a specific invitation from the PM to a meeting but I am not willing to be 'used' by him. There would need to be an agenda – a reason for meeting. It all depends on what the PM wants. If he really wants the party to unite around a broadly Eurosceptical position, I would try to help. If he is merely asking me to keep the lid on things while he openly abuses us – that is different. We agree to talk again.

I go on to the Garrick where I talk in similar terms to William Rees-Mogg.

Saturday 29 July
Christopher and Marjorie Lawson's fiftieth wedding anniversary in their lovely Cotswold home, south of Cheltenham. Not a cloud in the sky – temperature high eighties, if not nineties. Talk to Cecil and Ann Parkinson. We agree about the threat of Heseltine during the leadership election (Parkinson anti Hezza, which is surprising given that he was Hezza's PPS). We both agree that despite our support for Major, he heartily loathes us and assumes it is reciprocated. He had once said to Cecil that he assumed he would not want to come down to Chequers. His answer was that 'Margaret didn't own the place'. All very revealing of Major's view of us – confirmed by what Cranborne said to me about Major assuming even the soft sceptics disliked him.

Monday 11 September
Dinner at Michael Howard's official residence. Heavily guarded by police. Present: Portillo, Cranborne, Howard and me. Two areas of discussion:

Is there anything to be done about Europe from within Cabinet? I argue there is.

More philosophical discussion about the divisions on the right, e.g. between protectionists and free traders, moralists and libertarians, business-men and philosophers. This matches the debate on the left in the first half of the century.

Robert Cranborne says later that on the morning of the leadership vote he was waiting to see the PM. In the ante-room outside the Cabinet room, Michael Heseltine, who has presumably been summoned, is waiting and getting very restless. When he goes in he is there for several hours.

After the meeting have a private chat with Howard. We agree he must make a personal effort to start meeting a lot of individuals on a one-to-one basis.

Tuesday 12 September
Long planned dinner with Peregrine Worsthorne (formerly editor of, now columnist in, the *Sunday Telegraph*). He is a total romantic. We agree the choice for the future is personified by Murdoch (ambitious, competitive, lower middle class, trampling over everything mercilessly in the cause of self-preferment) and Delors (European socialism). I settle for Murdoch, he for Delors, because I say socialist protectionism could not last against the competition from the orient. We would come to Murdoch in the end, whether we like it or not. Conservatism, he says, is about more than competitive survival; it's about maintaining traditions and institutions. 'But', I ask, 'can you keep the traditions without competitive survival, i.e. is this a choice? Is not the choice between competitive survival and short-term socialist protectionism leading eventually and painfully back to competitive survival?'

Tuesday 19 September
Pratt's. Charlie Morrison[*] bemoans the obituaries for his brother. Bruce Anderson (late of the *Express*) and friend of Major, (a) buys me a drink and (b) congratulates me on my leadership campaign![†] Mark Lennox-Boyd invites me to dinner with Thatcher during the party conference.

Wednesday 20 September
Drink in the Savoy with Frank Johnson. He claims that Norman Lamont was always ready to accept Heseltine as leader (very much at variance with what he used to say to me when he was Chancellor of the Exchequer but in line with the position he is claimed by Alan Watkins to take at the start of Major's first leadership bid). Johnson also mystified by why Heseltine failed to 'go for it'.

---

[*] Charles Morrison MP for Devizes. His brother, Sir Peter Morrison MP, died on 13 July 1995.
[†] See Alan Clark, *The Last Diaries*, Weidenfeld & Nicolson, 2002: '23 March 1994: Bruce Anderson rang … Who's going to lead them? [The Thatcherite rump]. Bruce said, "Michael Spicer."'

Tuesday 10 October

Arrive in Blackpool. Bump into Major on the stairs of Imperial. He is very civil to Ann, calling her by her Christian name. Evidently the long telephone conversation with her earlier in the year has made its mark. Portillo arrives on the scene. Major congratulates him on his speech.

Tebbit, having joined us on the stairs, says to Major, 'Have said we mustn't rock the boat in tomorrow's *Sun*.'

Major replies, 'It's not so much a question of not rocking the boat, Norman, as your helping us to push the boat off the reef.'

Wednesday 11 October

Many delegates at the conference seem to be against Portillo – he is beginning to look rather extreme. All the rhetoric of the conference is anti-European but it's all hot air. It costs nothing and means nothing as the federal boat moves on, aided by the European constitution. Some discussions at Alexander Hesketh's party with Peter Lilley – who had spoken quite well to conference – about whether or not Labour would truly adopt Alan Howarth. I thought not, he thought they might.

Thursday 12 October

Michael Howard makes a good speech. More measured than usual, also the only speaker to claim a good record and specific action for the future – a new Crime Bill.

Drink with Mark and Arabella Lennox-Boyd at their baronial mansion outside Lancaster. Margaret Thatcher, Maurice Saatchi, Neil Hamilton, Archie Hamilton, Gerald Howarth present. Thatcher signs a copy of her book* I have brought and asks what I think about the attitude of delegates towards Europe. 'Hot air,' I say. I'm not sure she fully understands, but she has had a good day at the conference – much cheering of her. She is looking much better than a few months ago when apparently her health was causing her problems. Archie Hamilton gets me on one side. Says he is thinking of masterminding Portillo's campaign – what do I think? I say I think it is a bit premature. What about Howard? We agree to talk again.

Tuesday 17 October

Visit Ma for lunch at the Sailing Club at Lymington. Discuss our forebears. This was inspired by the fact that on Saturday we visited the site of my

---

* Margaret Thatcher, *The Path to Power*, HarperCollins, 1995.

grandfather's* home at Whitley Bay with Annabel and Ann. At Annabel's insistence we were determined to track down my grandparents' home. The trouble was it had long ago ceased to be called Lyndhurst. Annabel looked up 'Spicer' in the 1928 street register in the local library and found Edwina Spicer at Lyndhurst with the street name. We went round and found that Lyndhurst had been a college and had been pulled down three months previously for a housing development.

Meet Michael Howard in his room after 10 p.m. vote. Tell him Archie Hamilton has said was thinking of backing Portillo. Michael Howard says he tried to ring me over the weekend and he will try to have a drink with Archie. I say, 'You had better start quick with "getting your ducks in place" because time will run out pretty quickly now.'

Thursday 19 October

Michael Howard does well defending himself in Parliament against charges of having misled the House. Turns the debate into an attack on Blair. Shows his mettle for opposition!

Saturday 21 October

6 p.m. Michael Howard rings to thank me for my note after the debate, which had one word, 'Superb'. I say he must capitalise on it all by making as many friends as possible on the back benches.

Sunday 22 October

Howard not really getting a very good press – grudging admiration for his performance on Thursday summed up by the headline to a piece in the *Sunday Telegraph* by Petronella Wyatt: 'Right but Repulsive. It's his "smug" smile and funny vowel sounds which he will have to do something about. He has greater stature than Portillo but not his charisma – a good debater but bad orator.'

Saturday 28 October

Fly to Washington for what will probably be the last Bighorn conference on free trade, organised by Senator Wallop.

---

* My paternal grandfather, who died in 1925, ran a string of private banks along the Tyne. He was a close friend of Sir James Knott and a director of his shipping line.

ABOVE My parents' wedding, 1940; one guest distracted by the Battle of Britain overhead. My maternal grandparents had been given military clearance to attend the event only a few hours earlier.

BELOW Aged 3½, I take the salute beside my father as troops of the Sudanese Defence Force march by (Queen's Birthday Parade, Keren, Eritrea, 1946).

ABOVE I have painted from the day that I could hold a brush.

MIDDLE My mother, my sister Angela Jane and I meet Field Marshal Montgomery (Hamburg, 1950).

BELOW Firmly together, my parents sweat it out in post-war Khartoum (1946).

ABOVE Asking a question on behalf of *The Statist* to Alec Douglas-Home (general election 1964).
BELOW LEFT Ann and I emerge from Easington Colliery, 1965.
BELOW RIGHT With Edward Heath at Upton-upon-Severn: he tells me that I am to fight the by-election in South Worcestershire (1973). Later he changes his mind and calls a general election.

ABOVE Confronting Emanuel Shinwell, Easington, general election 1966: oldest and youngest candidates in the land fight it out.

BELOW Ann and I with the Queen in Malvern soon after I became an MP in 1974.

BANX

"YOU'RE JOINING ME FROM MICHAEL SPICER'S IN TRAY."

ABOVE Visiting troops at Heathrow after I had announced the posting of armed soldiers and police at the airport (1986).

BELOW LEFT My in-tray during the IDS debacle, as seen through the eyes of Banx in *The Times* (2003).

BELOW RIGHT Cutting the first sod at Stansted Airport with local MP Alan Haselhurst (1986).

OPPOSITE Playing tennis against the US Senate. I captained the parliamentary tennis team between 1997 and 2007.

ABOVE Putting a question to Gordon Brown (2009), by permission of the Parliamentary Recording Unit.

BELOW LEFT Jessica Chessher, Ann, Desmond Swayne, David Cameron and Patrick McLoughlin prepare to invade Committee Room 14 on my last meeting as Chairman of the 1922 Committee (2010).

BELOW RIGHT The result of the 'invasion'. David Cameron presents me with a silver salver from the Parliamentary Party.

ABOVE General election 2000. Behind Ann and me from the left: Richard Weatherill, Paul Swinburn, David Watkins and Jessica Chessher.

BELOW The House of Lords 2010. Family lines up with Lords Cope and Goodlad and Garter King of Arms.

Monday 30–Tuesday 31 October
Conference comprises usual Peter Ramshaw, Malcolm Wallop – no longer a senator, sadly – and itinerant congressmen and government officials. Not the calibre or commitment of the past. I probably speak too much, too fanatically about free trade.

Washington is superficially a beautiful place – especially on the Mall. In fact it's a bit of a dump with no soul.

Tuesday 7 November
Last day of the parliamentary session; very few people around. Those that are there are very miserable about Nolan vote on members' interests. Government now 40 points behind Labour. Have a drink with Nick Bonsor and Richard Shepherd.

Sunday 12 November
Michael Howard calls. He has won the *Spectator* debating competition. MH had lunch on Friday with Archie Hamilton. 'Advised' him not to come to a premature decision as to whom to back for the leadership. Archie said, 'Spicer is a key man these days.' MH apparently agreed.

Wednesday 15 November
I don't feel like a 'key man' when I speak at 7 p.m. on our side in the Queen's Speech debate. For once I have put quite a bit of effort into the speech, which is received in rapt silence by a House comprising four MPs (two whips, one minister, and David Nicholson, who is waiting to speak after me). A flavour of the speech is as follows:

> On the theme of loosening up the market, I would certainly abolish the Housing Corporation and all aid to housing associations. The Spicer Budget would give all the money saved directly to those who needed it through housing benefits, which would be managed in the manner that my Right Hon. Friend the Secretary of State for Social Security is rightly proposing. In other words – in response to some of the mockery from opposition members – I would give the money to those genuinely in need of help with housing, rather than spending it on bricks and mortar, which benefits the deserving and the undeserving alike. I suspect that, after fifty years of resisting such attempts to focus money on those who really need it, the Labour Party is beginning to change its mind. Some of the mockery may die on the lips of some opposition members fairly soon when the Labour Party, after all these years, at last begins to realise that, if one is going to help poor people, one should do so directly.

That is my view and the perfect instrument is housing benefit, rather than by spreading money across the board through the Housing Corporation and housing associations.[*]

Tuesday 21 November
Meeting with Michael Howard after the 10 p.m. vote. Press him again to get a campaign going of touting round backbenchers. He agrees to write a foreword for the pamphlet attacking Labour's views on Europe. Less keen on speaking to our conference on the European court.

Thursday 23 November
Arrive at Evesham station 1.45. Collected by Ann, who says, 'There is nothing interesting waiting in the post.' I find a letter marked 'Prime Minister' under a pile of envelopes on the round table in the middle of the hall. Open it and out pops an offer of a knighthood.

Monday 27 November
Go home with Archie Hamilton after the 10 p.m. vote to his flat in Tufton Street. Archie elated after being voted onto 1922 executive, now plans to go for the chairmanship. Archie had been spurned by Portillo; he went to see him and had expected to be welcomed with open arms. He got the same treatment as I did. Michael Howard did much better – inviting him for lunch, then ringing him up to congratulate him on getting onto the executive.

Friday 1 December
Conservative Political Centre annual dinner at the Pershore Civic Centre. The chairman, Richard Devenish, a man of few words and no gush, gives the vote of thanks, saying, 'Michael is his own man in Westminster and our man in Westminster.'

Monday 15 January 1996
The back-slapping in the lobby and the congratulations re the knighthood are a wonder to behold – bearing in mind that a few years earlier during the Maastricht revolt hardly anyone would speak to me. The only people now who don't speak to me are the hard right – my erstwhile Fresh Start chums who think I have deserted them. What they don't concede is that I have always felt that the issue was to recapture the party for the centre right and then to move it against federalism. You don't/can't do that from the wings.

---

[*] Hansard, HC Deb, 15 November 1995, vol. 267, col. 91.

Lunch at the Garrick, where in some strange way all the staff seem to know I was a 'Sir'; also members whom I have never seen before came up to congratulate me. Sit next to Robin Day and Giles Gordon, the literary agent. In taxi back to the House with Michael Mates (Heseltine's right-hand man), he says Hezza did not compete out of a sense of loyalty to Major. He accepts that Hezza's greatest flaw was inability to keep friends happy. (Hadn't talked to Peter Temple-Morris for months, despite frequent reminders from Mates.) Mates's final words are, 'He might yet surprise us all by standing for leadership before next election.' God knows what he means. 'Was there a Major–Hezza deal after all?' I ask. Mates says emphatically, 'No!' I wonder.

Michael Howard's stamina is formidable. He came back from India last evening, launched a debate on security and was due to go on BBC's *Today* at 7.30, as well as a punishing schedule before Christmas. He looks and sounds fine.

Tuesday 16 January

Lunch with PM and a mixture of parliamentary colleagues. I interrupt Major in a rather weak summary he makes of the debate on Europe, which takes place around the Number 10 dining table. 'What about the law court, PM?' 'Yes, we must tackle that; remove retrospection etc.' 'The real controversy is between those who want to tidy up the law court and those who want to reverse its powers to make law.' 'We are looking at the latter.' 'Wow.'

Major seems to be pleased with the lunch when I bump into him in the 7 p.m. lobby. 'Very agreeable atmosphere.' The fact that we were in debating terms at each other's throats has either escaped him or is something he chooses to ignore – probably the latter. What is so sad – and I made the point in my intervention at lunch – is that he continues to give equal weight to each side of the argument when the 'sceptic' cause is espoused by 90 per cent of the party and 60 per cent of the country.

Meet Brian Mawhinney on both Monday and Tuesday in the voting lobby to discuss the ERG pamphlet attacking Labour. The publication issue arose out of the fact that Michael Howard has sought his advice about whether or not to write a foreword. Mawhinney decides not to intervene and to leave it to Howard. Howard later decides to go ahead.

Wednesday 17 January

Strange evening. Amongst other things, meet up with Hugh Dykes and Bill Cash – opposite ends of the Euro spectrum. Hugh obviously upset that having voted for Major he seemed to get nothing out of it. Bill, having voted for Redwood (and disgusted at me for not having done so), was preparing a peace pact whereby the right and the left would try to find common ground; he has been talking to the chairman of the party about this.

Thursday 18 January

Geoffrey Parkhurst of the *Glasgow Herald* comes up to me outside Committee Room 14 and a very badly attended 1922 Committee. 'What do you make of *The Times* story that the grandees are out to get Major? Are you one of the grandees?'

I laugh and say, 'It sounds to me as if Peter Stothard and Nick Wood got together and made it up because they hate Major so much.'

Geoffrey says, 'I was at a party at Number 10 last night and Major was very low. I cracked a joke and he responded, "The steel goes very deep." Clearly he'd had word of the next day's press and was very depressed by it.'

The problem is we are still 40 points behind in the polls and we have the May elections and two by-elections ahead.

Friday 19 January

By train to Birmingham to IoD lunch to be addressed by PM. Meet him briefly before lunch. He looks grey and haggard. His performance to what could have been a very enthusiastic audience is tired and lacklustre. At the end, only a few people of the 1,000 or so present stand to applaud him. I was sitting next to Chris Miller* and we both agree it was not a very uplifting performance.

Afterwards one of his aides invites me up to the hospitality room where the PM is. Already there are Norman Fowler and Bill Cash. The conversation naturally turns to Europe. 'Why are those who should be in favour of my firm stance in Europe so against me?' the PM asks. 'Because I'm afraid they don't trust you,' says Bill.

We talk about the story of the plot to get rid of him which *The Times* had run the day before. 'It was put about by someone in the Lords,' the PM says, 'not (as had first been rumoured) by Archie Hamilton.' I say it was almost certainly invented by *The Times*, which all goes to show you must work through one or two chosen people in the press – in this case Nick Wood and Peter Stothard, but also Charles Moore (*Telegraph*), Trevor Kavanagh (political editor, *Sun*), and even Simon Heffer (*Mail*). 'I do,' says PM, 'but it doesn't work. What is so ironic is that if I went, there would be even more rows in the party.' Bill says, 'Say "no" to a single currency in the next Parliament. That would do it.' 'No it wouldn't,' says Fowler. PM says, 'We could still lose some

---

* Chief executive of Wassall plc.

of the left.' I say, 'Only if we continue to look like losers. The key thing is to start doing better in the polls.' We talk about factors which might strengthen the Deutschmark and so bring down German interest rates. 'Then we could bring ours down,' says Major. 'Do ours anyway,' I suggest. He gives me rather a dirty look. We clearly are shadowing the Deutschmark a bit.

On the train back to London, Bill and I agree it was all pretty hopeless. He still balances 5 per cent possible deserters and Heseltine and Clarke against the rest of the party – shades of Balfour. He is not prepared to give a proper lead. Bill feels there is therefore nothing to be lost by his going now – almost whoever takes over. However, Bill seems to have gone somewhat off the boil on Redwood.

Sunday 21 January

Sunday papers still full of the 'plot' to get Major. *Sunday Telegraph* calls it Old School Tie plot and names Archie Hamilton. PM makes it clear to me in Birmingham he doesn't believe this. 'Not in the Commons but the Lords.'

Ring Archie Hamilton to tell him PM doesn't believe the stories about him. Archie is very relieved to hear this. He has apparently been ambushed by Nick Wood, who said Heseltine would get it if Major went. Archie said he didn't believe Major would go and if he did Heseltine wouldn't get it. This was portrayed as part of a plot! The problem is that the state of the party has been so febrile that we are sitting targets for any roving journalist – especially when the only story that will win the approval of the editor (as in *The Times*) is one about Tory dissent.

Wednesday 24 January

Supper with Bonsor. We agree that the next leadership contest might be between Rifkind and Howard. I thought he would back his friend Rifkind – but interestingly he says Rifkind is too left wing and would go for Howard.

Monday 29 January

ERG lunch with Michael Heseltine. He makes no attempt to disguise his views in favour of a federal state of Europe and especially of the desirability of single currency. When pressed on a referendum, he agrees 'something would have to be said about it in the manifesto.' I ask, 'Since you don't want one, will you press to have it specifically rejected in the manifesto?'

He says, 'No, we will stick to the formula of "wait and see what circumstances come up".'

Wednesday 31 January

Walk home with Richard Ryder. Such a pleasant man but rather a sad lonely character now; troubled with back problems. We talk about how the party might split in opposition over Europe – especially if Labour took us into the single currency. He says, 'Whatever else happens you will enjoy yourself, Michael!'

Friday 2 February

Two bits of news relevant. First, the 1922 Committee decided last night (I couldn't make the meeting) that there will be no opportunity to challenge Major in November. So he's now his own man until the election – I wonder whether that will make a difference. The more I think back on the meeting with Heseltine the more convinced I am that he sees himself as the power behind the throne. The question is, is he? Major has this knack of letting everyone think they run him – and then letting them down, not so much because he knows his own mind but because he does not – he plays everything by ear. This means that although no one moves against him, everyone grumbles and generally feels let down.

In any event, Heseltine carries weight – although perhaps less so now that the 1922 Committee has made its decision. Heseltine is certainly more important in this administration than Rab Butler was when in the 1960s he played a similar role under Macmillan.

The second piece of news is that Neil Hamilton has said he will stand against John Townend for the chairmanship of the 92 Group. Whether or not he wins, this makes Hamilton a serious player again. I back Townend – much more straightforward (and a member of ERG). However, Hamilton has the charisma and may well win. He will then become an influential figure, not least because of his No Turning Back connections. NTB is both a social and a political group – very formidable. It may not produce a king but it will be important in making one. Names: Hamilton, Michael Forsyth (SoS Scotland), Gerald Howarth (my former PPS and PPC Aldershot), Christopher Chope (PPC Christchurch), Bernard Jenkin, Francis Maude, possibly Iain Duncan Smith (though he probably stands more aloof). Maude, Jenkin, Forsyth all live very close together in Kennington. They used to back Portillo but I think they would probably now go for Redwood.

Friday 9 February

ERG conference at Café Royal. Especially good to see Jacques Myard, the warm-hearted and intelligent Gaullist who is about five feet tall and speaks perfect English. Malcolm Rifkind the guest speaker at lunch. We discuss the government's position at the IGC. He says we would make the court more sensible. I say, 'Tinkering with it would be to miss the point. The IGC needs to reform it, to take away its law-making powers and "recover the *Acquis*".'* 'Impossible,' he says. I say we need to do just that by treaty amendment if we are to delay implementation of the single currency.

TV present but the 'Spicer curse' works again. At 7.01 the IRA blow up Canary Wharf and our conference is blown off the media.

Friday 16 February

Open BBC's new Wood Norton conference centre near Evesham. Sit next to the deputy head of news broadcasting, who says that although the government thought it had 'got away with Scott'† the Sundays will pursue it and so will the newspapers and BBC in the following week.

Sunday 18 February
They do.

Monday 19 February 1996

Looks as though my friend from the BBC on Friday may be right, though have now been told he is merely head of admin – i/c cameras etc. This means he doesn't know about news but he does know about how camera crews are allocated. As Peter Jay says, the only bias in the news may be in favour of what is plannable in advance because of sophistication of kit, difficulties of logistics, cast contracts etc.

Wednesday 21 February

Walk back after the 10 p.m. vote with John Taylor, deputy leader of the Ulster Unionists, who lives across the road in Maunsel Street. He points out that all the new IRA activity is coming from south of the border. This confirms what lay behind my question to the PM last week, asking him whether he had received any requests from the Dublin government for help with security (and after which the minister, Michael Ancram, had said to me that the question had been helpful and presumably sending signals to Dublin). Conservative MPs are becoming restive about lack of security south of the border. It's the southern Army Council which is initiating the current round of bombing – according to Taylor.

---

*   *Acquis* is the ccondition in the Treaty of Rome by which all European law must point one way, towards a federal state of Europe.

†   The Scott Enquiry was set up in 1992 to investigate alleged mis-selling of arms to Iraq.

Thursday 22 February

By coincidence leave my house at around 9.20 at the same time as Taylor is leaving his. We walk in the slush and snow past the Horseferry Road coroner's office, which is surrounded by cameramen waiting for the body of the IRA bomber who blew himself up on a bus last week.

Friday 23 February

Association AGM in the district council offices in Pershore. I am unanimously adopted as the candidate for the new constituency of West Worcestershire. I make a speech which goes down well, half read and half 'from the heart'. On the surface all is well but the officers elected are all sympathetic to a closer Europe.

Monday 26 February

Scott report debate. Government wins by one. Quentin Davies, who lives opposite us in Maunsel Street and who was particularly rude about me at Maastricht for 'destabilising' the government, votes against HMG.

Thursday 29 February

Lunch at the Garrick. My table full of judges, one of whom expresses the view that we need a coalition government, not only for Northern Ireland but also for a common policy on education, the health service etc. I argue that, on the contrary, the greatest mistakes in history – certainly in this century – have been when the two major parties have agreed with each other: Gold Standard, appeasement and Maastricht.

Monday 4 March

Right-wing art party! Gail Lilley (Peter's wife) painting exhibition at 33 St James's restaurant. Robin Day and lots of luvvies present. Chris Miers* on very good form on Northern Ireland. Everyone thinks he has been in military intelligence so listens to him attentively. 'There's no solution,' he says, 'so the only answer is to take out the IRA, especially south of the border.' Walk home after the vote with James Cran. We agree that Ireland is a ticking time bomb inside the Tory Party.

---

* Lt Col C. J. P. Miers, with whom I was at both prep and public school (see diary entry from 13 April 1959 on p. 5). Having won the Sword of Honour at Sandhurst, Christopher joined the 60th Rifles and retired from the army early to become a professional landscape painter.

Wednesday 6 March
Rather traumatic AEP* meeting at which decide that I should write a letter to the Electricity Association offering a merger.

Question to minister of agriculture, Douglas Hogg, demanding that we retrieve powers from the European court; goes down well with our side.

Bump into Bonsor; we decide to go out for dinner to discuss the options for the leadership and the emerging European situation. I ring Sandra Howard. Would Michael like to join us? He does at about 8 p.m. in the dining room of White's.

Bonsor swears allegiance to Howard. When he goes to the loo, Howard thanks me. We decide to rope Hannan in. The plot very definitely thickens. Bonsor evidently makes his mind up with Cranborne; so Cranborne on side – good.

Friday 8–Sunday 10 March
Staying at a small hotel near Rye. Pick up an early edition of *Charles Kingsley: His Letters and Memories of His Life*, edited by his wife. Flick through in between walking and running. What intrigues me is that she only gives two lines in the whole book to *The Water Babies*, which is the only work he is now remembered for by the general public. Her book is all about his sermons at Cambridge and, indeed, Eversley and his correspondence with Benson, who was then founding Wellington College. Such is the unpredictable nature of the effect and the memory of what we do on this earth.

Back in London on Sunday – call from Michael Howard to thank me for fixing supper with Bonsor. Ask him whether he has any business supporters. 'Yes, but I keep them at the back of my mind.' *Sunday Telegraph* has a list of hopefuls ready to take over from Major, who has been speculating on his departure and succession. (Would Major resign his seat for Chris Patten if we lose general election?) Howard is not listed amongst the potential leaders; this is bad journalism but very good for Howard. It is still all a bit early.

Tuesday 12 March
Publication date of government's White Paper on Europe. Do a bit of telly in the morning – problem that my voice is disappearing. 12.00: visit Malcolm Rifkind, at his invitation. At this meeting and in his statement he makes two opening points: (1) the competence of the court could be questioned;

---

* Association of Electricity Producers, of which I am president. A few years later the Electricity Association closes down and the AEP takes over its functions for electricity producers.

(2) HMG willing to question the *Acquis Communautaire* and to suggest that directives are reversible; this is new and important and I comment on it on TV when my voice allows it. Sadly I can't do *Newsnight* because my voice not up to it.

Friday 15 March

Down to Wellington for governors' meeting overnight. Call in on Fergus Russell* on the way. With his legs amputated, he is so brave and good-natured. Gives me review copies of his friend Mark Baker's collection of Kingsley's letters to Benson.

Tuesday 19 March

Approached in the lobby by Elinor Goodman, political editor, *Channel 4 News*. Who would I back for leader? 'I think you will be the king maker.' I say, 'Thanks, Elinor, but no thanks! He must be of the right but have some appeal to the rest of the party; that's as far as I will go.'

Thursday 21 March

Early into the House to reserve a seat at the top of the gangway for the European debate; this is swamped by mad cow disease news and by PM's statement on Northern Ireland. After breakfast bump into Iain Duncan Smith, who says he has list of speakers (from Speaker's office) and I am at the bottom of it. I point out it was in alphabetical order and they only work things out at 12 noon. Also says he wishes Bill Cash and I got on better. Apparently I was main topic of discussion at the 'selection' meeting for speakers for the debate. I have bullied and bombarded the chair about not being called in previous debates. In the event am called before several PCs. Make an acclaimed speech in prime time; one of my best – better for being limited by ten-minute rule.† I speak for eight minutes, including an interruption. Much

---

*　My housemaster when I was there as a boy.

†　My description of the powers and status of the European Court of Justice remains as relevant today as it was then: 'It has four specific federalist features. Since the Defreme case of 1976, the court has been able to make law; since the Factortame case of 1991, that law has had the makings of being superior to the law passed by the House of Commons. Because of the principle of direct applicability, the European Court's law may bypass the national institutions of each country and directly affect its citizens. Because of the fourth principle of Acquis Communautaire, that superior law compounds itself and occupies territory from which it cannot be dislodged; there is a compounding one-way process towards federalism. The problem is that a government who no longer control their law and who no longer control their money are no longer in control of the nation.'

of it was about what should be HMG's tactics, to which the minister (David Davis) responded. By fluke I had met him and had had good discussion in the tea room at both breakfast and lunch.

Walk home, after a good day, with Chris Gill. I say, 'It won't be as much fun as we think in opposition; we won't have any influence. We must get Labour hooked on a referendum so that they will split soon after being in office.'

At one point bump into a rather worried Malcolm Rifkind at the back of the chair, when I was going off for a cup of tea. He is conferring with his officials after having made not a brilliant speech for him and having, I suspect in his own mind and no doubt that of his officials, given away one or two hostages to fortune. I pat him on the back and say, 'What you've got to realise is that these European debates are a "club"; we all go back a long way with each other. There are all sorts of in-groups and in-phrases. You will need about three rounds with us to get into practice.' He laughs; he's a nice chap. I know him because I recruited him to PEST, and our daughters were friends at Durham University.

Late news tonight is that Peter Temple-Morris in serious trouble in his constituency. Tebbit is apparently saying in tomorrow's *Daily Telegraph* 'Good riddance'. Government's majority could be down to one.

Friday 22 March
ERG meeting at Archie Hamilton's mansion outside Guildford. Discuss leadership. I toss in Howard, which goes down like a lead balloon. Probably a mistake to push him. The consensus, of which I am not part, is that Redwood is increasingly the man. Some 3¼ hours to Worcestershire for evening meeting – Kempsey, which, for once, goes well.

Saturday 23 March
Times has a piece saying Cash has set up an umbrella group incorporating ERG. This is rubbish. BSE is dominating the news. I have a feeling the panic is over-reactive.

Tuesday 26 March
John Redwood to one of our regular ERG lunches at Wassall in Victoria Street. He is remarkably awkward in the circumstances, given that we are twelve ostensibly like-minded parliamentary colleagues of his. He is also less clear minded about European matters than one might have expected. Perhaps the explanation was that he thinks himself 'on parade' re a future leadership bid – which indeed he is. At the end he asks rather revealingly, 'Did I pass?'

At least we agree on the principle, e.g. on variable geometry, but he is very coy and fudgy in his answer to my question, 'If it came to a federal Europe versus pulling out – which would you be for?' Michael Howard had no hesitation in answering this point ('No question we should pull out').

After PM's Questions, have rather a 'straight' talk to Iain Duncan Smith, who is a friend of Bill Cash, about the article in *The Times*, clearly the result of briefings from Bill, where he claims to be running an umbrella group which comprises ERG. I say to IDS that there are three options: we let 'all flowers bloom' with lots of separate Eurosceptic groups; we have a genuine umbrella group, in which case we would need a neutral chairman like John Biffen; Bill presumes to speak for all of us, in which case we have a row.

Teddy Taylor, sort of leader of the former whipless, seems to be equally concerned that Bill has been proclaimed leader of the whipless.

Norman Lamont comes up to me and rather kindly says how much he enjoyed my speech in the Euro debate last week. 'It was not just the content; your delivery is good too.' Looking back on it, it really was a good debate.

Thursday 27 March
Take Daniel along to meet Michael Howard. We agree that Daniel will help him with a speech on Europe to be delivered to an ERG conference in May (about court's powers to make laws) and that Howard will send us a list of where he has spoken in the last year and where he plans to speak.

Thursday 28 March
David Davis says, 'Good speech last week' over breakfast.

I reply, 'You congratulated the member for Worcester in your speech. Peter Walker is still basking in the glory!'

Monday 1 April
Howard, Portillo, Bonsor to supper at Maunsel Street. Discuss the possibility of Clarke resigning on the issue of a referendum. This seems increasingly likely, although consensus is that he is engaging in brinkmanship.

Tuesday 2 April
Tennis at Queen's with Ann and the Russian ambassador. Luckily he and Ann won the second set and relations with Russia ended very amicably.

Wednesday 3 April
Drive with David Martin to Wimbledon to play with him, John Hannam and Michael Morris. Martin v. hot on Redwood. He says, 'We must have a

clear standard-bearer.' I say important that someone from the right wins the leadership – need to try to keep the party as 'one'. DM doesn't rate Howard at all – not trustworthy. Gave way on QMV – always protecting Major. I do think Howard has got to say something outrageous about Europe soon.

Monday 8 April
Bank holiday. Call Michael Howard; he rings me back. We agree to meet soon. Then prepare a detailed assessment of his chances under different scenarios. Redwood will be his main opponent throughout. If Rifkind enters, it could be very difficult for him.

Thursday 11 April
My letter (lead) in *Times** prompts 'supportive' calls from Budgen and Marlow – each smelling trouble. I say I am not out to screw the government, but if I can get Jim Spicer, Geoffrey Johnson Smith and Mark Lennox-Boyd – Ks of the shires – to stiffen the resolve of HMG on the beef crisis and our approach to it in Europe, I will. We may be able to use the Luxembourg compromise.†

Tuesday 16 April
Dinner at Carlton Club with Michael Howard. Put to him my thesis: party = 40 per cent hard right, 40 per cent soft right, 20 per cent left. First round: Redwood 30 per cent, Portillo 10 per cent (= hard right), Howard 25 per cent, A. N. Other 15 per cent (=soft right), Clarke/Dorrell 20 per cent. Next round: Redwood 45 per cent, Michael Howard 35 per cent, Clarke 20 per cent. Third round: Redwood 45 per cent, Howard 50 per cent, abstentions 5 per cent. Howard says I am too pessimistic about his vote on right and too optimistic about soft right. We agree to ask Cran and Bonsor whether they would like to join future discussions about post-election scenarios. Possibly Daniel Hannan later. As we come out into the street, two plain clothes policemen stand guard. We leave in Howard's bullet-proofed Jaguar, followed by a police Range Rover, for the 10 p.m. vote in the House.

Monday 22 April
Meet Peter Riddell (*Times*) and Alastair Goodlad (Chief Whip). I say to Alastair, 'I like the sound of the PM's new toughness on beef' – threats were

---

* I suggested that Britain should kick up rougher about the EU ban on British beef due to an outbreak of BSE.

† The agreement with de Gaulle in 1966 where an essential national interest overrode the Treaty of Rome – legally increasingly dubious.

to 'retaliate' for the EU ban on British beef, either by turning away their exports or holding back new contributions. Alastair said he must not do a Duke of York – import ban would be illegal.

Wednesday 24 April

Sit next to Alastair Goodlad at lunch. He asks my advice as to what he should say to the Cash group when he meets them. I say, 'Tell them what the plan is for dealing with beef. You have said we will only kill 40,000 cows and you know this will not satisfy the French and Germans. What are you going to do when they reject our plan? You must know; tell us all and we will follow.'

In the meantime that afternoon Major makes an anti-Eurosceptic speech to the IoD to make up for his 'sceptical' position on beef at the beginning of the week.

Saturday 27 April

Small drinks party at the Easington home of Patricia Lawford with one or two old stalwarts from the Easington candidature days – probably the last time I will ever really get together with them. I had a very good relationship with them in the past.

Quick word with Howard about Tuesday's meeting. He agrees that it should comprise Cran, Bonsor and me. MH has not managed to contact Cran. I say I will.

Tuesday 30 April

3.30: Meet Howard, Cran and Bonsor. *The Guardian* this morning proclaimed MH's challenge for the leadership if Major went and Bonsor as his campaign manager – all pretty quick as I only properly recruited Bonsor last week! I had a drink with him at my home last Thursday evening to explain exactly why in the lobby the previous night MH had invited him to meet him. At PMQs George Foulkes[*] asked a mischievous question about the leadership referring to the *Guardian* article. This is the first topic we discuss at the Howard meeting. The disturbing bit is that only six people know of our existence: Bonsor, Howard, Spicer, Cran, Hannan and Patrick Rock, political adviser. Probably the latter told *The Guardian*, but it could have been Bonsor in a moment of over-excitement.

Bonsor opens the discussion (clearly having taken on board the *Guardian* piece that said he was the new campaign manager!). He says we must be very

---

[*] MP for South Ayrshire 1979–83, Carrick, Cumnock & Doon Valley 1983–2005; MoS Scotland 2001–2; created 2005 Lord Foulkes of Cumnock.

robust and proactive. Cran says we must be cautious, especially in the light of the *Guardian* article. I say we must be focused and deliberate. Should consider MH's speaking engagements and should construct a list of 'good bet' PPCs to tackle. I will talk to Daniel about this. This is agreed. I become the repository of MH's only list of engagements. All in all a good first meeting.

5.15: Good chat to Cranborne in his room. He volunteers Lilley and Howard as possible future leaders.

Wednesday 1 May

Agriculture committee meeting. Douglas Hogg is getting nowhere with the Europeans on BSE.

Ask Daniel to prepare a list of suitable PPCs.

Thursday 2 May

Paul Goodman (*Daily Telegraph*) commissions an article from me re Goldsmith. He wants this to go wider than my book* on trade and attack Goldsmith on a wide front. Daniel rightly warns against looking like splitting the right.

Sunday 5 May

Bank holiday weekend. Michael Howard rings in the evening. He says the local election results on Thursday (when we lost 600 seats out of a maximum of 1,200) were not quite bad enough to throw out Major. We must plan now for the long haul. He had that morning refused to answer the question on the BBC *Today* programme as to whether or not he could ever envisage us pulling out of the EU!

Wednesday 8 May

ERG breakfast. We decide to move in the direction of studying the costs/benefits of European membership. Later at the 10 p.m. vote Michael Howard comes up to say we could meet for supper on Monday 13th. Still no word of whether the *Daily Telegraph* are to publish my article on Goldsmith.

Friday 10 May

In Prague for Congress on greater Atlantic unity. Many of the usual suspects gather under the chandeliers of Rudolph's Gallery in the Castle. Some 200 or so people listen to Václav Havel's opening address, the main point of which is

---

* Michael Spicer, *The Challenge from the East and the Rebirth of the West*, St Martin's Press, 1996.

to warn us not to be put off by the Russians in allowing former eastern bloc countries to join NATO.

At the buffet afterwards Conrad Black, Thatcher, Irwin Stelzer, Alan Chalfont and many others. John O'Sullivan the organising genius behind it. Apparently he only knew he had the money two months ago. Thatcher looking rather old. 'I am the only international figure who can put all this over.' There is concern amongst the organisers that she will go OTT tomorrow; however, as I walk over Charles Bridge – one of the most romantic places in the world – with John late at night, he says it's 'now all under control'. He should know; he wrote her autobiography.

John also has a copy of my book *The Challenge from the East*, which I hope he will show me tomorrow as I haven't seen it yet! He has brought it direct from the publishers (St Martin's Press) in New York, where he works.

Saturday 11–Sunday 12 May

Conference winds its way on. Thatcher dominating the scene with a powerful speech at the lunch. She talks of her 'second favourite PM', Václav Havel. Her 'favourite' is presumably John Major! She lives in a bit of a fantasy world about her premiership. 'We cut expenditure.' We didn't. As always she is magnificent but perverse, and totally self-absorbed. Perhaps all great people are.

Monday 13 May

Dinner chez Michael Howard. Present: Nicholas Bonsor, James Cran, Tim Collins, Rachel Whetstone, Sandra Howard. Debate between me (he must develop identity) and the rest (he must continue as middle of the road). I say the danger is that he would never establish a constituency.

When we leave at 11.15 I walk back to Pimlico with Cran, who says he is not very happy that Tim and Rachel stayed behind. I say that is why I wanted Daniel in and that is one reason I argued hard for focus to be given on the speeches (identity). We also agree to construct a list of sympathetic MPs.

Wednesday 15 May

Speak in a debate on agriculture in the midst of the beef crisis, which the government has all but acknowledged is out of its control. MH rings up when I get home to say my piece on Goldsmith really is 'brilliant' and I must get it published.

Thursday 16 May

Ring Paul Goodman at the *Telegraph* from King's Cross station about the Goldsmith piece. He says, 'Be patient. We may do it next week.'

Lady at the window in front of me in the queue for tickets complains about the fact that her destination is 'not a very nice station'. The man behind the counter is surprisingly sympathetic. He will pass her views 'up the line'.

Friday 17 May

Chair conference on future of European court at Inner Temple. Michael Howard opens the meeting and speaks to about forty lawyers and MPs from here and abroad. It is a tough speech touching on 'repatriation' and indicating he will have none of a federal Europe. Mainly written by Daniel Hannan and receives much publicity – on *Evening Standard* billboards. Just what we need, so long as tomorrow's papers don't say it is a leadership bid.

Saturday 18 May

Talk to Howard on the phone in Kent. He is slightly shocked by the massive coverage he has had. Downing Street is apparently in a bate about it. *Telegraph* says he's now a serious contender for leadership. *Mail* says he is merely interpreting government policy. *Times* says it's a start, but isn't really specific enough. Net effect: to have started process of winning right-wing editors to his side and making him a serious player in any leadership stakes after the general election. I think he needs to do it again when things have cooled off; but this is not the moment to say so.

Sunday 19 May

Drive (four hours) to Michael Howard's house in east Kent. Pass through a barrier of police armed with automatic guns. Michael and Sandra superb hosts. Also there – editor of the *Mail on Sunday* and his wife, Jonathan and Vivien Holborow. Sun shining. A very relaxed day. MH delighted with the way the publicity went on his speech – especially that the story was about Labour divisions and not Tory. Get him to agree to bring Daniel into the circle and to focus his next European speech on attacking Labour. The *Daily Mail* later agree to take a piece from me attacking Goldsmith. Overnight stay in her Kent house with Ann's friend and our neighbour in Maunsel Street, Fiona Hancock.

Tuesday 21 May

Major makes his 'we've had enough in Europe' statement in the House of Commons. I am hijacked by the BBC at St Stephen's Entrance and say something supportive (first item on 6 o'clock news). 'Eurosceptics support Major's new stand…'

Dinner in evening with Tom Dunne (St Martin's Press) at the Ritz. We don't have a proper plan to publish *Challenge from the East* in the UK. Tom and I end up arguing vehemently about Britain's role in Northern Ireland. He has a Catholic Irish background and takes the predictable line that the Brits must get out. I say I don't really care in emotional terms but I am not prepared to face anarchy and mass bloodshed on our back doorstep. I say he and the rest of the Yanks completely under-estimate the force and anger of the Protestants. This would erupt if the British withdrew and create a bloody civil war of Bosnian proportions.

Tuesday 28 May
Daniel puts the whole Howard business rather nicely. 'A year ago it was mad to be supporting Howard; now it's just eccentric.'

Wednesday 29 May – Sunday 2 June
In US promoting book. Lunches in New York (Manhattan Institute) on Thursday and Washington (American Enterprise Institute) on Friday. Some radio and dinner Friday night with John O'Sullivan. Quite good attendances and thought by publisher to be worthwhile – but they are only paying for the Washington bit.

Gloriously sunny weekend. On Saturday I am sitting in a bar in Greenwich Village where I ask for pen and paper. Just seen the most hilarious wedding. This is what I write:

> Unlikely time of 8.30 – warm late spring evening. Bride comes out of what looks like a synagogue with thick painted lips and smoking a cigarette. She tries to pick a fight with one of the guests on the doorsteps of the church. The groom, dressed entirely in white, intervenes to separate them. They then all proceed into the crowded street to find a taxi. Someone asks, 'Why isn't the maid of honour carrying the dress?' (a white Elizabethan-looking affair in which the bride, who must be at least 40, looks as though she is stifling). The bridee shouts, 'Because she is eight months pregnant and can hardly carry herself.' A slight man prances about chanting through taxi windows, 'My sister has just got married. Can I have your taxi?' No one obliges.
>
> The bride carries on into the street and is lost forever. The barman who lent me the biro and paper tells me the church has plastic flowers by the saints and candles which light up with electric bulbs.

The next day I am sitting in the same café in the village. Next to me two men are kissing; later I talk to a middle-aged woman whose daughter is a beautiful barmaid. The mother tells me she has come to New York from LA to have a tattoo on her left bum. She already has one on the right cheek. On the other side a 30-something professor of mathematics is blubbing quietly because she can't get 'tenure'.

Life in the raw. I wish I had the time to write the play.

Tuesday 4 June

MH asks me to have a drink with him in his room. Apparently Derek Conway (whips' office) is offering his services. MH has had him to lunch. Conway is in touch with Greg Knight (deputy Chief Whip). I urge MH to go as high profile as possible in his speeches, e.g. the one next week attacking Labour on Europe – but be very cautious about being seen to run too much of an operation for the leadership – the party won't like that. He agrees.

We discuss Portillo. General agreement he is a busted flush. Rumours about him too strong, even if untrue, especially as he is not denying them. We have to pick up the NTB gang, formerly Portillo, now Forsyth. Told MH of a conversation with Gerald Howarth when he said there were 3½ good men in the Cabinet – the ½ was Howard.

Wednesday 5 June

Go to Winston Churchill's engagement party. On the way Tony Marlow tries to get me to agree to vote for Bill Cash's Referendum Bill. I say, 'No. If you want I will write you a letter giving my reasons. A referendum on "in or out of Europe" is pandering to Goldsmith, premature and would be one we would lose at present.'

Marlow smiles and says, 'I won't trouble you again.'

At Churchill's party Jim Spicer says to Ann, 'Your husband is being a statesman; things are beginning to go his way.' Bump into Bernard Jenkin and Iain Duncan Smith. Tell them about offer from Downing Street to join a working group with federalists to discuss fraud in Europe. They agree with me that we should say no unless at least equal number of Eurosceptics. I don't really want to do it anyway.

Sunday 9 June

MH rings. Thinks we had better steer clear of the *On the Record* programme due on 23 June. Likes Hannan's new speech – may be difficult to clear with Number 10 and FCO. I ask his advice on voting for Cash's Bill; we decide, unless I can explain why not in, say, an article in the *Standard*, it would look churlish not to vote for him. Portillo gets very bad press, especially from Peter Dobbie in *Mail on Sunday*. He gave a rowdy party in his flat in Admiralty House which disturbed beating of the Retreat in Horse Guards Parade. General view is Portillo has had it. Question is where will his few supporters go? Can they be got for Howard?

Monday 10 June
'Philosophy'* meeting at Jonathan Aitken's. Much press interest prompted by a leak in the *Sunday Times* that James Goldsmith would be pitted against Bill Cash (with whom I had temporarily made peace by agreeing to vote for his Referendum Bill the next day). Richard Shepherd and I set out in Bonsor's government car. In the few minutes' drive to Lord North Street I tell Bonsor of the *Sunday Times* piece and that Aitken's house would no doubt be staked out by a mass of journalists. He asks the driver to take a right turn off Millbank and to park in Smith Square, from where we walk round the corner. Sure enough a pack of journalists. We march towards them in a phalanx which gives us a sense of security.

Inside Lamont delivers 45-minute paper giving three ways of pulling out of Europe: European Area (meaning complying with EU rules), Swiss-type negotiated arrangement and new arrangements based on GATT. Meeting packed with usual culprits.

Tuesday 11 June
Chair lunch meeting of ERG with Malcolm Rifkind at the Wassall offices in Victoria Street. Rifkind tries to get away with flannel. We probe and probe. What do you mean by variable geometry, repatriation, eastern expansion, controlling the cost? He says, 'Give us a chance', then, 'Our job is to hold the fort. Surely you don't want us to pull out?'

I say, 'More and more people will unless you have a coherent strategy.'

He says, 'It's early days.'

Malcolm Pearson asks, 'Have you looked at the cost and benefits of staying in?'

Rifkind begins to feel uncomfortable. On his way out he says, 'I wish I had brought my private detective rather than my PS.'

Vote with Bill Cash's Bill, not because I approve but because I do not wish to break ranks with Eurosceptics.

In evening dinner with Michael Howard. James Cran, Daniel Hannan and MH's two aides for guests.

---

* A large political discussion group run at the time by Jonathan Aitken.

Sunday 16 June

Ring MH. Put to him that he must continue to establish his European position. He says, in effect, 'I've done enough of this. I will not risk being disloyal.'

I say, 'Being loyal and being firm about Europe are not incompatible.' This is a matter to which we will have to return.

I am concerned that he will be lost in the crowd, and that the Eurosceptic centre right won't believe him. The problem will be the first round of the leadership contest.

Monday 17 June

David Howell has seen the amazing *Wall Street Journal* write-up of my book* (probably because he works for a Japanese firm) and wants to buy a copy.

Thursday 20 June

MH incandescent with rage about an article by Donald Macintyre in *The Independent*, saying he has backers for the bid for leadership, but that lack of real position on any issue makes him an implausible contestant. James Cran rings me to say, 'Howard should be "small" on plots/operation and "large" on speeches.'

Sunday 23 June

Drive to lunch at a big garden party given by Andrew Alexander. Peter Lilley and David Davis amongst the many guests. Davis has been in the weekend press as apparently having threatened to resign because he had not been offered a PC or Cabinet post. When I get home Paul Goodman from the *Telegraph* rings to say my article anti Goldsmith going in the paper the next day.

Monday 24 June

My anti-Goldsmith piece very prominent. My main point is that he is two faced: federalist when he writes in French and anti-federalist when in English. Much chat about it – on the whole complimentary – in the tea rooms.

Sunday 30 June

MH rings to congratulate me on the Goldsmith piece. MH and I are not quite at one at the moment. Apparently at a meeting I missed last Thursday

---

* Michael Spicer, *The Challenge from the East and the Rebirth of the West*, St Martin's Press, 1996. It opens with the accurate, but at the time implausible, forecast that China would be building one new large power station every week in 2010.

(because of Annabel's graduation) James Cran and Nick Bonsor took the view that there was no need for MH to make spectacular speeches, especially on Europe, but they would start to jog people's elbows. I take exactly the opposite point of view. I am worried about another article like Macintyre's in *The Independent* appearing. MH says it's all about the actions he takes in government, not words.

Monday 1 July

Bump into Howard and have two or three minutes in his room. My position is the following:

Key battle in early rounds of a leadership contest will be for the support of the centre right (two-thirds of the party).

Defining issue is Europe.

MH has some way to go in establishing a fair and credible position on this.

No necessary conflict between being loyal and credible on Europe.

Later that night walk home with James Cran. He and I remain at one that MH must not be seen to be plotting but he has a long way to go in fixing his credentials on the right.

While we are walking by the new loos near my house, Julian Brazier comes bouncing up about his rebellion on the privatisation of homes for servicemen. I say I sympathise with his anger that the services are being let down but the specific issue, a sale and leaseback of service property which would bring in money to defence and improve living conditions of servicemen, is a good thing.

Tuesday 2 July

Lunch with Alan Chalfont at Mark's Club. He has a government amendment in the Lords next Thursday on servicemen's houses and is going to see Portillo. I ring Portillo after lunch to tell him Chalfont personally quite friendly disposed to him.

Dinner at Number 10 – 200th anniversary of the Farmers' Club. Commons a three-line running whip with lots of votes. I am told that there is no need for Commons members to wear black tie (usual custom for Lords to wear black tie and Commons lounge suits). However on this occasion everyone turns up in a DJ except me. PM comes up to me and seems to take pity. 'Do you want to borrow a dinner jacket from me?' I say, 'I think you're taller than me, Prime Minister, and if I changed now I would miss the dinner!'

Drive home late with Alastair Goodlad. Say will support him on the sale of army homes coming – in a vote the opposition plan to force next week (Tuesday) when they hope to defeat the government.

Thursday 4 July
6 p.m. Meet Iain Duncan Smith in members' lobby. We go off to the smoking room to pick each other's brains. He runs Redwood's campaign. I sort of run Howard's. Neither of us gives anything away except to agree that Portillo is out of the race.

Friday 5–Sunday 7 July
Michael and Amanda Dobbs to stay. MD is the annual dinner speaker at Birtsmorton Court. Jolly, friendly evening. Nineteen people to lunch the next day. MD is such a pleasant, interesting man (with great ability).

Tuesday 16 July
A Michael Howard day. Chair a lunch of ERG at which he is guest speaker. He goes down pretty well, saying there would certainly be circumstances in which he would advocate pulling out of Europe. Sadly John Townend, Norman Lamont and Jonathan Aitken are not present.

Later that evening have dinner with MH in his heavily guarded Ebury Street house. Present: Whetstone, Hannan, Cran, Bonsor. MH doesn't want to say or do anything to rock the boat. However, prepared to take a bit of Daniel input to his speech to the party conference.

Sunday 21 July
MH calls. Heathcoat-Amory resignation from HMG story breaking. He's a friend of MH. We discuss how to involve him. I say I mean to get ERG to adopt him; he's in for a bit of a shock when he finds the ex-minister Eurosceptic beat rather crowded.

Tuesday 23 July
Michael Howard rings me late at night to congratulate me on *Newsnight* performance supporting David Heathcoat-Amory's pending resignation. I was reluctant to do this for two reasons:

David was a very tough deputy whip against us during Maastricht. James Cran actually walked out of a 'discussion without coffee' with him about voting. DH-A, ostensibly then a sceptic, had been holier than the Pope in his pursuit of government's policies.

I don't like arguing with Conservative MPs on *Newsnight* – this time it was Tim Rathbone.

However, it goes off reasonably amicably and I am able to re-emphasise my thoughts on Europe.

Monday 5 August
Jonathan and Vivien Holborow (Jonathan is editor of highly successful *Mail on Sunday*) to stay in Cropthorne. Such a nice couple. Brian Mawhinney joins us for tea on his way to Malvern. At that point polls still turning in our direction. We all agree in the midst of the summer fragrance (mainly lilies) of our courtyard that there is still enough to play for. Two opposite forces: wish for a change v. conservatism of British people and economy moving our way. I say a firm position on Europe would tip the balance.

Friday 9 August
'Snap shot' Gallup poll in the *Telegraph* shows gap widening with Labour.

Saturday 17 August
MH rings to thank me for my calls to Sandra the two previous days to warn her that a story was breaking in the *Daily Telegraph* that MH's new (and, in my view, undesirable) ID cards were carrying the EU flag. I have tried to stress that MH is fighting to include the Union Jack. Daniel is writing a critical leader for Monday as it is company policy to do so.

On the other subject, Howard says he is very keen to get our list of MPs sorted out. He would like someone to be the sole guardian of a single list. Would I think carefully about who should do this?

Tuesday 20 August
I call MH back to say I will do the list. He seems relieved and grateful. The ID storm has broken but he seems to be winning the Union Jack battle.

Saturday 24 August
Another Michael Howard storm breaking just as I leave for holiday. This time it's about a faulty calculation of sentences which has resulted in the beginning of a mass release of prisoners. Howard puts a stop to this, having just learnt about it on Thursday and pending a court decision next Tuesday. The issue is whether remand time should be set against total time of sentence or each of a multiple sentence (the latter very much to the benefit of the prisoner).

Sunday 22 September
Usual weekend phone conversation with MH. He has got Christopher Chope, chairman of the candidates, to invite in candidates in a systematic way to meet Howard on Home Office matters. CC, however, did not commit himself to MH. I say he is probably stuck with Portillo or with Forsyth perhaps. MH says he is apparently not doing a similar exercise for them.

We discuss the forthcoming ERG pamphlet, *Legal Agenda for Europe*, and MH's contribution. Does he want it hyped up or should I stress it is a report of his earlier speech? 'Without hesitation the latter,' he says; he was trying to have 'a go' at Ken Clarke at the Thursday Cabinet on the single currency. Clarke has been getting close to breaking the Cabinet truce with the formula 'Wait and see until after the election'. On BBC's *World This Weekend* Clarke comes close to advocating an entry into the single currency and to coming off the fence, which he apparently describes as a 'pathetic' position.

Tuesday 24 September
Up to London for lunch with Emmanuel Kay, Stanley Kalms, John Craven, former chairman of Morgan Grenfell, and someone from the CBI to whom I give a pounding on the single currency and the CBI's fence-sitting. Conversation moves to Ken Clarke, who was said in *The Sun* to be baring his teeth at the right for the party's position on single currency. Nick Bonsor has come out accusing him of breaking ranks – pretty remarkable thing for one minister to say of another. First story on BBC and ITV. Clearly Bonsor has gone to earth because no live footage of him – instead library footage on ITV of yours truly, Cash and Shepherd appearing rather sheepishly at Jonathan Aitken's party in the summer! This followed PM at Number 10 with Israeli PM in attendance, saying something to the effect of Clarke having been misrepresented.

Wednesday 25 September
Dinner at Ebury Street, MH's claustrophobic safe house. The whole of the ground floor is occupied by police. Much talk at the start about Bonsor's flirtation with political death by attacking Clarke in public. At one point he thought he was a goner. Onto Howard's speeches at the party conference. The main one is pretty straightforward. We try to add some spice to the one he is giving to the Conservative Way Forward. Eventually we settle for a CCO pamphlet-type speech packaged into the theme of 'patriotism'.

Wednesday 2 October
Jonathan Holborow phones from Pembroke Hotel where he is 'imprisoned' at the Labour Party conference in Blackpool. He asks whether I will do a piece attacking Neil Hamilton, who 'has to go'. I say it's not my scene.

That evening to a party given by Howard Flight at Royal Academy. Bump into the chairman of YCs, who is fighting Easington!

Prior to this had talked to Rachel Whetstone about MH's conference speeches. Put the point that it's important for him to appeal more to the right (to come out well in any future ballot) and to look more consistent. I suggest quoting the bits from the European White Paper which talk about reforming the Court of Justice. She says we wouldn't get it cleared by Number 10. 'He wouldn't be allowed to quote the White Paper?' I ask. 'Probably not. There is jealousy of anyone who tries to upstage on Euroscepticism.' Presumably because PM feels he can't do it himself. The fact that PM won't come off the European fence is a tragedy. To do so could still be one way of winning GE.

Monday 7 October

First day of party conference in Bournemouth. 9.50 *Panorama* on Goldsmith; they have dropped an interview with me in which I had warned right-wing Conservatives that voting for Goldsmith's Referendum Party would (a) be voting for a phoney (he is a federalist in France etc.) and (b) be putting in Labour if there were sufficient Tory defections. Instead *Panorama* show Alistair McAlpine deserting to Goldsmith and Redwood declining to say whether in some instances he would support a Goldsmith candidate against a Tory one.

Talk to Michael Howard on the phone in his hotel bedroom (he has two big speeches tomorrow). Decide Redwood has shot himself in the foot. Problem is to prevent loyalist sceptics all drifting off to Portillo or even Ian Lang, who has tried to make some sceptic noises.

Tuesday 8 October

MH's speeches OK, given that he doesn't want to be more Eurosceptical. Mood at the round of parties more jolly than might have been expected.

Wednesday 9 October

MH gets good leaders in *Times* and *Telegraph*. I meet him for a cup of tea. Very convivial. I say he must get someone to help him improve his presentation. He and Sandra agree. Also he must make his scepticism more passionate and believable. Apparently he goes on *The Andrew Neil Show* immediately afterwards and does just that.

Meet Jonathan Holborow and Peter Dobbie and work at more details on my *Mail on Sunday* pieces for the weekend. Michael Dobbs also there. He is a gun waiting to be hired by MH.

Meet up with Simon Jenkins at *Times* party – also a short but amicable chat with Peter Stothard. Off to dinner with Ann outside Bournemouth at a hotel in Ferndown.

Back at the conference get-together with *Target* people, on whom I try to press myself for some more work.

On to BA party. A bit of a spat with George Jones of *Telegraph* about party unity – he lectures me on it (a bit worrying since am writing a piece for *Mail on Sunday* on exactly this subject). Tell Redwood what I think of the *Panorama* piece. He says they faked the question. He was set up. I say I will remove criticism from my *Mail* article.

Talk to Brian Mawhinney and say he has to get tougher with Goldsmithites.

Friday 11 October

Up at 6.30 – having been to bed at 2 – to write first draft of my *Mail* piece. Leave Ma's flat in Milford-on-Sea on a lovely sunny day at around 12 noon for home. Meanwhile at the conference in Bournemouth Clarke apparently makes an amazingly popular speech.

Much toing and froing with the *Mail on Sunday* about my piece on the single currency. Complete my version in the late morning and go home and from there to *La Traviata* at Covent Garden. On returning from the opera find a piece on the fax machine completely rewritten by Jonathan Holborow, which sharpens up the point that with a Conservative government we would never enter a single currency and with Labour we almost definitely would. I decide to 'go' with this, with some changes.

Saturday 12 October

More work on the article with Peter Dobbie and Jonathan Holborow himself.

Talk to Michael Howard in the afternoon. He is nervous about the article, which he has discussed with Holborow.

Sunday 13 October

Article finally appears. No great reaction except MH rings to say how impressed he is by it in its final form.

Worcester Evening News rings me at about 10 p.m. Do I have any comments on Goldsmith's outburst against me on *On the Record* when asked by John Humphrys, 'Why are you putting up a candidate against the avid Eurosceptic Michael Spicer – if you say it's all about standing against the federalists?' He said, 'Michael was a Heathite.'

I tell the *WEN*, 'In that case so was Lady Thatcher.'

Monday 14 October

Parliament back and yet it isn't. One line whip and no one around except a few journalists. First day of two of debate on defence.

Dinner chez Cranborne. Discuss what to do about MPs' misdemeanours. If we give so many powers to Parliamentary Commissioner that we destroy sovereignty of Parliament, everything is lost.

Tuesday 15 October
ERG lunch – Alastair Goodlad attending.

92 Group dinner at St Stephen's Club. Much buzz about the 'slate' for 1922 election. Present: Portillo, Redwood, Marcus Fox – who claims this year will be his last one if re-elected chairman. David Evans comes up to congratulate me on my first 92 dinner. Says we have disagreed in the past but welcome. I say I did not realise we had disagreed. I think he is talking about his support for Redwood, whom he is apparently deserting. Since Redwood is standing beside us, it is a little awkward.

Wednesday 16 October
Lunch at Garrick. Alistair McAlpine at the big table looking a bit sheepish now he has joined the Referendum Party, which is opposing me. We meet later for a glass of wine. We agree to differ and to keep in touch. He is vehemently opposed to Michael Howard for his illiberal views re the police etc., but says he might change his mind when the dust settles. He was 'miffed' to have been edged out from the *Mail on Sunday* by my article 'because I was a friend of the editor'!

Tuesday 29 October
Bump into Townend and Cran. Apparently PM has been tough with Townend on the matter of personalised election address re single currency. Major is toughening up with the right. Is this because he is about to ditch the left on something? – or just that he has given up on us?

Wednesday 30 October
Take David Martin to Pratt's. David is very active with Redwood. I say it's unfortunate that Townend and Major trying to dig in about single currency and election addresses. It begins to become an issue. What I will do is say 'We will never enter single currency', and focus on need to reform process of the court, which paradoxically is much more important but not seen as relevant to the rebellion!

Sunday 3 November
Woken up at the Haven Hotel (Poole), where we are staying with Ma, at 6 a.m. by a firework display over at Studland – strange time for fireworks. Ma enjoys her usual war with the hotel receptionist. We are getting quite expert at it. All the news is about a Major caning row. Gillian Shephard says on BBC Radio 4 she would like to bring back the cane to deal with lawlessness in schools. Major is reported to have rung her on her mobile to warn her off this line.

Sunday 10 November

Out all day on the Remembrance Sunday circuit. Howard rings in evening. I spend quite a lot of time grumbling about the proposed gun laws and the fact that we did not follow Cullen's advice.* I say this is going to leave rather a trail in the press.

Wednesday 13 November

Talk to Rachel Whetstone. MH very tired and dispirited after gun business. Still more to come on Monday; I say if they can get opportunity to agree on a guillotine motion they should do it. Get it out of the way instead of prolonging the agony. MH wants to allow a free debate to make up for not having consulted before. I say, 'You can't mend that fence. Best to get rid of the issue quickly and cleanly now.' Rachel and I discuss dates for the new year.

Bump into Douglas Hogg in the voting lobby – having asked him a rather 'rude' question during the afternoon. I say, 'Well done not being rattled, for no purpose, into the extra cull of cattle.'

He says, in effect, 'We're going to have to do it in the end to please the Northern Irish' (and keep a majority together until the spring – we only won the vote by one, with the Irish voting against us). Things are never quite what they seem to be in politics.

This parliament is eking out its last days. Shades of 1978–9. This government digs its feet in, often on relatively minor issues which nevertheless cause controversy; just when the controversy is dying down, they abandon it. Child support, no doubt 48-hour week, presidency of the Commission, cow culling etc. They allow through all the big stuff: QMV, Maastricht, EMU conditions, without much hesitation.

Monday 18 November

Europe dominates everything – even when this wretched gun business is going through. Rachel Whetstone says she thinks we ought to get out – nothing else really counts. Bump into Dennis Skinner, 'Beast of Bolsover'. He says there's everything to fight for about Europe. 'We must pull out.' I say, 'You and I will fight shoulder to shoulder one day.'

He says, 'Blair's a piece of cake; he stands for nothing so you can push him over with ease.'

---

* Following the Dunblane shootings, Lord Cullen of Whitekirk held a public inquiry which made many recommendations, including stricter rules on the control and use of firearms.

Wednesday 20 November
The ultra-sceptics have been out in force today – in Committee Room 13 where the government defeated in John Whittingdale's vote on the issue of approving certain EU documents relating to conditions to be imposed on states not part of EMU. Cash, Duncan Smith, Marlow and Heathcoat-Amory stirring things up. I would join them if there was anything to achieve in terms of stopping the government.

Talk to Gill and Townend. The latter is chairman of 92 Group and certainly worth winning over, especially as he is a member of ERG – which we hope will be a Howard platform.

Not many people in the parliamentary party talking of winning the election now.

Thursday 21 November
Speak at 1922 Committee. I say there is confusion over Tory briefing about Ecofin;* December 2 stability pact† will go ahead, affecting Britain even though we have opted out of single currency because convergence conditions; but PM says at PMQs there will be no decision. Whom do we trust? We must have it out 'on the floor of the House before Ecofin'.

Repeat this to Alastair Goodlad, who says nothing will happen at Ecofin. Meanwhile the storm in the party grows. Tony Marlow has even threatened to resign the whip, which means we are in a minority.

Marcus Fox winks at me as he goes into Chief Whip's office, he says to put over my views and those of others.

Sunday 24 November
Sad day. Clarke pulls wool over eyes of the House of Commons on negotiation at Ecofin. Speaker calls far more Euro federalists than sceptics, thus giving the sense that the party going soft – which is the reverse of the case. Lamont takes up one Euro slot arguing that the currency 'opt out' is foolproof; people like me worried that EMU will come in by the back door in the sense that those with opt-out will still have to conform to EMU rules. I ask Lamont what was the point of his intervention. If all hunky dory at Ecofin, why join in the demand for a debate about it?

---

* The Economic and Financial Affairs Council, commonly known as Ecofin, comprises the economic and finance ministers of the EU member states, as well as budget ministers when budgetary issues are discussed.
† The arrangement agreed at Maastricht whereby EU can impose fiscal constrains on member states.

Wednesday 27 November
Dinner meeting at Maunsel Street with Michael Howard, Nick Bonsor and James Cran. MH determined mood. Needs to be a change of leadership even if result of GE is narrow.

Sunday 1 December
MH rings to thank me for the supper last Wednesday – also to talk about Francis Maude, who was a key figure in Major's election in 1990. Should he be campaign manager for Howard? I advise, 'Not so fast'. Maude has been out of Parliament for five years. Could upset the fragile group we are collecting. MH promises to 'pick his brains' but not to offer him anything. We agree to meet before Christmas.

Tuesday 3 December
Question to PM pressing him (unsuccessfully) on his IGC in Dublin. Meeting with MH during votes on the Budget. He wants me to lead his campaign. Give him the chance to think about it. He seems happy. Says he has fallen out with Major 'probably because the PM thinks I am engaged in an operation to succeed him. His intelligence is very good; it is how he survives'.

Meet Clarke in the loo during the voting. He and I agree at least on one thing, that as practically the only Eurosceptic to sign the (ineffective) letter supporting Nick Scott before his (deselection) committee, I was right to do it 'because I don't like mob rule' – my words.

Wednesday 4 December
Lovely clear autumn day. Walk through St James's Park to East India Club in St James's Square for Wellington governors' meeting. Clearly PM and Foreign Secretary have same idea because I literally bump into them crossing The Mall. They are on their way to a conference on Bosnia. I say to them, 'This could be embarrassing. People may think this is a conspiracy!' Then as we reach some crash barricades I say, 'How do ordinary people get out of this?'

Malcolm Rifkind says, 'That's your problem!' Both nice chaps – pity they're not better at running the country.

Thursday 5 December
Ann's birthday. Give her breakfast in bed then off to Hampton Court on a bright clear autumn day.

Frightful row at the 1922 Committee* when I get back. Edward Leigh leads the charge, accusing Major of being out of step with the party and therefore totally undemocratic.

Friday 6 December
Government's position going from bad to worse. PM backs off earlier in the week from his (leaked) position on a single currency. Polls show, unbelievably, Labour 40 points ahead. If true, I will go down the tube. BBC Radio 4 ask to interview me for the *Today* programme. I agree to suggest a compromise of 'no single currency in first wave'. Ring Alastair Goodlad to see if this is any sort of a runner. He says 'No' but would like me to go on the programme. I decline. I am not willing to waste my time on this one. Better the running be made by the left (Yeo, Dorrell), who are talking about not going in while the convergence conditions are being fudged.

Sunday 8 December
Michael Howard rings. Have I seen the papers – especially *Sunday Telegraph*: 'Howard seen off in fight with Clarke'? Apparently what happened is that Howard prepared a paper on the effect of 'fudging' the convergence conditions on our negotiating position. This was accepted after some argument by the Cabinet, although Major ended by saying, 'The policy of wait-and-see must not change.' Howard – far from losing – won the day.

Talk to Daniel (at home in Bath), who says he will ring Charles Moore about it.

I refuse all bids for TV, comments in paper etc.

Monday 9 December
Talk to Nick Wood (*Express*), Elinor Goodman (ITV), Robin Oakley (BBC) in the lobby, pointing them to the Cabinet paper on convergence. Woods intent on building it into a 'Michael Howard threatens to resign' story. I do my best to rubbish this.

MH rings me 7 p.m. at Maunsel Street, very worried: '*Express* going over the top.' I call Jon Craig on the *Express* to say not true that MH will kick up the dust. He says 'Don't worry.' I tell MH, who says, 'I just hope it's OK.'

---

* 'Described by some [MPs] as the worst 1922 meeting of their careers.' Anthony Seldon, *Major: A Political Life*, Weidenfeld & Nicolson, 1997, p. 688.

Tuesday 10 December

3.30: Meeting with Emmanuel Kay, Michael Edwardes, John Craven. Kay reads out a letter he has received from Thatcher backing a general referendum on Europe but saying she couldn't do it publicly.

On to a dinner at the Carlton Club, chaired by John Cope. Speaker Ken Clarke. Ask Clarke whether he has revised his view in the light of the stability pact that there is no relationship between single currency and single fiscal policy. He doesn't answer the question.

Talk of the old days not being quite so rosy. People punched each other. Jerry Wiggin winked at me. 'Like you with Tom Swain.'*

Amazed he remembers. I say, 'You should have been Chief Whip, Jerry, with that sort of memory'.

Francis Maude at dinner. I approach him, saying, 'I gather you had a meeting with Michael Howard and said you reserved your position.'

He says, 'I think we might still win; but if we don't MH is my man.'

Wednesday 11 December

Meet Tony Wedgwood Benn at ITV party. We both agree that left and right might one day have to combine to protect the democratic sovereignty of our country. He says there is always a sequence of leaders: 'dreamer, fixer and straight man'. He thinks Blair is bound to do a deal with Liberals whatever his majority after the next election.

MH emerging as the heavyweight on our side. Talk to him in the car on the way home. Tell him Jonathan Holborow has rung me to say he couldn't get through to MH. Wants reassurance about his article on Clarke. MH agrees to ring him at home at 11 p.m.

Thursday 12 December

Jonathan Holborow rings to say MH seeing him late tonight. His information is that Redwood is gaining in strength. He wants to help MH. I say these things come and go. MH's job is to get through the first round; then he could gain in strength.

---

* Labour MP for North East Derbyshire 1959–79 and a former fairground boxer – at least by repute. I had a contretemps with him during the Heseltine mace-waving episode. Conservatives felt cheated of a vote in the Commons, as a result of which the government survived, which the Conservatives felt they should not have done. It was the last time (1976) violence erupted in the chamber of the House of Commons.

Tuesday 17 December
Lunch with Aitken, who was at a dinner last night with Goldsmith, who has been plotting the destruction in his constituency of MH. MH must have done something to him at the DTI, or whatever. Very odd of Aitken to have accepted invitation. All very gloomy about election prospects.

Bump into Temple-Morris in the canteen before 10 p.m. vote. He is clear about his objectives – and 'those of about thirty others' (doubtless an exaggeration – probably only ten at most). Will try to split the right and get Heseltine, Clarke or Dorrell as leader. Failing this will 'vote with Labour' in Europe and, if necessary, form another party. Is he aiming for House of Lords?

Sunday 22 December
Daniel rings at about 10 a.m. when I am still in bed sorting out some notes. Have I seen the front page of the *Sunday Telegraph*? 'No.' 'Michael Howard is said to be launching his leadership campaign on the basis of "We may have to get out of Europe".'

I ring MH. 'What's going on?' Apparently his PPS, David Lidington, briefed David Wastell of the *Sunday Telegraph*, who was doing a story on the number of visits Cabinet members had made to MPs' seats. MH was second to Redwood (not in Cabinet). Hence the leadership story. Lidington has tried to damp it down but has achieved the reverse.

Howard angry – wants to ring all editors to say he is in favour of staying in Europe. I advise against anything so proactive. I don't think that Howard will take my advice.

Monday 23 December
Sure enough, denial stories appear.

Friday 27 December
Mail on Sunday lobby man rings to ask if I have anything to say about leadership campaign. I say, 'Not today, I'm afraid, however short of copy you are. Main objective is to put heads down and win the election.' Ring MH to check that he runs the same line. He says 'Absolutely'. Starts to talk about need not to look too 'extreme' on Europe. I say no fear that he will do this; problem is the other way, that he won't win enough Eurosceptics in the first round.

Sunday 29 December
MH rings to wish me a good holiday in the Canaries. The Cabinet on the

Thursday before Christmas (19 December) was a strange one. There was a narrow majority in favour of the wait-and-see policy on the single currency. Howard led the attack, which failed (weakly supported by Portillo). Rifkind argued vehemently against changing the policy. At the end of the meeting Major blurred matters by calling for another paper from Clarke on the question of whether other countries would 'fudge' the criteria. (Clarke had presented a paper saying it was too early to tell – hence the need for wait-and-see and no clear commitment not to go in.) 'Wait and see' is the new euphemism for 'We want to go into the single currency'.

Chapter 14

John Major: final days

Sunday 5 January 1997

Article appears in the *Sunday Times* to say Michael Howard could be backed by Margaret Thatcher and William Hague. I wonder where that is coming from.

Sunday 12 January

MH rings in London. 'We do need to work out our strategy.' Invites me and Ann to lunch on weekend of 24–26 January.

Tuesday 14 January

Bump into MH at David Davis's party at the Foreign Office. All the buzz is about several articles saying MH is now the front runner to take over from Major. The press, especially a lady from *On the Record*, Kim Catcheside, know about my involvement. MH indicates he wants to see me after 10 p.m. vote in his room. We meet and agree that cold water must be poured on all this before it gets out of control.

Wednesday 15 January

Article by Bruce Anderson in *Daily Mail* links me to Howard and talks of balloons bursting:.

> A new balloon has now appeared in the skies over Westminster. For some months now Michael Howard's friends have been making discreet soundings on his behalf, a process organised by the former Minister, Sir Michael Spicer.
>
> Yesterday, the first hint of their activities reached the press. This will not have pleased either Mr Howard or Sir Michael. It is even possible that the leak came from another aspirant in the hope that the Howard balloon will deflate.

Daniel Hannan talks of air war with no troops on the ground.

MH rings in the morning. Should he go on *On the Record* on Sunday? I warn him about Kim Catcheside and a Portilloite called Robbie Gibb, who works on the programme. Over lunch Robin Day, who has read Bruce Anderson's piece, introduces me ironically as MH's campaign manager.

Meeting in MH's room to agonise over *On the Record*. He decides to go on.

1922 Committee has been moved to 5.30 on Wednesdays; no whip given because business not announced till following day. I get up and suggest we go back to Thursday because the whip is the main attraction. People laugh and bang their desks. All very good natured and rather irrelevant.

Iain Duncan Smith says National Union are being disloyal by suggesting new way of electing the leader. Should be talking about the election victory – not about leadership. (National Union people are always accusing MPs of being disloyal and disruptive.) David Shaw says BBC will show a secretly made film of National Union discussing leadership on *On the Record*.

On the way home on a foggy night, bump into Stephen Dorrell and Peter Luff on corner of Cowley Street and Great Peter Street. As I pass them I say, 'What a right-wing Eurosceptic cabal.' They laugh. Dorrell and Luff on the left but Dorrell recently said that we may have to come out of Europe – his position to that date had been Euro-fanatical. This is now known as 'doing a Dorrell'. He has lost the left and made no friends on the right. Rumour has it he is still Major's choice as successor.

Sunday 19 January
MH does pretty well on *On the Record*, mainly about Home Office matters. When asked about the leadership he replies that his only real concern is to win the election. *Sunday Times* has a gossip piece by Simon Sebag Montefiore blaming me for all the hype about MH. He seems rather friendly with Tristan Garel-Jones. MH and I talk on the phone later in the evening and I agree not to stir matters up further. I say we may have a chance of winning the air war but not yet, I fear, the war on the ground, i.e. with MPs. MH ought to try to be more proactive with the target group.

Wednesday 22 January
My birthday. Ann prepares a lovely breakfast in the drawing room in front of the fire. MH rings the office. Rumours going round that he has given up pressing in Cabinet for firmer position on Euro currency. Could I scotch it without stirring up stories of leadership bids?

Friday 24 January
Chair ERG conference at French Assembly. Eleven UK MPs and PPCs present. Some good Germans this time. We manage to keep together and finally agree to meet again to look at problems of secession. Over a meal with

Michael Fabricant (one of our contingent), he says doesn't really like the look of MH. Would like me as leader! I say I am not exactly on the menu.

Sunday 26 January

Get off the Eurostar train with Ann at Ashford and taxi to MH. Arrive 10 a.m. and plunge into a discussion with him about the idea of trying to broker a compromise on the wording for candidates' election addresses. He suggests 'I agree with government's line and will not personally vote for a single currency'. I say that won't wash but 'I understand the government's line' might. I also say I'm adopting a rather different tack. He tries the revised version on the party chairman, Brian Mawhinney, on the phone, who likes it. (Later that night, on my advice, he tries it out on John Townend, who doesn't.) Also at lunch, Charles and Carla Powell, Nick Lloyd (former editor of *Daily Express*), Jonathan and Vivien Holborow and Alan and Jane Clark. Alan has just got Chelsea and I say to him, 'It's a good day for us shits.' He laughs. I add, 'A good day for us oldies; it has prolonged my shelf life by twenty years.' I ask Carla Powell what her leader (of the Referendum Party) thinks about everything. She feigns to be out of her depth and Charles feigns to be above it all. After lunch play table tennis. MH takes it very seriously and beats everyone.

Monday 27 January

Walk home with James Cran, who last week had lunch with Redwood, who apparently went out of his way to denigrate Howard. This reminds me that before lunch with MH I discussed a conversation I had in Paris with John Townend, the chairman of the 92 Group. He said he thought there should be no 'beauty parade' between right-wing candidates at 92 but that they would not support anyone who if he lost in early rounds of the leadership contest would not support the other right-wing candidate(s). Howard told me he would support Portillo but not Redwood. This mutual antipathy between Howard and Redwood bodes badly if one or the other wins.

Walk into the Commons with Redwood for the vote at about 6 p.m. I say to him in reference to a widely quoted remark of John Major to the *New Yorker* that he wouldn't like to be a Chancellor who put up interest rates because of the single currency, 'If you or I had said that, John, we would be in trouble.'

He says, 'I have.'

Redwood says to Cran, 'MH never took a strong stance in the Cabinet; he just did the PM's bidding.' This may have been true till after the last leadership election. MH changed his tune when Major was seen (at least by MH) to do all his deals with Heseltine.

Thursday 30 January

Brian Mawhinney slumped in the corner of the members' lobby looking pretty washed out. Rumour is that they are deciding whether or not to call a general election soon. Walk back with Daniel and Rachel Whetstone from my office to my home. Rachel says they are speeding up with the manifesto. News from the Wirral by-election front is very bad. They are mad to be distracted by that. Who cares if we lose another by-election at this stage? The important thing is to go in the spring. Major probably won't. Shades of 1974 – then it was my potential by-election.

Rachel, Daniel and I decide to advise MH that we should become more proactive – as there is now nothing much to lose. The press have already said there is a campaign and Portillo and Redwood are now hard at it. We must find a hardcore of about twenty helpers.

Sunday 2 February

Howard rings. We agree to my suggestion to collect twenty helpers asap. He says we must all meet for dinner very soon. 'What about next Thursday?' 'OK.' 'As long as you and I can do it!'

Tuesday 4 February

Meet Bonsor at 1.30 – we will play the 'campaign' to collect a few more trusties for MH very carefully; we will only move in on those who 'swear allegiance' to MH off their own bat. At dinner in members' dining room – talk with Edward Leigh. He says he might not vote for MH but thinks he will win: non-factional Eurosceptic.

MH asks me to invite David Maclean during one of the votes to come to the dinner on Thursday. David says he will if he can. On the way home with Cran bump into Chris Storey, who is standing against Peter Temple-Morris as 'the real conservative'. I hear my Referendum candidate may be standing down because she* realises I am more of a Eurosceptic than Goldsmith.

Wednesday 5 February

Theme of all the meetings I attend (especially '22) is the parliamentary party's wish for the latest possible date of election.

6.30: 1922 Committee erupts into banging desks and stamping feet when someone suggests 1 May to Mawhinney. Patrick Cormack advises 'caution'

---

* Diana Pollock, whose husband, Ken Pollock, became chairman of the West Worcestershire Conservative Association in 2008.

on this and is listened to in silence. At 92 Club in St Stephen's Club, guest speaker is Alastair Goodlad. Again the theme is 1 May election.

Thursday 6 February

Dinner at MH's home – present: Daniel, James Cran, Sandra, Rachel Whetstone, David Lidington. Not one of the best evenings. Michael wants to concentrate on administrative matters: offices etc. I want to focus on strategy: what would be his real position on Europe? What types of MPs do we go for?

Conclusion: (1) MH will not make an anti-federal pitch likely to appeal to Redwood/Portillo supporters. (2) No campaigning before the election. Therefore I believe we must identify the 'soft Eurosceptic vote' and really get them to know him, e.g. by setting up occasions when he can involve them.

I think he will need to write to each one after the election, suggesting a private meeting and participation at meetings on Europe and domestic affairs. At these meetings will invite people to sign up as 'helpers'.

Friday 7 February

Gallup shows a turn in our fortunes. Now 15 per cent behind Labour – and still counting!

Monday 10 February

'Philosophy' Society evening with Jonathan Aitken at his home in Lord North Street. Tebbit speaker. I intervene to agree with Lamont in Q&A that we will have to go very far – e.g. into questioning free provision of Health Service – if we are to keep taxes down.

Tuesday 11 February

MH comes up to me openly in the lobby – first time – and says, 'I want a word.' We discuss structure of his office and names of potential supporters. Agree to meet again tomorrow.

Wednesday 12 February

Breakfast with Malcolm Pearson at Victoria Square. Test him out on his interest in MH. He is mildly interested but fighting MH in Lords on gun control. Malcolm incandescent with rage against Bill Cash for trying to torpedo his anti-Europe Bill in Lords.

Lunch with ERG to discuss leadership. Heathcoat-Amory mentions Howard when question arises as to who would be best to renegotiate Treaty.

Over dinner Archie Hamilton says he will vote for Howard.

In lobby, Henry Bellingham* comes up to me. 'If MH wants support in leadership, he will need to review gun Bill – five PPSs thinking of resigning.' I mention this to MH; he says 'No go'.

Tuesday 18 February

Bad day for MH. Fourteen Tories vote against his gun Bill. I only vote for it out of loyalty to him. My appointment to see him has to be postponed because Michael Heseltine (deputy PM) and Tony Newton (leader of the House) slip in to see him.

Beginning to pick up a bit of support for him amongst PPCs.

Wednesday 19 February

Day starts with Malcolm Rifkind being cornered by BBC *Today* to say HMG 'on balance hostile to single currency'. I ring PA to say 'great' but it is not much reported. Row breaks with Clarke saying 'It was a "slip of the tongue"' and Rifkind saying 'It wasn't'. Clarke comes to the 1922 Committee where he does not answer questions. (However, he says he will have a 'word with Michael Spicer afterwards'.) Very desultory speech on 'the economy, stupid', which is the sort of speech any of us might just have made to our WIs on an off night. No preparation, no thought.

Earlier in the day MH fell out with Alastair Goodlad, who, together with Tony Newton, was upset not to have been present at a meeting chaired by PM and including Heseltine, Dorrell, Clarke, Rifkind and MH which had decided on a legal package of reforms of European Court procedures. Goodlad told Howard, to the latter's rage, 'It cannot go ahead without proper Cabinet sub-committee approval.' PM nowhere to be seen despite the fact that he had chaired the committee which took the decision.

Sunday 23 February

Howard rings 8ish: have I seen the papers? 'Yes.' Large article by a man called Lewis† whom MH sacked from being head of the prison service.

Monday 24 February

I accost Liam Fox and secure him for the cause. He agrees to come to the next dinner.

---

* MP for North West Norfolk.
† Derek Lewis, director-general of the Prison Service 1992–6.

Sunday 2 March

MH rings as usual around 7 p.m. He is quite worried about the potential threat from Rifkind; agree to watch it. Dominic Lawson, editor of
Sunday Telegraph, and, apparently, William Hague, are on side. Agree that
William is someone MH should ring very early on in campaign – after the
general election.

Wednesday 5 March

Very agreeable dinner with Alastair Goodlad. Steer off politics for most of the
time. AG seems genuinely to believe that if we all calm down we can win the
election – at least, that's what he says.

I'm beginning to think the final battle for leadership will be between
Howard and Heseltine.

Saturday 8 March

George Gardiner on the TV announcing he is to join the Referendum Party
as their first MP.

Sunday 9 March

Norman Lamont rings up to point me to an article in the *Spectator* by Bruce
Anderson, which repeats the stuff about me 'campaigning' for Howard. MH
and I talk later to decide nothing much can be done about it as it's true!

In the morning am rung up by Ralph Harris, on the advice of Malcolm
Pearson. RH says he is leaving Bill Cash's operations because of his disloyalty
to Pearson during the latter's 'pull out of Europe' Bill in the House of Lords.
Harris is also contacting Jim Miller to advise him no longer to spend money
on Cash. I say in effect that I can have nothing to do with undermining Cash.

Monday 10 March

Dinner in Admiralty House – Portillo host. His flat has the appearance of
having been stripped of all personal possessions and of his being 'on his
way'. Furniture, cushions, pictures, cutlery, glasses, clearly belong to the
government.

Tuesday 11 March

Michael Mates at a Unionist dinner confirms that Heseltine will be standing
to replace Major if we lose GE. Pass this on to Portillo, who laughs and says
it is ridiculous (not my view). William Hague is the speaker at the Unionist
do. His speech is surprisingly badly constructed – in view of the audience
(ex-ministers) rather patronising, heavy on loyalty. Walk home with Archie

Hamilton. Michael Howard rings to say Derek Conway probably coming over. Hope he's right. Conway is pairing whip and would be a good catch.

On 17 March Parliament was dissolved, with the general election date set for 1 May.

Wednesday 19 March

Howard rings, involved, as on the night before, with clearing up Home Office business, doing deals with Libs and Labs. Finally catch up with him in the cafeteria at about 11 p.m. Go through a number of administrative matters.

Thursday 20 March

Last real day of this parliament. The place has an eerie feel about it; members come and go and coyly wish each other well or bid farewell. Then they leave, blinking in the bright early spring sunlight. My last political call of the day is to Nicholas Bonsor in his new flat in Westminster Gardens. He agrees to have a go at Aitken with a view to hoping to get him to let us have his house for the Howard campaign. Bonsor rings Aitken; they agree to have dinner at the Turf Club. (I have fixed to take Ann out to the latest film, *The English Patient*.) After the finish (c. 11.30) I ring Bonsor, who does not have good news. Aitken 'undecided' between Howard and Portillo. Portillo is gaining ground on the right. It is probably what Derek Conway's hesitation is in part about.

A lot will now depend on whether MH can personally attract some 'big hitters' on the Friday/Saturday after the election, e.g. Lilley and Hague, and then Lamont, Maude, Heathcoat-Amory – Conway if he will do it. Increasingly it looks as though Redwood has peaked at the old whip-less and Duncan Smith and possibly Cash and Wintertons. Portillo is moving fast and Howard's vote is untested. If he comes after Portillo in the first round but in front of Redwood, it's probably worth trying to get Redwood's vote; but more likely it will be necessary to strike a deal with Portillo.

Monday 24 March

Ring Archie Hamilton to see if he would let us have his flat. 'Yes, as long as I am not chairman of the 1922 Committee by then.' At last some sort of a breakthrough – which I report to MH. He is delighted. Rings me again that evening (twice), once to say has had a good chat to Daniel re his regurgitated pamphlet. He will write a foreword. And should he ring Archie to thank him? I say 'Yes'. He rings back to say all is well.

Election going a little more our way today; economy rather than sleaze makes the running. Labour always look rather petty on the economy – whereas we have a problem on sleaze because Major is open to the charge that he fixed prorogation to avoid Parliamentary Commissioner's report on Hamilton et al. reaching privileges committee.

Tuesday 25 March

Apparently MH will be nowhere to be seen during the election campaign – which is bad news for him. Talk to MH early in the morning to discover he has bought a house in Pimlico which we will be able to use as his HQ.

More ghastly opinion polls.

Tuesday 1 April

Easter is over. Grannies have gone home. It's been an exceptionally lovely weekend; now we have to get back to the election.

Evening phone call from MH. He is bullish about what he is finding on the doorsteps (apparently *Guardian* will say tomorrow we are only 14 points below).

Monday 7 April

To London on the 9.05 from Evesham to clear up in the office – last full day as an MP. London looking lovely in the spring sunshine – blossom and daffodils everywhere – especially in St James's Park.

Lunch in the Millbank canteen with Daniel Hannan and Nick Bonsor.

7 p.m. To Daniel's new flat in Marsham Court for a glass of champagne and then on to dinner with David Porter and Daniel downstairs at Shepherd's. Michael Heseltine and Richard Ottaway come in. They are clearly plotting his campaign.

Tuesday 8 April

Weather still lovely. Lunch with Sir Emmanuel Kay, who pledges a five-figure sum for MH subject to Jim Miller doing the same. 2.30: Cease to be an MP. 3.00: Move fax and computers to Maunsel Street by taxi, then off to Paddington and Evesham. At Paddington I bump into Paul Tyler (Liberal) in the first-class lounge, where one can use telephones and fax machines. He and I happily chat side by side to our respective secretaries/agents about our election campaigns, attacking each other's party!

Dinner with Ann and Douglas Barrington at Lygon Arms where exactly thirty years ago had two days' honeymoon.

Sunday 13 April
Day after my adoption meeting, which went well. 120 or so present. Gave speech without notes and it came off.

Today go to point-to-point near Gloucester. Archie Smith-Maxwell announces on the Tannoy that I am there. Point-to-points are good canvassing for us since the fear is that Labour will abolish hunting and therefore point-to-points.

Ring MH. Relieved to hear he is doing the press conference on Tuesday as he has been, noticeably, hidden so far. The press today comments on this. He seems quite chirpy, though his seat is seen as not entirely safe. Says the doorstep reaction is good. I will find out for myself tomorrow when I go to Malvern for canvassing.

Monday 14 April
First day of my campaign. Masses of previous Conservative 'don't knows' in Malvern. Good attendances at lively meetings in Dursley (33) and Great Whitley (50).

Talk to Daniel – apparently *Spectator* (Frank Johnson) coming out for Hague.

MH not very brilliant on *Newsnight* (not assertive enough against aggressive questioning from a studio audience).

Tuesday 15 April
Small meetings around Bredon Hill/Sedgeberrow (22), Beckford (30), Overbury (12). MH meant to be doing the daily press conference but obliterated on TV by Major in West Country trying to work up the fishermen – 'We will not give way on abolition of quota hopping' – not very credible in view of BSE. Also several junior ministers rebelling with impunity on Europe.

Wednesday 16 April
A defining day. Major extols virtues of single currency and attacks sceptical ministers after meeting Clarke and Heseltine. What's going on? Presumably Major has given up and is huddling together with Europhiles in anticipation of the debacle to follow. Increasingly I feel there is a deal between Hezza and Major. The latter will back the former for the leadership.

Meanwhile *Daily Mail* talk of sceptic MPs grows. I am in it today. God knows what the electorate is making of it all.

Tonight Major blows any chance of narrowing Labour's majority. We are heading for disaster. A strong position on Europe was our only chance.

Major exacerbates the divisions in the party, and undermines my case that a single currency is impossible/unattainable under the Tories! It's all over now – perhaps even for me.

Earlier on *Newsnight* there were Conservative heavies almost manhandling the BBC to keep them away from PM – unbelievable. It looked very sinister indeed.

Thursday 17 April

Another day of Europe. Major answers a question from Elinor Goodman that a free vote might be given in the House over single currency. Heseltine/Clarke pour doubt on the certainty of this. I am rung up by *PM* to see if I will join in a debate with Edwina Currie. 'No. I will not debate with a colleague.'

Meetings at Birtsmorton (18) and Corse Lawn (28, v. lively on Europe). Europe is becoming more and more prominent.

The effect of these Tory rows on Europe is to heighten interest in Europe, which is supposedly in our interest. The mood is slightly better today, but polls still show gap of around 20 per cent.

Friday 18 April

Quiet day. Good meetings at Hanley Swan (18) and Malvern (54). Deal done with UK Independence Party at the Malvern meeting. I will be firm about Europe, they will not stand against me. MH calls just before I leave. Still bullish. Says that he is to do a number of high-profile appearances. My worry is that he is being lost vis-à-vis Portillo and Redwood. Redwood is coming over as disloyal, Portillo a bit too loyal. On second thoughts, maybe MH not in too bad a position.

Saturday 19 April

Reaction in the town centres of Upton, Pershore and Malvern surprisingly friendly given Labour's continuing massive lead in the opinion polls. Meet a chap in Malvern who claims to have seen me last when he was a patient in St Wulstan's Mental Hospital – twenty-two years ago, when I fought to keep the hospital open.

Sunday 20 April

MH rings in the evening. We agree that Sandra should phone through lists of 'target' MPs and telephones.

Monday 21 April

MH on phone on Radio 4 – pretty anodyne. He is not having a very glamorous election. My election meetings at Clifton, Martley and Shelsley not well attended. The councillors fighting their own campaign almost to the point of snubbing me, e.g. refusing to hand out my literature.

Tuesday 22 April
Polls stuck in the rut of Tories 32ish, Labour 48ish. Looks like a Labour majority of 100–150. (I can't believe it will be much over 100.)

Main excitement today – poster battle between Spicer and Luff supporters on land owned by Peter Strickland. He is mine but the land is Luff's. Row between Richard Mumford (chairman of Mid Worcestershire), who pulled down our posters and put them in the back of his car without telling anyone, and Richard Williams (my chairman), both estate agents and competitors!

Matters resolved: posters facing Evesham = me (as one approaches Pershore), facing Pershore = Luff (as one approaches Evesham)!

Thursday 24 April
Polls back to 'normal' – Labour lead of 20 per cent, which is wipe-out for us.

Saturday 26 April
5 p.m. Meeting with the team – Richard Williams, Chris Sanderson, Bill Allington, Paul de la Pena, Ann, Susan Burlingham, Anthony Ogilvie. I spell out the implication of canvass figures so far: we could lose. This impression confirmed when poll figures produce a vast swing against us, unimaginable 13 per cent, which if it were straight from Conservatives to Liberals would do for me. Richard Williams says as a keen European if we want to win we must say 'No' to single currency, then rat on this later. Everyone agrees but also accepts it won't happen.

I pass all this on the phone to MH, who says he will try to have a word with Robert Cranborne – but says he (MH) no longer has any clout with Major. 'He won't even listen.'

Sunday 27 April
Talk to Howard several times about life after the general election. Good news that Francis Maude seems to be coming over to MH's cause. Also talk to Bonsor, Gill, Cran, Townend. Bonsor apparently bullish but no one really knows what is going on. He still thinks the polls are wrong.

Telephone conversation with Cranborne in the morning. I rang him to say the only hope is to sharpen the rhetoric on the single currency (the symbol of the Europe debate). He says: (a) no hope now of policy change, (b) I am preaching to the converted, (c) Major is unlikely to be very receptive. I say there has to be a question now as to whether Major is more concerned about his future position in the party than with winning a few extra seats. Cranborne says, 'No comment.'

Monday 28 April

Rather hostile feel on the streets of Pershore. I think we are going to be very hard pushed to keep this seat. Postering in the fields better, the farmers seem to be staying with us – though I have some worried questions from farmers at a meeting in Longdon. David Kleeman and George Docker have kindly come down from London to help canvass.

Three or four calls backwards and forwards with Howard. Tell him of a conversation in the morning with Cran, who says Derek Conway willing to join us.

Tuesday 29 April

Heavy atmosphere in the constituency. Work out that could lose the election with 13 per cent swing to the Liberals if the Labour vote does not hold up.

David Kleeman canvassing with me – Upton-on-Severn. Masses of disaffected Tory 'don't knows', even amongst young mums.

Wednesday 30 April

Several morning conversations with MH and Tim Collins. We have a choice either to back or sack Major but not to fudge it by saying 'It's up to him'. This would look silly and shifty. 'If you are going to back him,' I say, 'you are free to say what you like on policy.' MH asks me to talk this over with Tim Collins. This I do. MH then agrees. This is our strategy. I agree to talk to Sunday newspapers.

People a bit chirpier on the streets, perhaps because the sun is shining and hot. Canvassing in Malvern and getting sunburnt.

Good eve-of-poll meeting in Upton. High spirits rather dampened by a call from Rosalie Dawes to report 75 per cent 'don't knows' in Birtsmorton.

Thursday 1 May – polling day

Beautiful clear warm morning. Ann and I have postal votes. Thank goodness they have arrived at Cropthorne so I deliver them as part of my round of the polling stations, with Richard Williams, at the Wychavon offices, all adding to a rather panicky start to the day. The sense that something is missing grows during the day and reaches a climax when we get to Malvern, where our organisation is appalling. Committee room after committee room manned by a few old ladies working with no proper canvass returns. You can feel the Liberal vote pouring out.

All this is reflected later at the count, where Ann and I arrive at 3.00 a.m. Our deepest gloom has lifted after we received a relatively optimistic call from my agent, Susan Burlingham, who was working off what the scrutineers had reported to her to have come out of the boxes. When the count starts this optimism is not entirely vindicated. We are the victims of the tidal wave of anti-Toryism surging through the country.

Majority slashed to 3.9k; at one time it looked as if it might disappear altogether. Saved by high Labour vote.

The 1997 general election resulted in a Labour victory, with a majority of 178. John Major immediately resigned as leader of the Conservative Party. Amongst those who lost their seats were Michael Portillo, Malcolm Rifkind, Michael Forsyth, Ian Lang, Norman Lamont, Jonathan Aitken, Nicholas Bonsor and Derek Conway.

Reflections – the end of parliamentary democracy?

Who won the civil war about Europe, which raged within the Conservative Party between 1991 and 1997? And, more importantly, what was the historical significance of the outcome?

John Major won the votes in Parliament for the Bill ratifying the Maastricht Treaty. Possibly the best opportunity to halt the process towards a federal state of Europe was lost. But in the process the Eurosceptics arguably captured the soul of the Conservative parliamentary party. Archie Hamilton, William Hague, myself, Iain Duncan Smith, David Cameron and later Graham Brady all won our respective elections in the parliamentary party by appealing in large measure to the Eurosceptics. Eighty-one of them re-emerged on the night of 24 October 2011 to vote against a three-line whip in favour of a referendum on the future of Britain's relationship with the EU. Both Fresh Start and the ERG are still active in the parliamentary party.

Despite my best entreaties to him as his campaign manager, Michael Howard in 1997 decided not to make full use of his Eurosceptic credentials; he came last of six candidates in the leadership ballot.

Major's skill was in playing one end of the political spectrum against the other. How seriously did he take the several, on the whole, friendly meetings with me during the course of the rebellion? The answer, I suspect, is 'Not very'. He makes, for instance, little mention of our talks in his autobiography. Nor did he make any changes to his policy on Europe to accommodate anything I had suggested, either directly to him or through his excellent Chief Whip, Richard Ryder.

My belief is that his objective was the exact opposite to that of making peace between the main factions. Possibly subconsciously, he aimed to stir up each side against the other. To the Garel-Jonesites (who on at least one occasion entered his room as I left it) we were represented as the 'bastards'; to us the federalists were portrayed as unwelcome obstacles (in the case of Michael Heseltine and Ken Clarke as the 'big beasts'). Talk of a federalist Europe he would describe as 'Eurocrap'. In this way, by stirring the conflict between the two sides, he made his own role as peacemaker the more necessary.

Did the Maastricht affair cause the downfall of John Major's government? My own view is that, despite all the fury and furore, it played at best a marginal role in the defeat of 1997. It was a symptom. The disease was Major's handling of the economy, especially his policy on exchange rates, which of course did have a strong interplay with the European issue. By keeping interest rates high, in order to 'shadow' first the Deutschmark and then the Euro, he created unemployment and an economic recession in the early 1990s; it was a policy for which he and the Conservatives were eventually punished. It was, in other words, the delayed effect of economic developments which was the real cause of the declining fortunes of the Conservative Party and of the subsequent long years in opposition.

None of this alters the fact that the Eurosceptic failure to defeat the Maastricht Bill, in particular the paving motion which preceded it on 4 November 1992, was historically and intrinsically a pivotal event. It made possible a gear-change in the process of the transference of critical powers from Westminster to Brussels. By the end of 1992 the undermining of British parliamentary democracy was firmly under way.

The *coup de grâce* for Parliament came over a decade later in a wholly unexpected form which was not directly connected to the European issue. The so-called parliamentary expenses scandal arose out of the theft of MPs' personal data held by the House of Commons authorities. When this data was published, several cases of fraud were revealed and these resulted in prison sentences.

For the overwhelming mass of MPs, the accusations focused on the use they had made of allowances specifically designed to support one of two homes necessary to carry out work in two places: Parliament and the constituency. This was portrayed in the press as an outrageous abuse and was believed as such by a demoralised and politically disillusioned public. The consequent powers given to the Independent Parliamentary Standards Authority finally brought Parliament to its knees.

Now acting as an agency of the European government and under the boot of an outside controller, the British Parliament has virtually ceased to have a practical function in the governance of Britain, save to provide a pool of ministers. Symptomatic of this is one idea* floating around to turn the Parliamentary Estate into a subscription-based club.

That all said, the Maastricht rebellion did help to maintain Britain's options in Europe. The effect of this on the Conservative Party in opposition will emerge in the final section of this book. It forms the background to the massive issues facing the Cameron administration in its relationship with Europe.

---

* *Sunday Times*, 18 December 2011.

Part III

Opposition: chairman of the 1922 Committee

Chapter 15

William Hague: a new age

The diary notes now focus on my relations with the four leaders of the Conservative opposition between 1997 and 2010 – William Hague, Iain Duncan Smith, Michael Howard and David Cameron. For the last three I was the chairman of the 1922 Committee, in other words, chairman of the Conservative Members of Parliament.

Account must be taken of my bias. My notes make it clear that at the time I judged the four leaders largely by the degree of their Euroscepticism or, to be more precise, the extent to which they stuck to their proclaimed Eurosceptic credentials. This at least has the merit of being one way of assessing their credibility and their trustworthiness – not unimportant qualities in a leader.

Even here, however, I consider that the flipside of 'trustworthiness' may not be a simple 'untrustworthiness'. If, for instance, you support further integration in Europe, you may wish to consider Hague, Duncan Smith and Howard as being 'shrewd', 'flexible', 'balanced' and 'holding the middle ground'. In so doing you would, I am sure, have their total agreement. This also is not an irrelevant factor. What they themselves were trying to achieve, in the context of Conservative Party unity and modernisation, is certainly part of the final mix by which they should be judged.

Hague changes his mind and wins

Friday 2 May 1997
Return home from the count in bright daylight with our old friends the De la Penas, who have been so supportive. Loll around the house taking calls from friends and then up to London for meeting with Michael Howard at Rachel Whetstone's flat in Lennox Gardens. Very rambling, rather tired and rather unsatisfactory meeting, dominated by Francis Maude, who gives us his view on ERM and what we should do – at great length. (He was the man who signed the Maastricht Treaty.)

A desire emerges (pushed by Maude) to delay launch of Howard campaign until Major – who resigned today as leader – is properly 'buried'. Nothing much discussed about organisation. I leave rather depressed.

Monday 5 May

Masses of phone calling. Twenty names pledge to Howard. Arrive in London. MH calls at 7.30 p.m. 'Come round'. Reveals to me that William Hague will join us if he is to be chairman of party. We have the makings of the dream ticket. Do we tell Francis Maude, Norman Lamont et al. at dinner? No. I leave Howard's home by pre-arrangement at 9.20 p.m. I go to a phone box and ask Howard if 'all clear'. 'Yes, come back.' Hague and I arrive at same time at the government house (Howards are due to hand this over to Mo Mowlam[*] tomorrow). Deal consummated.[†]

Champagne flows. I return to Daniel Hannan's flat in Marsham Court to drink more champagne and discuss details of volunteers.

We are close to victory. Arrange to meet – all of us – at my house in Maunsel Street tomorrow. There are the makings of real stability and continuity at the top of the Conservative Party. Hague would be well placed to follow MH as leader.

Tuesday 6 May

MH rings at 7.30 a.m. disaster – possibly fatal. Ghastly mistake not to have issued a joint declaration at once. Hague has rung MH to say he has changed his mind.

In retrospect we should have issued a joint statement last night. At the time it was all so certain that the imperative was to achieve the maximum impact at the press conference today.

It never occurred to me that Hague would rat. Decision taken to let the press know. MH very hesitant about this and angry when it goes high profile in the news. This causes another Tory squabble – what a tragedy. MH's press conference at the Institution of Civil Engineers well attended but distorted by what has happened in the last few hours. We may never recover from this. MH looks rather old and hesitant on TV.

Wednesday 7 May

Meeting in my house. MH overrules me on almost everything. Grab him on his way out and suggest that he takes over campaign co-ordination

---

[*] SoS Northern Ireland 1997–9.

[†] Those present were Michael and Sandra Howard, William and Ffion Hague and myself. It is important to note that the meeting was over very quickly. There was no negotiation, merely agreement to go ahead as a team, MH as leader and WH as party chairman. There was some discussion about the arrangements for the next day's joint announcement and the press release I was asked to draft. Otherwise it was all a fait accompli.

himself. He says 'No' and asks me to carry on, but has to rush to a meeting of shadow Cabinet.

Meet MH in my home later and we decide to plough on as normal.

Thursday 8 May
Papers full of Hague and his successful launch campaign under the slogan 'Fresh Start'. Where have I heard that before? Good cartoon in *The Times*: 'I support, er, Michael Howard – no, I'll start that again, etc.' The whole episode has, however, done us more harm than him.

Morning meeting in my home, which is becoming the centre point until we move into Aitken's. No real movement of MPs signed up; in fact we are beginning to meet resistance.

Ann and I drive to Soar Mill Cove Hotel in Devon for a brief rest – we are exhausted following the general election and its traumatic finale.

Friday 9 May
Phone never stops in my room. So much so the hotel allows us to stay in after check-out through to 3 p.m. Main issue fixing plan for Aitkens to move out. On to David and Judith Porter's at Herodsfoot – pursued by the phone and bleeper.

Saturday 10 May
Bad press for Howard. No chairman in the country can be found to support him. Steel ourselves for more bad news tomorrow – Sunday press polls. Talk to Richard Williams (my chairman) – to make sure I am not in too much trouble in my constituency for not having consulted them. He is arranging for a write-in and then to say advice was 'conflicting' – resisting a special meeting of the Executive – so far. Hope he stays firm – assure him will consult in later rounds if MH falls early, as he now looks as though he might.

Sunday 11 May
Mixed news for MH which I read at David Porter's house before driving six hours to London. Good bits – Garel-Jones backing Hague! Bad bits – Hague reported as having a bandwagon going for him.

On the car phone start to learn of Ann Widdecombe outburst against Howard; then phone breaks down! Ring MH and *Times*, *Telegraph*, *Mail* and *Sun* from a service station on the M4 to say it's a personal spat on her side. David Maclean loved working for him as his No.2 at the Home Office. Pouring with rain. Back in Maunsel Street at 6 p.m. Prepare for the week ahead.

Monday 12 May

Very bad press for MH re Ann Widdecombe outburst; accuses MH of having 'something of the night' about him. Splash stories in *Times* and *Telegraph*. I start to take view MH needs to take a new initiative, e.g. offering to be reselected as leader if the rules for election are changed. After consulting with Tim Collins and Rachel Whetstone MH disagrees. I chair the morning meeting, when we cover a lot of ground in MH's absence. Mechanics of campaign fixed – especially the move to Jonathan Aitken's house in Lord North Street.

Wednesday 14 May

7.30 a.m. In House to claim my seat at the top of the gangway. The parliamentary party huddled mainly on the Speaker's side of the gangway. Liberals all over the place but Heath holds his own below the gangway. You've got to give it to the old boy.

8.30: Meet Margaret Bottomley outside Aitken's house to move in telephone lines.

In early afternoon meet Jonathan Holborow outside St Stephen's Entrance, to discuss his giving 'splash' treatment to a Howard initiative to offer himself for reselection if rules changed after he gets the job.

Later that night after a successful reception for MPs, MH puts same proposition to Conrad Black at dinner in Black's house. Again he (Black) agrees to go with it.

Thursday 15 May

After intervention from Francis Maude and David Davis, Howard changes his mind. Likes the idea but refuses to go with it. I remonstrate. Later that evening he says, 'Sorry we disagree about this.' I say the problem is in the manner of changing as in anything. Daniel and I retire to Pratt's. Howard rings on Daniel's telephone to suggest we go round to him for supper. I suspect we will simply agonise over his refusal to change his mind. Daniel and I pretty depressed.

Wake up at 3 a.m. and write desperate letter to Howard. Read out to him in early morning. He refuses to budge. When I get in office, Francis Maude and David Davis have in effect taken the campaign over. I tidy up one or two loose ends organisationally and return to the Garrick to survey the new bedrooms with former BBC reporter Michael Charlton.

Ann Widdecombe very much around. Sadly, it's all falling apart.

Friday 16 May

Story breaks in the evening that Hague and Dorrell showing willing to listen to the voluntary party about the leadership process. They have in other words beaten us to it. I am spitting mad.

Saturday 17 May

Frantic and multiple calls to Howard to see whether we can do anything to retrieve the situation. Talk to Jonathan Holborow; he says that the leadership and the party story is now dead. I offer a story on 'Europe' with Michael's pamphlet coming out. Joe Murphy interviews Howard. Jonathan comes back to say it's not strong enough and there are a lot of 'government' stories about, e.g. Frank Field is 'going for single mothers'; and utility companies are lobbying re windfall tax. News switching rapidly to the government.

I press Michael, as do Tim Collins and Rachel Whetstone, aided by Daniel, to harden his position (on Europe), at least to deal with the question of what happens if we don't get our way, e.g. will need to amend Treaty of Accession unilaterally. Michael won't do it and becomes increasingly angry at being pressed. I tell him that with the Ann Widdecombe story still running and since he was not prepared to come out on the 'put myself up for reselection if the rules change' line, unless he goes for Europe he has had it (he has lost the libertarian right, lost the traditional right with guns; all he has left is the anti-Europe right). He's got to gamble on this one, but he won't. This is the moment I realise it's pretty well all over. Two or three years of wasted effort. I don't think he will get past the first round. Best guess: Dorrell 10, Howard 20, Redwood 20, Hague 25, Lilley 35, Clarke 55.* Lilley looks the winner. Only hope is for Howard and Hague to come together again.

Sunday 18 May

Newbury races with Jonathan and Vivien and Holborow. Lovely day away from the battle scene. Brief and slightly frosty talks to Howard on the phone. He sounds very tired. Let's hope he does well against Widdecombe tomorrow; apparently he was OK on *On the Record* at lunchtime. His views on Europe were picked up on the news bulletins later in the day.

Monday 19–Thursday 22 May

The week has its ups and downs. MH performs reasonably well on TV and in the Commons but is probably damaged by the Ann Widdecombe affair. Charles Wardle is on the horizon. MH continues to interfere in the office in such a way as to upset most of his 'staff', including me. On Wednesday he reverses the decision – to invite Dick Body, who is considering coming over

---

*   In the event not far off the mark, if one assumes all Dorrell votes went to Hague.

to us, to lunch. Dick told not to come on the day because MH worried about his meeting with Michael Ancram, who is definitely not voting for him.

Monday 19 May
92 Group dinner at St Stephen's Club. Sit next to Gerald Howarth, who has just come back to Parliament, and Bill Walker, who has been kicked out. I get onto 92 slate for '22 Committee Executive.

Tuesday 20 May
7.50: I am on *Today* programme defending MH.
    Elected 'captain' of tennis at AGM, which includes Richard Weatherill, Pam Sharples* and Rhodri Morgan.

Wednesday 21 May
Lunch at Boodle's. Try (unsuccessfully) to get Richard Shepherd to vote for MH. He is a libertarian and not with MH; though Dick Body trying to get former 'whipless' (Teddy Taylor, Shepherd, Gorman, Gill, Wilkinson) to vote as a bloc for MH.
    At 1922 Committee voted on to the Executive, then back to Lord North Street for reception.

Thursday 22 May
MH removes me from lunch list presumably because I am too right wing. Lunch with Cran to try to sort out accounts and target MPs. Cran to produce a detailed paper.

Friday 23 May
Drop in to Lord North Street at around 9.30. MH with former press chief from CCO, Brendan Bruce. His advice: (1) play to MH's strength, e.g. one-to-one interviews; (2) get him to be his natural self, e.g. at football match, even if 3rd Division Swansea, a club he has always supported. Don't get him to play a ping-pong match, except in his own home.
    Lunch at Garrick. Meet Alistair McAlpine accompanied by aborigine from Australia. On to Ritz to discuss a book on China in a rather desultory way with Tom Dunne. By coincidence meet Alistair again, who walks off with some glamorous fashion 'expert'.
    Train to Worcestershire for long bank holiday weekend. Ponder on the train as to whether will join in *Panorama* programme on the Euro rebellion

---

*   Baroness Sharples.

and its effect on Tory fortunes. My theory is that Major could have 'done a deal'; part of me wants to say this. The other part of me knows that I will simply come across as disruptive; it will not help with the Howard campaign. I am disinclined to do the programme, even though Douglas Hurd will get away with his view of history.

Saturday 24–Tuesday 27 May
Hot bank holiday weekend. Everyone relaxes a bit, though a lot of phone calls backwards and forwards to MH/Cran/Whetstone. MH decides to follow in Lilley's footsteps around the regions. I argue that it would be much better to follow up his attack on Labour's devolution plans in Parliament next week.

As usual in this campaign, my view does not prevail.

Wednesday 28 May
Meeting at 10 a.m. in Lord North Street. Tim Collins, whose father was tragically killed over the weekend by electrocuting himself, bravely comes – and says to MH 'You are too cautious for your own good' – in the context of trying to get MH to take a punt on a referendum on devolution for England. Despite all this the word is that one or two may be coming over to us – e.g. Alan Clark and John Stanley. Ken Clarke looking like walking it at present, but I cannot see the party settling down with the guy who was completely out of step with the party under Major.

Good party at Lord North Street for association chairmen, about sixty of whom show up. As usual we were over-cautious about inviting in the press. MH speaks quite well and says to me, 'You think I'm too cautious, don't you?'

I say, 'Yes, you're behind and you must take risks to catch up and to be heard at all by the press.' Repeat all this to Sandra.

Thursday 29 May
Goodish piece in *The Independent* shows MH in the pack in terms of supporters.

Friday 30 May
MH off on his wild goose chase around country. (Daniel and I had advised him to restrict it to Wales, Scotland, Ireland and limit it to his attack on Labour's devolution bill next week. This would have given a clear story for the journalists. As usual our advice ignored.) I go to Cropthorne and spend some of the afternoon ringing the Sunday journalists to say MH's position not too bad (say we rather agree with *The Independent*, except that they have

given to Hague Taylor and Swayne, who are 'ours'). Also warn that Clarke is the man to beat and Howard the only man to do it.

Saturday 31 May

Ring MH early at Ivan Lawrence's house in Burton. Talk to Douglas Carswell, whom MH had taken on his helicopter trip around the nation in preference to Daniel, whom I had suggested. Apparently Northern Ireland was OK but in Birmingham there were only twenty-five. MH grumbles about 'no publicity'. I say, in effect, 'I told you so.' Tell him that journalists are asking about what Charles Wardle is going to say in his adjournment debate next week. He says, 'I really haven't a clue.'

I say, 'That's what I told them.'

In the car driving back to London James Cran says *Telegraph* are going to put MH second. I wonder if that's my story regurgitated?

Sunday 1 June

Once-in-a-lifetime visit to Kew Gardens. Not beautiful but impressive; then for picnic with Annabel, Ann and Thea in Richmond Park.

That night (11 p.m.) telephoned by MH hotfoot back from his wasted tour of the Union. I think the penny is beginning to drop that he's not doing too well. Indeed, he will probably fall at the first fence. He gives me, surprisingly, the go-ahead to try to negotiate a deal with Redwood, who is, apparently, doing even worse. This has all arisen out of a conversation I had in the afternoon with Daniel Hannan.

Monday 2 June

Early into Lord North Street. Fix to see Redwood's manager, Iain Duncan Smith, in the smoking room. Then off to spend an hour with Ma over lunch in Brockenhurst.

6 p.m. Meet Iain Duncan Smith. He listens to my points that an 'alliance' between Howard and Redwood would trample over all else. Seems to think Redwood is better placed than others do – so can see no reason for his man not going through the first round and then discussing later. I say Redwood may get sidelined at future discussions. Now could offer good shadow Cabinet post for Duncan Smith. IDS appears not very interested in this as he says that he must get out and make money to educate his children. Not sure how serious he is about this.

Tuesday 3 June

Much time around the House of Commons. Later in the members' dining room – mainly trying to woo Owen Paterson – with the help of Desmond Swayne. Also Teresa Gorman; remind her of the dinner we had together when we discussed the future reform of the Conservative Party.

Wednesday 4 June
Chair meeting of some fifteen MPs in the team. Dorrell 'surrenders' to Clarke. David Faber* comes over to us. MH sees a lot of prospects – I hope successfully. Things may be picking up for us.

Thursday 5 June
Up and down day. Hot and muggy; slight rain in the evening a relief, especially as it does not stop us watching the Beating of the Retreat. Howard good at 92 Group – as was Redwood. MH says, 'We must not screw it up on the right.' They like that. Bump into Tony Bevins of *The Independent*, who lets me have his list of supporters being published the next day. Daniel and I gave him our list, on which MH came second to Clarke. MH objects especially to my 'outing' the whips and Archie Hamilton. I put him in touch with Holborow and Conrad Black on the phone. We are (vainly, I suspect) trying for an endorsement from *Sunday Telegraph* and *Mail on Sunday*.

Friday 6 June
Breakfast with Peter Oborne (*Express*) at Ritz. Discuss Tony Bevins's 'figures', which are much as we agreed with him the night before. Oborne accepts that MH is on a comeback. He and Holborow due to write anti-Clarke stuff on Sunday. Off to Paddington station for train for Evesham and lunch with local businessmen. Ring campaign office and speak to Margaret Bottomley. *FT* has my chairman, Richard Williams, backing Clarke. When I get to Upton-on-Severn and lunch he is upset because he is mandated by association to back Hague. I couldn't be more at odds with my association. Only consolation – so is everyone else with theirs!

Saturday 7 June
Stay in London to pop into the campaign office where there is much excitement. Bonsor staying with Archie Hamilton, Malcolm Pearson and Lady T working themselves up for MH. Lady T apparently says she will do some calls for us. Sadly this has reached the ears of the press – something I learn when I get off train at Evesham. This apparently sends the lady into a great bate and she refuses to do the deed.

---

* MP for Westbury 1992–2001.

Sunday 8 June

Day of phoning – mainly around the campaign team to give ourselves therapy. One or two real voters contacted. Sunday press on the whole gives impression of MH doing better than Lilley.

Monday 9 June

Up early to catch 7 a.m. train to London. Newspapers full of leadership contest. MH seen to be coming up from the outside. Just as we were wrongly written off before, now the strength of our position is being exaggerated. It remains parlous according to my figures (two votes between us and Lilley).

Meeting at 11 a.m. in Lord North Street well attended with MPs. Everyone in a quite bullish mood. Even more so after the champagne party attended by all the great, good and beautiful and much TV. Annabel Spicer was wonderful. On TV later in the evening: on *Newsnight* to make our pitch against John Whittingdale and Iain Duncan Smith.

Tuesday 10 June

Into Committee Room 14 for meeting of 1922 Executive. Bombshell result of poll of constituency chairmen: Howard bottom by a long way, Clarke miles on top. Meeting with Howard late in the morning. Despite a brave face from the team that are there, this is a knock-out blow. Meet various 'marginals' like Teresa Gorman and Owen Paterson. They do not look me in the face. It's the general election all over again (written one hour before the results are announced). I know we will lose.

Sit in Room 14 to hear the results: Ken Clarke 49, William Hague 41, John Redwood 27, Peter Lilley 24, Michael Howard 23. Ann Widdecombe and the constituencies have taken their toll.

5.45: Gloomy meeting with MH and about fifteen MP members of the team. MH has bilateral with Lilley and they decide to go across to Hague pretty well unconditionally except for a few words on Europe.

Bump into both Redwood and Lilley later. Refuse to come out publicly for Redwood. Conversation with him acrimonious. We owe him nothing. He refused to do a deal before the vote. I may well vote for him but it will be in secret. Take what remains of the office staff to a gloomy supper in the private room at Shepherd's.

Wednesday 11 June

Drinks party given by Sky at Whitehall. Townend and I have good chat about life. I refuse to reveal my voting intentions.

Thursday 12 June
Opening of a herb garden with Holborows at Royal Hospital, Putney. Back to see Hague at 4 p.m. He has double booked me with John Hayes. I make my pitch on Europe: if you want to repatriate powers you will need to have a bottom line – renegotiate Treaty of Accession. He doesn't buy this. On thinking about it, what Hague actually says is, 'Yes, we might have to pull out; but I'm not going to make a speech saying this. I might do so in answer to a question.' Maybe someone will have to ask him the question.

Friday 13 June
Ring Jonathan Holborow early with offer of an article, 'What it would take to make me vote for Mr Hague'. MH rings to discuss list of 'thank you' letters – all very sad. He is having a big lunch party in Kent on Sunday 22nd.

Saturday 14 June
Howard lost for four reasons:
   Widdecombe.
   Failure to consolidate Hague as No. 2. Should have kept the team on to meet him; would have made it more difficult for Hague to rat.
   Not brave enough on Europe in the first round. His soul wasn't in it.
   Failed to get enough constituencies by going for my idea of an announcement on willingness to be reselected. (There was a brief moment when this would have had news value.)
   It'll be Hague now. The right has blown it again by failing to rally round a winnable leader.

Wednesday 18 June
Story so far: Hague, Redwood and Clarke played off on Thursday. Clarke 64, Hague 62, Redwood 38. Redwood out. Hague and Clarke closer than anticipated.
   Redwood announces will support Clarke. I have a long chat with Redwood, for whom I voted, in members' lobby. He seems to have made his choice on the basis of Clarke allowing him to say 'Never' to a single currency. Redwood's fury was directed against Howard and Lilley, especially Lilley.

Thursday 19 June
Hague wins. Sixteen- minute wait – with careers in the balance – in Room 10 for 4 p.m. when ballot closes. Result: 97-71 plus one abstention and one spoilt ballot paper. Afterwards Cran pretty agile at getting himself on TV and

radio as Hague team player – amazing; must annoy the real Hague team. He will get something from Hague, I have no doubt.

Friday 20 June
Jonathan Aitken 'lie' story breaks. Talk to Malcolm Pearson in Scotland. He confirms it will be 'bad news' in court today. Hints that JA will have to withdraw and face prosecution for perjury.

Ring Howard to warn him. He suggests that all press queries about our relationship with Aitken referred to me. Rather predictably I say, 'Certainly not.'

Saturday 21 June
Day in Cropthorne watching shadow Cabinet being formed – at least it looks quite Eurosceptic. Try unsuccessfully to get through to Parkinson (new party chairman).

Sunday 22 June
Drive to Howards' for a rather dreary lunch party to 'thank the team' and to celebrate his job as shadow Foreign Secretary. I leave after lunch and before the ping-pong. Massive thunderstorm breaks as I escape through the armed police barrier for London.

Tuesday 8 July
Dinner with new Chinese ambassador at the embassy. All the talk of Hong Kong – 'We will stick by the agreement if only because of Taiwan etc.'

He says China has four bogeys: (1) British and Hong Kong, which is now no longer relevant; (2) Russia, with 1 million square miles of disputed territory, although relations are apparently now much better about this; (3) Japan – 'We will never forgive the atrocities of the war'; (4) US/Taiwan – 'We resent the arrogance of the 7th Fleet.'

Wednesday 9 July
Walk home with Peter Temple-Morris. He seems almost to have given up. 'I'm out of tune – probably forever – with the present party.'

1922 lunch at Savoy for Hague. I sit at his table at Archie Hamilton's invitation. Hague says, 'We must listen and work hard' – does not strike me as a great battle cry.

5.45: Growing row at 1922 Executive committee about Parkinson's/Archie Norman's and Hague's incipient attempts to cut parliamentary party down to size. Especially worrying if they give themselves powers to sack us for supporting our constituency associations re central lists etc.

Thursday 10 July

Interview with Sarah Neville of the *Yorkshire Post*, who is writing the official biography of Hague. Give her my view of the abortive Hague–Howard pact. It will probably annoy the new establishment when it comes out. In the early morning join the rally for fox hunting in Hyde Park.

At an evening party given by Carlton TV in College Garden amidst glorious evening sunset bump into Howard. He is concerned to wrap up his declaration of expenses for his leadership campaign fund. Also discuss an incipient backbench rebellion if CCO and National Union league up against parliamentary party.

Friday 11 July

Hague speaks at our constituency association annual dinner at Abberley School (fulfilling a long-standing arrangement). The evening itself goes off well. Hague says his catchword is 'listening' – sounds good and enables him to avoid talking about policy. For me it's all rather awkward.

After the event I drive Ann and Hague to our home for the night, where we have a couple of whiskies and go to bed. Main points of conversation:

He in effect advises me that the game is up; unity is all that matters now. Policy differences are out. Single currency issue 'decided' – he will sack anyone who steps out of line on this.

I, equally obliquely, advise him that there would be trouble if he uses the Hamilton affair to suppress the parliamentary party – double trouble if he does what he says he might do, which is to abolish much of the National Union.

After a few whiskies the conversation becomes lighter. We joke about Heath, Thatcher and even about Major's gross photos in *The Sun* of himself with pot belly looking like a lager lout on holiday.

I float the idea of ERG 'pathfinding' amongst other right-wing parties in Europe. Hague says he will think about it, i.e. he doesn't like it. Over dinner he told the headmaster of Abberley, John Walker, he wanted policy ideas to move on, e.g. on education neither private nor public sector good or bad. Need to 'amalgamate' through a voucher system. On party organisation/how to deal with recalcitrant MPs, he was pretty vague. Some form of central control needed but not sure how to distinguish between rebels and scoundrels. Also unsure how to prevent central membership lists from destroying constituency autonomy.

On the Howard–Hague meeting at the start of the leadership election, Hague gave as his reason for changing his mind about Howard that he began to believe overnight that Howard would not win.* 'If I had gone in with Howard, several of my people would have gone elsewhere, e.g. James Arbuthnot would have gone with Lilley. I was beginning to feel out on a limb.' I say my view is that the combined ticket would have been pretty overwhelming, not just for the short run but for the longer-term future, were we, for instance, not to win the next election and the baton needed to be passed on smoothly.

Hague determined to stamp his authority: 'I'm almost looking forward to the opportunity of sacking one of my shadow Cabinet for stepping out of line.' He is a young man determined to play it differently from Major. I wonder if it will work. Will depend on opinion polls and how the public takes it.

Saturday 12 July

Leave Cropthorne at 4.30 for a dinner-dance in Wiltshire given by Edward's friend Charlie Reece. Lovely to be with Edward and his new and highly suitable girlfriend Lulu and Annabel and Jonathan. Weather coldish but dry. Edward arranged for us to stay in a ramshackle stud farm B&B. Great adventure and great fun. Wonderful break from politicians.

Sunday 13 July

Back to normal – charity lunch in Kemerton, having driven back early in the morning; I have a row with a lady who accuses me of being rude because I talked to constituents rather than to her, who did not vote Conservative at last GE. We Conservative MPs are not quite ready yet to take it on the chin from people who voted against us on 1 May.

Tuesday 15 July

MH rings early; off to see Hague. How did I get on with him? 'Pretty well, but you may remember I didn't vote for him!' Walk home after the vote with Chris Gill. He would not vote for Howard because of MH's action on guns at the Home Office.

Wednesday 16 July

Lunch with Alastair Goodlad at his house in Lord North Street. Pass the photographers and TV crews waiting for Jonathan Aitken's return home to his house on the opposite side of the road. Over lunch Alastair congratulates me on being given the 'overseas office' in CCO. I say this is the first I have

---

* Several years later I learnt that Brooks Newmark (MP for Braintree) had played an important part in changing Hague's mind (see the entry for 1 April 2009, p. 594).

heard of it. He is much embarrassed; says that MH had approached him about it some weeks ago in his capacity as shadow overseas development minister. Thought it was all sewn up. I assume that was what MH was off to see Hague about on Monday but nothing has happened.

Later at 1922 Executive we begin to discuss the growing rift between the shadow government and backbenchers. I make the point that when we were last in opposition there was a spectrum from backbench to leader because the No. 2 spokesmen were the elected backbench vice-chairmen of party committees.

Tuesday 22 July
MH rings. Do I want the CCO job (deputy chairman, Foreign Department)? 'No. Don't want to be a deputy again.'

Question Gordon Brown (Chancellor of Exchequer) in select committee. Try to get him to admit that he has blown the reserves; also attack his policy of making the Bank of England responsible for monetary policy. Lunch with Emmanuel Kay; he agrees to keep funding ERG.

Walk home with Jeffrey Archer, who wants to stand for mayor of London. Since he flopped with Lilley I've got to like him a bit better. I said, 'At least you got it right twice [Thatcher and Major]. I've got it wrong three times – good for character building.'

Wednesday 23 July
Holborow asks for a piece by me for the *Mail on Sunday* on the trampling over of Parliament.

Governor of Bank of England speaks to select committee. I lead with question as to whether he feels 'comfortable' managing the nation's interest policy on the sole criterion of inflation. He says 'Yes', or words to that effect. On to the 1922 Executive, where Cecil Parkinson talks to us – says something flattering about how I sorted out the party's finances, which are now in a perilous state and in his – and Hague's – view reason for controlling the party. I lead a critical line of questioning about this. Alan Clark is very forthright on MP disciplinary procedures, which, despite assurances, would be used to get rid of awkward customers, and on leadership. We should retain right to sack leader and most of rights to elect him.

Thursday 24 July
TV interview on Major years which will be screened during the party conference. I will no doubt irritate people by sounding divisive.

Write piece for *Mail.*

Monday 28 July
Archie Norman has issued a questionnaire 'about relationship between MP and his association' to associations. What is the purpose of this other than to upset colleagues and volunteers alike?

Sunday 31 August
Woken at 6 a.m. by 'Bear' radio with the news of Princess Diana's death. All day TV/radio reports Diana's coffin's return from Paris. If any good comes from this, I hope the monarchy will go back into mysterious obscurity. It is symbolic that one of its members should in effect have been blown up by a photographer's flashbulb. My main concern is for my 83-year-old mother, who worshipped the ground Diana walked on.

Saturday 6 September
Watch Princess Diana's funeral from a bar in Formentera. With the assistance of the one pro-British barman, overcome the resistance of another anti-British colleague and capture Sky TV from Germans and Italians who want to watch in their languages. The service and the subsequent scenes of the crowds lining the routes especially in north London are memorable and moving. The day, however, has left very big question marks. Did Diana save the monarchy by making it more accessible, glamorous, 'caring' and 'loving', or did she seriously undermine it by attacking it, and by forcing it to lift its veil and its mystique? I incline to the latter view. Lord Spencer's eulogy was at the heart of this riddle. On the one hand he lent support to the view that Diana could be 'queen' ('of hearts', her words) without being part of the monarchy; on the other hand he wanted to protect her offspring – presumably in part so they could ultimately add to the monarchy. Actually this is all being too fair to him. It was a pretty blatant attack on the Windsors and the clapping it received had the makings of being revolutionary. Blair is helping to whip all this up.* It will be useful to him when he destroys the Lords. Monarchs who are tribunes of the people are rivals to politicians. Perhaps the matter is best summed up by a policeman who (on the TV screen) approaches a drunk tottering about with a beer can in his hand, with the words 'This is Princess Di's funeral and you are out of order.'

Tuesday 16 September
Hague's reforms seem to be in real trouble. Michael Howard seems to

---

* I suspect this is the reason why many years later Blair was not present at Prince William's wedding.

have fallen out with him on the strength of some comments MH made in Washington, where he talked of the next victory being not so much a matter of scaling Everest but of climbing Snowdon. (MH had in fact included this in a speech during his leadership bid but it was dropped on the grounds of being rather weak, not to say obscure.)

Hague apparently takes it as a slur on the need for the great reforms and MH is in the doghouse!

Wednesday 17 September
Back in Worcestershire. Take Susan Burlingham (and Ann) out to riverside restaurant for lunch. We sit on the veranda overlooking the Avon as it winds its way towards Stratford; we discuss the local Conservative association, which is apparently coming round to the view that all the reforming stuff, which was seen as a good smack in the eyes for MPs, is in fact a threat to constituency autonomy.

Alan Clark rings to say he is planning a letter to the press attacking Hague's reforms (faxes me a copy of this the next day).

There is no doubt these are disturbing times. All institutions are under attack from left and right. Monarchy, Parliament, the law, the form of voting etc. A vacuum is being created which will be filled by undemocratic Europe. No one seems to mind or be capable of doing anything about it. The Labour and Liberal parties fan it on and so, to an extent, do we.

Sunday 21 September
Talk to Archie Hamilton about Alan Clark's letter, published in *Times* yesterday.*

Archie asks, 'Should I try to rein Alan in?'

I say, 'You won't succeed and anyway he's struck a chord with which most people agree.'

Tuesday 7 October
Leave Cropthorne 8 a.m. and drive to Blackpool. Meet Jonathan Holborow at the Pembroke Hotel (only really modern hotel in the Blackpool hotel

---

* In his letter Clark criticised the method by which William Hague sought a mandate to bring forward his six 'principles of reform'. Linking grassroots endorsement of him as leader with approval of his reform programme in the ballot question to all party members would, said Clark, 'confer a blank cheque on a small coterie of management consultants to proceed as they think fit'. He also drew attention to the danger inherent in endowing the centre with the 'powers to impose de-selection by edict'.

desert). Jonathan tells me things are pretty fraught with Lord Rothermere[*] – which explains why my anti-federalist and pro-Tory article was not published the week before. J says he has been given three years more; then he must go.

Change of policy on Euro currency

Wednesday 8 October 1997
Michael Howard's speech uses words 'No single currency into the foreseeable future'. The story is that Hague wasn't willing for him to go ahead with his usual words 'over the lifetime of this parliament'. Things are slipping again.

Friday 10 October
Drive down from Sellafield having visited the Thorp and MOX plants the day before. On the radio Hague delivers his commitment to no single currency 'in the foreseeable future'. I rather hope Blair brings it all to the boil soon so we can sort the whole thing out one way or the other.

Monday 13 October
Bump into Geoffrey Howe at the Spanish embassy (lunchtime reception). He thinks we will go into EMU and the Tory Party will then split. He may be right.

Tuesday 21 October
Travel to Eastbourne. 144 Conservative MPs stay at the Grand Hotel. At last moment I am asked to chair the meeting with the press; Peter Tapsell has bowed out because he wouldn't recognise anyone's name!

The microphones play up to begin with, causing a certain amount of jeering. However, things settle down. I suggest, 'Anyone who hasn't had a message and wants one should ring my secretary and she will help.'

Afterwards find myself dining next to Hague. He promises to be tough on EMU and not to fudge. Talk to David Heathcoat-Amory after dinner. He is very keen to use ERG business contacts to help fight an EMU referendum if this comes about. I say, 'Fine; but the first thing is to ensure the message comes across loud and clear.' He agrees. Cecil Parkinson and I have a good and friendly chat at the bar. Apparently he is to lunch with Alistair McAlpine (head of Referendum Party) next week.

---

[*] Chairman of Associated Newspapers, publishers of the *Daily Mail.*

Wednesday 22 October
Visit Bank of England with Treasury select committee and then formalise our
report. My main input is to ensure that if the Bank is to have responsibility
for inflation, its instructions from the government must be clear.

Thursday 23 October
Lunch with Emmanuel Kay and Daniel Hannan. Emmanuel big subscriber
to ERG. Claims that Blair has been persuaded by some businessmen not to
shut off EMU option. Daniel says this squares with what he has heard, that
HMG might drag its feet on EMU next week in the promised announcement to Parliament when it gets back.

   In the evening it is announced that shadow Cabinet has toughened up
its stance – no EMU application in the next parliament. For the first time
Conservatives sounding clearer than Labour on this matter.

Sunday 2 November
Lunch at Cropthorne. Conversation focuses on Conservatives and Europe.
Michael Howard against turning Clarke/Temple-Morris out. His immediate
worry is whether to take them on in the forthcoming debate on the proposed
Treaty of Amsterdam. I advise 'Yes' strongly. Hague has got to win his way
through with argument. Howards stay on overnight, when discussion continues. A good day. MH still playing the role of the insider, not really a happy
life for him; still surrounded by security police, two of whom stay up all night
'guarding' him from the TV room.

Tuesday 4 November
ERG breakfast at Garrick Club. Agreement that Hague is on the right track
and needed 'supporting'; we can help with our industrial contacts, indeed
already have.

   This is taken up in the evening at a 92 dinner at St Stephen's addressed by
Hague. I ask him what he is doing to win business to the anti-EMU cause.
His answer in part is to use the list 'you, Michael, are providing'. Hague is
good and goes down well. In the voting lobby at 4 p.m. talk to his aide Alan
Duncan; we agree next job might be to absorb the Referendum movement.
We say we might have a word about Alistair McAlpine and how we might
approach him.

   After 92 dinner, walking back to the Commons is eerie; for first time in
years there is nothing to complain about. Even Bill Cash gets up to say he
agrees with all that has been said and sits down to cheers. Hague says, 'How
remarkable.' After the 10 o'clock vote walk some of the way home with Virginia

Bottomley, who has made the transition from Cabinet to the back benches. She says she now hates the party's policy on Europe. All these people who have been controlling our lives are now out and miserable. How long will it last? We've been in rebellion mode for so long, it's going to be hard to adjust!

Wednesday 5 November

1922 Committee Executive up in arms about the proposed constitutional changes. I say jokingly, 'I'm part of the establishment now and will go along with most that Hague suggests if it is in the interest of European policy.' In the main committee Ken Clarke comes in looking rather miserable, especially when the whip on duty (the recycled John Taylor) announces three-line whip next week to vote against the Treaty of Amsterdam. How the wheels of fortune move round in politics!

Tuesday 11 November

Malcolm Pearson rings to tell me about his intention to form 'No to Europe' campaign.

Wednesday 12 November

Dinner in the House. Andrew Mackay (Northern Ireland spokesman) and I agree proportional representation could come before next election – in which case we would be snookered.

Tuesday 18 November

Lunch at Garrick with William Rees-Mogg. We have coincided with each other in the ups and downs and swings and roundabouts of political fortune. Long talk with a judge who is clear that nothing can impinge on the sovereignty of Parliament – he says, '"Irrevocable" is a meaningless word.' He will send me one of his recent judgments about this. That evening who should I bump into and sit next to but John Major (also Michael Ancram and Alastair Goodlad). Alastair and I swap stories about playing rugby against each other for our respective schools. Major looks a bit nonplussed. Then it is my turn (to look nonplussed) when I hear Major say, 'Politics is about luck; when a person is cut down in his political prime – it may not be because he is bad at the job but because of chance.'

Later we talk about Peter Temple-Morris's possible defection. Major says, 'I hate people who deal with the other side.'

I say, 'I did certainly talk to Labour members about trying to defeat Maastricht – not quite the same thing as defecting.' 'Quite,' says Major. All amicable.

Then we talk about Scotland. I say, 'I seem to be leading the charge on the select committee to try to get financial "fairness" for England but am a bit inhibited by my desire to keep the Union going.' Major says, 'Stuff that. We've been blackmailed by the Scots for too long and it hasn't done either the English or the Conservatives much good.' Later in the conversation Major seems to become more concerned about the Unionist point. It is an agreeable evening. Major has been down to Winchester and says we could win the by-election on Thursday.*

Wednesday 19 November
Visit Hague's rooms behind the Speaker's chair. His office is reached up two flights of stairs and along a rather poky corridor.† I raise with him the question of his attitude to a 'no' to the Euro campaign. He says, in effect, 'Fine – go ahead. I'll join in if it works.' Should just about give us enough 'cred' to get on with it.

Tuesday 25 November
Attend a meeting convened by Phil Bradley, chairman of West Midlands Conservatives. He has a go at 'elitist' MPs. I say we seem to be joining the class war – just when the real socialists have given up. The real problem is that MPs are losing all control. Dine with Nick Bonsor. He is bearing up well (after his astonishing defeat at the general election). He says Michael Howard is probably going to leave politics. (He was staying with Bonsor last weekend.)

Friday 28 November
Lunch in the members' dining room. Michael Heseltine joins us after making rather a good speech in favour of unity. Have a long sensible conversation with him.

Heseltine starts by saying that Europe 'is going to be his main topic for the rest of this parliament' (having been prompted by me). I say that means he is going to be at odds with the party – at least he and Ken Clarke would now have to justify their position – which has not been the case heretofore. I ask what is the point of a federal Europe; he says so that we can punch harder.

---

* Mark Oaten, Liberal Democrat, won the Winchester by-election with a majority of 21,556.

† This office became mine when I was chairman of the 1922 Committee between 2001 and 2010. The room itself is grand, with two chandeliers and three large windows, looking east along the Thames towards the City. It was once part of the Serjeant-at-Arms's flat and is, I believe, after the PM's office, the largest in Parliament.

I ask, 'Punch who?' and would we really if we were economically weaker, which would be the case if we have to pay higher taxes and suffer the 'wrong' exchange and interest rates? We all agree that the nation state is not necessarily a fixture, but I argue with Douglas Hogg and Robert Jackson my position that the nation state is still the best unit of loyalty and hence of accountability and so the base for democracy.

We leave in a reflective truce to go back into the chamber for the wind-up speeches on the Hunting Bill.

Wednesday 3 December

Day of discussing the proposed reform of the Conservative Party. Start with a presentation in Central Office by Cecil Parkinson and Archie Norman. I get up to leave after the main presentation. Parkinson follows me out and suggests a cup of coffee upstairs – much to the horror of his secretary, who has at least two appointments lined up; *plus ça change*! We sit in a side room upstairs and gossip for about half an hour – until the poor secretary looks as if she might resign on the spot. He clearly likes Hague despite press rumours to the contrary and despite some of his public implied criticisms – that 'Hague has a lot to learn', commented on by Daniel in yesterday's *Telegraph* leader. However, he does seem to be awkward with Hague's young staff. We discuss a referendum campaign on which Conservatives need to try to have a handle without being seen to run it.

Lunch with Norman Lamont at Gran Paradiso. He makes the good point that if we are to have a controversial policy, e.g. no EMU for ten years, we must push it and argue it and not be fearful of being 'extreme'. At the moment it's a popular policy but this may not last. In some ways the more controversial the better – Hague needs to be burnished.

Later that day subject of referendum taken up at the 1922 Executive and the full committee. There is a rebellion going on amongst the new intake against us old fogies who want to keep things much as they are so far as the selection of a leader is concerned. A lot of them want one-man, one-vote in the party. Will get an electoral college with 30–40 per cent votes to party members. The Executive digs in against Hague's wishes to make a challenge (vote of confidence) totally public. We are all off to see him next week (except me, who has to be with Chancellor of Exchequer at Treasury select committee).

Thursday 4 December

Lunch with *FT* (David Wighton) about select committee business.

Spot David Lidington behind Speaker's chair. Tell him that ERG, which includes three members of shadow Cabinet, has now written to Hague twice

– with no answer. He looks wearily at me as if this is not his first encounter with this sort of thing. It's crazy that Hague's office should be run in this way.

Monday 15 December

Longish talk on the phone to Robert Cranborne. He, like others, wants to set up an 'umbrella' movement for the 'no' campaign. Claims to have secured Murdoch. Certainly he will have Black on side as he works for his board.

Tuesday 16 December

Give lunch to my secretary, Emma Wells-Cole, at the Garrick. She tells me several people in my association (whom she names) are being pretty disloyal to me. They are ganging up with the officers to produce a pro-Europe phalanx. I tell Anthony Ogilvie in the evening to make sure he is standing for chairmanship. He is the only officer even vaguely on my wavelength.

Wednesday 17 December

10.30–11.30 a.m. Quiz Gordon Brown about welfare reform. I and one or two Tories on the Treasury select committee reticent to ask questions because we like what he is doing, or at least is thought to be doing (financial prudence and welfare reform). Labour members silent because they don't like what they think he is doing.

11.30–1.00: Attend board meeting of Association of Electricity Producers (AEP). Members, especially big players, beginning to wobble on 'competition' and return to old wheeler-dealer arrangements behind closed doors.

5.45: Argue for more toughness on party reform at 1922 Committee.

6.30: With Ann to Hague's wedding party at the Carlton Club.

9.00: Speak, not very well, in the truncated debate on the Treaty of Amsterdam.

10.30: Join Jonathan and Vivien Holborow at a pub in Notting Hill for *Mail on Sunday* office party.

Home at 1.00 a.m.

Monday 12 January 1998

Back from fourteen days in the Canaries, where Archie Hamilton faxed me to say there was a majority of the 1922 Executive who wanted a vote of confidence for the leadership to be done with a raised threshold to 25 per cent of the party or forty-five MPs.* I fax back to ask when we reached this decision.

---

* Making it more difficult for a leader to be challenged than is the case with the present 15 per cent threshold.

Tuesday 13 January

Raise the above at 1922 Committee Executive. Archie says he has telephoned round to get the majority. When pressed on this it turns out that the 'majority' was Hague. The real majority on the 1922 Executive was for a much lower figure. No doubt Archie was protecting the leader. I might well have done the same in his position; in this case we would both have been wrong – not the job of 1922 chairman to give priority to protecting the leader. That's what Chief Whips are for.

Wednesday 14 January

Another 1922 Executive meeting to discuss rules for leadership ballot.

Monday 19 January

Dinner at Malcolm Pearson's place in Victoria Square. Present: Malcolm, Robert Cranborne, David Stoddart (Labour, chairman of Campaign for an Independent Britain and Anti-Maastricht Allowance) and me (chairman of ERG). Lots of rambling tirades against Europe. Cranborne says we must get more lefties, trade unionists etc., and he will help light the fuse and withdraw. I say he must be part of it (we all must) or withdraw now. I agree to talk to Alan Simpson, left wing Labour Eurosceptic, and RC says he will find some money. Agree on a general title of 'Save the Pound'. Malcolm Pearson thinks this is too narrow. RC and I agree it is simple and will draw the wider arguments.

Tuesday 20 January

Meet up in my office with Alan Simpson. He is very keen that we should find 'resources' for him, but doesn't want to be formally represented in the Congress for Democracy* as he wants to base part of his attack on Blair that he has done a Ramsay MacDonald and sold out to us. If he, Simpson, joins up with us formally, that would compromise his position.

Lunch with Daniel at the Garrick, where I propose him for membership. 'We need a fund with lots of lolly. He who controls the dosh controls everything,' I say.

92 Group dinner with Cranborne as the speaker. Townend, the chairman of 92, says that Cranborne is an astute politician. I came into Parliament

---

* The Congress for Democracy was set up by the ERG later in 1998 as an all-party group to bring together campaigners for an independent pound and against British entry to the single currency.

same time as him. He joined both Blue Chip (left) and 92 (right) at the same time; left the latter under Major and got put in his Cabinet; now that the wheel of fortune has changed direction, he has begun to back 92 position.

[This passage about Robert Cranborne has reminded me that there are at least two ways of reaching the top in politics: stand like a rock and let the tide of fashion swirl around you, or swim with the tide. Each approach can be as effective as the other. Which one wins is usually a matter of timing and the convergence of circumstances.]

Wednesday 21 January
Did two *Targets*, one on Europe with Ian Taylor and one on agriculture with a man from the NFU. Good fun. Malcolm Pearson wants to set up his 'Global Britain'. I want to collect money for Save the Pound. A meeting is fixed with Cranborne.

1922 Committee, which because of *Target* I did not attend, has voted for a complex solution to what should trigger off vote of no confidence in the leader. Hague has now announced he wants to see the full committee tomorrow.

Thursday 22 January
6 p.m. Hague meets 1922 Executive and effectively agrees to the proposal hammered out by the officers and approved by us in the Executive committee in the morning. They comprise 15 per cent triggering-off mechanism (as opposed to 25 per cent he wanted) and he cannot stand for reselection if simple majority against him. It would have been a bad day for the parliamentary party if he had rolled over us. In the event he doesn't. Later Malcolm Pearson and I agree to focus on a money-raising operation re Europe. We need a million this year and ten million over next four years. Malcolm has suggested that I should chair his lunches.

Tuesday 27 January
Chair ERG breakfast at the Garrick. Very high-powered group. Excellent discussion which is later reported to shadow Cabinet, according to John Redwood, whom I meet in the corridor. Main topics: Hague's visit, and how to link business to 'No' campaign.

Discuss this later with Stanley Kalms, who agrees to support ERG's business conference but says that wants to do 'No' campaign through Central Office and IoD.

7.30: Meeting at Pearson home with Stoddart* and Cranborne. In true Salisbury style, Cranborne announces that 'his friends' do not want to be associated with the Tories and will do their thing as friends of Cranborne. In other words he wants to hijack the operation and get on with it himself. Meanwhile Pearson wants to send out invitations to his lunch which I am meant to be chairing!

Later bump into Peter Tapsell in the vote in the House. We agree that he and I and Bill Cash and Malcolm Pearson really ought to get together.

Wednesday 28 January

The Cash/Tapsell/Spicer/Pearson meeting takes place in Room J – the former site of the Maastricht meetings. We agree after lengthy and amicable discussion:

The fault lines in the Tory Party need to be sorted out before we go on to the multi-party meeting on Europe.

To launch anything we do with Hague.

To convene a meeting of the twenty key Eurosceptic parliamentary Tories – no chairman.

Thursday 29 January

Lunch at Victoria Square with Pearson, Christopher Booker and Stoddart. Booker concedes that the case for leaving Europe comes at the end of the process. Not much doubt in his and Pearson's minds that it's part of it; they are not keen on isolating the EMU issue

Back at the office Hannan has returned from Central Office, where he has been having talks about their lists. Apparently Cranborne is the key man to deal with on this.

Sunday 1 February

Drive from London to Kent to the Howards'. Phone call from Pearson to say CCO backing David Heathcoat-Amory's umbrella group and Heathcoat-Amory supporting his (Pearson's) efforts.

After lunch Ann and I stay on for an evening of bridge, TV etc. MH very assertive on the subject of Europe. Says the party line is absolute and it does not matter who runs the 'No' campaign. Thinks it ought to be Cranborne or himself.

---

* Lord Stoddart of Swindon, Labour Peer, former MP for Swindon and Labour Government Whip. Chairman of the Campaign for an Independent Britain and of the Anti-Maastricht Alliance. Independent Labour Peer from 2001.

Treasury select committee

Tuesday 3 February 1998
Paris with Treasury select committee. Main visits to Minister of Economy, Finance and Industry* and governor of the Bank of France.

6.30: Meeting with governor, rather significantly back from his meeting with (taking instructions from?) his German opposite number whom we are seeing next week. Room painted in grey-green and lined with tall tapestries. The governor says in answer to a question from me, 'Ecofin has more power over the budget than US Treasury over the states or German Ministry of Finance over Bavaria.'

I say, 'If you control the budget you control the money.'

Governor looks a bit nonplussed.

Main conclusion of the visit: French are going ahead with EMU whatever the pain (12 per cent unemployment and misery).

Wednesday 4 February
To Birmingham for Jim Miller's memorial service. Roman Catholic service with Welsh accent (Howard flies in by helicopter to read the lesson). Vast Eurosceptic congregation come to say farewell to one of its own. On the return, lunch on the train with Daniel Hannan and Bill Cash.

Dinner at Cranborne's home. Present: Howard, Cranborne, Bonsor, Portillo, me and Conrad Black. Heated discussion of the party's policy of refusing to say 'No' to single currency for next parliament. Portillo and Howard say EMU will collapse because it is innately unstable. I say, 'But governments, especially Germany and France, are backing it.' 'Doesn't matter,' say Portillo and Howard. 'They are out of touch with the people.' 'I've been fighting "out of touch" governments for the last seven years, and they have a tendency to win in the short run!'

Prior to this I was quite vociferous at 1922. There seemed to be a good hearing for my argument that 1922 should keep control of the power to change leadership rules.

Thursday 5 February
Lunch with Cecil Parkinson and Jonathan Holborow. CP clearly wants to leave CCO asap once reorganisation of the party done.

---

* Dominique Strauss-Kahn, later managing director of the International Monetary Fund.

Tuesday 10 February
Bonn. Lunch with select committee and Herr Tietmeyer,[*] – probably future governor of ECB. Germany is going ahead with EMU. Nothing will stop them, neither the Court nor the Bundestag. It is their way of preventing another Hitler, that's how Kohl sees it; that's how all the political establishment see it.

Wednesday 11–Thursday 12 February
Germany and Italy. Treasury committee visit finance ministers and governors of central banks.

Lunch on 11th in Bonn with Bundestag members. I ask, 'Isn't the German parliamentary vote on EMU conditions going to be a farce? They are meant to insist on the strict adherence by all countries to the Maastricht criteria but everyone knows that they will not be complied with even by Germany.' Much staring at plates and muttering of '*Nein, nein, das ist keine Farce*', but they know it's true.

Germany and Italy are heading for the single currency in May. Britain is going to be out on her own.

At lunch on the 12th at the Rome embassy sit next to Antonio Martino, former Foreign Minister and Forza Italia foreign affairs spokesman and liberal economist. He and I defend the free market line as best we can in front of federalist Brits and Italians.

Daniel comes round to Maunsel Street at around 10 p.m. on my return. Nick Wood of *The Times* on the warpath – knows that Robert Cranborne and I are up to something re the referendum. Ring Robert – he is working very close to Hague. Discuss with him how to play the forthcoming meeting between Hague, Tapsell and Cash.

Monday 16 February
Tapsell, Cash and I discuss tactics for meeting with Hague tomorrow. Tapsell wants a gung-ho approach: 'We need umbrella group, cross party etc.'

I say, 'Hague will laugh us out of court, or rather, be very polite; we will be the third such group to approach him in the last week, Pearson and Cranborne being the other two. What we need to do is listen to Hague; see what he says.'

---

[*] Hans Tietmeyer, president of the Deutsche Bundesbank 1993–9.

Tuesday 17 February
Meeting with Hague, Cash, Tapsell. Cash complains about being left out of what is going on. Hague says Cranborne is in charge and getting things off the ground; agrees to keep Cash more in the picture. I argue that he can't just drop Malcolm Pearson. He is considering the question of principle and the question of the effect of Britain staying outside the single currency.

Thursday 19 February
Charles Moore, editor of *Daily Telegraph*, speaks on EMU to IoD. I encourage Alan Simpson, very left-wing Labour pal, to ask an anti-EMU question; 200 people clap. AS well pleased.

Monday 23 February
Chair ERG lunch. Discuss our forthcoming EMU booklet and conference. How far to go down the may-have-to-come-out road? Rodney Leach says must look at the question of principle, which is becoming a euphemism for may have to come out. Michael Edwardes says Malcolm Pearson's emerging group are lone outers and go too far. Malcolm looks a bit miffed, especially when I tell him privately that Hague is backing Cranborne.

Later that evening walk back with Alan Duncan, Hague's right-hand man. Alan says that the Conservative Party's EMU cause demands that Cash, Pearson, Cranborne and I hang together, otherwise there will be chaos. I wonder if he is talking with his master's voice?

Tuesday 24 February
Bump into Cranborne at a Centre for Policy Studies lecture given by Hague: Cranborne says we must meet about referendum umbrellas. I say, 'Fine – you fix it.' He claims to be coming close to getting a permanent person to run a secretariat.

Thursday 26 February
Lunch in the Cholmondeley room in the House of Lords given by Malcolm Pearson, who is trying to set up his 'Global Britain' group. Christopher Booker and Bill Cash clash over the proposal to set up an all-party think tank. Cash claims to be it. Nigel Vinson* says, 'You're not because you are Cash and Tory. What we need is the European Foundation without Cash.' Bill says he'll think about it – clearly implying: not beyond the second course.

---

* Baron Vinson, co-founder of the Centre for Policy Studies.

Friday 27 February
Talk to Malcolm Pearson on the phone before going off to my AGM in Worcestershire. He says he's going to go it alone with a come-out-of-Europe event to 'set the pace' – point the direction in which the rest of us can follow when the time is right – in other words, when it's safe? We think we are trying to keep the movement in some sort of kilter with public opinion – timing is everything etc.

Malcolm a mixture of great decisiveness and great indecisiveness; much like the rest of us, only he does it with so much more energy.

Monday 2 March
Hague to lunch with ERG. John Bercow very impressive, as is Hague. I start questions with: Can you oppose single currency on economic grounds only? Hague says 'No' and he is going to make a speech about the political implications of entry (loss of sovereignty etc.) but without words like 'it's a matter of principle'.

Tuesday 3 March
Bumped into Hague in the 10 o'clock vote. He seemed to have enjoyed the lunch.

Dinner with Michael Howard at Pratt's: his first night as a member of the club. Apparently the Queen had lunch there two days ago.

Eurosceptic umbrella group

Friday 6 March 1998
Ring Robert Cranborne re Eurosceptic umbrella group. He says, 'It's all sewn up' and 'My donors do not want anything to do with Tory politics.' I say it all could become very remote – to be characterised by a few civil servants and backroom boys funded by Rupert Murdoch and Conrad Black, i.e. two foreign proprietors. He says, 'I hope you won't badmouth it.'

At Malcolm Pearson's lunch I warn against the campaign being got off by a bunch of bankers behind closed doors. Someone quotes 'Michael Spicer's phrase', 'Let all flowers bloom'. (Chairman Mao's, actually.) Stanley Kalms says he has heard of the bad time I gave the CBI yesterday in the select committee – hopes I won't do it to him next week.

Ruth Lea rings from the IoD. 'Can we change our mind and give evidence to the select committee?'

I say, 'I fear it's a bit late.'

Wednesday 11 March
ERG lunch. Chat around familiar subjects: how to get businessmen against the single currency and how to marshal wider forum on EMU referendum. Some of the MPs – notably Chris Gill and John Townend – linger afterwards.

At the 1922 Executive I am rather out on a limb re Cranborne's presentation of his deals with Labour on the hereditary peerage. 'Is there not a danger', I ask, 'of our seeming to connive with Labour in the destruction of hereditaries?' No one seems especially interested. Cranborne presents what he is doing as 'being seen to be reasonable' in the press; he mentions people like Hugo Young being impressed with his tactics. I think to myself, 'If Hugo likes what we are doing, it must be wrong.' Others on the 1922 Executive do not see it quite like this. But then Alan Clark is absent and it isn't about Europe. Townend and Gill switch off their earphones (metaphorically!).

Thursday 12 March
Dinner at whips' table with David Heathcoat-Amory. Find myself more and more in tune with him; he is very shrewd about people. Also invited to the table by the whip John Taylor is Ann Widdecombe. After a difficult beginning, we agree very much that the job of opposition is to oppose, not, à la Cranborne, to do deals with the government.

Monday 16 March
Bill Cash fretting in the lobby about the need to combine forces in the parliamentary party against the 'mainstream' people who are having it all their own way. Bill makes a reasonable point – good time to get together when there is meant to be 'peace' and it is all going our way (on the surface).

By coincidence Hague comes up to me in the lobby. I ask him if he has got my letter. 'Not yet, I've just got back from Australia.' Tell him Cranborne and I are having lunch tomorrow. I tell him about our worries. He says, 'Let's talk again after your lunch and I have read your letter.'

Tuesday 17 March
Budget day. Arrive 7.15 at the House to book my seat. Then on to Treasury select committee to discuss the EMU report. Lunch with Cranborne at White's. He still feels he can set up his umbrella group with financiers (many of whom don't like the Tories) behind closed doors. I stick to my view that we Tories cannot be ignored. We need to be part of it all – as we are the best organised anti-EMU political group; also Tory Eurosceptics getting restless because they don't know how to join in and are tired of the growingly effective

operations of Heseltine and Clarke, who are running seminars for the party faithful and the City. Feeling is it is time to stand up for Hague's position.

Talk also on the phone to Malcolm Pearson; suggest he goes ahead with his think tank.

Speak in Budget debate.*

Wednesday 18 March

People seemed to have liked my speech – at least that which they read in Hansard – Jacqui Lait, Alan Clark, Owen Paterson all come up and say it was enjoyable.

Meeting with Cecil Parkinson and other MPs at CCO in the morning. Attend 1922 Committee Executive at 5.45. I lead discussion about need for Hague to commit himself against obligatory reselection of MPs.† Archie Hamilton says he will report this. Theatre with Ann (*Amy's View* with Judi Dench, v. funny) then to the Garrick for supper.

I'm rather enjoying being an ex-minister, ex-rebel with menace – the jokes are flowing; so are the arguments.

Tuesday 24 March

Twenty-five ERGites in Dining Room B. Discussion afterwards lasts till about 11 p.m. Complete agreement: leader needs to have an internal referendum on his policy to stay out of EMU, which is being increasingly challenged by the so-called 'mainstream' Clarkeites.

Thursday 26 March

Lunch with Clive Bossom‡ as host at the Carlton Club. Jonathan Aitken turns up. Says he will probably go to prison for three years for his perjury; remarkably calm about it all. He will confess in order to try to save his daughter and wife, who are being charged with conspiracy to pervert course of

---

* The following passage from Hansard (vol. 308, col. 1141) gives a taste of my fairly relaxed style at this time.

  Sir Michael Spicer: The best that can be said about this Budget is that it is not as bad as some people feared. That is why all the left-wing Labour members rushed out of the chamber to report the Chancellor to the press.

  Mr Bill Michie: Not all of them.

  Sir Michael Spicer: I exonerate the Honourable Member for Sheffield Heeley. If other Labour members want to raise their hands they should do so now.

† By which all sitting MPs would automatically have to go through a formal reselection process.

‡ Sir Clive Bossom, MP for Leominster 1959–74.

justice – apparently easier to get a conviction than perjury. When he leaves, which he does early, he says, 'Come and see me in Wormwood Scrubs.' One cannot help but feel deeply sorry – so unnecessary; he might have been leader of the party.

Saturday 28 March
Off to Harrogate to hear Hague at the last Central Council before the new-fangled party is born. Hague repeats his commitment to no single currency in the next manifesto but then proceeds to pander to the left with constant references to 'one nation' and jibes at 'blue Trotskyites'. I decide to clear off after his speech and find Alan and Jane Clark at the station doing the same thing.

Tuesday 31 March
Chancellor up before the select committee. Teddy Taylor and I are pretty fierce. Teddy is a man whose bite is worse than his bark. Sounds all meek and mild but if crossed can go bananas. Committee significantly barring itself from discussing the rights and wrongs of EMU and restricting itself to looking at the technical facts of being out and in. Teddy wants me to join in with a minority report he has drafted saying how awful EMU is. I could certainly have drafted something similar but it misses the point. This report is not about the rights and wrongs – if it was the majority would say we must go in. We want to avoid that.

Friday 3 April
Malcolm Pearson rings. Has finally fallen out with Bill Cash.

Creation of Business for Sterling

Monday 6 April 1998
Main splash story in the *Telegraph* about the ERG conference of 3 July with a supportive leader:

'Business leaders unite to defeat the Euro'
More than 100 captains of industry* are to launch a campaign against the introduction of the European Single Currency, with a manifesto setting out

---

* The 100 names, which were published in the ERG pamphlet *The Euro: Bad for Business*, provided the core membership for Business for Sterling when it was eventually formed.

the economic case against monetary union. William Hague will address the group's first conference…

The campaign, organised by the European Research Group, headed by the Tory MP Sir Michael Spicer, will be a serious blow to Tony Blair and Gordon Brown, the Chancellor. The launch at the Café Royal in London on July 3rd is likely to be embarrassing to ministers, who claim that there is a wide support for EMU among businessmen.

Tuesday 7 April

Malcolm Pearson's lunch at the House of Lords. Key figure present: Alan Duncan, Hague's sidekick, who makes a little speech saying 'It's all about focus groups'. Malcolm tells us that Cranborne has handed over his file for the umbrella group to Richard Marsh. I ask by whose authority, and how representative is his operation to be? Malcolm replies, 'We will find out at a meeting to be held with him at 5.15.' Sir Michael Edwardes says, 'Spicer should be at the meeting, as should Rodney Leach and David Stoddart.'

At 5.15 Marsh arrives in a committee room in the House of Lords. I offer to support him; he says he is not ready to start an umbrella group. He says he is financed by Lord Hanson* and wants to set up something new. Makes some disparaging remarks about the Conservative Party. I, on the other hand, am determined that the Conservative Party should be part of the operation for its own good and for that of the cause. I walk out before the end of the meeting, not in a huff but because I think it's all becoming a waste of time.

Dinner at Pratt's with Daniel Hannan; Michael Howard joins us. The idea is beginning to firm in Daniel's and my minds of acting as a catalyst to a real umbrella group with John Banham as the chairman – but make it really representative: trade unions, major parties, Federation of Small Businesses, IoD etc. Let's see if we can pull it off.

Thursday 9 April

Breakfast with Tom Arnold. Daniel and I decide to go for it with Banham. Support pouring in from businessmen. How we deal with this is a big problem. Spend night at Manor House, Moreton-in-Marsh, because massive floods prevent train from getting through to Evesham. Peter Tapsell tells me that Thatcher said Malcolm Pearson was behind the *Telegraph* story. Tapsell said I was. She didn't seem too receptive. *Plus ça change*. I think Thatcher now resents (rather than regrets) not having promoted me.

---

* Industrialist and co-founder of the Hanson Trust.

Saturday 11 April
Ring Malcolm Pearson in Scotland. Ask him to hold off going firm with Marsh until I see him on Monday week (by which time will have sounded out Banham).

Monday 20 April
12 noon: Visit John Banham, chairman of Tarmac and Kingfisher, with Hannan. Offer to make him our leader; he is flattered. Agrees on EMU, but must put it to his board. He is former director-general of CBI and chairman of Boundary Commission. Treasury committee accepts more of my amendments to EMU report, which just about makes it acceptable. The majority would have liked it to be a paean in praise of EMU.

Tuesday 21 April
Bump into Peter Temple-Morris after 10 p.m. vote. He thanks me for speaking to his constituency AGM; only problem is that it wasn't his AGM. He's left the party and is seemingly thinking of formally joining Labour, to assure himself of a place in the House or Lords, and to be able to dine alongside someone in the members' dining room. Currently he seems rather lonely. Very sad. Socially he's a nice chap.

Wednesday 22 April
Talk at some length to Stanley Kalms on the phone. He is setting up a businessmen's club to control the anti-single currency movement with Dick Marsh in charge. My job is to hand over the names of our businessmen once we have had one conference!!

Tuesday 28 April
Terrific row over Treasury select committee report on EMU published at 3 p.m. I am accused of leaking it over weekend. Reports, especially by David Wastell in *Sunday Telegraph*, very favourable to Eurosceptic point of view, e.g. 'at least five years' before we will know whether economies converged sufficiently. Giles Radice (chairman) furious, as is our lad Quentin Davies, both Eurofederalists. As a matter of fact I did not leak. Wastell rang me up with the story. I did not comment on it but neither did I deny its accuracy. Similar story appeared in *Observer*, to whom I did not speak.

Tuesday 5 May
Help Daniel Hannan to stuff 250 envelopes for the businessmen's conference. Then we chew over life in the Rochester Row Indian restaurant. Daniel

hopeful of becoming an MEP. With his views (we should pull out of Europe) he may have to give his salary to a Eurosceptic cause and earn another salary writing or something.

Monday 11 May

Distress call from Nicholas Budgen, who has been turned down by the Euro Parliament sifting committee in the West Midlands. All very predictable because of the nature of the selection committee but also because of the nature of Budgen. He says he has talked to Charles Moore of the *Telegraph* and together they will blow the lid off the whole selection process. My own view is that the avid Eurosceptics are being rather absurd going for the European Parliament (the list apparently now includes Lamont, who is also being turned down).

I tell Budgie he won't have much hope of getting reselected elsewhere if he is too rude.

Wednesday 20 May

Lunch at *Times* with Edward Pickering (vice-chairman of Times Newspapers). Rupert Murdoch joins us briefly at lunch. When I appear on Sky TV late that afternoon, I warn the studio boys that Murdoch was watching. Bump into Chris Buckland (*Express*) a few minutes later at the Members' Entrance to the House of Commons. He is an amusing fellow and evidently has a keen nose for what is going on. 'How's your pal Murdoch?' he asks about a meeting which happened only minutes before.

Most of week spent ringing businessmen who had said they would give us money for the ERG conference. Banham seems to be backing off. No signs of life from him.

Thursday 21 May

Take governor of Bank of England apart at the Treasury select committee. 'Why are you always wrong? Your job is to keep down inflation. It's not working, is it?' Labour hates this line of questioning; they want to get off the hook of the inflation target.

Meet David Lidington at launch of Douglas Hurd's book at Politico's. DL is now Hague's PPS. 'Why can't Hague get himself better organised?' I ask. 'Can't afford a proper staff,' says Lidington. 'I'll get the money for him, if that's the problem.'

Tuesday 2 June

Lunch with Tim Melville Ross, very suave and rather astute Eurosceptical chief executive of IoD. He is part of the new business group which is being set up under Kalms and Dick Marsh in its own mind to take over the 'No' campaign. What our relations will turn out to be with all this is as yet uncertain.

9.30 p.m. See Hague with Townend and Eric Forth (chairman of Conservative Way Forward). Townend kicks off by referring to stories in today's papers that Stephen Dorrell, having come out of the shadow Cabinet, is on the rampage in the Eurofederalist cause. Hague must take a grip and hold his 'internal referendum' within the party sooner rather than later.

I speak next and make three points:

If the issue is left to the next general election it could 'explode' in our faces.

Hague's policy needs the legitimacy of party support. I make the point that Dorrell is meant to be coming to West Worcestershire; if I try to disinvite him I will be told his speech is part of general discussion on Europe leading to a future decision, even if his talk is against the leader's position.

Hague will vastly strengthen his position if he comes out of a battle on this victorious. At the moment, I say, he is doing well in private and in Parliament but not making any dent on the public – a row would give him much higher profile. Only reason for not going early with referendum is that it could stir up the pro-Euro faction – but they are stirred up already.

Forth makes additional point that whereas he would win now, he might not win so overwhelmingly later.

Hague says these are all important points and he will chew them over seriously. Forth asks afterwards whether he is just becoming clever at fobbing people like us off. He was certainly very friendly and apparently in agreement with us.

Monday 8 June

Washington with the Treasury committee. Usual round of congressional and executive meetings. Group led by Giles Radice. Dinner at embassy, more impressive than ever. Gardens looking beautiful with June roses and herbaceous border. Christopher Meyer, the ambassador, very professional. I have a contretemps with GR over dinner about Europe, much to the apparent amusement of the Americans and the ambassador's wife.* CM proclaims her to be Eurosceptic.

Tuesday 9–Wednesday 10 June

Meet, amongst others, James Wolfensohn (president, World Bank) and Alan Greenspan (chairman, Federal Reserve). Two prime areas of discussion:

---

* The lovely Russo-French Catherine.

Will US economy, currently on a remarkably strong and prolonged climb, eventually have a soft landing? Greenspan is talking about low inflation, high employment, high growth and being 'beyond history'. I wonder.

In light of Asia/Russia economic crisis, do we need new worldwide formal monitoring and rescuing organisation?

Thursday 18 June

Meet Michael Howard in the smoking room. He says, now that Marsh et al. have announced that they want nothing to do with politicians, may be time for Conservative Party to take more of a lead. I say if we are given the go-ahead we could turn our Euro conference into something more connected with the party.

He says he will talk to Francis Maude. I say, what about talking it over with Hague? He looks a bit glum about this.

The businessmen's conference

Tuesday 23 June 1998

ERG breakfast in Commons Dining Room D. We decide to press ahead with 'political' dimension after business conference.

Discuss whether Hague should hold his internal referendum on EMU. Two shadow Cabinet members defend position of delay. I and Bercow and the rest lead the charge to 'get the matter sorted out'. More talks later on the phone with businessmen, money pouring in from our conference.

In the constituency am calling for Irish tinkers to be repatriated when they terrorise law-abiding Brits.

Bump into Iain Duncan Smith in the 'No' lobby. Has just come back from talking to Stanley Kalms. Idea emerging of leaving Kalms to run businessmen, and we organise the politicians. IDS wants to keep in touch.

Wednesday 24 June

Meeting at Dean's Yard between myself, Stanley Kalms and Richard Marsh. We agree they will do the businessmen and we will do the politicians.

Sunday 28 June

Bill Cash rings me to ask whether he can come to ERG businessmen's lunch. I tell him he must talk to the others. My preference would be to have him on our committee. Others may have different views. Probably should be a member before he comes to a public meeting.

Monday 29 June
Lunch with Malcolm Pearson. He is hell-bent on setting up a 'pull out of Europe or renegotiate' movement.

Thursday 2 July
Eve of the ERG businessmen's conference. Up to the US ambassador's residence for bun fight in unusually cold and damp weather. Ann told by someone that the Liberal member for Hereford (Paul Keetch) could be a closet Eurosceptic – might be important information if we set up all-party group.

On to late-night champagne party given in his flat in the Albany by Peter Tapsell – most of Eurosceptic crowd there including Thatcher and, interestingly, Austin Mitchell. Thatcher seems to blame me for getting her out to speak so late at night. Actually it was Cash wot done it!

Friday 3 July
Off to Café Royal at 7.30. Over 100 top businessmen turn up. Lamont suggests a march. Everyone calls for umbrella group. Perhaps we will have to do it – if I can get Labour and Liberal people to join in. It's all a great success. Sadly Hague ill. Lilley substitutes. Redwood, Maude, Heathcoat-Amory join in.

Saturday 4 July
Nigel Dawes's sixtieth birthday. Birtsmorton Court beautifully lit up for the occasion. All the drives and tree walks lined with firelights. The lake beautiful in the late summer light.

8.30: A Spitfire flies over several times in salute to Nigel. Clowns and magicians everywhere. I argue with a couple of devout Catholics about the deity of Christ, of which I have increasing doubts – but have increasing faith in his interpretation of a loving God. Makes much of the Christian service hard to go along with – though, like others, appreciate the protective structure, the safety net, and the discipline it provides.

Monday 6–Thursday 9 July
Monday morning: Call Emma at the office on my way down to have my monthly lunch with Ma. She says she is being flooded out with calls about EMU (and the pamphlet in particular) following the conference.

Story of the week is the sale of *The Euro: Bad for Business*. Every time the phone goes down it rings again with another order. We are going to have to pursue this success with a big all-party conference in December.

Thursday 23 July
Malcolm Pearson lunch in the Attlee room. Thatcher sits at the far end of the table. Every so often she calls out that she can't hear. Cuts in to repeat, 'We don't want the detail; it's the broad picture that matters.' I mutter at one point, 'But it was the small print in the Single Act wot done us.' Malcolm asks me to give a résumé of the ERG business conference. I do this, saying we are now moving on to constitutional and political matters; Richard Marsh (sitting opposite me) and Business for Sterling are taking on the business case. Marsh agrees, 'as soon as we have an office'.

Wednesday 29 July
7.45 Dinner at Simpson's-in-the-Strand with Austin Mitchell, Alan Simpson and Daniel Hannan. Sit in the secluded seats at the far right-hand corner. Everyone comes on time in between votes at 7 p.m. and 10. Paul Keetch (Liberal) has been running scared all week about coming – saying he would turn up then making implausible excuses for not doing so. Finally he says he has a party meeting and might come late. He doesn't. By coincidence we pass him in our taxi at the main gate to Jubilee Court – after the dinner. We open the window and wave to him; he looks back sheepishly and avoids me later in the evening. So much for our brave Eurosceptical Liberal Democrat.

The rest of us decide to do without the Liberals. I put forward the idea for an all-party Congress for Democracy. Simpson gives us his usual line about not wanting to co-operate openly with the Conservatives; he wants a covert operation in order to take our money. Mitchell supportive of overt co-operation at a congress on 18 December. We decide to try to involve Major(!), David Owen and Tony Benn as speakers. Mitchell says he will give his help with Labour people (e.g. Denzil Davies, Benn). I will get the money. We also agree on a covert liaison group which would include Simpson.

It is a beginning, though how firm a one remains to be seen. Simpson says, 'We don't want to help the Conservatives by giving credibility of a multi-party show.'

I say, 'Conservatives would benefit from being on their own; the general cause, however, might not.'

Thursday 30 July
Lunch at Wilton's with Jonathan Holborow. He is getting close to Hague (dining à quatre with wives next Tuesday) – which is good.

Thursday 17 September
Everyone in the party is a Eurosceptic now because Hague has taken a firm stand. If only Major had done so.

Friday 25 September
Lunch at IEA. Sam Brittan main speaker. Good chat with him beforehand. He had hoped that Ken Clarke would be present (which until ten minutes before he intended to be) – as he wanted to witness a scrap between me and Clarke on Europe.

Sam is trying to sell a modified inflation target à la USA. I say in a question (a) we aren't the USA and our Bank is less independent, (b) politicians only understand single constraints – fudge them a bit and that would be the end of the constraint. Sam says, 'Point taken, but the answer is to make the Bank more independent.'

Monday 28 September
Early train to London for lunch with David Owen as my guest at the Garrick. Fail to get him to agree to be a speaker at our Congress for Democracy. This is a severe blow. We are trying to make it cross-party; so far we have no serious big political speaker. Owen's reasons for not joining – very convoluted. Felt Europe and the prevention of a single foreign policy the only important issue in town and the only one he wanted to play a part in – but not yet. Seems to think Blair may back off if left to work it all out for himself. Would play a major role in the actual referendum campaign. Sees the need for effort before then but doesn't want to be part of it – especially with politicians. Will try to get a line-up of Major, Denzil Davies, Lawson.

Monday 5 October
Party conference in Bournemouth. Major on TV side by side with Hague. Outside Highcliffe Hotel Major says Heseltine is a good man; 'the real troublemakers are the ultra Eurosceptics.' Major in his true colours. Hague looks a bit nonplussed; says Heseltine et al. speak for themselves.

Monday 12 October
Off with the parliamentary party for 'bonding' in Eastbourne. Beautiful day, lovely room overlooking the sea.

Despite his agreeability I find it hard to make conversation with Hague – although he joins in about USA, where he wants to visit every state capital.

Perhaps I am the problem; certainly he doesn't answer my letters written on behalf of ERG.

Tuesday 13 October
Drive back to London with John Redwood, who gives me another round of the story of his relationship with Portillo. He gave Portillo every chance at the second Major leadership contest to take the lead, which he (Portillo) didn't take up: 'I will come in at the second round.' Redwood not willing to accept this. Redwood still 'in the race'.

Summing up current position of Hague, Redwood, Portillo: Hague is brave, clear on Europe and in situ; his presence is all we have between life as we now know it on Europe and a Clarke-led counter-revolution. But Hague does not appeal; so the position of the Conservative Party and of its current policy towards Europe is very fragile. If Hague loses both the election, badly, and the single currency referendum, for which, inevitably, he will be the leader of the 'No' campaign, he will be a goner. Redwood is still ambitious to be leader but will never make it because of his history of lifting the dagger in the past. Portillo is charismatic but not in Parliament and probably won't get back till the next election. It is possible, thereafter, that he will replace Hague, but unlikely. If Hague goes so will the case against the single currency. In will come some compromiser like Maude, probably backed by Clarke or someone completely new.

In the meantime I am doing my best to build up a national anti-EMU movement.

Wednesday 28 October
Dinner with Jonathan Holborow. Seems to be recovering from the shock of being sacked as editor of the *Mail on Sunday.* In deep dialogue with Hague about coming in as director of communications. He insists (rightly) must report to Hague directly, not to chairman.

Thursday 29 October
Bump into Norman Lamont at Turkish embassy. He continues with his view (with which I agree) that Hague should be more consistent and proactive with policy. If we attack high interest rates it must be because we say they are brought on by fiscal profligacy not because we want to risk seeing inflation back. NL thinks on Europe especially Hague must be more gung-ho. I agree and tell NL he is the closest of many of us to Hague and should tell him all this.

Wednesday 4 November
Manage to produce quite a good speech in a short economic debate in the House, despite a bad cold.

Thursday 5 November
Breakfast at Hyde Park Hotel with Rodney Leach, shrewd behind-the-scenes guru for Business for Sterling, and Robin Birley, Goldsmith's not very strong stepson, to see whether there is any meeting of minds. I think we can co-operate on specific projects. As long as Birley is boss of the Democracy Movement, the self-important Paul Sykes will go along with it. Drive with Rodney in his car to give AEP president's speech at the Barbican.

Monday 9 November
Early train from Evesham 8.00. Lunch at Garrick. Robin Day at the table. He watches the House from a Sky TV channel which shows permanent coverage of Parliament. Referring to my speech in the House on Wednesday he says, 'I didn't realise you were such a good speaker. What impressed me was that you made a coherent argument without notes.' Quite an accolade from the great TV inquisitor. He adds, 'I haven't a clue what you said.'

Gordon Brown, in front of us at the Treasury select committee. Lots of Brown-bashing. We have a spat over money supply figures. I feel I won. 'You're good on invective and rhetoric – not so hot on the small print,' I say. Brown has a technique of giving long answers and in effect talking over his questioner; for the present it's quite effective. At the end Liz Blackman (nice, harmless Labour MP) says, 'You are a terrier, Michael.'

Afterwards bump into Michael Ancram; ask him when he will make a decision about Jonathan Holborow. He says, 'Hopefully later this week.'

Wednesday 11 November
Hague article in the *Telegraph*, answering Portillo's yesterday (who accused Hague of not being proactive enough with his European policy). Has a swipe at quarrelling Eurosceptics. Hague seems to be changing his views a bit; like Major he doesn't seem to feel comfortable certainly with the old, battle-hardened Eurosceptics. This fits with his refusal in a letter to me last week to have lunch/breakfast with ERG, although he has offered a meeting with me.

Thursday 12 November
Ring Paul Sykes. He thinks he can run the 'mass movement' himself. Still he says he's coming to the Congress for Democracy. We will see whether we can do business there.

4.30: Chat over European matters with Chief Whip, James Arbuthnot. I tell him there are two problems: (1) Paul Sykes – Will he defer to the Tories? (2) The usual ineffectiveness of Business for Sterling; hopefully that will eventually be put right by kicking Marsh 'upstairs' to the presidency.

Friday 13 November
Malcolm Pearson rings. Tells me that a new anti-Euro party is being formed in Malvern. That won't please Sykes. I ring Anthony Ogilvie to say we must kill it with kindness, e.g. by inviting Geoff Southall* to the congress.

Tuesday 17 November
Malcolm Pearson rings early in the morning to say that Dick Marsh is planning to convert Business for Sterling into Britain for Sterling and to take over all the Eurosceptic groups. Checking this with Rodney Leach later in the day, he says it's nonsense and time Marsh 'was pushed upstairs'. What we need is a more effective Business for Sterling.

Speak in Teddy Taylor's Southend East constituency. Drive down and back with him. He is the ultimate loner.

Thursday 19 November
Drinks with Maurice Saatchi in House of Lords. He is something of a weather vane, given his trade; seems to feel that 'it's inevitable' is beginning to gain ground on the Euro currency issue.

Friday 20 November
A rather disconsolate Bill Cash asks how can we co-operate? I say I will think hard about it.

Wednesday 25 November
1922 Executive go off to see William Hague at 7 p.m. Rather a good meeting – not too sycophantic. Marion Roe says don't forget the oldies – Hague looks a bit nonplussed. Alan Clark glares but doesn't say anything, which is rather disappointing given all the rude things he says about Hague and his entourage when we meet as a committee. Archie Hamilton raises all the necessary points. I encourage Hague to fight to the end if the Euro elections Bill is chucked back at us by the House of Lords.

---

* Geoffrey Southall, Midlands regional agent for the Referendum Party at the 1997 general election, formed the Democratic Party in 1998.

Monday 30 November
ERG dinner. Good combination of old/new, pro-pull-out/anti-pull-out. First time have had pull-out argument so forceful amongst a coherent group: Forth, Hannan, Bercow, Bonsor, Pearson.

Cranborne resigns

Wednesday 2 December 1998
All hell breaks loose after Hague's question to PM at 3 p.m. Blair asks Hague whether he accepts deal done by Robert Cranborne in Lords to the effect that Lords will go quietly if 100 hereditaries out of 1,000 remain. Hague says 'No'. Later at 1922 Executive emerges that RC called a meeting of 200 Lords to consolidate his position: all done without Hague's knowledge. Halfway through 1922 Executive, around 6 p.m., a flustered David Lidington (PPS to Hague) arrives to say RC has resigned and Hague will address full 1922 at 6.30.

This Hague does rather well, explaining that what lay between him and RC was: RC had negotiated unilaterally; and he had not complied with shadow Cabinet policy, which was to note what was offered by government but not to agree to roll over and give them the Bill in return.

Thursday 3 December
Bump into the mysterious James Arbuthnot while 'booking' my seat. He asks me whether I would have a word with one or two editors to try to put right the disastrous press Hague is getting. I say I will certainly do my best. Thereafter talk to Paul Goodman on *Telegraph* who says the next day's paper will be more supportive.

Later talk to Jonathan Holborow. Hague has offered him a job, two days a week, but as yet he has no contract.

Go on Radio (*Week in Westminster)* to defend Hague against Peter Fraser,[*] who resigned that morning. Fraser seems to agree during the interview with Hague's position – all very bizarre.

By chance have a scheduled meeting with Hague about Europe at 5.45. He is v. charming and cool. We discuss Fraser's position and Holborow's lack of a letter.

Impending Congress for Democracy (9 July). Hague says will try to come. Strange day ends with dinner with David Porter.

---

[*] Lord Fraser of Carmyllie, MoS Scottish Office 1992–5, MoS Trade & Industry 1995–7, deputy Leader of the Opposition in the Lords 1997–8.

Monday 7 December
Meet Malcolm Pearson, who is on the phone to Margaret Thatcher in a room off the Lords' members' lobby. He is briefing her for a dinner party she is giving tomorrow. Malcolm trying to persuade her to make a 'mea culpa' speech 'to clear the decks'.

Wednesday 9 December
Decide overnight Monday not to stand for '22 Executive. Tell Alan Clark, whom I bump into in the members' lobby, that I want to get back to the European 'gutter'. This seems to please him. Heath puts his head round the door of Room 14 when Executive meets before the main committee. He is about twenty minutes early for the vote.

At 6.30 the room is packed with Heseltine, Heath, Clarke et al. They are clearly targeting one or two key right wingers/Eurosceptics. First John Townend (chairman of the once feared 92 Group) is voted down, as is one of the secretaries against the leftish Michael Mates. Then he and the hard right (but otherwise harmless) Andrew Hunter, are voted off the committee. In comes the Euro-enthusiast Jacqui Lait.

Wednesday 16 December
Bank of England cocktail party. Governor Eddie George very friendly; I think he rather likes me being direct to the point of rudeness in the select committee about inflation; he is able to balance me against the socialists.

Back to dinner at a little Italian restaurant in St James's with Bill Cash to set up a truce in anticipation of the Congress for Democracy.

Thursday 17 December
Having established a modus vivendi with Cash, surprised to see faxed press releases from his office claiming credit for the Congress for Democracy. Give him his due, he's contrite when I ring him and offers me to go on *Today* show instead of him. I reckon this would not be *politique*. Eventually Sir Michael Edwardes – of British Leyland fame – does it.

Friday 18 December
Quite an achievement at Church House. Some 300 people gather together from some 50-odd groups in Congress for Democracy. I introduce Austin Mitchell to chair first session; I chair second.

We agree:

  1. a statement on EMU;

2. to meet again;
3. to engage in focus group research;
4. to produce a possible structure for an umbrella group and to consult on this.

Many of TUs present as well as businessmen. Afterwards meet Mark Reckless – who wrote *Business for Sterling* – at Paddington station. He says, 'You are the only person I know who could call a delegate "a charming communist" and not sound condescending.'

Sadly we are wiped off the news by the bombing of Iraq, and by the vote in Congress to impeach President Clinton. This is called 'the curse of Spicer'.

Sunday 20 December
Bill Cash rather charmingly rings up to commiserate on the lack of publicity for the Congress for Democracy. Malcolm Pearson also rings to say he is going to keep up his campaign to seek alternatives to the Single Market and to get Thatcher to apologise for having set it up.

Saturday 2 January 1999
Bill Cash rings. We must all get together quickly. He is upset (with some reason) by the way the first day of the Euro is being portrayed as a great European triumph on the BBC. Fireworks in Frankfurt etc.

Saturday 9 January
Article by Simon Heffer in the *Mail* saying Hague is useless: there will be a battle for second place between us and the Liberals. Gallup in yesterday's *Telegraph* has Labour slipping 2 points – after all their travails over Christmas (resignation of Mandelson, Charlie Whelan, Ron Davies etc.) with Liberals up 2 points. Is this a portent of things to come?

Friday 15 January
Bill Cash wants more talk of co-operation and tells me has put my name at the top of an EDM list calling for a White Paper on the political and economic effects of entry to EMU. I tell him OK as long as not factional within Conservatives. He says it is not: Peter Luff has signed as have David Trimble and Austin Mitchell.

Monday 18 January
Back in London. Meet Rodney Leach at a Commons reception. He says he is about to become chairman of Business for Sterling. Good news – we

will find it easier to co-operate with him. He knows the network so much better than Marsh. Agree to set up joint working party to monitor the focus group work.

Sunday 24 January

Dinner at New Zealand House with the Prime Minister, Jenny Shipley (Jenny's first constituency chairman and sponsor was David Tripp, Ann's cousin, who lives in Ashburton in NZ, which Shipley represents). Richard Grant, the high commissioner, rather wishy-washy in his views on EU. Shipley was much more outspoken in favour of us retaining our own currency as, she said, NZ would expect to do with hers, with a population of three million. Little wonder that she has posted Grant to Paris and put a political appointee in London.

Tuesday 26 January

Telegraph has splash story that Hague about to sack Howard and Redwood. All looking very authentic. Has Hague been talking to Charles Moore? At Treasury select committee, Industry Secretary, Patricia Hewitt, gives unequivocal answer to me that there will be no withholding tax and no loss of the abatement. We shall see.

Jonathan Holborow round to my office when I get back to tell me of the panic in CCO about the *Telegraph* piece.

Wednesday 27 January

Walk home with Archie Hamilton. Discuss latest hoo-ha about *Telegraph* leak that Hague plans to sack all his oldies, e.g. Redwood and Howard. Ironic that Redwood claimed to be his best ally on the way back from Far East tour. Had to be someone close to Hague to make the story credible to the (experienced) journalist Robert Shrimsley. Amazing to have a reshuffle crisis when we are in opposition.

Friday 29 January

Meet Doug Nicholls, general secretary of the Youth & Community Workers' Union, in Abbey Hotel, Malvern. Agreed to co-operate in various ways. He will try to get us in touch with Unison. I will try to fund a pamphlet which hopefully will be entitled *The Euro: Bad for Trade Unions*.

Saturday 30 January

Lunch meeting at home in Cropthorne. Agree to run a large anti-Euro rally in Malvern in the autumn. On to an anti-Euro meeting at Little Comberton Parish Hall attended by about forty people.

Sunday 31 January
Michael Howard rings to say he intends to see Hague tomorrow to say he wants to leave the shadow Cabinet. This follows all the leaks – in the *Daily Telegraph* and *Mail on Sunday* especially – that Hague wants him to go. It's going to have to be very carefully handled tomorrow. It must be seen to be Michael's initiative otherwise, coming on top of all the denials by Hague that he wants him to go, it's going to look a total shambles.

I tell Michael it will be sad and there is the risk of more faceless men; but we are going to be out for the next ten years* and there is a need to build up new faces. MH would make a good EU Commissioner. MH asks me not to speak to anyone in case something changes overnight.† I say, 'Shades of the night of the Hague deal.' He thanks me rather emotionally 'for all I have done'.

Tuesday 2 February
I vote (minority of one) against publishing the Treasury select committee report on more formal regulation of the City. Ruffley and Teddy Taylor vote with government.

Wednesday 3 February
Attend Nick Budgen's memorial service – full of Eurosceptics and resounding music. Charles Moore, now editor of the *Daily Telegraph*, ends his eulogy with 'He was a great Englishman and therefore a good Tory.' Afterwards bump into Norman Lamont, who is writing his autobiography – says that on the day of the Danish referendum result in 1992 he rang Major saying we must now change our tune. Major was non-committal but Lamont was summoned to a meeting when the policy of 'business as usual' had been pre-determined – discussion was of presentation. Also Hurd had gone on radio saying the same thing. It had all in other words been stitched up by the Europhiles in the Cabinet.

Tuesday 9 February
First meeting of focus group committee. Nick Herbert (new CE of Business for Sterling), Marc Glendening (Democracy Movement), Doug Nicholls and Research International.

---

* In fact it was just over eleven years.
† Michael Howard announced on 9 March 1999 that he would retire from the shadow Cabinet at the next reshuffle, which took place in June 1999.

We make sure that the 'it's inevitable' line is tested and 'may be kicked out'. Herbert looks glum – worried Congress taking over from him. Have got to sort out 'one telephone number' with Rodney Leach next week. Malcolm Pearson (have drink with him later in the Pugin room) happy that Congress should be umbrella as long as Global Britain given its own separate status.

Bump into Chris Gill, Richard Shepherd and John Townend in 10 o'clock vote. Shepherd has heard that there was a letter from Hague's office throwing doubt on our fisheries policy. Signed by Patrick Nicholls (rejected by his boss, Tim Yeo, but supported by Howard), it affirmed that we would insist on getting back our rights to control our own fishing limits, thus driving a ramrod through the Treaty of Rome. Now apparently we don't know where we stand. Gill and Townend saw Hague today, who said, 'We must speak with one voice on this' – whose voice?

Wednesday 10 February

The fisheries issue is brewing up. Drink with Christopher Gill in smoking room. He saw Michael Howard today to solicit his support on the Nicholls line (repatriation of fishing rights) – no luck. I see Archie Hamilton, chairman of 1922 Committee, to warn him there could be a major split on this. The answer's to stick to the objective but to say will negotiate towards it. The worry is that, although we are such a small party, press still obsessed with ridiculing us. They should be concentrating on the government two years into this parliament – but Blair, who was good in PM's Questions, is still walking on water.

Tuesday 16 February

Breakfast with Rodney Leach and Robin Birley. Agree to try to set up a joint operations office. Chair Treasury select sub-committee. Daniel meeting other paid people from Eurosceptic groups. Nick Herbert says what Rodney, Birley and I have agreed to is wrong. He is trying to set up his own operation. Speak in debate on House of Lords.

Wednesday 17 February

Breakfast at the Goring Hotel with Michael Portillo. Michael P. in relaxed and rather charming mood. 'My fantasy is to lead the country out of Europe.' Wants to come back for a London seat at the next election but not before. Looking for a big project. The question arises, if party unity is the purpose – unity for what? Portillo certainly retains his magnetism and yet there is something crude about him. 'Don't worry, I'm not looking at your seat' isn't entirely a joke.

Dinner with Chevron at the Institute of Petroleum dinner at Grosvenor House. Redwood speaks well and amusingly without notes. Denis Silk* is even better – very funny. Had no idea he was an MCC player as well as an important rugby player. He always seems so mild at Wellington governors' meetings.

Must ask the following onto a steering group for Congress for Democracy: Cash, Leach, Birley, Mitchell, Stoddart, Doug Nicholls, Green Party.

Thursday 18 February

Christopher Gill says he is writing a letter to *Telegraph* on fishing policy – forcing the issue of Patrick Nicholls versus Yeo. Will I sign? Not unless we have reached desperation or we are going to win.

Dinner at Garrick with Donald and Diana Sinden and our neighbours Michael and Ann Reddington (actor/producer), who have all known each other since rep days in Brighton during the war. On return to Maunsel Street ring Michael Howard to warn him (with Gill's agreement) of the forthcoming letter. He says, 'We are near agreement.' 'In that case for God's sake tell Gill,' I say. Reluctantly he agrees to ring the Chief Whip and send him into action tomorrow. I will also ring Gill.

Friday 19 February

Ring Gill, who is very cagey. Eventually tells me that the Chief Whip has rung him to say Michael Howard will be speaking to him over the weekend. Gill now has the bit between his teeth. Cran gets the Chief Whip (James Arbuthnot) to ring me. I say if the policy really is aligned with Patrick Nicholls, then someone should tell Gill quickly. It is left that Michael Howard will have another go.

Talk to Redwood. He says if a letter goes off half-cock it won't help the position he is arguing in the shadow Cabinet, which is that the option of tearing up the treaty unilaterally must at least be left open. Ring Daniel. He has rung Gill, who has agreed to look at the policy which emerges on Wednesday from shadow Cabinet before going ballistic.

Saturday 20 February

Howard rings before he phones Gill. I say, 'Gill will hold fast on the assumption that the right policy will be produced on Wednesday.' Howard says, 'I think it can.' 'It had better. Otherwise I will join in the public row and so will others who will feel we have been taken for a ride.'

---

* Warden, Radley College 1968–91; Chairman, Test & County Cricket Board 1994–6.

Sunday 21 February

Talk to Eric Forth and John Townend about the ERG supper on Wednesday. Eric says if we are duped we will have to vent our fury on Hague on Wednesday. Townend agrees – and we won't take much on trust in the future. The problem is that this is the first real flashpoint where rhetoric 'about regaining control over fisheries' meets the reality of the treaty. Gill has brought things to a head. We are giving Redwood/Howard etc. the benefit of the doubt – all hell will break loose if we are duped.

Monday 22 February

Drive to London with Ann on a blustery winter day. Daniel rings from the *Telegraph* to the office, which I reach at about 2.30. 'Where is Patrick Nicholls? He is meant to be restating his policy and the *Telegraph* is going to support it and thus put it into stone.' 'No idea. Ring his constituency office.' When I see Patrick in the lobby, turns out he has been in Brussels: yes, he made the speech – yes, Daniel caught up with him. Yes, the *Telegraph* are supporting the speech. (Gill still out of sorts with me. This is not his style; he wants his letter out.)

As I leave the lobby I hear Michael Jack, former agriculture spokesman and very federalist, in effect accusing Yeo – also very of but going along with the new fisheries policy. Walk back with Archie Hamilton – we question whether the party can in effect hold together. Nicholas Soames shouts to me across the corridor, 'The Euro is inevitable – you people have lost.' Alan Duncan says somewhat same thing as I walk in to the House.

Tuesday 23 February

Morning questioning Eddie George about Bank's policy on the Euro. Valedictory speech at Savoy to P&S.[*] Sit next to Duke of Edinburgh. He asks me whether 'right to roam' Bill will go through. I say, 'I sincerely hope not.'

Back in Commons, question to PM about Euro. 'Will he shadow it downwards?' 10 o'clock vote, Paterson, Townend, Bercow and inevitably Gill all in a huddle talking about tomorrow's shadow Cabinet discussions on fishing rights. I will join Gill's letter if the decision goes the wrong way; let's hope it doesn't. Daniel has written a leader in today's *Telegraph* saying, in effect, 'Well done, Hague, you're on the right lines with fishing – they'll be drinking a glass of rum to you in every pub' etc. We'll see tomorrow.

---

[*] Parliamentary & Scientific Committee, of which I was chairman.

Wednesday 24 February

Tennis at Queen's for Lords and Commons. Play rather well with Lord Naseby (formerly Michael Morris). L&C won – unusually.

Party for ERG at Archie Hamilton's home. Hague and Arbuthnot attend for a while. Specific issue is the fishing question. Patrick Nicholls joins us. Hague says we have gone further than ever before to say we will regain control while keeping the party as one. Nicholls suggests Heseltine, Clarke and Heath are going to break away one day: why not let them do it now? Gill is all for having it out. My view is that as long as the commitment is there, there is no need to be too explicit at this stage about the implications for the treaty; that will come up in good time. Others refer to Hague's performance in the House the day before when he did say going into the Euro was a constitutional matter as well as economic. Why then, asked Blair, is Hague only committed to it for one parliament?

A jolly, if slightly intoxicated, evening by the end. Much ERG bonding. Howard Flight very helpful on finances. He wants to be more proactive. Townend was heard saying 'Spicer has done more for the cause in a quiet way than anyone else I know.' I say, 'If you want to be effective, don't go for recognition.'

Wednesday 3 March

At the 1922 I argue against universal reselection by secret ballot (being proposed at the party convention on Sunday week). Archie Hamilton is trying to stand out against it without much hope of being able to do so. I make two points against it: it is divisive, and it encourages 'entryism'. But apparently under new constitution, Hague has no powers to stop it. Hague has set up a monster in the form of the constitution, whose effect is now completely out of control.

Thursday 4 March

Bump into Alan Clark at prayers. Alan says, 'If he were any sort of a leader he would stop it anyway. Proper leaders get their way whatever the constitution.' He has a point, but we must try to keep Hague. There is no one else in the running who would continue his European policy so firmly. Ken Clarke would probably take over if he fell.

Thursday 11 March

Fascinating trip to Cambridge to inaugural PEST dinner. White tie, lovely nostalgic occasion in St John's. Tudor buildings – sense of continuity. (It's not the old PEST: they are using the name for a social club to have some fun – good for them.)

Saturday 13 March

Down by train to Reading to listen to Hague baring his soul and that of the party (we are still 20 points behind in the polls). Not my style, I'm afraid.

Announced on the news that Colin Marshall to be the leader of New Europe, i.e. the federalist movement. What a turn-up for the books.

Tuesday 16 March

The whole EU Commission resigns because auditors refuse to clear their books – implication is corruption.

Wednesday 17 March

Suggest to 1922 Committee that Hague should write a letter to party saying compulsory reselection bad for the party. Archie Hamilton disagrees. I go down like a lead balloon.

Thursday 18 March

Good Pearson lunch. It seems to be established that the Congress is the umbrella organisation. Much talk of going into a common building. Tebbit in good form. Several important journalists there: Michael Gove, Matthew d'Ancona, Alice Thompson, Rachel Sylvester.

Saturday 20 March

After governors' meeting at Wellington meet Fergus Russell, my former housemaster, in his old people's home. Amazing man; still very coherent at ninety-two, despite losing both his legs.

Tuesday 30 March

Meet Daniel off Victoria Street to look round offices which might be suitable to house the main anti-federal HQ.

Tuesday 13 April

Parliament back after Easter (mainly spent canvassing for the local elections). Meet Peter Shore (beginning to show his age and poor health) to discuss pulling the anti-EMU people together.

On to see Michael Howard, who is about to retire as shadow Foreign Secretary. He wants to set up an Atlantic Trust – with John O'Sullivan.

Lilley's speech

Tuesday 20 April 1999
Leave Maunsel Street at 6.30 to drive to Worcestershire where Hague is arriving by helicopter to support local government candidates. Drive him to Wychavon offices. About 200 people there to welcome him. In the car brief him on local issues. Peter Lilley's 'we don't believe in market forces' speech breaking; warn Hague he may get question on this; says he can cope. Speak in Finance debate on withholding tax.

Wednesday 21 April
Together with Robathan, Townend, Bercow, Hannan, Howarth, choose new 'Dan' to replace Daniel Hannan as secretary to ERG. At 1922 Committee Forth raises concern about Lilley speech. Walking back from supper with Ann from 10 p.m. vote, bump into Alan Duncan. We agree parties win from opposition by (a) destroying government's reputation for economic competence and (b) establishing an ideology of their own. Lilley has not helped.

Alan says Hague has 'lost the plot', which is quite something coming from the guy who ran Hague's campaign. But then Forth ran Lilley's campaign and is now his main opponent. Amazing in the circumstances that Howard and I have remained reasonably friendly.

Michael Jack nails PM to commit to veto withholding tax if necessary. We have won. Next question to PM will be 'What are his views on *corpus juris?*' (ie about EU having *locus* in criminal laws).

Tuesday 27 April
ERG breakfast. Main subject not Europe at all but split in party following Lilley's speech and that we must apparently apologise yet again for the past and take on Labour's spending plans for health/education for the future.

Switch to a conversation about who should replace Howard as shadow Foreign Secretary – Heathcoat-Amory our choice. I am deputed to talk to the whips about this. Do so later to Cran – very receptive.

Wednesday 28 April
Another day of shambles. Hague tries to calm things at 1922 Committee by saying we are in favour of private and public control of health/education. The fact is that it is crazy to launch this debate before next week's local elections. Nicholas Soames talks about a 'fiasco' at the 1922. He must smell Hague's death and the resurgence of Clarke, who is currently nowhere to be seen. Cran confirms that word has gone up the line that ERG would like

Heathcoat-Amory to take over from Howard. Ironic in view of the way H-A used to bully everyone, especially Cran, from the whip's office in Maastricht days. Bercow has also warned Chief Whip against appointing a lefty. Apparently we have sunk further in tomorrow's Mori polls. These are bad times for the opposition, mainly because the enemy is doing so well.

Going through the lobby at 10.00 p.m. it is noticeable how in a crisis the party breaks into a mosaic of different factions. Very sad, but probably inevitable until the government's credibility for running the economy goes.

Monday 3 May
Bank holiday. Glorious weather for the Cropthorne walkabout.* Tory Party still in the doldrums. Waiting on next Thursday's local elections, which if we do badly will be the end of Hague. He has managed to alienate both the left wing and (since the Lilley anti-market forces speech) the right, which in today's press he seems to be threatening to sack from the shadow Cabinet. From a talk with Michael Howard it seems that the sniping in the right-wing press and from people like Duncan Smith has got to Hague as it got to Major. If so he is very silly. He was made by the right and could be destroyed by it; in this case like a queen bee it will destroy itself by putting in Clarke. The anarchists like Alan Clark and Gorman on the right are quite capable of doing that – though MH says he thinks Alan Clark hates Ken Clarke more than he despises Hague. Everything hangs on Thursday. Even if we do reasonably well, Hague has got to sort himself out – and realise he must:
 - hold the right;
 - work out a way of attacking the government's economic credentials and do so by improving our own through a credible low-tax policy;
 - play it long, certainly through the next election, and target the referendum. If he plays a leading part in running this, there could be everything to play for.

Tuesday 4 May
Give lunch on the Terrace to Malcolm Pearson and Kim Bolt (VP of the Republicans in London). Vague talk of trying to get the Hoover Institution, of which Kim's mother is a director, to look into US policy towards Europe with the idea that it would be in US interests to have to deal with a Europe of nation states rather than a one-telephone-call Europe.

Dine with Patrick McLoughlin, deputy Chief Whip – discuss the febrile nature of the party and the potential takeover by Clarke.

---

* During which many hundreds of people come round our garden over two days.

Wednesday 5 May

Lunch with Angela Knight, chief executive of Private Clients Investment Managers and Stockbroking, late CE of British Bankers' Association, and former Tory MP and Treasury minister. Apparently the City willing to do a deal on withholding tax – they are mad given the hook on which the government hangs, much due to my efforts on the floor and in committee.

Big issue in the office is whether to allow the Communist Party to come to the Congress for Democracy. I draft a letter saying 'No' but I will take advice from Austin Mitchell and Dan Hannan. Let all flowers bloom or keep it to democrats? Are the commies democrats?

Thursday 6 May

Early morning train to the constituency to tour committee rooms with the excellent Anthony Ogilvie, my chairman and kindred spirit. Crucial for Hague's survival that we do reasonably well in these local and Euro elections.

Sunday 9 May

Celebration drink for the new Wychavon District councillors, who are part of a new Conservative administration. Reasonable success repeated elsewhere up and down the country.

TV news of riots in China – reaction to NATO bombing Chinese embassy in Belgrade. Ring duty officer at FCO to express anxiety about Annabel and Jon, who are in Tibet. He says VP of China has been on Chinese TV to say that of course the crowds are angry but they must not break the law. According to the FCO man things are dying down. Presumably the Chinese authorities don't want crowds to get out of hand in case they turn against the government. Will try to ring Annabel tomorrow.[*]

Tuesday 11 May

Jonathan Aitken and others to lunch at Maunsel Street. JA remarkably calm and controlled in political conversation. He leaves a little early, presumably to write his book. Who would think this is the day he is made a bankrupt and in two weeks' time he will be sent to prison? Walk home after 10 p.m. vote with Chris Gill. Try to persuade him to postpone his speech to '22 tomorrow, when he intends to indict Clarke and Gummer for treachery during the election (revealed in Donald Macintyre's book on Mandelson).[†]

---

[*]   Annabel and Jon return home safely a few days later.

[†]   Donald Macintyre, *Mandelson and the Making of New Labour*, HarperCollins, 1999.

Monday 17 May

Thought Hague's speech last Wednesday in Budapest – written largely by Daniel Hannan, on ERG variable geometry/à la carte choices/rewrite of the treaty etc. – set a new tone which was being gratefully received by my constituents and well written up in Saturday's *Times* and *Telegraph*. Bill Cash says he went to a meeting today where it was stressed there was no change of policy. By contrast, Andrew Lansley comes up to me in the lobby (he's apparently involved with the policy) and asks, 'What do I think of the new policy?' 'Fine, as long as he means it and sticks to it,' I say.

Tuesday 25 May

Breakfast at Institute of Directors. IoD wobbling from its previously firm position against Euro.

That evening I meet Tom Dunne, my New York publisher and long-standing friend, in the Ritz. Take him round to Pratt's, which rises to the occasion and presents a caricature of Tory establishment in exile from the Lords.* Other countries chop off the heads of their deposed aristocrats; we send ours to Pratt's.

Wednesday 26 May

7.50 plane to Frankfurt. Wait on tarmac at Gatwick for one hour while a slot is made available at Frankfurt (heavy traffic at US air base related to Kosovo war). Thanks to a manic taxi ride (120 mph on the motorway) I arrive just in time to meet fellow members of the Treasury select committee visiting Wim Duisenberg, the president of the European Central Bank. We arrive on the day that the Italians decide to break ranks on the stability pact. I talk to WD about this. He has to leave the room at one point to take call from Italy. Labour MPs' reaction to the meeting more interesting than his reaction to us. They are genuinely surprised at the lack of democratic accountability at ECB and the reason given for it, the danger that people would espouse national causes or be thought to do so. I say to my Labour colleagues (Jim Cousins, David Kidney, Jacqui Smith, Liz Blackman), 'That's what it's all about – federalism.' David Kidney is heard to suggest to our chairman, Giles Radice, one of the early figures in the Eurofederalist movement, that maybe Blair should tread water a little longer. Giles Radice cannot have been best pleased with the view.

Returning to London, bump into Malcolm Pearson, who is in a tizzy about the Democracy Movement's unwillingness to join the Congress committee. He has talked to Rodney Leach. He gets Rodney to say it's a top priority

---

* Following the partial abolition of hereditary peers in the House of Lords.

of his to meet me. [Our secretaries later fix for a breakfast meeting on the Monday I get back from a week's holiday at St Mawes.] Also run into Francis Maude. I am delighted he (and in future Tim Bell) is formalising the Conservative campaign against a single currency.

Tuesday 1 June
Papers full of new Hague–Maude committee against single currency. Quotes from someone near Maude as saying, 'We don't intend to take over other groups.' Tim Bell says everyone should join us from no party and all parties.

The importance of my meeting with Rodney grows. If I can't do a deal with him will have to try to involve Portillo/Freddie Forsyth; this will make it almost another group rather than one which embraces the others.

Wednesday 2 June
Hague seems to be becoming firmer on Europe, while the Euro collapses. Whether this is all too late for next Thursday remains to be seen. He is getting a good press in *Times* and *Telegraph*. UKIP is lurking round the corner; they had a professional party political broadcast last night. The problem is that the Conservative MEPs who will, ironically, be elected on this tide of Euroscepticism are all Europhiles; they want to join the European People's Party, which is avowedly federalist. This will be the first real fight after next Thursday and Daniel will be at the centre of it.

Thursday 3 June
Papers full of concern for security in Tiananmen Square, Beijing, for where Annabel and Jon leave the day after tomorrow. Blair on the defensive on Europe.

Monday 7 June
Breakfast at Hyde Park Hotel (as it's now to be called) with Rodney Leach. He says 60-40 chance against BFS joining the Congress committee, now that Democracy Movement don't want to join in. His young men have got at him (they want to run their own empires – can't say I blame them). My letter of invitation being used as an excuse – I mentioned gearing up for the 'No' campaign in it. This is being taken as implying an ambition that the Congress wants to take everything over. Rodney says he will get back to me later in the week. We will plough on with the Congress and see what happens.

Tuesday 8 June
Breakfast with Portillo at the Goring Hotel; he is hotfoot back from a

pilgrimage to Spain, which was widely covered in the press. Reading between the lines, I guess he may be offered some senior post by Hague – perhaps chairman of the party. Says he saw Carol Thatcher and others of Jonathan Aitken's friends outside Malcolm Pearson's house (opposite his) last night. Transpires from *The Times* today that there had been a last lunch before Jonathan went to prison today. Whatever he has done wrong, he is a brave man.

My purpose in seeing Portillo was to sound him out about coming on our committee. He said he was not against it in principle but would need to wait to see whether a job came up for him in the next week or so. On to Queen's to meet Ann, both of us guests of John Crowther of the LTA, for Stella Artois. First day it hasn't rained for what seems like months; in fact it's been raining pretty persistently since the Stella Artois last year.

Thursday 10 June
Ring Malcolm Pearson, who has been deeply involved supporting Aitken as he goes to prison for eighteen months. Apparently JA has now been moved to a secure wing for his own safety. Malcolm says he will do anything to help the anti-federalist cause, e.g. joining the Congress committee. In the afternoon John Hoerner, chief executive of Arcadia (which Malcolm warns me is not doing very well), also says he will do what he can to help – said as much at yesterday's meeting with Business for Sterling, which decided not to join us on the basis that we were a rather disparate crowd. We do not suit the likes of Nick Herbert.

Polls close at 10 p.m. for Euro elections – very low turnout, even lower at Ed Wild's by-election in Leeds – sadly he comes third.

Jonathan Bush asks me if he can marry Annabel, having proposed to her two weeks ago on the Yangtze. We all go mad with excitement.

Friday 11 June
Bombshell in the form of a letter from Rodney Leach saying Business for Sterling will not be coming to the Congress for Democracy. I write back to this effect: 'God help the idea of co-operation between the various Eurosceptic groups if we can't even get together two or three times a year to talk things over.'

Thank goodness to be able to spend most of the day in the Royal Box at Wimbledon.

Chapter 16

William Hague: the EPP row 1999

Saturday 12 June 1999

Michael Howard rings to say cannot afford to join ERG. I say we will try to work out some 'associate' status for non-payers. I warn him about emerging crisis with the European People's Party. He says a deal could be done with EPP. I say they are opposed to the Conservative position, e.g. they are pro federal policing, army, currency, foreign policy. If Daniel forced out of the party because of his unwillingness to sit with EPP there will be one hell of a row.

Sunday 13 June

Meet MEPs John Corrie and Edward McMillan-Scott. The latter indicates they are bound to join EPP, which he says is basically his decision. That evening at our regional count the figures are roughly Conservative 9,500, Liberals 3,500, Labour 2,500, UKIP 1,500, Greens 1,500. Result repeated throughout the country.

Monday 14 June

Eurosceptic lunch at House of Lords. Rodney Leach, who had travelled up on the train with John Hoerner, very friendly. 'We must find a formula for not being seen to fall out.' Peter Shore says he will make a full-blooded speech at the Congress: he could replace Frank Field. I say we may as a result of Euro elections be deprived of a referendum on currency – in which case we will have to choose another battlefield for a clash of arms. Somehow the future of our relationship with Europe must be brought to a head – so we can win and reverse the trends.

That night drive down to Thames Ditton for a focus group with women aged 20–30. They are much the same as everyone else – very sceptical of Euro currency but don't want 'to leave Europe'.

Daniel Hannan confirms on the phone that he will stand firm on EPP. Malcolm rings Thatcher's office from the car phone to make sure she is 'on side' on EPP issue and will happily talk to Hague.

Tuesday 15 June

More talking on phone with Daniel, who sees Hague in the afternoon. DH says he will not sit with EPP whatever happens. Hague says there must be unity. He leaves the impression that he wants a compromise, e.g. MEPs do not join EPP but an alliance which involves EPP. Daniel would have to accept this. Daniel also wrote the leader in today's *Telegraph*, in effect supporting himself.

At dinner in members' dining room, whips' office gets a blast from me. 'If Daniel expelled from party, it will be "dust the sword and don the flak jacket" for me,' I say.

Wednesday 16 June

Big discussions at 1922 Committee about EPP. Chris Gill leads off. We mustn't join them. I wade in, 'They stand for the opposite to that for which we fought the Euro elections, e.g. they are in favour of federal police force, army, foreign policy and money.' Archie Hamilton agrees we should meet MEPs to discuss further with them. Later in the smoking room bump into new shadow Foreign Secretary, John Maples. He says he has persuaded the MEPs to put off the meeting to decide on the matter till next week. Later Daniel rings from Brussels to say Gaullists are coming round to not sitting with EPP. Many of them are waiting for the sign from us. Archie Hamilton gives his view that the reorganisation of the party is going to be 'bad news'. The weakness of 1922 Executive in this matter is one reason I left it. (When Archie leaves Parliament at next election, I might try to stand for 1922 chairmanship myself.)

Thursday 17 June

Bump into Eric Forth in members' lobby on my way out of chairing the sub-committee of the Treasury select committee. He says people like Tim Boswell (fairly senior former minister) must be a bit sickened by reshuffle announced on Wednesday. Theresa May came into Parliament this time and is now in the shadow Cabinet. Experience counts for nothing now. The emphasis is on newness – perhaps rightly so, given we are unlikely to be in government for another five or six years; anyone older than forty not much use.

Saturday 19 June

Major on the *Today* programme extolling the virtues of three members of the new shadow Government – Theresa May, Damian Green, Caroline Spelman. Major really is beginning to appear in his true colours.

Sunday 20 June

Daniel rings to say that John Maples has fixed to go to Bonn and Paris tomorrow to see the CDU and EPP people to try to form a loose confederation. The problem is – according to Charles Pasqua's office – Maples will not see Pasqua's people, the thirteen Pasqua-ites being the largest and most Eurosceptic Gaullist group in the French Parliament. Clearly Maples is being led by McMillan-Scott into trying to avoid the real Eurosceptics who would ally with twenty-six Forza Italians – possibly forming a Eurosceptic Gaullist–Conservative–Forza group. Apparently Daniel has told Maude and Heathcoat-Amory, who are supportive. I pass all this over to James Cran. He repeats my little speech to the 1922 Committee when he says ideally we don't want anything to do with the EPP, who are pro Euro army, Euro foreign policy, Euro police and Euro currency – which, as I said in my speech, is the 'opposite of what we stood for at the Euro elections'.

Monday 21 June

Supper in members' dining room. Eric Pickles and Geoffrey Johnson-Smith at the table; both pretty Europhile but both pretty subdued on the subject. Both want a deal with EPP. Geoffrey argues in effect for negotiating an alliance on the basis of 'what we agree on'. The problem is we don't agree on very much. Eric says can we even give it another name – probably the solution that will be chosen. Talk to Daniel later that night; he seems to agree with the Pickles proposal.

Tuesday 22 June

A day of bubbling up towards the special 1922 on whether we should join the EPP. Daniel rings to say things are not going well. I say I saw Maples briefly before Question Time and before I went on TV. He said that he was in touch with Pasqua (the leader of the thirteen Eurosceptic French Gaullist MEPs). Daniel says that was not the case according to Pasqua's own office. I ask Daniel what is his bottom line. His reply: (1) can't join EPP, (2) can't have a more Eurosceptic conservative grouping of which we are not members. In either case he would resign the whip. I say, having taken this position, his whole credibility now depends on his seeing it through. David Heathcoat-Amory comes up to me as I am on my way to Treasury select committee. He is shadow Chief Secretary. 'We must talk,' he says.

At the special 1922 Committee I'm the first to speak from the floor. About 100 members there, including Edward McMillan-Scott, who starts off by saying 'I'm here to listen' and then counteracts every Eurosceptic speech.

I say:

EPP not just difficult for us, they are the opposite; we cannot negotiate with them.

If we must lock up with anyone, let's do it with someone we agree with, e.g. Pasqua, Forza Italia, etc.

Above all, don't rush things.

I get a very favourable ovation. The whole meeting (with divisions in the chamber) goes on for 1½ hours.

As I go out Maples beckons me over. 'I am trying my best; we have talked to Pasqua.' I say, 'At office boy level,' whereas Hague has talked to Chirac, who only has six MEPs.

People come up to congratulate me in the voting lobby. Iain Duncan Smith says he will try to hold the fort at shadow Cabinet tomorrow, as does Michael Ancram, who says he will argue for talking to all the groups and not being rushed. I walk back with Owen Paterson. Laurence Robertson tells me he will stand for 1922 Executive, following Bercow's promotion. I say I will back him.

I tell a number of people Hague's future lies in the balance. If he is a man of steel and leads his MEPs, he could just win the next election; if he bows to them and is a man of straw, he is a goner.

Wednesday 23 June
Lunch at Cranborne's home. Pre-lunch drinks in the sunshine in the garden for which Cranborne is late. When he does arrive, he takes a drink and sits himself down next to Alastair Goodlad, who is wearing an Australian-type straw hat, no doubt in anticipation of taking up his duties as high commissioner in Australia.

When I return to the Commons a number of people come up to me about the EPP matter, including Iain Duncan Smith and David Heathcoat-Amory, each of whom feels that the answer is a deal with the real Eurosceptics. In the voting lobby, Hague says there will be no compromise over the manifesto on which we fought the Euro election. I say, 'That's all very well, but EPP have no desire at all to negotiate away their platform – what is more, they don't even seem willing to discuss an umbrella group.' Hague says the problem is that the other parties – even the Gaullists – have some 'funny' people amongst them. I say, 'That's just propaganda by our enemies.' Hague looks a bit concerned about this. He also mentions that he is talking to Pasqua; I say, 'That's just as well because his office were claiming that they had not had their calls returned for the last week.' Hague indicates that the EPP will modify their position – I say that isn't my information. Why should they change their ten-year-old stance on a federal Europe? According to Heathcoat-Amory there was no discussion of this subject at shadow Cabinet. He is off to see Hague about it all later in the evening.

Thursday 24 June
Daniel rings to say that the deal with EPP is going ahead – he saw Heathcoat-Amory today, who had a very unsatisfactory meeting with Hague yesterday. Daniel intends to refuse to sit with EPP almost come what may.

Friday 25 June
Daniel rings to ask what we will do if he is thrown out of the party for refusing to sit with the EPP, which is the likely outcome of the shadow Cabinet's impending decision next Wednesday to sit with them. I say, 'All hell will break loose.' 'What does that mean? Will it mean shadow Cabinet resignations and people resigning the whip?' 'Not for many,' I caution. 'Iain Duncan Smith and Heathcoat-Amory might leave and so might Gill, but for most people where we sit in the European Parliament is not the great test.'

Sunday 27 June
Daniel rings to say he thinks that some new 'fudged' umbrella group will be founded with the EPP and he will have to go along with it. John Whittingdale rings to say that Hague is being warned about rumours that Business for Sterling and the Democracy Movement have pulled out of the Congress for Democracy. I tell him Nick Herbert lies at the root of this. There are many individual members of both groups coming; he says it would be difficult for Hague to come if UKIP MEPs are there. I say I won't disinvite them now. ERG members will take it very seriously if Hague pulls out at this moment. Whittingdale says there is no intention to do that; I suspect there is.

Monday 28 June
Michael Holmes, chairman of UKIP, rings to say he is coming. I tell John Whittingdale, who puts this to Hague, whose response is he will not come if Holmes does. I have to pass this on to Holmes, who says he will make some publicity out of it, saying Hague is completely two faced. I go back to Hague's office and suggest that Hague opens and Holmes is not there. Hague leaves and Holmes arrives. Whittingdale says that might work.

Whittingdale also checks with me my views on the proposed EPP compromise: one umbrella but no common purpose. I say it will have to do – probably guided by Daniel Hannan's report that Hague said in Whittingdale's presence if it was a choice between fighting the left and fighting the right, he would fight the left, i.e. not against Daniel.

Wednesday 30 June

Times reports EPP row is all about Francis Maude's leadership bid. Judging by his appearance yesterday at the ERG breakfast, he is probably getting a bit too active for his own good.

While I am talking to Michael Howard in the lobby, John Maples comes up – deal is to have an umbrella called Alliance of EPP and Conservative Parties. I say this is very bad – gives all the wrong signals; however, opportunity missed when we did not form our own group. Howard says it was never on the cards: Silvio Berlusconi, leader of Forza, told him before Euro elections they would join EPP. I say they could have been invited anyway. The die is cast – as I say to Michael Ancram, 'We will acquiesce sullenly in the knowledge that an opportunity has been missed to give a lead in the European Parliament.' In fact it may be for the best as the party will never really settle for this arrangement – whereas they might have been sucked in securely to something more sensible.

In evening meet Rodney Leach, chairman of Business for Sterling, on Terrace, along with his chief executive. We agree to go our own ways in a friendly manner – nothing new, although Leach requests a meeting.

At 1922 Laurence Robertson gets onto the committee and bizarrely John Townend does not. Especially sad as I had persuaded Gerald Howarth to stand down so as not to split the vote.

Incidentally, Prescott gets away with Question Time. Silly lengthy questions to him from George Young on the front bench and heavily prepared answers. I am not called. Had I been I would have asked him, 'What is the government's policy on *corpus juris*?'* May have had the same effect as my withholding tax question. Prescott was very cocky on the terrace afterwards.

Wednesday 7 July

Roger Helmer MEP leaves a message with Emma, my secretary, that the EPP deal is off: he rings from Marbella where they are all sweating it out. I ring Daniel, who has not gone to Marbella; he confirms that it looks as though EPP will insist we join them, with no frills.

Talk to John Whittingdale during 10 p.m. vote. He says it's all a question of spin. There may be a short period during which we join EPP in order to fragment it a week later. William Hague has flown down to try to settle matters on our terms.

---

*   i.e. on the criminal law becoming part of the Treaty of Rome.

Annabel waits for me on the Terrace. We walk home on a very hot night (still in the 70s) meeting friendly MPs all the way home – notably John Bercow, recently promoted to his first frontbench job (Education).

Thursday 8 July
EPP issue rumbles on. The leaders of the EPP – Germans, French and Hague – have agreed to set up a new body but this needs to be ratified by the MEPs themselves. Many of them are saying they won't do it.

Friday 9 July
Day of second Congress for Democracy. Daniel sees Hague before this; is initially threatened with the removal of his party membership but apparently holds out. Hague arrives at the Congress; looks worried on this issue over coffee but speaks well. Luckily no real trouble with Michael Holmes. Congress passes resolution to meet again and to set up a committee and bank account etc.

Later that day, John Whittingdale suggests to Daniel that under the new rules of the party if you don't obey, may have to be thrown out.

Sunday 11 July
Talk to Christopher Gill on the phone. He has told James Cran that he will no longer be voting until the EPP thing is sorted out. Whittingdale has told him that this should be on Monday – we will see. I may have to put down a marker at the 1922 Committee.

Tuesday 13 July
Bump into Hague in the lobby. He thinks we have 'sorted out' EPP. 'We will affiliate and will keep our programme; how it all works out will depend on whether MEPs toe the line. We are setting up a liaison committee to try to ensure this. Francis Maude said something similar at a party.' We shall see.

Wednesday 14 July
Lively 1922 Committee. Eric Forth leads the charge with an ironic speech. 'It can't be true, it surely isn't, but rumour has it that we are still part of EPP. I assume that this is not true.' The subject now turns to equally sore matter of automatic reselection. Indeterminate vote. Walk home with Hamilton. He says we must vote in the postal ballot for the proposed changes to selection process. The alternative would be real 'open' selection. There is nothing we can do about it since the changes in the constitution. I say this is one reason I came off the Executive committee. The others were that Hague had let us

down on the reselection of MPs – promising that in this area he would keep his veto.

Some people are getting themselves reselected under the old 'acclamation' regime. I think I will let things run their course. The new system will allow an MP to choose timing of his reselection and if he loses to have a secret ballot of whole membership.

Thursday 15 July
The EPP row rolls on. Daniel tells me that the name has been changed but all else remains the same.

Chapter 17

William Hague: his last period as leader

Monday 19 July 1999

Ann and I depart – with five-hour delay – for Washington with the British American Parliamentary Group.

Wednesday 21 July

Amongst the meetings visit the Pentagon: down miles of corridors (almost literally) and up two floors; shown by a smart air force officer into a darkened ops room where we meet a two-star general. Prompted by me he expresses anxiety about the way in which the Europeans are developing European Security and Defence Identity with different goals from NATO. The other anxiety is that the rhetoric will be stronger than the troops on the ground. There is further concern about the increasing gap between Europe and US in communication systems. There is now a real danger of our not being able to talk to each other.

At a later meeting at the Old Executive Office (which has the appearance of a Habsburg castle) with Tony Blenheim, special assistant to the President on the National Security Council, I say that the threat to the Atlantic alliance is in part the fault of Washington pushing the Europeans together and in particular their present apparent desire that Britain should join the single currency. Rivalry between US and Europe inevitable. Indeed, jealousy of the US was part of the French motivation for setting up the EEC in the first place.

Thursday 22 July

More talks in Washington ending with a glittering evening at the Congressional Library. Meet Senator Smith at a lunch at the embassy and Senator Bond at the dinner, both potential Eurosceptics/NAFTAites.

Friday 23 July

Fly from Andrews Air Force base by USAF to Greenbriar Conference Centre with half a dozen senators trying to put up a show of Anglo-US solidarity but really off for a day's golf with their wives. Most senior of them is Robert Byrd (82½), former Democrat majority leader and currently ranking member of the Senate appropriations committee, whose chairman is the Republican Ted Stevens, our host for the occasion – tough little man, also in his eighties.

Saturday 24 July

Unfocused talks with three senators who were not playing golf. We are led by Michael Meacher, MoS at Environment, on edge about reshuffle going on at home. Blair would be silly to sack a tame lefty like Meacher who would be a nuisance on the back benches but who, I would have thought, has value on the front bench. Norman Lamont also with us. He and I speak as one on free trade, pro-NATO (thus against European independent defence initiative, which I argue undermines NATO and does not complement it as the government would have us believe). Norman sad to be in the Lords and not 'where the action is' in the Commons.

Sunday 25 July

Discover Meacher rather good at tennis, which we play at 8 in the morning before the intense heat arrives. America is having a heatwave – 100 degrees in most places.

Monday 26 July

Ann and I leave for six days in Key West.

Thursday 2 September

Speak to Freddie Forsyth on the phone about the Congress for Democracy sub-committee under his chairmanship to consider forthcoming legislation on referendum. Agree that this will be wide-ranging, considering the wider political context within which a referendum on single currency might take place. This committee will be formidable – loaded with QCs and high-powered lawyers.

Tuesday 7 September

News of Alan Clark's death. Apparently he died without the press knowing on Sunday and was buried today. We never really hit it off. I thought he was untrustworthy. During the Thatcher political collapse he wrote speeches for her and attended Tristan Garel-Jones's plotting sessions. He was pro-Soviet Union during the cold war (when he was a defence minister) because he was so anti-American, and yet he was a moderate Eurosceptic. He was pretty irritated with me when I refused to stand again for the 1922 Executive, where he and I were allies in the attempt to stop the break-up of the constituency party organisation.*

Fax Portillo to ask him what line with the press he wants to take about his future (the BBC has already been on to me). I say so far I have said that he would be an excellent colleague and Hague would be leader at the GE. We agree to stick to these two points. He has said that he would like to go ahead and try for Chelsea,[†] though this was less than ideal from his point of view. (Very difficult as before with Major for him to steer a line between being his own man and looking as though he was challenging Hague.) I say, 'All you can do is play the chips as they are dealt to you.' Rifkind likely to be his main rival for selection. Hopefully the European card will play in his favour; hopefully there really are no skeletons in his cupboard, despite what some informed people are saying.

Wednesday 8 September
Am told at about 6 p.m. that a story is breaking in *The Times* tomorrow that Portillo has admitted to a homosexual relationship at university. The BBC missed the story right through *Newsnight*, although they had a large feature on Portillo. Some producer will be in for the chop. Showed BBC up as total asses. ITV rounds off with a confirmed item as their lead story at 11 p.m. Michael says categorically, 'No further affairs since entered public life.' What is certain is that every tabloid in town will be after him to see whether his statement 'nothing after university' stands up.

Thursday 9 September
Portillo declares he is going to stand at Kensington & Chelsea.

Friday 10 September
Daily Telegraph argues Portillo has made a mistake; tabloids are not going to give up looking for former boyfriends. It's very unpredictable as to what Chelsea electors will think of all this. Interesting that Portillo is being defended publicly almost exclusively by the left: Nick Scott (former MP for Chelsea), Tim Yeo etc.

---

*   I have kept a letter from him written in December 1998. His scrawl at the bottom reads, 'Can we vote for each other? You get mine…!' Alan, by his own admission, had form for dodgy voting at '22 elections.
†   Kensington & Chelsea, the seat which Alan Clark had held.

Thursday 16–Sunday 19 September

By train with Ann to Scotland to stay with Malcolm Pearson in his nine-teenth-century officers' mess at Rannoch, built for the suppression of recalcitrant Scots and known as The Barracks. Deerstalking was the main item on the agenda on this occasion. What a primevally skilful sport it is. Some rules of the game:

Dress in camouflage (my blue denim hat would not do).

Always approach quarry from downwind, stand motionless if you can be seen, watch out for stray deer, especially hinds, who may give you away.

Crawl on your belly to rifle butt position.

Make sure you choose the right stag, i.e. heaviest with best horns (preferably about eight points). This is more difficult than it sounds in the week before rutting, when we are there, because herds are keeping together and they're very alert. During rutting, stags and hinds break ranks and are distracted!

I find out the difficulty of choosing the best target on Saturday when after five hours stalking, and lying prone waiting to fire, I shoot my first stag (great rejoicing and blooding etc.) and then go to shoot another after a short stalk later in the day – around 6 p.m. On the second occasion I pick the smallest stag (12 stone) from a choice of four targets, one of which was a 16-stone beast, according to Malcolm. This leaves a slight dampener on the day, which ends with a two-hour tramp back to the car – while Malcolm goes off in a mini-tank to collect the carcasses. Secretly I am pretty pleased that after not shooting a rifle since prep school (fifty years ago) I hit both targets perfectly.

Monday 20 September

Down to Leeds (Oulton Hall) for annual gathering of Conservative MPs, via Edinburgh, where I attended a meeting of AEP (Scottish branch). Policy is discussed. Archie Hamilton and I press for greater clarity and willingness to accept risks. Hague agrees with this in a good round-up speech, in which he says there are two ways of working back from opposition:

Lying prone and waiting for the government to trip up (the classic approach).

Striding out bravely with a policy which fires the imagination of the electorate.

Given Labour's popularity and the strength of the economy, we have to take the second path. The problem is that I'm not sure he is really willing to carry this out, e.g. on Europe the consensus is to engage in bold rhetoric but to be cautious in practical terms. Archie Hamilton and I press for radical tax cuts and injection of private capital into improving public services, pensions etc.

James Cran relates to me an interesting tale after dinner. Apparently as a whip he was shepherding stragglers (including Major) into the 'No' lobby in the last session. Major turned towards his friends and, pointing at Cran, says, 'He may be part of the new establishment but he helped to cause havoc in my time.' The tone was bitter and uncompromising. We are going to hear much more of this sort of thing in the days to come when Major's book is published.

Sunday 3 October
Eve of the Conservative Party conference in Blackpool; papers full of a poor speech made by Blair calling forces of conservatism 'evil'. According to Blair 'radical change' (whatever that means) is good – never mind what the change is to, e.g. House of Lords reform: abolishing the hereditary peerages good – providing for the alternative is unnecessary.

An interview with Hague by the will-o'-the-wisp former Conservative MP Gyles Brandreth in the *Sunday Telegraph* catches my eye. Hague says, 'I did think about teaming up with Michael Howard, we didn't finalise anything, we didn't shake hands on it.' In fact, so settled was the matter that all we discussed on the night we met was how to run the joint press conference the next day, when we would meet etc. There wasn't any need for histrionics, we were in business; even the glass of champagne was superfluous as it was getting late and we had a pretty momentous day ahead of us.

Several of Hague's pronouncements are beginning to cause concern, such as his commitment not to send his children to private schools and his hope that his shadow Cabinet would follow suit. What does that say for encouraging more private capital into schools, hospitals, roads, pensions etc. – the only way forward if taxes are to be contained and services are to be improved?

Wednesday 6 October
Conference is going rather well; distinctive policies on Europe and taxation beginning to emerge. Next step is to make them add up. Will we go for private capital into public services/pensions, thus creating the savings from which to get the tax cuts?

Monday 18 October
Drinks at Thatcher's office with some two dozen 'Thatcherites' – Tebbit, Parkinson, Tim Bell – and some new boys – Bercow, Bernard Jenkin, Redwood etc. Thatcher has grown old. Says she would 'come out' of Europe. If only she had taken a real stand when she had had the opportunity to do so.

Hague makes a little tactful speech – saying words to the effect that the party has reverted to Thatcherism. 'We're going to win, win, win,' she promises.

Friday 12 November
Chair Keep the Pound rally in Malvern. About 250 people show up in the new theatre. Amongst the speakers are Doug Nicholls – extols the virtues of the Congress as the best umbrella body for anti-EMU campaign. Michael Edwardes also a speaker – stays the night with us. Driving home with him he agrees that the Congress and Business for Sterling (which he accepts I was instrumental in founding) should link arms and perhaps set up some form of trust. I agree. The idea grows. There must be no one chairman. Edwardes agrees to report back to me after next Business for Sterling meeting.

Monday 15 November
Leader in *The Times* suggests that Blair may put off single currency referendum – possibly in return for giving up further powers on other matters in Europe. This will undermine Tory position on the one issue where we are currently strong. *Times* also prints a Congress for Democracy letter on referendum by our 'sub-committee on the constitution' as a lead letter.

All in all a good weekend for the Congress – but need to get our numbers up for the next meeting on 10 December.

Patrick Nicholls has written to me to say he is resigning his frontbench position because his policy of renegotiating the fisheries policy has been ditched.

Tomorrow plan to canvass with Portillo at Earl's Court Tube station at 7.30 a.m.!

Friday 26 November
Lunch at IEA. Trevor Kavanagh, political editor of *The Sun*, asserts that Blair will not have a referendum on single currency. I ask, 'Shouldn't we try to force him to battle? Otherwise the federal state of Europe will come about by default.' He responds tartly, 'You will just have to persuade Blair that he will win.'

Sunday 28 November
Joe Murphy, political editor of the *Sunday Telegraph* and formerly of the *Mail on Sunday* (great friend of Holborow) has a remarkable scoop. Stolen diaries of Paddy Ashdown have details of potential deal between him and Blair to form a coalition. Blair named Malcolm Bruce as unacceptably hostile to Labour and in need of going back to his family. This ties up with Bruce's outburst to

me in a train coming back from Brussels – when he claimed Ashdown and Blair and their wives sat down to dinner alone for Blair's birthday.

Tuesday 7 December
ERG breakfast. Nearest we have come to a consensus that we may have to get out of Europe. We agree to prepare a paper for a meeting with Hague in the new year to discuss amendments to the Treaty of Accession so that we guard certain areas for our Parliament.

Friday 10 December
Around 250 people meet under my chairmanship in Church House. Good speech by Senator Gordon Smith (Republican, Oregon), a presidential aspirant. Warns against decoupling Europe from NATO and losing independent currency. Gets standing ovation. Good speech also from Doug Nicholls. This coincides with his pamphlet (produced by Congress): *The Euro: Bad for Trade Unions*. Usual demands for us to turn ourselves into an umbrella group. Problem with this is that Business for Sterling and Democracy Movement not with us – will discuss this further with Rodney Leach when I meet him for lunch in the new year.

Tuesday 14 December
Hear Thatcher at a twenty-fifth anniversary celebration of CPS praise Keith Joseph as one of the most 'marvellous' men of this century. Joseph bowed out of the leadership race in preference to her.

Interesting comparison between her fulsome rhetoric, 'marvellous, marvellous', and Blair's 'actually, actually'. Each has a limited command of language; each vies with the other as the century's most powerful PM.

Thatcher says, 'We must all work hard to cut down the [Labour] majority as much as possible next time and eliminate it altogether as soon as we can.' This will be interpreted as 'We can't win the next election.'*

Wednesday 15 December
I speak at 1922 Committee at a meeting addressed by Francis Maude. I say we must have a tax-cutting policy which is both dramatic and credible, i.e. must add up with expenditure – only way will be through introduction of private capital. Anti-tax-cutters are Nicholas Soames, Douglas Hogg and Peter Tapsell.

---

* It was, in the *Sunday Times* of 19 December.

Thursday 16 December

Meet Malcolm Pearson for lunch at White's. Rodney Leach has told him that he is very suspicious of me wanting to take the whole thing over. We argue 'the thing' has moved on from the Euro because Blair won't hold a referendum he will lose anyway.

Malcolm also says he had been offered the leadership of UKIP but has turned it down on the basis that what really matters is converting the Tory Party through the ERG etc. I agree that what we are doing with ERG is probably more important than Congress at the moment.

Sunday 19 December

Just manage to catch Douglas Hurd on the radio saying that if Hague goes on with present policy direction other defections might appear in addition to his successor in Witney, Shaun Woodward.*

Tuesday 21 December

Stand talking to James Cran in the members' lobby after the last vote before the Christmas break. James is doing his 'we must back William at all costs' bit. I agree: 'We must prop him up at least until the next election.' 'Michael, you must do what you can to restrain the right going after the left as Laurence Robertson has done in Monday's *Telegraph* re Shaun Woodward.' 'OK, but what about our policy stance from now? Is this going to be a backing off on, for instance, tax to pander to all those like Douglas Hurd who are saying we have gone crazily right?' 'No, absolutely not,' says James. I say, 'We are back to the old proposition of Hague's at Leeds: we have two options, "do nothing" or "make ourselves conspicuous". If the latter, we must start building up and selling a coherent programme of policies, e.g. reduce tax and encourage private capital into public services. Needs clear thinking and good selling.' James seems to agree.

The New Millennium

Friday 31 December

Last few hours of this millennium. Dressed in white tie and ready to go to the Pears'. We are providing puddings and Sauternes.

Saturday 1 January 2000

Gloriously sunny start to the new millennium. Up in mid-morning after a white-tie-and-medals dinner party generously hosted by our close friends

---

* Shaun Woodward, Conservative MP for Witney, joined the Labour Party. He became Labour MP for St Helens South at the 2001 general election.

the Pearses. (Also there – Stoneses, Kelleys, Carters, Lewises). We told stories and jokes around the glistening mahogany dining room table until the early hours of the new millennium. Then we went outside and watched the dawn of a new era rise above Birmingham on the far horizon to the north.

Tuesday 11 January
Lunch with Rodney Leach in the Riverside room at the Savoy. We hit it off on this occasion. We develop the idea of a trust to come into operation as the statutory 'umbrella' group if a referendum takes place on the single currency. We agree that Business for Sterling would do the businessmen and Congress would do the politicians (we need to do more work on the left). RL agrees to put all this to his committee and come back to me.

Back in the Commons bump into Major. 'Why weren't you ruder about me in your book?' I ask. He replies, 'I thought about it but decided it's not in my character to do it.' 'Probably just as well.' Apparently he is about to join Britain in Europe.

6 p.m. Meeting with John Maples. Paradox remains that Eurosceptics are meant to be mainstream in the party but people like Christopher Gill have an enormous capacity for making us look extreme and marginalised.

Thursday 13 January
Lunch in the City with Henry Angest, Swiss chairman of Arbuthnot banking group. Helps the Congress generously financially. Complains that regulation was driving him out of business. 'Socialism on the sly,' I say.

Fascinating dinner at the Churchill Hotel with the Swedish Central Bank committee. I am stand-in for the chairman of the Treasury select committee, Giles Radice. Manage to make an off-the-cuff speech which seems at least to live up to their idea of a British funny after-dinner speech. Before dinner talk to two of Gordon Brown's closest advisers, Ed Balls[*] and Gus O'Donnell[†]. Balls gives me his view that the five economic conditions for entry to the single currency are real. He indicates obliquely that they will not be met. This is in answer to my question 'Given what you guys want to do, why didn't you hold the referendum two years ago?' Balls says, 'Because we only want to go in if it's in the national economic interest.' This may indicate that there is a rift between Brown and Blair on this issue.

---

[*] MP for Normanton from 2005, Secretary of State, Department for Children, Schools and Families from June 2007, shadow Chancellor from 2011. .

[†] Later Sir Gus O'Donnell, appointed Cabinet Secretary and Head of Home Civil Service in 2005.

On the other hand it may suggest that the government really are going cold on the whole idea. Maybe it's because Brown realises that he gets a place at the top tables whereas these days his German and French opposite numbers don't. This happened in Tokyo last week. The EU were there, Japan, UK, US, Canada and that was it. Germany and France came in for coffee after lunch!

Tuesday 1 February

Hague comes to the 92 Group dinner at St Stephen's Club. The questions are astonishingly tough. John Bercow (with one eye perhaps on a future Portillo leadership) congratulates Hague for having appointed Portillo to shadow Chancellor an hour before but criticises his sacking Redwood, to which there are loud 'Hear, hears' and thumping of tables. David Wilshire backs this up saying Hague's justification (there has been some) for sacking Redwood is 'inadequate'. I ask what our response on Europe will be if Blair shoots our fox by backing off from the single currency. Hague says we will attack future integrationist moves and Blair for being two faced; but this, as Bill Cash points out, begs the question of whether we will renegotiate the treaties. Altogether a less than bland evening with the press crowding round the front door of St Stephen's.

Monday 7 February

Winter Ball at the Grosvenor Hotel. Seated with the Steens. Hague makes a good speech, fluent and well paced but with little hard content; no real warmth in the audience's response despite the fact that they have had a few glasses of wine before he speaks. Anthony Steen's chairman – a sensible lady presiding over a majority of a few hundred against the Liberals – says, 'The trouble is he offers no coherent alternative.'

Wednesday 9 February

Rumour sweeps the back benches that we are going to change our policy on the EU veto (only keep it for core issues). The thought is that Francis Maude is behind this potential U-turn. I approach David Heathcoat-Amory, who has heard nothing but promises to keep in touch after afternoon meeting of shadow Cabinet. Comes up to me after 6 p.m. vote. 'Michael, you are right, there is talk of this from Maude.' I say, 'In that case there will be a riot.' Duncan Smith is the only honourable fellow in the shadow Cabinet; he's a bit too intense to make much impact. People come up to me all evening (Paterson, Cash, Gill, Townend etc.) – the message is apparently getting to Maude that the right is on the rampage.

Tuesday 22 February
ERG breakfast. Maude shows more sympathy for the idea of amending the Act of Accession to ring-fence tax, law, immigration, defence and foreign policy than I anticipated. We agree to have a joint meeting (me, Maude and Martin Howe QC).

Sunday 27 February
Portillo interviewed on *The Frost Programme* and indicates that our policy of 'no' to single currency could one day be up for grabs: 'I am not a "never" man.' (Though Hague had said earlier in the week, 'We will never leave the EU.') I tell the press, 'I cannot imagine any possible circumstances in which we would enter the single currency and I would expect Michael Portillo to think likewise.'

Monday 28 February
A number of ERG people hopping mad about Portillo's attitude – not just publicly but how he is treating us privately.

On the way home bump into James Cran, who says 'We must be ever-vigilant, otherwise things will slip away from our side of the argument.' I say there are only three people in the shadow government I trust: him, David Heathcoat-Amory and Iain Duncan Smith.

Friday 3 March
Suggest to Portillo's secretary – who says he can't come to the ERG breakfast because of meetings with Hague – that we make it 8.00 a.m. 'I hope he is not running away from us,' I say.

Tuesday 28 March
ERG breakfast. Portillo, our guest, is quite evasive on the single currency. Twice he says, 'I suggest you lot would want to come out of Europe.' Finally I chip in, 'What about you?' He says, 'I would rather be thought of that way than the reverse' and the rising tension eases. Eric Forth certainly thinks Portillo's heart is in the right place but he is dismissive to a fault of his erstwhile Eurosceptic allies. Having fallen too precipitously perhaps his course back has been too sudden. It has all left him (and us) disorientated.

Saturday 8 April
Annabel's wedding. Gloriously sunny day following three lovely days of preparation of marquee – fabulous flowers in the church.

Take Annabel a cup of lemon and ginger tea in bed. She had not slept and has a bad cough but is looking radiant. Dresser, make-up and hair people begin to arrive. Ann's planning has been meticulous. Antonia looking so pretty in her bridesmaid's dress (Chinese style) made by Charlotte Trevelyan.

2.30: start to walk with Annabel, both very emotional. Lots of villagers outside gate. Sun still shining. Warmest day of the new century, certainly warm enough for Annabel and me to walk arm in arm to the Norman church next door.

Peter Williman (helping in the house with Jill, his wife) rushes up just as we are about to emerge outside our gate. Where is the key to the garage? Jazz band have locked their equipment there. I ask Annabel whether I should go back to show them. 'Absolutely not. I can't believe you are thinking of leaving me at this point, Daddy!' Annabel remembers, 'Garage keys are in a bucket in the outhouse.' Problem solved by the bride. Two vicars in the distance by the church door (one to preach and the other to preside). We pause for photos. Masses of villagers on the grass outside the church. Annabel says to me, 'I want to get on and be married now.' They laugh. Someone goes ahead with a plastic bottle of water for her cough. She is looking beautiful. She is so in love and everyone is trying to control their emotions. This finally becomes impossible when she chokes on her marriage vows. Someone says later that even grown men were passing handkerchiefs to and from their wives. Annabel's hand stretches out for mine on several occasions in search for the big white handkerchief she had given me that morning; eventually she keeps it. When she and Jonathan sit down together after the vows she sends a message to me via the vicar, Ken Boyce, that she wants a Fisherman's Friend for her cough from my pocket. The vicar comes over to me with an open service sheet asking for the lozenge. I place this in the service sheet and he takes it over to Annabel in her front pew. The congregation presumably thinks this is an obscure part of the service! (Meanwhile the water bottle is being passed up and down the line from the best man via the groom to the bride.) When the prayer which they have written is read out, it is all too much for me. Tears are rolling from my eyes when I stand up. Afterwards Annabel appears oblivious to all the emotional upheaval she has generated. Everyone I talk to afterwards – in a sunlit garden outside the marquee – says it has been the most 'meaningful' service they have ever attended.

The next day even Ron Williams, my former government driver, is welling up when Annabel sobs just before she finally leaves with Jon, 'I'm so happy but I don't want to grow up. Mummy, please don't change my room round too quickly.' You've got to know Annabel to know that when she cries a lot she really is happy!

Monday 8 May

Sit with John Major after dinner in the smoking room. He is recovering from a back operation. He is also angry/worried about an investigation into his earnings from writings and lectures by standards committee, which he set up. Ironically Archie Hamilton joins the conversation. Archie fought Major tooth and nail in the last parliament against allowing standards committee to insist on publication of amounts earned. Major says to me that he now regrets agreeing to this. He indeed says his main interest these days is preserving the integrity of Parliament. Says he has been reading the chapter by me in *The Rape of the Constitution?*.* Very ironic. What/who is the real Major?

Tuesday 9 May

ERG breakfast. Martin Howe gives a summary of his work for Maude on retrieval of powers in a new Act of Accession. Iain Duncan Smith and David Heathcoat-Amory amongst those who say we should get our meeting with Maude to 'steel him up' before we have dinner with Hague later in the summer.

Thursday 11 May

ERG dinner with three Danish and three Swedish MPs/MEPs, including Pia Kjærsgaard, to discuss tactics and help we could give to the Danish 'No' campaign for their referendum on EMU in September. Agree that John Townend will open a bank account for donations.

Walk home with Daniel Hannan and stop for half pint of Guinness in the pub on Horseferry Road. Daniel's close friend Mark Reckless has done some research which shows that the good results by the Conservatives at the local elections were due to switching from Labour to Tory rather than differential abstentions – if so, good news and suggests Hague should plough on with populist 'right-wing' causes: Europe, asylum seekers, crime, rather than search for something called the 'middle ground' as advised by Peter Riddell in *The Times* and elsewhere.

Wednesday 24 May

Linger on over dinner in the members' dining room with John Major. I say to him at one point, 'Historians will puzzle over where you really stood on Maastricht.' He smiles and makes no audible response. I suppose that is how he became Prime Minister in the first place.

---

* Keith Sutherland (ed.), *The Rape of the Constitution?*, Imprint Academic, 2000. In my chapter I discuss the decline of Parliament.

Friday 2 June
The Times reports that Major has persuaded his constituency association to make all applicants who want to succeed him fill in a questionnaire, one of whose questions is, 'Would you have supported the Maastricht Bill?' Anyone who says 'No' will be turned down automatically.*

Saturday 3 June
The papers are full of the Franco-German plan to incorporate a European constitution into domestic law.

Tuesday 6–Wednesday 7 June
Visit Germany (Frankfurt and Berlin) with the Treasury select committee. Only real point of note is that the President of the European Central Bank, Wim Duisenberg, says that he is responsible to the public in general but to no one in particular – although he thinks it a good idea that from time to time he should make report to the Parliament. He and his board set the monetary constraint and the appropriate interest rate. Their only broad objective under the Treaty is 'to maintain low inflation'. They can interpret this how they like, and in secret. I ask whether they think a central fiscal authority will one day be necessary. Otmar Issing, the economist on the Board, accepts that it probably will in order to maintain 'stability between regions and to ensure that monetary policy and fiscal policy are compatible with each other'.

Tuesday 20 June
ERG breakfast in Dining Room C. Francis Maude – who is a member of ERG – present. Says his speech in Berlin, made on Friday 9 June, committed party to an amendment to Act of Accession (1972) so as to protect parliamentary sovereignty over certain matters including tax, law, defence and foreign affairs. Open question as to whether this will be retrospective, i.e. will require rejecting bits of the Treaty of Rome as currently in place.

Thursday 22 June
Chair meeting of sub-committee of Treasury select committee. Witnesses: Ken Clarke and Lord Barnett.† Good clean fun. Barnett talks of need to

---

* Jonathan Djanogly, a Eurosceptic, was selected.
† Formerly Rt Hon Joel Barnett MP, Chief Secretary to the Treasury, 1974–89, Chairman Public Accounts Committee, 1979–83. Created Lord Barnett in 1983.

reform Barnett formula, by which Scotland these days gets more than its fair share of public expenditure.

Afterwards the whole (main) committee repairs to the residence of the French ambassador, Daniel Bernard, for lunch with him and the German ambassador, Hans-Friedrich von Ploetz. Bernard pretty rude about the British. 'Up to you whether you join the EMU: we would like it but it is not essential. Meanwhile we will build our alliance with the Germans.' Ploetz says much the same thing but more politely. Indeed at one point he says that Bernard's comments 'bordered on the hostile'. Germany making excuses for French disdain of the Anglo-Saxons.

I intervene twice, once to dispute the Germans' view that the EU has been a benign influence on world trade. I say that at the Uruguay round of GATT it was the opposite. I also comment that centralists have a political objective, for which they accept there is an economic price; we by contrast have an economic objective for which most of us accept there is a serious political price, i.e. democracy. I also ask whether fiscal centralisation would follow monetary centralisation. Ploetz says 'No' and later modifies this. Bernard says 'Yes' – it is called harmonisation.

Altogether a rather significant lunch with a full cross-section of parliamentary opinion on the EMU and the German and French ambassadors getting together to try to nobble us – realpolitik in action.

I also say that for the French to call their proposals for their presidency and the Treaty of Nice 'modest' 'is like calling this delicious lunch a fast food picnic'. Menu: fish in puff pastry, pigeon, sorbets, white and red wines.

Monday 26 June

Meeting in Hague's room with the Leader. We discuss Europe. I say that the strong economy would probably prevail as the main determinant of the outcome of the next general election, but we have nevertheless to have a big idea – low taxes and better public services with private resources. Hague seems to agree. I say the problem is it would take eighteen months to put our ideas around and we don't have that time.

Tuesday 27 June

Hague comes to dinner with ERG. Usual cocktail of bonhomie and menace at ERG dos. Hague reasonably convincing that he is on our side but so was Major when he came to see us. Hague said that our MEPs would never join the EPP in its present form and they did. He promises to retrieve powers that have already been given away but doesn't seem to appreciate this means tearing up the *Acquis Communautaire* and with it the Treaty of Rome. Maude, who is also present (and signed the Treaty of Maastricht), mumbles something about 'renegotiating'. He hasn't a cat in hell's chance of this with the present state of the EU.

Monday 24 July
Freshly returned to Parliament after two-day fourteen-country inter-parliamentary tennis tournament which I organised on Friday and Saturday at Wimbledon with reception in Speaker's House on the Thursday. Busy day. Chair Treasury sub-committee, give dinner to key workers for the tennis tournament and chair Congress agenda committee. Decide to plough on as a focus for cross-party build-up against Euro rather than set members up as a campaigning group and so upset all the other groups.

Tuesday 25 July
Robin Oakley's goodbye party (he is leaving the BBC). Gordon Brown is there. I grilled him this morning in the Treasury select committee beginning with the question 'Do you still want to be Prime Minister?' I tell him he just about won on points, which pleases him. Malcolm Bruce, Lib Dem spokesman on the economy, tells me as a follow-up to his Blair/Ashdown birthday party story, that he was in Charles Kennedy's office the day he was elected leader. The telephone rang and it was Blair: Would he like to come round for a quiet dinner with Cherie? Kennedy said, 'Terribly sorry; I'm already fixed up.' That would never have happened under Ashdown.

On to St Stephen's Club for 92 dinner presided over by John Townend. Portillo the speaker; I ask a question/make a statement about using private resources to make public services work better. Portillo says, 'I know it's frustrating for people like Michael but we have got to be cautious.' Something has happened to him since he came back to Parliament.

Wednesday 26 July
Good work in the morning voting against Treasury select committee paper on Euro. In the afternoon Speaker gives her farewell speech in the Commons. People run out of thanks after about an hour. Most of the later speakers are candidates for her job. I think the plan is that it should be a Labour person, probably Michael Martin – a weak but decent Labour man.

Peter Lloyd* says to me, 'If you stood you'd probably win.' I wouldn't because I wouldn't gain many Labour votes, but it bodes well if I stand for

---

* MP for Fareham 1979–2001.

1922 Committee chairman next year to replace Archie Hamilton – I would be hopeless as Speaker as I can't remember anyone's name.

Thursday 27 July

End-of-term scenes in the whips' office, where the odd glass of wine is being tasted. Owen Paterson has been made a whip, which is good, as has Graham Brady, which is also good. Graham is the youngest Conservative MP and was on Howard's campaign team.

Dale Campbell-Savours, a Labour member, tells me in the members' lobby that he has a good head of steam over a potential Liberal Speaker. Despite the best efforts of Alan Haselhurst, Nick Winterton, John Butterfill and George Young, it will be the Labour Party which chooses the next Speaker. Big argument going on between the clever chaps who want a Liberal Speaker and the others who want one of their own, e.g. Michael Martin. I fear our boys won't get a look-in.

Wednesday 1 November

ERG breakfast. We debate whether or not we should go ahead with opinion research on whether Britain should pull out of EU. I take a vote, which is carried 9-3.

Tuesday 7 November

Lunch with Irwin Stelzer at Mark's Club. Sit opposite Lord Weinstock, GEC MD. Remarkably he knows exactly who I am, especially that I once went to Florida as a minister and came back 'knowing all there was to know about the electricity industry'.

Stelzer tells me that Gordon Brown has invited him to lead a seminar next week on competition. He will tell him (at Number 11) that this means lower taxes and benign labour laws.

Wednesday 8 November

Robin Day* memorial service at Inner Temple; share a taxi with Tapsells. At a subsequent party at St Stephen's Club given by 1922 Committee, Howard Flight says his letter has gone off to potential donors for a study of public opinion of Britain 'renegotiating' in Europe. At our age he says one does what's right. I agree. I like Howard, who has apparently made a lot of money but hasn't allowed it to go to his head.

---

* Sir Robin Day died 6 August 2000.

Tuesday 21 November
Go to a meeting in Francis Maude's room. Question under discussion is whether we will reverse Treaty of Nice if ratified. FM refuses to have word 'renegotiate', writing 'open up'. Edward Leigh and I ask what happens if they say 'Stuff it up your jumper' (my expression). Do we say we want to reopen discussion on treaties? No answer from Maude.

Thursday 23 November
Michael Portillo agrees via secretaries to host a dinner in January! At the start of the Euro debate get Robin Cook (Foreign Secretary) to say they want to sign Treaty of Nice in December and ratify in new year. The clouds are rolling in – unless Nice is a damp squib, which I doubt that the other countries will allow.

Friday 1 December
Iain Duncan Smith comes to the annual dinner in Malvern and stays the night. Nice man, heart in the right place, but no orator.

Monday 4 December
Meeting in my room in the House with Research International, Margaret Bottomley, Mark Reckless, to discuss qualitative study of effect of coming out of Europe.

Then on to chair agenda committee of Congress to discuss *Declaration of Democracy* with Mike Woodin (Green), Jacqui Johnson (Trade Unionists against Single Currency), Austin Mitchell, Henry Angest, Malcolm Pearson, David Stoddart, Peter Shore, Brian Prime (Federation of Small Businesses). Decide to include a reference to retrieval of powers.

Monday 11 December
Blair returns from Nice summit. During the statement I ask him why he agreed to a compensation tax; he said he didn't, claiming there was some opt-out; we haven't been allowed to see the small print yet. No one knows who is right.

Tuesday 12 December
ERG breakfast. Decide to proceed with the focus study. John Bercow asks (after he has left) whether Francis Maude carries too much 'baggage' from the past to be effective, especially on European matters.

Chapter 18

Candidate for 1922 Committee chairmanship

The 1922 Committee was originally formed from those backbench Conservative MPs who came into Parliament in 1922. Over the years it has come to embrace all Members of Parliament who take the Conservative whip. When Parliament is sitting, and while I was chairman, the committee met once a week, at 5.30 p.m. on Wednesdays, when views were shared on any matter (usually about party policy, organisation or pay and rations). It is the job of the committee chairman to represent these views to the leadership of the party.

Wednesday 13 December 2000
Interviewed on *Today* on Europe. Do it from Cropthorne where I have driven in haste to assist at yet another flood in Upton-upon-Severn. Back in London the broadcast has gone down well. *Times* has me as one of four candidates for the 1922 Committee chairman; glad this is in circulation. The others are Michael Mates, Gillian Shephard and John Butterfill – just the right line-up for me. Will try to get David Ruffley, Gerald Howarth and Michael Fabricant as assistants. Hague tells 1922 Committee that our private polls show us only single figures behind, unlike public polls where we are some 15 points below.

Sunday 17 December
Malcolm Pearson rings me in Cropthorne. Says that UKIP have been in touch with him. They want him to collect £2 million for them. He says he might do it if they call off candidates in seats like mine where there is a strong Eurosceptic. He tells them he will take soundings in the Conservative Party especially with 'people around Hague'. I say I wouldn't touch it: (a) they weren't able to deliver after similar conversations with Pearson; (b) they will harm the Conservative Party whatever deal is struck and the Tories are the only real hope for Euroscepticism. Malcolm is unconvinced.

Monday 18 December
Marion Roe asks me if I am going to stand for 92 Group chairman. I say that I am more interested in 1922 Committee. She does not react to this except to say she is not standing herself. Agree other candidates – Mates,

Butterfill, Shephard and also Eric Forth – all have their weaknesses. Walk home with Archie Hamilton, present chairman of 1922. Agree that it's too late for a massive new policy initiative, e.g. on reforming the welfare state/NHS and bringing taxes down.

Wednesday 20 December
Sitting on the back benches during the Hunting Bill with Redwood and Archie Hamilton. Redwood accepts that Malcolm Pearson may be able to help by buying off UKIP from some seats. I disagree with him. Talk to Gerald Howarth about his helping me with my operations re the chairmanship. He says he is close to Forth but not actually committed to him. He says he will take soundings on the right and come back to me after Christmas. He adds, 'We go back a long way.'

Butterfill says, 'Gillian hasn't a hope. They're all going for me.' The final line-up will be me, Mates, Butterfill, Forth, Shephard, Simon Burns and no doubt others.

Thursday 21 December
Bump into Archie Hamilton at Pratt's. 'If you want to be chairman of 1922 your campaign should have started months ago. Get a team. Gillian Shephard is miles out in front at the moment.'

Saturday 30 December
Snow overnight. Norman Blackwell, former adviser to Lords and chairman of the Centre for Policy Studies, writes in *Times* saying we should get out of Europe if we want Thatcherite policies at home. Chris Gill rings to ask if he can make a formal speech at the Congress saying we should come out. I tell him he can say what he likes from the floor but I have no mandate to put a 'come out' speech on the programme. The *Declaration of Democracy* would, however, provide a peg for him to say if we want to repatriate powers we have at least to threaten to come out. He accepts this – it is a sign of the way things are going. The pace seems to be hotting up.

Wednesday 10 January 2001
Eric Forth, who, I assumed, according to press reports, would stand for chairmanship of 1922 Committee, comes up to me in the 'No' lobby and offers to support me if I stand. I say I intend to do so. We agree we should try to keep the 'right' vote united. Eric says he will raise the matter at the next 92 dinner on 31 January. Gerald Howarth very pleased by this and says he will raise it at NTB next week. Also we will meet to discuss tactics more generally, e.g.

how to win a few votes from the centre and left and what to do about new Members in next parliament.

Eric indicates that his leadership loyalties have switched from Portillo to David Davis, 'if Hague does badly at the election'.

Sunday 14 January

Daniel Hannan rings to discuss plans for lobbying PPCs who might support me for the '22 election. We agree to meet, hopefully with Gerald Howarth, in two weeks' time. Need to discuss proposer and seconder and how to get at new Members – first to identify who is likely to get in. Get lists off Margaret Bottomley of those who have responded about the Congress for Democracy invitations. Discuss future of Hague, assuming we don't win the election. There would need to be very strong reasons/pressures for replacing him. What is needed is a commitment from him to be strong on Europe and strong on public spending/tax.

Tuesday 16 January

ERG breakfast – not well attended. Those who are there are very hostile to Malcolm Pearson's idea of giving money to UKIP not to fight certain seats – and quite rightly so.

At 6.45 go to a place in Savile Row for the first of the focus groups on whether we should come out of the EU. Young, lower-middle-class, Labour-inclined taxpayers. Four men say we should come out. Four women say uncertain but if pressed should stay in. When asked what would be their opinion if taxes went up for UK in EU and trade would still be possible outside EU (under WTO rules) seven of the eight said 'out'. Malcolm is elated.

John Redwood comes up to me with John Townend and says, 'Congratulations, I will back you for 92 chairman.' I say many thanks but I don't want to stand because I want to do the '22 chairmanship. Redwood says he will have to think again!

Wednesday 17 January

First meeting with Gerald Howarth in my room after '22 Committee to discuss how to set about the campaign. Plan to form a small team to canvass MPs. Daniel to deal with new Members. At 10 o'clock vote on banning hunting; Gerald says he had good vibes for me from two members of NTB.

Friday 19–Saturday 20 January

Birthday weekend with the family in London. Saturday night champagne at the Savoy and on to *Importance of Being Earnest* at the Savoy Theatre.

Sunday 21 January
Guards Chapel with family; lunch at Maunsel Street (Annabel and Jon, Lulu and Edward, Antonia), on to Tate Modern and Globe. Tennis at Queen's with Ann and Malcolm Pearson. Malcolm still flirting with UKIP. Nigel Farage* rings him to say for £2 million he will call off candidates in some Tory seats, including mine. I tell him again – don't touch them. Malcolm says he has put out feelers to Hague.

Monday 22 January
My birthday! ERG focus group in the evening. Same story as before. Latent desire (below the surface) to leave Europe. Feeling of frustration because none of political parties want to do so. First meeting in my room with David Ruffley and Gerald Howarth to discuss chairmanship of '22 Committee. Current parliamentary party about 50-50 Gillian Shephard and me. Long talk to Dan Hannan late at night on the phone: his main message – must get at the 'undecided' new boys.

Thursday 25 January
David Davis rings to offer his support. He feels '22 chairmanship will go to the centre right candidate. Michael Howard agrees to be my proposer. Eric Forth says I should show my face more in the tea room: 'Butterfill was on the rampage last night,' which I know.

Davis and I agree that next parliament will be about need for Conservatives to be very proactive in shaping up policies, for instance on health reform and the mix of private and public monies – also pressing need for involvement of backbenchers in policy groups like when I first came in in the 70s.

Monday 29 January
Dinner with Dan Hannan, David Ruffley, Gerald Howarth. Agree to approach Alan Duncan, John Bercow and David Maclean to see if they will join the 'team'. I will also see Howard Flight. DH is working up a programme with new intake. Will include Mark Reckless in this. Will also try to get endorsement of 92 Group.

Have a drink with Archie Hamilton; apparently he didn't do much campaigning last time.

Wednesday 31 January
Maude very difficult at '22. Says we should be cautious on Europe. Edward

---

*   MEP for South East England since 1999, leader of UKIP 2006–9 and since 2010.

Leigh asks, 'What do we stand for?' Later at 92 dinner Hague much more robust in pointing direction we are taking. Gerald Howarth elected chairman of 92 Group in place of Townend. I go on the 92 steering committee. Agree 92 will only have one candidate for '22 chairman. Steering group will choose him. No one seems to want Butterfill, the only other candidate. Way seems clear for me.

Thursday 1 February
Just before my adjournment debate Bercow claims he will vote for me but will not campaign because it might upset Butterfill.

Friday 2 February
Congress day. Pass a declaration calling for repatriation of powers. Andrew Robathan agrees to join my team for '22 campaign.

Thursday 8 February
92 steering group meeting under Gerald Howarth's chairmanship. Decide to back me for chairmanship of '22. Julian Lewis advises me to have five 92 parties in my room before the end of this parliament for the next new intake. Marion Roe joins my team. Peter Tapsell says, 'You would be on my shortlist but you are probably too factional.'

Monday 12 February
Meeting in my room at 6.15: Mark Reckless, David Ruffley, Gerald Howarth, Daniel Hannan. Gerald says he should keep his distance a bit as the new chairman of 92. I say, 'We've got to start somewhere; there are 60-odd votes up for grabs.' After 7 p.m. vote, on to Room W4 for meeting of 92 Steering Group: Howarth, Townend, Robertson, Lewis, Forth – the real hard right. Decide to hold a 92 party before the election and three or four smaller sessions in my room (a) to promote 92 and (b) to promote me – if I am supported at a meeting of 92 in two weeks' time.

Tuesday 27 February
Meet in my room re '22 campaign: Fabricant, Robathan, Ruffley, Michael Fallon, Anthony Steen. Each comes up to me afterwards and says how barmy the others are – marvellous!

Wednesday 28 February
Somewhat unsatisfactory meeting of 92 which selects me rather than Butterfill as their candidate. All other positions – except '22 chairman nominee – to

be elected democratically; this doesn't go down well with Butterfill. I think I would have got the vote easily if it had been secret ballot. As it was there was a show of hands with one candidate, me. Butterfill walks in late and complains after the vote. Nick Winterton comes in even later and also complains.

Friday 2 March

Up to Harrogate for the Central Council to try to corner some prospective candidates. Malcolm Pearson and UKIP story breaks. *Times* has me as one of his close friends – could be rather a setback. I say 'No comment' to papers who ring me. Madly search for support amongst candidates. Seem to be getting some. Butterfill also active but no sign of Shephard.

Saturday 3 March

Pearson story rumbles on with me in tow. *Guardian* talks of my alleged involvement with the deal – not true.

Wednesday 7 March

Budget day. Queue for my seat at the top of the gangway. Spend morning in the Library writing my speech. 12 noon: 92 meeting to elect people for jobs other than chairman of '22 Committee. Butterfill voted off the vice-chairman ticket by secret ballot. Useful article by Ben Brogan, Daweses' son-in-law, in *Telegraph*. Looks as if there is momentum behind my campaign. Speak in Budget on public spending.

Tuesday 13 March

Jonathan Holborow rings to say he has just had lunch with Michael Ancram, who says he thinks I will become '22 chairman but 'hopes I won't be too political'. Whether I get the job will depend on the mood of the party.

5 p.m. visit Hague with Oliver Letwin to talk him through the ERG report on the focus study of 'Should we come out?' Tell him (a) people don't see much difference between parties on Europe, (b) they think going further is inevitable especially if Blair wins the election. Hague says in that case we must hype it all up more. He seems to be totally unshakable, 'The credibility problems are inherited from the past.'

Archie Hamilton offers his flat for my '22 campaign meetings after election. James Cran will check out the whips' office.

Monday 9 April

One of the aspects of campaigning for '22 chairmanship I rather enjoy is that people talk to you about their problems. I regularly invite a few supporters to my room* to put them in the picture and to spread the word. This time: Julian Lewis, David Wilshire, Michael Fabricant, Marion Roe, and Patrick Nicholls – last two also standing for '22 officership. My campaign going quite well. The right is solidly behind me – no real surprise anywhere else, except that Sydney Chapman is not for me.

6 p.m. see Hague to assure him my campaign has nothing to do with leadership – on the whole support him 'except thought you were too young, but that's a fading liability'. He seems to think this quite funny. As I go in Tebbit is coming out. 'I've warmed him up for you,' he says. Tebbit still has a column in the *Mail on Sunday*. Later, while I am playing bridge, the deputy Chief Whip comes in to say the Chief Whip would like to see me. Turns out Christopher Gill won't renew his membership of the party and they are thinking of withdrawing the whip – will I talk to him? His old friend and mine, James Cran, has already had a go at him. I say I will walk home with Chris but hold out little chance of changing his mind – remembering the whipless days. It turns out I am right. I say to Chris his defection will be an embarrassment to the right; he says, 'I will just be thought of as an eccentric and no one will notice much unless the powers that be blow it up, in which case I will fight back!' He's probably right and the powers that be probably will be daft enough to fight him – and it will then be a bigger event than need be.

Tuesday 10 April

Archie Hamilton agrees with me: leave Gill alone. Bump into Portillo. When I ask if he will vote for me, he grins. I can't relate to him at all and will do without his vote.

Ring Angela Browning.† Despite Redwood's words of assurance, she is not for me – not at present, anyway. Claims not even to know she is allowed to vote. At the moment I am on the brink of winning but it all depends on what the new parliament looks like.

Back in Cropthorne on the phone to Malcolm Pearson – he tells story of being at a Conservative ball last week. Bercow brings Portillo up to his table. Portillo says 'You are too extreme for me' and moves on.

---

* A cabin on the roof of Parliament.
† MP for Tiverton 1992–7, Tiverton & Honiton 1997–2010; shadow leader of the Commons 2000–2001; later created Baroness Browning.

Wednesday 11 April
Julian Lewis rings with more names of parliamentary candidates who may win and will vote for me if they do. I am teetering on the brink of winning in the first round.

Sunday 29 April
James Cran rings me to see whether I can get John Townend to agree to pipe down about his 'right-wing' views – threatening seriously to damage Hague's leadership. I say that Gerald Howarth likely to have more influence with him. Talk to GH, who does ring Townend and gets his agreement not to say more.

Monday 30 April
Anti-capitalist riot day. Tommy, bald window cleaner, having his head shaved when I reach Pepe, my hairdresser, in Marsham Street. As I arrive Tommy says, 'These riots are becoming annual events, like the Boat Race.' More one-to-one meetings with potential supporters in the '22 vote. Andrew Hunter and Philip Hammond* both say they will vote for me. I am on the verge of getting it on the first round – if I keep my seat.

Thursday 3 May
Polls very bad – Labour to increase its majority – unbelievable. Townend row has left its mark. The public hate disunity in a party, especially in one like ours which has no idea where it is going.

General election

Saturday 12 May 2001
First Saturday of the national election campaign which has started rather well for us – except for the incidental fact that we are 20 points behind in the polls. Talk is of tax (our subject) and health (their subject). Peter Tapsell all over the headlines for saying 'never' to the Euro and for comparing propaganda from the government on the subject to events in Nazi Germany. When I ring him in the afternoon he is delighted with his new fame. 'Someone I hadn't heard of for years has just rung me from Australia to say he saw my picture on TV – wonderful. It's what we are in politics for – to have our views published

---

* MP for Runnymede & Weybridge since 1997; shadow Chief Secretary to Treasury 2005, 2007–10; shadow SoS Work & Pensions 2005–7; SoS Transport 2010–11; SoS Defence since 2011.

– even Hague pleaded with me not to make adoption speech – but I got a standing ovation. An old lady in her eighties had to be helped to her feet.'

Tuesday 15 May

Parliament dissolved. First serious day's canvassing for Wyre Forest, a seat we hope to win back from Labour. The polls are appalling; the received view is that we can't be doing quite as badly as they show. Maybe it's not fashionable to say you are voting Conservative; eventually one person whispers when I call, 'I'll be voting for you,' as if frightened that her neighbour might hear.

Tuesday 22 May

Polls are getting worse. Spoke to Daniel Hannan, who is involved with Hague's speeches. Must get some anger into him, especially against Liberals and their economic mismanagement. DH says, 'If you spoke to Ancram you might get somewhere on Liberal point, but you can't budge him on the rest.'

Wednesday 23 May

For the first time I am seriously concerned as to whether I will keep the seat. Hague is clever but his speeches are lacklustre, no passion. In my case I would like him to attack the Liberals for having most in common with the Arthur Scargill party. On the doorsteps it's all 'Don't know', which means 'Not you, mate'. We now have to reckon we are not going to win this election and stop playing it safe. We need to come on hard and angry about the economy.

Thursday 24 May

Poll position being confirmed on the doorsteps and by talking to other colleagues The bonhomie which we experienced over the weekend in shopping centres has been replaced/hardened into a 2–4 point swing against us from the last election. On this basis I may not hold this seat and will go down with 60–70 existing Conservative MPs. We may even lose our position as the official opposition. Talk to Archie Hamilton, former chairman of '22 Committee and currently with some sort of role at Central Office. 'Forget trying to win,' I say. 'Forget all the clever focus/issue stuff. Take the gloves off and attack Labour and Liberals on generalities. Scare the people as to what it would be like with no effective Conservative opposition.' Archie implies Hague will not do it. The colleagues whose seats are most at risk – e.g. Ruffley – are getting very angry about this.

Friday 25 May
Hague a little better today; seems to believe in what he is saying. Maybe my chats to Hannan and Hamilton are getting through.

Saturday 26 May
Polls still diabolical but people still friendly in the shops and in the streets. This is borne out by Conservatives like Bill Cash, Peter Luff, Geoffrey Clifton-Brown, John Redwood, Michael Howard. All say lots of 'Don't knows'; Hague's lack of inspiration the problem.

Friday 1 June
I am becoming convinced all those 'don't knows' are going to vote for that nice Mr Kennedy and that I am a goner. Ann and I begin to discuss life after politics. If I do lose the important thing is to do so gracefully. Transmit all this to John Whittingdale, Hague's PPS, who seems very sanguine and says we will be picking up seats.

Monday 4 June
Things look pretty grim but not yet quite enough to unseat me, despite the UKIP candidate whom I meet in Malvern High Street on Saturday and who claims (wrongly in my view) that he is taking as many away from the Lib Dems as from me. No signs of the critical 3–4 point swing away from me to Liberals.

Geoff Southall, Democratic Party, advises people to vote Tory on Europe. Pass this on to Nick Wood at CCO who asks me about the campaign. I say I don't think that polls will be catastrophic here but there hasn't been enough passion – reasons for voting Tory from the heart. Polls still slipping away from us. Best bet is still that we will hold on here. Torbay – an early result – will be a key one for us, although as it is held by a Liberal we will probably do 1 per cent better in swing terms.

Tuesday 5 June
There is a drift away from Labour – most of which will go to Liberals. I will lose about 2 per cent to UKIP. This gives the picture:

Conservative	Labour	Lib Dem	Others	Majority
43% (−2)	12%	41% (+4)	4%	1,000–2,000

Wednesday 6 June
Polls much the same – drift to Tories and Liberals. Above looks local worst result. National poll looks bad:

Conservative	Labour	Lib Dem	Others
30% (–1)	44% (0)	19% (+3)	6% (–2)

Thursday 7 June
Polling day. Weather rather better than hoped for. Liberal voters may come out. (They don't). Tour twenty-four polling station committee rooms. Atmosphere in the villages good. By the afternoon it is becoming apparent in places like Bredon and Eckington that our vote is coming out. Malvern not so hot – some places nothing is happening at all. By the time Ann and Chris Sanderson (chairman) reach the office at around 3 p.m., they (Ann in particular) reckon it is time to stir things up. She is on the phone roping in anyone she can find. (One person says she is in a depression; Ann asks her whether that can wait till tomorrow. If she is physically OK she should come in – she does).

Everyone is asked to bring a mobile telephone. The whole place is set up into a buzzing ops room the like of which has not been seen in Malvern before. Ann has much the same impact in Pershore when she gets there – though things are in much better shape there. It really has been Ann's campaign.

However, polling night is, in the words of the young, 'really scary'. Torbay falls early on to Liberals with a swing of 8 per cent and Guildford goes later with a swing of 4.5 per cent; these swings would have ended me. Phone Chris Sanderson, who is in the count; he tells me he is generally confident about my position. Nevertheless Ann and I arrive at it about 3.30 a.m., shaking a bit. Wonderful surprise to find Edward there; he has come out of the blue to give support in the event that disaster strikes. As it happens, get a pro-Tory swing of 2.5 per cent rather against the national trend, especially to Liberals.

Friday 8 June
Breakfast with those who want it from the count at Cropthorne. Two hours' sleep then begin to think about the '22 Committee. Do radio interview on *World at One* about this. Life begins to creep back to normal.

1922 chairmanship contest

Monday 11 June 2001
Lunch with Tapsell and Cash at the Athenaeum. Agree that the most likely Eurosceptic contenders for the party leadership are Duncan Smith and Davis.

Thursday 14 June
Curse of Spicer strikes again. Profile of me in *Telegraph* all but wiped out by 'Portillo to stand for leadership' story. Still Ben Brogan has written a very friendly piece saying I will win. Very good party for about forty last night at Archie Hamilton's flat. I am about six short of outright victory now.

Tuesday 19 June
Eventful day before opening of Parliament. See two doubtfuls for '22 election (John Bercow and Andrew Murrison*). John Taylor rings to say Butterfill thinks he is winning with twenty-five 'definites'. I think I have seventy-five.

At 92 dinner will try to say what I would do with leadership timing if I become '22 chairman. Portillistas want rapid election – view put by John Bercow, contra view of Davisites and Duncan Smithites – who want time. Ultimately the decision is mine. Redwood walks home to advise caution – 'You manipulate the party and they will become very angry.' I am not quite sure what game Redwood is playing. The irony would be that I appear too close to the anti-Portillistas and lose the 'Portillo' vote, e.g. Bercow, Fabricant, Duncan. Will invite them in tomorrow. Conversely Bernard Jenkin (for Duncan Smith) says in an aside that I have taken sides in the way I have presented the leadership programme. I hear him and say he has misunderstood me – I am merely presenting options.

Monday 25 June
My numbers of definite pledges have gone to eighty-two, including Peter Luff, which is over the margin of 50 per cent. Everyone seems to be talking in terms of my having got it. Still two days to go till the actual vote. In a way I will miss the combat but it's really what I want to do.

Tuesday 26 June
Telegraph carries a wonderful leader supporting me. Daniel Hannan

---

* MP for Westbury 2001–10, South West Wiltshire since 2010.

pressed hard for this, according to Paul Goodman. Eventually Charles Moore agreed – 'It would be nice for once to be on the winning side!' Definitely strengthens one or two wobblier brethren. Around midnight go to Victoria Street to get early edition of _Telegraph_. Find interview previous day with Ben Brogan has been compressed by night editor to say opposite of what I said. I told Ben on the subject of timing of elections that I do not want to be bounced into decision before I am chairman. 'Keeping options open' becomes 'Spicer presses for early election'. Get copy changed for third and fourth editions but headline stays. Worried that I may be thought to be backing Portillo position. Have to assure all other camps that I am not.

Wednesday 27 June

1922 Committee elects me as Chairman: me 79, Shephard 66, Butterfill 11. By one vote, no need for second ballot. John Butterfill says, 'Your campaign was done with military precision.' In acceptance speech outline procedure for election of leader, also say intend to raise status of backbenchers and policy groups.

8 p.m. Meet leadership candidates' managers together. Four want delayed election. Maude for Portillo goes along with this reluctantly – trick was to get them into room together on what was highly emotive subject.

9 p.m. Clear with Executive committee. 'Punish' _Times_ by not responding to their photographer but do it for _Telegraph_.

10 p.m. Publish decision to MPs on whip to go for Thursday 12 September.

10.30 p.m. Tell David Prior, Michael Ashcroft and John Taylor about this in my room in the House.

Leadership Contest

Thursday 28 June 2001

Evening Standard says I was overridden on the timing decisions by '22 Executive committee – not true.

Michael Portillo is first of the candidates to come to my room.

Monday 2 July

Meet David Davis and Ken Clarke in my room.

Tuesday 3 July

Meet Iain Duncan Smith and Bernard Jenkin. Jenkin threatens a legal challenge if I don't reballot if there is a tie in the first round.

Wednesday 4 July

First regular '22 meeting. Discuss leadership schedule and the fact that party policy groups will be set up.

Over dinner in members' dining room Andrew Mackay calls over David Trimble, leader of Ulster Unionists. Trimble dines with us. Afterwards Andrew explains to me that negotiations are going well for UU to take Tory whip.

Thursday 5 July

Andrew Tyrie for Clarke's team aggressively suggests he doesn't like the agreed timetable. At present looks as if his man may not get through to final two. With all this nastiness around, decide to call in managers of all candidates for Monday.

Friday 6 July

150 to celebration party in Hanley Swan. Ann looked radiant in a yellow dress. She has become such a star. Who would have thought it twenty-two years ago? Given a bunch of flowers by the committee. I present Anthony Ogilvie with an eighteenth-century picture of Magna Carta. Go home to see Malcolm and Caroline Pearson, who stay weekend. Malcolm will pursue 'come out of Europe' tack and is hoping to persuade Thatcher to make a speech in the autumn to that effect.

Monday 9 July

Meet campaign managers in my office: Bernard Jenkin (Duncan Smith), Andrew Tyrie (Clarke), Patrick McLoughlin (David Davis), Stephen O'Brien (Ancram), Francis Maude (Portillo). I say one reason for calling the meeting is that campaigns are becoming litigious. Big issue is campaign expenses limit. I am minded to keep them at £100,000 but will discuss it with two 'successful' candidates. Hustings meetings will not be in cost limits as long as all candidates invited. Public meetings OK if 'by invitation'.

Tuesday 10 July

First ballot opens at 1 p.m. in Committee Room 14. Count managed by the formidable Marion Roe. Three votes slip through cracks in the table; Marion crawls underneath to find them – thank God. A tie between Ancram and Davis (21 each; Portillo 49, Duncan Smith 39, Clarke 36) makes me decide to call a reballot. At a function given by the *House Magazine* afterwards at the Churchill War Rooms, Michael Mates says he has a gut feeling that Ancram will pull out – not what he says later in the news. Media starting to treat the whole process as a bit of fun – they have nothing much else to report about. Jeremy Vine says on *Newsnight* what a strange system where there is a reballot because no one came last. 'Did Michael S. make the right decision?' he asks Maude, who hums and hahs a bit. I don't think I had a choice. If I had wiped out Davis and Ancram at a stroke (a quarter of party) there would have been a hell of a row.

Thursday 12 July

Another ballot day. Early into breakfast in the tea room. Julian Brazier says, 'If you are successful no one will thank you; if you fail everyone will blame you.'

Second ballot goes off without any crisis. Portillo 50, IDS 42, Clarke 39, Davis 18, Ancram 17. Ancram goes out.

Friday 13 July

Congress steering committee decides to take on Business for Sterling by putting ourselves up as the statutory umbrella group – at least to force BfS to talk to us seriously. A number of organisations previously hostile to this move – e.g. Campaign for an Independent Britain and Democracy Movement – give in because of BfS arrogance.

A note reaches me saying David Davis has withdrawn. Now we are left with Clarke, Portillo and IDS.

Saturday 14 July

Michael Portillo rings me in Cropthorne 'as a voter'. I tell him I can't blink an eyelid. He says, 'I'm just ringing you out of courtesy.' Ho ho. 'Have you got any questions for me?' I say, 'No.'

Sunday 15 July

Ancram says his people are dividing between Duncan Smith and Clarke – very few for Portillo. (Same seems to be true of Davis's lot.) Portillo is in real trouble. Will find it hard to get the fifty-five he needs. Talk to Nick Lyell QC just before catching 9.15 p.m. train to London. Discuss legal position of (a) a tie, (b) voting arrangements in the country. Pray that there is no tie. Before leaving for London watch Amanda Platell's* devastating attack on Portillo/ Maude for their disloyalty to Hague. She looks pretty plausible and therefore damaging to Portillo.

---

* Journalist; press secretary to William Hague 1999–2001.

Ring Archie Hamilton in the afternoon; he says if there is a tie for second place you must put all three to the Party membership – the parliamentary party would have in effect failed to make its mind up.

Monday 16 July

Meet remaining candidates in my room: Clarke, Maude (for Portillo), Jenkin (for Duncan Smith). Main question: if there is a tie do we reballot or give three names to the country? Clarke and Maude: give three names. Jenkin: reballot.

Jenkin follows this up with a written opinion from Sir Sydney Kentridge QC, then rings me late at night to warn me (letter to follow) against abusing my position by not taking sufficient advice. Kentridge in effect says you can't put it to the country without changing the rules because the balloting mechanics does not exist. I will get alternative written/formal opinion and seek views of the board.

Tuesday 17 July

9.30 meeting in CCO very ably chaired by David Prior. Meet Tom Strathclyde, Michael Ashcroft, Stephen Gilbert, Chris Poole. Phone conference with the rest of the board. Party reps all press hard for three candidates to be put to the country. However, other board members say rules are paramount. Agree with board members at CCO to take formal legal advice. I decide, with the support of legal advice, that we will reballot in the event of a tie.

Result: Clarke 59, Duncan Smith 54, Portillo 53. I am let off the hook by one vote. If I had had to implement my decision it would have split the party from top to bottom – which may well yet happen.

Wednesday 18 July

It is beginning to dawn on me how pivotal my role may be and how brittle is now the state of the party. In the tea room at lunchtime, Forth is explicit as to how quickly he will bring forward a challenge to the leadership if it's Clarke (he needs to collect twenty-nine votes whose names only I will know). At a reception in the evening in College Garden, Ruffley (who voted for me and whose constant encouragement for me to stand was a first indication that my support stretched a little further than the Eurosceptic right), Clarke's former political adviser, makes a similar threat in the event of IDS winning. The Portillistas are very angry.

Another straw in the wind – at the Executive of the '22 which I chair at 5.45, there is some feeling (on the left) against my suggestion that the policy groups, for which I plan to press, should report back to the full '22

Committee. 'The leader', it is felt by this group, 'must make his own policy.' But what happens if this is out of tune with the parliamentary party?

Whips try to throw Andrew Robathan off the International Development select committee because he has conspired against the choice of chairman, Edward Leigh. I argue against Robathan's dismissal, because (a) he has been on the committee (and very assiduous) since its inception, and (b) it would blunt our current attack on the government for manipulating the select committees – the cause of a government defeat on Monday.

My question (No. 3) to the PM results in long cheers from our side who seem content, no doubt pro tem, about the way I have conducted the leadership ballot. We all know (or I do) just how big a part luck played in the last round. There would have been a riot from one side or other whatever I had done on Tuesday had there been a tie – which is why I decided to keep as close as possible to the rules. At least I would have had the shield of the law even if this did not protect me against the blast of political outrage by the party at large, who would have wanted three candidates.

Thursday 19 July

Civil war already breaking out on the *Today* programme: Teddy Taylor/Julian Lewis v. Heseltine. Will I as a Eurosceptic really be able to hold the fort? Depends who wins. Pick up Alan Simpson by Vauxhall Bridge and drive him to Wimbledon for annual match against AELTC.* Simpson – on the left of his party – confirms the vehemence of his colleagues' resentment of Blair and of the need in his view for an alliance between left and right to 'get Blair'. There is a need to 'get tactics right'. Example of how not to do it was last night when there were three amendments to European Communities Bill on a referendum, one from Labour, one from Bill Cash and one from Francis Maude – all very similar. We voted for Maude, not the Labour one, which might have prevailed.

Got back from Wimbledon at 3 p.m. to meet the two remaining candidates. Clarke there but not Duncan Smith or Bernard Jenkin. Sort out timetable for ballot. Then on to the 'thank you' party at Maunsel Street, which I give mainly for people who helped/supported me for my election to '22 chairmanship.

Monday 23 July

Dinner with the splendid Henry Angest. Apparently his loan to the Conservatives at the last election has now been returned to him.

---

* All England Lawn Tennis Club.

Day spent waiting for Edward and Lulu's baby. They have both been in Salisbury Hospital all day – and an unusually hot day it's been. Looks as though 'its' birthday will be 24 July – let's hope all will be well.

Tuesday 24 July
Alexia born at 12.30 a.m. (Ann rings me from Cropthorne at 1 a.m.) Wonderful news.

Board meeting starts at 10 a.m. and ends at 5 p.m. at St Stephen's Club. Hague comes for a 'goodbye' buffet lunch. Ashcroft, the retiring treasurer, talks about the need for the centre to take over declining associations. I argue vehemently against this – suggest that in view of the perilous state of the party's finances, we should plan to cut back at the centre. Jean Searle (this year's chairman of the party conference) seems to have inherited Robin Hodgson's[*] hatred of MPs. She works it in at every contribution. Whole discussion conducted in the absence of a leader, chairman, or money.

Antonia and I toast the baby at the Garrick.

Wednesday 25 July
It's Andrew Tyrie's day to read me the Riot Act on behalf of Ken Clarke. Arrives unannounced in my room to complain about IDS using a helicopter which 'has not been properly declared'. 'Either we go public about this or the expenditure limits are put up to accommodate this extravagance.' David Maclean says, 'We are declaring it and we don't want more money so there is no need for a meeting.' Tyrie rings David Prior (acting CEO at CCO) to say he demands a meeting but is too busy to ring me back. I go ballistic with his secretary and leave for a drink in the Garrick with Michael Ashcroft, who wants to touch base before flying in his private plane from Luton to New York that evening.

Thursday 26 July
David Prior indicates I am wrong to be going on holiday next week – but I haven't stopped since January. He insists I give him my hotel telephone number. In the meantime I send out three-page letter to candidate managers with dates on which ballot papers to go out – very controversial. Clarkeites (Andrew Tyrie) want it later so Clarke can have a good holiday. They don't thank me for leaving it at 20 August. The main advantage of my holiday during the leadership election is that once I have taken decisions, the party

---

[*] Chairman, National Union 1996–8; chairman, National Convention 1998–2000.

officials must stick to them. When I'm on holiday they won't be able to gnaw at the bone any more. They'll just have to get on with it.

Friday 10 August
Return from ten days in Canaries sleeping and reading. All seems quiet on the leadership contest front. Main bone of contention is the use to which candidates can put party membership lists. David Prior has said that for reasons of impartiality and data protection, they may not have the lists. IDS people say this is unfair as Clarke is better known and does not need to mail out. Luckily this is more one for Central Office than for me.

Monday 10 September
Was readopted in the constituency last Wednesday.
Return from a week in Formentera. Clarke camp clearly trying to undermine credibility of leadership race. I suspect they may end up challenging the whole process if they lose. It could all turn even nastier than it has already been. It's a question of what is practicable.

Tuesday 11 September
Driving up the M40, Jessica, my secretary, rings to tell me about the terrorist attacks in America. Literally unbelievable. David Prior comes on the phone to say we must discuss plans for the leadership count the next day. We decide immediately that the main event must be cancelled. Big issue is whether we continue the count at a low-key level. I am inclined to this. David says he will talk to Clarke, Duncan Smith and Hague before I get to London. Drive straight to Central Office. Mood is hardening to postpone everything. I am moving towards this view as the ghastliness of the whole business unfolds. It's Pearl Harbor without a known enemy. All the talk on the US media is of war, but against whom? My job is to take the final decision abut the leadership election timing. I walk into CCO in white trousers and open-neck shirt. Talk to Hague, then to Clarke and Duncan Smith; we reach an agreement that Hague will make low-key announcement of a 24-hour delay in the count. I put out a message on the pager to colleagues.
Ann is feeling unwell with the strain when I get home. Go alone to Robin Oakley's book launch. He says the crisis will give the Conservatives a chance to recover out of the limelight. Michael White says this is a story which has yet fully to explode. We have yet to hear the casualty figures. Both he and John Pienaar (BBC) agree we made the appropriate decision.
Cecil Parkinson apologises for his letter supporting John Butterfill. Says he did not realise I was standing. I say he should have rung me to tell me;

he accepts this. In return tells me Thatcher did not want to keep me in her government in 1987. He 'persuaded her'. Funny she promoted me a few years later. She was simply careless and uncaring about her middle-level colleagues/appointments.

Try to get Tom Dunne on the phone. All lines to New York are busy.

Hague was very good and firm on TV. I said afterwards, 'Makes me wonder why you are going.' He grinned and said, 'Don't start that, Michael. I am glad we decided to do what we did.' He grows in stature by the day; even his voice sounds deeper and more mature.

Chapter 19

Iain Duncan Smith

Thursday 13 September 2001

CCO at 9.30 when we decide will have to take a view before 2 p.m. about whether to amend new programme for announcing leadership result. If it is likely to rain, will need to bring the press in and put the announcement meeting upstairs. Take 45-minute taxi trip to somewhere in north London where Electoral Reform Society counting the votes. Meet a rather glum Oliver Heald (head scrutineer for Clarke) and rather more cheerful John Hayes (ditto for Duncan Smith). Two points become clear: (1) the vote will be over by about 2.30 and therefore there is a strong likelihood that the result will leak; (2) IDS in the lead by a substantial margin (percentage result in the end 61-39). Return to CCO and take decision to bring the announcement inside. Go to my office in the House where results phoned through at 3.30; at 5.00 I make the announcement first to MPs on the 3rd floor of Central Office and then to the press in the conference room. Before this have to tell Clarke, who is sitting in chairman's room, that he has lost. Takes it pretty well – probably knew it already. IDS says he knows 'nothing definite' when I tell him. After announcement, join IDS and his triumphant team for a glass of champagne in the leader's room. He tells me most of his appointments – seems especially pleased about Michael Howard at shadow Treasury. Rather surreally, Annabel comes through on my mobile to ask result – says 'Wow!' when hears 'IDS'; pass this on to him and he laughs.

Afterwards off to a rather noisy film called *Moulin Rouge* with Ann.

Friday 14 September

In *Telegraph* Frank Johnson describes my statement as lacking usual 'show off' character of these occasions. In *Times* Matthew Parris calls it 'gentlemanly'.

Left-wing press, including Max Hastings in the *Standard*, very hostile to IDS. Event sadly largely ignored because of drama in the US. 'Curse of Spicer': whenever I am involved with an announcement an event takes place which wipes it off the press. Daniel Hannan reminds me of one occasion when an article had been written (about an ERG meeting at the Café Royal when Business for Sterling was formed) in the *Telegraph* and the newspaper office was blown up by IRA before it could come out on the streets!

In the Commons, IDS makes a low-key speech notable mainly for the number of times he says he agrees with the Prime Minister about anti-terrorism. Not sure whether IDS or PM more damaged by this. House full: absent Forth and Cran in US (Forth to be made shadow leader of House). Don't know what will happen to Cran. Portillo, Clarke, Norman, Lansley, Maude – all the careerists from the last administration – have been left out of this one for one reason or another. At around 4 p.m. run into Michael Howard in the members' lobby; he has just been appointed shadow Chancellor, thus displacing Redwood, who wanted the job and now refuses to take Trade and Industry. This is all very odd as IDS was Redwood's manager; perhaps they fell out over the Redwood–Clarke deal last time round. Anyway, Howard doesn't seem particularly worried about what job he takes (he's not standing next time) but Redwood does – so trouble ahead looks likely.

Have a cup of tea with Howard behind the screens in the tea room. He asks, 'What's your advice?' I say, 'Your job is (a) to exploit the government's troubles over the economy, (b) to create a distinctive low-tax strategy of your own linked to reform of health etc. I am going to have to try to push things along with the backing of the '22.' Later Richard Ottaway comes up to say he thinks the leadership rules will need changing. I tell him the voluntary side will want more choice – I will resist it. More than two candidates to the wider membership means AV, which we must try to resist so far as general elections are concerned. It would be a bad precedent if we introduce it for the leadership battles. Also constitutional leader needs support of parliamentary party (which three candidates might leave in some doubt).

Send letter to all candidates reminding them to let me have their accounts to be published. I wonder if they will comply.

Three principles which I will develop in speeches on how we can win the next election:

1. Back international attack on terrorism including those who operate here.
2. Exploit Labour's growing vulnerability – the economy.
3. Decide our view on low-tax/insurance-based strategy for maximum impact in public services.

Monday 17–Saturday 22 September
By night sleeper to Rannoch: two days' deerstalking with Malcolm Pearson. Down to Edinburgh for AEP meeting, then on to the Lowlands for two nights with Mervyn Pike, who is getting very old and doddery.

Time to reflect on the political scene, which has been somewhat clouded by the ghastly events in America. IDS's shadow government includes – probably understandably – all the red rags to the leftie bull – Bill Cash, Lawrence Robertson, Eric Forth. Sense trouble could lie ahead if the left can find a champion and if they combine with the defrocked Portillistas. They will be inhibited by my chairmanship of the '22 from giving me the necessary twenty-nine names to start another contest. So the first part of the game plan must be to try to get rid of me in a year's time.

Sunday 7 October

Arrive in a windswept Blackpool, pouring with rain, to receive the news that the US has attacked Afghanistan. IDS offers support of opposition. Parliament to sit tomorrow but most MPs are asked by IDS at agents' dinner to stay on in Blackpool 'in the interest of democracy'. Much discussion in the corridors of the rights/wrongs of party centralisation – central membership etc. John Taylor, chairman of the Convention, assures me that we must put a stop to all the moves towards centralisation. We agree on the importance of not destroying the voluntary side of the party.

Monday 8 October

Meet David Maclean, new Chief Whip, after breakfast. Agree that whips should give more meat at their '22 reports, that policy groups will be set up, that I will discuss EPP with Iain Duncan Smith. Maclean wants to suppress everything European. I sit on platform during IDS's short speech to the conference before he flies to London for the emergency debate on Afghanistan.

Tuesday 9 October

Daniel Hannan on the warpath with one or two other MEPs at reception given by US ambassador and Canadian high commissioner. DH wants to leave the federalist EPP in the European Parliament, saying IDS agreed to this during the leadership election. 'Now it is a test of his sincerity.' However, IDS faced by the problem that (a) the majority of Conservative MEPs don't want to sever the ties, (b) he doesn't want to stir up the left in the parliamentary party. I'm left trying to decide whether to call a '22 meeting on this with a left of centre Executive and left of centre backbench party. (IDS has stripped out the right for his shadow administration.)

Wednesday 10 October

IDS makes an adequate speech. Because of the international situation he has survived the conference without too much blood being spilt. However, I get a possible flavour of things to come when I bump into Andrew Tyrie, who is clearly out for a row with the leadership.

Thursday 11 October
IDS speech panned by Matthew Parris, who accuses him of not being able to read and putting the wrong emphasis on words.

Monday 15 October
Drinks with Thatcher. She is looking drawn, white and rather old. Still takes keen interest in contemporary politics e.g. Railtrack renationalisation. 'Railtrack is like roads and should perhaps be kept in the public sector.' I pointed out that we could have taken the same view about airports.

Tuesday 16 October
Meet IDS. One of his characteristics is that he talks without interruption. Nevertheless agreeable mood music between us. I agree to keep lid on EPP issue for a week or so while Michael Ancram explores a solution. IDS says Ancram 'has a nose for the centre of gravity in the party'. Agree also with setting up of policy groups in the parliamentary party. He says MPs will be a part of policymaking; I say they cannot be an appendage to it – must be at the centre.

Wednesday 17 October
Present Hague with a map of America at '22 Committee. Executive committee discuss policy groups/centralisation. Agree to have a longer meeting next week.

Walk home with James Cran, who has just resigned as shadow deputy leader of the House, which he accepted last week: 'non-job, not for me'. Says the parliamentary party in a febrile mood. This is confirmed by dining with Douglas Hogg, who says he and others will always be 'irrevocably opposed to IDS'. Marion Roe, deputy '22 chairman, agrees this is a problem. At PM's Questions IDS seems to have choreographed himself to act as the PM's alter ego. I know they met beforehand so they probably did plan the Q&A – all a bit disorientating for us backbenchers – opposition leader involved in planted questions.

My weekly do with Association of Conservative Peers (ACP). Encourage them to join the policy groups we are setting up in the Commons. Mark Schreiber (Lord Marlesford) asks whether the Conservative Research Department will be involved. I say, 'My Lord, the CRD is not exactly what it was when you and I were in it.' Much clapping at the end.

Friday 19 October
Visit Ma (87), getting old and forgetful, Milford-on-Sea. Jessica, my secretary, rings to say there is another security scare in the House. Nothing on the news so presumably all OK.

Monday 22 October
Start meetings over tea/drinks with new MPs, including Andrew Selous. Agree that MPs need to be involved – and new ones need to be guided. I tell Selous he will be amazed how quickly he and his contemporaries pick it all up. In the meantime, I will be happy to act as 'agony uncle'.

Hand over ERG at a dinner to David Heathcoat-Amory. Present: Pearson, Heathcoat-Amory, Margaret Bottomley, Lamont, Forth, Swayne, Bercow, Maude.

Wednesday 24 October
Executive committee meeting. Subjects: central membership, leadership rules, policy groups. One member, who has had a good lunch and wants to make trouble, says wants to discuss why we lost the election under Hague.

Monday 29 October
Supper with Michael Fabricant at Chimes in Pimlico. Fabricant is a mixture of eccentric and increasingly savvy politician. He says IDS already in trouble with party because of his poor performances. Forth saying that if he's no good will have to go. IDS will look stronger as economy weakens and government falters.

Michael Fabricant has consistently thought I should be leader! Can't think of anything worse these days.

Tuesday 30 October
Meet IDS to discuss his speech to '22 tomorrow. Cover other subjects, e.g. appointment of treasurer and party finances, balancing left and right, setting up policy groups (total agreement on this), how to contest referendum. IDS looks tired. Says he was expecting a long rest after the general election. It has been 'non-stop' instead; he finds speech-making especially tiring and difficult. I say, 'You must take a good rest at Christmas; opposition leaders who take good holidays frighten PMs.' Things will get better in the new year as our policy meetings get into action and the enemy falters.

Wednesday 31 October
On *Today* IDS starts to criticise the way government is getting over the message

about the war. 'We need to win hearts and minds of the British people.'

IDS addresses '22 Committee. Apparently neither he nor I can be heard. Will need to get amplification at least on busy nights.

Thursday 1 November

Discuss a draft letter from IDS to colleagues with his new head of the Policy Unit, Greg Clark. I suggest a paragraph which relates policy exercise more directly to '22 Committee. This is accepted.

Friday 2 November

Give a eulogy at Anthony Ogilvie's funeral in Malvern Priory. He was a very good and loyal friend. As chairman and president of the association he helped me to secure the post-Maastricht period, in particular to be readopted as candidate and to have a good base from which to become chairman of '22. He acted as my agent at the last general election.

Friday 9 November

By train to Grantham to speak in Peter Tapsell's constituency of Louth. He's apparently already the longest serving member of the '22 Committee. When Peter shows me to my room in his lovely house, he points to the fitted cupboards and says, 'See those cupboards, Spicer? None of them are for you because they're stuffed full of Gabrielle's clothes.' Dinner attended by about seventy people – about par for the course these days. There are only forty booked so far for Ann Widdecombe at my annual dinner in two weeks' time. The town hall at Louth is a magnificent and very large room; luckily I am given a microphone. The editor of the local paper wins the draw prize so the evening should get a good write-up.

Monday 19 November

Put my foot down at Conservative board* meeting about finance. We are getting very close to the overdraft limit and all board members are liable for the party's debts. I insist that at next meeting – in January, I assume – we consider options, such as massive cut in expenses.

Tuesday 20 November

Bump into IDS in the 'No' lobby. I have an empathy with him; in fact, he is the first leader with whom I have a genuinely easy relationship. Neither wants

---

* I became an ex officio member of the board of the party when I was elected Chairman of the 1922 Committee.

anything from the other and we are agreed on policy. Suggest to him that he takes care over whom he appoints in charge of candidates. What about Chris Chope? He seems to want a woman in the job and says all will be OK as long as the admin officer is on the ball; I say I'm not so sure. It's a role where the top man matters.

First breakfast meeting of ERG to be chaired by David Heathcoat-Amory. Francis Maude: 'Soundness on Europe not only quality for membership of ERG.' I say, 'Maybe not, but it should be one of them.' Francis looks rather glum.

Wednesday 21 November

Launch policy groups at '22 Committee. Douglas Hogg is supportive.

Address ACP. Big issue is unsurprisingly government's White Paper to 'reform' House of Lords. Lords want to keep things as they are, except Strathclyde, the shadow leader. At the back of the room sits Eric Forth, shadow leader of the Commons, who wants a fully elected Lords and will be very proactive about it. Later that morning, John Bercow drops into my vast offices for a drink. He too, I suspect, wants to 'reform' House of Lords.

Monday 26 November

Meeting at CCO under chairmanship of John Taylor with proposition from Edward McMillan-Scott (leader of MEPs) that '22 Committee should no longer run leadership contest and MEPs should be included in first round. Vetoed by me!

Wednesday 28 November

Four issues at '22 Committee:

1. Constituencies want share of new allowances. I point out that could only be for services specifically given to us as MPs.
2. Data protection laws worrying more and more.
3. Pension: government seems to be ratting on Commons resolution to raise pensions.
4. Perks – e.g. airport car park passes – under fire.

Friday 30 November

Ann Widdecombe stays the night in Cropthorne and speaks to the association annual dinner at Bransford Hotel. She believes Major was badly wronged. I take the opposite view. We don't quarrel but we don't see eye to eye on Major.

Friday 7 December

Meet Beryl Hickling at meeting of county councillors at Shire Hall. She tells me that Richard Weatherill wants my job. (I say it's not on the market for a few years.) She wants to be president of the WWCA. The anti-Spicer/pro-Europe group is re-forming. I have to decide whether to mount a counter-operation or ride it out in the knowledge that I can't be touched for eight years.

Dan Hannan rings. He has fallen out with IDS about position of MEPs with EPP, which is the federalist umbrella to which we are joined. DH plans to leave EPP, much to IDS's fury, as the latter is trying to ignore the European issue to maintain unity.

Monday 10 December

Meet IDS at a cocktail party for Conservative wives at John Gummer's home/office in Queen Anne's Gate. Discuss EPP (issue centres on its federalist constitution and our membership of it) and Daniel Hannan. 'He should trust me,' says IDS. 'He claims that is what Major and William Hague used to say; he would accept anything in writing,' I reply. 'The issue is one of timing.' 'The problem is that a clear-cut position has become "wait and see".'

Tuesday 18 December

Run into Stanley Kalms (new treasurer) at CCO Christmas party. Tell him I will back him on the board if he insists on massive cost cuts.

Wednesday 19 December

Blair mocks IDS at PMQs for having written EPP a letter making demands that they alter their position to one which was anti-federalist, which was rejected, prompting IDS to ask for further time to resubmit his demands, which was granted. I hear Blair say to the Foreign Secretary (Jack Straw), who is sitting next to him, 'It's quite true!'

Relations with David Davis and David Maclean becoming a bit strained. Neither really keeps me in the picture about '22 matters. Each is wary of me because I strike an independent posture for MPs and refinance in CCO. David Davis cut me out of CCO meetings from the start. It may all be for the best: I do have an agenda for the parliamentary party.

Thursday 27 December

Talk to John Taylor on the phone. We discuss leadership rules amicably and then go on to talk about party's finances. JT says that David Davis et al. are keeping me at arm's length because they know I am a hawk on what needs to be done, i.e. a massive cut in costs, for which I am backed by the Executive of the '22. He himself is 'on the fence'; he sees the need for action but wants to try to go along with DD's approach – to ride it out with minimal sackings. We both agree the budget committee should be re-established with chairman of party, chairman of '22, chairman of Convention and Treasurer. Finally we touch on question of the press – who is leaking (he probably suspects me). *The Times* today has a cartoon showing collapse in our finances on a graph with the caption 'People vote for the party they think will be best on the economy'. It looks like an interesting new year ahead.

Wednesday 9 January 2002
'22 Executive very concerned party rushing unnecessarily into a position of pressing for an elected House of Lords just to outflank Labour. Also people speak against elected House of Lords at main committee.

Wednesday 16 January
IDS defends to '22 Committee his policy announced over the weekend of largely elected House of Lords. There is a lot of concern at the way he has managed this.

Thursday 17 January
ACP sullen when I am asked about whether '22 Executive consulted by David Renton. I say 'No' but there was a meeting of a policy group about it before Christmas. IDS to speak to their Lordships next week. Not a happy event. I tell the Lords New Labour has lost its way on the issue of private/public ownership of railways and health.

Tuesday 22 January
Minor crisis in Commons re election of a Conservative representative to European Convention. Discuss with David Maclean and Eric Forth how to stop Redwood and Heathcoat-Amory fighting each other. (Heathcoat-Amory rings to ask if I will sponsor him. I say 'No' because of my '22 job.) Bump into Austin Mitchell, co-chairman of Congress for Democracy. He says we must find a form of words which heads off the clash with Business for Sterling – even if they won't co-operate.

Wednesday 23 January
Voting for our representative on Convention: David Heathcoat-Amory 88, John Maples 33, Patrick Cormack 5.

Saturday 2 February
Letter from Rodney Leach which says Business for Sterling/'No' campaign have cornered the market and there is no room for Congress for Democracy in any team.

Sunday 3 February
Talk on the phone with Malcolm Pearson; he agrees that if I push him he will take over Congress for Democracy – but very reluctantly. He also agrees it should remain a forum for discussion about matters other than Euro – wants me to stay on but this will be very difficult with my role as '22 chairman.

Monday 11 February
Meeting of agenda committee of Congress for Democracy. Russell Walters (Democracy Movement) and chairman of Green Party confirm they have come to an arrangement with Business for Sterling. I persuade rest of meeting that Congress should stay in business but as a talking shop going wider than the Euro, e.g. to the next IGC (*corpus juris*) and the Convention. Am asked by David Stoddart what I intend to do. I say chair the next Congress and decide on my future as co-chairman thereafter.

Sunday 17 February
Malcolm Pearson calls to 'check in' about Congress meeting next Friday. He plans to say that Business for Sterling don't want anything to do with 'come-outery' – so we had better have our own show. (Ironic that BfS have just hired a former UKIP man.) I warn him against a situation where the press presents Congress as a Trojan horse with a 'come out' agenda, which then frightens off Conservative Party, Democracy Movement et al. The situation especially difficult for me, as I am planning to hand over Congress to Malcolm.

Thursday 28 February
Dinner with Cita and Irwin Stelzer. Melanie Phillips (*Daily Mail*) and husband Joshua Rozenberg (former BBC, now *Telegraph*), Michael Gove (deputy editor, *Times*) and his partner. Bullish right-wing conversation.
   General view is that there will not be a referendum on the Euro because it is felt that Brown 'has no motive' to withdraw his opposition to the single currency. I am asked about the state of the Conservative Party and answer, 'Better than in '97; we have started to think a bit in a cohesive and relatively disciplined way.' Important issues are how to deal with taxes and improve public services. On Iraq – general agreement we will have to take out Saddam

Hussein but this could put a million lives at risk in Israel. He is much better armed these days.

Friday 1 March
Chair Congress for Democracy. Manage to steer a course between setting up a rival campaigning organisation to BfS and ceasing to exist.

Wednesday 13 March
Sullen meeting of '22 with IDS. Virtually no questions. He made same speech as at 1992 dinner two weeks before. Storm clouds could be gathering. The feeling is growing that he is making no impact.

Monday 18 March
Conservative board. Clash with Stanley Kalms over finances. I request the board sees the debt figures. SK refuses. I say we cannot sign away the 'budget' without knowing the financial position. Get nowhere; no one else backs me. One board member says as a new boy my 'hysterics' unjustified.

Thursday 21 March
Michael Ashcroft, former party treasurer, calls in at my office. Says that he has heard about my spat with Kalms. My worries are well founded: commercial debt repayable in year's time. Getting too high. He advises me to say will not agree to total debt rising above a predefined ceiling. Kalms will leave in a year's time.

Tuesday 9 April
CCO board meeting this afternoon. My suggestion of a limit on our borrowing rejected. However, I ask for this to be minuted. Board accept that finance sub-committee should be put on ice.

Wednesday 10 April
Full '22 meeting on Iraq. Ten people get up and express concern/caution.

By chance sit opposite IDS at dinner in members' dining room. Recently I have found my relationship with him more difficult, as I now have with Maclean and Davis. Perhaps it's all a legacy of the leadership battle or, more likely, the contrasting nature of our various roles. In fact the only members of present establishment I get on with reasonably well are Forth and Ancram. IDS and I discuss relationships with MEPs in anticipation of my visit to them – he wants to be shot of European issue.

Tuesday 16 April

Good 1992 dinner. Everyone very supportive of Liam Fox view of NHS: must break up state monopoly and give purchasing power to consumer. Sit next to the doughty Ann Winterton. She is determined that we are going to press for renegotiation of Treaty of Rome re fisheries. We must support her.

Wednesday 24 April

Meet Greg Clark in my office. Several matters concern me about policy-making process; Ann Winterton under pressure about her defence of our policy to repatriate fishing.

Later, after '22 Committee, have a spat with David Davis. He has said he cannot come to Executive committee to discuss new candidate election arrangements. I say, 'I hope it is not because you do not want to meet us.' He says that he cannot understand why I should think he wouldn't want to meet the committee. Davis and I have had a difficult relationship since he barred me from his morning meetings when he got the job at CCO. I have been fighting for financial transparency on the board, which has clearly annoyed him.

Sunday 5 May

News coming through that Ann Winterton has been sacked for remarks in a rugby club – sad because she was bravely fighting the corner for fisheries policy.

Tuesday 7 May

Attend meeting of foreign affairs policy group. Not many people there: Michael Ancram's speech confirms worst fears that we may retreat on fishing policy repatriation. He does, however, promise an alternative European Convention. The European clouds could be gathering again in the Conservative Party.

Bump into David Lidington, Ann Winterton's successor. He says he has been 'instructed' to keep faith with fisheries policy; we shall see.

Thursday 9 May

IDS and David Davis present 'strategy' in CCO to parliamentary party. Right wing is becoming restive.

Sunday 12 May

Kelvin Mackenzie, former editor of *The Sun*, writing in the *Sunday Times*, writes off the Tory Party in general and IDS in particular for having no identity on Europe, transport, trade, health to which people can relate.

Monday 13 May

Conservative board meeting in a tatty hotel on a roundabout outside Oxford which Ann and I have happily driven past every weekend for twenty-five years. Voluntary side of the party very restive – no leadership, no message etc. IDS has to do better or he's in trouble. The irony is that the government has had a bad few weeks thanks to Byers[*] and our position in the polls seems to be getting better – at least according to private polls. David Davis seems to accept my view that we need more identity and bite. On behalf of '22 I insist that constituencies retain sovereignty re selection of candidates.

Wednesday 15 May

The splendid Peter Tapsell gets up at the end of a debate at the '22 on candidate selection and says the main four criteria when he was selected were: (1) commission in HM Forces, (2) not a woman, (3) not a Catholic, (4) over thirty-five years old – number of candidates came down from 144 to 17. He brings the house down.

IDS at IoD dinner at Aston Villa. Not a brilliant speech. He agrees (we talk amicably afterwards over dinner) that we need direction – 'centre right'. I have agreed to do an 'in depth' interview in *Financial Times*.

Monday 20 May

I give lunch to Nick Soames. 'We're rudderless and sinking.' I point out that opinion polls are going up for us. 'I don't believe them,' he says. What he is reflecting is the mood of the party in the country. He is very much 'in touch', speaking to more associations than most shadow ministers.

Tuesday 21 May

Try to contact Central Office about the *FT* interview on Thursday. Dominic Cummings, so-called strategy man, refuses to talk to me, puts me on to Nick Wood, who is pretty bland. Bump into IDS in the tea room. I raise *FT* interview; he says there is the decentralisation and power to the patients/consumers etc. 'That will do me for Thursday,' I say. 'Walk with me to my office,' he offers. 'I'll give you a copy of the relevant policy statement.' 'I'm rather relieved about this because the troops are beginning to want some red meat.' 'I know.'

In the voting lobby at 10 p.m., Robin Cook, Leader of the House, grabs

---

[*] The Rt Hon. Stephen Byers MP resigned as Secretary of State for Transport.

me to say he is making progress with data protection.* I say, 'Good, I was going to ask you about this on Thursday across the floor. I still will in a gentle way.' 'We are making good progress,' says Cook. 'In that case I won't say anything to embarrass you,' I reply.

Wednesday 5 June

Newsnight reports that Dominic Cummings (who refused to discuss *FT* piece with me) has said the only thing more unpopular than the Euro is the Tory Party; this view supported by Business for Sterling. This has been a story simply waiting to erupt. *PM* and *Today* programmes have been trying to speak to me – I have kept and will keep well away from them.

Wednesday 12 June

Further disquiet at '22 Executive. Touchy-feely phase has run its course – need identity to which everyone can relate.

Thursday 13 June

5.30 p.m. Meeting with IDS in his rather poky suite of rooms on the ground floor at the back of the shadow Cabinet block. I begin by saying that his 'all-embracing, unfocused charm offensive' has in many colleagues' view run its course. What is wanted now is some real identity for the party, a sense of direction and commitment to firm principles – perhaps by giving some flesh and bones to his 'power to the people' idea, for instance by saying we will give power to the patient through a health insurance scheme.

He says the 'Compassionate Conservative' campaign will go on, not just to appeal to the under-privileged themselves, but to give middle classes a warm feeling about us. We can move on to economic matters at a later date. IDS argues that this strategy, espoused by Cummings, is beginning to pay off – we have risen from 29 per cent to 33 per cent in the polls. Hope he's right; a lot hangs on it for him and for us. Meeting rushed at the end; we leave his room together having been told there is a vote, finding Ann Widdecombe in the room outside understandably impatient to see him. Just before I leave he says, 'Policies are well advanced.' I say, 'I hope not because it would mean the parliamentary party aren't involved.' He claims, 'If the parliamentary party aren't involved, that's their fault because they don't turn up to meetings.' I say, 'Not true' (it's a myth being put around by Chief Whip, who wants to close down policy groups) 'except for education.

---

* Data protection legislation clashed with laws governing freedom of information. As we shall see, with respect to MPs, FoI laws won.

The problem is the shadow Cabinet don't invite them'. IDS replies, 'I want to know more about that if it's true'. Owen Paterson steps in and suggests he and I talk.

Sunday 16 June
John Taylor, chairman of the Party Convention, rings me on the train going up to London. The voluntary-side members of the board, having not supported me over the board's financial loss of control, are now unhappy about their loss of control of the party conference, which had previously been their fiefdom. They want my support at tomorrow's board meeting. I say I certainly agree there was a convergence of views between voluntary party and MPs (a) that CCO is there to serve and (b) that voluntary constituency autonomy should be maintained – though in the past many volunteers have also been centralisers. Apparently there is now a change of heart about this because they see the way CCO is taking over.

Monday 17 June
Board meeting. The voluntary side of the party, which outnumbers MPs by ten to one and theoretically dominates the board but which has remained supine on such matters as the finances of the party, financial contributions etc., revolts today on the proposed removal from them of chairmanships at the party conference. I say, 'Join the club; MPs had everything removed from them five years ago.'

 Much later meet up with them as Ann and I are coming out of a Vietnamese restaurant in Churton Street. They are all in very good spirits.

 Earlier have good talk at parliamentary wives party with Owen Paterson, IDS's effective PPS, about our membership of EPP. He says we're going to leave but at a quiet moment.

Tuesday 18 June
Run into David Davis outside IDS's office beneath mine. He congratulates me for being 'gutsy' at the board meeting.

Wednesday 19 June
Discuss EPP with Dan Hannan on phone. I say talk to IDS at Conservative meeting in Seville before you decide to jump ship. Owen Paterson has said IDS will deal with EPP in his own time.

Thursday 20 June
2.15: ACP meeting. Tell them of the formation of Reform of House of

Lords joint committee. They are all pretty glum, especially Geoffrey Howe – in particular when I say in answer to a question from David Renton that majority of House of Commons parliamentary party in favour of elected Lords, though not I.

Wednesday 26 June 2002
Post-'22 meeting with Chief Whip (David Maclean). He is hell bent on trying to do a deal with Labour on modernisation of Parliament. I tell him, 'Modernisation means castration. Don't make same mistake as was made with the Lords of tangoing with the government; we're not in office.'

Thursday 27 June
Breakfast meeting with IDS. He speaks at length about how we must be all inclusive. Members of the Executive are sceptical. Role of an MP to represent his constituency in Parliament not, as IDS suggests, to do good works around the country.

Wednesday 3 July
David Davis addresses '22 in total silence. Two rather hesitant questions at the end.

Friday 5 July
Ring Eric Forth on a matter to do with data protection. He says he is becoming increasingly alarmed by IDS and Maclean's strategy of being nice to everyone without a sense of direction. Willing to give it a go till the spring then may have to take some action. I say I hope the direction will begin to emerge in the autumn at the party conference. By the spring will be half way through this parliament. Forth says David Davis thinks as he does. I say I fervently hope we don't have to have another revolution. Forth says we can't leave it like we did with Hague last time.

Ring Chris Poole (secretary to CCO board) about apparent removal of veto powers from MPs over changes in constitution to do with leadership rules. He says he will think about it and come back next week.

Sunday 7 July
Lunch party at Cropthorne for nineteen people including Angela and Michael Brinton (Lord Lieutenant), and Rosalie and Nigel Dawes. Some of the guests say they 'like the look of David Davis'. I say, 'No comment; if thirty MPs give me their names as wanting to dismiss Iain Duncan Smith, I have to hold a vote of confidence.' The DD

band-wagon could be rolling faster and wider than I thought. IDS may be in serious trouble.

Monday 8 July

Several people come up to me during the day to grumble about the state of the party. Daniel Hannan rings from Brussels to say that unless IDS carries out his promise to leave EPP by 26 August, he will leave the Conservative Party. At a Sky party at the Cinnamon Club Norman Lamont says, 'I don't know what we stand for. It's no good concentrating on being liked; we've never been liked. When we win we are respected.' James Cran says same thing.

People are talking up David Davis. I ask Edward Leigh whether he has been directly confronted by David Maclean about his letter to the *Telegraph*, calling for clear policies, of three weeks earlier. Leigh says, 'No.'

Wednesday 10 July

Someone expresses the view at breakfast in the tea room that scrambling to join the shadow Cabinet at this time is like applying to join Doenitz's government in 1945. IDS gives a lacklustre performance to the '22 to half the party (only two questions). I say, 'We back you because it is our intent that your strategy thrives.' Afterwards David Maclean says to me, 'The party is in a very nervous mood' – and so it is.

Thursday 11 July

Dinner for '22 Executive at Garrick, old card room. Thrust of the discussion is depressing. Party is a mess, no direction, no identity. What are we for? But we must back IDS. I say Thatcher did not shine in opposition. We agree to discuss all this again in the autumn and to see the leader, possibly informally over dinner. Fabricant says (again!) would like me as leader! He must be joking.

Saturday 20 July

Owen Paterson rings about an article in *Times* saying great controversy has arisen about appointment of a communications director. We agree no point in meeting before summer but need to arrange a dinner date in late November for informal get-together. If disquiet persists and is widespread in run-up to Christmas it will need a very serious talk, say I.

Sunday 21 July

Owen Paterson rings (again) to ask if David Davis stays in our house in Florida. He can't reach him on the phone. I say we sold our house several years ago.

Tuesday 23 July
David Davis sacked as chairman of party while on holiday in Florida. In one stroke IDS has attempted to kill off his chief rival. Whether it will work will depend on how the party now performs and how ruthless Davis is with his ally Forth. Briefing against Davis has either come from IDS or Portilloites – as presumably was the rude piece about me in Black Dog in the *Mail on Sunday* the weekend before last. John Taylor comes to my room to say I am invaluable as chairman of '22 and that he wants to be as supportive as possible at board meetings.

Wednesday 24 July
I arrive in the tea room for breakfast. Everyone feeling a bit 'morning after the Night of the Long Knives'. No one laughs very much. As it happens, I bump into IDS after PM's questions. I say, 'Party not happy with the way 'twere done.'

Thursday 25 July
Times has a piece saying reason asylum seekers want to come here is because they think Thatcher is still in charge and that means we are a rich and strong country.

Friday 26 July
'Anonymous' briefing in press (by Eric Forth?) in defence of Davis. Tory Party must stop 'consuming its own vomit'.

Battle for the soul of the party

Sunday 28 July 2002
David Davis returned from Florida yesterday. He and Forth all over the Sunday press; they are very angry and on the rampage, blaming Dominic Cummings and IDS for briefing against DD. I ring Owen Paterson. He says, 'We are going to get to the root of this; it is by people who want to stir up trouble between DD and IDS.'

Thursday 15 August
First half of August spent at Cropthorne. Post still high despite it being the holiday period. People write all the year round these days*. Tories still getting consistently bad press following the David Davis debacle. Battle between

---

* If one takes account of emails, they write all day and all night.

so-called modernisers ('mods'), whose mantra seems to focus on more women candidates and welcome to minority groups, and the 'rockers', who say what we want is a re-establishment of our identity/principles – choice, small state, decentralisation of decisions and appropriate policies (health insurance, low taxes etc.). I suspect we will get a bit of all that at the party conference.

Monday 19 August
IDS was put there for one reason – to give the party a distinctive theme. (Tebbit has articles in *Sunday Times* and *Telegraph* quoting Churchill's 'pudding with a theme'.) He was thought to represent a clear point of view. He is fast losing that reputation.

A new battle has started in the emerging vacuum of weak leadership: libertarians v. the rest.

Sunday 22 September
407,000 people march for the countryside. At CCO IDS gives Ann a kiss on the cheek and tells her (and me) the party conference is going to be an amazing success.

Monday 23 September
Meet Michael Howard in his room; suggest to him that if the polls do not improve – and with the economy apparently still set fair and war looming they may not – rebellion may be afoot. Chair meeting of the party on Iraq; about sixty there from Lords and Commons. As long as the policy is to try the UN route first, party is pretty united. Douglas Hogg argues, like his father, for peace at any price, but this is Labour's problem.

Saturday 28 September
Story breaks about Edwina Currie and Major. From my point of view interesting bit is her fury when, having expected to take over from me as minister of housing when Major became PM, the job was given to George Young.

Sunday 6 October
Arrive at Bournemouth for party conference at 4.30. Beautiful clear early autumn afternoon. Agents' dinner at 7.30 transferred to the dreary Hilton from the Highcliffe because party chiefs do not want us to be seen about in dinner jackets! IDS comes for the speeches and lurks behind a pillar waiting for his turn to speak. He is dressed in a lounge suit. When he is called he makes a lacklustre speech; after this the master of ceremonies, the only

competent speaker of the evening (including Theresa May), invites everyone to rise 'in respect for the leader as he leaves'. What a dreary start to the 'defining conference'.

Monday 7 October
A number of MPs say they want time with me: Brian Mawhinney, Sydney Chapman, Michael Jack. One comes into the drinks session in the Highcliffe for my constituents with a copy of the *Daily Mirror* in which Anthony Steen, 'committee member of the '22', calls for IDS to go. The two key speakers at the conference itself are Theresa May, the new chairman ('some people call us the nasty party'), and Liam Fox, who makes a respectable stab at a new approach to health. (People will be helped to go private and insurance subscriptions will be tax deductible.) These two speeches will characterise this conference. Policy and self-flagellation. Which will prevail in the public's mind I don't know. I suspect Theresa May's 'some people hate us' theme will prevail, which will be bad news as I doubt (a) whether her diagnosis of the party's travails is right (more to do with Blair's brilliance and the general second-ratedness of our leadership since Thatcher) and (b) whether self-doubt charms the electorate.

Thursday 10 October
Speech by IDS just saved by 'Never under-estimate the resolve of a quiet man'.

Wednesday 16 October
'22 meeting: Portillo listened to in stony silence when he defends the leadership's line that we should turn our back on the past and try to be loved, especially by minorities. Earlier at PMQs, IDS said that A-levels are no longer worth the paper they're written on – an inept attempt to censure the government for their inept management of A-level marking this summer.

Discuss all this in an evening meeting with David Maclean and Marion Roe. I say if leader is determined to pursue the strategy of self-hate, 'it had better work'.

Walk home with Owen Paterson. He is a nice man and his heart is in the right place. I say if IDS is going to mend fences with colleagues he must listen; he is becoming completely isolated.

Thursday 17 October
Walk back from a candidates' committee meeting in CCO with Peter Luff, the new pairing whip. He asks me, 'Why has parliamentary party suddenly become so fractious?' I say, (a) because we are doing so badly in the polls, (b) because their constituency parties are getting at them.

Monday 21 October
Conservative board meeting. Everyone says how wonderful the conference was and how we must have more self-flagellation. Bumped into Eric Forth afterwards; he seems to think a leadership challenge may be on the way.

Wednesday 23 October
I sense all is not well with my relationship with whips' office. Decide that X is only person I can trust there; invite him to my room. He confirms reluctantly that the whips are putting it about that I am being disruptive. Immediately ring Owen Paterson and fix an appointment with the leader for 7.30. IDS in a friendly mood. I tell him that even a semi-public row between me and the whips could be the match which lights the fire against him. IDS says he will talk to the Chief Whip and agrees he could do with my help. I say I see it as my job to do my best to stabilise things. Like so many others, I am faced with a dilemma: IDS not up to the job but anarchy could follow his departure.

Wednesday 30 October
Lunch with Chief Whip to patch up our relations and to discuss the deluge of press reports of unrest in the party about IDS. I tell him that my way of trying to dampen things down is to do so quietly on a person-to-person basis. I am not going to lecture the party on behalf of the leadership – not my proper role, which is more to report the view of the party to the leadership.

Later at '22 Committee meeting Edward Leigh leads a pro-IDS charge. I back the view that the briefing of the press should stop.

Thursday 31 October
Guardian carries front page story that Keith Simpson will stand against me for chairmanship. Ben Brogan rings me to warn me of this. Andrew Robathan offers help. Advises me to see Gerald Howarth, who is on frontbench team with Simpson. Find Howarth in the chamber; sit next to Gerald on front bench. He readily agrees to help. Simpson joins us and says he has absolutely no intention of standing and went on *World at One* to say so.

Sunday 3 November
Long mid-morning phone call at Cropthorne to IDS. I put the following thoughts:

In the short term you are probably OK because colleagues are coming up for reselection and won't want to be seen as regicides by their associations. When they are reselected it could be different.

Continue with short sharp questions at PMQs.

More raw meat on policy e.g. low taxes, enterprise.

Set up advisory 'council of elders', e.g. Clarke, Portillo, Widdecombe, Mawhinney, Hague, Redwood, me.

Recruit PR supremo.

Monday 4 November

Meet Owen Paterson in my room to finalise list for advisory council. List of twelve. Agree, when IDS is content, that I should approach them. Later in the lobby IDS says he wants to call it a 'panel'. I say OK but it must be 'advisory'. Bump into Ann Widdecombe and say, 'All is going well with your plan to form a council/panel of elder statesmen.' She is pleased. Eight Tories, including Clarke and Portillo, vote with the government on a three-line whip (thirty-five abstain, which was permitted) on the Adoption Bill. John Bercow resigns from the shadow Cabinet on this issue.

Tuesday 5 November

First letter comes calling for a vote of confidence in IDS. IDS issues a statement amidst maximum publicity from CCO blaming those who voted against the three-line whip as an attack on his leadership. This is a major blunder. Portillo issues an immediate response saying in effect that he's tried to be loyal but no more.

Gloom everywhere – tea rooms, dining room – even in the whips' office. Talk late at night with Owen Paterson. I think even he thinks IDS has blundered; apparently IDS was determined that the secret briefing and contra-briefing between leader and Portilloites, which he feels destroyed Hague, should not be repeated and should be flushed out. One effect may have been to put the kybosh on the idea of a panel of senior advisers including Portillo and Clarke.

Wednesday 6 November

IDS gets appalling press. Arrive in the tea room at breakfast time. Find myself sitting with Michael Portillo and Brian Mawhinney. We start to talk about the council of elders when the fire alarm goes off. The three of us pile out and stand out of the rain in the archway to Speaker's Court. Portillo agrees – despite everything – to join what we decide should be a breakfast club.

Chair '22 Committee: start with a statement calling for restraint. IDS people, including Chief Whip and IDS himself in 10 p.m. lobby, thank me. I say I am under no illusion about this. The party is sullen and very troubled.

I stress my job is to try to calm things down, especially vis-à-vis the press, but to be a conduit for party opinion to the leadership – not the other way round. In the lobby at 10 p.m. IDS bangs on again about Portillo's disloyalty.

At the Executive there are three criticisms: bad advisers, bad PR, bad man management. Lords agree when we join up with ACP.

Early in the morning run into Andrew Lansley (Portilloite), one of those who voted with Labour on the Adoption Bill – furious to have been designated as disloyal to IDS. I tell him that I think an exception has been made for him. He is known to have been consistent on this – not so Portillo.

Thursday 14 November
Discuss advisory group with Owen Paterson. He has the bright idea of dividing it into two groups and varying them between Chief Whip and IDS. Can you imagine Portillo or Clarke agreeing to this? It just shows the penny really hasn't dropped. Man management is not the strong point of this leadership.

Monday 18 November
Another MP-bashing session at the Conservative board. Voluntary party in full flood for the shenanigans of last few weeks. Senior volunteers lost touch with the voluntary side of the party years ago – that's the irony. MPs are more in touch with the rank and file than they are.

Wednesday 20 November
Re-elected without opposition to chairmanship of '22 at 6.30 meeting.

Tuesday 26 November
Chair very successful meeting of party on policy. Good debate between Nick Gibb[*] (centralisation of standards especially education) versus Redwood et al. (real choice).

Wednesday 27 November
'22 Executive dinner at Garrick for IDS. Begins with a surreal moment when there is a choice between ordering the soufflé and waiting for IDS (who I know is having a hurriedly arranged meeting with Ken Clarke). Instant decision is to order the soufflé, which will take fifteen minutes to do. Only point of real debate is about EPP membership. A very relaxed and agreeable evening.

---

[*]   MP for Bognor Regis & Littlehampton since 1997; MoS Schools since 2010.

Tuesday 3 December
'22 officers' meeting with IDS in his room at 6 p.m. He gets quite stroppy when we discuss leaving EPP and whether his 'notice to quit' will do.

Tuesday 10 December
Letters of thanks for Garrick dinner 'and your personal support' from IDS. Chief Whip asks me to sign a letter jointly with him asking MPs to keep their engagements when they have committed themselves.

Wednesday 11 December
Good meeting between '22 Executive and senior members of the voluntary party; we agree to help to get more MP speakers. CCO party given by Stanley Kalms as the treasurer. Come across Christina Dykes (i/c candidates) and Christabel Flight arguing about whether I am a rottweiler or a pussycat.

Tuesday 17 December
Breakfast in the House. Deputy Chief Whip, Patrick McLoughlin, tells me not to read *The Guardian* – ICM shows us only 3 points ahead of Liberals. We are in a mess. Goodness knows what IDS will say to '22 tomorrow.

Wednesday 18 December
Fractious '22 Executive.
    IDS speaks to 100 peers and MPs at the main committee. I thank him at the end for 'his hard work for the party – and it is hard to get our message over to a public basking in the prosperity we left behind. My new year wish is that this will be the year in which the shabbiness of Labour and its Liberal acolytes percolates to the consciousness of the electorate.' IDS thanks me for the involvement of the party in policy-making. I say in winding up, 'The message is becoming clearer and there is a good deal of agreement in the parliamentary party.'

Thursday 19 December
Good one-to-one meeting with IDS. He agrees that taxation and pensions should be focus of policy.

Monday 23 December
Telegraph splashes with story of IDS commitment to tax cuts. This is a repeat by Ben Brogan of yesterday's story in the *Sunday Times* and is being presented as a Tory split. Francis Maude goes on the media to rubbish it.

Tuesday 24 December

Papers full of row between Michael Howard and IDS about tax speech – some saying MH involved in leadership bid. Ring MH. He is furious: all untrue. Wouldn't do leadership if forced on him. Ring Owen Paterson, to tell him about Howard's anger. On substance IDS and MH seem to be agreed – Tory policy: low taxes and new ways of raising money for pensions and health.

Chapter 20

The fall of Iain Duncan Smith

We now move to the events leading up to the passing of a vote of no confidence in the leadership of Iain Duncan Smith.

All the names of colleagues whom I report writing to me demanding this vote are pseudonyms. In this way I comply with the party's constitution, which states that Conservative Members of Parliament may write such letters to the chairman of the 1922 Committee in secret; and that if 15 per cent of the parliamentary party do so, the 1922 chairman must call a vote of confidence in the leader.

The chairman of the '22 and his assistant (in this case me and Jessica Stewart – now Jessica Chessher) are thus the only people in the world who know the true picture, although I always worked on the assumption that in these litigious days I could be challenged in open court. I believe I nearly was. I certainly think that the shadow Attorney General at the time – Bill Cash – was working hard on this.

My greatest potential hazard was, however, forgery. I did indeed receive nineteen forged letters. Each was neatly typed and short, typically composed of two lines; five were written on Carlton Club paper.

I received a total of thirty-six genuine letters (a minimum of twenty-nine being required for the vote of confidence). Almost all of these were handwritten and usually discursive, typically using two sides of paper. To my certain knowledge others had been written but were not sent once I had announced that the vote of confidence would take place.

In all cases I checked directly with the sender to ensure that it was indeed his/her letter I had received. On one or two occasions tracking down the relevant person was easier said than done. Several were terrified of being found out and did everything they could physically to distance themselves from me.

The length to which some colleagues went to avoid recognition when delivering letters is documented in the diary. With representatives of Iain Duncan Smith and the whips' office sitting outside my room, it was for some a genuine problem. It was a concern for me too, charged as I was by the party's constitution to keep the names secret. Here is how the story unfolds in the diary.

Wednesday 8 January 2003

Parliamentary party in disarray. Portilloites in particular on the rampage, notably Bercow, Maude and Norman, but behind the scenes at least a dozen others. They seem to have no real agenda other than 'modernisation', i.e. social libertarianism. They are irreconcilably and viciously anti-IDS. Many of them were members of the Federation Conservative Students in the 1980s – closed down by Tebbit for being too outrageous, even violent. They are working increasingly as a pack. In the '22 Executive they are not well represented. Even here there is considerable opposition to IDS; but they are unwilling to put the dagger in immediately.

After a '22 meeting have a 1½-hour session with IDS. His PMQs were sharper this afternoon and exposed Labour divisions on Iraq; he intends to stick to his guns on tax cuts, law and order and immigration by appointing a new PR supremo (Paul Baverstock). So the things that are capable of rational adjustment are gradually being addressed. The questions of his persona and of his enemies persist and make him very (probably increasingly) vulnerable.

As I enter IDS's room he is on the phone to his thirteen-year-old daughter, who has just returned to boarding school. I gesture that I will leave but he waves me to a seat. I tell him – pity we wasted last year on trying to be loved ('compassionate Conservatives'). I concede, however, that because he was perceived as being so right wing, he may have had to soften himself up.

Thursday 9 January

Breakfast at 8.00 in IDS's room with Clarke, Widdecombe, Lilley and Mawhinney (Portillo backs off at the last minute). IDS spends a lot of time displaying new polls by YouGov which purport to show us to be in a better position than the public polls. These irritate Clarke and Widdecombe, who say all that matters is identity and robustness. IDS says, 'That is exactly what I am doing on tax policy.' Clarke says, 'And look what a mess that has been.' (Over Christmas IDS was regarded as wanting low taxes, Michael Howard as hesitating and Howard Flight as calling for 20 per cent cuts in expenditure – the latter mercilessly exploited by Blair at PMQs.) Altogether not much meeting of minds between Clarke and IDS. In general Clarkeites are letting Portilloites make the running and probably egging them on from the sidelines – ditto David Davis people, apart from various nods and winks.

The only current counterpoints are that Blair has lost touch with his party on Iraq and the economy is faltering.

Sunday 12 January

IDS rather good on *Frost Programme*: relaxed, effective in exposing split in

Labour Party on Iraq, and firm on Conservative policy e.g. on tax. If he goes on like this he may survive.

Monday 13 January 2003
IDS seems to have lost control of the party. In the morning his PPS, Owen Paterson, comes to my office to say that the leader is very keen that Nikki Page should be reinstated at the board meeting this afternoon as a London mayoral candidate. (She has not been chosen to go to the hustings by a nine-man sifting board and there is suspicion that this was an anti-IDS move). I assume Paterson will have a word with other members of the board. When it comes to the meeting, the board, led by Theresa May, the Chairman, who presumably knows IDS's wishes, votes 11-3 against reinstating Page.

I mention this afterwards to IDS, who simply looks bemused. In the voting lobby, Robert Key says he is under growing pressure from his association to vote IDS out. I say that in that case, 'the constitution of the party provides for you to write me a letter in secret.'

Tuesday 14 January
Chat to John Redwood in the chamber. He is pretty irritated about Nikki Page. However, he thinks the Clarke people are backing off in their challenge to IDS.

Wednesday 15 January
Breakfast in the tea room. Peter Tapsell says that the peace movement is growing in the Conservative Party. Our job, he says, is to oppose the government, not to support it, however noble our motive. Tapsell is interesting because he is a Macmillanesque supporter of IDS.

At '22 David Heathcoat-Amory presents a chilling picture of the European Convention: European citizenship; foreign affairs and commercial law no longer intergovernmental; Convention on Human Rights becomes part of UK law. Peter Lilley asks, 'Is it amendable?' to which DH-A replies, 'No.' In this case we are either for it (the new Europe) or against it. The decision point is approaching. Previously there was another go at analysing IDS in the Executive committee which now meets at 4.30 (full committee at 5.30). A view expressed by two members that I should lead a team to IDS to ask him to fall on his sword and be replaced by a single 'compromise' candidate (i.e. Clarke!) is knocked on the head by me for these reasons: (1) I have a constitutional role which I cannot prejudice; (2) IDS will only go if defeated in a vote of confidence; (3) there can then be a bloody battle for the leadership with great bitterness on the part of the loser.

Tuesday 21 January
Go to listen to Norman Tebbit at a dinner at the Athenaeum. He is pretty caustic about the IDS regime. Claims to want him to survive but feels that time may be running out for him. (IDS is Tebbit's successor at Chingford.)

Wednesday 22 January
'22 Executive drinks my health (60) in champagne bought by Michael Fabricant. Unanimous against compulsory all-women lists.

Tuesday 28 January
Have long meeting with IDS. I say that he has a breathing space. This gives him an opportunity to shuffle his shadow Cabinet. Needs to bring back some notable figures (e.g. Widdecombe and Redwood) and sack the invisible ones. He seems to agree.

Wednesday 29 January
Bump into Tam Dalyell, Father of the House, at around 8.30. He thinks matters in the Labour Party are heading towards 'Ramsay MacDonald territory'. By the end of PMQs (at their new time of 12 noon) this is manifest. Blair now at odds with his party on four issues: Iraq, firemen's strike, House of Lords reform (he wants wholly appointed), university top-up fees. His backbenchers almost in open revolt today. Meet the charming Alan Simpson in the lobby afterwards. He says Blair has become a frightening megalomaniac. I wonder if we are heading for a national government with the Labour left in opposition. The trouble is the Tory Party is smaller than the government's majority.

Tuesday 4 February
8 a.m. Breakfast with IDS and Executive of '22. Pretty hostile questioning which he parries rather well – polls beginning to go our way etc.

5–7 p.m. House votes down all government options for House of Lords reform – result is chaos. HM's opposition, which wanted fully elected Lords, also with *oeuf sur visage*. I vote with about forty other Conservatives for a fully appointed Lords.

The Legg affair

Thursday 13 February 2003
Owen Paterson (IDS's PPS) comes to my room to tell me that tomorrow they will sack CCO chief executive, Mark MacGregor, and Stephen Gilbert, his deputy; this is apparently much to the annoyance of Theresa May and is a reversal for the Portillistas (Maude, Lansley, Norman, Bercow and Mackay) and the 'let's be all-inclusive at the expense of everything' brigade. I warn Owen they may well send me letters demanding IDS goes. Hans Blix* is pronouncing on Iraq at UN tomorrow; hope is that this will wash out the CCO news.

Friday 14 February
Owen Paterson rings: MacGregor sacked; Barry Legg offered job but Stephen Gilbert to stay pro tem.

Monday 17 February
Staying with Lulu and Edward. Piece in *The Times* talks of revolt at Conservative board level. Chris Poole (board secretary) rings my office to say an emergency board meeting being called. Later speak to Chris, who confirms Don Porter, John Taylor, David Trefgarne,[†] Theresa May, Caroline Abel Smith, will be meeting. (Apparently Stanley Kalms told Owen Paterson earlier in the day that he and I are the only two members of the board who matter – an exaggeration, I fear, but flattering.)

Owen apparently tells IDS, 'This is not important: people are dropping in for a cup of tea.' I say, 'You must be joking,' to OP. The leader's team once again seem totally out of touch – this time with the party's constitution, which says board must have a say in senior appointments at CCO. I talk to Trefgarne and say nothing is currently worth a massive party constitutional row as the country goes to war and when we are calling for a united government.

This is all very sad as a combination of greater unity, break-up of the Labour Party over Iraq and the failing economy had looked as though it might improve our fortunes. Now nothing but internal tension seems to lie ahead.

---

* Chief UN weapons inspector.
† 2nd Baron Trefgarne; MoS Defence 1985–9; MoS Trade & Industry 1989–90.

Tuesday 18 February
Drive to Royal Crescent Hotel, Bath. A whip rings to say that colleagues he has talked to in the whips' office are 'gobsmacked' by Legg appointment.*

Wednesday 19 February
Still in Bath. *Guardian* says I am angry. Can't think where they got that from as I have refused to talk to the press. Several MPs ring to say they are very angry. Another whip rings to ask what is going on. No reports on the BBC of the 'informal' meeting of the board, though journalists ring to ask whether I was there – 'No comment'. Great thing about the mobile – no one knows where you are. Meanwhile the nation is poised for war.

Thursday 20 February
Owen Paterson rings to see whether I know what happened at board meeting. I say, 'No, but I intend to ring Chris Poole.' Chris not very informative – agrees to ring back later but says some proposition to be made to the leader. Ring Chris from the car driving back to Cropthorne – cannot speak, will talk tomorrow. Nicholas Soames rings, ostensibly to voice concern (and that of about twelve others), but in reality to find out what is going on. I tell him as much as I can. 'Why did IDS do it?' he asks. I say, 'Presumably because he wants a clearer sense of direction than CCO under Mark MacGregor was offering.'

Friday 21 February
At last find out the score from Chris Poole (which in any event is all over the *Daily Telegraph*) courtesy of angry board member. There was a row with some board members saying they could not work with IDS. 'Compromise' proposed that IDS would divide Barry Legg job in two and appoint him chief of staff with someone else at CCO.
    Phone call from Stanley Kalms from ski slopes at midday. We agree board cannot stand out against the leader. There must be a quick board meeting next week, hopefully before '22 on Wednesday, to put this right. Kalms says he will talk to Taylor and Porter.
    Owen Paterson agrees with early board meeting but who will call it? Presumably not the disaffected Theresa May. Portillo has put out a statement today saying her position now impossible. I suggest IDS may need to talk to '22. Owen says I could report on the board meeting – 'True,' I say, 'but I

---

* Barry Legg, Conservative Member of Parliament for Milton Keynes South West, 1992–97. Conservative Party chief executive, February–May 2003.

could not do a full-blooded defence of what the leadership has done.' He says he will talk to IDS and come back.

Talk again later to OP. Idea now is to have a statement agreed on the phone by the board members setting up a sub-committee to look at future organisation of the party. Confirm with Stanley Kalms that this is what is happening.

Ring CCO to ask Paul Baverstock (new communications director) to copy me with statement. Apparently it was Baverstock's incompatibility with Mark MacGregor which led to all the fuss.

Speak to John Taylor; he talks about putting Barry Legg back in his box. I say you cannot have the leader losing and expect him to survive; answer is to promote Baverstock, not to demote Legg. He seems to agree (sort of!).

Anthony Steen rings from Austria. He is not planning to abscond to the Liberals (as reported in one newspaper).

Mark Mardell says IDS in real trouble on BBC evening news. Mardell is not given to hyperbole.

Saturday 22 February
Portillo's attack on IDS front page in all major newspapers. I now have to decide whether long-planned meeting of '22 Executive on Wednesday with board top brass will look like an anti-IDS War Cabinet. May consult Chief Whip about this.

Several conversations during the day with Owen Paterson, David Maclean, Paul Baverstock, IDS himself and a representative number of MPs. Picture emerging of anti-Portillo mood in the party at large, which seems to be supporting IDS. If this is reflected in the press tomorrow, he may be in the clear, especially as there is to be a substantive vote on Iraq on Wednesday. IDS is certainly bullish when he calls me at around 9 p.m. I am impressed by how calm he sounds after all he must have been through.

Sunday 23 February
Press full of expletives from IDS supporters against Portillo. 'All this venom must stop,' I say. Maybe Maude should replace Portillo in the breakfast group. As yet have no sense that letters demanding vote of confidence are coming in.

Monday 24 February
Lots of angry phone calls and excited colleagues – e.g. half an hour of Bercow – but no letters calling for a vote of confidence.

Tuesday 25 February

Breakfast with IDS, Clarke, Redwood, Maude, Widdecombe, Lilley, Mawhinney. Clarke treats IDS with disdain, Maude accuses IDS of briefing against Portillo. IDS dogged but pedestrian.

Later meet IDS alone. He is almost in tears with rage, threatens to resign if board do not let him have his way about Legg.

5.30 p.m. Meet with Theresa May, Stanley Kalms, John Taylor, IDS. It is agreed Legg will be chief executive, to be ratified at next board meeting. (I have previously primed Taylor (from my room) that unless IDS gets his way, his position as leader will be intolerable and he may leave, brought down by voluntary party.)

Wednesday 26 February

Acrimonious meeting between '22 Executive and IDS. Issues raised appointment of Legg, 'lies' about Stephen Gilbert's 'sacking'/'unsacking', briefing against members of the party. Nick Winterton ends on a high note saying grateful for IDS's apology. IDS later says to me he didn't realise he'd given one!

At full '22 Committee I suggest we discuss all these matters next week 'because colleagues will be wanting to take part in the Iraq debate'. In fact 120 of them are in the room – biggest turnout in this parliament! I say also 'because it would surprise the press stacked up outside the door'; this was met by much banging of desks. When I ask for any other business there is dead silence. To much relief I say, 'The meeting is closed.'

Back in IDS's room I tell him, 'You have bought breathing space but I'm afraid that's all.'

Friday 7 March

Eightieth celebration of 1922 Committee – dinner with 150 MPs and ex-MPs at Haberdashers Hall. Beforehand find IDS wandering round the House looking for the Chief Whip to help him with his speech – two hours before the event. I suggest his office get on to the two previous chairmen (Archie Hamilton, Edward du Cann) for some jokes/anecdotes; also keep it short. Keep it about yourself. What comes out is muddled, without substance and ill prepared. IDS's speech is not good. He should have been better prepared for such a key speech to his MP electorate.

My speech somewhat contrasts with this (at least in so far as it was heavily prepared), so makes him look even worse. (The '22 itself is eerily quiet. I am probably now at the peak of my career/influence in the party. It will no doubt be downhill now.) This is very unfortunate. Sitting next to him at dinner

I realise he seems to have no idea what deep trouble he is in with MPs. I think – the war aside – there will be a putsch after the May elections and that will be very messy. I don't think he understands what is about to hit him; he complains again about having to work too hard, with not enough breaks and time to see his family. All very unsatisfactory. He's just too new to the game.

However, politics is in a state of great flux. Apparently Blair's whips ring ours every day to make sure we are still onside over the war. IDS tells me over dinner there is no question, however, of a coalition. (At the end of the dinner I ask whether, as at a Quaker meeting, anyone feels inspired to tell a joke. No takers!)

A lot of MPs come up – even the cynics like Brian Mawhinney – to congratulate me and, I'm afraid, to disparage IDS.

[This looks rather self-serving. I have left it in because I believe it was his performance at the dinner which marked the real beginning of the end for IDS. I was merely the foil, a metaphor for doing it right.]

Sunday 9 March

Malcolm Pearson rings me on the car phone. 'John Redwood, Barry Legg and Nikki Page are aiming to oust Theresa May as chairman of the party and replace her with Redwood.' I say IDS will never agree to this while he is in his present weak position (IDS told me at the dinner on Wednesday that he was very irritated by Redwood's machinations: 'Redwood not a team player' etc.) Unlikely Redwood will get anything for the time being. Anyway it would create too much of a row with Portilloites and Clarkeites – already fuming about MacGregor/Legg affair.

Ended up in a Q&A session at Annabel's church in Hambledon. Very high-powered panel chaired by Jeremy Paxman (lives in the next village), with John Mortimer and Melvyn Bragg. I ask whether Labour will implode over Iraq. Paxman says afterwards he thought I was a Spicer lookalike because the real Spicer was in Worcestershire! Had he realised it was me, would not have let me get away with my 'opportunistic' question. Audience, including Paxman, largely anti-war.

Monday 10 March

Meeting of board very hostile to IDS, partly because a letter from him offering chief executive and chief of staff to Barry Legg circulated with a letter from Legg refusing to report to the chairman. I insist IDS must get his way. Finally this is agreed but a sub-committee is set up to hedge the appointment around with conditions, including whether BL can do the two jobs. (Theresa May says this is the main issue.) I say we cannot have a stand-off with leader as Labour implodes on Iraq. Board agree to water down conditions and remit of the sub-committee.

In the evening board meet IDS for dinner at St Stephen's Club; atmosphere sullen when IDS speaks after dinner.

Tuesday 11 March
Meet IDS 6 p.m. Tell him the potential clash between him and the board about Barry Legg is serious, i.e. that they want to split Legg's jobs of chief executive and chief of staff. IDS says Legg is taking legal advice and is considering suing the party for constructive dismissal. I say he must be mad; it is what the board wants. IDS says, 'My position is not strong. It could seriously affect me if he walks. Could you talk to him and say how vulnerable I am?' I agree to try to tell him he must report to chairman. I ring the number IDS gives me but Legg refuses to meet me: 'It's all gone too far and is not of my making.' I let IDS's office know that he will not meet me. Perhaps it is best if Legg goes. His appointment doesn't make IDS look good.

(IDS previously said he would tell Theresa May that I must be on the special subcommittee looking at the future organisation of Central Office. I say, 'Don't do that. I will get on myself.')

Meanwhile, according to a small piece in *The Times* we are level pegging with Labour 34/34, with Lib Dems on 24. The war effort is falling apart: US Defence Secretary, Donald Rumsfeld, says, 'We can go it alone without the Brits.' Perhaps these two facts will save IDS.

Saturday 15–Sunday 16 March
Just as well that I go to the spring conference in Harrogate. MEPs complain there are no MPs. IDS points out to them that Spicer is here. However, I don't plan to go next year. IDS makes a passable speech on the Sunday and a rather good, seemingly off-the-cuff, one about the forthcoming war on the Saturday. Tell Bernard Jenkin (shadow Defence and close friend of IDS), who is forever fiddling with his pager, that IDS should let Barry Legg go.

Check with Chris Poole that he has minuted that parliamentary party should be represented on the special committee looking at the future of CCO.

Monday 17 March
IDS comes to the '22, which meets at 10 p.m., after Jack Straw makes statement to the House saying US and UK give Saddam Hussein forty-eight hours to comply or leave Iraq. IDS speaks for rather too long, listened to in silence – no questions.

Tuesday 18 March
IDS's enemies out in force against his speech on Monday. Blair makes superb speech and I tell him so in the lobby. He looks tired but relieved by the vote. John Butterfill, who I know has thought of challenging me, tells me a wide cross-section of the party say I am doing OK as '22 chairman. Long may this view last! [It won't. Everything in politics always ends in tears.] Supper with Henry Angest in the canteen. We agree that replacement of IDS unlikely to improve matters, therefore must try to make IDS regime work. He has the policies but not the technique.

Tuesday 25 March
Meeting with IDS at 6.15 follows sandwich meeting in my room with Raymond Monbiot – new chairman of the Convention – who wants IDS out. 'If you can find a simple way of doing it, I will help.'

Wednesday 26 March
Meet Owen Paterson in my room. Stanley Kalms has now apparently turned his back on IDS. Refuses to have his name printed on Carlton Club dinner invitation for the autumn saying it will be a waste of money because IDS will no longer be leader then. OP recognises (a) almost the whole board against IDS, (b) there will probably be a challenge in May.

The IDS campaign team to win a vote of confidence is now gathering (Bill Cash, John Hayes, Bernard Jenkin, Owen Paterson). Factors in its favour are the war and better opinion polls. Re Europe, IDS has a majority in favour of his views on this highly significant issue; also there is a fear of a chaotic and incoherent leadership contest and rivalry between potential challengers. Against him is the fact that most of party now think of him as a liability. I fear we may be heading for a damaging contest.

People have written IDS off. In the tea room today hardly anyone took any notice of him when he proclaimed that his personal poll ratings were rising rapidly.

Monday 31 March
Melissa Kite in *The Times* says new intake MPs back Michael Howard for leader.

Tuesday 1 April
Meet James Cran in Jubilee Court. He is very bitter about IDS, having been sacked by him; seems to believe that IDS should be challenged at once before the end of the war and May elections. He is leaving at the next election. Talks

of 'some people … saying we must move in on IDS at once'. Bitterness is very debilitating. At one point Keith Simpson passes us; he from the left and Cran from the right seemed from their eye contact to be in some sort of touch with each other.

Wednesday 2 April

Bridge evening at Maunsel Street with Sandra and Michael Howard. MH says he has no intention of standing for the leadership but unworried about *Times* report. 'It may put David Davis off. Hope must be that none of the warlords feel they can win.'

Slightly odd encounter with Ann Widdecombe while waiting at Members' Entrance for Sandra and Michael to pick me up. I say to her, 'I'm waiting for the Howards.' She retorts, 'God help you.' I say, 'I thought you two had made it up.' She says, 'We behave like grown-ups,' and makes off to catch her taxi. Afterwards I worry she may think, in view of the press reports, that I am plotting with MH. Must put her right.

Monday 7 April

Conservative board meeting. As usual me versus the voluntary party. Raymond Monbiot suggests that representatives of the voluntary party be put in charge of 'chasing up MPs to visit other people's constituencies'. I say that would be inappropriate. 'That's my job, or the Chief Whip's.'

I propose MPs be offered more to do at party conferences. This is taken as some sort of threat by, for instance, Gordon Keymer, who says volunteers will not work for MPs. 'In that case', I say, 'there's no point in them.'

Tuesday 8 April

Summoned to chairman's office and told voluntary party upset by my attitude to them. 'They don't like the parliamentary party,' she says. I say, 'We're fed up with being kicked by them, especially when they seem to be trying to take over the management of the party.' Theresa, of course, has her own agenda with the leadership.

When I see IDS that evening I tell him again he must sort out the board and the chairmanship, knowing, however, he is too weak to do so at present. His mind is on the Budget tomorrow. Also he is minded to withdraw his engagement with the '22 next Monday. I say, 'If you want to postpone till after Easter, you must have a foolproof reason. In any event, you must appeal to your natural supporters in the parliamentary party.' I offer these two messages:

- Policy is lower taxes, tighter control over asylum seekers and anti-Europe.

- Warn them that a trail of blood will follow another leadership contest: may all lose our seats.

Bump into Tam Dalyell, Father of the House, who has just called Blair, his leader, a warmonger. He is now threatened with expulsion from the PLP. He says, 'Extraordinary how one can represent three-quarters of the party's view and still be in trouble.' 'I know,' I say, 'it happened to me at Maastricht!'

Wednesday 9 April
Budget day. All eyes on the fall of Baghdad.

At '22 Executive relate experience with board. Colleagues start to become angry. One member says the problem is the weakness of the leadership. Another member says leader will side with the volunteers (who voted for him) against the parliamentary party (who didn't). I say Barry Legg affair showed it was not quite like that: board were challenging the leader. Someone else says in that case perhaps we should ally ourselves with the leader. Take all this up with Chief Whip and IDS, both of whom Theresa May has seen about my visit to her yesterday. People are beginning to dread a bloodbath. However, IDS could be a goner if there is another cock-up.

Monday 14 April
First bad meeting of '22 for some time. Forty-eight people turn up to hear IDS at 5.30. 133 vote later on the Budget votes. Various reasons given – too short notice (it's been on the whip for two weeks), wrong time, 'he comes too often' (last time I think was before Christmas). The truth is three-quarters of the party didn't want to hear him. Gerald Howarth (chairman of 92 Group) comes to my room later. 'Michael, you may have to sort things out to avoid blood-letting.'

Where will the present crisis end? We certainly should be moving ahead of Labour by now, whereas today's poll in *The Times* shows Lib 22, Con 29, Lab 44. Two colleagues from opposite ends of the political spectrum want Howard. They think any change would be better than what we have now. I am less sure – a bloody leadership battle could be the worst outcome, certainly between now and the election. Paul Swinburn, my deputy chairman in the constituency, thinks this does not matter because the next election is written off. What matters is the one after that.

Tuesday 22 April
Warm weather in Cropthorne. Peace is going wrong in Iraq. Question should ask PM: 'What is to be done to prevent a Shia theocracy in Iraq linking with Syria and Iran to form not so much an "axis of evil" [Bush's words] as an axis

of nuclear powers?' This losing of the peace must be a further blow to IDS, who was such a supporter of Blair's war.

Sunday 27 April

The Sunday papers, e.g. Matthew d'Ancona's piece in the *Sunday Telegraph*, are full of comment that IDS is not to be challenged after all. They may be right. The Clarkeites are currently busted flushes, Clarke having been anti-war. The Portilloites remain determined to get IDS but they are too few in number.

Monday 28 April

First day back after Easter. Party still in turbulence. Two journalists (Rachel Sylvester and Michael White) say Howard–Letwin axis emerging. Forth tells me Yeo's party tomorrow is part of a leadership campaign.

Jack Straw tells Commons that trains are running for the first time for three years between Basra and Um Qasir. One wag on our benches: 'What about trains from Haywards Heath? You haven't got that sorted out yet.' Straw smiles and says he will tell Department of Transport.

If there is a challenge it looks as though it will be impossible to stop a fight – Yeo (left) v. Howard (right)?

Tuesday 29 April

Board sub-committee in CCO determined to humiliate IDS over Barry Legg. Paper produced to say they do not want a chief executive. Party at Tim Yeo's flat full of journalists. 'Is this the start of a leadership campaign?' everyone asks.

Wednesday 30 April

IDS has a bad PMQ. The PM runs circles around him. Not a good day to have a bad day. Owen Paterson thinks I may get letters from up to eighteen MPs mainly Portilloites.

Thursday 1 May

Win a debate at the Cambridge Union on Euro with John Bercow on my side; he was brilliant. In the car driving back to London, hear (a) Crispin Blunt has resigned calling for IDS to go, (b) we have done badly in Malvern at local elections – as have all councils where there is a straight fight with Liberals. However, picture is masked by a reasonable showing against Labour, who are suffering from mid-term blues. National picture: Liberals 30 per cent, Labour 30 per cent, Tories 34 per cent – enough to save IDS – but the party is not in good shape. Bercow says I am seen as too pro-IDS. He also expresses his intense dislike of Michael Howard.

Wednesday 7 May

Crispin Blunt makes his statement to the '22. Two basic points: (1) 'If you write to Michael Spicer you can do so with impunity because he kept the secret of my letter to him for six months.' (2) 'I will give up my campaign against IDS by the end of May.' I precede this by saying to the committee (about 100 present): 'I humbly advise everyone not to prolong the discussion as this will be interpreted outside as yet another squabble in the Conservative Party, which will cause consternation in the party at large.' Everyone except Peter Bottomley remains quiet. Some call it 'stunned silence'.

At the Executive main subject is forthcoming battle with the board about independence of associations.

Later advise IDS not to preach to the party at the 'awayday' due on Friday but to confide in people and to pick their brains.

Will Crispin Blunt's speech turn into some kind of turning point?

Friday 9 May

133 members of parliamentary party take off to Latimer House hotel in Buckinghamshire to 'bond'. Sit next to IDS over dinner; he is in good form following good local election results against Labour (if not Liberals). IDS points out that he has the best-looking press secretary – at least he is human. Prior to all the good humour over dinner, I have a tiff with Theresa May over restructuring of the party. I warn her publicly of major rows ahead if board attacks associations' autonomy. She implies I am wrong and premature to raise the issue.

Monday 12 May

Another awayday, this time for the board, another pretentious (and expensive – £175 per night) hotel, this time Eynsham Hall, in Oxfordshire. Frightful row between me and rest of board. This follows presentation of paper stripping associations of all real powers – money, membership and agents etc. I vehemently oppose this; the argument spills over into dinner with IDS.

Tuesday 13 May

All this spills out into Spy column of the *Telegraph* – probably from MPs' discussion as opposed to board meeting.

Wednesday 14 May

'22 Executive discusses issue of association autonomy. I have to be careful not to be too specific about board's position. This slightly irritates several members of the Executive.

Meeting afterwards with IDS. I explain the position and say I will have to ask him to give us a steer of his views at breakfast next Tuesday (he was hoping to sit on the fence and watch the fun – it can't be quite like that, I say).

Friday 16 May

Simon Walters of the *Mail on Sunday* has the whole story of the row. Sad, because I will not now be able to trust '22 Executive. Tell Owen Paterson to warn IDS. 'They even know about the breakfast.'

Monday 19 May

Eric Forth comes to see me about leaked story in *Mail on Sunday*'s Black Dog column re 'power-crazed' Theresa May taking over constituency associations. Forth says, 'If she is allowed to succeed I will not only resign from shadow Cabinet but will write you a letter calling for IDS to resign as he is in charge – or meant to be.'

Tuesday 20 May

Breakfast with IDS and '22 Executive. We are unanimous that the constituency associations must be strengthened and reformed rather than stripped of their powers. IDS sits and listens. Says we must see May; he has limited powers with the board – has no vote on it. Clearly he is enjoying watching the Executive shape up to the board.

Later that morning Crispin Blunt comes to see me. 'Have I received any more letters calling for vote of confidence in IDS?' I say I cannot tell him (I haven't) but 'people in our business tend to work in gangs more openly than is the received view, so you can work it out for yourself' – all said very politely. He says, 'I will probably write a letter to colleagues saying I will back off.' (He does: 'In view of the lack of support I have received I will henceforth be playing my part from the outfield rather than the slips.')

Tuesday 3 June

2 p.m. '22 Executive meets Theresa May to make it clear to her that we will defend constituency autonomy. Agree to meet again when board is more certain about its intentions on 23 June. Also we will prepare our own plan.

5 p.m. Liam Fox reveals radical plan for reform of health service to a small policy group meeting. I say, 'First understandably Conservative policy for years, but needs to be squared with low-tax policy.'

6 p.m. Meeting with IDS. He is in a perky mood. While I am there he receives a letter from Blair in response to his demanding an immediate statement on intelligence reporting leading to war with Iraq. Blair's letter in effect says wait for my statement tomorrow. IDS has a *petit problème* – since he backed war with Iraq he cannot now rubbish it. We agree on policy; this should be limited – health, pensions, tax, schools – and, he says (in my view more questionably), abolition of university fees, which at best is a detailed policy rather than part of a theme.

Monday 9 June
Gordon Brown's non-statement on the Euro. Michael Howard gives him a good drubbing. I ask a question about the 'correct' exchange rate: what is it? Brown accuses me of asking detailed questions when I'm opposed in principle.

Monday 16 June
Another frightful board meeting. This time I am outnumbered on the issue of primary elections for candidates, which parliamentary party are dead against.

Tuesday 17 June
Polls in *The Times* much better. We're only four points behind Labour and the Liberals are nowhere.

Stanley Kalms resigns as treasurer. All very sudden given his general demeanour at his party last night. Kalms is a prima donna without being mega-rich, so his departure can probably be quickly absorbed.

IDS in good form when we have our fortnightly meeting. Likes the idea of '22 Committee doing battle with the board over autonomy of constituencies. Says May takes the view that '22 Executive out of touch with the party. We shall see in two weeks' time when she comes to the full committee and faces the wrath, for instance, of Douglas Hogg.

Wednesday 18 June
Poor performance by IDS against PM. (He goes on for too long provoking the Labour Party and giving Blair the chance to ridicule him – he really doesn't have a natural feel for the House.) Provokes renewed grumbles on the back benches from all parts of the spectrum.

Tetchy meeting of '22 Executive, ostensibly directed against CCO and Theresa May, whom we are seeing next Monday. Still feel there will be no outright revolt against IDS if trend in the polls is maintained.

Monday 23 June
'22 Executive meets Theresa May and gives her a bad time in defence of constituency autonomy. According to Owen Paterson, the whips are blaming me for creating trouble about this in the party.

Wednesday 25 June
Owen Paterson comes up to my offices to discuss our membership of the EPP. Dan Hannan thinks the IDS team are bungling/ratting on their commitment to come out and form a new anti-federalist alliance. Owen denies this.

Thursday 26 June
Frank Field (Labour) and John Burnett (Lib Dem) come to see me to say anti-Euro-convention cause is lost if IDS leads it.

Sunday 29 June
Bruce Anderson in *Sunday Telegraph* says IDS must go.

Monday 30 June
Dinner with Patrick Cormack (anti IDS), says cannot afford the row of getting rid of him. In the lobby Douglas Hogg flies at Theresa May, IDS, me and David Maclean (Chief Whip), re primary election for candidates. Is told by all of us that the board, which is all-powerful in this, has sold the pass. He demands a resolution of '22 Committee deploring the fact that the parliamentary party was not consulted; then he says will not be there for next three weeks because he has a murder case in Leeds!

Wednesday 2 July
Theresa May given a cool reception at '22. A dozen questions, mostly hostile; she seems surprised by this.

Monday 14 July
Final meeting with IDS before the summer break. Polls show us narrowing the gap with Labour but Liberals coming up on the outside. I say it will all hang on the economy. IDS says Howard Flight is pessimistic about the economy. I say, 'I know he has been for some time.' 'What do you think,

Michael?' 'None of us really knows, but sadly for us the stock market is improving, as, importantly, is the American economy.' IDS looks wistful.

Wednesday 16 July
IDS addresses an almost empty '22 Committee (forty people). No questions. Dead silence. Sad and amazing. Where will this lead? Later that evening Robert Key says the whole event a disaster.

Friday 18 July
Blair looks ghastly on TV after death (suicide) of the former UN weapons inspector David Kelly. For the first time can imagine him resigning.

Monday 21 July
Last board meeting of the summer. Parliament has already disbanded. Everyone very conciliatory. I present '22 paper defending constituency autonomy. No one remonstrates. I think we have won and a great row has been averted.

Tuesday 4 August
Polls confirm downward trend in Labour and improved position of Liberals. The parliamentary party will not like this. IDS could be in trouble again.

Meanwhile we are basking in one of the hottest summers ever. The current issue, which will affect the government's popularity and may undermine IDS's, is whether there was any point to the Iraqi war. The impression one has is that the powers that be know they will find evidence of WMD. This will be good for Blair, quite good for IDS (he will survive as leader) and bad for Charles Kennedy (took an anti-war position). The reverse will be the case if no WMD are found.

Monday 8 September 2003
Ann Widdecombe says IDS is hopeless and she plans to raise her view that he must do better at '22.

Wednesday 10 September
Meet IDS, who is bullish. Agrees must tidy up our policies, e.g. tax. I tell him he must take firmer grip of CCO. He says he will attend next week's board.

Tuesday 16 September
Gordon Keymer rings me at office. 'Things can't go on like this,' he says. I say I will have to look at options of cutting £1 million and £2 million. Tell this to

Raymond Monbiot, who puts it in writing to the chairman as my view that we should cut everything at CCO except propaganda and work financed by Short money, i.e. by the state.

Friday 19 September 2003
We have been knocked into third place at Brent East by-election, which Lib Dems won.

Monday 22 September
Finance committee, 11 a.m., CCO. Raymond Monbiot, George Magan (new treasurer), me, Stephen Gilbert. Everyone very nervous following disaster at Brent East. Agreement that we will look at implications of taking several millions out of budget.

Friday 26 September
IDS has apparently called for Blair's resignation but no mention of this in the press – extraordinary. It really does look as if they want to ignore IDS whatever he does.

Monday 29 September
Owen Paterson rings to say that *Independent on Sunday* has run a story saying that IDS due to appear on a platform at the Congress for Democracy with Pia Kjærsgaard (leader of Danish People's Party), who has been reported as making some racist remark. I tell OP I will pull her, which I do by ringing her office. Pia is out but I speak to her sidekick. They have seen *IoS* report; happy for her not to come to the Congress on 7 November as long as it's her initiative not to do so. I say 'No problem' and the deal is done.

Sunday 5 October
Arrive at dreary old Blackpool – why we still come here I cannot imagine. Howling gale. 2–3-minute talk with IDS, who is surprisingly bullish and bouncy given the appalling press he has been getting. I question him on his giveaway policy on pensions – how does this square with our intention to cut taxes? 'It's part of a package which saves money' (e.g. cutting out welfare-to-work programme). Later he speaks well at the agents' dinner – showing passion and for once stopping at the right moment. Unlike last year, he is introduced properly.

Monday 6 October
Mood growing to get round Michael Howard. I tell Cathy Newman (*FT*)

at dinner and Edward Garnier afterwards that MH will never challenge IDS. One informed colleague says the left would do a deal with the right for Michael Howard.

Howling gale throughout the day. Could hardly stand in front of the hotel.

Tuesday 7 October
Outbreak of rumours that a large number of MPs have written me 'IDS must resign' letters (they haven't – yet). BBC news (Andrew Marr) full of it. Fifteen messages from press for me to ring back when I get back to my room at 5.30. I don't. I do ring Owen Paterson, to say I make no comments on the letters to anyone ever. They are meant to be written in confidence to me. Leader's office, i.e. Nick Wood, not too happy about this.

At conference David Davis makes a clear pitch for the leadership – hardly talking about his subject (local government) at all.

Wednesday 8 October
No let-up in IDS crisis. All national papers have rumours about my having received at least twelve names in writing. Everyone from Chief Whip downwards tries to find the true position. 'Doorstepped' by BBC TV as I come off conference stage from chairing plenary policy session. All get same answer: 'I never comment on this issue to anyone.' *Press Association* ask, 'Does that mean there is no point in ringing you up?' I say, 'Yes.' David Maclean says, 'There is a rumour going round that you are taking legal advice and things are getting serious.' I say, 'Bollocks.' (I have still received no letters.)

Much of drama played out on TV. IDS getting more tetchy and caricatured. Andrew Marr asks him, 'What will you do if Michael Spicer gives you twenty-five names?' 'Tell him to put them in a phone box.' Not very clever. Looks as if he wants to ignore constitution of the party again. Nervously pats me on the back when I pass him at Imperial Hotel. John Maples caught in the camera and asked, 'Are you plotting?' Says, 'No.' He probably is, as is Francis Maude.

Raymond Monbiot accosts me behind stage as I prepare to chair the policy discussion in main auditorium. Repeats what he said several months ago – if there were one candidate from MPs, he would help to ensure his smooth adoption. RM hates IDS, as is proved by the fact that he has talked to Peter Oborne for this week's *Spectator* about IDS's 'promise' of 5 per cent rise in the polls after party conference.

Thursday 9 October
Funny old day. IDS makes a speech at Blackpool which prompts twenty

or so standing ovations. But on telly it looks contrived and unreal. If he is pushed out he will be remembered for what he did to develop party's policy on tax, health (choice), pensions, education and Europe. He has gone way beyond his predecessors on this. Chief Whip on the warpath to out the five or six MPs who destabilised the conference. He goes on 10 o'clock BBC news to tell rebels, 'If you want to give your names to Michael Spicer, do so now or shut up.' Presumably he feels this is the moment to smoke them out.

Strange encounter with Vanessa Gearson* in the bus coming back from the conference hall to collect car from Imperial Hotel. She sits glumly, only speaking to answer my question about what her job is these days: 'Liaising between leader and CCO.' Strange she makes no comment on leader's speech. (I saw him hugging her earlier in the week.) She once (two years ago) reported me to the Chief Whip for 'disloyalty' in a speech I made in her would-be constituency of Cheltenham. (I had said there were some problems and here's how we would deal with them.)

Friday 10 October
Mixed press for IDS. *Times* and *Sun* (Murdoch) hostile; *Telegraph* and *Mail* praise him. Rebels have probably been frightened off, in which case the grumbles will probably go on till Christmas.

I am sure I will be under increasing pressure from the whips to say what is going on. There are several reasons for keeping quiet – the main one being that the rules say 'shall be given in confidence'; a public running total would be very destabilising and would possibly have its own momentum.

Gloucester Echo ring to ask why I am heading the rebellion – following Chief Whip's advice to write to Spicer or shut up! *GE* comes back to me to apologise for getting it wrong and to ask me how many names I have. I say if I told them that, having fended off the entire national press on the subject, they would have a world scoop.

Saturday 11 October
First item on the news: David Maclean to write a warning letter to 'guilty' men and to copy letter to their chairmen. Otherwise a quiet day in the press

---

*   Former chief of staff to IDS and deputy director of the Conservative Party. An email from her querying payments made to Betsy Duncan Smith prompted the 'Betsygate' investigation by the Parliamentary Commissioner for Standards, who exonerated Iain Duncan Smith of any improper claims of office costs allowance.

and beautiful cloudless day in Cropthorne. What a contrast in every sense with the stress in Blackpool. Is this the lull before the storm?

Towards the vote of confidence

Sunday 12 October 2003
Phone calls from three members of the '22 Executive – all wanting to find a painless solution to IDS issue without getting blood on their hands. I say, 'There isn't one.'

Mail on Sunday has a little diary piece headed 'Spicer is no whipping boy' about a discussion I had with David Maclean in the Winter Gardens at Blackpool when he said there was a rumour that I had taken legal advice on the leadership issue – to which I said 'Bollocks'. The only other person around at the time was Eric Forth, who has his own agenda on behalf of David Davis. (The *MoS* story says that Maclean had asked me to give him the number of letters so far – he didn't – and that I said, 'Don't even think about it, David' – I didn't.)

Monday 13 October
Tough board meeting. I advise to budget for a deficit and to underwrite the debt. Great sigh of relief around the table.

Tuesday 14 October
Parliamentary Standards Commissioner announces he will investigate IDS payments to his wife Betsy.

Tom sends me a letter. His secretary comes furtively into the office and nervously places it on Jessica's desk. All is very frenetic but no real substance yet to the rebellion. Journalists say rebels are holding back until case against IDS resolved.

Eric Forth also confirms that there was no way that David Davis would back off for Michael Howard. There would be a bloody battle and that is that. In any event, he thinks a proper contest would be a good thing for the party.

Wednesday 15 October
Great disquiet at '22 Executive. Those against IDS (ten members) try to get the committee to write him a letter telling him to go or hold a vote of confidence. For him: seven members. I say we will have to play it by the rules.

DICK has sent me a letter. This makes three. Jessica and I agree to use a simple code both when speaking in the office and on the phone – in case of bugging – about the letters, which we now call 'constituents' letters'.

One shadow minister says he would write me a letter if he were not on the front bench. I say that is of no interest to me; I cannot 'work with background noise', only to the rules – which require secrecy for names who write to me.

At '22 Committee I say, 'The management of our business today is for the committee. All I say is that the entire press lobby is camped outside our door' (it was) 'and that therefore there is a low probability of anything we say remaining secret. Any other business?' 'No.' 'The meeting is closed.' Cheers. Very irritated press. I say afterwards, 'The 1922 Committee has lived up to its reputation of never discussing anything interesting.'

Friday 17 October
Daily Telegraph carries a leak from Wednesday's '22 Executive that the majority of the committee wanted to write to IDS telling him to hold a vote of confidence. I am accurately reported as wanting to stick to the rules. Owen Paterson rings me on my mobile at the Japanese self-service restaurant at Paddington. He asks, 'Is the story true?' I say, 'All I can say is I don't like leaks.' He is upbeat about report in *Times* about Tory association chairmen backing IDS. They always do back any leader. It's the MPs he needs to watch. I am beginning to feel he is a goner but only four letters so far: Crispin Blunt (went public himself), Tom, Dick and Harry.

Evening meeting at Cropthorne with my officers. Dreary talk about the state of the party and IDS.

Saturday 18 October
Patrick Cormack breaks cover on radio saying IDS must stand for vote of confidence. Edward Garnier on the news says, 'He won't.' Nicholas Soames rings to ask what is going on. I say someone has leaked. He says, 'Bloody fool.'

Sunday 19 October
Sunday press full of IDS's troubles with his office. *Times* and *Telegraph* have two-page spreads. How long can he (we) go on like this?

Tuesday 21 October
Matthew's letter makes five.

The party in the country seems to be sticking with IDS and no sign yet at my end of a major revolt. Matthew Parris in yesterday's *Times* says the moment for successful revolt may be passing. IDS may gain from (a) increased recognition,

(b) sympathy, (c) admiration for his toughness. But MPs may simply be wait-ing for the outcome of Betsygate (some hoping it will topple him); some may also come to the view that things will never settle down under him.

Meanwhile Liberals are falling away in the polls and we are level pegging with Labour. One thing seems certain: any idea that IDS will be persuaded to go is for the birds.

That evening we have a dinner party at Maunsel Street. Michael and Susie Ashcroft, Colin and Janet Marshall, Anthony and Caroline Steen. Ashcroft says IDS was a mistake but the only way forward now is to back him and build him up and unite behind him. Steen says he is an electoral disaster, will never be anything else. While he is there, there will always be a void at the top. Anyone would be better.

Wednesday 22 October
Day begins with Stuart Wheeler on *Today* programme saying IDS must go. (Wheeler gave £5 million to the party at the last election). Large piece in *The Times* (plus cartoon about me) and my ability to keep a secret – which they say is a good reason to write to me. The paper's Philip Webster says I am playing a 'blinder'. On the way up the stairs to my office, IDS's second PPS, Alistair Burt, tries to get the picture from me. I say it would not be in IDS's interest for me to give a running commentary.

MARK rings to say he wants to send a letter in strict confidence. It is arranged for Jessica to meet him at 10 a.m. at the ticket barrier at Westminster Underground station. When he arrives he is very nervous; hands her the letter, enclosed in a magazine.

Patrick McLoughlin (deputy Chief Whip) comes to see me in my office. 'You probably won't agree to this, Michael, but we desperately need to know what is going on.' I say, 'I can't help, (a) because the constitution says the letters I get are given in confidence and (b) because I could be legally challenged if I take sides.' He says David Maclean has advised IDS to go (later denied in public) and IDS very nearly did but later changed his mind and decided to wait for the twenty-nine letters. I say, 'I will intervene if this all drags on beyond Christmas; they must put up or back him.' Patrick says, reasonably, 'We simply can't wait till then. By the way, we know that MATTHEW and LUKE have been to your office with letters.' They have and I am surprised he knows. I don't blink an eyelid but when he is gone walk out onto the staircase to find Jonathan Hellewell from IDS's office sitting in an open room facing the stairs and reading a book. He grins sheepishly at me. I say, 'You must be getting pretty bored, Jon.' He says, 'Yes.' I ring MATTHEW and LUKE to tell them what has happened. The letter tally is now nine.

At '22 Executive another attempt is made to get me to lead a posse to IDS to tell him 'on behalf of '22 to go'. As per last week I resist this as being unconstitutional and prejudicial to my neutral position. The noisiest anti-IDS people still haven't written to me.

Another silent but full main '22 Committee, though I give them plenty of opportunity to speak. Peter Tapsell complains about the crush of press outside our doors.

I leave to go to see Annabel and Harry, born twenty minutes earlier at High Wycombe Hospital.

Thursday 23 October

Day begins (and ends) with Derek Conway attacking IDS. (He hasn't written to me yet). PAUL rings to say he will be bringing round a letter. GEORGE writes. RINGO also brings round a letter. JACK arranges to meet Jessica in central lobby and, speaking out of the side of his mouth, tells her to walk with him towards St Stephen's Entrance; he peels off into Westminster Hall.

Gillian Shephard bumps into me in Victoria Street when I am coming back from lunch with Edward in Japanese restaurant in Strutton Ground. She says she has been in the tea room, where there was an eerie silence at the Tory tables. 'I wish to goodness the loudmouths would either shut up or write you a letter.'

By the evening we have fifteen – all individuals. Still no apparent concerted operation, though Joe Murphy in the *Evening Standard* says that is coming on Monday.

Ann Widdecombe asks, 'How on earth did we get here when things had looked so rosy in the early summer?'

Sun carries a piece about journalists being confused when I came out of '22 brandishing a paper, to discover it was a note about Annabel's baby.

Friday 24 October

Ben Brogan in the *Telegraph* full of anonymous people saying my mailbag will be full of names on Monday.

Chief Whip rings me to ask: in the event that I get twenty-nine names – and I say there is no certainty about that – how will I get hold of the leader? He advises going through Tim Montgomerie – IDS's political secretary – who is presumably a trusty of his. I ring Owen Paterson about this. 'Could I have a number for IDS in case press reports that I will get an avalanche of names on Monday are true?' He says he will see what he can do but does not give me a number – suggests going through him, which I say may not be what I want to do.

Saturday 25 October

Ring Archie Hamilton to check exact status of the rules: how they came about. Archie says '22 voted on them in the last parliament; agrees to send me the appropriate record/minutes.

Constituency meetings in Upton (yesterday), Berrow & Pendock (today) confirm the view that members want us to sort the matter out one way or another quickly.

Sunday 26 October

John Greenway latest non-letter-writer to say publicly in *Sunday Times* that there should be a vote of confidence. Owen Paterson rings to say IDS does not want to give me a direct telephone number. I think I have one in the office anyway.

Derek Conway waves his letter to me on the 10 p.m. news. He says, 'It will all be over in forty-eight hours.'

At some point I may have to say, 'This can't go on forever.'

Monday 27 October

Jim Naughtie on *Today* says I will give IDS a 'civilised' chance to resign. The only person I have discussed this with is the Chief Whip.

Owen Paterson in my office for no particular reason. I like him and tell him I admire his cheerfulness.

BBC TV 'doorstep' outside Maunsel Street. During the day letters rise to twenty-three. BILL BREWER, JAN STEWER, Derek Conway, JILL, PETER GURNEY, PETER DAVY, DANIEL WHIDDON. (Jessica meets JILL in ladies' loo outside cafeteria).

Michael Fabricant rings to ask whether confidential really does mean confidential! 'Yes, at our end.'

Anthony Steen on the phone (twice). 'Why won't IDS see a delegation?' I say, 'Why don't you ask him?'

Surreally, Malcolm Pearson arrives at Maunsel Street with the head of the stag I shot two years ago!

HARRY HAWKE comes up in the lobby – his letter on the way makes twenty-four.

IDS comes up to me in the chamber. 'Am I allowed to speak to you?' he asks, smiling. 'Of course,' I say, also smiling. 'I talk to anyone who is willing to chat to me. I just have a problem about one subject.'

Newsnight's Martha Kearney says it's all gone off the boil! What an extraordinary position I am in. Ann Widdecombe says, 'You have amazingly kept everyone equally frustrated.' 'That's why I'm Michael No-Mates,' I say.

Bump into Tim Montgomerie outside leader's room. I say, 'Can we have a word?' We go into shadow Cabinet room. I say, 'If I ring you to say I have the names, you must only tell IDS – and not, for instance, the Chief Whip – do I have your word on this?' He looks shifty and nods. Maclean is up to something.

To avoid prying eyes of the press watching me as I collect my mail from letter board in members' lobby, arrange for a messenger to meet me with five letters in central lobby. Furtively take letters from him – none of them to do with leadership contest!

Relief that we will not go to twenty-nine tonight. Better a new day tomorrow.

Tuesday 28 October
Leave Maunsel Street with Ann in her tennis kit hotly pursued by BBC TV crew. ERG breakfast then up to the office where Jessica has the necessary five votes. Alert Owen Paterson. IDS comes up to my room at 10.30. Very impressed by his courage. Tell him Jessica has been in tears; he shows real concern.

Decide not to release the news of an election till 2 p.m. to give IDS chance to get his team together.

Chief Whip comes in at 12.30. Agree to arrange vote of confidence the next day.

1.45: Bill Cash arrives with brief from learned counsel saying vote of confidence rules *ultra vires*. I hold up proceedings when IDS bursts in and says, 'I want to get on with it.' I agree.

Outside CCO at 2.20 IDS says, 'I welcome this vote of confidence. I always said I wanted the boil of dissent lanced.' He gains in stature by the minute. More meetings with Chief Whip.

3.00: Meet '22 Executive in my room.

Dinner party at Maunsel Street: Roe, Irwin Stelzer and Dan Hannan. Three issues which we have to decide next day are:
- When to hold ballot if IDS loses.
- Do we give the figures for the vote?
- What happens to spoilt papers?

Wednesday 29 October
Last day of TV doorstepping.

Meet '22 Executive in my room. Decide after some discussion, which I lead, we will publish numbers of vote of confidence and will leave close of nominations till Thursday 6 November if IDS loses. Both points I had suggested.

IDS makes best speech of his life to the '22 but too late. 75-90 when vote taken. I make announcement in Room 14.

Meet Theresa May at CCO to discuss what to do next. Michael Howard seems to have the field to himself. A Liberal MP comes up to me in the lobby saying, 'Those letters you have must be worth a few bob.'

David Maclean tells me he is retiring as Chief Whip. Patrick McLoughlin will take over temporarily.

Thank Phil Webster for his comment about me, which seems to be entering political mythology – 'playing a blinder'.

Thursday 30 October
Denis Thatcher's memorial service. Beautiful music in the Guards Chapel. Margaret in tears as she walks down the aisle with her grandson. Afterwards at marquee reception in Wellington Barracks. Michael and Sandra Howard move about like the unanointed King and Queen. (He declares later in the afternoon.) David Davis, who has surrendered unconditionally to Howard, looks like a PoW (all the stuffing out of him).

Friday 31 October
Patrons' do. Everyone delighted that it looks as if there may not be a leadership battle.

Saturday 1 November 2003
Talk to Michael Howard on the phone. He wants to abolish CCO and 'take on the board'. 'Money will be no problem – we will borrow more if necessary.' 'What about the liability of board members?' 'Tough; they shouldn't do the job if they are worried about that.'

Monday 3 November
Anthony Steen explains to me that he has been pulling the strings on 'anti-IDS groups' 'behind the scenes'.

John Bercow comes up to me at Queen's in the morning when I am captaining Lords and Commons tennis team. 'Are you sure the names will never come out?' 'Not from me – or I will be before a judge.'

Tuesday 4 November
Visit MEPs in Brussels with '22 Executive. Chew over with them the issue of whether they should leave EPP, on which they are bitterly divided. Jessica

rings to say Theresa May seeking board's advice on some relatively minor changes at CCO. Also says we have received another five letters late in post (mail strike)!

On return journey on Eurostar, Cormack, Roe, Nick Winterton, Garnier and I try to work out best way of announcing Howard's leadership if it comes to that. Decide to make it as instant as possible.

Dinner at Mosimann's with Henry Angest, Pearson, Ann et al. Angest makes the same point as I made to Michael Howard: If we sell CCO we will have lost our asset base for borrowing. ('I say this as a banker.')

Wednesday 5 November
Michael Howard rings to discuss how we will present him tomorrow when I announce him as leader. He says he would rather not be there if it is to be a small attendance (with light whipping). During the day whips work out that we will get 80–90, so we will go ahead. No signs of any challengers.

IDS insists on coming to Congress.*

Talk to Rachel Whetstone for first time in six years. Michael Howard off to do touchy-feely stuff in the East End after I announce him tomorrow. Here we go again. Blimey O'Reilly.

---

* On Friday 7 November, Iain Duncan Smith was guest speaker at the Congress for Democracy's Rally for a Referendum at Church House, Westminster.

Chapter 21

Michael Howard

Thursday 6 November 2003

Day of decision for the leadership succession. A bit of nail-biting in the office at around noon waiting to see if there are more nominations. Alan Duncan arrives with a nomination from Michael Ancram, which is to become operational if there is a genuine second nomination. There isn't. Down to Committee Room 14 (about 100 in the room), which I enter to the sound of loud desk-banging. (Michael Howard had taken his place in the body of the kirk just before me.) I say, 'Thank you.' Lots of laughter and then dead silence. I say, 'Keep on chatting; there are four minutes still to go' (before we go live on radio and, for the first time, on TV, for which Speaker has given exceptional permission for my head and shoulders to be shown just doing the announcement that 'Michael Howard has been elected leader of the Conservative Party and of Her Majesty's Opposition').

Afterwards interviewed on BBC *PM* and speak in a rather relaxed way at a well-attended meeting in Windsor.

Monday 10 November

Strange pall hangs over party as Michael Howard announces his cut of the shadow Cabinet by a half. Duncan Smithites especially unhappy. Owen Paterson says that David Maclean, now mysteriously back as Chief Whip, was part of the 'plot'.

Drinks at Buckingham Palace, where the Royal Family has had a tough week too.* Howard Flight, a former Michael Howard loyalist, says the new Cabinet structure is 'mad'; he, surprisingly, has lost his place. Christabel Flight looks rather glum. Nicholas Soames happy as shadow Minister of Defence.

The one problem I have is that Bill Cash and his friends, now on the outside, believe there is a legal problem with the rules by which IDS was deposed.

Howard's Day of Long Knives

I am deeply worried. For the first time since John Major the Eurosceptics

---

* The courts had that week issued injunctions preventing newspapers from publishing allegations made by former Royal servants.

feel themselves on the outside and they are (visibly) networking fast. People I meet during the day who have become disaffected include Tapsell, Chope, Flight, Shepherd, Paterson, Hayes. To their number should be added Teddy Taylor, Jenkin, Whittingdale, Heathcoat-Amory, Forth, IDS himself and, above all, Cash. Cash is the most effective because he is the most uncompromising and persistent – proactive and knows where the legal bodies are buried. I must see him asap, as well as Howard himself – though I have no idea what is to be done. The shadow Cabinet is up and running. May, Yeo, Curry – no sceptics. The thing about the Eurosceptics is that they relate to a large chunk of the party who will feel deprived of involvement this time. MH should have bent over backwards to appease them: he hasn't. The people he should be especially wary of are those who feel kicked out by a coup.

To raise all this would simply annoy MH and would not achieve much. The possibility of a legal challenge is another matter.

November 10: From *The Times*
'Sometimes, you have to lose a job to find a voice' by William Rees-Mogg

On Friday morning, Gillian and I went to Church House, Westminster, to attend the Congress for Democracy's rally for a referendum; the MPs Sir Michael Spicer and Austin Mitchell were sharing the chair. We went – and this should be treated as a declaration of an interest – to listen to Annunziata Rees-Mogg, our youngest daughter, who was speaking as chairman of Trust the People; that is, in effect, the youth wing of the referendum movement. I am not impartial, but notoriously a proud papa, second in this role only to Gordon Brown. I thought her speech was brilliant – which it was.

She followed a speech by Iain Duncan Smith. This was the day after he had left the Tory leadership – he had originally accepted the invitation to speak as the Leader of the Opposition. Leaders who are freed from office often speak better because they are no longer chained by their responsibilities. That notably happened in the cases of Harold Macmillan, Ted Heath and John Major.

The same thing happened on Friday with Mr Duncan Smith. He has not suddenly become a gifted orator, like William Hague or Michael Howard, but he spoke from the heart, without any of the Blackpool artifice, and was rewarded with two non-artificial standing ovations. It was a very good speech.

… However, there is some unease even among the Tory Eurosceptics. They greatly value Michael Howard's experience and ability. They want the party to be united. But they do not want the party to be united at their expense, let alone at the expense of their European policy. They know that Europhiles, who had never wanted Mr Duncan Smith, helped to vote him out. They know that his Eurosceptic majority in the constituencies was overturned, with the help of the old pro-Maastricht brigade. They feel bruised.

…There is disquiet about a possible weakening of European policy in the electorate and in the Tory party itself. Yet, so long as Iain Duncan Smith continues to give the Tory policy on Europe his seal of approval, Eurosceptics are likely to accept that as valid.

Tuesday 11 November

Fulsome endorsement of Michael Howard by Heseltine on *Today*; congratulates Howard for all-embracing shadow Cabinet – what he means is pro-Europe.

Michael Howard leaves a message on my office voicemail asking me to ring him. Wants to see me in the Chief Whip's office, which he is occupying temporarily till he takes over a suite in Norman Shaw South. How he will cope so far away from the House I can't think. He wants my agreement to sell CCO – which I am reluctant to give. 'Can I have time to think about it?' I tell him about the rules problem. He says, 'Sit tight and wait to see if anything happens.'

MH relaxed but purposeful and decisive chairing his first board meeting (so different from IDS). We sack Paul Baverstock and Nick Wood (sad) and Vanessa Gearson. Walk back to Commons with Gillian Shephard. We are interrupted from discussing the reshuffle when MH's car goes by and Liam Fox gets out to walk with us.

Later MH admits that a lot of decisions he has taken in last two days were out of a desire to have excitement, momentum and change. I say, 'It's a gamble.' He agrees. I'm beginning to think he may be right; it's what Blair did in the early days of New Labour.

Bump into Jack Straw, Foreign Secretary, whom I like. 'You must be relieved,' he says. 'Back from being a parish clerk to being a normal obscure politician,' say I. 'You do yourself an injustice,' he says.

Wednesday 12 November

To Pratt's for a committee meeting. Georgina, the excellent manageress, says, 'You were wonderful,' as does the Duke of Devonshire. Tom Strathclyde says, 'You fixed it, didn't you?' Bizarre – it won't last.

At '22 Executive indecisive discussion about the need to change constitution to amend leadership rules. I am for caution (I don't want to raise *vires* point about the last leadership battle). Three colleagues gung-ho to take on the voluntary side. Three urge caution. (Raymond Monbiot, chairman of Convention, also does not want to discuss this before an election.)

View gaining ground that there was a whips' plot to get rid of IDS. It may explain why David Maclean resigned and then came back to the fold and why senior posts in whips' office have remained intact.

Thursday 13 November
Good meeting with Maurice Saatchi in CCO. Talk later to Bill Cash, who says he will make big trouble if Howard comes off the European policy laid down by IDS. I believe him. Gerald Howarth says that there are growing concerns on the right about direction Howard may take us. John Whittingdale (demoted from shadow Cabinet) especially restless.

Hugh Robertson (a whip) accosts Jessica in the lift to ask about 'the letters'. Where were they kept? Jessica says, 'Only Michael knows.'

Monday 17 November
Meet MH in the shadow Cabinet room – Alistair Burt also there. I say, 'IDS had to worry about the left; you have to worry about the right, who can be far more dangerous because they hang around, unlike the left, who simply go off and sulk.' MH thanks me and says we must meet more often and less formally.

Gerald Howarth comes up to me and says he is thinking of handing over 92 chairmanship to Eric Forth. I say that would mean 92 Group would start living dangerously.

The tension between left and right remains real because of Europe.

The leadership rules

Tuesday 18 November 2003
Patrick McLoughlin (deputy Chief Whip) comes to my room. My reputation has apparently 'gone through the stratosphere'. He tells me that he voted for MH last time. I had forgotten this. Main purpose of his visit to pressure me to speed up change of leadership rules to give greater power to parliamentary party – perhaps through an electoral college where we have 75 per cent of vote. 'Now is the time to strike while your reputation is high and party in the country wants it. You should chair a committee to look at this.' Richard Ottaway makes the same point in the lobby – as does Douglas Hogg (interestingly all on the left of the party).

Wednesday 19 November
Excitement moves to the chamber where government under pressure on foundation hospitals (wins by seventeen votes) and jury system. 11.30 p.m.

in the smoking room MH comes in in white tie from dinner at Palace with Bush. Loud cheers all round. This really is like old times, or perhaps new times.

Monday 24 November

Board meeting at CCO. Talk to Raymond Monbiot afterwards about leadership rules. Agree process needs to be speeded up and MPs need to have final say. I go along with his idea: (1) MPs elect, (2) all those with 15 per cent+ go to Convention, (3) Convention ranks and gives list back to MPs, who (4) do the final vote. Will put this to '22.

Later talk to Michael Ashcroft about his offer to spend several millions direct in constituencies of his own choice without reference to CCO. Party has turned it down but Ashcroft won't back off. I think we should let things cool off and return to the issue after Christmas.

Tuesday 25 November

Dinner at Mosimann's with Henry Angest, who has just become one of the party's bankers. Angest is well pleased with the change from IDS to Howard.

Monday 1 December

Back from an idyllic long weekend in Vienna, where visited Rosen Villa* for first time in fifty-five years! Gerald Howarth rings to ask me to 'look after' Margaret Thatcher at tomorrow's 92 Group dinner. He is handing over chairmanship to Forth – unlike in IDS's time, he does not feel he can be in the shadow government and chairman of 92. He says this is the first time since 1975 that we have had a leader who is not a member of 92.

Tuesday 2 December

No one at 92 opposes me for chairmanship of '22. Cheered when Marion Roe announces this at 92 dinner at St Stephen's Club. Sit next to Margaret Thatcher. Where once she would put you down, now she listens and nods and repeats herself. I tell her she was the greatest peacetime PM of the twentieth century. She says like a kindly old aunt, 'It's very kind of you to say so.' Gerald Howarth, the chairman, tells her Denis's memorial service marked the rebirth of the Conservative Party.

Later pick up my coat from Howard Flight's house. He is shadow Chief Secretary. Discuss tax cut policy. I say the reason why it's so important

---

* Where we lived when my father was second in command of British occupation troops after the war.

is that Labour is putting taxes up. But incomes are also going up with a strong economy.

Wednesday 3 December

Meeting with Chief Whip and deputy, and vice-chairmen (freshly elected) Marion Roe and Nick Winterton. Discuss leadership rules. Agree Monbiot proposition too good to refuse despite Michael Howard's objection. Tell his PPS (Alistair Burt) will need to put the issue to the new '22 Executive. Hope MH won't dig in against the Monbiot plan.

Monday 8 December

Party for treasurers in CCO. Michael Howard good but looking tired; must take a good break at Christmas. Henry Angest concerned we should not blow proceeds of sale of CCO. He asks what about renting it out? Brief talk with MH. He asks, 'Do I have the power to stop change in leadership rules?'

Wednesday 10 December

2.00: Meet Michael Howard. He is still firmly against moves 'until after GE' to change leadership rules. To do so would be 'a distraction'. Ominously he has talked to Monbiot about this. (As it turns out, so had the joint chairman Liam Fox, who had spoken to me in identical terms to MH, on the phone at about 12 noon). MH in favour of 80 per cent elected House of Lords. Will not attack European constitution in principle.

4.30: '22 Executive agrees we should welcome Monbiot's offer.

Thursday 11 December

Ring Raymond Monbiot to tell him about the Executive's decision. Having been got at by Howard and Fox, he curtly says, 'I will not be bounced on this; leave it till after the election.' I write to him to record this conversation so that the blame for lack of action is clearly established. That seems to be the end of the matter. MH has thwarted the '22 Executive.

2.00: Meeting, by coincidence, with Monbiot in George Magan's office at CCO. Discover a flustered and sweating Monbiot, who has just been given the job of cutting £1 million from CCO budget, and a very angry Magan, who has resigned as treasurer.

Saturday 13 December

Talk on the phone to MH's PPS, Graham Brady. Tell him all is well on the surface; MH has developed a sense of reawakening for the party. Behind the scenes dust has been stirred up. The Lords are unhappy, the '22 Executive

will be miffed about the leadership rules, and the board is unhappy about
not having been consulted (as the constitution says it must be) about major
changes at CCO and the money situation, which is worrying. I suggest a
quiet chat to MH over dinner rather than a formal meeting next week.

Wednesday 17 December
'22 Executive irritated by Monbiot's delaying of changes in leadership rules. I
am asked to write to him about this.

Friday 19 December
YouGov poll has Tories 39, Labour 38, Lib Dems 18. Publicly MH is off to a
good start.

Tuesday 6 January 2004
Populus poll in *Times*: Labour 40 per cent, Conservatives 35 per cent, Lib
Dems 18 per cent. Discuss this with Michael Howard at a regular meeting.
He is disappointed that, after all the open splits in the Labour Party, they are
still doing so well, though 'it's good that the Libs are being squeezed'. I say,
'It's the economy – and people's gross incomes. We should keep reminding
them of their net incomes, i.e. after tax, and that means having a low-tax
policy of our own.' MH says, 'I agree as long as it's credible. We must also
keep plugging on about poor public services.' I say, 'But no one believes we
will be better at providing public services. We would either have to commit
more money to them or radically reform them.' MH says, 'We will do the
latter.' 'That will be dangerous,' I say, 'although it's what I would do on health,
pensions, transport and education.' He says, 'I know it will be dangerous but
we'll do it.' So in effect MH has said, 'We will have a low-tax, radical reform
of public services policy.'

Sunday 11 January
Michael Howard on TV. Very coherent and forceful in attacking government's university top-up fees scheme – but in my view very misguided.
Top-up fees after all are aimed at making students contribute towards their
own education on very generous terms – as opposed to all the brunt being
borne by the taxpayer. Good Conservative policy. We are being pretty cynical about this – as with our pension policy of throwing more taxpayers'
money at it.

Monday 12 January
Strange board meeting. Agonising discussion on how to keep CCO within

budget. Decide to keep finance sub-committee after I argue we either run it properly or shut it down.

Tuesday 13 January
Meet in Chief Whip's office to discuss policy groups. Michael Howard comes in at one point looking for a telephone. Looks white and tired. It occurs to me at that moment that one reason he is going soft on Europe (change of IDS policy to come out of EPP), plus passionate attack on university fees, plus no commitment on lower taxes, may be a deal he may have done with Ken Clarke.

Wednesday 14 January
I tick David Ruffley off for missing '22 Executive. 'Attending '22 Executive', I say, 'is not optional.' He replies, 'Executive meetings are serious and the only really interesting regular activity in my present life.' I am rather disarmed.

There is disquiet around the party about tuition fees but, like Labour in the nineties, we are now more interested in denting the government than in policy initiatives. Perhaps we have finally learnt how to be an opposition.

We are all being told the policy will be changed after the great vote, when we hope to defeat the government, on the 27th.

Monday 19 January
Lunch with Cecil Parkinson. Glorious trip down memory lane. Discuss influence of Clarke on Howard. I say MH could do with a bit of steeling up. CP, who is looking in tremendous form, seems a bit disconnected from contemporary politics. He doesn't speak much in the Lords. His forte is not the set speech – as we recollect from party conference days. He's good at the light, off-the-cuff, after dinner-speech.

Tuesday 20 January
Meet MH. Fail to persuade him that our policies need to be more clear cut, e.g. council tax and pensions. Suggest he makes better use of Redwood – to which he seems to agree. Also get his agreement that, if we drop leadership rule changes till after election, he will stay on long enough as leader for us to sort things out.

On to the Garrick where I have a drink with Alistair McAlpine. Alistair is great friend (and biographer) of the secretive Barclay brothers. He is concerned by *Times* reports that their agreement to buy *Telegraph* from Conrad Black could be hostile to Conservatives. He says 'They are great supporters – pass it round.' The contrary view could be damaging to the *Telegraph* deal, which is presumably why *Times* are on the case.

Prior to all this attend a meeting in Speaker's House with Privy Councillors and head of MI5* – she proposes a screen shielding public gallery from the chamber. She is a formidable lady.

Wednesday 21 January

Tim Yeo, now shadow Education, speaks at '22 about our top-up policy – or lack of it (parliamentary party getting restless about this). We are to cast off the fig leaf that we will pay for abolishing top up by cutting back on university expansion. It looks like we have another tax commitment. No questions to Yeo at '22 but several worried colleagues came up to him afterwards.

I am out of tune with MH's policy on Lords, pensions, council tax and university fees and therefore probably tax. Ken Clarke was sitting beside him at PMQs and made a 'guest' appearance at the dispatch box – all very symbolic.

Yeo under great pressure on *Newsnight* about where we would get the money from if we abolish top-up fees. Has no real answer. The Clarke– Howard friendship is becoming quite a factor – they are old mates (and sparring partners) from Cambridge.

Thursday 22 January

My birthday. Nice piece about me in *The Times*. Bill Cash rings to say 'Happy birthday' and to say how worried he is about rising influence of Ken Clarke over MH. I say must wheel in Cecil Parkinson and Norman Lamont as antidotes.

Monday 26 January

Owen Paterson accosts me. 'Very worried about way party policy on Europe developing.'

Tuesday 27 January

At ERG breakfast concern expressed at our (MH's) position on party's constitution. Michael Howard refuses to declare our position on our membership of EPP.

All this a sideshow to debate on second reading of University Bill – government wins 316-311. Blair now in real trouble. Best result of all from our point

---

* Elizabeth Manningham-Buller, director general of MI5 2002–7. Created 2008 Baroness Manningham-Buller in June 2008.

of view. He gets his Bill, which most of us really want (allows for student top-up charges), and falls out with his party.

Wednesday 28 January

It's not been a very good two days. MH and David Cameron went to the Cabinet Office to read an advance copy of the Hutton report* and found the government had been totally vindicated. MH makes the best of a weak hand in Commons but it was Blair's day.

I ask a question at PMQs: 'Why are the balance of payments deficit and the fiscal deficit so horribly out of control?' Blair says it was worse in our day. Christopher Chope says, 'A classic Spicer one-liner.'

Thursday 5 February

Parliamentary & Scientific lunch at the Savoy. Chris Patten lambasts the Tories for their attack on government's top-up policies. For once I agree with him (the next chancellor of Oxford). It really is strange how the left have made the running on this one.

Monday 9 February

Dan Hannan rings to say that Howard has caved in on EPP membership. Life will go on as before; he has rejected Dan's and eleven other MEPs' demands in their letter to MH. Now Dan will leave EPP, so will one or two others. Will I see Howard to ensure they are not driven out of the party? In return Dan will go without a fuss and at a time of Howard's choosing. I say, 'I will.' Later this evening Alistair Burt comes up to say Howard would like to see me tomorrow.

At board meeting I insist that under the constitution (which I don't like but which exists) the board is sovereign on financial matters. Maurice Saatchi, in the chair, does agree to reconsider the sale of 32 Smith Square. 'With lawyers', he says, 'we must be able to protect the proceeds from the sale of the offices.' I say, 'This is a matter for the board, not lawyers.'

Tuesday 10 February

Meeting in my office with officers of the Executive and Maurice Saatchi. Maurice tells me after the meeting that he talked to an estate agent this morning about my suggestion last night not to sell the offices. To his surprise, the

---

* The Hutton inquiry was a judicial inquiry chaired by Lord Hutton, who was appointed by the Labour government to investigate the circumstances surrounding the death of Dr David Kelly.

agent agreed with me. Now we will have to find the money to do them up. Saatchi says MH's heart is not in keeping it; but I say, 'Nor does he mind if we keep it.'

On to meeting with MH. He says that his deal with EPP 'better than Iain achieved'. I say, 'Let's not debate that. My real aim is to ensure you do not persecute those who leave EPP. That really will stir up the right.'

Wednesday 11 February

Very successful meeting between the '22 Executive and the voluntary members of the board, led by Raymond Monbiot, followed by dinner in 1 Parliament Street.* All in total agreement that final say in leadership election must be with parliamentary party. Rather a historic moment. Monbiot and I to pursue the details. At the main '22 Committee, Cash, Howarth and Forth publicly express concern about EPP arrangements/sell-out. Rumbles on the right are growing. Unlike the left, the right doesn't take its bat and ball home.

Thursday 12 February

Evening Standard full of Howard's speech in Berlin where it is claimed he will ditch IDS's Eurosceptic policies. Later, on the BBC, it is not so bad: 'no constitution' and 'renegotiation of agriculture and fisheries' are kept. Howard puts forward his variable geometry idea – let the others go on a 'fast track' without us. Trouble is they won't allow us to stay behind. As Andrew Marr says, 'Fat chance.'

In sum, Howard is making the fatal mistake of upsetting his right wing à la Major.

'William Bray' MP

After much thought I have decided not to give the real name of the MP from another party who is the subject of what follows.

Sunday 22 February 2004

William Bray comes round to Maunsel Street at 8 p.m. very nervous, as well he might be, to be having supper with chairman of the 1922 Committee to discuss his future. That would look bad for him if ever it leaked out. He will resign his whip if Liberals do a deal with Labour in the Lords on the European constitution. Will not move earlier, though we agree to have supper again in

---

* Part of the Palace of Westminster.

a month's time. Open to the idea of fighting his seat for us but WB not specially keen to come back to Parliament.

I agree to do what I can to make sure none of this gets to the press, and that I will tell all to Howard in private.

Tuesday 24 February

With Michael Howard for my regular meeting in his office; at my request see him alone without PPSs. He has been thinking a lot about William Bray following meetings with Chief Whip. MH wants to move fast. I say WB not ready to jump yet: totally focused on Europe, does not want anything from us. MH asks, 'Should I see him alone?' I say, 'That might work.' Agree that I should try to get a meeting between the two of them. MH says I must be able to tell Chief Whip. I say I will try to get WB's agreement to this. MH suggests, 'We may fix an opposition day debate on Europe to give WB a cause to leave.' I say, 'It will be hard to press him to step up his pace.'

Later I phone WB. He agrees to meet MH; wants to meet in my home. Will come back with a date. Agrees to our Chief Whip being told.

Tell MH all this during 7 p.m. vote. He says we must move fast. Next week is the last 'opposition day' before Easter. I say, 'This is probably too early. I must wait for WB to come back with a date for a meeting.'

MH agrees to keep CCO 'as an asset' so long as we move out for the election.

Thursday 26 February

Meet WB while walking into Commons. He says, 'Don't let MH try to push me too fast. I like your laid-back approach.' MH will push him, probably rightly. Later he rings me to agree 11 March as the date to meet MH at my house.

Patrick Cormack drops into my office to ask me to mediate with MH to ensure whip restored to Ann Winterton. (It was removed from her when she made a remark at a private dinner about 'Morecambe Bay Chinese'.)

Sunday 29 February

Michael Howard rings me in Cropthorne to ask what is going on about WB. I tell him all is organised through his chief of staff. Then we discuss Ann Winterton. I say I understand that she had merely been repeating a joke she had picked up on the internet 'as an example of the awful jokes circulating around'. MH says, 'This could have been sorted out in a low-key way at the start.' Now he will have to insist on an apology – otherwise he will be in an impossible position.

Monday 1 March
Meeting with Don Porter and Raymond Monbiot (plus Marion Roe) in my room. We agree on principles for new rules for leadership. MPs to have final say, voluntary party to give 'an advisory' ranking to list given by MPs. I am to write to Monbiot confirming all this, plus a streamlining of our rules.

Wednesday 3 March
'22 Executive agrees new leadership rules whereby MPs take control of the selection process again. I say, 'This is a great step backwards,' to laughter. '22 Committee discuss Ann Winterton's withdrawal of the whip. Some say MH could not have done otherwise. More take opposite view, that action was not proportionate to the 'crime'. Very civilised, rather significant debate.

6.25: Meeting with David Maclean, Patrick McLoughlin and Nick Winterton to discuss Ann Winterton. I am to be the 'go-between'. Somehow face must be saved all round – probably impossible unless AW allowed to say, 'I did not do anything wrong but if others are hurt of course I apologise.' But I doubt if MH would buy that.

7.30: Adjournment debate on trains in Worcestershire.

8.15: Dinner at Wolseley for all MPs in for 30 years – me, Michael Ancram, John Stanley, Anthony Steen, Peter Viggers, George Young – all with same wives.

Thursday 4 March
Call from Maclean while I am at AEP board meeting. I return call, to be told that there is a verbatim report of yesterday's '22 in *The Times*. I say, 'It's very sad, but I cannot stop conversations such as the one we had yesterday. I stressed the need for secrecy.' The report is so accurate; it is as if someone had been there with a notebook.

Friday 5 March
Literally bump into William Bray in the tea room after lunch. Asks to come to my room. Should we postpone meeting with MH? 'No.' Can he bring his son-in-law? 'Yes.'

Saturday 6 March
Up to Harrogate for spring conference. Bump into Michael and Sandra Howard in frightful Moat House hotel. Tell him about Bray. 'Is he trying to set us up?' 'He would have nothing to gain by it,' I say.

Liam Fox performs well at the conference. He has charisma, intelligence and appeal to the right. But he is not especially easy to get on with.

Gavin Barwell tells me that a special board meeting this morning which I could not attend took my advice to keep and restore the offices – and was offered a donation to do so. I say, 'Someone needs to thank Gordon Keymer as well as me!'

Sunday 7 March
Slip away down the back stairs of the hotel to catch an early morning train to London so that I can be with Annabel for her thirtieth birthday tea party – find 100 or so other people at the station also with previous engagements.

Monday 8 March
Marion Roe comes to my office She had meeting with Speaker on Monday last week who told her that, on the basis of my support for a damehood, her name was now before the PM.

Wednesday 10 March
ERG meeting with Howard in his room. MH turns his back on using threat of coming out of Europe if constitution put in place, 'because we must stay in Europe to keep it from being anti-American'. Howard has believed this for years. Forth says afterwards this is clear and disastrous. Generally this meeting upsets Eurosceptics. Prompted by me, MH does say would come out of EPP if they break faith with his agreement with them.

At '22 Committee I assume that (contrary to the wish of Chief Whip) shadow ministers can speak at '22. (Last week Anne McIntosh fell foul of Maclean by joining in in support of Ann Winterton – all of which appeared in next day's *Times*.)

My guess is that MH will have had a much easier ride with the left than with ERG, just as Major was more comfortable with Chris Patten and Tristan Garel-Jones. Major was a coup from the left as, it increasingly appears, was Howard.

Thursday 11 March
MH arrives 5.45 p.m. on the dot at Maunsel Street. We discuss how to play William Bray. MH will stress to him that if he hates the idea of a European constitution, the best party for him is the Conservatives. Then we switch to Ann Winterton – no give: 'She will have to make an unreserved apology.' I say, 'That will be very difficult for her, given that her firm view is that she has done no wrong.' WB arrives with his son-in-law at 6.00. Champagne is accepted all round. Very amicable conversation. WB agrees to think over what MH has said, which included the offer of a debate on the constitution.

He agrees to talk to his family and keep in touch with Michael and me. MH leaves at about 6.40.

Sunday 14 March

Phone MH at his home in Kent. Suggest to him that our Achilles heel is the perception that the economy is doing well and that Gordon Brown is a great success. Need Malcolm Rifkind to do a hatchet job on Brown, which means an early by-election at Kensington & Chelsea* – Portillo would have to go early. MH says he is reluctant to do this. 'By-elections are very unpredictable; also I would be nervous about moving Oliver [Letwin]. It is the job he wants and he is a credible alternative Chancellor.' I say, 'That's not quite the point. What we need is someone who will destroy government's economic credibility.' 'Too dangerous.'

Tuesday 16 March

At finance committee meeting at CCO, Raymond Monbiot and Gavin Barwell very excited because MH has approached Colin Moynihan apparently to build a target seats operation behind the back of CCO. This comes on top of discussion of a multi-million cost to move offices for the election – with not much money coming in. Agree to arrange a multi-million-pound overdraft with three banks, including RBS and Arbuthnots.

Liam Fox, who is upset by Moynihan idea ('If I am chairman I must be in charge'), tells me we are level pegging with Labour – means Labour majority of forty – and doing badly v. Liberals. Moynihan himself comes up to me in the smoking room. He says MH very keen on moving marginal seat campaign out of CCO.

Wednesday 17 March

At '22 Executive strong feeling that compromise should be struck between MH and Ann Winterton. Edward Garnier offers to mediate (he is a libel QC). I say, 'MH won't budge without "apology" in the letter from Ann, whatever the context.'

Thursday 18 March

Moynihan comes into my office while I am going through my speech for the Budget. MH and Maurice Saatchi have come to a deal about the new target

---

* Michael Portillo had announced in November 2003 his intention to stand down from the Commons at the next general election.

seat campaign. Later joined in my room by Winterton and Garnier. Work out a formula for Ann to apologise. Hope I can sell it to MH.

Monday 22 March
Board meeting. MH's proposal to hand over running of target seats to Colin Moynihan under fire. 'Who is in charge? Monbiot, chairman or Moynihan?' I ask: 'Where is the money coming from?'

Tuesday 23 March
Meet Ann Winterton in my room at 12 noon.

4 p.m. MH for regular meeting. Present him with a proposal for Wintertons where she 'apologises for involvement' in the episode at a private dinner. MH says this will not do. 'She must apologise for what she said.' I say I don't think Wintertons will agree, that many in the party will think he is being unreasonable, and that the '22 Executive will probably wish to see him. I also say some people will connect his views against Winterton with a weak stand on Europe. MH responds firmly that his Berlin speech most Eurosceptical ever from a party leader.

There's a vacancy on the '22 Committee with David Curry's resignation from shadow Cabinet and David Ruffley's consequent promotion to whip's office. Blunt and Amess put their names in. Amess retires because of his affection for Blunt's late father. I discover Blunt's Defence select committee clashes with meeting of '22 Executive and get him to stand down – so Amess goes ahead.

Wednesday 24 March
More telephone conversations and meetings with Wintertons, who want to remove 'unreservedly' from MH drafted apology letter, which accepts reference to 'repeating' bad email joke. MH will not budge. I get (I think) Wintertons to accept this but they will sleep on it. Tell '22 Executive. 'Should be OK' – as agreed with Ann Winterton.

Thursday 25 March
Graham Brady rings to ask if Ann Winterton has sent letter yet. Nick Winterton tells me in the chamber, 'On Monday.' William Bray rings to ask to meet me, 6.30 Monday at Maunsel Street. I tell MH's office must put down motion on Tuesday on Europe.

2.15: At ACP, Michael Jopling, Geoffrey Howe, Tom King all say we must be 'cautious' in manifesto about Lords reform – I agree. Trouble brewing here for MH.

In the car driving back to Worcestershire, Rachel Whetstone rings from MH's office to say MH will put down tough motion on Europe. I say I will find out WB's reaction on Monday evening.

Monday 29 March
At his request, meet WB at Maunsel Street. He now envisages following plan: assess final constitution on 17 June; we put down tough motion. He votes against it and promptly resigns as an MP.

Tuesday 30 March
MH excited by the WB news when I tell him at 12 p.m. He asks what will happen if all this gets out. I say WB will merely say, 'I talk to Eurosceptics of all parties.'

Thursday 1 April
Daniel Hannan rings to say has had letter from Howard via Liam Fox threatening to sack him from the party if he does not write him a letter by next Monday agreeing to join EPP; another call from Martin Callanan saying same thing.

Talk to MH on phone, who agrees will accept a letter which makes the proviso that he will consider his agreement with EPP invalid if ED* members not allowed to join EPP. Hannan and Callanan say this is meaningless because EPP members can veto ED membership for an applicant party.

Wednesday 21 April
It's all back to Europe in the 1922 following Blair's announcement yesterday that he will after all hold a referendum on the European constitution. There is a great deal of unhappiness on our side about the EPP issue. Liam Fox writes the ultimatum to Conservative MEPs on behalf of MH (that they have to agree by Monday 19th to sit with EPP or be deselected). The view of the '22 Executive is that if this has to be, it should be even-handed, i.e. should mean everyone signing up to the attack on the constitution as something wrong in principle.

---

* The European Democrats group was formed in 1979 by British Conservative, Danish Conservative and other MEPs. From 1999 to 2009 it was allied in the European Parliament with the pro-EU, centre right EPP forming the EPP-ED group.

Thursday 22 April

Bump into Liam Fox while claiming my seat in the chamber at 9.00. Rather startled when he says that MH wants to see the '22 Executive at 10.00 to discuss last evening's events – clearly Alistair Burt has stirred up MH. Ring Stephen Sherbourne, who confirms this. I say this all seems rather unnecessary and, to say the least, short notice! In the event four say they can do it in response to an email from me. Patrick Cormack leaves the dentist's chair to return to the Commons only to find MH has postponed the meeting till Monday.

Later in the afternoon I meet MH for regular session. He apologises for not having properly consulted me about the proposed '22 Executive meeting. I say if he had, I would have advised against it, as last night was a 'letting off steam' session. 'Things have moved on a bit since Blair's announcement of a referendum on the constitution.' MH says, 'I quite agree. My inclination if I see trouble is to move quickly to meet it; sometimes this leads me to over-react. This was probably one such occasion. Can we cancel the meeting altogether?' I say, 'No, that would look very erratic.' He agrees and we decide to hold the meeting on Monday evening. I say, 'You must not make the meeting too bland or everyone will wonder what the attempted "urgent" meeting this morning was all about.' MH agrees and we part on good terms.*

Specifically on the Daniel issue, when I ask how it is going, MH says, 'Negotiations about this are now secret. I am hopeful but we are not there yet.'

Wednesday 28 April

Liam Fox rings me to say all the EPP 'rebels' have written 'acceptable' letters. He accepts not much can be done if they rat on the agreement after the election.

Wednesday 5 May

Last committee meeting (for me) at Pratt's. One minute's silence for the Duke of Devonshire's death earlier in the day. He was a good man. A journalist once asked him, 'Do you belong to Pratt's?' Without hesitation he replied, 'I think you will find Pratt's belongs to me.'

Tuesday 11 May

MH comes up to me in lobby. 'Where are we with WB?' he asks. I say, 'Have just had a call from him. Wants to meet next Monday.' MH says, 'We really must land him now.'

---

* The meeting does take place without incident the following Monday.

Monday 17 May
Meet WB at Maunsel Street which, as I have warned him, is a building site. We sit in chairs in the drawing room covered in polythene. He will contemplate coming over only when he knows the result of Dublin IGC on constitution in mid-June. However, he wants to talk freely to one or two senior Conservatives in his constituency.

Tuesday 18 May
Message from Jessica while in a board sub-committee on future of party conference (should we continue with Blackpool?). Apparently Michael Howard has been on the phone to her. When I ring him back he asks, will WB jump before the local elections on 10 June? I say 'No' and report yesterday's meeting.

Wednesday 19 May
Fifteen members of '22 Executive meet MH for dinner at the Garrick. He agrees to lift his veto on the leadership rule changes going to the board but not on an elected House of Lords as a manifesto commitment. This causes much disquiet. With three exceptions, everyone in accord with ACP, with whom we met on 5 May, that we want an appointed Lords.

Monday 24 May
Poll in the *Daily Telegraph* has UKIP at 18 per cent on the Euro poll, ahead of the Liberals. At a short routine meeting with MH he offers the view that 'whereas Blair will never ultimately say "No" on European matters, because he does not want to upset his Euro friends like Bertie Ahern [Irish PM], I would if I disagreed. It's one big difference between him and me.'

This arises in the context of WB's determination to jump only if the constitution becomes a reality at the IGC next month. MH thinks it will because of Blair's compliance in Europe. I'm not so sure now that Blair has boxed himself in on the referendum. We shall see. MH easy about making a presentation to IDS when he gives his end-of-term speech to '22.

Monday 31 May (Bank holiday)
Gerald Howarth rings. He is very upset about MH's pending attack tomorrow on UKIP. I agree it will give them more publicity and serve little purpose. We will certainly need a major debrief after the Euro elections on 10 June.

Ring Graham Brady, MH's PPS. We agree it's too late to change tack at this stage but will need a serious reappraisal later. Ring back Gerald Howarth to confirm all this.

Sunday 13 June
Euro result: Conservative 27 per cent, Labour 23 per cent, UKIP 16 per cent, Lib Dems 15 per cent.

Monday 14 June
I chair special meeting of '22 to discuss aftermath of Euro and local elections. MH speaks. Tells 100 or so present – 'No intention of changing Euro policy despite UKIP success.' Says, 'In any case your views are of no account' – pause – 'nor are mine unless I become PM, which I won't if we all quarrel in public.' First leader we have had in recent memory who tells us to eff off. May be good for us.

Tuesday 15 June
Bump into IDS in central lobby. Tell him we have collected over £1,000 for his present. Would he like this to be given to him same day as MH addresses us, when there will be a good turnout? MH happy about this. IDS says he will think about it. Then adds, 'The UKIP vote would not have been so high if I had been leader because Eurosceptics would have trusted me.'

Monday 21 June
Board agrees to the principle of new leadership rules, e.g. MPs have last say.

Thursday 24 June
I get back from Wimbledon – message from Chief Whip. Would I cancel next three weeks' 1922 so we can all go off and canvass and fight the by-elections (Birmingham Hodge Hill and Leicester South)! The next day I tell Gina (David Maclean's assistant), 'We didn't do that even during the Second World War; in any event, we would look ridiculous bearing in mind we haven't much chance of winning either Leicester or Birmingham seats. I will, if Chief Whip wants it, put the idea to the Executive'. Gina comes back to say Chief Whip has changed his mind – keep the '22 meetings.

Saturday 26 June
Daily Express has an article (which has Eric Forth's fingerprints on it) saying MH out of touch with middle England and some Conservatives are calling for David Davis (EF's protégé) to take over.

Sunday 27 June
Visit Ma in Bricklehampton nursing home. She is eating almost nothing and is in a semi-coma. Today may be the last time I see her alive.

MH rings, 'Any news about WB?' 'I am meeting him the week after next – refuses to give me any clue as to how his mind is working – I am not hopeful.' MH asks whether he should speak to him direct. 'Why not?' I say. 'I will try to put him in touch via his pager.'

Wednesday 30 June
MH rings early to ask again about WB. I say I will not meet him at home next week unless he has something positive to say.

Saturday 3 July
Daniel Hannan rings. Should he have one more go at MH before jumping ship from EPP? I say MH thinks EPP honouring its side of the 'deal' about accepting new Eurosceptic parties and giving them some autonomy within the group. If this is not the case, Daniel should tell MH to his face – MH has always maintained that the deal would be off if they (EPP leadership) did not honour their side. Daniel says he will try to see MH.

Sunday 4 July
WB rings to say he won't jump. 'I'll wait to be pushed.' End of saga. WB's warmth towards us has varied according to our position in the polls – currently on the slide.

Monday 5 July
Bad day. Polls back to where they were before MH took over (Labour 33 per cent, Conservatives 29 per cent, Lib Dems 24 per cent). Next Monday's board meeting may be a decisive one. We may have to call a halt to all spending.

Tuesday 8 July
Regular meeting with MH. I become heated and say the parliamentary party is becoming restive (polls etc.) and he knows about the perilous financial position. It would be as well to finesse the EPP issue at least by offering to become personally involved in forging a Eurosceptic bloc of parties within EPP. MH thanks me. He comes into his outer office and says to an assistant, 'I will follow MS's advice.'

Thursday 8 July
Battle bus to Birmingham Hodge Hill for by-election at which whole parliamentary party is being thrown rather heroically but, one suspects, hopelessly. Except for Damian Green, very Eurosceptic mood which even he went along

with. Canvass poorer areas. Every fifth house has a cross of St George, put up for the Euro 2004 football championships but left on display. Very nationalistic mood, with which we are totally failing to connect.

General view on the bus coming back is that we are wrongly 'me-tooing' Labour on health and education and totally missing out in 'our' areas of crime, immigration, low taxes and Europe. We're lucky UKIP aren't fighting these by-elections.

Sunday 11 July
DH rings to say that MH has written to him to say that if a fully fledged independent body is not formed within EPP, we will leave. He will write to parliamentary party to this effect. My contribution was to get the two sides talking, which before I saw MH last Wednesday would not have been the case.

Tuesday 13 July
Rebellious 92 dinner. Forth, Leigh, Redwood, Wintertons all furious with MH over defence. (Report in *Evening Standard* suggests he does not know where he is on defence.)

Wednesday 14 July
Bump into Tony Benn at a private viewing of the ghastly Royal Academy Summer Exhibition.* He divides the political world into 'weathercocks' and 'signposts'. 'You are a signpost,' he says kindly.

Monday 19 July
Meeting with MH in his room in Norman Shaw South. I say, 'Parliamentary party restive and anxious. We need to recapture *Sun* readers of the Thatcher (and Disraeli!) years and from whom we were totally disconnected at the by-elections. We must reconnect with the patriotic working class, who have left up their crosses of St George on their semi-detached houses and white vans. Policies on immigration, Europe, crime need to be toughened up.' As the son of an immigrant, MH in a good position to do something about this. MH quiet, thoughtful and quite receptive to this. Agree that the game plan is to crush Labour first.

---

* My views of the Summer Exhibition may be influenced by the fact that over the years the hanging committee have turned down several of my paintings!

Tuesday 20 July
Officers of '22 Committee (Steen, Butterfill, Roe, Winterton) meet Liam Fox in my room in the Commons. Press case for policy hardening. Fox agrees but unable to clarify how policy will be decided. 'Your meeting yesterday with MH was very helpful,' he says to me.

Wednesday 21 July
Presentation to IDS.

MH virtually apologises to '22 for a 'bad week' personally. No questions, I think because people do not want to be thought to be rocking the boat, which according to the opinion polls is becoming leaky again.

Thursday 22 July
Parliament breaks up for the summer recess. It has not been a good week. I warned MH on 19 July against making too much of Iraq (he backed the war). He tries to make a distinction between backing the war and being tricked into voting for the precise wording of the relevant motion. I say you are either for or against the war; the rest is playing with words. MH disagrees.*

Saturday 31 July
Ma dies at 5 a.m. Her last words to me when she was fading fast were 'Boo to you' in response to my 'Boo!' (A few days before she had spoken to me in German to tell me that I had too much of an Austrian accent!)

Politics has gone from bad to worse for us. At the start of the week Portillo and Alan Duncan attacked the party for not being 'nice' enough. By the end of the week a spat was raging between the oldies ('bed blockers') and the forty-somethings, MPs and candidates. All absurd – shows how press still hates us and how we hate them and ourselves. What a mess and it's high summer before a general election next May.

Thursday 19 August
Bizarre finance committee meeting in CCO new offices in Victoria Street. Someone from 'Marketing' made a 'presentation' of how we should start to spend a million pounds a month from September of money we don't have. (We are already at our debt/asset limit.) I remonstrate and say that, far from increasing costs, we will have to cut them, if necessary taking the discretionary election budget to zero.

---

* This was as much an issue of timing as anything. Five years later the MH approach would no doubt have been highly effective.

Wednesday 8 September

The issue today has been 'bed blocking', the term derived from press reports in the *Telegraph* and *Mail* that the leadership is tired of old farts who play no part in Parliament. Several are mentioned who have come up to me today and the issue is heavily discussed at '22 Executive, where I am deputed to see the Chief Whip to remonstrate with him. This I do at a meeting with him, McLoughlin and Nick Winterton. Maclean swears he is not source of the story. (He says he would have put out a very different list of names.)

Monday 13 September

Fund-raising dinner at Marco Pierre White's Drones. Don Porter says that Raymond Monbiot did not get agreement at a meeting last week of Convention officers about leadership rule changes.

Tuesday 14 September

Meeting with Maurice Saatchi (party chairman), and officers of '22 (Nick Winterton, Marion Roe, Anthony Steen, Paul Beresford*). Maurice expresses the view that we will only win GE if we are 10 points ahead of Labour (at present we are 2 points behind). A lead of between 3 points and 10 points would mean a hung parliament with all that would bring (PR etc.) – a nightmare for the Conservatives, who may not share power for years unless they do a deal with Liberals or perhaps Blair faction of Labour. British politics is about to become fragmented. This may also mean GE later than next May.

Wednesday 15 September

The day the chamber was invaded:[†] I was taking part in a meeting in my room of the board's finance committee. We decide to allow borrowings to rise, leaving the remainder to be raised in cash and only spent when raised. The board will probably agree on Monday 30th.

4 p.m. Chief Whip asks me to give him advice as to what to do if a Conservative MP involved in the attack in the chamber. I say it would depend on what his role really is. Is Maclean fishing to see if I know more? I do not, but later learn that a senior colleague's name was on a forged letter of introduction held by the invaders.

---

[*] MP for Croydon Central 1992–7, Mole Valley since 1997.

[†] Parliament was suspended as five pro-hunt campaigners invaded the House of Commons while MPs were debating whether to ban hunting with dogs. The ban was later approved.

Monday 20 September
Board meeting. I lead the fray against further unbudgeted expenditure until we pull in the money. This is agreed: visible relief around the board table.

Wednesday 22 September
Talked to Stephen Sherbourne (MH's very able chief of staff). MH needs to make one interesting and specific new policy point, e.g. abolishing inheritance tax. Canvass in Hartlepool on the way to AEP meeting in Scotland. Find no MPs there except Michael Fabricant and George Osborne dressed in a dark suit. Going back to Darlington station, Osborne asks whether I would reveal the letters re IDS. I say, 'Never the names. Indeed, I have forgotten most of them.'

Friday 24 September
Press (*Mail* and *Telegraph*) has reports that at last we have come off the fence on tax and will raise the inheritance tax threshold to £1 million.

Saturday 25 September
This is all denied. Letwin and Howard don't want a specific commitment. Maurice Saatchi and I do. Meanwhile Labour are plummeting in the polls – the economy is off the boil, house prices are falling, Iraq is a major embarrassment to Blair and people are switching, not to us, but to the Liberals, who are making specific commitments on many policy areas, e.g. to abolish DTI.

Friday 1 October
Fourth, behind UKIP, in the Hartlepool by-election. To quote Soames – 'A bloody awful disaster!' MH has been a strong leader but in my view his judgement has been wrong on a number of important issues: EDP, UKIP, Euro elections, calling 'temporary' supporters 'mad', Iraq, wobbling in his support and, above all this week on taxation, especially on inheritance tax, seeming to support a £1 million threshold and then backing off. He has also mishandled individuals, e.g. Ann Winterton, John Bercow (probably impossible to please). Is running the party into a serious financial mess – confronting the board – by over-spending and failing to sort out the treasurers.

MH seems to be driven by polls, which are telling him how distrusted politicians are. His conclusion from this is that he must be more cautious and consider the legal niceties of everything. This serves only to make him look more shifty. What he should be doing is hook himself to one or two strong pledges which are so bold that people will have no choice but to hold him to them and thus believe him.

Sunday 3 October

First night of Bournemouth party conference. As usual wet and very windy at the Highcliffe. Brief private conversation with MH. Try to persuade him that 'credible' tax policies can mean brave ones which arise out of our philosophy and on which we are 'hooked'; he thinks that it means the opposite, i.e. being cautious and not giving any hostages to fortune. Sandra Howard says to him, 'Michael Spicer doesn't think the policies go far enough.'

He speaks well at the agents' dinner, brushing aside bad press and bad polls and concentrating on the opportunities from collapsing government due to failing economy (falling house prices), Iraq and Blair's announcement that he will go in next parliament. Question is where will defecting Labour votes go? UKIP or Lib Dems, unless we appeal to their pockets through tax/pension promises.

Monday 4 October

Oliver Letwin makes a point in his speech to the Conference of saying that he will not be specific on tax cuts because people will not believe us. My view is the reverse. No one will listen to our platitudes. We are becoming sidelined, an irrelevance. The way to be trusted is to make promises which you look as though you will keep, not to avoid making any promises at all. I think this may turn out to be the point at which we blew the conference.

Tuesday 5 October

MH makes a good and at times tear-jerking 'trust me' speech. Only trouble is I am not sure whether he looks credible.

Wednesday 6 October

MH gets good press.

I contemplate further this 'trust me' line. Take Europe: who really believes we can negotiate powers back from the EU when it would require unanimity? Howard says we would 'trade', allowing others to go ahead at their own, faster, pace; but this is out of date (the *Acquis* ensures the automatic movement towards European centralisation enforced by the European Court). There is no need for them to 'trade' anything. The truth is that our position on Europe is not credible.

Sunday 10 October

ICM poll shows us 9 points behind Labour with the Liberals catching up. Our conference has not worked. Portillo says in today's *Sunday Times* this is because we are failing to capture the 'middle ground', which he does not define. I think he is talking rubbish. What we have to do is to make people think we will make them better off than the government will. This is not easy when the economy still looks strong.

Monday 11 October
Bump into John Taylor, who now wants his party (Ulster Unionists) to join us. Agree to discuss this with MH.

Wednesday 13 October
MH addresses '22. Totally uncompromising. 'Don't believe the polls and stay rigidly on message.' He is probably giving the party the one thing in his grasp: discipline. Briefly mention to him John Taylor conversation. We both agree to be wary. The Ulster Unionists are approaching us from a position of weakness.

Thursday 14 October
Raymond Monbiot and Don Porter in my office to discuss how we sell the leadership deal (MPs get the last say) to the voluntary party. Agree that MPs should have the first and last vote, voluntary party to rank the candidates presented to them but no vote. RM agrees to begin selling this at a meeting of chairmen on 4 December. At the end of the meeting says he could not be controlling finances of the party without the two Rottweilers (me and Gordon Keymer) in the background!

Monday 18 October
Don Porter rings to say Monbiot now wants volunteers to eliminate leadership candidates at an early stage.

At a dinner meeting of 92 Group, Oliver Letwin, under questioning from me, says we will produce 'specific tax cuts' but later. I say don't leave it too late. He says (a) we don't want Labour to pinch our policies (I say, 'Unlikely for tax cuts' – he demurs) and (b) we want to make sure tax cuts match expenditure proposals. I say OK but get on with it, otherwise all will be lost in 'noise' of an election. It's all we have to match Labour's economic 'competence'.

Thursday 21 October
Regular meeting with MH. He sticks rigidly to the point of discussion (no gossip). Tell him that leadership rules issue could reach the press. MH says, 'You may have been right. Perhaps we should have put the matter to bed last year. Must suppress it now.' Also briefly discuss party's finances:

no more loans, large gifts very rare. Try, unsuccessfully, to press for less cautious tax policies.

Sunday 24 October
Ring Dan Hannan, try to persuade him to stand in Surrey seat to be vacated by Archie Hamilton. He is disinclined to do so.

Friday 29 October
Talk on the phone to Simon Eardley, my agent. He says there is no 'fizz' in the party's posture. I agree with him and say MH must be more adventurous. He must above all excite the Conservative vote. The next GE may be all about who can get their own vote out.

Monday 1 November
Regular meeting with MH. I raise issue of polls, which are trending against us. (For me to lose my own seat now only requires a 3.5 per cent swing to Liberals.) I ask, 'What are we going to do about it?' and answer my own question. 'All we can do is to be more adventurous – especially on tax.' 'I agree with the first but not the second,' MH says. I say low taxes are a defining Conservative issue and tell him about the canvassing experience – 'no identity'. MH says, 'But I remember you sitting on that chair three months ago and saying immigration was the pivotal issue.' 'That was because I knew you were unbudgeable on tax!' This breaks the tension. 'We are going to consult on lower taxes.' 'That's better than nothing,' I say, 'but Letwin must become nasty on the economy.' We break up in good humour. He says his new Australian spin doctor (Lynton Crosby) says Australian election won in last three days. Rather disarmingly MH ends the meeting by saying, 'Who knows, Michael, you may turn out to be right. Only history will tell.' I am reminded of the debate we had about Europe – and how he should project himself – during his abortive leadership challenge.

Tuesday 2 November
'Invited in' by the Chief Whip to witness John Bercow threatened with having the whip withdrawn. In the event he surrenders and agrees to apologise for being publicly rude about the party, especially in Monday's *Independent*, and also to declare he will 'never' cross the floor of the House. Great relief: his departure would have created a furore. This time MH's toughness pays off. I see myself as being there to ensure fair play, as JB's shop steward.

Sunday 7 November
MH, interviewed in *Sunday Telegraph* by Dominic Lawson, refuses to congratulate Bush on his victory. Blimey.

Monday 15 November
Splash story in *Daily Telegraph* effectively says I am changing the leadership rules. Bill Cash quoted as saying this is a Euro federalist move because their candidates will never win a popular membership vote.

At my meeting with MH remind him of his blockage of 'dealing with' leadership rule changes last autumn. I say, 'As I guessed then, it is going to be much more difficult now.' 'You may be right,' he says.

Wednesday 17 November
Regular meeting with MH on a bad opinion poll day – Conservatives 30 per cent, Labour 39 per cent, worse than days of IDS. 'Tell the party not to believe polls,' he says. 'It's in their blood to do so,' I say, adding, 'We need to do more to sex up one or two policies.' 'We've wasted too much time already trying to find a silver policy bullet,' says MH. Lynton Crosby seems to have cheered him up by having reminded him that John Howard came from behind in recent Australian elections – but he was already PM.

Monday 22 November
Gordon Keymer and I as usual arm in arm to stop spending beyond the budget. Start to worry about post-election debts.

Wednesday 1 December
Very outspoken '22 meeting. Nick Winterton, Howarth, Heathcoat-Amory and Leigh all speak for greater sharpness in policy, especially re low taxes. Letwin defends the view that it is 'too early to give hostages to fortune'. This does not go down well as we are some 8 points behind Labour in the polls. Bizarrely MH sits at the back of the room listening. At beginning I was elected chairman unopposed.

Thursday 2 December
Raymond Monbiot rings to say that MH was given much the same treatment by the officers of the Convention as Letwin last night at the '22. There is agreement between the voluntary side and much of the parliamentary party (and, I suspect, Maurice Saatchi) that the only real initiative we hold in our hands is tax policy. The problem, as today's pre-Budget statement confirms, the economy – on the surface – is too strong for us (à la 1980s for Thatcher).

Tuesday 7 December

'22 Executive meets MH in his room at 3 p.m. Subjects:

State of polls – bad. He says our private polls are good. No one really believes this.

Policy: Nick Winterton calls for immediate policy to reduce taxes. MH says to wait till after Budget so Brown won't pinch our policies. (Ridiculous idea that Labour could appear more dedicated tax cutters than us.)

Party finances and organisation (*Times* said yesterday that we were bust). MH asks for my comments, which I refuse to give as I do not wish to air my anxieties in detail. I just say, 'Debt is debt and it's far too high.'

That morning opened the ballot box for spare '22 Executive places. One of the names is Damian Green, proposed by Keith Simpson.

Tuesday 14 December

Finance committee in my room in the House. Agree that we are likely to be many millions of pounds short this year and to recommend immediate cuts in the election budget.

On to drinks party given by Lady T. at Canning House, Belgrave Square. She tells me, 'We should give more of these parties.' She is going to South Africa at Christmas to see Mark, who is under virtual house arrest there. Norman Lamont said, 'Howard is far too worried about upsetting anyone and so fails to please anyone.'

Wednesday 15 December

Private meeting with MH. He appears to listen to me when I say we will have to pull in our horns financially. He is still determined to put a whip on identity cards next Monday. I say I will probably abstain.

Later he addresses '22 Committee. Usual appeal for unity – re identity card issue. MH makes the – in my view unconvincing – argument that when he was Home Secretary the police wanted them. 'And I always gave them the tools they wanted.' Douglas Hogg pleads that he take account of 'liberal' view in the party.

Monday 20 December

Pairing whip, Peter Luff, told me on Thursday night that if it were to be a free vote on identity cards, a slight majority of the party would vote 'No'. It looks as if over 100 Conservatives would have done so. I warned MH that this might be the case when I saw him on Wednesday. 'I hope you're wrong,' he said. 'The whips tell me we will get a good vote.' I say, 'They may be right; it's their job to count. I do my counting in the tea room.'

Friday 24 December

MH rings in the middle of our annual Christmas Eve *Glühwein* party in Cropthorne. Take the call in my bedroom. MH plans to announce over Christmas that he wants to cut the Commons by 120 MPs. I say the '22 Executive have discussed the issue – understand that it would work to our advantage but there are no votes in it. MH says it's part of a wider package of small government. We exchange pleasantries and leave it there.

Chapter 22

Michael Howard:
general election and massive rows

As the diary notes make clear, the early part of 2005 was dominated not just, as might have been expected, by preparations for what turned out to be a pretty disastrous (for the Conservatives) general election on 5 May, but also by a massive internal row about the future shape and structure of the party. It reached a climax on 24 May, shortly after the general election. This was when the advocates of central membership, amalgamation of constituencies and head office control of the selection of candidates were brutally routed at a meeting mainly of MPs in the Grand Committee Room of the House of Commons. The seriousness of the attack on leaders of the voluntary party and the Central Office apparatchiks was not mollified by their offer to return the process of electing the party leader exclusively to MPs, an offer they were in any event unable to deliver.

Saturday 1 January 2005
Week's holiday in Canaries; chilly wind, filthy cold – otherwise all is well!

Learn in the English papers that Michael Howard has issued a bland pre-manifesto – nothing to get your teeth into. With the terrible Indian Ocean tsunami, not surprising it receives scant coverage. He has made a great mistake leaving tax commitments so late – probably four months till GE. (Apparently Oliver Letwin is going to say something specific to the '22 when we get back.) We enter the new year making no real electoral progress despite the surface unpopularity of the government.

Tuesday 4 January
Canaries version of the *Daily Mail* reports that Michael Howard said in reply to a radio interview that he might not go as leader if he lost the election.

Thursday 13 January
Meeting with Raymond Monbiot and Gordon Keymer in CCO. Agree that many millions will need to come off the election budget. Tell MH about this;

he looks blank. His only comment is, 'Let's wait and see what comes in.' (But then, what else could he say?)

He confirms to me that Letwin's talk to '22 on Monday will say nothing specific about tax. That should irritate some of the brethren. We are agreed that we have probably missed the boat on presenting an exciting policy image. Must now wait for HMG to implode.

Monday 17 January

MH speaks well at fund-raising dinner given at Frankie's in Knightsbridge by Marco Pierre White. Michael is fluent, witty, passionate and paces himself well – all on a day of fielding questions about Robert Jackson's defection. Meet Rachel Whetstone outside the loo. 'Do drop MH a note to congratulate him,' she says. 'It would mean a lot to him if you said his speech was noticeably better/different. We have been practising all afternoon.' I say, 'I will.'

Tuesday 18 January

Write the promised note to MH. Bill Cash in my room for 1½ hours. Warns me against stirring leadership rules issue after the GE. (He does not want MPs to have final say because he thinks that this will work against Eurosceptics. I disagree.) Anyway, what about our constitutional arrangement whereby a Prime Minister must have the support of over 50 per cent of the House of Commons in order to survive in office?

Monday 24 January

Win argument at the board that we should knock millions off election budget because we don't have the money.

Wednesday 26 January

Meeting with MH. Congratulate him on his clear stance on immigration policy. Try to encourage him to do same thing on tax and pensions (e.g. cut taxes for pensioners). He has never been passionate about taxes, which explains some of his problem with activists in the party.

Meeting with Gerald Howarth, chairman of 92 Group. He thinks, despite Forth and Cash, we should retrieve final say in leadership elections for MPs – mainly because of the time and delays involved in the present system.

Tuesday 1 February

Share a taxi (with Ann) with Peter Luff back from Nick Scott's memorial service (Chelsea Old Church packed out). PL thinks Blair will go early – 21 April.

Wednesday 2 February

Chair '22 Savoy dinner: 300 PPCs, MPs, peers, old boys. Organisationally a great success. MH's speech competent without being inspirational. Rather curt responses to questions, e.g. Toby Jessel asks 'Why can't we have a 25-year commitment to abolishing income tax?' and Paul Marland, 'What do we tell them on the doorstep?' MH replies, in effect, 'I've just told you!' He has a specific go at Alan Duncan, who has apparently told the *Telegraph* that he will stand for leadership one day. MH effectively tells him he is too short to appear to be standing at all, let alone for leadership.

Despite MH's remarks, Alan Duncan comes up and says he has enjoyed the evening. Liam Fox presents a view that polls are over-estimating Labour lead and under-estimating our propensity to vote.

Sunday 6 February

We now plan officially to abstain on next week's vote on ID cards.

Tuesday 8 February

Canvass with other MPs in Guildford. Anne Milton, the PPC, is impressive but I am not sure we are making much headway against Liberals. George Osborne, the dry but intelligent (and ambitious) son-in-law of David Howell, a one-time Member for Guildford, encourages me to press ahead with changes to the leadership rules 'as my shop steward'. Is this part of a plot to play for time after the GE to prepare the ground for David Cameron, George's ally?

Saturday 12 February

Rather a damaging programme by Michael Cockerell on BBC on Michael Howard. He comes out looking old and without much direction. Sad.

Saturday 19 February

Cold but relaxed day in London. Light lunch at Wolseley, then to a matinee of *Blithe Spirit* with Penelope Keith; back to Maunsel Street to see *La Fille mal gardée* on TV. Papers full of pre-election boom.

Thursday 24 February

Bump into Jack Straw in the corridor leading towards my office and outside his. 'The travelling is beginning to weary me,' says the Foreign Secretary. Doesn't sound like a man going on in his job in the next parliament.

Wednesday 2 March

MH tetchy at a meeting over sandwiches in his office with nine members of

'22 Executive. I ask, 'Our Achilles heel remains the perception of the strong economy. What will be our attack on the Budget?' He replies, 'It's all in the literature we put out every week. The government will put up taxes by £18 billion. We will reduce them by £4 billion.' Fair enough.

Wednesday 9 March

Walk through lobby with MH. He is angry about Francis Maude's list of modernists v. 'Forgets' (includes me).* Talk to FM. He is apologetic but accepts that he sent out paper, which reached *Mail on Sunday*.

Bump into Chief Whip in lobby. He says continuity of his job, leader, and my job should be maintained after election. 'We will need time to sort ourselves out.'

Wednesday 16 March

Alan Duncan tells me in the tea room over breakfast that there was no plot when Hague changed his mind in the first leadership campaign. AD knew nothing of the deal between Howard and Hague. Using Brooks Newmark he did help 'unwittingly' during the night to change Hague's mind by encouraging him to stand. Duncan, who seems to have become distanced from Hague, says, 'He always keeps his cards close to his chest. No one knows what he thinks.'

After '22, hold regular meeting with David Maclean, who says '22 meetings no good. '22 needs to do more campaigning 'on the streets'. I say, 'Whips' office would no doubt like to disband '22 altogether.' Maclean realises he has overstepped the mark. As I leave the room, I say, 'Don't worry, David, the '22 will become more interesting in the next parliament when we start discussing the leadership rules and when the party is bigger.'

Thursday 24 March

Bump into William Bray near Maunsel Street; walk with him to Commons. Briefly he says he could 'switch' after the general election (i.e. when he is no longer an MP), in which he thinks we will do well, e.g. pick up sixty or so seats; brilliant end to the WB saga.

News full of Howard Flight's resignation from his non-job (deputy party chairman) – absurd that it should have come to this and deeply distressing for the Flights.

Brilliant article in *The Times* by Anatole Kaletsky. Argues that our continuing travails are the result not just of the apparently strong economy, but more

---

* A heading Maude had used in a leaked list of, in his view, hopeless cases of obstructers.

of the fact that we are not engaging with Blair in the substantive political debate: more state intervention v. less. Instead we operate at the margin: gypsies, £4 billion savings (better value) for tax cuts, cleaner hospitals etc. – exactly my view.

Howard Flight issue

Friday 25 March 2005 – Good Friday
News starts with Howard Flight's resignation. *Times* leads with the story. (*Telegraph* has us neck and neck with Labour in the polls.)

Later in the morning Labour says that Howard Flight's 'gaffe' shows there is a secret Tory agenda to slash public spending. MH responds (disastrously in my view) by sacking Howard Flight as an MP. HF refuses to go, saying it is a matter for his association, which will back him. Gerald Howarth, Nick Winterton and Don Porter ring to say Michael Howard must change his mind. HF's crime seems pretty small – has said we may need to go beyond James[*] in government – a sacking but not hanging offence.

On the evening news looks as if MH may get his way with HF's association.

Saturday 26 March
Back at Cropthorne, Howard Flight rings. Claims seventy MPs supporting him. I question the number and ask him how many want to reverse Michael Howard's decision to sack him. He becomes rather vague and asks my view on the constitution. I say that however much one sympathises with him, the priority now must be to protect the reputation of the leader – in the interest of the party – on the eve of a general election. He says he is minded to fight for his seat, if necessary to the High Court. I say that this will alienate the party, whereas if he acts nobly could become a man of stature in the party. 'Too problematic,' he says. We agree to sleep on it.

Nick Winterton rings to say he is incensed. 'Michael Howard must compromise.'

Sunday 27 March – Easter Day
HF rings at 9.20 to say he intends to fight to the finish and if necessary stand as an independent. I say, 'What about your future in the party – say as a big figure on the voluntary side?' 'Not for me. I am going for it with nothing to lose.' I ring MH: 'As you know, my view is that it was the wrong

---

[*] David James, economist and 'company doctor', appointed by the Conservative Party to review government spending and waste.

decision. What is your view on a compromise with HF?' MH says, 'It would be madness. I have the powers to sack him and must now see it through.' We agree that, if possible, he should address the '22 next week.

Redwood rings. We agree we would not have played it like MH, but we are where we are. MH must now win. Redwood says he will speak to HF, as does Marion Roe. However, HF goes public, threatening to go independent. When Nick Winterton rings I say bridge-building is now over – at least for the time being. We will need to back MH.

Monday 28 March
Christabel Flight rings with a question about amendments to the constitution. The danger now is that each side miscalculates the position – MH the strength of his case under the constitution/law of unfair dismissal/human rights and HF MH's potential to be bullied into a compromise.

Gavin Barwell (CCO chief executive) rings to ask for my agreement as member of the board to sack the Slough candidate (Adrian Hilton). I say, 'We are sacking people like flies. I want Andrew Mackay (deputy chairman, candidates) to talk to me direct – to confirm he has exhausted all diplomatic means with the Slough association – before I agree.'

Tuesday 29 March
Howard Flight on *Newsnight*. 'Let's see whether an EGM backs me.' But this will be two weeks out into the middle of a general election. Although MH can probably sack HF, much more doubtful is that he can appoint someone else – certainly not without board approval. No mention of this in the constitution.

Wednesday 30 March
HF rings. His legal opinion on the way. What he requires is a vote on 'de-adoption' at his general meeting. If he wins he will contest the seat without the whip.

Telephone Maclean and Barwell to transmit all this.

Thursday 31 March
Still no Labour candidate in West Worcestershire – without one it will be very close.

Friday 1 April
Chief Whip rings to ask that I phone HF to ask him to surrender. I say there is no point in that but I will find out his mood. HF very angry. 'MH has

taken politeness at my meeting with him as weakness. I have not brought the party into disrepute. I intend to pursue the matter as far as I can with my association and possibly in the courts'. I transmit this to Chief Whip. '22 Executive divided on question of whether MH should give way.

Monday 4 April
At last a Labour candidate in West Worcestershire.

Eric Forth comes to my room. 'MH is in real trouble after the election re Flight affair unless we win 225 seats at least.' Alistair Burt, MH's PPS, also comes over. 'Could I have another go at Flight?' I say, 'No point.'

Tuesday 5 April
Four good polls today. Looks as though I may win my seat after all!

Fury everywhere in the Commons about Howard/Flight.

Meet Raymond Monbiot in my office for breakfast. We agree:

- Leadership rules: MPs to have final say but first ranked from volunteers; will go through to MPs' final round.

- Whip can be removed only temporarily.

- Selection/deselection of MPs by local association.

General election

Sunday 10 April 2005
MH rings up to say he has been in the area and has been told that my seat is under siege – Liberals are moving people down from Ludlow. I say all you can do is to play up your record as a good MP and get out your vote – and hope the polls go our way. I wish CCO would stop bugging me – and go away too.

Monday 11 April
Based on the polls (today) here is my forecast majority in West Worcestershire: worst 2,000, best 5,000, probable 3,500.

Wednesday 13 April
Another panicky call from the whips: this time from David Ruffley about my refusal to appear with Tom Wells* on a BBC debate. DR says, 'You may be upsetting the Beeb.' I say, 'If the BBC and the Conservative Party were the same thing that might be bad, but they're not. They are opposites and

---

* Liberal Democrat candidate for West Worcestershire.

I'm not willing to give the Lib Dems an airing, which is the one thing they want.' DR agrees.

Thursday 14 April
First day of canvassing. One lady tells me she will vote Conservative if I stop her grandchildren having to bring back homework 'because the teachers are too lazy to teach them'. We are now flat-lining in the polls, having lost all momentum after the Howard Flight affair.

Saturday 16 April
Appalling polls: worse than 1997. Libs creeping up. MH had better have something dramatic up his sleeve or he will lose his own seat. What about pensions?

Sunday 17 April
I must be psychic: we're doing pensions this week!

Friday 22 April
Half-way point. Things may be on a bit of a turn. People much friendlier towards us. Polls showing some modest improvement. MH good with Paxman. Our view on immigration beginning to take off, especially with lower middle classes. Foolishly the PM attacks back on this issue.

Sunday 24 April
Our momentum seems to have ground to a halt and we are going backwards, certainly against the Liberals. It looks again like 'it's the economy wot won it'. I should just scrape home unless there is a seismic movement next week.

Thursday 28 April
With the Iraq War now the prominent issue, Labour is on a slide, Libs on the up. We shall have to see whether this will do for me. Seats like Luff's, where Labour is second, will have relatively large majorities. I chose the wrong one in 1992!

MH not brilliant on special leaders' *Question Time*: fails to justify tax cuts and says we would have attacked Iraq for reasons of 'regime change plus'.

Sunday 1 May
Patrick Cormack rings to say his Lib Dem candidate has died; his campaign is aborted. Will have to fight a by-election in June/July. Poor chap.

MH has attacked Blair as a liar. Any 'distrust the PM' benefit has gone to the Liberals. Perhaps this is the plan for Labour marginals where Liberals are third. Meanwhile our policies don't seem to add up to a theme. Hopefully Liberal momentum won't gather more pace this week.

As of today, my best guess (for my seat) is: Conservative 46%, Lib Dems 38%, Labour 10%. Majority 8% = 3,500.

Monday 2 May

The polls are running away from us. It looks worse than 1997. I shall be lucky to hold on. Best guess now: Conservative 45%, Lib Dem 38%, Labour 11%, others 6%. Majority 7% = 3,000.

Tuesday 3 May

Nothing seismic (yet) but polls still drifting away from us. Today looks like: Conservative 44%, Lib Dem 39%, Labour 11%, others 6%. Majority 5% = 2,000.*

Friday 6 May

Actual result: Conservative 45.39%, Lib/Dem 40.03%, Labour 10.71%, others 3.87%. Majority 5% = 2,500. (Total collapse of Greens and 30% fall in Labour.)

National result: Labour 35.2%, Conservative 32.4%, Lib Dem 22.0%, others 10.4%.

Saturday 7 May

Roger Gale and Nick Winterton ring to express their distress about MH's sudden announcement that he will go as soon as leadership rules have been sorted out. Gale asks, 'Has there been a stitch-up? If so, it will upset the volunteers'.

Sunday 8 May

Speak to MH on the phone. He will stay until the party conference. He thinks campaigns in the future will all be local/pavement politics. I disagree. They will be about the positioning of parties and the economy. I tell him his legacy will be to have plugged the leaking Conservative ship (provided a semblance of unity) and to have set it sailing again.

Wednesday 18 May

Voted in unopposed as chairman of '22. Dinner with Henry Angest at Mosimann's. Henry concerned about the 'control freakery' of the party. (He

---

* This turns out to be the most accurate pre-poll forecast I have ever made.

offers to resign two days later as a party treasurer when told by Jonathan Marland he cannot have a view about the leadership contenders when he is backing David Davis. Subsequently he agrees to put the Treasurership into abeyance for the duration of the leadership contest.

Thursday 19 May

Meet most members of new '22 Executive. Great concern about Chief Whip's rumoured new rules of behaviour and new constitution being linked to leadership rule changes. Lack of dialogue with leadership resented. Talk to Monbiot. Ask why I have not seen draft paper on constitution. Says it's on its way. Agrees to meet '22 on Monday before board meeting.

Sunday 22 May

Nick Winterton rings to say he will stand for vacant position of treasurer, having failed to retain his position as vice-chairman.

Francis Maude, new party chairman, phones Maunsel Street, basically to complain about Damian Green's public criticism of leadership rule changes (DM is a member of the '22 Executive).

Monday 23 May

Michael Howard rings from Monte Carlo on a line which keeps breaking up. 'What do you think about the constitutional changes?' I think it's a bit late to consult me now. I say, 'I've only been put in the picture in the last twenty-four hours.'

Raymond Monbiot gets a rough time at '22 Executive. I get a rough time at the board, where I argue that we should uncouple leadership rule changes from other changes and I refuse to sign the consultative document which goes out from the board collectively.

Disastrous meeting in Grand Committee Room

Tuesday 24 May 2005

David Maclean (Chief Whip) rings me at home to tell me MH has arranged a meeting of parliamentary party in Grand Committee Room. I say there will be 'even more of a row if I do not chair this under the aegis of '22 Committee'. DM says he will convey this to the leader; MH later agrees, as he does to meet the '22 Executive in his room. This is a tough meeting poisoned by Howard Flight affair. Eric Forth leads off saying, 'Never again must one man be allowed to deprive a colleague of his livelihood on a whim and just because he disagrees with his views.' MH defends himself. Rachel Whetstone looks as if she might burst into tears. Others speak in a similar vein, though in a more moderate tone.

All this is nothing to the mood of the meeting which I chair at 6 p.m. in the Grand Committee Room. About 200 MPs and peers present. MH introduces Raymond Monbiot, who starts to speak on proposed leadership rule changes and constitutional changes. All is relatively quiet until Monbiot says this is a take-it-or-leave-it, no-cherry-picking package, which no one who wants to win the next general election will dare change. The room electrifies. You can feel everyone is spoiling for a fight. Douglas Hogg begins. He launches into a vicious attack. 'We are being bounced. The leadership rules and the changes to the structure of the party are two totally different things which do not require each other. If necessary we should throw the entire package out!' Massive cheers. Even more so when Edward Leigh launches into a pretty personal attack on MH for Howard Flight affair.

After six more attacks, I close down meeting and say we will meet again tomorrow!

Brief word with MH. I suggest a redrafting committee with parity for MPs and volunteers. He likes it.

Wednesday 25 May

Take morning call from Rachel Whetstone. She says, 'We may have done things wrong in the past but we have never been this incompetent before.'

Summoned to meet MH in his office. Suggests a drafting committee with MPs. I say there would need to be equal numbers of MPs and volunteers. He agrees. Stephen Sherborne comes back later with a proposal for three MPs and three board members, with Francis Maude in the chair.

'22 Executive meeting later in the day (4 p.m.) doesn't like this – especially if Maude has a vote. Forth out to create anarchy, from whose ashes Davis will rise. Mood maintained, though not quite so electric as night before, at full '22. MH on platform is glum when I tell him about Executive's decision for the moment to throw out drafting committee idea. Threatens to issue press release about this. I advise against.

Thursday 26 May

MH calls a telephone conference of the board; proposes decoupling leadership rules from the rest. After much discussion, decision eventually taken to decouple.

Later I try to email this to Executive members and, after talking to McLoughlin, to page the party. MH blocks this on the phone, saying 'It was my initiative. I want to send a letter.' I say, 'I have already told the Executive.' MH replies, 'I wish you hadn't.' It has come to this.

Wednesday 1 June

Ring Gavin to confirm that if any part of the reform package is voted down by MPs, the 'veto' applies to it all and the whole lot falls. He says, 'Michael, you are the only person who can bring the parliamentary party back into some kind of dialogue with the board'. I say, 'I have two problems: (1) I will not know, until we get back [from a short recess], whether the Davisites will try to force MH out early,* (2) the way Monbiot has tried to force the package of reform on MPs has left them with a deep suspicion of being forced into surrendering further powers/freedoms over their own actions.'

Monday 6 June

Party still in a febrile state on return from the short recess. Peter Tapsell asks me how it would work if I received thirty letters demanding a vote of confidence in MH. I say if MH lost or withdrew, leadership election would go ahead under present rules.

Tuesday 7 June

'22 Executive meets at 9.30 to discuss constitution, especially leadership rules. Evenly divided on alternative of ranking by the Convention; eventually agree on 'soundings'.†

Beginning to weld '22 Committee into more of a team. At one crucial moment in the proceedings Nicholas Soames belches; Peter Luff jumps.

Wednesday 8 June

Interesting meeting of '22. Committee in a thoughtful mood – determined to take leadership rules separately from organisational ones. Discuss leadership rules in detail. (Tapsell, Cash, Gale, Quentin Davies want immediate election. They want me to ask Howard to go at once. If I did I would be taking sides – pro Davis.) Six proposals emerge. Will vote next week.

Much booing of whips when Forth asks why no whip on the platform.‡ I

---

* A *Telegraph* poll on this day showed Davis had support of 54 per cent of the party membership.

† MPs would take 'soundings' of the voluntary party before they finally voted for the leader. For the volunteers it was the weakest of the options.

‡ The Chief Whip had decided to end the age-old practice of a whip giving the next week's business, much to the chagrin of the '22 Committee.

ask Maclean to reply as he is sitting at the back. He does so by saying, 'There are lots of whips dotted around the room.' Why he wants to quarrel with us on such a trivial matter I can't imagine. David Wilshire (ex-whip) comes up to say that he has written evidence that the whips want to cut down '22 to size. The eternal tension between whips and '22 goes on!*

Thursday 9 June
ROMEO brings up first letter calling for a vote of confidence in MH and says to Jessica that my move with the Chief Whip at '22 last night was 'brilliant'. David Wilshire shows me a memo Maclean wrote to his whips telling them of his plans to bypass '22 by setting up a planning meeting on Tuesdays where the whip would be announced. Rachel Whetstone comes to my office to ask my view about whether MH should go early. I say that to give a view that he should would be in effect to back the position of one of the leadership candidates (David Davis). Quentin Davies indicates he will be writing to me.

Lunch with Maurice Saatchi (peers' dining room). MH really thought he would win the general election. Focus groups had told him the only issue that mattered was immigration – Tories were *numero uno* on this.

Geoffrey Clifton-Brown (pairing whip) tells me there is a growing mood to move fast on leadership and to 'acclaim' one man. I wonder.

Tuesday 14 June
Two more letters, from HAMLET and MACBETH – the latter given to me ostentatiously at my seat at the top of the gangway in the chamber! No real move from the Davis set yet.

Meeting between '22 Executive and seven members of the board. Billed in the press as a gladiatorial clash, it is all rather muted. I give them list of eight leadership rule options on which we will vote tomorrow. Stress we do not want a decision on organisational changes until new leader emerges. Ominously, Forth stays silent. I wonder what, if anything, he has up his sleeve.

Wednesday 15 June
Interesting times at the '22. About 140 members present. We vote on eight alternatives to leadership rules. Howard, Maude and Maclean only three

---

*   For the genesis of this tension, see Philip Goodhart and Ursula Branston, *The 1922: The Story of the Conservative Backbenchers' Parliamentary Committee*, Macmillan, 1973.

who vote for board's proposals. '22 Executive proposal carried by about 2:1.* Davisites and ex-Duncan Smithites furious because (a) they want chaos, out of which DD will rise like a phoenix (it was all too 'slick' according to Bernard Jenkin), and (b) they don't want final say to rest with parliamentary party, which let down IDS. IDS himself comes up to me outside Room 14 and says vote not decisive enough. IDS looks calm. He had a good PMQ. MH had a bad one. We are rudderless.

Hence letters demanding vote of confidence in MH beginning to arrive – total of almost ten tonight, including two new boys. My proposition to MH a year ago is turning out to be so accurate. Leadership rule changes were bound to become entwined with ambitions of rival factions.

Whetstone thinks I will get thirty letters but MH will win vote of confidence. It's been such a humiliation for MH, who sat on the right in the body of the hall; anything could happen now.

Steen, Tyrie, Simpson, Soames, all say to me before the meeting, 'You must push through the '22 Executive proposal for new rules.' Clearly they were in concert and worried about the tactics of the Duncan Smithites. At bridge dinner afterwards, Robathan reveals himself as a Cameronite. It's going to be Cameron v. Davis. Cameron wants delay. Davis wants to go now.

Friday 17 June

Another letter in, from OTHELLO; makes ten. Still the individualists and the disaffected; no real sign of a concerted move by Duncan Smithites or Davisites. If it doesn't happen next week, may not happen at all. Time is running out for those who want a change in leader before party conference.

Monday 20 June

Acrimonious board meeting. I refuse to join discussions about future organisation until there is agreement on an end date after we have a new leader. Jonathan Marland blames 'antics of MPs' for money drying up. I say, 'Leaving aside the abuse and the excuses, are we going bust?' Ashcroft smiles. Everyone else very po-faced and quiet.

Tuesday 21 June

Tyrie and Steen ring up to say, 'I hear you had a tough time on the board,'

---

* About 100 of the 180 backbenchers who attended the meeting endorsed a motion drawn up by the Executive of the 1922 Committee. This proposal included a consultative period with all local associations, but the choice of leader would ultimately be decided by the parliamentary party.

which means a board member is getting to them. Francis Maude in the division lobby trying to work on members of the Executive, especially Ottaway, Soames and Tyrie.

As we file past the voting desks, Keith Simpson shouts out, 'There are twenty-nine letters in your pigeonhole because Eric Forth can't count.' Roger Gale says, 'In that case he has thirty because I've written one.' Things are a bit more open this time (although JULIET beckons me out of sight in the corridor leading to PM's office behind the Speaker's chair to give me her letter).

Wednesday 22 June
Open rebellion at main committee. Poor Geoffrey Clifton-Brown booed when he says, in answer to Steen's request for a written whip, that most information is on the electronic whip. (This can't go on: up to thirteen letters and still no concerted operation.)

Re Howard Flight, Peter Tapsell tells committee how Churchill rebelled against the party on the India Act and nobody called for him to lose the whip. 'Yes they did,' I say. 'The 1922 Committee did, but nobody took a blind bit of notice of them.' I am not sure this is quite right but it breaks the tension for a moment.

At Executive I say MH wants to row forward with reforms whereas we want to row back! What I suppose I'm doing is allowing everyone to let off a bit of steam in as orderly a way as possible. Forth never speaks at the Executive except to say, 'I want a leadership election now.'

Cameron catching up on the outside, according to gossip.

Monday 27 June
Meeting with MH. He is still bent on pushing through his 'reforms' by 27 September. I say party won't be bounced. This view confirmed at a planning meeting in my room of the working group set up to negotiate with board (Chope, Green, Ottaway, Tyrie).

Wednesday 29 June
More open discussion of the constitution at '22, most of it firmly anti board's proposals, but sensible. Then Laurence Robertson proposes abolition of the board and gets enough 'hear, hears' for me to feel encouraged to bring forward a firm motion next week. Am I allowing all this to get out of hand – or are we just letting off steam in high summer?

Thursday 30 June
Extraordinary meeting at CCO in Victoria Street. Present for board:

Maude, Monbiot, Porter, Barwell, Ashcroft. For '22: me, Ottaway, Tyrie, Chope, Green. Agree on all our main demands: leadership rules – voting back to MPs with consultation for the rest of the party; other contentious rule changes only by agreement or when new leader in place. Maude admits he misjudged most of parliamentary party – which was soured by Howard Flight affair, Monbiot bouncing, and past history of being bashed by voluntary party.

Tuesday 5 July
Second meeting of the working group in my room in the Commons. Last Thursday's meeting really was too good to be true. Maude clearly sees the need to row back. Says he will write a paper for next week which will be a way through. It will no doubt attempt to relink leadership rule changes with the rest and we will have to turn it down. However, we do agree an amended leadership rule change to provide for a candidate to go out for open consultation, with MPs having the final choice. At a meeting afterwards, '22 Executive accepts this.

Wednesday 6 July
'22 Executive, having exhausted itself on leadership rules, reverts to usual pay and rations agenda. Main committee a dry tinder box, just avert a motion from Laurence Robertson being put to the vote abolishing the board! The former Duncan Smithites (Cash, Jenkin, Hayes) try to disrupt everything on leadership rules; they want their revenge on parliamentary party and to keep the rules as they are. Next week we will have to decide whether to have a serious vote on leadership rules, e.g. secret ballot.

Thursday 7 July
London attacked by terrorists. Walk from Westminster to Paddington. No buses. Crowds of pedestrians with mobiles to their ears scurrying home in the afternoon sun.

Wednesday 13 July
'22 Executive decides to go for a full ballot on leadership rules with a ballot on Tuesday/Wednesday.

Thursday 14 July
One-to-one meeting with MH, who accepts that rule changes may not now get necessary two-thirds vote. Meeting is short and rather cold. He must be pretty fed up; he certainly seems so.

Friday 15 July
Telegraph leader talks of 'Howard's rule changes' – which they are not – saying they are 'retrogressive' and should be voted down next Wednesday in favour of an electoral college.

Monday 18 July
Meeting of CCO property company. Great deal of latent unhappiness/ anger for having wasted several millions of the party's money moving HQ to Victoria Street and leaving 32 Smith Square to rot. Decision taken to get on with refurbishing 32 Smith Square and to get rid of Victoria Street asap.

Tuesday 19 July
Letter in *Telegraph* from Ancram, May, Leigh et al. (ten in all) disowning leadership rule changes on which we are now voting. MH very downhearted at drinks he gives after Buck House garden party. Wants to quit his job asap. At the moment this looks as if it will be around Christmas.

Wednesday 20 July
Count in the little office on right of Chief Whip's office. Nick Winterton shouts the total number of votes as he pulls ballot papers from box. Butterfill counts yeses (127), Chope noes (50). So motion to change leadership rules carried with over two thirds. All rather surprising as I announce results to full committee – as there had been quite a 'No' operation. Looks as if MPs will take control again.

Thursday 4 August
Board meeting. Board agrees to put new leadership rules to the constitutional college. Francis Maude states simply, 'That's that – we are all agreed!' and no one demurs. I consider it best not to say much.

Next subject introduced by me – Howard Flight. Board agrees to meet him on my suggestion.

Chapter 23

David Cameron

Tuesday 16 August 2005

David Cameron comes to see me at his request in Cropthorne to 'ask my advice' about the leadership rules. Sit on the lawn on a lovely clear midsummer's evening. Everything fresh and green after yesterday's rain. Herbaceous border in full bloom. Cross of St George fluttering in a warm breeze above the church tower and against a pure blue sky. I sit in my tennis clothes after a morning game. Relaxed and at peace with the world.

Cameron begins by asking me several technical questions about rules of expenditure for candidates – when I will call the election etc. On the latter point I say, 'I assume MH will formally announce his departure on last day of party conference. I will follow immediately to call for nominations.'

Cameron tells me his key supporters are Andrew Robathan, Peter Luff, Greg Barker[*] and George Osborne.

Briefly we talk politics. He says, 'What we want is people to vote for us. This will mean changing some of our past emphases.' I say, 'We also need coherence. Policies must add up to a set of clear objectives. Above all we must be able to answer the question "What is the Conservative Party for?"' The conversation is very agreeable. We part on good terms.

Wednesday 24 August

Nicholas Winterton rings to say Daniel Hannan MEP has rung him to seek his support as a leadership candidate. Subject to legal advice, I will have to rule against this. The constitution says that the leader must be chosen from Parliament. I will assume this means the British Parliament, from which the Executive is drawn.

Friday 26 August

Very difficult '22 meeting in CCO, to discuss proposed leadership rules changes – meeting demanded by the constitution 'to discuss and debate' rule changes but not to decide them. Those who show up – Ann Widdecombe

---

[*] MP for Bexhill & Battle since 2001; MoS for Energy and Climate Change since 2010.

and stroppy Duncan Smithites – don't like proposals to give decision on leadership to the parliamentary party, which they resent for having given IDS the push. They stage what is clearly a planned demo, complaining about timing and notice of the meeting. Their strong point is that the ballot papers only reached MPs' offices the day before. I say meeting was called at the beginning of the postal ballot so that votes would be able to be influenced (the only point of the meeting) prior to their being sent in. However, I accede to the request that the meeting be adjourned to late in September. I expect more trouble then.

Saturday 27 August
Letter in the *Telegraph* from Cash et al. attacking yesterday's meeting and the new leadership rules. I agree on the phone with Gavin Barlow to strengthen my letter to colleagues about the suspended meeting, pointing out that this could not amend or change the ballot, which is now under way.

Sunday 28 August
All the talk in the Sunday press is of the rise of Ken Clarke. The Cashites believe the new rules would help him. I wonder.

Friday 2 September
Peace on the balcony at St Tropez broken by a stream of faxes from Jessica, e.g. Howard Flight wants a copy of '22 report (rejected by board) recommending his case goes to ethics and integrity committee. After talk with Richard Ottaway I agree. Also certain amount of flak from Peter Luff about changed date of leadership rules meeting for MPs. Tell Luff if I hadn't agreed we would have lost the vote and probably faced legal challenge from Cash et al.

Sunday 4 September
British papers full of the meeting of Conservative chairmen (last Tuesday) hell bent on throwing out proposed leadership changes.

Wednesday 7 September
St Tropez. Worst storms that I have ever witnessed overnight.

Times is full of association chairmen wanting Clarke and the old rules; ironic that Cash thinks new rules will benefit Clarke. Equally ironic is that Andrew Tyrie, Clarke's manager, should have been pressing hard for a change in the rules to give MPs the final say. It's all based on a wrong assessment of the IDS election. Portillo at that point split the right, not the left. He became leftish later. The right did have a majority amongst MPs.

Friday 9 September
Talk to Jessica on train between Nice and Florence. Dan Hannan has rung her for a copy of the leadership rules.

Sunday 11 September
Florence. Saturday's *Telegraph* confirms topsy-turvy nature of Conservative politics. Party at large beginning to support Clarke (he is better known). MPs seem to favour Davis – exactly the opposite to what each camp expected.

Monday 12 September
Panzano, Chianti. Talk to Francis Maude about what to do if there is a vote to stay with old rules. He says that if we are to get through by Christmas may have to have flawed membership lists (I don't like this). Also I say not inclined to alter consequential rules if we go with old rules.

Tuesday 13 September
Ring Maude and tell him I do not think it desirable to rush the leadership election knowingly without adequate membership data. He says he will look into the details of the trade-offs and we will talk again.

Monday 19 September
Last day in Panzano. Jessica rings to say Chris Grayling has been on to her to ask if Liam Fox can have list of association chairmen, as Ken Clarke has got one.

Wednesday 21 September
Bill Cash raises legal point arguing that I have not complied with constitution in calling meeting of '22 (reconvened for today – about forty present at CCO). Doesn't seem inclined to press his arguments.

Friday 23 September
Bill Cash writes enclosing a legal opinion from a QC to say I have got it all wrong in the leadership rule change process – especially with respect to MPs' meetings. A lot seems to hang on the meaning of 'convene', which according to the dictionary has two senses – to arrange a meeting or to arrange to arrange a meeting. Bill's lawyer takes the second meaning and says I acted prematurely in writing to MPs to fix a meeting (re Article 9 of the constitution); needless to say I take first meaning. Bill disagrees with the leadership rule changes and is trying to wreck the whole process. (I bumped into him in the Garrick on Wednesday; he said then that he admired my cool.) I have

written to him to say that I have played it right. I wonder what he will do next – take me to court? (Francis Maude, a lawyer, has said he has no case but party would pay my legal fees.)

George Osborne is producing good speeches arguing, amongst other things, that we were wrong to produce minor tax cuts 'like rabbits from a hat'. What was needed was a confident and coherent rationale of low taxes. Meanwhile Cameron courts the left.

Tuesday 27 September
4 p.m. Result of the leadership rule change ballot produces a majority in favour of change of about 61 per cent, which is not enough (63.6 per cent needed) – MPs over 70 per cent in favour. MH being said to have 'lost'; he could easily detach himself from the whole process, in which he has no real locus. He is in a sombre mood when I ring him at home to discuss mechanics of his resignation. (He will write me a letter on the Friday after next week's party conference.) 'I agree,' I say. 'It will give a clear run for your valedictory speech.' He adds, 'Actually I will probably write to you on the Thursday, dated Friday.'

Wednesday 28 September
MH rings me at Maunsel Street. He is in a chirpier mood and ready to involve himself in organisational matters to do with the ballot (my job). 'You should run off the last ballot of two so that everyone knows the parliamentary party's real views,' he says. I say, 'That may be difficult to get through the '22 Executive at this stage.' Later in the day the board rejects the idea and I decide to drop it in favour of going for as little change to our rules as possible. Board broadly agrees with this.

Howard Flight comes to the board and is very charming and says he could be conciliatory, although he is accompanied by his lawyer. After his departure, I support Michael Ashcroft that he be restored to the candidates' list.

Thursday 29 September
Bizarrely Ken Clarke rings me to lobby me. I tell him, in my role as referee, I can't even blink an eyelid. (I go back a bit with KC, to the days when he would have drummed me out of the party over Maastricht.) I wonder if the rest of his lobbying of MPs is as insensitive. He might be joking – ends up with 'Treat yourself as lobbied'. Talk to Gavin Barwell about what we will do if Davis gets majority of the party in the early rounds and the rest drop out; in this case there won't be a public ballot.

Saturday 1 October

Michael Howard rings to press his view, rejected by the board, that there should be a run-off between last two in the MPs' ballot. I say this could be construed as getting the new rules by the back door, especially if the person who comes second backed out of the membership ballot; however, if he wishes me to do so, I will canvass the leadership candidates. MH says he will sleep on it and ring me in the morning.

Sunday 2 October

MH rings back to say he has thought about my views overnight and will not press the matter of an extra final ballot of MPs.

Talk in the papers of Ancram standing as the candidate of hard right – Christian family values, moral majority – backed by Bill Cash: Catholics' last stand.

Monday 3 October

Off to Blackpool for party conference. Meet MH to confirm he will be giving me a letter of resignation this week, post-dated Friday.

Dramatic *Newsnight* focus group showing Cameron miles ahead (of Fox). No votes published for Davis, Clarke, Rifkind.

Tuesday 4 October

Wake up with Cameron newsletter outside our door underscoring *Newsnight* programme. Excellent speeches by Cameron, Osborne and Clarke.

2 p.m. Meeting of 1922 Executive in Ascot room in Imperial Hotel. We agree to keep our rules broadly as they are, with four minor drafting changes.

Decks now cleared for MH resignation.

Wednesday 5 October

While waiting in the sunshine for the shuttle bus from the Imperial to listen to David Davis and Liam Fox, MH's driver comes up to me with handwritten letter of resignation from MH. Wonder what my fellow passengers on the bus would say if they knew what is in the envelope!

DD's speech wooden; he's slipping. LF's speech good; he's rising.

Chris Hutton (treasurer's department) rings me to ask if I was involved with the details in 1983 of sale and leaseback of 32 Smith Square. I say I was around but Cecil Parkinson and Alistair McAlpine knew details.

Owen Paterson, Bill Cash and Edward Leigh eating together in the main dining room. They ask: when is last moment for nominations?

Thursday 6 October
Walk to Commons at 10 a.m. Met by BBC camera outside St Stephen's Entrance. Say, 'I can't say much now but it looks like it's going to be a busy day in the office.' 12 noon: issue press release, which says roughly, 'I have received MH's letter of resignation. I now call for nominations, which marks the start of the leadership campaign.'

MH rings me in Cropthorne. 'Furious' with '22's idea to delay the count by one day so new leader would not have to do PMQs at once. 'I don't want to do it for one week longer than I have to.' I say that is important and I will try to get the decision reviewed. Press full of Davis's fall and Cameron's rise.

Tuesday 11 October
Dan Hannan rings to say he will vote Cameron (has various Eurosceptic assurances from him, including that we will leave EPP 'on day one') – mainly because only Cameron will beat Clarke. Cameron's man, Robathan, comes to my office with his nomination papers, which exclude the necessary commitment to 'abide by 1922 rules and regulations'. Has to take the papers away. Will have to warn other candidates not to leave it too late.

Wednesday 12 October
Chris Grayling comes in with Fox's nominations. Clarke and Davis still to submit papers. Rifkind leaves the race and declares for Clarke. Ancram going for Cameron, 'I'll have to take my tie off.'

Jessica rings on her way home; has seen Ottaway coming out of a Davis drinks party 'so he must still be running'. Pass McLoughlin. He hopes to be Cameron's Chief Whip.

Thursday 13 October
Eightieth birthday party for Thatcher at Mandarin, Hyde Park, attended by the Queen. One wag says, 'The Queen looks regal, too.' MT makes a good response to speech by Peter Carrington. Afterwards I tell her her speech was 'excellent'. 'No, it was adequate,' she says.

Friday 14 October
Papers full of Cameron's unwillingness to come clean about drugs he took at Oxford. Anthony Steen (for Clarke) rings me to ask whether it would be 'helpful' to Cameron if the '22 officers asked to see him 'to clear his record'. I said words to the effect of 'You must be joking. It's not our job to protect

or expose candidates.' Steen persists (he is a lawyer). 'Couldn't we be got for negligence if he were found out later?' 'Only if it was our job to vet the candidates and to give them a clean bill of health – which it is not,' I say. The matter takes on some significance when Damian Green (DD) rings me to say a senior lobby man has told him that I am summoning Cameron for 'a vetting'. Is Steen at the bottom of this and, if so, what on earth does Clarke's 'no dirty tricks' campaign think it is up to?

Tuesday 18 October

First ballot day. Davis bandwagon slows down, Cameron–Fox accelerates. Prescott comes up to me in the lobby: 'Keep that man Davis going. We don't want a bloody Blair Mark II.' IDS votes last in the ballot five minutes before close at 5 p.m.

Unbeknownst to me, Ann apparently saw MH last week about a PC for me. MH gave her a polite brush-off, saying his quota with Blair was full. (Come to think of it, I must be one of a very few ex-ministers of state not to be a Privy Counsellor and probably the only chairman of the '22 Committee.)

Result of first ballot: David Davis 62, David Cameron 56, Liam Fox 42, Ken Clarke 38. Clarke is eliminated.

Wednesday 19 October

Liam Fox comes up at the 7 p.m. vote with his campaign manager, Oliver Heald, who says he is taking legal advice as to whether CCO has prejudiced tomorrow's ballot. He is upset by a BBC story that CCO is planning a 'coronation' of Cameron on Friday. I heard about this earlier in the afternoon. At 5.40 I ring Francis Maude about it. He says it is completely untrue. (Confirmed by Gavin Barwell in a telephone call from Maunsel Street.) BBC runs story again at 10 p.m. Davis very weak when asked, 'Will you pull out if Cameron well ahead?' He says, 'I think I will,' which seems to confirm BBC story.

Thursday 20 October

Day of second ballot. All talk on the radio is of whether Davis will withdraw if he does badly. I ring Francis Maude at 8.00 to say I will give my consent to this (which is required by the constitution) only if the party at large is in some way consulted first. Maude agrees enthusiastically.

A senior colleague comes to my room to say that he has tried, unsuccessfully, to persuade DD unequivocally to stay in the race if he comes a bad second. The MP is agonising as to whether to switch from Davis to Fox. His problem is that by doing so he may further weaken DD's resolve without getting LF in the last two. Bill Cash tries to see me 'about the rules'. I get Jessica to tell him, 'After the ballot.' He apparently says, 'Too late.' He is last to vote at 4.55. Result: Cameron 90, Davis 57, Fox 51.

Davis makes a fair point on TV: 'If LF had gone out in first round I would have been in the nineties.'

Friday 21 October
Meet Cameron and Davis with Andrew Mitchell, George Osborne, Maude, Gavin Barwell in CCO. We agree to eight hustings. Atmosphere relaxed. You sense DD team not really in it – they aim to 'keep in with DC'.

Monday 24 October
Board gives dinner to say goodbye to MH at hotel next to MI5. MH raises with me across the table the issue of a run-off by MPs of last two candidates – a suggestion of his I had rejected some days ago. I say jokingly, 'If I had changed the rules at this stage, I would risk going to jail.' MH gives me a short legal dissertation as to why I might have faced damages (which interests me) but why I would not go to jail.

Wednesday 26 October
Andrew Robathan asks in division lobby if OK for Cameron to come to my office on Friday. I say, as far as I am concerned, this is OK so long as I am not being lobbied.

Wednesday 2 November
After '22 Committee, Cameron comes to my office, prompted by Andrew Robathan. We agree, if he wins, parliamentary party will not settle down easily. Key positions will be Chief Whip (he seems to favour the experienced McLoughlin) and chairman. DC asks me whether I have any suggestions for a chief of staff. I suggest a colleague's name. He seems to quite like the idea.

Thursday 3 November
DC and DD head to head on TV. Young idealist v. experienced politico with commitment to hardcore policies (tax, Europe). DD may have made up some ground. We shall see.

Friday 4 November
Press comments boost DD.

Wednesday 9 November
Blair defeated on ninety-days clause in Terrorism Bill.

Tuesday 14 November
Richard Ottaway tells me that while driving DC to his constituency of Croydon South, gets strong feeling Maude will be left as chairman.

'22 Executive agrees to three changes in the constitution: more MPs on board, some board intervention with associations, appeals for 'sacked' MPs.

Monday 5 December
Receive a call from MH, who insists that he speak first at the winner's announcement.

Ring Electoral Reform Society to find out how opening of envelopes going. Told in effect that Cameron has won overwhelmingly.

Tuesday 6 December
Day of the announcement. One last glitch. Arrive with Jessica in government pool car at around 2.40. (Walk last 200 yards because of the traffic.) In theory I am the only one who knows the result, having received the figures by fax in my office at 2 p.m. But the result has leaked to the two candidates. DC seems surprised by the extent of his victory when I tell him. DD has been told the exact figures by his campaign manager, David Wilshire, whom, together with James Gray, Tobias Ellwood (both DC) and Mark Prisk (DD), I allowed to leave the count room at 2 p.m. on the personal assurance of each that they would not reveal the result. So far as I know Wilshire is the only one to break the arrangement – he confirms this to me just after I leave DD.

DD himself is preparing himself for his concession speech, which he is to make after I have given the results and before DC makes his speech. I hear that he plans to end this with 'I now give you the next leader of the Conservative Party'. I say, 'That is meant to be my job.' DD insists he will do it himself and that Cameron wants it. I say, 'Maybe we should both do it,' and leave the room. A moment later I come back and say, 'That's a bit silly. You can do it.' Outside I tell Michael Salter (excellent Central Office man who is running the show) what I have decided. He must have told George Osborne, who rushes up to me and says, 'There has been no agreement about this with DD. As returning officer you should introduce DC.' It is now five minutes before the announcement, scheduled for 3 p.m. I say, 'I have no wish to quarrel with DD at this point. I am quite happy to leave the stage after I have given the result.' GO consults his PR man (Steve Hilton), who agrees that a handshake between DD and DC and a warm departure from

DD would be a good thing. We agree the change of plan and move down the back stairs with MH, DD, DC and me for the event which is the biggest show in town that day.

The result I gave was:

Candidate	Votes	% of votes cast	% of eligible voters
David Cameron	134,446	67.61	53.00
David Davis	64,398	32.39	25.38

Majority: 70,048 (35.23%). Total vote: 198,844. Total electorate: 253,689. Turnout: 78.38%.

David Cameron is elected leader.

Wednesday 7 December
DC addresses '22. Afterwards his chief parliamentary lieutenant, Andrew Robathan, comes up to me at a small party in Maunsel Street, where we both live, and tells me that he is not to be in the shadow Cabinet (whereas Andrew Mitchell, DD's campaign manager is). He is to be deputy Chief Whip under Patrick McLoughlin.

Monday 12 December
Desmond Swayne, Cameron's right-wing and independent-minded PPS, whom he inherited from MH, comes to see me in my room in Commons. I say '22 Executive needs to see DC asap (this is fixed later for following Monday).

Tuesday 13 December
A good deal of anxiety expressed at ERG breakfast about delay in leaving EPP. DC originally said it would be done overnight. We agree to write to Cameron.

At meeting of candidates committee, Bernard Jenkin, new deputy chairman (candidates), says the legal advice is that the constitution prevents the imposition of women candidates. The formula being used is that associations are 'expected' to adopt them.

Monday 19 December
'22 Executive meets Cameron. Well-structured meeting which he handles well. Four issues at meeting:

1. Links to policy groups
2. Changes to constitution, especially more MPs on board
3. Policy on candidates
4. Pensions: Cameron wants to be tough on public-sector pensions; must include MPs.

Afterwards to party at CCHQ.

Saturday 7 January 2006

According to the *Telegraph*, we're going to win the general election with a more interventionist approach to big business, health (more spending on a monopoly service), education (less choice) and Lib Dem policies on the environment and on aid, especially to Africa. Meanwhile Blair opts for a more Tory approach to the above.

Thursday 12 January

Meeting with DC in his room. He accepts that communication with parliamentary party not all it might have been during these 'dynamic days' but is totally confident about the essence of his 'new' policies – support the Health Service with more cash, protect comprehensive education and do not emphasise low-tax objective.

Later in the day, at 1 o'clock in my room, have 1½-hour meeting with Oliver Letwin, head of policy. I say, 'We won't win unless we beat the government on economics – by destroying their credibility and/or with a believable policy of our own, which in my view starts by reducing taxes to stimulate growth and personal well-being.' 'We've done that before,' says Letwin, 'and it didn't produce results'. 'That is because we were half-hearted and incoherent about it,' say I. 'You have to do better than Labour's approach to engineering growth through education and public-sector expansion; the secret has to be in personal and corporate motivation, i.e. low taxes.'

Wednesday 18 January

1922 Committee – fullish house for election for one vacancy for the Executive. Victory for politically incorrect right-winger – Mike Penning, press secretary to IDS. Afterwards Francis Maude runs into flak about special treatment for potential women candidates. 'Why pick out women? Why not go for the toffs?' asks an outspoken new MP. 'Give special treatment to working class.' Much cheering; the troops are restless.

I assume Maude briefing against me – as he used to do against William

Hague, with Portillo – in last Friday's *Independent*. In the last parliament his blacklist of anti-modernisers (I was defined as beyond the pale) reached the press and he had to apologise.

Monday 23 January
Meeting with Cameron OK. He takes note about FM.

Tuesday 7 February
ERG breakfast. Agree to press William Hague on leaving EPP.

Wednesday 8 February
PMQ: Cameron has a bad day: accuses PM of flip-flopping on policy on the day he (DC) is reported to be agreeing with Liberals on Iraq. Labour Party roars with support for PM, who squeezes every drop of political juice from the moment.

I politely eject Roger Helmer MEP from '22 Committee as he has (temporarily) had whip removed. (I walk the length of the room to chat to him in almost total silence.)

Tuesday 14 February
Candidates committee in CCHQ. Two hundred and two men have applied for 50 places on A list; 63 women have applied for same number of places.

Wednesday 15 March
1922 Executive meets Cameron in shadow Cabinet room at 3 p.m. One issue is whether or not DC is right to support government tonight on Education Bill. Cameron is robust in his own defence: 'Leadership means taking decisions which not everyone will support.' I sum up by saying, 'The more radical the change of policy, the more we need to be kept in touch.' Although the polls are beginning to turn against us, he is still on his own high, as were IDS and MH at this point.

Tuesday 28 March
Meeting with Cameron in his room; also present, as usual, his PPS, Desmond Swayne. Subject: the 'cash for coronets' crisis besetting Labour. Cameron's response to this has been to propose more state funding. I say if this is his final position, he will have to sell it to the party.

A number of colleagues come up in the votes on the Budget to say I must stay on as chairman of '22. John Butterfill, who thought of challenging me, says, 'You have my full support.' Andrew Robathan: 'You must stay on.'

Gerald Howarth: 'You are the only one who has been above the leadership battle who can give Cameron sound advice.'

Saturday 1 April

Michael Ashcroft's party at the Grosvenor House Hotel. Tom Jones, Lulu, Cliff Richard, Denise van Outen, cast of *Chicago*, Band of Scots Guards, indoor fireworks etc. – all compered by a slightly ageing and forgetful Jasper Carrott. What a wonderful evening.

David Cameron gets up from his table to talk to me as I return from the gents. 'You were right at our meeting the other day, Michael. Central Office is going to have to radically cut its expenses.' Loans and large gifts are 'out'.

Wednesday 19 April

Restive Exec meeting. Complaints about not being kept in touch re new candidate selection rules, policies etc.

Wednesday 26 April

Bump into Speaker at 8.15 in Lord North Street – doing an early morning walk as part of his recovery from his heart op. He is hopping mad about Charles Clarke having made his 'I've lost over a thousand foreign prisoners' confession by way of a written statement.

Friday 5 May

We got 40 per cent of the votes at the local elections. This presages a Lib–Con government at next election with us agreeing to 'discuss' PR and to abolish existing Lords. If Brown believes this, it also means another four years of Labour.

Wednesday 10 May

Walked home with Graham Brady, very agreeable, youngish shadow minister for Europe, one of our few MPs representing a northern seat. We agree that a strategic choice lies between appealing to middle-class Liberals and working-class former Tories.

Monday 15 May

Meet DC in his room to discuss various proposals:

1. appeal procedure for MPs who have lost the whip;
2. intervention from the centre on constituencies;
3. restructuring Board to allow for more MPs;
4. leadership rules to allow MPs the final say when we are in government.

I suggest, following a meeting with volunteers previous Wednesday, that we should try a voluntary approach to (1), (2) and (3). Cameron wants constitutional change – especially re being able to intervene with constituencies. I say '22 Executive likely to agree only with board change to include more MPs. DC accepts this.

Wednesday 17 May
Sit next to Thatcher at dinner given by 1922 Committee to mark her eightieth birthday at Four Seasons Hotel. Good speeches by Cameron, Parkinson and Brooke. I do a short welcome.

Monday 5 June
Meeting with Cameron and Swayne. Cameron prepared to sign agreement on appeal system for MPs who lose the whip near an election.

Tuesday 13 June
ERG fixes to meet Hague on Thursday when I am lunching with the Queen! Conservative Euro politics beginning to hot up.

Patrick McLoughlin and I open the ballot box in the whips' office to find one nomination for replacement of Eric Forth* on '22 Executive: arch-right-winger/Eurosceptic new boy Phil Davies!

Word has it that Hague has decided to postpone EPP exit. If true this is very serious. Desmond Swayne, who has warned DC about this in a note for his box tonight, shows concern when I see him in voting lobby at about 7 p.m. The change in mood about EPP confirmed when I talk at about 8 p.m. with Graham Brady. He is being kept out of the loop but confirms that difficulties with Czechs now a new 'reason' for not leaving EPP.

Wednesday 14 June
1922 Exec meets Cameron 3 p.m. in shadow Cabinet room. About EPP, DC says it's all a question of who we sit with (Czechs playing hard to get). This makes left on the Exec very happy; right are absent.

Thursday 15 June
St Paul's Cathedral for Queen's eightieth birthday service. Afterwards lunch given for the Queen by the City. Tony Blair, Menzies Campbell† and I

---

*   Eric Forth died on 17 May 2006.
†   MP for North East Fife since 1987; deputy leader, Lib Dems 2003–6; leader, Lib Dems 2006–7.

represent our various parties. Cameron at St Paul's but for some reason could not be at the lunch.

Thursday 22 June
See Cameron in his office 9.45. Desmond Swayne also present. Subject EPP. I make two points: First, this issue cannot be 'finessed'. We either stay in or come out. No one is interested in the whys or wherefores. There is no acceptable fudge. To say we will come out in 2009 (the next EP election) will be to stay in. Second, the fury of those who want to come out if we stay in will be far greater than that of their opposite numbers if we come out. A majority of the parliamentary party want out and at least twelve (I give the names) will rush to the media saying faith has been broken if we stay in. In discussion I make the point that to come out of the EPP was DC's one major promise during his election campaign. DC says, 'To get more women candidates was another.'

Thursday 29 June
Tennis with Swayne et al. on a glorious midsummer morning at Vincent Square – afterwards David Lea, former deputy secretary general of TUC, and Swayne came back for coffee on the roof terrace at Maunsel Street. Swayne tells me privately that only he and I know of Hague–Cameron trip to Czech Republic today (to meet leader of ODS, major Czech centre-right party). Purpose of this trip to persuade ODS to join our proposed group in European Parliament. Meanwhile Gerald Howarth girds the loins of 92 Group by getting them to sign a letter to Cameron telling him not to break faith on EPP issue.

Wednesday 5 July
Howarth tells me thirty MPs have signed his anti-EPP letter.

Sunday 9 July
Desmond Swayne all over the *Sunday Times*. Someone has hacked into his computer to reveal his very derogatory personal views given to Cameron about Theresa May, Francis Maude and others. I ring him to advise him not to resign.

Thursday 13 July
Cameron summons the parliamentary party to Room 14 ('22 room), 9.30 a.m., to tell us he will sign a deal with ODS to come out of EPP in 2009. David Heathcoat-Amory calls it a broken promise. The left are happy; David Curry says this gives us plenty of 'wriggle room'.

Friday 14 July
Predictably critical leader in *Telegraph* about Cameron's EPP 'sell-out'.

Friday 18 August
'Conference call' board meeting with Cameron participating. He overrides reservations/objections against positive discrimination in favour of women applicants for seats; at least 50 per cent of total in the final round must now be women. DC has a mandate for this, having fought his leadership campaign on 'more women MPs' and 'leave EPP'.

Monday 21 August
Up to London for the day for the finance committee. Agree, with my prompting, to report the actual financial position to the board and to seek its agreement to delay several millions of 'discretionary' expenditure.

Wednesday 25 October
Secret ballot by '22 on three extra places (for MPs) on the board. Draw between left and right. Victors – Ottaway (left) and Whittingdale (right), Graham Stuart (new). Disappointed: Luff (left), Chope (right), each only just missing.*

Thursday 16 November
I pop across road with a decanter of port for a gossip with Robathan. Not much port left when I take decanter home.

Monday 11 December
Right becoming very restive. (Polls tomorrow will show UKIP up 2 per cent, us down to 34 per cent, Labour 33 per cent.)

Monday 15 January 2007
Saw Cameron by myself in his room (regular fortnightly meeting). We agree that he will keep out of MPs' pay claim and I will keep our submission to SSRB† confidential.

Wednesday 21 February
Unveiling of Margaret Thatcher's statue. She makes a good joke: 'I would have preferred iron, but bronze will do.'

---

* I had successfully fought for three extra places on the board for MPs.
† Senior Salaries Review Body.

Monday 5 March
Regular meeting with Cameron, who is now riding high in the polls (8-point lead over Labour). He confesses to having 'had his eye off the ball' re the Probation Bill. 'We should have backed the government's plans to open the service up to competition against their left wing.'

Tuesday 6 March
With help of our front bench, Parliament votes to abolish the House of Lords in its present form.

Monday 26 March
Walk back from Committee Room 4, House of Lords (meeting on Cotswold line) with Cameron to his room in Norman Shaw. Along corridor beside the library, left at Speaker's Palace, right behind chair past PM's office, through two doors (my office two floors up), down one flight of stairs, out back door, right into cloisters in Jubilee Court, under tunnel, up escalators, across Portcullis House atrium, up two floors in lift to leader's suite. We are doing even better in the polls (15 points ahead in ICM). My job is to point out to him that there remain points of tension in the parliamentary party. 'Nothing nasty', I say, but (1) probation officers' issue (we voted against competition), (2) House of Lords (shadow government v. seventy-five Tory MPs), (3) Catholic adoption agencies to be forced to use homosexual couples, (4) announced tax on aviation, (5) U-turn on Manchester casino, (6) whip put on communication allowance vote, against '22 advice. Cameron takes note of this and agrees to meet '22 at 5.45 this Wednesday. Nevertheless, agreeable meeting.

Wednesday 28 March
Jacqui Lait, from next-door office, tells me '22 meetings 'much more informal these days'. Cameron addresses the '22 meeting; later back to Maunsel Street (after 11.30), where Ann still playing bridge with Rachel Robathan, Rosemary Lamont and Cecilia Goodlad.

In intervening weeks minor contretemps with Chief Whip about his office taking over major meetings between leader/chairman and parliamentary party. Chief Whip agrees there is a problem. I chair good meeting with Francis Maude after local elections.

Tuesday 24 April
Oliver Letwin (head of policy) comes to my room in the Commons. We agree on the following:

1. Policy papers to be produced at start of September for debate at party conference.
2. Sifting committee (me, OL, McLoughlin, Whittingdale, Ottaway) meet at party conference to select twelve controversial policies.
3. Debate these for six weeks in October/November.
4. Shadow Cabinet consider our deliberations.
5. Continue process, if necessary, next year.

Wednesday 2 May
Process described above goes off the rails with the sudden announcement of internal flight aviation tax completely out of the blue to the parliamentary party. Rumblings at '22.

Monday 14 May
Good meeting with Cameron. He is still doing well in the polls and it has given him confidence. He is more relaxed. Issues: DC wants to make a 'let's clean up politics' speech and to talk of MPs' pay being determined by third party. I say idea must come from MPs. This is a shop floor matter. He agrees. We say we will meet again to see how we can work this out.

Wednesday 16 May
Rumblings become outbursts at '22 on grammar school attack by Willetts. One hundred and ten at '22. Twenty-four speak, twenty-one essentially against Willetts.

Grammar schools

Thursday 31 May 2007
Grammar school issue rumbles on. Graham Brady forced to resign last week because he wants to build more, especially in and around his constituency. Dominic Grieve* allowed to stay on after writing in his local newspaper that more grammar schools should be built in Buckinghamshire if 'demographic trends warrant it'. Willetts agrees with this, somewhat implausibly, on *Newsnight*. So OK to expand in Bucks but not OK to expand in Sale.

---

* MP for Beaconsfield since 1997; shadow Attorney General 2003–9; shadow Home Secretary 2008–9; shadow SoS for Justice 2009–10; Attorney General since 2010.

Saturday 2 June
Grammar school debacle gathers pace in the press. Greg Clark (Kent) has added his voice to those saying party policy allows for building more grammar schools where they exist already. I call John Whittingdale, who turns out to be in Egypt. He is furious not to have been consulted about appointment of Andy Coulson (the other row story running). The Culture, Media and Sport select committee, of which JW is chairman, are about to produce a critical report on Coulson's role in the 'Royal bugging' affair (when he was editor of *News of the World*).

Sunday 3 June
Sunday papers (especially *Telegraph*) very critical of grammar school issue and Coulson appointment. Polls are beginning to narrow. We are 5 points ahead in ICM, down 2 from last time.

Tuesday 5 June
3.15: Short meeting with Cameron prior to 3.30 meeting with him and Exec. Discuss grammar schools. At the main committee Ken Clarke gives us a preview of a paper which he is publishing tomorrow on parliamentary reform and which, like the Maastricht Treaty, apparently he hasn't read.

Monday 9 July
Party's fortunes up and down. Down at present so all talk is of an election; don't believe it.

Tuesday 10 July
DC asks me to have a word with a colleague he has sacked. 'He is a close friend of mine,' says Cameron. 'He needs to know there will always be a way back.'

Friday 20 July
Day after appalling by-election results at Ealing Southall and Sedgefield. Leaked story in *Telegraph* re Cameron rows with '22 Executive – not true but damaging.

Sunday 22 July
Papers full of stories about me receiving up to six 'letters'. Actually I have one, from a bitter colleague.

Wednesday 25 July
DC addresses '22 Committee. One hundred and fifty people there. Does not take my advice to answer questions.

Thursday 26 July
David Cameron visits Upton-on-Severn following floods. Arrives at 6 p.m. at the memorial hall, an hour late. Meets civic leaders, fire chiefs etc. As he leaves we agree to meet over the summer recess.

Monday 24 September
Chair finance committee in the morning. All afternoon at board meeting where we discuss little else but (assumed) impending GE.

Dinner for board and Cameron at City Inn. Generally he is lively (shirt-sleeves), bullish, 'I'm looking forward to the election.' Impressive.

Tuesday 25 September
David Cameron comes up to me at end of a 'pre-election' presentation to MPs. 'I enjoyed last night,' he says.

Tuesday 2 October
Visit Blackpool conference to give sandwiches to association officers (for the last time?). Travel to Preston with Michael and Sandra Howard. She wants him to stay as MP. He claims to want to go.

Daily Telegraph publishes article by Iain Dale titled 'The right's 100 most influential personalities':

46. SIR MICHAEL SPICER MP
Chairman, 1922 Committee

Sir Michael has announced he is standing down at the next election but until then his influence remains. A shrewd tester of the political tea leaves, he has now had to preside over three leadership changes. He knew Iain Duncan Smith was in trouble before IDS himself did.

Wednesday 3 October
Cameron makes a good speech to the full '22 Committee and without notes. Enough to stave off a general election?

On 7 October Gordon Brown announced that he would not call an early general election.

Tuesday 9 October
Cameron in good form at our regular meeting. Says, 'Now we are riding high is the time to make friends.' Agree to proceed with programme of consulting party on policy, as previously planned.

Monday 15 October
Another Cameron meeting. Both he and the right are claiming the credit for the change in our fortunes. The right say it is because of the inheritance tax announcement. Cameron says (a) his 'greening' has made us likeable, (b) his performance, especially at the party conference, has made the next election winnable. The position of the right is made clear at a well-attended policy meeting to discuss 'priorities for tax cuts'.

Saturday 3 November
Liam Fox is speaker at my association's annual dinner. On the way to his car he says, 'Now Cameron is doing rather well in the polls, he is determined to use the opportunity this gives to make friends, e.g. in the parliamentary party.'

Monday 5 November
Friendly meeting with Cameron. Ed Llewellyn and Desmond Swayne also present. Discuss Cameron's next speech to '22, probably after Executive committee vote, Monday week.

   Also discuss question of patronage and one or two long-serving colleagues. It is agreed that there is a blockage at Number 10, but a willingness to set up a vehicle for sifting political honours. We agree that Cameron will be proactive in pushing for such a body made up, say, of former party leaders and Speakers.

Wednesday 14 November
Bump into John Prescott. 'Was it the withholding tax?' he asks. 'Crumbs, John,' I say, 'your memory is long.' At '22 I am reinstated unopposed.

Sunday 16 December
Announcement made that a new community hospital will be built in Malvern.

Monday 28 January 2008
Meet Cameron 4.30. He is troubled about whether to remove whip from Derek Conway, who has been censured by standards & privileges committee. I advise against.

Raise budget issue as chairman of finance. DC is determined to go ahead with an advertising campaign. I tell him if he does we may not be holding a war chest for the election.

Friday 1 February
Talk to Cameron on the phone. He says he would like to test ideas he has for controlling/releasing more details of MPs' expenses on parliamentary party. I suggest he meets '22 Executive next week. He agrees. Cameron tells me gardening and cleaning no-noes for claim under additional costs allowance. I say mortgage interest is the real no-no. Shows how hard whole disaggregation process is going to be.

Monday 4 February
DC calls me in to say he's decided to go ahead without consultation with his programme for releasing expenses information. He has called shadow Cabinet for 9 a.m. and '22 Exec for 9.45. He will tell us that we must publish details of all our expenses from 1 April.

Monday 18 February
Meeting with DC. Discuss formation of working party on declaration of allowances. Cameron agrees this should be advisory.

Tuesday 26 February
Speaker Martin invites in twenty or so elderly Tories for discussion of allowances. Ken Clarke: 'Put it all out to KPMG.' Rest of us: 'Leave ultimate control with Parliament.' Speaker seems in a muddle.

Wednesday 27 February
Talk to Speaker at the chair. Hopefully persuade him to go for an appeal procedure on 'retrospection' (retrospective disclosure of allowance claims).

Monday 3 March
Meet Patrick McLoughlin in my bank: says he is looking forward to our next dinner. 'We must work even closer together.'

Wednesday 5 March
Private meeting with Speaker; tell him '22 Executive in process of appealing against retrospection. Also invite him to speak to '22, which he declines. Virtually tells me he intends to stay till end of this parliament.

Monday 17 March
Chair finance meeting. No cash headroom at bank next month. Report this to the board and then leave for meeting with Cameron, where we discuss how to finesse members' allowances (transparency) issue and party finances.

Wednesday 19 March
Discover there will be full (three years') retrospective revelation of members' allowances.

Tuesday 1 April
Entertain Patrick McLoughlin at the Garrick. Very agreeable evening. He wants me to stay as chairman of '22 until election.

Wednesday 23 April
Good meeting with Cameron. He asks my view about future appointment of a CEO (Andrew Feldman) at Central Office. I approve.

Thursday 8 May
DC's diary secretary, Kate, tells Jessica that he wants to cancel my meeting with him on Monday and does not want to meet '22 Exec. He could meet me tomorrow, but I am in Worcestershire. Sensing something is up, I decide to go back tomorrow.

Friday 9 May
Arrive back in London on the train. Cameron confirms he has cancelled meeting with '22 Executive. I give three reasons why he should come to Executive: (1) he has said he would, (2) the attack on the Climate Bill is mounting, (3) colleagues are not happy with his involvement in pay and rations matters. He agrees to see Executive 'after Crewe & Nantwich [by-election]'.

Tuesday 13 May
Visit Crewe & Nantwich. Everyone very bullish. There are many 'For Sale' signs on the housing terraces – indicating private ownership and mobility.

Friday 23 May
Conservative Edward Timpson won Crewe & Nantwich yesterday with a 7,860 majority – a 17.6 per cent swing against Labour.

Tuesday 10 June
Meet with Cameron to prepare for meeting whole Exec tomorrow.

Wednesday 11 June

'22 Executive decides that modified ACP* scheme should be 'run through' standards in public life committee.[†] Cameron goes along with this in a hard-hitting but friendly meeting at 3 p.m. with '22 Exec.

Tuesday 17 June

Meet Speaker and Tony Lloyd, chairman of Parliamentary Labour Party. Shown advance copy of allowances report.

Memorial service for Francis Pym. Chris Patten gives the eulogy – pedantic and takes a swipe at Thatcher for sacking Pym after Falklands War.

Wednesday 18 June

Ask PM: 'Why are there always so many strikes at the end of a Labour government?' *Evening Standard* says I brought the House down. I also know that it is all so transitory and capable of sudden change.

What was good about the question: it was short (fourteen words) and did not allow PM to think up an evasive answer; strikes should be lower under Labour; 'always' refers back to the Winter of Discontent; 'end' implies Labour will lose next GE.

Monday 23 June

Latest in my meetings with Tony Lloyd. Prepare to see whether there is a motion on pay which we can jointly sign. He won't accept Baker in its entirety (3.5 per cent + £650 for three years and public-sector average earnings) nor can he accept government's rejection of it all.

Friday 27 June

Awayday at Latimer House. At dinner Keith Simpson does another of his funny turns. He masquerades as the Headmaster of the rather lefty Latimer College. I am supposed to be the Chairman of the Parent/Teacher Association. Keith is very good; totally captivates a potentially cynical audience of fellow MPs.

---

* Association of Conservative Peers

† This was eventually adopted by the House of Lords and is the scheme currently operational there; it comprises a per diem attendance allowance plus travel to and from the main home.

Saturday 28 June
At lunch Ed Llewellyn asks me to join Cameron to discuss MPs' pay debate next Thursday. On pay DC is voting with the government for restraint. I tell him '22 Exec voted in favour of fully accepting Baker. DC says, 'Why don't you vote with me? That would be really useful.' I say, 'It would also be surprising.' We then move in from our table on the lawn to a room set aside for his use.

Tuesday 1 July
Meet reps of PLP with Chope, Ottaway, Whittingdale. Agree to back Don Touhig's compromise amendment on MPs' pay.

Wednesday 2 July
Full Executive agrees and signs Touhig's motion to take full 'Baker pay increase' but delayed till next year.

Thursday 3 July
With shadow Cabinet support, Touhig amendment defeated. Recommendations of John Baker thrown out. The exact opposite has happened from what was required – more allowances, less pay. All because of shadow Cabinet and split in PLP. Tony Lloyd took a largish bunch with him with the encouragement of his whips. Our meetings with PLP were a waste of time.

Thursday 2 October
In a speech at party conference, Cameron attacks MPs' pension rights.

Monday 6 October
Parliament back. Stock Exchange collapses (7.9 per cent). We are in the middle of a financial crisis which is set to turn into an economic crisis.

5 p.m. Together with the Chief Whip I chair an emergency meeting of the parliamentary party which George Osborne addresses. He manages to sell the strategy of co-operating with the government in the eye of the storm. There is an underlying concern about this – most strongly held by people such as John Redwood and Philip Davies* – especially if it leads to our assisting in the wholesale nationalisation of British banks. Capitalism is seen to have failed and the left is on the attack. We must be careful not to give them (the socialists) cover, especially at the point when the real economy is about to turn.

---

* MP for Shipley since 2005.

The same dilemma faces the Republicans in the US presidential elections. It is one reason why Obama is forging ahead of McCain. Try to transmit all this to Osborne in the corridor outside the meeting. We both accept the need for him to keep closely in touch with parliamentary party in the weeks ahead. Agree to discuss again in a week's time.

Tuesday 7 October
Government commits £500 billion to save the banking system – almost doubling public expenditure in one day. AT PMQs David Cameron says, in effect, 'We support you so long as you crack down on the greedy banks.' Labour jeers – what a day. Stock market crashes again (5 per cent), nears 4,000 points – started year around 7,000. Great deal of unhappiness in parliamentary party. The concern is felt across the party.

Douglas Hogg says at '22 meeting that Parliament should probe more into what government are doing. He is representative of a wider view.

Wednesday 22 October
All goes well with the '22 dinner at the Grosvenor Marriott Hotel. Cameron says he wants me to continue to chair the finance & audit committee up to and including the election. He thinks Brown will stay. He speaks well. We have an interesting three-sided discussion with Patrick McLoughlin. Cameron not too pleased that Patrick and I think Speaker will stay till end of parliament. (I say we could do without a divisive election for his successor.) Patrick says, 'If he does go, Michael and I will have to do hard work on his successor'. (I open my speech from the rostrum: 'For those who have never heard of the 1922 Committee, all you have to know is that it was founded in 1923.')

Discuss with Cameron and McLoughlin next week's Climate Change Bill, over which there is an incipient rebellion: Redwood and Tyrie – opposite ends of the spectrum. I advise a two-line whip with relaxed view of those who abstain.

Friday 24 October
Stock market down again. 0.5 per cent fall in GDP. These are very bad economic times indeed.

Monday 27 October
Chair a meeting of finance committee at which it is reported that the financial crisis and narrowing of our lead in the polls are combining to dry up our funding in the City. Report this to the board.

Wednesday 29 October
Nicholas Winterton gets up at dinner with '22 Executive and officers of National Convention (chaired by Don Porter) and says I have been the best chairman of '22 in his life in Parliament (thirty-seven years)! Long may all this last – it won't.

Monday 17 November
My question to PM (who had refused to answer similar one from IDS): 'Why has the pound collapsed? Surely this is a reasonable question to ask a Prime Minister?'

Meet Cameron. He is tired. He has had a bad week – with polls narrowing and George Osborne under fire. Osborne coming to '22 this week. Cameron and I get on, even when we disagree.

Tuesday 18 November
DC meets parliamentary party. Tells them he has reversed previous policy to 'match Labour's' spending plans in 2010, thus allowing him to cut taxes to stimulate demand, and that they should be more focused at PMQ, 'like Michael Spicer'.

Wednesday 19 November
150ish people at '22 to hear George Osborne. He uses my question on Monday as a distraction: 'MS was spot on'! Two new colleagues, Ed Timpson and John Howell, to dinner.

Wednesday 26 November
Invite Ed Llewellyn to my room for a drink. Tell him we run out of money in January!

Friday 28 November
News of Damian Green's arrest.

Sunday 30 November
On *Andrew Marr Show*, Jacqui Smith, Home Secretary, apologises for Damian Green's arrest. Bill Cash rings me. We agree the prime issue is what role Speaker played, what he was told (Green says he was informed and not consulted), who gave permission for Green's room to be searched.

Wednesday 10 December
Don Porter threatens to resign from board and to take £4 million of loans

from the constituencies unless his helper at CCO is reinstated in the budget. The chairman, Caroline Spelman (still being investigated by standards commissioner), consults me. I advise that she should give in to Porter. There is a whiff of an early general election in the air (Brown is coming back fast in the polls; he is having a good credit crunch and we are not).

Wednesday 17 December
Meeting with Cameron 4 p.m. Discuss timing of general election. He thinks it could be very soon. I don't – too much at stake for Brown. I tell DC that from my experience with Thatcher, decisions about GEs very personal to the interests of PM. DC says at one point to Desmond Swayne, 'Michael and I very rarely disagree about anything' – nice, but not totally accurate! More a question of respecting/understanding the reasons for the other chap's point of view. In the modern jargon, each of us understands where the other 'is coming from'. For a start he is management; I am shop floor – except when I am chairing the party's finance committee.

Tuesday 13 January 2009
Patrick McLoughlin comes to see me in my room to alert me that we were shaping up to attack Harriet Harman's* plan to make us publish our expenses to the level that the Conservatives now do, by category heads. We now want to 'go further' and to publish in greater detail.

Sunday 18 January
McLoughlin rings me at Maunsel Street to say that the intention is to vote against government's motion to modify Freedom of Information Act re MPs' allowances and publication of receipts. My view is that advantages likely to be short lived, whereas disaffection on back benches could rebound for some time. I may ask to see DC this week (vote is on Thursday). Meanwhile restiveness on the right caused by appointment of Ken Clarke as shadow Business Secretary.

Wednesday 21 January
Dinner for parliamentary party. Samantha Cameron and Ann also invited. Sit opposite David Cameron. Good talk to him. Apparently he had tried to get me on the phone over the weekend about Ken Clarke appointment.

---

* MP for Peckham 1982–97, Camberwell & Peckham since 1997; SoS Social Security 1997–8; Solicitor General 2001–5; leader of Commons 2007–10; shadow SoS International Development 2010–11; shadow SoS Culture since 2011; chairman, Labour Party since 2007.

We discuss ups and downs of the week. DC says wishes he had more time to involve me. I say, 'I see a lot of the Chief Whip; he is very loyal to you and much liked by the parliamentary party, though needless to say we don't always agree.'

Tuesday 3 February
11.45: Meet DC. Andrew Mackay in attendance, as Desmond Swayne away at army camp as a TA major. Points raised by me:

MPs' pay. DC confirmed party policy that this should be set and implemented by an independent body by statute after the GE. But until then he reserves the right to interfere if Brown does.

Policy groups to be revived. Where policy has to be made rapidly, I am to be involved.

On further appointments to the Lords DC says, 'I will have to make a batch of working peers.'

Wednesday 25 March
11.10: Meeting with Cameron. He suggests MPs should make a declaration of their homes once a year. This goes down like a lead balloon when I put it to the Executive at 4.30 this afternoon.

Wednesday 1 April
Have a very interesting conversation (in the smoking room after '22 Committee) with Brooks Newmark (Braintree) about the 1997 leadership election. After Hagues left Howards and me, Brooks heard about the 'deal' from Alan Duncan. He went straight round to Hague's flat in Dolphin Square 'in the pouring rain' and met Hague just before midnight (Brooks was a close friend of Hague at Oxford). They spoke for over an hour. Brooks's argument was that if he went ahead with Howard – who BN felt would never win except with Hague on his ticket – Hague might never have the opportunity again to be leader. At around 1 a.m. Hague agreed with this. Asked later by BN why he felt able to rat on the Howard deal, Hague answered rather curiously, 'Because we never shook hands on it.' BN semi-fell out with Hague during his campaign, which was effectively taken over by Sebastian Coe,[*] Alan Duncan and Phil Harris.[†] But BN is revealed as having single-handedly turned Hague around on the critical night.

---

[*] MP for Falmouth & Camborne 1992–7; created Lord Coe 2000.
[†] Lord Harris of Peckham.

Wednesday 22 April
The only subject of the day is Prime Minister's suggestion of replacing living allowances with a per diem. DC comes to the '22 Executive and proclaims himself against it, as is the Executive for different reasons. They think Prime Minister being too draconian. DC thinks the reverse. Late that evening I join Patrick McLoughlin, Alan Duncan* and DC in a discussion of how we will amend the PM's motion. DC shows me a piece of paper he left with PM at meeting with him and Nick Clegg. This states, amongst other things, that overall value of package of allowances must come down.

Wednesday 29 April
Question 2 to PM, 'Now that fiscal probity is back in vogue, why do we need a Labour government?', seems to confuse PM and is enjoyed by our lot.

Later to Cameron, to whom I talked at the Carlton Club board dinner last night. Then he was adamant about taking a different line on MPs' allowances from the parliamentary party but after talking to me said maybe he would 'sleep on it' – especially how to vote on standards and privileges committee motion to refer whole thing to independent standards in public life committee. He has decided to vote for this and calls me in to tell me.

Tuesday 12 May
Telegraph splashes with me and seven other 'grandees'; says I have a helipad and chandelier.

DC calls meeting of '22 Exec (1 p.m.) and whole party (2 p.m.). He says to me, 'I've been to your house and did not see a helipad.' 'That's because there isn't one.'

Tuesday 19 May
Both Chief Whips 'outed'.

Wednesday 20 May
A voluble new member rushes out of '22 Exec saying, 'I can't stand this any longer.' Anthony Steen announces he will leave at next GE, after being attacked in *Telegraph*.

---

* Shadow leader of the House

Thursday 21 May
Another colleague rings – can't stand being treated like a crook. Intends to resign and fight a by-election. I advise against this. The whole thing is a catastrophe of massive proportions.

Wednesday 3 June
Start the day with a parliamentary visit to Picasso exhibition at National Gallery. Joke in circulation, attributed to Michael Mates: 'This is the first time MPs have rushed to the newsagents to make sure they are *not* in the newspapers.'

3.15: See DC. I suggest to him that people in the parliamentary party, senior ones, are becoming pretty restless about (a) fairness and (b) legal status of the Conservative scrutiny committee and its powers, backed by threat of removal of the whip to five MPs. We effectively agree on three matters, which are later picked up by Patrick McLoughlin when he joins '22 Executive in my room:

Fairness between mortgage payers and maintenance people, also within categories, e.g. gardeners, cleaners.

If possible scrutiny group which meets MPs must be restricted to Chief Whip and assistant Chief Whip.

Statement of payback of money must not imply MPs' guilt.

As I leave DC says, 'Always pop in whenever you want to see me. It is vital we keep in touch.'

A shadow minister rings – resents being treated as a potential criminal by scrutiny committee.

Monday 8 June
DC gives a party for colleagues. Asks me whether he should make a speech. I say, 'Yes.' He makes an excellent 'also *mea culpa*' speech – exactly what I have advised him to make. I tell him it was just right.

Wednesday 10 June
Meet DC in the 10 p.m. vote and walk with him to Speaker's Palace. He wants the paybacks from the scrutiny panel to be announced next week in one big bang. I say there are now diminishing returns from this exercise and more colleagues could be hurt if payback seen as punishment. 'Why not allow individual MPs more control, especially on how it is treated locally?' He says 'No', but will think about it over the weekend and come back to me. Agrees to make it clear 'payback not a sign of guilt'. His policy has been successful against Brown so far; the unhappiness is with MPs.

Thursday 11 June
Osborne in *The Times* for 'flipping'.* Andrew Robathan rings to say how important my meeting with DC is.

Tuesday 16 June
At a party meeting DC tells MPs that he meets me every week to keep in touch with the parliamentary party.

Wednesday 17 June
3 p.m. Meet DC to discuss how to (a) ensure that when paybacks are published they are not seen as punishment, (b) end the overt threat of a removal of the whip if people do not comply with payback. DC agrees to (a) but not (b). However, he does join '22 Executive committee at last moment (on my suggestion) and says he will try to remain silent about removal of the whip.

Monday 22 June
John Bercow wins Speakership – whatever next?

Tuesday 23 June
Tomorrow is payback day and I have been asked to approve DC's press release.

Wednesday 24 June
Many colleagues in a terrible state about paying back. First of all, it's wrong – unsupported by the law. Second, it's expensive for some people. I reword several passages in the press release, e.g. 'unacceptable' replaced with 'disproportionate', add 'payback not any indication of guilt', take out reference to colleagues who have 'estates'. People are still going to be very upset.

Thursday 25 June
Having refused '22 invitation last night, DC calls his own meeting at 9.15 for 10 a.m. About sixty present. DC talks about 'what had to be' to keep our lead in the polls and of 'rough justice'. Says I twice approved press release.

We meet in his room at 1 p.m. for a few minutes. I say, 'I'm doing everything I can to unite the party behind you. It does not help this effort if you undermine '22 by bypassing it when you have something to say to the party.' He listens to this and we part on good terms.

---

* 'Flipping' implies changing the designation of a member's second home in order to maximise the benefit from the additional costs allowance.

Friday 3 July
Patrick McLoughlin comes to my constituency to speak to about eighty association members at home of Archie and Patricia Smith-Maxwell in Welland. Archie is a former constituency association president. Atmosphere potentially explosive because of MPs' expenses. Patrick is very supportive of me – says I have been a central stabilising force within the party for the past eight years. I say, in thanking him, he is that rare phenomenon, a popular Chief Whip.

Wednesday 8 July
Over a hundred colleagues and their wives to a 'cheering-up' party sponsored by the '22. Cameron made his 'I feel your pain' speech. I was more specific: 'MPs are not corrupt, especially Conservative MPs. They are traumatised, hurt and damaged; they will welcome David Cameron's words of comfort to help them to keep buggering on, in the words of one former statesman.'

Wednesday 22 July
Parliament broke up for the summer last night.
    12.15: meet Cameron. I alert him to the fact that there could be four flashpoints in the autumn, affecting his relationship with parliamentary party:

1.   Kelly report*
2.   SSRB report on MPs' pensions
3.   Legg audit of allowances
4.   Publication of '08/'09 figures.

We agree to keep in touch over the summer.

Tuesday 28 July
Ann driving while I talk to Edward Llewellyn (DC's chief of staff) about Anthony Steen. Steen has drafted a letter appointing himself as 'ambassador' for DC on the issue of human trafficking for DC to sign. AS feels that once he ceases to be an MP (as he has been a serious casualty of expenses crisis), no one will take much notice of him. He is probably right and needs a platform. EL reads out a letter which falls short of what AS wants but asks him to report 'direct to me', signed DC. Talk to AS, who will accept this but will write a responding letter saying words to the effect that he hopes this will be the start of a long and fruitful relationship (between himself and DC).

---

*   The report produced by Sir Christopher Kelly, chairman of the Committee for Standards in Public Life, originator of a new system for MPs' allowances.

Monday 10 August
Discuss with Chief Whip cases of some ten colleagues, who have typically unfair but pressing expenses problems.

Sunday 20 September
I saw Cameron last night at Ashcroft's party. He said that for once he had had a good break. Alan Duncan is there with his 'other half': very pleasant man who knows our son, Edward. Duncan is taking his demotion well. I say, 'Keep at it. The wheel usually comes full circle if you hold your nerve and don't get bitter. You probably had to have a bit of a knock back at some point.'

Tuesday 22 September
Meeting with Chief Whip. Raise Anthony Steen issue. I say, 'What he needs above all is an acknowledgment from the leader's office to the letters he sends DC about human trafficking.' We also discuss expenses. He says he hopes that Legg report will settle matters and that the party will not need to intervene again.

Saturday 3 October
Edward McMillan-Scott (former leader of MEPs, constituent of mine and I suspect keen over the years to get my seat) emails me to seek my help having had his membership of the party removed. I ring him. (I am sympathetic to his case that whip removal for his 'crime' of being rude about the Polish leader of our new grouping in the European Parliament would have been enough.) What I say to him is that if he apologises and effectively withdraws his attack, I will see what I can do to get his party membership restored. (I am seeing DC Monday week.)

Sunday 4 October
Cameron on *Andrew Marr Show* before the party conference, looking strained. Difficult questions on Europe (what if Czechs and Poles ratify?). Will public expenditure cuts create more unemployment? What is his personal wealth? Not surprisingly, DC struggles a bit with his answers. Foretaste of what is to come in government.

Saturday 10 October
Edward McMillan-Scott comes round for a cup of tea at Cropthorne. Shows me a letter from William Hague which has three conditions for a return of the whip:

1. Apologise for his accusation of anti-Semitism against Michał Kamiński, Polish leader of the new group in European Parliament.
2. Resign as vice-president of European Parliament.
3. Agree to be a loyal member of new group.

Since evidently this is all too much for him, I agree to advise DC to keep in touch with him, as long as he doesn't stir matters up again, and let matters heal. EM-S doesn't much like this as he wants a recognition from the board that he has been badly treated – something he won't get.

Monday 12 October
Meeting with DC at 2.30. He says that whatever individuals do to query Legg about his letter, they must ultimately settle, even if the whole process is arbitrary and retrospective.

Then he asks what do we do if Czechs settle re Lisbon Treaty.* I say, 'Agree to hold a referendum on "in" or "out". That would shaft everyone because they all expect to win – UKIP, Lib Dems, Eurofanatics, Eurosceptics, the lot'. He does not dismiss this but asks, 'What happens if the "outers" win?' I say, 'Then either come out or threaten to do so as a strong bargaining counter. Either way a referendum should clear the air – especially before the election.'

Wednesday 14 October
Much better day. Just get in at question no. 10 in PMQs; ask: 'Would he confirm that he will soldier on to the bitter end?' The House, I have to say, loves it, after a rather sombre session on Afghanistan.

Afterwards chair '22. Bill Cash very long-winded, though on the ball about the legal minefield Legg is stumbling through. Retrospective and legally very dodgy. I say, 'On behalf of the committee I will listen to Bill's full speech afterwards.' Chatted to Bill in the tea room after.

Much dissatisfaction amongst colleagues for once again being threatened with loss of the whip if they do not eventually stump up for Legg. The appeal procedure if an MP loses the whip six months before an election is that I have to appoint 1½ of three members of the appeal committee. National Convention chairman appoints other 1½.

Sunday 18 October
Papers at one against MPs and pro Cameron's stance, backed up in the

---

* The Lisbon Treaty required all member states to ratify; only the Czechs were holding out at this point.

case of the *Sunday Times* by a very decisive poll. General line: 'gardeners/ cleaners' pretty awful – no sympathy for retrospective limits. 'Flippers' and property speculators have got off scot free from Legg.

Monday 19 October
Manage to persuade the officers at a sandwich lunch in my office that nothing to be gained by being too confrontational with DC.

At 4.30 meet DC in his office (preceded by a delegation from China). I begin by saying we support his attempts to bring the expenses issue to a close, but there has to be natural justice. People must be given time to appeal and question Legg. DC says OK but they mustn't be allowed to hold things up. We then raise Kelly,[*] to which DC says, 'The pass has been sold,' and adds, 'My job is to appeal to the public over the heads of the parliamentary party.'

Wednesday 21 October
DC reluctant to come to '22 even when I invite him direct. He does, however, come at last moment to the Executive and sits at the back of the main committee.

Tuesday 27 October
ERG breakfast 8.30. Question: What should be our policy on Europe if the Czechs cave in and ratify Lisbon Treaty, as they look like doing? I say: hold referendum on in/out: would shaft Lib Dems and UKIP.

Afterwards Dennis Skinner comes up to me to say, 'Your question to Brown last week was by far the sharpest.' Quite something from a man who always called me 'the gaffer' (from the days when I was minister for coal) and who anyway never used to talk to Tories.

Sunday 1 November
Dan Hannan rings. 'It is quite clear from the [ERG] breakfast and subsequent conversations I have had that they are going to sell out on a referendum following the coming Czech collapse on Lisbon. They will offer "repatriation of the powers given away" and a referendum if there are any more intergovernmental moves to federalism. This is clearly meaningless since repatriation is impossible because of the *Acquis* and the Brussels government said they have enough federal powers for the present. So there will be no referendum despite promises.'

---

[*] Sir Christopher Kelly, chairman of the Committee for Standards in Public Life, author of a new system of MPs' allowances.

I say, 'I agree. The question is what you do now. Remember one day there will be a decisive clash and the Eurosceptics will finally be put to the test. You can't achieve much at the moment. (Parliamentarians are obsessed with expenses and with the coming election.) Keep your powder dry; the day will come.'

Tuesday 3 November

Summoned to see DC at 3.45. He tells me will speak to '22 tomorrow to say on Europe, 'Thus far and no further.' I ask, 'What about the ratchet effect?'* He agrees to address this. He will also promise repatriation of powers. I say, 'What about the *Acquis*?'

Wednesday 4 November

Two full meetings of '22. DC addresses the first at 2.45. No referendum on Lisbon Treaty but offers to amend 1972 Act of Accession to permit unilateral retrieval of powers and possibility of referendum in Parliament after next.

Second meeting at 5.30 discusses Christopher Kelly, who has published his report on future of MPs' allowances. I tell '22 that the Executive is focused on establishing an appeal from Legg.

Friday 20 November

Michael Gove speaks at my constituency association annual dinner. Legg has not demanded a payback from him for his assisted housing loans. In the car driving home from Malvern he calls the whole system 'capricious'.

Thursday 26 November

Peter Luff tells me he has had his Legg letter. A pattern seems to be emerging where everything is negotiable except gardening and cleaning claims. Interest on money borrowed to buy a house is OK but maintaining the house is not (although it was at the time the claim was made).

Sunday 6 December 2009

Polls are narrowing. Much talk in the press about hung parliament. Brown had a good PMQ last week and it has percolated through. People say PMQs don't matter. I have a feeling that they do when PM performs particularly well – or badly.

---

* The process, endemic to the Treaty of Rome, whereby all European law moves irreversibly and exclusively towards the creation of a centralised federal state.

Wednesday 9 December
At PMQ DC attacks Brown for not being tough enough re the expenses saga.

Later I see DC in his room. He says he wants shorter summer hols. I say, 'I hope you will give the skiers a better deal at Christmas.' 'You mean less Umbria and more Verbier?'

Friday 11 December
Last hospital visits in the constituency.*

Tuesday 22 December
Last party at the West Worcestershire Conservative offices. I feel – perhaps over-sensitively – a frosty reception, though Ken Pollock, the chairman, very friendly.

Monday 4 January 2010
Bump into John Major at the bar of the Trafalgar Studio Theatre in the interval of Agatha Christie's *A Daughter's a Daughter* – her only non-crime play: excellent. I congratulate JM on his robust defence of backbench MPs on the radio last Saturday (need for stronger select committees etc.). He adds that he would take every opportunity to attack the 'outrageous' Legg approach to MPs' expenses.

Wednesday 6 January
Ask a question at PMQs. 'Now we are facing stagflation, what's he going to do about it?' Prescott comes up to me afterwards and says, 'Still asking trick questions.' We laugh again about the withholding tax; it still gets to him. Bump into Bercow in the Jubilee room. I ask him, 'What are you doing in our humble bar?' He says, 'I'm reforming,' and then, 'You asked another of your short crisp questions.'

Sunday 10 January
Meet Frank Field after evensong at Westminster Abbey. Frank tells me how he wrote to complain to Legg after being charged for cleaning. Legg's response was to reduce it. This makes Field even more 'furious' because it further highlighted just how arbitrary and dictatorial the whole system is. We can only hope that Paul Kennedy will be radical in his appeal approach. The hope is pretty muted in the light of all that has gone before.

---

* Every year since I entered Parliament I have visited hospitals and care homes in my constituency in the run-up to Christmas.

Tuesday 12 January
Invited by Patrick McLoughlin to join him and Simon Burns (assistant Chief Whip) at his table in the corner of members' dining room. When asked by Simon if I am writing an autobiography/keep a diary, I gurgle into my soup. Patrick laughs and says, 'That's not an answer.' 'I say, 'If I were writing an autobiography, I would begin with "I was not at the height of events but I was at the bottom of many of them."' The subject changes.

Thursday 19 January
Meeting between '22 reps and Sir Ian Kennedy, chairman of IPSA.* I begin by asking him what he means by MPs having been 'on the take'. He replies that it was other people's perception that they have been. I say, 'You don't raise the status of Parliament by dumbing down its members.'

Monday 1 February
2.30: Meeting with DC in his office. Polls are narrowing and pointing to a hung parliament.

Wednesday 3 February
Dinner at Garrick for '22 Executive and Patrick McLoughlin, Peter Tapsell, Jessica, Ann. I speak about '22–whip–leader relationship – all problems at the beginning of '22. Chief Whip speaks and says I kept party together when it was virtually leaderless. Nick Winterton says I have been best chairman 'ever'! (He has been wonderfully supportive in good times and bad – and there have been both.)

Thursday 4 February
Sir Paul Kennedy says, in effect, we have been wrongly traduced for claiming gardening and cleaning, which were both eligible to be claimed in full from allowances at the time. But his terms of reference did not allow him to intervene on this matter.

Monday 22 February
Meeting with Catherine Fall, second in charge in DC's office (Ed Llewellyn off sick), to discuss DC's speech to '22 on Wednesday. Catherine says he will give the main points that MPs need to know for the election. I say what is important is the link; there must be a theme. Repeat this in the tea room to Desmond Swayne.

---

* Independent Parliamentary Standards Authority.

Wednesday 24 February

About 150 at '22 to hear DC speak. Spends first five minutes saying that he and I have met every week for the past 4½ years and what a wonderful chappie I am.

Unanimously decide that only backbenchers can vote for '22 chairman and Executive in next parliament. DC wants whole parliamentary party to be part of '22. Makings of a row.

Friday 26 February

Peter Tapsell speaks at my farewell party in Malvern, starting, 'Anyone from Cameron downwards in the parliamentary party would have considered it a very great honour to have been asked to speak at Michael's farewell dinner.' 176 present of the great and good from the two constituencies of South (now defunct) and West Worcestershire. Evening ended with a brilliantly funny speech by Edward 'on behalf of the family'. He described three episodes: (1) Annabel's cactus, which (aged about two) she accidentally pushes up the bottom of the dignitary at the opening of a hospital wing in Evesham. (2) Antonia (aged six) rumbling the tombola – wins all the prizes, which she has to return. (3) Ann's canvassing: two eyes through the letter box, 'Mummy... in bed having a tickle.'

Wednesday 3 March

Dinner with Patrick McLoughlin in Carlton Club, then on to Pratt's, where Michael Heseltine about to leave to do a eulogy on *Newsnight* for Michael Foot. We agree we must focus on the economy to stop the rot in the polls. Patrick McLoughlin also confirms that dissolution will be on 12 April.

Monday 8 March

See Cameron for what may turn out to be last time. Give him the 'Spicerian' view of how to win election. I was in managerial charge of the most success-ful election for us in modern times (1983). Then as now it was based on 'the economy, stupid'. He listens to me politely, showing signs of fatigue.

Wednesday 10 March

Another go at asking PMQ in a 'free' slot. Bercow has now ignored me for three weeks running. Three weeks ago I wanted to ask, 'What is the date of the next General Election?' which would have been quite funny then. Redwood was called. Last week I wanted to ask, 'Why do Labour govern-ments always run out of money?' This week Ann Widdecombe was called. I wanted to ask, 'Why *are* there always so many strikes at the end of a Labour government?' referring to BA strike.

I suspect Speaker doesn't like me since I was brought into a meeting in the last parliament to read him the Riot Act to avoid the threat of his crossing the floor of the House. Also at Business Questions last week I asked an anti-Speaker question: 'Why won't next parliament be able to vote for Speaker – as for his deputies – in a secret ballot?'

Monday 22 March
Last board meeting. The chairman, Eric Pickles, almost forgets to say 'Goodbye' to me after nine years. (However long you are in politics it is an extraordinarily transitory career. In this case I am almost forgotten *before* I leave!) Patrick McLoughlin invites me into a meeting with a colleague who has gone to pieces after the expenses business – no longer goes to his constituency, and drinks all day. Patrick wheels in a friendly doctor and tells the colleague he is having a severe breakdown and needs help. Patrick is very good. This is a medical casualty of the expenses affair.

Tuesday 23 March
Lunch in the House of Commons with Pollocks and Ann. Ken Pollock (my constituency chairman) has been very supportive.

Dinner (last?) in Strangers with Patrick McLoughlin and Nick Winterton.

Wednesday 24 March
Begin to chair my final '22. Just after I call for the minutes and they have been read, Cameron bursts into the room with Ann and Jessica. I am prepared for the latter two but not for DC. About 100 people present. The desk-thumping goes on for several minutes. Then DC speaks, saying this is a genuine applause. I have kept the party united for nine years etc. etc. He then presents me with a magnificent (1922) silver salver, the funds for which I learn afterwards have been collected from the entire parliamentary party. I am sufficiently prepared to make a speech of general thanks (below). Almost break down at last sentence.

> This is probably the last meeting I will chair. Perhaps I might be permitted a word of thanks to the committee before I open the formal proceedings.
>
> I am enormously grateful that you have allowed me to be your chairman for nearly nine years. During this time I believe I have chaired some 288 meetings. I know now that you do not need necessarily to be mad or drunk to speak at the '22 Committee. Many of our meetings have been first-class discussions – and usually they have been secure – for which heartfelt thanks, colleagues.

I wish to give special thanks to the Executive committee. Covering a wide spectrum of views, they have been a wonderful team. I want in particular to mention two retiring officers: (1) the retiring treasurer, Sir Nicholas Winterton, one of the most honest men in modern politics and a great servant of Parliament over many years; (2) the retiring joint secretary, Anthony Steen. He has done tremendous good works throughout his political life, often unrecognised. Thank you to both of them.

We have had our excitement over the past nine years, three leadership elections amongst them. We also had our successes, most noticeably changing the constitution to allow three extra MPs on the board and successfully pressing for appeals procedures for Howard Flight-type situations and with respect to the Legg report.

But I suspect the real excitement lies ahead; with half of the next parliament full of new people and half of colleagues traumatised by the previous parliament, it is not going to be boring.

In this context may I wish the very best of good fortune to my successor, whoever he or she may be.

Afterwards Executive, Patrick McLoughlin and DC come round to my room for champagne. Quiet word with DC. He has taken on board my advice to focus on the economy and on a tax cut.

Supper at 'Grumbles' with Ann, Patrick and Jessica.

Thursday 25 March
Our slide in the polls goes on. *Evening Standard* claim we will no longer be the largest party. At the start of the year we were 26 points ahead.

Tuesday 30 March
Last full day in Parliament as an MP for thirty-six years.

Thursday 1 April
Ring Ed Llewellyn. I say, 'Things [the campaign] are going better.' He says, 'It's up and down.' I say, 'David is following what we discussed on two matters (attack on the economy and have one major tax cut commitment – e.g. commitment not to raise national insurance as Labour are proposing) but we have not yet seen any pithy one-liners in the ad campaign.' He says, 'Can you suggest any?' I suggest 'Why do we always have so many strikes at the end of a Labour government?' and 'Why do Labour governments always run out of money?' Ed says, 'I will feed them in.'

Monday 5 April (Easter Monday)
Harriett Baldwin* rings and, rather surprisingly, says she wants me publicly involved in her campaign. She will build an event around me.

Wednesday 7 April
Emergency meeting of '22 Executive at 3 p.m. to meet chief executive of IPSA, Andrew McDonald, to discuss IPSA's general attitude to MPs. On the way to the meeting in the shadow Cabinet room bump into Tony Lloyd, chairman of PLP. Suggest he drops in on our meeting for five minutes so we can share our thoughts. He does so (this is probably a 'first'). In the end both his appearance and the holding of the meeting turn out to be productive. IPSA agrees to discuss policy matters on a regular basis with '22 Executive (and, by implication, PLP). I pass this on to Tony Lloyd, who agrees to keep in touch with Richard Ottaway about it.

Sumptuous dinner at White's with Nicholas Soames our generous host. Soufflé, spicy lamb cutlets and lavish wines. Lots of 'Goodbye, Michael'. Several flattering remarks about my chairmanship. Walk home on a beautifully clear night through St James's Park with Andrew Robathan.

Thursday 8 April
Parliament prorogued.

Sunday 18 April
Ever since Clegg starred in the TV debate last Thursday the wheels seem to have been falling off the Conservative bandwagon, at least so far as the polls are concerned. Three polls now put the three parties neck and neck, which would have been unimaginable a week ago.

Monday 19 April
Liberals top with 33 per cent, us 32 per cent, Labour 23 per cent for a YouGov poll in *The Sun*. Bump into Michael Portillo in the street. He thinks Lib Dem 'bubble'/swings will last a bit. There is a surreal air about all this.

Wednesday 28 April
Piano recital at Michael Portillo's lovely house in Vincent Square. Also there: Heseltines, Bakers, Parkinsons, Jessels, Mackays. Much talk of Brown's gaffe with Mrs Duffy – 'bigoted woman'. General view is that Brown is finished and that Cameron will be next PM, with or without Lib Dem support.

---

* Conservative candidate for West Worcestershire, my excellent successor.

Thursday 29 April

Last of three leaders' debates, the first of which catapulted Nick Clegg into prominence and his party to 30 per cent in the polls. I don't think the effect will last. If it does it will be the first time that personality has had a long-term effect on the polls.

Tuesday 4 May

Portillo says on Andrew Neil's *Daily Politics*, 'Cameron didn't finish the sentence which began "We must change". Change to what?'

Wednesday 5 May

Eve of poll. Cameron rings me at Cropthorne after his all-night campaigning. 'David here.' 'David who?' 'David Cameron. Would you be prepared to go into the Lords?' 'Yes please.' 'Good – well deserved.' I take the next train to London after saying, 'Don't get so tired that you can't form a government at the weekend.' 'I won't.'

Following the general election on 6 May, the Conservatives were the largest party in the House of Commons, but with no overall majority. A coalition of the Conservative and Liberal Democrat parties was formed on 11 May, with David Cameron at its head.

Wednesday 19 May

First the Chief Whip and then the Prime Minister ring me to tell me they plan that afternoon to meet the parliamentary party to say there will be a secret ballot to determine whether the 1922 will comprise the entire party, including the payroll. What is my position? I say presumably they realise there will be considerable resistance to this. I personally want to give my support to the coalition's attempts to put the nation's finances right. On the specific issue raised by Cameron I have mixed views (later expressed in the *Daily Telegraph* of 21 May). I think it is a good idea, for instance, for the entire parliamentary party to meet under the aegis of the 1922 Committee. Later in the day and before the meeting at 4.00 p.m. I ring and speak separately to Kate Fall, Ed Llewellyn and Patrick McLoughlin to say that, after a little reflection, I think DC should say he has 'discussed' the matter with me but go no further.

When I was phoned by Cameron I took the view that on balance bringing the whole party under the chairmanship of the 1922 chairman was a good thing. Ministers voting at the 1922 for the Executive was an entirely different matter. In the end, ministers were told not to vote for the election of officers on the 1922. I do not think it would have made much difference to the result had they done so, but this complied with what the '22 had decided in the last parliament.

Thursday 20 May

Daily Telegraph ask me for an article on the '22 issue, which I give them by 4.00 p.m. The position I have tried to maintain since the Maastricht days is for the right to be clear on vital issues but to do its best to be in the mainstream of the party. This has had variable success (e.g. with the single currency), but has often been misunderstood – particularly on the right – as being weak.

Wednesday 26 May

At '22 election, Graham Brady wins, as do Christopher Chope, Mark Pritchard,[*] Charles Walker[†] and John Whittingdale. Clean sweep of '22 officer positions for the Eurosceptic right. By coincidence, bump into Richard Ottaway (the loser) outside my flat; take him off to Pratt's, where I get six votes for his membership application. I have not agreed with his politics over the years, but he was a good vice-chairman of the '22.

Wednesday 4 August

Dinner with the Herfords in my former constituency. Sit next to Meriel Darby, the daughter of Sir Alec Douglas-Home and wife of a local Liberal councillor and former Oxford don. Effectively I apologise for what I did almost half a century ago to undermine her father's leadership of the party. Thus have we come full circle, a good point to end.

On first sight the Lords[‡] looks a good place to settle old scores! You meet up with everyone from your past, and then you realise they have all mellowed and that you yourself are older and wiser and you want to begin the process of scrubbing out the nasty bits in your published diary. Some you do; others you leave, on the grounds that they are part of history and arguably deserve to be in the public domain.

This is the last entry I will make in my diary, which I began in a fashion almost sixty years ago.

---

[*] MP for The Wrekin since 2005.
[†] MP for Broxbourne since 2005.
[‡] To which I was 'introduced' on 12 July 2010.

A last word

So what does it all add up to? I will permit myself one last long sentence by way of response. It is this: If the English language continues to be spoken freely in North America, India and Africa and by air traffic controllers around the world and it is the language of the internet, if we build one PWR nuclear power station each year for twenty years, if we remain a democracy, if the climate stays mild, if we have a health and education system able to cater for around seventy million people, if we retain control of our currency, our borders and our defences, if we trade freely, if we keep inflation below two per cent, if our pensions are largely funded, if business can be conducted with profit, if the City of London remains a premier financial market, if industrial and other protest stays within the boundaries of the law, if our international airports (especially Heathrow) and docks are developed with appropriate infrastructure, if London remains the cultural capital of the world and, above all, if we retain our values and free speech, we will be here as a nation and doing fine; but as I close the last page and rest my pen, these are big 'ifs'.

As for me, I have my new coat of arms with its three lions, red box, quill pens, two tennis racquets and paintbrushes. Underneath is inscribed the motto *Et facere et pati fortia*, loosely translated as Churchill's 'KBO'* – a thoroughly Conservative ambition.

---

* 'Keep buggering on.' The literal translation of Livy's quote is 'Acting and suffering bravely'.

Index

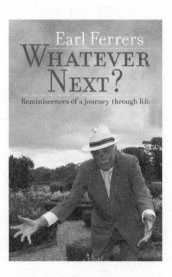

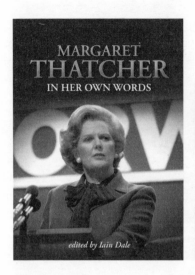
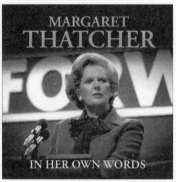